13

FINANCIAL REPORTING ENVIRONMENT

Navzar Taraporvala

Published by Certified Accountants Educational Projects Ltd

Credits for the second edition

Subject consultant Barry Elliott

Commissioning editor Jane Elliot

Managing editor Linda Auld

Copyeditor Linda Auld

Proofreaders James Griffin, Andrew Lewis

Indexer Indexing Specialists

Production Frances Follin, Petra Green

Text design Carla Turchini

Cover design Fielding Rowinski

DTP layout Eirini Mutzuris, CCTS

Acknowledgements
Past exam questions are reproduced with the kind permission of the Chartered Association of Certified Accountants and the Institute of Chartered Accountants in England and Wales.

First edition published 1993
Second edition published 1994

Certified Accounts Educational Projects Limited
29 Lincoln's Inn Fields
London WC2A 3EE

ISBN 1 85908 077 4

Further information on Certified Accountants Educational Projects Limited products and services may be obtained from Certified Accountants Educational Projects Limited, 29 Lincoln's Inn Fields, London WC2A 3EE.

British Library Cataloguing in Publication data
A catalogue record for this book is available from the British Library.

Printed in the UK by: Page Bros.

Table of Contents

Overview

The syllabus for this paper may, conveniently, be broken down into four parts

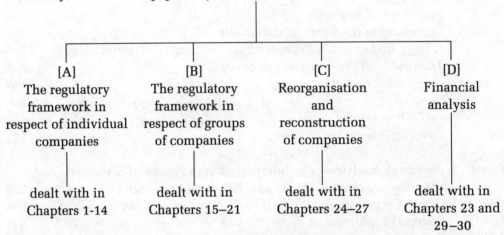

[A] The regulatory framework in respect of individual companies	[B] The regulatory framework in respect of groups of companies	[C] Reorganisation and reconstruction of companies	[D] Financial analysis
dealt with in Chapters 1-14	dealt with in Chapters 15–21	dealt with in Chapters 24–27	dealt with in Chapters 23 and 29–30

[A] The regulatory framework in respect of individual companies – you will have covered much of the ground in this area in your studies for earlier accounting papers. Thus, you will already be familiar with the accounting treatment of, for example, goodwill, depreciation, post-balance sheet events, contingencies, stocks and continuing and discontinued operations. These topics are dealt with here again insofar as they remain relevant to overall analysis in (D) and given that, in some cases, fundamental problems remain to be resolved in respect of accounting treatment.

Chapter 1 serves as a useful introduction and, most relevant to following chapters, introduces the ASB's Statement of Principles that you must always bear in mind in considering the relevance and usefulness of various accounting solutions to various accounting problems.

Chapter 2 introduces the international dimension and serves as a reminder that GAAP varies in different parts of the world.

Chapter 3 introduces the audit dimension and concludes with a section on the auditors' report. You should bear in mind, when working through subsequent chapters, the impact of alternative approaches to recognition, measurement and disclosure on the audit opinion.

Chapters 4–8 deal with the accounting for tangible fixed assets, intangible fixed assets, tax in company accounts and pension costs. The main problems arising here are to do with:

▶ no standard accounting practice as to revaluations
▶ alternative accepted treatments of goodwill
▶ the variations that can be introduced into financial statements given the judgements necessary in accounting for deferred tax under SSAP 15
▶ variations from regular cost in respect of pensions.

It would be unusual for an examination paper not to deal with some of these problems.

Chapter 9 is most important in that it covers the requirements of, at the time of writing, the ASB's two most recent reporting standards, FRS 4 and FRS 5. Both have had a long development period. Reflecting the substance of transactions is relevant to most other chapters in this textbook. Standard reporting practice for capital instruments has a fundamental bearing on analysis in terms of Debt and Equity, the relationship of one to the other and the recognition of the cost thereon in the profit and loss account. It is to be expected that the paper will be concerned, in good measure, with most current issues and your learning and revision time should be weighted accordingly.

Chapter 10 on leasing has been often examined in the past and accounting by lessees and lessors and for sale and leaseback transactions must be covered in depth.

Chapter 11 deals with the innovative FRS 3 and reporting financial performance and how this may best be achieved to be most useful to most users. FRS 3 is fundamental to financial analysis.

Chapter 12 on cash flow statements is best approached after covering the regulatory framework in respect of groups of companies.

Chapter 13 covers what, in my view, is the subject matter of a typical Paper 13 question, that is one which spreads its requirements over vast swathes of the syllabus. Almost all of the ground of Chapters 1 to 11 is relevant to the question of a company's maximum legally distributable profit.

Chapter 14 deals with the effects of changing prices and is, therefore, of crucial importance in financial analysis.

In reading and working through the first 14 chapters you may, initially, be overwhelmed with the detail and question the relevance of what some may argue is an over historic approach adopted in getting to where we are now. The past has been included in an attempt to explain the present; you do not need to spend much time on it. Suffice that you read it through quickly bearing in mind the three-fold question put by Harrison Ford in the film *Blade Runner*:

▶ where are we coming from?
▶ where are we going?
▶ how much time do we have?

[B] The regulatory framework in respect of groups of companies – I see this section as central to the examinable syllabus. Groups are introduced in Paper 10 but the major problems arising in consolidated accounts are deferred to this paper and must be seen as a timing difference that will reverse, to use the terminology of SSAP 15.

Start with Chapter 15 as an introduction to the regulatory framework in this area. Chapters 16 and 17 deal with the mechanics of consolidation and the time you require to spend here will depend on the level of your previous exposure to the preparation of consolidated accounts.

Chapter 18 moves into the more rarified atmosphere of accounting for changes in the composition of a group, disposals and step-by-step acquisitions. There is much to examine here and you need to be fully aware of the legal rules involved and the FRS 2 interpretation of these rules.

Chapters 19 and 20 deal with mergers, acquisitions and goodwill and the ASB's response to SSAPs 22 and 23. The issues dealt with are these:

▶ which method to use on consolidation?
▶ if the acquisition method is used, what should be the treatment of goodwill arising on consolidation?
▶ what is the fair value of a subsidiary at acquisition?

The first question is addressed by the ASB in FRED 6, the second in a Discussion Paper and the third in FRED 7. This is the stuff of which a typical Paper 13 question will be made.

Chapter 21 describes the alternative methods of accounting for investments in consolidated accounts and in particular, accounting for associated companies under the equity method. The problem areas arising are expressed in terms of questions as follows:

▶ is the 'single line' equity method appropriate for associates?
▶ does compliance with SSAP 1 give a true and fair view?
▶ how do we account for a change in the status of associates?

Chapter 22 deals with the very often previously examined area of overseas transactions. It would be exceptional, given that there are no more extraordinary items, for Paper 13 not to have some requirement in respect of overseas transactions and exchange differences arising.

[C] The reorganisation and reconstruction of companies –

this part of the syllabus is dealt with in the textbook as follows:

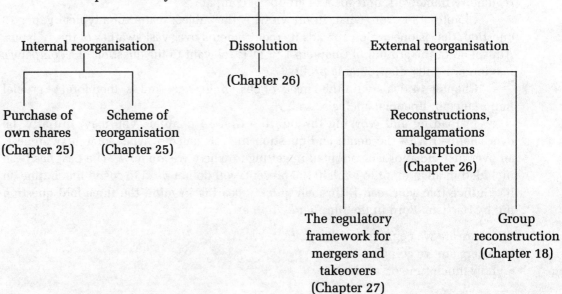

The principles of share valuation are relevant here and are dealt with in Chapter 24.

[D] Financial analysis – this draws on the whole of all previous sections. Certainly we are concerned here with ratios and with trends but we are also concerned with:

▶ the impact of changing prices
▶ the impact of different accounting policies on earnings and position
▶ the relevance of related party transactions
▶ analysis of the going concern
▶ corporate failure prediction.

These areas are dealt with in Chapters 29 and 30.

Chapter 23 deals with the preparation of additional reports. Thus, in the context of financial analysis, we are also concerned with segmental reporting and profit forecasts and accountants' reports in share circular.

Enjoy

The Syllabus for Paper 13

1 The accountant as a professional

a Interpretation and application of all extant SSAPs and FRSs.

b Critically appraising; evaluating proposed changes and promoting changes in
  i) accounting theories and principles
  ii) concepts
  iii) Accounting Standards
  iv) Financial Reporting Standards
  v) Financial Reporting Exposure Drafts
  vi) discussion drafts
  vii) guidelines
  viii) major pronouncements of the Urgent Issues Task Force and the Review Panel
  ix) accounting aspects of company law.

c Monitoring and evaluating
  i) international issues
  ii) ethical issues.

d *Managing the audit relationship*
  i) negotiating provision of services
  ii) discussion of administration and results of audit.

2 Preparing financial statements and reports

a Preparation of financial statements and reports under conditions of stable or changing prices.

b Groups of companies
  i) explaining statutory and professional requirements relating to the preparation for publication of consolidated accounts for groups and the audit thereof
  ii) accounting for the following organisational situations
    – foreign subsidiary undertaking
    – mixed and vertical groups.

c The preparation of reports for a variety of users, including
  i) shareholders relating to offers for sale, rights issues, profit forecasts
  ii) lenders to assist in decisions relating to company loan obligations
  iii) employees
  iv) assessing the valuation of shares in unquoted companies for balance sheet purposes
  v) calculating and appraising the impact on profit reporting and balance sheet of the available methods of valuation.

3 Accounting for reconstructions, mergers and combinations

a Accounting for changes in organisational structures
  i) single companies
    – reconstruction
    – capital reorganisations

    – amalgamations and absorptions
  ii) groups
    – changes of parent company interest.

b Explaining the major features of reconstructions, mergers and takeovers, their principal aspects and the legal and audit consequences in relation to
  i) control of mergers and the public interest
  ii) regulation of takeovers; statutory procedures
  iii) obligations on directors
  iv) minority rights

c Explaining the major features of dissolution, its principal aspects and the legal consequences in relation to
  i) administrative receivership
  ii) voluntary winding up
  iii) compulsory winding up.

4 Analysing and appraising financial and related information

The analysis and appraisal of implications of financial and related information for accounting purposes and for the auditor's analytical review to include

a Evaluating internal consistency and validity of the information collected/produced for the accounts.

b Identifying matters for further interpretation in the information produced (eg by comparing it to other information such as prior years, budgets/targets, industry norms, state of the economy).

c Interpreting and analysing accounts and statements (eg by ratio analysis) for indications of aspects of business performance (such as value for money, quality, long-term solvency and stability, short-term solvency and liquidity, profitability, efficiency, growth, failure prediction using, for example
  i) inter temporal analysis
  ii) intra and inter-firm comparisons
  iii) multi-variate analysis
  iv) trend analysis.

d Assessing the impact of price level changes on the analysis.

e Assessing informational weaknesses/limitations of statements and analyses.

f Presenting financial and related information and analysis in reports taking account of
  i) sources of information for the purpose of comparisons, such as financial statements for previous periods, industry norms

---

ii) background to the organisation (eg market, sales, profits, capital investment, management structure,

employees and industrial relations)
iii) future trends affecting the organisation (national and international)
iv) types and relevance of different ratios and trends
v) levels of ratios expected for the organisation/sector.

Guide to Syllabus Coverage

Paper 13: Financial reporting environment

CHAPTER TITLE	SYLLABUS SECTIONS
1 Introduction	1(a),(b)
2 International issues	1(c)
3 Managing the audit relationship	1(d)
4 Tangible fixed assets	1(a),(b)
5 Intangible fixed assets	1(a),(b)
6 Stocks and long-term contracts	1(a),(b)
7 Tax in company accounts	1(a),(b)
8 Accounting for pension costs	1(a),(b)
9 Post B/S events, contingencies and off balance sheet finance and accounting for capital instruments	1(a),(b)
10 Leasing	1(a),(b)
11 Reporting financial performance	1(a),(b)
12 Cash flow statements	1(a),(b)
13 Realised and legally distrubutable profits	1(b)
14 Accounting for the effects of changing prices	2(a)
15 Consolidated accounts 1	2(b) (i)

CHAPTER TITLE	SYLLABUS SECTIONS
16 Consolidated accounts 2	2(b) (i)
17 Consolidated accounts 3	2(b) (ii)
18 Consolidated accounts 4	3(a)(ii)
19 Consolidated accounts 5	2(b), 3(b)
20 Consolidated accounts 6	2(b), 3(b)
21 Associated companies	2(b) (i)
22 Overseas transactions	2(b) (ii)
23 The preparation of additional reports	2(c) (i)–(iii)
24 Share valuation	2(c) (iv) and (v)
25 Changes in organisational structure – single companies	3(a) (i)
26 Accounting for cesssation and dissolution of companies	3(c)
27 The major features of reconstructions and mergers	3(b)
28 Earnings per share	1(a), (b) and 4(c)
29 Financial analysis	4(a) to (e)
30 Financial analysis continued	4(a) to (e)

Preface

This is a lengthy textbook. It is written specifically for students preparing for Paper 13 in Module F of the professional stage of the Association's exams. As its title makes clear, we are here concerned with the Financial Reporting Environment and the impact of statute, accounting standards, stock exchange rules, the audit requirement and Directives on this environment. These regulations are ever expanding and at a rate more rapid than ever before. We will look at here some of the ground that you will have covered during your previous studies and more. At this stage we are also concerned with more recent developments and the proposals as to changes in the regulations governing the Financial Reporting Environment. We look not only at the going concern but also at the causes of, and the accounting for, failure of companies.

The chapters in the book divide into fairly compartmentalised sections. The first fourteen chapters deal with Accounting Standards, audit management and current developments affecting the form and content of the annual reports of companies. Chapters 15 to 22 deal with consolidated accounts and Chapters 23 to 27 with various aspects of the reorganisation of companies. Chapters 28 to 30 deal essentially with the interpretation and analysis of accounts. The chapters follow, as closely as is reasonably possible, the published syllabus for this paper.

Chapter 3, on Managing the Audit Relationship and the going concern section in Chapter 30 are written by Andy Perkins of the MAP partnership who is also a teaching colleague at Emile Woolf Colleges. Chris Welch, also a teaching colleague at Emile Woolf Colleges, wrote the auditors' report section in Chapter 3. I am grateful to Barry Elliott for his critical though always incisive comments made with courtesy and to Jane Elliot for devotion to duty in keeping me at my task. Thanks also to Linda Auld and the proofreaders for their editorial input and fine sense of detail. The shortcomings that do remain are wholly mine.

Lastly this would not have been written without Anne who cared and Zara who is pleased that I can now return to my preferred role as storyteller to the very young.

Introduction

The major part of this textbook deals with the regulatory framework of accounting. The framework, with which you will be familiar from your studies at Paper 10, has evolved over time and consists of a mass of rules and regulations. Paper 10 will have covered both the statutory and non-statutory frameworks of accounting. The statutory framework changed following the introduction of the provisions of the 1989 Companies Act into UK company law; the non-statutory framework changed with the replacement of the Accounting Standards Committee (ASC) in 1990 with the new three-tier system of setting accounting standards, consisting of the Financial Reporting Council, the Accounting Standards Board (ASB) and the Review Panel.

You will also be generally familiar from your earlier studies with the regulation of accounting from a wider national and international perspective. You will know that in the UK it is not only the requirements of the Companies Acts and Accounting Standards that must be complied with by companies; listed companies must also observe the regulations of the Stock Exchange. The programme of harmonisation of company law throughout the European Community has introduced a wider, international horizon. Thus, the Companies Act 1989 introduced the provisions of the 7th and 8th Directives into UK company law and the International Accounting Standards Committee (IASC), even though its accounting standards carry no legal force in the UK, brings together the accounting bodies of ten countries, the aim being to improve comparison between companies within the international community. The Accounting Standards and other statements and drafts of the UK standard-setting bodies, Stock Exchange rules and regulations, the requirements of International Accounting Standards and those of EC Directives are all dealt with within this textbook on the basis that you 'know little of England if England is all you know'.

This chapter will briefly examine the role of company legislation, the Stock Exchange, the ASC, the ASB, the Review Panel, the Urgent Issues Task Force (UITF), EC Directives and the IASC in the development of the UK regulatory framework. We will discuss the areas in which Statements of Standard Accounting Practice (SSAPs) have been successful, identify the areas of weakness of the now defunct ASC and describe the factors that should ensure that the ASB overcomes these weaknesses and discuss the effect that the Review Panel has had on audit quality. In this context we will need to look again at the conceptual framework and the benefits to standard setters, preparers and users that a conceptual framework would bring. Here we will have to define the elements of financial statements and their objectives, and discuss the stated intentions of the ASB regarding the role and development of a conceptual framework that is the development of its Statement of Principles, which underpins many of the accounting procedures dealt with throughout this textbook. Lastly, we will look at the interrelationship of the characteristics of useful information, including the role of the materiality concept and look at the role of the audit function in the financial reporting environment.

Contributions to UK accounting regulations

This section looks at the significance of the contributions made to UK accounting regulations from different sources and the effectiveness of the UK regulatory framework of accounting. It is intended to serve as a reminder of your previous accountancy studies and gives an overview of the UK regulatory framework of accounting.

The significance of the Companies Act

The overriding requirement for published accounts to give a true and fair view was introduced into UK company law by the 1948 Companies Act. The true and fair requirement is now enshrined in S.224 of the 1985 Act. The term 'true and fair' is deliberately not defined in the Companies Act, as its meaning is specific to a particular point in time; where the law does lay down the essential framework of accounting, the definition of the technical detail is left to the accountancy profession. Company law lays down the form and content of company accounts subject to the true and fair override taking precedence. Either historical cost or alternative valuation rules (see Chapter 14) may be applied and the accounts must be audited. The Department of Trade and Industry (DTI) now allows public companies to provide shareholders with summary financial statements in the place of full statutory requirements. Company law requires that accounts state whether they have been prepared in accordance with Accounting Standards. The reasons for and details of any departures must be given.

The significance of the Stock Exchange

Until January 1991, the Stock Exchange operated a three-tier system consisting of the Stock Exchange, the Unlisted Securities Market (USM) and the Third Market. The Third Market has now been phased out; the USM may also be phased out in the future. The Stock Exchange is self-regulated within the legal framework of the Financial Services Act which, through the Securities and Investment Board, regulates the investment industry. The system is designed to protect both investors and the companies being invested in and attempts to ensure that information is equally available to all interested parties. The rules and regulations of the Stock Exchange have been incorporated in substantial measure in company law and Accounting Standards, although some requirements, such as the need for interim accounts and the publication of information in the national press, emanate solely from the Stock Exchange.

All shares that are quoted on the Stock Exchange are included in the Official List and are given an official daily quotation. Listed companies must conform with the rules of the Stock Exchange as incorporated in the Stock Exchange (Listing) Regulations and its *Yellow Book on Admission of Securities to Listing*. Some of these rules are dealt with in Chapter 27, which deals with the major features of reconstructions, mergers and takeovers.

The significance of the ASC and, now, the ASB

You will already be familiar with the reasons for the creation of the ASC and the introduction of accounting standards, the criticisms made of the ASC, the setting up of the Dearing Committee and the three-tier system of non-statutory bodies that replaced the ASC in August 1990. This development is summarised below:

▶ The absence of relevant disclosure and the wide variety in accounting practice led to criticisms of the accountancy profession in the late 1960s and early 1970s.

► The Accounting Standards Steering Committee (ASSC) was formed with the objectives of increasing the level of disclosure in accounts and reducing the variety of accounting practices in use. It was also intended to improve accounting standards.

► The ASSC became the ASC in 1976.

► The task of the ASC was to review financial reporting, publish consultative documents and prepare statements of standard accounting practice.

► Over two decades the ASC issued 25 SSAPs and two Statements of Recommended Practice (SORPs) (see below), the former being mandatory for statements intended to show a true and fair view.

► Criticism of the accounting profession continued, as it was considered that Accounting Standards were too formal, there was too much subjectivity and inconsistencies remained (see below).

► Reasons for these shortcomings included the lack of resources available to the ASC and the need to have the unanimous approval of the Consultative Committee of Accounting Bodies, which led to compromises in the setting of accounting standards.

► The Dearing Committee was formed in 1987 as a response to the criticisms above. The Committee recommended a total reorganisation of the standard-setting process.

► The Financial Reporting Council was established to provide good accounting practice, to provide policy guidance and to establish budgets for the new standard-setting systems.

► The ASB prepares and issues standards on its own authority, subject to only two-thirds majority support.

► The Review Panel was set up to investigate alleged breaches of accounting standards by companies and has statutory powers to ensure that companies comply with the requirements of UK company law.

► The ASB's work programme includes the preparation of Financial Reporting Standards (FRSs) and also the preparation of a Statement of Principles, the intention being to form a foundation and framework of accounting.

► The UITF was created to give authoritative guidance on newly emerging issues in order, in the words of R.E. Dearing (1991), 'to safeguard against opportunism or unwisdom.'

► The work of the Council, Panel, Board and Force above is underpinned by the legislative provisions of the Companies Act 1989 (now incorporated into the amended 1985 Act) as follows:

   – Accounting standards have statutory recognition and the ASB has the power to make, amend or withdraw them on its own authority.
   – large companies are required by law to state in their accounts whether or not they have followed applicable Accounting Standards and to give reasons for any material departures from them.
   – an application may be made by the court to the Secretary of State for an order requiring revision of a company's accounts; the Secretary of State has authorised the Financial Reporting Review Panel to use these powers.

Accounting Standards, some problems and solutions

The reasons for the setting up of the ASC were dealt with briefly above. Twenty-five accounting standards were issued, three (7, 11 and 16) were withdrawn and 22 adopted by the ASB. The ASC failed in achieving its objectives, given that it was essentially a fire-fighting tool – it did not define a conceptual framework and non-compliance with Accounting Standards did not, at that time, result in legal penalties. Before addressing the issue of the significance of the ASB, let us look again at the SSAPs of the ASC, identify the accounting problems that remain despite them and, in so doing, look also at the output so far of the ASB.

Accounting standards, exposure drafts, abstracts, principles
The ASC has issued the following statements of standard accounting practice and exposure drafts.

SSAP 1	Accounting for Associated Companies
SSAP 2	Disclosure of Accounting Policies
SSAP 3	Earnings per Share (amended by FRS3)
SSAP 4	The Accounting Treatment of Government Grants
SSAP 5	Accounting for Value Added Tax
SSAP 6	Extraordinary Items and Prior Year Adjustments (superseded by FRS3)
SSAP 7	Accounting for Changes in the Purchasing Power of Money (*withdrawn*)
SSAP 8	The Treatment of Taxation Under the Imputation System in the Accounts of Companies
SSAP 9	Stock and Work in Progress
SSAP 10-	Statements of Source and Application of Funds (superseded by FRS1)
SSAP 11	Accounting for Deferred Taxation *(withdrawn)*
SSAP 12	Accounting for Depreciation
SSAP 13	Accounting for Research and Development
SSAP 14	Group Accounts (superseded by FRS2)
SSAP 15	Accounting for Deferred Taxation
SSAP 16	Current Cost Accounting *(withdrawn)*
SSAP 17	Accounting for Post Balance Sheet Events
SSAP 18	Accounting for Contingencies
SSAP 19	Accounting for Investment Properties
SSAP 20	Foreign Currency Translation
SSAP 21	Accounting for Leases and Hire Purchase Contracts
SSAP 22	Accounting for Goodwill
SSAP 23	Accounting for Acquisitons and Mergers
SSAP 24	Accounting for Pension Costs
SSAP 25	Segmental Reporting
ED 46	Related Party Transactions
ED 47	Accounting for Goodwill
ED 48	Accounting for Acquisitions and Mergers
ED 49	Reflecting the Substance of Transactions in Assets and Liabilities
ED 50	Consolidated Accounts
ED 51	Accounting for Fixed Assets and Revaluations
ED 52	Accounting for Intangible Fixed Assets
ED 53	Fair Value in the Context of Acquisition Accounting
ED 54	Cash Flow Statements
ED 54	Accounting for Investments

The ASB has issued the following

FRS 1	Cash Flow Statements
FRS 2	Accounting for Subsidiary Undertakings
FRS 3	Reporting Financial Performance
FRS 4	Accounting for Capital Instruments
FRS 5	Reporting the Substance of Transactions
FRED 1	The Structure of Financial Statements – Reporting of Financial Performance
FRED 2	Amendment to SSAP15 – Accounting for Deferred Tax
FRED 3	Accounting for Capital Instruments
FRED 4	Reporting the Substance of Transactions
FRED 5	Amendment to FRS3
FRED 6	Acquisitions and Mergers
FRED 7	Fair Values in Acquisition Accounting

FRED 8	Related Parity Tranactions
FRED 9	Amendment to SSAP 19
UITF Abstract 1	Convertible Bonds – Supplemental Interest Premiums
UITF Abstract 2	Restructuring Costs
UITF Abstract 3	Treatment of Goodwill on Disposal of a Business
UITF Abstract 4	Presentation of Long Term Debtors in Current Assets
UITF Abstract 5	Transfers from Current Assets to Fixed Assets
UITF Abstract 6	Accounting for Post Retirement Benefits Other Than Pensions
UITF Abstract 7	True and Fair Override Disclosures
UITF Abstract 8	Repurchase of Own Debt
UITF Abstract 9	Accounting for Operations in Hyper–Inflationary Economies

The ASB's statement of principles will eventually comprise seven chapters on the following subjects:

Chapter 1	The Objective of Financial Statements
Chapter 2	The Qualitative Characteristics of Financial Information
Chapter 3	The Elements of Financial Statements
Chapter 4	The Recognition of Items in Financial Statements
Chapter 5	The Measurement of Items in Financial Statements
Chapter 6	Presentation of Financial Information
Chapter 7	The Reporting Entity

We will now look very briefly at the statements of standard accounting practice.

SSAP 1 and accounting for associated companies are considered in Chapter 21 of this textbook. The standard deals with the equity method of accounting for such investments in the consolidated accounts of an investor. The area is topical and of interest in that changes introduced by the 1989 Act remain to be dealt with in a Financial Reporting Standard and because joint-venture accounting, increasingly popular in the construction industry, remains an area of accounting difficulty. Equity accounting for investments under SSAP 1, the so-called single-line equity method, is also of current interest in that in some instances it may result in assets and liabilities that are controlled or significantly influenced by the group being left off the consolidated balance sheet, which may impair the true and fair view given by the consolidated accounts. Further, SSAP 1 does link with FRS 2 in that the equity method is the appropriate method for inclusion of some subsidiaries from consolidation in the consolidated accounts; this aspect is dealt with in Chapter 15.

A revised Accounting Standard is to be issued on accounting for associates and it is expected that it will provide guidance on the treatment of deficiencies in associates' net assets and also on joint ventures now that they have been distinguished from associated undertakings.

SSAP 2 and the disclosure of accounting policies, with which you will be familiar, was issued in 1971 with the aim of facilitating the understanding of the assumptions that form the basis of financial accounts. In the absence, until recently, of a conceptual framework this Standard concerns the very basis of the regulatory framework of accounting. Thus, accounting *concepts* are defined as the 'broad basic assumptions which underlie the periodic financial accounts of business enterprises'; these are defined as the four accounting concepts of going concern, accruals, consistency and prudence and are regarded as being of general application. Company law also contains these four accounting concepts and adds a fifth concept (or principle), which is that of the separate determination of items.

Accounting *bases* are the methods developed to apply accounting concepts to financial transactions and, given a variety of bases that may be suitable, accounting *policies* are specific accounting bases adopted by companies in preparing their financial accounts. Prior to the development of the ASB's Statement of Principles the

Dearing Committee, which was formed in 1987 to undertake a review of the standard-setting process, identified the need for a conceptual framework of accounting – this is dealt with below. SSAP 2 was the one statement of the ASC that can be construed as an attempt to establish a conceptual framework by that body. Even so, given the inconsistency between the concepts – for example, between accruals and prudence – subjectivity will remain until the completion of the ASB's work on the development of a Statement of Principles makes SSAP 2 no longer necessary.

SSAP 3 on earnings per share (eps) is in Chapter 28, where we look at stock market ratios, and has been amended by FRS 3 – Reporting Financial Performance. As explained below, in respect of that Standard the ASB has shifted the emphasis in reporting financial performance away from merely a focus on the profit and loss account and eps to a more complete information set including other recognised gains and losses and items dealt with within reserves. With the effective abolition of extraordinary items under FRS 3, eps is likely to become more volatile in that the earnings on which it is based will now include one off-items previously excluded as extraordinary.

SSAP 4 on accounting for government grants is looked at in Chapter 4. The main issue here is the question of the recognition of such grants as income. The standard has been revised to take account of the growing relevance of revenue grants and the basic principles are:

▶ re capital-based grants, to recognise them as income over the life of the asset to which they relate
▶ re revenue-based grants, to pass them through the profit and loss account when the conditions attaching to the grant have been satisfied by the company and so as to match the benefit with the expense as and when the latter is incurred.

SSAP 5 deals with VAT and is unique among Accounting Standards in that it has been free from criticism. The Standard is not dealt with in the chapters that follow. Its essential requirements are:

▶ turnover in the profit and loss acccount should exclude VAT
▶ irrecoverable VAT allocated to fixed assets and other items that are separately disclosed should be included in their cost where practical
▶ the net amount due to or recoverable from the Customs and Excise should be included as part of debtors or creditors.

SSAP 6 on extraordinary items has now been superseded by FRS 3, and the problems and current solutions as to how best to report financial performance are dealt with in Chapter 11. The extraordinary impact of these developments is that there are no longer any extraordinary items and what is relevant to any assessment of financial performance is not the distinction between ordinary and extraordinary results, but the separate analysis and disclosure of results deriving from continuing and discontinued operations and an analysis of total recognised gains and losses wherever they are recognised in the accounts. The thrust of the current argument is that it is not possible to have one unfudgeable performance indicator such as eps, and even where such an amount is disclosed it should not be relied upon to the exclusion of other factors that may well be excluded in its calculation. FRS 3 represents a fundamental change in the reporting of financial performance and is a prime example of a standard-setting body establishing itself as an agent of change.

SSAP 7 was issued as a provisional standard and has been withdrawn. It dealt with inflation accounting and the preparation of accounts, as is permitted under the alternative valuation rules of the Act, on a current purchasing power basis. This area is looked at in Chapter 14.

SSAP 8 on the treatment of taxation under the imputation system is covered in Chapter 7. The Standard concentrates on the breakdown of the corporation tax liability between advance corporation tax (ACT) and mainstream corporation tax (MCT). There is a link between this Standard and eps, and Chapter 28 addresses the question of whether unrelieved ACT or ACT deemed irrecoverable is an appropriation of profits or a part of the tax charge for a year.

SSAP 9 on stocks and work in progress is considered in Chapter 6. It has been revised, principally in relation to accounting for contracts following a conflict between the then applicable 1981 Act and the original Standard. Given that the accounting rules of the Act recognise that an asset be carried at the lower of purchase price or production cost and net realisable value there was a conflict between the valuation rule of statute and the requirement of the original Standard that long-term contract balances in the balance sheet include an amount for attributable profits. This conflict was removed following revision of the standard and an integrated approach to accounting for contracts that removed attributable profit from the carrying value of work in progress in the balance sheet.

SSAP 10 has now been superseded by FRS 1 on cash flow statements, which is discussed in Chapter 12. To use the language of a conceptual framework, cash flow statements are deemed superior to funds flow statements in that the former are more relevant, understandable, reliable and objective, complete and timely than the latter.

SSAP 11 has been withdrawn, see SSAP 15 below.

SSAP 12 on accounting for depreciation, which is examined in Chapter 4, remains a problem area in accounting in the context of revaluations and the absence of any standard practice in accounting for revaluations. ED 51 deals with some of these problems and the ASB has issued, in 1993, a Discussion Paper on the role of valuation in financial reporting. If the ASC's output in this area can be criticised it is that its proposals were not based on any agreed conceptual framework. The ASB's proposals may be considered more useful in that they are based on Chapter 5 of the draft Statement of Principles, 'Measurement in financial statements'.

Before standard setters can usefully pronounce on the practice of valuation they first need to examine the conceptual issues that arise in various systems of valuation for accounting purposes. David Tweedie, chairman of the ASB, in the press notice accompanying the release of the Discussion Paper has challenged anyone to find any logic underlying the British balance sheet that 'adds together assets at original cost with assets at a range of valuations made at a range of times'. This hybrid system can have important consequences for the reporting of financial performance and questions are raised as to when an increase in the value of assets should be reflected in accounts; in the period in which the asset is sold (strict historical cost accounting) or in the period in which the increase in value takes place (modified historical cost and current value reporting). It is in the answering of questions such as these that the significance of the standard-setting bodies and their contributions to the effectiveness of the UK regulatory framework of accounting needs to be examined.

SSAP 13 on accounting for research and development costs is dealt with in Chapter 5. Again, the problems that arise from the absence of a conceptual framework come to the fore. Can development cost be regarded as an asset, and if so should it be capitalised, and if capitalised what are the principles that should apply in amortising such costs? SSAP 13 does not provide an answer to these questions in that it permits – as opposed to requires – capitalisation of development costs and in allowing this option does not contribute to the usefulness of financial information and detracts from a fair comparison of the accounts of different companies.

SSAP 14 has been superseded by FRS 2 on accounting for subsidiary undertakings, which is looked at in Chapters 15 to 18 and Chapter 20 of this textbook. Useful points can be made here as to the significance of the ASC/ASB and the effectiveness of the UK regulatory framework as follows:

▶ Under the 1948 Act subsidiaries were loosely defined so as to give rise to situations where the 'legal form' indicated the existence of a subsidiary while the 'commercial substance' was no effective control or where, legally, there was no subsidiary but, in substance, there was effective control.

▶ Thus it was possible to have subsidiaries with ineffective control and non-subsidiaries with effective control.

▶ The consolidation of the one and exclusion from consolidation of the other could not possibly result in the consolidated accounts giving a true and fair view.

▶ SSAP 14 dealt in part with the problem of ineffective control and required such subsidiaries to be excluded from consolidation.

▶ The legal definition of a subsidiary changed with the introduction of the requirements of the EC 7th Directive into UK law; the new definition is based upon control as opposed to ownership and is a solution to the old problems of non-controlled subsidiaries and non-subsidiaries that were controlled.

▶ Some problems – quasi subsidiaries – remain and these are considered in Chapter 9, where we look at the problem of off balance sheet finance.

▶ There were other problems under SSAP 14, which prompted the revision of the Standard as FRS 2, in that answers to the following questions were required:
   – When should subsidiaries be excluded from consolidation?
   – Would exclusion of subsidiariti es under the Act always give a true and fair view, for example in respect of dissimilar subsidiaries?
   – How should changes in the composition of a group be accounted for?
   – Are there circumstances where a piecemeal as opposed to a one-off approach would be more appropriate in the event of step-by-step acquisitions?
   – How should disposals be accounted for and how should goodwill paid on the acquisition of a subsidiary be treated on its sale?
   – What are the principles that should apply in eliminating profit on intercompany transactions?
   – How should a loss-making subsidiary be dealt with in arriving at the minority interest therein?

UK Company law does not deal with detailed provisions to answer these questions. The answers are provided by the accountancy profession in the Accounting Standards issued by what is now the Accounting Standards Board. Has the ASB got it right with FRS 2? The standard is not a complete answer. Problems remain with 'special purpose transactions', the problem of the quasi subsidiary referred to above. Problems also remain in respect of fair values in the context of acquisition accounting. A solution has been put forward here in a Discussion Paper, which is looked at in Chapter 20.

As Dearing (1991) himself has said,

> 'change is needed if the present framework of financial reporting is to continue to meet in full measure the needs of the ever-developing market economy of the United Kingdom ... the period covered by this review has been one of increasing concern about the responsibility of directors in preparing reports and accounts, and of auditors in examining and reporting on them.

SSAP 15 on deferred tax, examined here in Chapter 7, is, like the Standard on goodwill and the development of a standard on current cost accounting, in the last analysis, a failure. What should be the basis for a provision for deferred tax? Should we fully provide or only partially provide for the tax effects of timing differences? Full provision was the conclusion of SSAP 11, partial provision the mantra of SSAP 15. Some mantras are not sacred. ASB has now taken the view, under the proposals of

FRED 2, that partial provision as an approach may result in material understatement of deferred tax recoverable on provisions for pensions and other post-retirement benefits. Such provisions reverse in the long term, while a partial provision approach to accounting for deferred tax is essentially short term. As a result, deferred tax that will be recovered, in the long term, on the setting up of such provisions will not be recognised in accounts. The ASB thus proposes that full provision for the tax recoverable on such a timing difference should be permitted, suggesting an eventual return to full provision in respect of all timing differences.

SSAP 16 and current cost accounting is covered in Chapter 14 and ranks as the overriding instance of the failure of the standard-setting process and the self-regulation of the accounting profession under the ASC. Not surprisingly, not much has been published on accounting for the effects of changing prices since the withdrawal of SSAP 16, other than the proposals of the Handbook on this area. The impact of price changes is crucial to an understanding of the performance and position of companies and the course of the whole of the debate since the early 1970s has been an illustration of the result of:

▶ the absence of a conceptual framework
▶ insistence on unanimous approval in arriving at Standards
▶ underfunding.

Given the impact on any assessment of the performance and position of changing prices, this area is also looked at in Chapter 30 on the further interpretation of accounts. In response to the often-asked question as to why current purchasing power accounting systems are included in the syllabus for examination when the system itself has been discredited and is not in use, the only answer, given by the examiner himself at ACCA Teachers' Meetings, is that there are key factors, such as gains or losses arising on the holding of monetary items, that are useful in interpreting accounts and that it is useful to be aware of alternative accounting systems and to be able to compare the strengths of one with another.

SSAP 17 and 18 are looked at in Chapter 9. They deal, given periodic reporting, with the impact of post balance sheet events and contingencies, and whether or not we should adjust for these items at the balance sheet date. In the context of events after the balance sheet date we should also be aware of the impact of what are referred to as window-dressing transactions.

Chapter 9 is mainly concerned, however, with accounting for the substance of transactions and the defining of and search for a solution for the problems of off balance sheet finance. The ASB has, following the ASC's ED 42 and ED 49, issued FRED 4, which looks at the impact of transactions including leases, quasi subsidiaries, sale and repurchase of assets, factoring and loan transfers, in the context of usefully reporting the substance or commercial viability underlying such transactions. It was the corporate confidence of the 1980s boom in the UK, together with the willingness of banks to lend and companies to borrow during this boom, that led to the growth of innovative accounting practices, such as off balance sheet financing, and the development of hybrid financial instruments designed solely to avoid an increase in reported company gearing. Dearing has stated (Dearing, 1991) that the strains of recession have given rise to attempts to show a company's results in as positive a light as possible and it is because of this that there is a need for stronger Standards. FRED 3 on accounting for capital instruments and FRED 4 on the substance of transactions are mere steps down that road. FRS 4 and FRS 5 have now been issued and are dealt with in Chapter 9. To achieve meaningful accounting standards the problems that need to be overcome are:

▶ the lack of a coherent body of thought on which individual standards can be based
  – the answer lies in the development of a Statement of Principles

► standards, such as those of the ASC, that rely too much on prescription as opposed to being clear statements of principles are vulnerable to innovations not anticipated when they were formulated – for example, classifying finance leases in accordance with the present value (PV) test of SSAP 21

► primary statements handed down from the 1948 Act no longer reflect current needs and add to the reliance placed on the notes to the accounts making accounts accessible only to experts – thus the need for a radical change such as that now brought about by FRS 3

► the pain of change that is strongly resisted by those who are disadvantaged by it.

SSAP 19 deals with investment properties and is examined in Chapter 4. It explains why such properties should be treated differently from other fixed assets – that is why investment properties should be accounted for by way of annual valuations without depreciation. ED 55 included some interesting proposals for recognition of gains and losses arising. FRED 9 amends SSAP 19 in respect of some deficits on investment properties.

SSAP 20 an overseas transactions is considered in Chapter 22 and covers the accounting for exchange differences in both the accounts of an individual company and a group. In the former there is a need for rules as to where in the accounts such differences should be recognised, whereas the method adopted for translation will have a fundamental bearing on the latter. The collapse of companies such as Polly Peck International (in the early 1990s) has brought into focus the treatment of foreign exchange losses and raises the question of how best to account for losses on overseas assets caused by the depreciation of a currency in an inflationary environment. In such circumstances:

► the group's reported profit may be overstated

► this will be so if there is no adjustment for the results of foreign subsidiaries in such an environment for the effects of inflation *before* translation into sterling

► translation losses would be dealt with in reserves rather than the profit and loss account.

► FRS 3 reporting would enable a better appreciation of the effects of such exchange differences.

SSAP 21 on leasing is considered in Chapter 10. The main impact of this Standard was the introduction of the requirement for lessees to capitalise finance leases, a finance lease being based on the 90% PV rule or quantitative test of SSAP 21. The ASB is now thinking, following IAS 17, of introducing qualitative tests for lease classification to eliminate the problem that can and has arisen under SSAP 21 of a lease falling to be classified as an operating lease by one party but as a finance lease by the other. Such qualitative tests could include questions such as:

► Is ownership transferred by the end of the lease term?

► Does the lease contain a bargain purchase option?

► Is the lease term for the major part of the asset's useful life?

► Is the PV of the minimum lease payments greater than or substantially equal to the asset's fair value?

The reason for this thinking is because there are schemes available where what should be reported as debt will not be included in the balance sheet of a lessee company. This can be achieved by a strict application of the 90% PV test of the standard – see Chapter 9. Given the artificiality of such schemes the ASB is likely to alter the requirements of SSAP 21 in this regard.

SSAP 22 on goodwill is examined in Chapters 5 and 20. The ASC issued a Standard, revised the Standard and then proposed, in ED 47, the re-revision of the Standard. Standardising the accounting treatment of goodwill is not on the list of the successes of the ASC. Its Standard permitted optional treatments for purchased goodwill, did not deal with goodwill when sold and did not address the very practical problems, in acquisition accounting, of:

▶ the use of merger relief in conjunction with the acquisition method of consolidation
▶ provisioning in a new subsidiary
▶ deferred consideration.

A discussion of the issues raised by these problems can be found in Chapter 20.

In its accounting standard on goodwill the ASC did not specifically deal with other intangibles such as brand names. The question of the distinction between internally created and purchased brands, the capitalisation of brands, and the amortisation of brands if capitalised, were dealt with in ED 52, but the proposals have not resulted in uniform accounting practice. This remains an area that does require urgent solution if the credibility of standard setting is to be sustained. Brand valuation was a big issue in takeovers (see Chapter 27) in the 1980s. The ASB has begun its development of Standards to deal with the problems of mergers, acquisition and goodwill and its proposals to date, in mid-1994, include proposals as to goodwill and other intangibles (see Chapter 20).

SSAP 23 on accounting for acquisitions and mergers is dealt with in Chapters 19 and 20. Merger and acquisition accounting have quite different effects on a group's balance sheet and profit and loss account. SSAP 23 permits choice and there has been criticism of the ease with which companies can adopt the treatment that results in the most favourable position. FRED 6, which is looked at in Chapter 20, seeks to remedy this situation.

SSAP 24 on pension costs is covered in Chapter 8. The Standard as is has attracted comment, given the continually changing nature of pensions and the existence of material surpluses in many pension schemes. Criticism has been directed at the Standard for the number of options and interpretations that it permits and the ASB is researching into implementation problems associated with the standard.

SSAP 25 deals with segmental reporting and is covered in Chapter 23. The rules of the Stock Exchange require segment reports of a sort for listed companies and the Standard is on expansion of information disclosed regarding turnover, results and net assets from geographical areas of operation and by class of business.

Much has been achieved in the standard-setting process, because there has been much *to* criticise. The source of all criticism of the standards set by the ASC is that they were developed in the absence of a conceptual framework and therefore lack coherence. Before we go on to look at the conceptual framework that is now being developed by the ASB, we will look at the different tiers of the current standard-setting process and comment on that most important, overriding requirement to give a true and fair view.

The functions of the bodies involved in the standard-setting process

Financial Reporting Council
This is the overarching and facilitating body through which appointments to the operational bodies are made and financial support to them is channelled. The role of the Council is to:

▶ promote good financial reporting, to make public its view on reporting standards and to make representations to government on current legislation and the development of legislation

▶ provide guidance to the ASB on work programmes and on broad policy matters

▶ verify that arrangements are conducted with efficiency and economy and that they are adequately funded.

Accounting Standards Board

The ASB took over from the former ASC the responsibility for making, amending and withdrawing accounting standards. The Board is independent, acts on its own authority and needs no external approval for its actions. The Board has formed two committees to assist in its work:

▶ *Urgent Issues Task Force* The main role of the UITF is to assist the ASB in areas where an accounting standard or Companies Act provision exists but where unsatisfactory or conflicting interpretations have developed or seem likely to develop. In such circumstances the task force will endeavour to reach a consensus on the desirable accounting treatment for the matter in question, for example:

– how to account for supplemental interest (prior to FRED 3)
– how to account for reorganisation and reconstruction costs (prior to FRS 3)
– how to account for post-retirement benefits other than pensions.

Where a consensus is achieved the intention is that it should be considered to be part of the corpus of practices forming the basis for what determines a true and fair view and the expectation is that companies will conform to it.

A foreword to UITF Abstracts was issued by the ASB in February 1994. It deals with the authority, scope and application of Abstracts which are expected to be observed by members of CCAB bodies. Any significant departures should be adequately disclosed and explained in the financial statements. Auditors are not expected to refer in their report to departures with which they concur provided adequate disclosure has been made in the financial statements. Further, UITF Abstracts may be taken into consideration by the Financial Review Reporting Panel in deciding whether financial statements call for review.

▶ *Public Sector Liaison Committee* The committee's task is to apprise the ASB of any points that they consider might be helpful in the development of their thinking, with the aim of minimising differences between private and public sector practices while recognising that final decisions on public sector accounting are taken by the government. The committee advises the Board on any proposed public sector SORPs.

Financial Reporting Review Panel (FRRP)

The panel was created in 1990 following the introduction into company legislation of provisions for the compulsory revision of defective accounts. The panel is authorised by the Secretary of State for Trade and Industry to examine departures from the accounting requirements of the 1985 Act and, if necessary, to seek an order from the court to remedy them.

The Panel's main focus will be on material departures from accounting standards where this results in the accounts in question not giving a true and fair view as required by law (see below). If a company's accounts are defective, the panel will endeavour to secure revision by voluntary means but can apply to the court for an order compelling revision. For example, as reported in *Accountancy* (November 1992, p. 10).

> After taking independent legal and accounting advice the Trafalgar directors refused to accept the Panel's view on two key issues – transfer of assets and the treatment of ACT – but in the face of a threat of legal action the Panel announced that 'the directors have undertaken to make the appropriate changes and adjustments in the 1992 accounts to meet the Panel's concerns.

Trafalgar's original treatment of transfers of assets from current to fixed assets was in part the reason for the issue of UITF 5, which rules against avoiding charging the profit and loss account with write-downs to net realisable value arising on unsold trading assets by revaluing them and transferring them to fixed assets.

Brian Singleton Greene, writing in the December 1992 issue of *Accountancy* (p. 117) states that the panel seems to have concluded in respect of Trafalgar not that it breached any of the detailed requirements of the Act or Accounting Standards, but that it failed to give a true and fair view. As to what gives a true and fair view (see below) is a question that is notoriously subjective: 'If the case had gone to court, it's anyone's guess what would have happened.' We are still waiting for the panel to find, in David Tweedie's words, 'a company to hang'.

FRRP pronouncements are examinable and, in addition to the Trafalgar example above, the FRRP has examined the accounts of a number of companies. A list of the cases on which it has issued comments is included on pages 42 and 43 of the August 1993 Students' Newsletter to which you should, particularly in relation to current accounting and auditing issues, refer.

The underpinning of the standard-setting bodies by the legislative provisions introduced by the 1989 Act

Accounting Standards are given statutory recognition and the ASB is empowered to make, amend or withdraw them on its own authority. Large companies are required by law to state in their accounts whether or not they have followed applicable Accounting Standards and give the reasons for any departures from them. The review panel is authorised to apply to the court for a revision of a company's accounts and directors may have to bear the costs of legal proceedings and accounts revision. Accordingly, director's may revise their company's accounts if it appears to them that the accounts did not comply with the requirements of the Companies Act.

The legal status of accounting standards

The ASB issued a foreword to Accounting Standards in June 1993. The foreword states that FRSs are based on the Statement of Principles currently in issue. These deal with the concepts underlying the information presented in accounts. The objective of the Statement is to provide a framework for the consistent and logical formulation of individual Accounting Standards.

Mary Arden, QC, in a legal opinion published with the foreword concluded that the courts are more likely than ever to rule that compliance with Accounting Standards is necessary to meet the true and fair requirement. When Miss Arden produced a joint opinion with Leonard Hoffman, then QC now Lord Justice, in 1983 on the relationship between Accounting Standards and the legal requirement to show a true and fair view, their joint opinion was that 'courts will treat compliance with accepted accounting principles as prima facie evidence that the accounts are true and fair', but they added that 'if there remains a strong body of professional opinion which consistently opts out of applying an SSAP, the prima facie assumption is weakened'. In her latest opinion Arden considered the changes in the Companies Act in respect to Standards as outlined above which, in her view, strengthens the status of Accounting Standards. Thus the granting of statutory recognition to the existence of Standards and the introduction of the procedure whereby the Review Panel can ask the courts to determine whether accounts comply with the true and fair requirement increases the likelihood that the courts, in general, will hold that compliance with Accounting Standards is necessary to meet the true and fair requirement. Further, the improved standard-setting process and the fact that the standard-setting body represents the views of a broad spectrum of opinion and not just those of the accounting profession must enhance the status of Standards, as will the ASB's practice of consultation and investigation in producing standards. Arden (1993), who has since become a judge (The Honourable Mrs Justice Arden) is of the view that the old assumption that non-acceptance of a Standard would have led a court to conclude that compliance is not necessary to give a true and fair view is no longer likely to be the case. The immediate reaction to the legal opinion is that it gives the ASB the go-ahead to issue and enforce controversial Accounting Standards where there is no universal consensus. David Tweedie, for example, was reported in the July 1993 *Accountancy* (p. 26) as being delighted with the opinion as it effectively means that on a controversial issue such as goodwill, where 'whatever we do, we upset two-thirds of the populace', the ASB can now proceed so long as it deals fairly with all points made to it. The accounting technical partner at Touche Ross, Ken Wild, agreed (*Accountancy*, July 1993, p. 26) that the new Arden opinion is 'a very considerable change', and something to draw to the attention of a recalcitrant client that refused to comply with a Standard.

Arden (1993) also warns that courts are likely to treat UITF Abstracts as of 'considerable standing', even though they are not envisaged by the Companies Act. This is even though, as indicated in the foreword to UITF Abstracts also issued in June 1993, nothing in UITF Abstracts is to be construed as amending or overriding the Accounting Standards or other statements issued by the ASB. The spirit and reasoning of individual UITF Abstracts are based on the ASB's Statement of Principles for Financial Reporting. These are dealt with after we look briefly at the international dimension, below.

The significance of European Community Directives and of the IASC

Members of the EC are committed to the harmonisation of company law throughout the Community. The IASC works generally for the improvement and harmonisation of regulations, Accounting Standards and procedures relating to the presentation of financial statements. Chapter 2 of this textbook deals with the issues of international comparisons and the aim of international harmonisation and you should look to that chapter for the international dimension as far as its significance is concerned in assessing the overall effectiveness of the UK regulatory framework of accounting. The 1993 foreword to Accounting Standards referred to above also states that FRSs are formulated with due regard to international developments and that the Board supports the IASC in its aim to harmonise international financial reporting.

The development of a conceptual framework

The point has been made repeatedly so far in this chapter that the lack of a conceptual framework was the signal factor affecting the effectiveness of the standard-setting process in the UK regulatory framework of accounting, and repeated reference has been made to the ASB's Statement of Principles in this regard. The ASB is undertaking the ambitious task of attempting to create a theoretical framework that it can use to guide the process of setting Accounting Standards. As at the time of writing (mid-1993) the Statement is not complete we will here first briefly review, as a reminder, the development of a conceptual framework, and then briefly look at the content of the Statements of Principles that have been developed to date.

A brief historical background

A conceptual framework for financial reporting is a theory of accounting against which the practical problems of accounting can be objectively tested. The ASC, as already noted, sought to resolve practical problems of accounting and reporting without such an accepted theoretical frame of reference with the result that its accounting standards were issued on a haphazard basis adopting what was termed a fire-fighting approach. As a result there are inconsistencies in UK Accounting Standards, given conflicts between matching and prudence and substance and form.

FINANCIAL REPORTING ENVIRONMENT

The US experience

The Accounting Principles Board was formed in 1959. In 1970 it approved Statement No. 4 – Basic Concepts and Accounting Principles Underlying Financial Statements of Business Enterprises. In 1971 two study groups were formed, resulting in the establishment of the Financial Accounting Statements Board (FASB) in 1973 and the Trueblood Report in 1973, which developed 12 objectives of Financial Statements, and seven qualitative characteristics, which information contained in Financial Statements should possess. The FASB has so far issued six concepts statements (Statements of Financial Accounting Concepts – SFACs) as follows:

SFAC 1   Objectives of financial reporting by business enterprises
SFAC 2   Qualitative characteristics of accounting information
SFAC 3   Elements of financial statements
SFAC 4   Objectives of financial statements of business enterprises
SFAC 5   Recognition and measurement in financial statements of business enterprises
SFAC 6   Elements of financial statements, replacing SFAC 3.

The UK experience

Although SSAP2, referred to above, does not set out to provide a conceptual framework, it does cover some of the issues involved as it seeks to improve user-understanding by seeking to promote improvement in the quality of information disclosed.

The Corporate Report, issued in 1975 was the first real attempt by standard setters in the UK to develop a conceptual framework. Its publication coincided with that of the Sandilands Report, which established the point that accounts presented on the historical cost basis alone could not meet the information needs of the different user-groups identified in The Corporate Report. You may remember from your previous studies 'continuously contemporary accounting' (Co.Co.A) and the merits put forward for cash flow accounting. In 1981, as a result of written submissions received in response to its consultative document, 'Setting accounting standards' the ASC commissioned Professor Robert Macre to form preliminary conclusions as to the possibilities of developing an agreed conceptual framework for setting Accounting Standards. He published his report in 1981, focusing on The Corporate Report and the FASB's conceptual framework project.

In Canada Professor Stamp produced a research project to provide a Canadian solution to the problem of improving the quality of corporate financial reporting standards and the Institute of Chartered Accounts of Scotland (ICAS) issued a discussion document in 1988 entitled 'Making Corporate Reports Valuable'. In 1987 the ICAEW decided to sponsor a project that resulted in the Solomons Report and in 1991 the ICAS research committee and ICAEW research board jointly published a discussion paper headed 'The future shape of financial reports'. The stage was set for the ASB's idea of a conceptual framework to underpin its Standards, that is its Statement of Principles for Financial Reporting.

The ASB's Statement of Principles

The purposes of the development of the Statement of Principles are to:

▶ assist the Board in the development of future Accounting Standards and in its review of existing Standards
▶ assist the Board by providing a basis for reducing the number of alternative accounting treatments permitted by law and Accounting Standards
▶ assist preparers of financial statements in applying Accounting Standards and in dealing with topics that do not form the subject of an Accounting Standard

- ▶ assist auditors in forming an opinion on whether financial statements conform with Accounting Standards
- ▶ assist users of financial statements in interpreting the information contained in financial statements prepared in conformity with Accounting Standards
- ▶ provide those who are interested in the work of the Board with information about its approach to the formulation of Accounting Standards.

Drafts of the six chapters that have been published are discussed below.

Chapter 1 – The objective of financial statements

This chapter confirms the need for financial statements to provide information to a wide range of users. The main financial statements should give information on financial position (balance sheet), financial performance (profit and loss account – see FRS 3 in Chapter 11) and financial adaptability (cash flow statements – see Chapter 12). These statements should provide information to assist external users in economic decision making but the chapter also confirms the need for financial statements to continue to fulfil a stewardship function.

Economic decisions should be based on assessments of future cash flows. Such assessments require the following financial statements:

- ▶ Balance sheets:
  - ▶ Shows the resources available to generate future cash flows.
  - ▶ Allows an assessment of management of resources in the past.
  - ▶ Indicates where future cash flows will be distributed, (for example, interest, dividends).
  - ▶ Shows liquidity (short-term cash) position.
  - ▶ Shows solvency (long-term cash) position.

- ▶ Profit and loss account:
  - ▶ Allows assessment of potential changes in resources.
  - ▶ Permits assessment of potential effective use of resources.
  - ▶ Shows potential to generate cash flows.

- ▶ Cash flow statement:
  - ▶ Allows an assessment of the ability of the enterprise to generate and use cash flows (see FRS 1 in Chapter 12).

The financial report should also include notes and supplementary statements that contain relevant additional information on the risks and uncertainties of the reporting enterprise (see FRS 3 in Chapter 11).

Compared with SFAC 1 of the FASB's conceptual framework this chapter is more specific on the type of statement required but the overall objective re information to assess future cash flows is the same. The IASC framework considers the balance sheet and profit and loss account in the same manner but discusses changes in financial position rather than cash flow statements, and does not discuss future cash flows specifically although the framework does emphasise the need to consider economic decisions of a wide range of users.

Chapter 2 – Qualitative characteristics

The complex interrelationship of the characteristics can clearly be seen from Figure 1.1, which you will have seen before in Paper 10 but is reproduced again in this textbook for completeness. These qualitative characteristics are considered by the ASB to be those that make financial statements useful to users. They should ensure understanding by a diligent user.

Primary characteristics

▶ Relevance:

  – Useful to the formulation of predictions.
  – Useful for the assessment of past predictions.
  – Shows all the suitable aspects of a transaction.

▶ Reliability:

  – Free from material error and bias.
    Valid description, that is, it represents faithfully what it purports to represent.
  – Complies with the substance over form concept.
  – Does not influence decision. Information is neutral.
  – Shows the exercise of prudence. This needs to be balanced with neutrality requirement.
  – Includes all the relevant aspects.

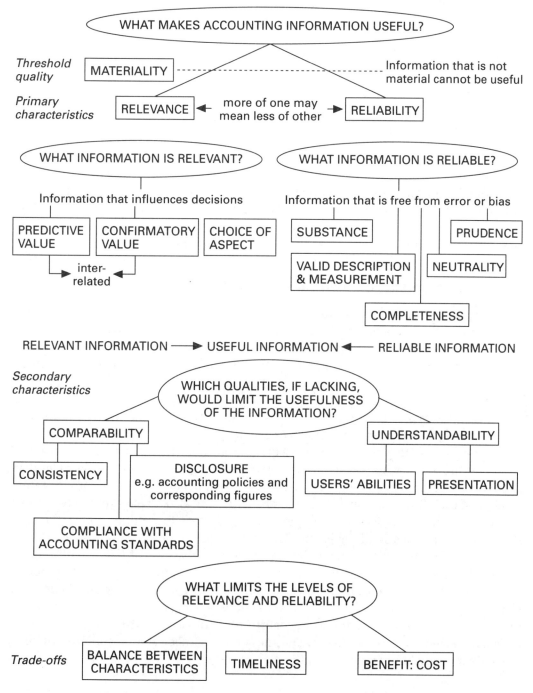

It is necessary to balance the need to be reliable with the need to be timely.

Timeliness should not override relevance, but management will need to consider the overall objective of providing useful information to decision makers. It may therefore be necessary to report at a time when reliability is impaired.

Secondary characteristics

Without these characteristics the financial statements will be of limited use.

▶ Comparability:

- Should be possible to compare financial statements of the same enterprise over time.
- Should be able to compare the reporting enterprise with other similar enterprises.
- Need disclosure of information on accounting policies adopted.
- Should not impede relevance and reliability by unnecessary emphasis on uniformity.

▶ Understandability:

- Should be readily understood by a diligent user.
- Should not eliminate the need to account for, and report on, complex technical issues.

There is also the need to consider the threshold quality of materiality. If any information does not meet the concept of materiality it should not be considered any further. Any item is considered to be material if its omission or misstatement could influence the economic decisions of users taken on the basis of the financial statements.

SFAC 2 of the FASB conceptual framework is similar to Chapter 2, but it does not consider the possible trade-offs between the characteristics as does the ASB statement. The ISAC framework has all the above categorised as principal characteristics, but it does recognise the need for compromise.

Chapter 3 – Elements of financial statements

This chapter sets out the definitions of seven elements of financial statements. These elements and their interaction form the basis on which financial statements present relevant information in a structured manner. Each element is fully discussed in the chapter; the following notes include the definitions and a summary of the discussion.

Assets

Definition: Assets are rights or other access to future economic benefits controlled by an entity as a result of past transactions or events.

The asset is the 'right or other access' to an item rather than the item itself. Examples are licences to partake in an activity and rights to use a factory. The item should provide future economic benefits, which will usually be in the form of future receipts of cash flows, although economic benefits may also be only indirectly related to the generation of cash – for example, use of a factory to produce goods, the cash flows relating to the sale of the goods. This cash flow should be within the control of the reporting entity. This includes the ability to restrict access of the benefit to other parties. The recognition of an asset is restricted to the position where the transaction or event resulting in the 'right' to the economic benefit has passed. An example is an order for goods being placed and the right to delivery being obtained. Legal ownership of an item is not essential for its recognition as an asset, but the right to future economic benefits is a requirement, and these benefits need not be certain providing there is some possibility of access to them.

Liabilities

Definition: Liabilities are an entity's obligation to transfer economic benefits as a result of past transactions or events.

A liability should be recognised only when the reporting entity is obliged to give up economic benefits, but this obligation need not be a legally enforceable one. The outflow of economic benefits can be in cash (or any other kind of property), or the provision of a labour service, or by refraining from an otherwise profitable activity. The obligation can only arise from an event or transaction that has passed. An example is placing a legally enforceable order for goods.

Assets and liabilities can be considered to be mirror images of each other and are in many ways complementary. Assets and liabilities should normally be reported gross and can be netted off only under special circumstances, for example, when the reporting entity has the ability to insist on settlement by paying a net amount.

Equity

Definition: Equity is the ownership interest in the entity; it is the residual amount found by deducting all liabilities of the entity from all of the entity's assets.

The amount of equity is dependent on the measurement of assets and liabilities. It is usually disclosed in a manner that shows the amount contributed by the owners and the changes in net assets resulting from trading and other activities.

Gains

Definition: Gains are increases in equity, other than those relating to contributions from owners.

Losses

Definition: Losses are decrease in equity, other than those relating to distributions to owners.

Financial statements distinguish changes in equity resulting from transactions with owners from other changes in equity. The latter changes are referred to as gains and losses.

As a result of the articulation of the financial statements (see Chapter 4), changes in wealth of an entity (that is, in net assets) depicted in the balance sheet are also reflected in its performance (that is, net gains in the period). Gains and losses may be of a revenue nature, for example sales (revenue gain), expenses (revenue loss). Such gains and losses are usually reported gross and all gains and losses should be presented separately. Adjustments to the gains and losses should be made to reflect the capital maintenance concept employed.

Contributions from owners

Definitions: Contributions from owners are increases in equity resulting from investments made by owners in their capacity as owners.

Such contributions are usually in the form of cash (although other property transfers can be made) and the consideration given by the reporting entity is the granting of equity rights in the entity.

Distributions to owners

Definition: Distributions to owners are decreases in equity resulting from transfers made to owners in their capacity as owners.

This definition includes payments of dividend and purchase of own shares but does not include a bonus issue of shares.

This chapter is similar to SFAC 3 in the FASB conceptual framework but the American statement does give further definitions of comprehensive income and revenues and expenses. The IASC framework also covers income and expenses but does not include definitions of gains and losses.

Chapter 4 – The recognition of items in financial statements

Recognition is the process of incorporating an item into the primary financial statements. It involves depiction of the item in words and in monetary amount and the inclusion of that amount in the statement totals.

General recognition criteria

An item should be recognised in financial statements if:

▶ it meets the definition of an element of financial statements; *and*
▶ there is sufficient evidence that the changes in assets and liabilities inherent in the item have occurred (including, where appropriate, evidence that a future inflow or outflow of benefit will occur); *and*
▶ it can be measured at monetary amount with sufficient reliability.

Where an item currently recognised ceases to meet any of these criteria it should be derecognised.

The recognition process

Recognition is triggered where a past event (before the balance sheet date) indicates that there has been a measurable change in the assets or liabilities of the entity. These past events can be:

▶ transactions – transfers of assets or liabilities to/from an external party.
▶ contracts – this is an enforceable, but as yet unperformed, promise given to or by an external party to transfer assets and/or liabilities in the future.
▶ other events – changes in assets and liabilities other than transactions and contracts.

To the extent a past event has resulted in access to future economic benefits (or obligations to transfer economic benefits) assets (or liabilities) are recognised; to the extent that it has resulted in previously recognised access to future economic benefits (or obligations to transfer economic benefits) being transferred or ceasing to exist, assets (or liabilities) are derecognised; and to the extent that it has resulted in a flow of economic benefits in the current period, a gain or loss is recognised (unless the flow relates to a transaction with owners, in which case a contribution from owners or distribution to owners is recognised). Recognised items are measured at the amount inherent in the transaction (that is, the amount of assets and liabilities given or received as consideration) and previously recognised items disposed of at other than carrying value will result in a gain or loss.

Effect of uncertainty

The environment in which entities operate is inherently uncertain and for many past events there is either a lack of certainty that there has been a change in the entity's assets or liabilities, or a lack of certainty as to the monetary amount of the change. It is this lack of certainty that gives rise to recognition problems.

Uncertainty is countered by evidence – the more evidence there is about an item and the better the quality of that evidence, the less uncertainty there will be over its existence, nature and measurement, and the more reliable the item will be. The exercise of prudence means that the evidence for the recognition of assets and gains should be more persuasive than that relating to liabilities and losses.

Evidence is required of both changes in assets/liabilities and monetary amount for recognition in the financial statements.

The IASC framework does not directly deal with recognition criteria and the FASB conceptual framework is more closely related to that framework's concept of comprehensive income.

Chapter 5 – The measurement of items in financial statements

This chapter provides a comprehensive overview of the many issues relevant to the measurement of assets and liabilities recognised in the financial statements and the significance of the associated gains and losses. It begins by contrasting the use of historical cost in financial reporting with systems based on current values. It notes that current values are generally more relevant (although, arguably, more subjective) than historical costs. It draws attention to the existence of several different bases on which current values may be assessed and explains how the concept of 'value to the business' provides a rationale for choosing the basis appropriate to particular circumstances. Use of the value to the business principle results in assets being stated at the lower of replacement cost and the amount that they will yield to the business through use or disposal. A section on the valuation of liabilities addresses inter alia the different implications of a change in value reflecting a general movement in interest rates and one caused by a change in the borrower's credit rating.

The chapter contains a discussion of the concepts of capital maintenance, which determine the amount and significance of both the 'total gains and losses' and the narrower 'profit and loss' that are recognised. A comparison is made between nominal money capital maintenance, current purchasing power capital maintenance, and physical capital maintenance, each of which is relevant only where an appropriate valuation system is used. The chapter concludes that all these concepts have potential user relevance, and points out that it is possible to combine different concepts of capital maintenance within a single financial statement using a 'real terms' system. (See Chapter 14.)

Chapter 6 – Presentation of financial information

This chapter is based on the objective of providing information to external users and considers the need to disclose financial information in the balance sheet, the profit and loss account, the statement of total recognised gains and losses (see FRS 3 in Chapter 11) and the cash flow statement. Presentation requires consideration of:

► aggregation – the need to balance the requirement to report condensed details with the benefit of disclosing more detailed information
► classification – items should be grouped with reference to their nature or function, and characteristics such as continuity or recurrence, stability, risk and reliability are highlighted
► structure – presentation should be in individual statements of financial performance, financial position and cash flows
► articulation – the financial statements should interrelate and be consistent thus collective, enabling analysis and interpretation
► accounting policies – to enable a suitable understanding of the financial statements it is necessary to disclose the accounting policies adopted, any changes in policy and the effect of such changes
► notes to the statements – these should be provided to amplify, explain or provide an alternative view of items included in the primary statements or provide information on items not included
► supplementary information – information positioned outside the primary statements may be used to provide a different perspective, or information useful to some users but not all.

This chapter also considers the importance of financial adaptability; the ability of the enterprise to take effective action to alter the amounts and timing of cash flows so that it can respond to unexpected needs or opportunities. As can be seen from the review of Chapter 1 of the Principles, all the primary financial statements provide information that is useful in assessing financial adaptability.

Lastly, highlights and summary indicators – such details are considered to be useful but they should avoid concentrating on the 'bottom line' or on eps, and, for complex businesses, cannot be expected adequately to describe an enterprise's financial performance, financial position and financial adaptability.

The Audit dimension

Any examination of the financial reporting environment must include an examination of the audit dimension. You will be familiar with auditing practice from your previous studies of both Paper 6 and Paper 10. Here in Module F of the Professional stage you are more concerned with the relevance of such practice to improving the financial reporting environment and with areas that are likely to pose particular problems for auditors such as off balance sheet finance dealt with in Chapter 9. Thus, auditors will be concerned with the principles of recognition of items dealt with previously in this chapter and with disclosure to support their true and fair opinion.

As with Accounting Standards the Statements of Auditing Standards (SAS) are currently being issued by the Auditing Practices Board as part of their revision of Auditing Standards and Guidelines; auditors have to operate in a rapidly changing and constantly expanding regulatory environment. Much of what you will have studied of previous Papers has already changed or is about to change. Thus, new SASs have already been issued in draft form.

Exposure drafts have been issued on:

▶ objective and general principles governing an audit of financial statements
▶ overall review of financial statements
▶ the work of internal audit
▶ the relationship between principal auditors and other auditors (relevant to groups)
▶ using the work of an expert (relevant to, for example, pension costs and their measurement)

You will have to keep in constant contact with the accountancy press to keep pace with these changes. See Chapter 3 for a description of the present position as to the ASB programme.

Summary

This chapter looks at the significance of the contributions made to UK accounting regulation from different sources

▶ the Companies Act
▶ the Stock Exchange
▶ the ASC and the ASB
▶ the EC and the IASC

and the effectiveness of the UK regulatory framework. In this context we also looked at various Accounting Standards and problems arising in their implementation and some solutions as proposed by Discussion Papers and Exposure Drafts of the ASB. This section of the chapter also serves as a useful introduction to the contents of the rest of the textbook and the problems you will face in understanding the financial reporting environment in the UK.

The chapter also looks at the interaction between Accounting Standards and company law and includes a section on the legal status of Accounting Standards and the current legal opinion, which is included in the foreword to Accounting Standards. Note the fundamental change in this legal opinion compared with that given in 1983 in respect of a true and fair view.

The role of the three-tier system of the standard-setting bodies was described and the chapter ended with a discussion as to the development of a conceptual framework in the UK – the ASB's Statement of Principles. So far the impact is to focus attention on the balance sheet – hence the importance of principles of valuation – and to measure performance by the total movement in equity.

Suggested reading

Financial Reporting 1992-93 Survey of UK Reporting Practice (Tonkin and Skerratt 1993)

This publication has a useful chapter on the impact of the ASB.

The Financial Reporting Council presents an annual review of the state of financial reporting – the most recent review will keep you up to date on developments.

UK GAAP (Ernst & Young, 1992).

Chapter 2 provides comprehensive coverage of the development of a conceptual framework and the ASB's Statement of Principles.

Self test questions

1   Define under the discussion draft, Statement of Principles, Chapter 3 – The elements of financial statements:

a)   assets
b)   liabilities
c)   equity.

2   State the general recognition criteria from the discussion draft, Statement of Principles, Chapter 4 – The recognition of items in financial statements.

3   Draw a simple diagram to illustrate the 'value to the business'.

4   Draw a simple diagram to illustrate the principle of the 'relief value of a liability'.

5   Outline the role of the Urgent Issues Task Force.

Exam style question

1   John Poor has been discussing with the directors of Fencing Ltd the steps taken by accountants to ensure that financial statements are useful. He mentioned that in the view of the accounting profession the usefulness of the information in the financial statements is determined primarily by two qualitative characteristics known as relevance and reliability.

Required
Explain to the directors the meaning of relevance and reliability.

*Adapted from ACCA Level 3
AFA, question 3(c), June 1992*

All answers on pages 625–626

International Issues – Comparisons and Harmonisation

Chapter 1 dealt with the impact of the UK regulatory framework on the financial reporting environment. UK companies are subject to Parliament, the ASB, Industry requirements, the Council of the Stock Exchange, the EC and the IASC. They are regulated to a greater or lesser extent by the Companies Acts, SSAPs and FRSs, SORPs, Stock Exchange regulations, EC directives and IASs. These regulations have, variously, statutory or non-statutory backing and may be either mandatory or non-mandatory. This chapter deals specifically with international issues, comparisons and harmonisations. Notes on the ACCA Teachers' Meetings held in March 1993 on the Association's new examination scheme state that:

> the intention is not for students to address international accounting standards but to make a comparison of each international accounting standard with the UK. Students will be expected to look at harmonisation and activities in relation to the IASC. A question could be set providing, for example, a set of accounts from America and asking students how they would appear in the UK. Students would not be expected to know any of the foreign presentations but could be provided with the foreign presentation and required to discuss the differences between that and the UK methods.

In the question and answer session at this meeting it was stated that a single question would not be set on this topic, but it could feature as a part of a question where, for example, students could be required to express an opinion in a case where the EC lead was not followed and to comment on the benefits of this.

The development of accounting practice in different countries

Several factors influence the development of accounting practice in any one country. Chapter 1 dealt with some of these influences in the context of the UK. This chapter looks at the factors that have affected the development of accounting practice worldwide. Some of these factors have a stronger influence in one country than in another, and will contribute to the differences existing between national accounting practices.

Factors leading to differences in national accounting practices

In 1968 Mueller identified a list of circumstances that resulted in accounting diversity, as follows:

- ▶ relative stability of the currency unit
- ▶ degree of legislative business interference
- ▶ nature of business ownership
- ▶ level of sophistication of business management
- ▶ differences in size and complexity of business firms
- ▶ speed of business innovation

- ▶ presence of specific accounting legislation
- ▶ stage of economic development
- ▶ type of economy involved
- ▶ growing pattern of an economy
- ▶ status of professional education and organisation
- ▶ general level of education.

To elaborate on some of the points in the list above let us consider, in turn, the effects of the degree of statutory regulation, tax assessment regulations, providers of finance and types of organisation, professional accountancy bodies and other environmental factors.

The degree of statutory regulation

In the UK, company legislation is written in general terms and is interpreted on a case-by-case basis. This 'common law' system also applies in other countries with strong historical ties to the UK. In such a commercial legal environment, where the emphasis has been on reporting to shareholders, it has been possible for the accounting profession to develop a strong influence on national accounting practice through the issue of statements of standard accounting practice or, as they are now referred to, financial reporting standards.

Elsewhere, company legislation is enshrined in what is termed 'codified law', where the legislation contains detailed rules often linked to ideas of justice and morality. In such an environment it is the law itself that establishes detailed rules for financial accounting and reporting; creditor protection is a dominant feature and the government tends to exercise a dominant influence. Such systems prevail in much of Europe, principally in Germany and France following on from the tradition of Frederick of Prussia and Napoleon.

The EC tendency has been to move towards a codified system of financial reporting but this has not yet occurred in practice. In the drafting of the 4th EC Directive the UK extolled the virtues of 'true and fair' while the essential thrust of the rest of the European view was that all accounts should be published in a common format. The UK insisted on alternative valuation rules, while Germany insisted on a reconciliation back to historical cost. As for America, see later in this chapter.

Tax regulations

Different countries have different fiscal rules, which differently affect accounting measurements. Thus, in the UK, The Netherlands and Denmark tax assessment and financial reporting – fiscal rules as opposed to accounting rules – are not closely linked and financial accounting practice can develop without the need to follow tax-based rules to obtain a tax advantage. By way of contrast, Sweden, Norway and Germany are countries where accounting practice is influenced by tax rules in that, for example, tax allowances can be claimed only if the relevant item is treated identically for financial reporting and tax purposes. In such circumstances, where there is no difference between accounting and taxable profit there will be no need for a deferred tax provision (see Chapter 7).

A further instance of the impact that tax rules can have on accounting practice arises in the context of the revaluation of fixed assets. In France, for example, revaluation surpluses are treated as taxable income, and tax allowances for future periods are based on the revalued amount. Arguably, there is less of an incentive to revalue fixed assets.

The strong influence of tax legislation on German accounting practice is achieved through the Mabgeblichkeitsprinzip or authoritative principle, which requires tax returns to be based on the figures published in the company's financial statements. Tax law can have an indirect effect on financial reporting, particularly in the areas of depreciation and inventory valuation.

The objective of accounting in different countries is therefore affected by tax rules; should accounts provide information for shareholders and other users or is the objective to show the most advantageous position from a tax point of view?

Providers of finance and types of organisation

In the UK the tradition has been for corporate finance to be provided by either private or institutional equity investors and, as a result, financial reporting has developed to meet the needs of such investors. Further, the development of large multinational companies has resulted in the development of financial reporting for, for example, groups and foreign currency transactions. The independent audit assumes a growing importance. In other countries, where companies are smaller and the need for finance is limited there is less scope for the development of detailed accounting regulations and the need for an independent audit is itself reduced.

Sources of finance can also affect the development of financial reporting in that where, as in Germany, extensive use is made of banks in raising finance, there is less of a need for extensive financial reporting and emphasis on external disclosure as the banks have access to internal financial data. So, too, in France, where there is substantial state capital investment, the fact that the providers of finance have access to internal financial information reduces the need for and development of external reporting.

Clearly, the greater the reliance on equity finance raised in the capital markets, the more important the role of accounting standards and Stock Exchange regulations in order to protect the interests of the providers of finance. The more extensive the use of banks, the more conservative accounts tend to be in terms of strict adherence to historical cost accounting and the use of reserves. Further differences will arise in the development of accounting practice in those countries where the state plays the major role in providing finance for companies in that in these countries, such as France, Belgium and Spain, there is likely to be a national accounting plan and a reduced need for the development of a conceptual framework for accounting or, as is being developed in the UK by the ASB, a statement of principles.

Professional accountancy bodies

The degree of influence that can be exercised by the professional accountancy bodies of different countries in the development of accounting practice will vary depending on the level of government intervention in each country. The less the intervention of the state, the greater will be the influence of the accounting bodies as in the UK and The Netherlands, where there has been considerable development of accounting standards or guidelines by independent accounting bodies. In such countries there will be a need for independent auditors and this, in turn, expands the influence of the accountancy bodies in preparing a body of rules that must be complied with in order for auditors to express an opinion on accounts.

In countries where there is government intervention such as with the *Plan Comptable* in France, professional bodies will not have a direct influence, but they are likely to have an indirect influence in the creation and development of the state accounting plan.

Environmental factors

As well as the legal and economic differences, dealt with above, that give rise to differences in the development of accounting practice, there are other environmental factors to be considered:

▶ *Educational standards* These will influence the complexity and extent of external financial reporting. Whereas this is not likely to be a factor that gives rise to differences in national accounting practice in Western Europe, it is likely to be an important factor in the developing countries of Eastern Europe. There is little point in developing financial reporting practices aimed at a large number of recipients who do not have the financial background that is necessary to make use of such information.

▶ *Political factors* As reporting in general becomes more open so will financial reporting. Systems that were developed to serve the needs of the controlling ministry are becoming increasingly obsolete and it is likely that a more West European/North American style of accounting and reporting will develop.

▶ *Cultural factors* These will affect the development of accounting practice in that cultures tending towards secrecy are unlikely to adopt full disclosure-based financial reporting practices and cultures with strong nationalistic traits are unlikely to willingly accept accounting practices from overseas. Cultural differences will also result in different levels of audit regulation.

Factors leading to similarities in national accounting practices

Despite the factors leading to the differences explained above, most countries adopt similar forms of bookkeeping, and there are several factors that have given rise to similarities in national accounting practices. These are dealt with below.

EC directives

These directives have led to some harmonisation in the development of the accounting practices of the member states of the EC. The EC directives that have a direct bearing on accounting practice through the EC are the 4th, 7th and 8th Directives. The 4th and 7th Directives deal with detailed rules governing the drawing up of accounts of individual companies and groups of companies. The 8th Directive deals with the imposition of an obligation upon member states to ensure that auditors are independent, the new minimum standards for the education and training of auditors, and the conduct of audits.

Where the introduction of standardised formats was a major change in UK financial reporting, such standardisation was already a part of the national accounting systems of France and Germany. The 7th Directive introduced only minor changes in the practice of consolidation in the UK, but considerably extended national accounting requirements on group accounts in other countries. In Germany, for example, the implementation of the 7th Directive resulted in the consolidation of overseas subsidiaries for the first time.

Where the effect of bringing together different national accounting practices through the EC by means of directives is regional it is not restricted to member states of the EC. Other countries, such as Finland, are adjusting their accounting practices to bring them into line with EC requirements and the need to source finance within the EC may force some non-EC countries into compliance with EC reporting requirements.

The rationale behind the harmonisation programme is to avoid distortions in the single market by establishing common standards in the domestic company laws of member states. The concern is that, unless the harmonisation programme is progressed, member states with relatively sophisticated company laws will be at a competitive disadvantage to those with more relaxed rules. Even so, there is some fear as to the method of harmonisation of company law by directive. As Cameron (1993) points out, detailed directives to ensure harmonisation may lead to inflexible and even fossilised company laws that will not easily be amended as business practices develop.

The globalisation of capital markets

In today's business environment cross-border trading is a fact of life. Investors can trade on capital markets throughout the world; they are not restricted to trading on their own national stock exchange. Such an environment requires the development of financial reporting practices that are meaningful to investors and their advisers. A further phenomenon giving rise to a growing similarity of accounting practices between different countries is the multinational company quoted on more than one stock exchange. Such companies would prefer to have to produce one set of accounts to file with these various stock exchanges rather than the various different sets that they currently produce. Other reasons put forward as to why multinationals will attempt to advance harmonisation include:

► to eliminate awkward adjustments on consolidation
► to make the appraisal of overseas companies for takeovers, mergers and joint ventures more efficient
► to make for easier management control in that harmonisation, helps in the internal communication of accounting information
► to make it possible to transfer staff to different countries without resorting to extensive retraining programmes.

These reasons are relevant today in the context of the growing number of joint venture appraisals being undertaken with the former Eastern Bloc of socialist countries and the fact that large accounting firms and trading concerns often transfer staff to countries throughout the world.

Harmonisation following from this factor is evidenced by the fact that French consolidated accounts do not have to comply with the national accounting plan and are often in a form that reflects UK consolidation practice. Further, Dutch subsidiaries with an EC parent may use overseas accounting principles to produce its (Dutch) accounts.

International organisations

There are several organisations that affect accounting and auditing on an international scale. These organisations are of significant influence in the development of similarities in financial reporting practices between countries. Some of these organisations have an effect on global accounting, whereas others affect only specific regions. In addition to the European Commission of the European Community, other organisations with which you should be familiar in the context of international accounting harmonisation are the International Accounting Standards Committee (IASC), the International Federation of Accountants (IFAC), the Organisation for Economic Cooperation and Development (OECD), the United Nations (UN) and other regional organisations. These are looked at below.

The International Accounting Standards Committee (IASC)
The IASC came into existence in 1973 as a result of an agreement by accounting bodies in Australia, Canada, France, Germany, Japan, Mexico, The Netherlands, the UK, Ireland and the USA. Mexico has now been replaced by Denmark and the main board has been expanded to include Italy, Jordan, South Africa and Korea. There are 95 member organisations from all the major countries around the world and the IASC, with a small full-time secretariat, has published 29 international accounting standards (IASs). It coordinates with the EC, the UN and the OECD. Its objectives, as set out in its constitution, are:

► to formulate and publish in the public interest accounting standards to be observed in the presentation of financial statements and to promote their worldwide acceptance and observance, and
► to work generally for the improvement and harmonisation of regulations, accounting standards and procedures relating to the presentation of financial statements.

Its members undertake:

to support the work of the IASC by publishing in their respective countries every International Accounting Standard approved for issue by the IASC and by using their best endeavours:

(i)   to ensure that published financial statements comply with IASs in all material respects and disclose the fact of such compliance;

(ii) to persuade governments and standard-setting bodies that published financial statements should comply with IASs in all material respects;

(iii) to persuade authorities controlling securities markets and the industrial and business community that published financial statements should comply with IASs in all material respects and disclose the fact of such compliance;

(iv) to ensure that the auditors satisfy themselves that the financial statements comply with IASs in all material respects;

(v)   to foster acceptance and observance on IASs internationally.

In the UK, while several IASs are covered by equivalent SSAPs and FRSs, IASs are not directly applicable in the UK. The ACCA *Members' Handbook* states:

In the UK (and Ireland) it is *only* necessary for members to be familiar with SSAPs. IASs which have not been incorporated into SSAPs have *no* authoritative standing in the UK (and Ireland), companies are *not* required to comply with them in their financial statements and auditors are not required to note departure from them in their audit reports.

Harmonisation has not yet resulted and the IASC has been criticised in that:

▶ it is a private sector body and cannot enforce its standards
▶ it is biased towards Anglo-Saxon accounting practice
▶ it allows too many options (but see below) in seeking to be all things to all countries
▶ it has only indirect application in many countries
▶ its standards leave too much scope for interpretation
▶ not all of its members are representatives of regulating authorities
▶ an increasing number of countries (including, for example, India) have started to produce their own national standards, making the task of harmonisation more difficult.

However, some countries (for example, Kenya and Pakistan) have adopted IASs and Canada gives them positive support in that the Toronto Stock Exchange requires quoted companies to comply with IASs.

The barriers to harmonisation, some of which have been dealt with above, include nationalism, different prominent user groups in different countries, different purposes of financial reporting (tax assessment versus investment decision making) in different countries, different legal systems, different needs of developing as opposed to developed countries and cultural differences.

In 1987 the International Organisation of Securities Commissions and other Organisations (IOSCO) was formed. One of its initiatives was to assist in multinational offerings and for this purpose it needed internationally agreed accounting standards. It decided that it could not accept IASs as they stood in that there were too many choices, guidance was inadequate in many instances and there were gaps in the overall coverage of international accounting standards. The gaps were largest in the areas most important to securities regulators such as interim reporting, eps and segmentation. Between 1987 and 1993 the IASC has doubled its budget, with voluntary support from the large accounting firms and multinational companies and set out to reduce choice (see below for the IASC's comparability and improvements project) in standard. Work has also started on outstanding areas such as eps.

The International Federation of Accountants (IFAC)

The IFAC was established in 1977 and works closely with, and has the same membership as, the IASC. The IFAC actually contributes 10% of the funding of the IASC and undertakes to support the work of the IASC in the field of international accounting standard-setting. The IFAC does not operate in the area of financial accounting standard-setting but does have committees that are an important part of the campaign to harmonise global accounting and auditing practices. The IFAC has the following committees:

▶ *Education Committee* Its objective is to develop guidelines on pre-qualification training and education as well as on continuing professional education for qualified members of the profession. It has so far issued nine guidelines on these subjects.

▶ *Ethics Committee* Its objective is to develop fundamental guidelines that are essential to an accounting profession irrespective of national background or conditions, and regardless of whether the accountant is in public practice or not. Issues addressed by the 'Guideline on ethics for professional accountants' include advertising, changes of accountant, fees and commissions, tax practice and handling clients' monies.

▶ *Financial and Management Accounting Committee* Its objective is to encourage the development of financial and management accounting by creating an environment that increases the level of competence and involvement of management accountants in the community at large, thereby achieving increased recognition of their professional contribution. The statements produced by this committee are aimed at management areas such as control of projects and foreign currency exposure and risk management.

▶ *Public Sector Committee* Its objective is to develop programmes aimed at improving public sector financial management and accountability. Its work to date has mainly concentrated on producing statements that cover the applicability of international accounting standards and international auditing guidelines to public sector enterprises.

▶ *International Auditing Practices Committee* Its objective is to produce generally accepted international standards on auditing, statements on auditing and guidelines on related services. There are 29 standards, three statements and four guidelines. The standards do not override national standards, but they do attempt to set standards of auditing practice that are accepted internationally. The standards cover the basic principles of an audit as well as several specific areas such as related parties. The statements include auditing of stand-alone microcomputers and the guidelines on related services includes one on engagements to compile financial information.

Organisation for Economic Cooperation and Development (OECD)

Membership is established by the governments of all EC countries, all nordic countries, Austria, Switzerland, Turkey, USA, Canada, Australia and Japan. The Council of the OECD has established a Committee on International Investment and Multinational Enterprises. This committee has established guidelines on disclosure of information for multinational enterprises and has also established a Working Group on Accounting Standards. The working group supports efforts to increase accounting standards' comparability and publishes reports as part of an 'Accounting Standards Harmonisation Series'.

United Nations (UN)

The UN has established a Committee on Transnational Corporations which, through its Intergovernmental Working Group of Experts on International Standards of

Accounting and Reporting, serves as an international body for the improvement of the availability and comparability of information disclosed by transnational corporations. This working group reviews developments in standard setting, with particular emphasis on the needs of developing countries. For example, in its annual review, *International Accounting and Reporting Issues*, of 1989, the working party included a section under the heading 'Ways and means of improving education, research and practical training in the field of accounting and reporting in member states: The special case of Africa'. This section typifies the type of project reported on by the working group on behalf of developing countries. The reviews published by UN are a very useful source of data for a global overview of the current developments in accounting and reporting.

Other regional organisations

There are many other organisations attempting to influence accounting on a regional rather than an international scale. These organisations include:

▶ *Federation des Experts-comptables Europeens (FEE)* This is the umbrella body for the accountancy profession in Europe. Its objectives include the promotion of co-operation among the professional accountancy bodies in Europe and to represent the European accountancy profession at the international level. FEE has close links with IASC, IFAC and OECD.

▶ *African Accounting Council (AAC)* This body has stated objectives, which include the standardisation of accounting among all African countries, the development of African teaching materials and an intra-African exchange of accounting specialists and experts.

▶ *Interamerican Accounting Association (Asociacion Interamericana de Contabilidad) (AIC)* The AIC is comprised of North, Central and South American accounting bodies. The organisation holds conferences to discuss Western Hemisphere accounting problems, with particular emphasis on the problems faced in South America. Its conference papers are published, usually in Spanish.

▶ *The Confederation of Asian and Pacific Accountants (CAPA)* Papers delivered at CAPA conferences focus on the accounting problems of Pacific Rim countries. There are currently 20 countries represented by the membership of over 30 professional accounting bodies.

International standard setting

The standard-setting process in the UK was described in Chapter 1 and the setting of accounting standards was described earlier in this chapter. To get some further insight into the UK standard-setting process this part of this chapter describes the process of accounting regulation in some other countries.

The United States of America

There is little or no legislation on the form or content of published periodic financial statements. Financial reporting is controlled by the government by delegated authority to the stock exchange body, the Securities and Exchange Commission (SEC). The complicated regulating structure is illustrated in Figure 2.1.

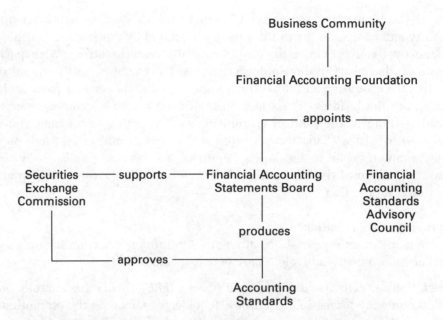

Figure 2.1 Regulating structure for financial reporting in the USA

The bodies making up the regulating structure are:

▶ *Securities and Exchange Commission (SEC)* Public sector body with delegated power to approve (or not) standards issued by the FASB. Members of the SEC are appointed by the President of the United States.
▶ *Financial Accounting Standards Board (FASB)* Technical body that issues accounting standards. *Not* dependent and not responsible to the American Institute of Certified Public Accountants (AICPA). The accounting profession (mainly the AICPA) plays only a minor role in regulating published financial statements.
▶ *Financial Accounting Foundation (FAF)* This is a board of trustees appointed by various other bodies. The main tasks of the trustees are to appoint members of the FASB and the FASAC, and to arrange funds for the FASB.
▶ *Financial Accounting Standards Advisory Council (FASAC)* This body provides the contact between the business community and the FASB.

Japan

The form and content of published financial statements are regulated by the government. This influence is exercised through legislation in the country's Commercial Code and the Securities and Exchange Law. The professional accounting body in Japan is the Japanese Institute of Certified Public Accountants (JICPA). The major role of the JICPA is the provision of professionally qualified auditors and tax advisers. The institute has only a secondary role to play in setting accounting standards and establishing accounting principles.

Both the AICPA and the JICPA are members of the IASC but they have little direct influence over their country's accounting practices. This presents problems for the IASC in its attempts to harmonise worldwide accounting practices. Contrast this situation with that of the FASB, which is a member of the IASC's consultative group, which allows it to comment at an early stage on the development of IASC projects.

Germany

It is German tradition that accounting regulation is governed by the law, with the accounting profession having a supplementary and subsidiary role. The detailed provision of accounting requirements by law has a long history, with much of the legislation being laid down in tax laws and regulations. In Germany there is a legal principle that values of profits and assets reported in financial accounts may be no higher than their counterparts allowed for tax purposes, and liabilities no lower. Financial accounting in Germany is almost totally tax based, inflexible and highly conservative. No attention is paid to the need to regulate financial accounting from a user's point of view.

The accounting profession in Germany tends to concern itself with auditing and tax matters, emphasising the application of legislative regulations rather than the development of accounting practices.

France

Accounting in France is regulated by the government using a 'National Plan' (the *Plan Comptable*). The plan originated in 1947; it was revised in 1957 and the current version is the plan that was developed after the implementation of the EC 4th Directive. The plan provides:

▶ a national uniform chart of accounts
▶ definitions and explanations of terminology
▶ details of debit/credit entries
▶ principles of accounting measurement (valuations)
▶ standard forms for financial statements (The introduction of standard formats for published accounts by the 4th Directive was new in the UK but not in France or Germany.)
▶ acceptable cost accounting methods.

The accounting profession in France has no direct influence on the content of the *Plan Comptable* but it does issue non-mandatory opinions and recommendations of accounting principles relevant to implementing the plan.

Neither France nor Germany has accounting standards as we know them in the UK.

The Netherlands

Accounting in Holland is regulated by the Civil Code, which contains the 1970 Act on Annual Accounts. The Dutch Institute of Registered Accountants has played an active role in developing recommendations on accounting (and auditing) standards to supplement the more general Civil Code.

These guidelines are issued by the Council for annual reporting, which is made up of the Dutch Institute plus representatives both of employers and of employees. These guidelines are broadly consistent with international accounting standards, and probably because of the large multinational companies in Holland, in line with UK/USA accounting practices.

Interested parties can take legal action to force a company to comply with the Act of Annual Accounts. Action is taken through the Enterprise Chamber of the Court of Justice of Amsterdam.

This brief review highlights the variety of influences on the accounting practices in different countries. The next situation describes specific cases of differences between the requirements of the IASC and US and UK GAAP.

UK GAAP and a selective comparison with the requirements of the IASC's accounting standards and with US GAAP

Certified Research Report 33 (Weetman, Adams and Gray, 1993) points out that there are over 40 UK companies that have to produce accounts under UK GAAP for home purposes and also under US GAAP where they report on Form 20-F using US GAAP. The Research Report measured profit under UK rules ranging from 34% below to 41 times higher than under US rules, while equity or net worth measured under UK rules ranged from 159% below to 150% above the value attained under US rules. The need for harmonisation was clearly stated by Hugh Collum, Chair of the UK Hundred Group of finance directors at the XIV World Congress of Accountants in 1992:

> I hardly need to explain to you why harmonisation is important. Running an Anglo-American multinational, registered in the UK and listed and reporting in the UK, the US and Japan, I live in a veritable Tower of Babel of conflicting accounting practices ... As an international business, one of our important requirements is access on the best terms and with the greatest confidence to the capital markets of the world. We currently have to present ourselves to different markets in different formats so as to comply with different requirements, and that in turn hampers our business. (Quoted in Weetman, Adams and Gray, 1993)

Tables 2.1–2.12 show these different requirements for various profit and loss account and balance sheet items.

Table 2.1 Different accounting requirements for goodwill

	IASC	US GAAP	UK GAAP
Described in	E 32	APB17	SSAP 22
Preferred treatment	Capitalise and amortise over a maximum period of 20 years	Capitalise and amortise over a maximum period of 40 years	Immediate write-off against reserves
Allowed alternative treatment	–	–	Amortise over economic useful life
Not allowed	Immediate write-off	Immediate write-off	–

Source: Certified Research Report 33 (Weetman, Adams and Gray, 1993)

Note: Accounting for goodwill is looked at in detail in Chapter 5.

Table 2.2 Different accounting requirements for deferred tax

	IASC	US GAAP	UK GAAP
Described in	E 33	FAS 109	SSAP 15, CA 1985
Preferred treatment	Liability method, full provision	Liability method, full provision	Liability method, partial provision
Allowed alternative treatment	Liability method, partial provision	–	– (Note, however, the alternative of full provision for tax recoverable on pension provisions under FRED 2.)
Not allowed	Deferral method	Deferral method, partial provision	Deferral method

Source: Certified Research Report 33 (Weetman, Adams and Gray, 1993)

Table 2.3 Different accounting requirements for extraordinary items

	IASC	US GAAP	UK GAAP
Described in	IAS 8	APB 30 and APB 16	FRS 3, CA 1985
Preferred treatment	No definition of exceptional or extraordinary items; refers only to 'unusual items'	Definitions are similar in the USA and the UK; FRS 3 in effectively abolishing extraordinary items brings the UK closer to the USA by establishing the rarity of extraordinary items.	
Allowed alternative treatment	–	–	–
Not allowed	–	–	–

Source: Certified Research Report 33 (Weetman, Adams and Gray, 1993)

Table 2.4 Different accounting requirements for valuation of property, plant and equipment

	IASC	US GAAP	UK GAAP
Described in	E 32	ARB 43 and APB 6	CA 1985 (ASB Discussion Papers)
Preferred treatment	Cost	Cost	No preferred treatment
Allowed alternative treatment	Valuation	–	Cost or valuation
Not allowed	–	Valuation	–

Source: Certified Research Report 33 (Weetman, Adams and Gray, 1993)

Table 2.5 Different accounting requirements for business combinations

	IASC	US GAAP	UK GAAP
Described in	E 32	APB 16	SSAP 23, FRS 2, CA 1985 (FRED 6)
Preferred treatment	Purchase method for acquisitions; pooling of interests method for uniting of interests		Acquisition and merger accounting, under SSAP 23, are not necessarily mutually exclusive (although they would be if FRED 6 were to proceed as standard).
Allowed alternative treatment	–	–	See above.
Not allowed	Purchase method for uniting of interests		–

Source: Certified Research Report 33 (Weetman, Adams and Gray, 1993)

Table 2.6 Different accounting requirements for borrowing costs

	IASC	US GAAP	UK GAAP
Described in	IAS 22 (Revised)	FAS 34 as amended by FAS 42, FAS 58 and FAS 62	CA 1985 (also ED 5l)
Preferred treatment	Write off all borrowing costs as incurred	Capitalisation compulsory for certain assets	No preferred treatment under the Act
Allowed alternative treatment	Capitalisation permitted in specific circumstances	–	Capitalise or write off immediately
Not allowed	–	Immediate write-off for certain assets	–

Source: Certified Research Report 33 (Weetman, Adams and Gray, 1993)

Table 2.7 Different accounting requirements for foreign currency translation

	IASC	US GAAP	UK GAAP
Described in	E 32	FAS 52	SSAP 20, CA 1985
Exchange rate for translating the profit and loss account			
Preferred treatment	Rate at transaction date or average rate	Rate at time of recognition or weighted average rate	Average rate or closing rate
Not allowed	Closing rate	–	–
Subsidiaries operating in hyper-inflationary economies			
Preferred treatment	Restate financial statements before translation	Temporal method	Restate financial statements before translation
Not allowed	Translate financial statements without prior restatement	–	–

Source: Certified Research Report 33 (Weetman, Adams and Gray, 1993)

Table 2.8 Different accounting requirements for capitalisation of development costs

	IASC	US GAAP	UK GAAP
Described in	IAS 9 (Revised)	FAS 2, FAS 68, FAS 86	SSAP 13, CA 1985
Preferred treatment	Recognise such costs as assets when specified criteria are met and write off as expense when the criteria are not met	Write off as incurred	May recognise as assets when specific criteria are met; choice of immediate write-off also permitted

Source: Certified Research Report 33 (Weetman, Adams and Gray, 1993)

Table 2.9 Different accounting requirements for dividends

	IASC	US GAAP	UK GAAP
Described in	IAS 10	Reg. S-X	CA 1985
Preferred treatment	Either provide for or disclose proposed dividends	Do not provide for dividends that are not declared at the year end	Must provide for dividends relating to a financial year even though not declared until after the year end

Source: Certified Research Report 33 (Weetman, Adams and Gray, 1993)

Table 2.10 Different accounting requirements for recognition of profit and revenue on long-term contracts

	IASC	US GAAP	UK GAAP
Described in	E 32, confirmed by E 42	APB 45	SSAP 9
Preferred treatment	Percentage of completion method	Percentage of completion and completed contract methods	Percentage of completion method
Not allowed	Completed contract method	–	Completed contract method

Source: Certified Research Report 33 (Weetman, Adams and Gray, 1993)

Table 2.11 Different accounting requirements for stock

	IASC	US GAAP	UK GAAP
Described in	IAS 2 (Revised)	APB 43	SSAP 9, CA 1985
Preferred treatment	FIFO and WAC	FIFO, WAC and LIFO	FIFO and WAC LIFO and base stock
Allowed alternative treatment	LIFO	–	–
Not allowed	Base stock	–	–

Source: Certified Research Report 33 (Weetman, Adams and Gray, 1993)

Table 2.12 Different accounting requirements for prior year adjustments

	IASC	US GAAP	UK GAAP
Described in	E 32	APB 20, FAS 32	FRS 3
Preferred treatment	Adjust retained earnings brought forward and amend comparatives	The cumulative effect is to be shown as a separate item in the profit and loss account	Adjust retained earnings brought forward and amend comparatives
Allowed alternative treatment	Include the effect in the income of the current period and present amended pro forma comparative information	In some circumstances a restatement of prior year amounts is permitted	SSAPs 22 and 24 allowed alternative treatments on a change of accounting policy re goodwill and pension costs
Not allowed	–	Restatement of prior year amounts except in some circumstances	–

Source: Certified Research Report 33 (Weetman, Adams and Gray, 1993)

The IASC comparability and improvements project

Given the need in international securities markets to establish confidence in the quality of accounts of companies raising capital in these markets, it follows that one way of establishing such confidence is to require all companies using the markets to apply international accounting standards (IASs). The problem here is the lack of confidence that follows from the IASC permitting too free a choice of accounting treatments in some areas.

The IASC published the first stage of its comparability and improvements project, E 32, in 1989. The likely benefits of enhanced comparability of accounts include advantages to standard setters in developing countries, multinational preparers, companies seeking to raise capital internationally and users including investors, analysts and regulators. The prime objective of the project was to reduce the number of alternative treatments allowed in IASs to date. Until E 32 most IASs had two acceptable alternative treatments, such choice being necessary in the past to gain acceptance of some standards. The increase in cross-border financing is seen as the main reason for seeking to reduce the choice available. Purvis, Gernon and Diamond (1991) identified three groups of countries as far as the development of accounting standards is concerned:

▶ countries with weak accounting professions with no formalised system for developing, issuing and enforcing accounting standards
▶ countries dependent on the IASC
▶ countries independent of the IASC.

It was found, not surprisingly, that the degree of conformity for the independent group was markedly lower than that for the dependent group.

Tables 2.1–2.12 show, in respect of the UK and the USA, the extent to which the GAAP of a particular country is not in harmony with the proposals of the IASC. It would appear from the above that the project will not achieve its objective of reducing the number of permitted alternatives unless it gets support from all the member bodies including those of the USA and the UK. If this support is not forthcoming and the IASC is not successful in reducing the number of permitted alternatives, it will not get the support of the major stock exchanges.

The reconciliation of UK GAAP-based accounts with accounts based on the GAAP of another country (or vice versa)

As a result of the different accounting bases adopted around the world it is unlikely that reported profit and shareholders' funds following the GAAP of a company's home country will be the same as those produced by following the GAAP of another country. It is, therefore, sometimes necessary to produce a statement reconciling the two sets of figures. This is particularly true of UK companies requiring to produce figures following US GAAP, either as a requirement to comply with the US stock exchange regulations or as voluntary additional information for US investors. Example 2.1 illustrates such a reconciliation and also highlights the technical differences that exist between countries.

EXAMPLE 2.1 Reconciling UK GAAP to US GAAP

A British company, Bulldog Group plc, has reported the following consolidated figures when following GAAP in the UK:

Net income   £130 million
Shareholders' equity   £(297) million

The following adjustments have to be made to comply with US GAAP:

▶ Goodwill from an acquisition made several years ago had been immediately written off under UK GAAP. Under US GAAP this should be capitalised and written off over 40 years. The amortisation charge for the year in question is £26 million and the unamortised balance at the year end amounted to £461 million.
▶ Interest incurred as part of acquiring fixed assets has been written off in previous years' profit and loss accounts when following UK GAAP. This interest should be capitalised and amortised over the assets' life following US GAAP. The additional amortisation cost is £3 million and the unamortised balance at the year end amounts to £37 million.
▶ Under UK GAAP dividends are accounted for in the fiscal year to which they relate. In the USA the dividends are included in the year when the board of directors

propose to pay the dividends. This would eliminate a proposed dividend of £50 million in the balance sheet.

▶ Deferred tax will have been provided on a partial provision basis under the liability method. Under US GAAP the full provision basis is required. This increases the deferred tax charge to the profit and loss account for the current year by £30 million and a cumulative charge to the balance sheet provision resulting in an increase of £61 million.

▶ Following UK GAAP the group has revalued some of its land, creating a revaluation reserve of £156 million. Such revaluations are not permitted under US GAAP.

▶ During the year there was a merger resulting in a change in the group composition at the year end. The merger was accounted for under UK GAAP and profits of £144 million attributable to the pre-merger period have been included in the consolidated profit and loss account. However, the combination did not meet the US requirements for the use of the merger (pooling of interest) method and it is therefore necessary to use the acquisition (purchase) method. This requires balance sheet adjustments of £104 million to tangible assets (increase in value) £2,665 million additional goodwill and £754 million to other intangible assets (increase in value). Additional depreciation and amortisation for the year amounts to £130 million.

Reconciliation statement:	£m
Income statement adjustments	
Net income per UK GAAP	130
US GAAP adjustments (assumed net of taxation):	
Goodwill amortisation	(26)
Capitalised interest amortised	(3)
Deferred tax	(30)
Elimination of results prior to 'merger'	(144)
Purchase accounting – additional depreciation and amortisation of goodwill	(130)
	(203)
Balance sheet data	
Shareholders' equity per UK GAAP	(297)
US GAAP adjustments:	
Goodwill	461
Capitalisation of interest	37
Dividend liability eliminated	50
Deferred tax	(61)
Revaluation reserve eliminated	(156)
Purchase accounting:	
Tangible fixed assets	104
Goodwill	2,665
Other intangibles	754
	3,557

This statement clearly shows the effect that adopting a different country's GAAP can have. In the above situation a profitable group has now reported a loss, and a group with a negative shareholders' interest of a few hundred million pounds now reports capital employed of over three and half billion pounds.

Summary

► This chapter, dealing with international issues affecting financial reporting, takes you through the determinants of the variety of accounting practices around the world and identifies the factors resulting in differences and those that result in similarities in the accounting practices of different countries.

► The chapter also deals with the organisations that form and influence global accounting, some of which have been formed by the accounting profession (the IASC and the IFAC) and others that are formed by the political processes of government (UN committees and the OECD). In addition we looked at regional bodies that have an accounting influence across national borders, the most important of which is the EC in terms of its directives.

► To put the UK and the international standard-setting process in context, the regulatory frameworks of five other countries were described, illustrating the great variety of regulatory systems that operate in the world. Differences between UK and US GAAP were highlighted and a further contrast drawn between these GAAP and the proposals of the IASC. Reference was made to the IASC comparability project and the increased relevance of international accounting harmonisation in the context of increased cross-border financing. The effects of using different GAAP were illustrated in an example reconciling UK GAAP to US GAAP.

Suggested reading

Certified Research Report 33 – Issues in International Accounting Harmonisation (Weetman, Adams and Gray 1993)
This is a comprehensive guide on the significance of UK/US accounting differences and the implications for the IASC's comparability project.

The European Handbook 1993 (LSCA 1993)
This provides useful insights into the different accounting practices of EC member states.

'Happy Birthday IASC' (Mitchell 1993)
This article is a useful account of the problems faced by and the achievements of the IASC.

'The crunch comes for international harmonisation' (Thompson 1992)
Georgette Thompson's article provides further information on the IASC's comparability project.

Self test questions

1 What are the objectives of the IASC?

2 Is the national standard-setting process in the UK a model of the regulating processes in other countries?

3 Summarise the arguments supporting global harmonisation of financial reporting.

4 Contrast the roles of the United Nations and the European Commission in the regulation of international financial reporting.

5 Compare and contrast the different accounting requirements for borrowing costs under the IASC, US GAAP and UK GAAP.

Exam style question

1 *Revenue recognition*

International Accounting Standard (IAS) 18 – Revenue recognition, was issued in December 1982. There is no equivalent accounting standard in the United Kingdom but it is considered that compliance with company law and other normally accepted practices will ensure compliance with IAS 18.

Required:

a) Briefly state the principles set out in the standard as to when revenue should be recognised, first for sales transactions and secondly for transactions involving the rendering of services.

b) Apply the principles stated in (a) above to the following transactions and indicate briefly whether (or not) and when and why you would recognise revenue arising on each transaction:

   (i) 'Bill and hold sales', that is, delivery is delayed at buyer's request but buyer takes title and accepts billing.

   (ii) 'Guaranteed sales', that is, where shipment is made giving the buyer an unlimited right of return.

   (iii) Publication and record subscriptions.

   (iv) Advertising and insurance agency commissions.

   (v) Financial service commissions.

   (vi) Franchise fees.

All answers on pages 626–627.

Managing the Audit Relationship

An audit requirement was first recognised as a social and economic necessity during the Industrial Revolution in the second half of the eighteenth century, when the limited liability company became commonly used as a business vehicle. The limited company arrangement enabled investors to commit a fixed amount of funds to a commercial venture in the knowledge that the funds committed represented the limit of their liability should disaster occur and the venture fail.

The nature of the 'vehicle' caused a division between the ownership of the company and the control of the investor's funds. The owners were the shareholders, the managers – now known as directors – were the controllers. To enable the shareholders to assess the performance of the company, it was necessary for the directors to produce accounts describing the use of the investors' funds and showing the profits or losses made by the application of these funds. For these accounts to have any credibility it was apparent that an independent review would be required. Thus, the concept of the audit was conceived.

The audit requirement was first recognised in law in the 1844 Joint Stock Company Act, which stipulated that limited companies should provide accounts to the shareholders and that those accounts should be audited by an independent 'auditor'. It was, and still is, the auditor's duty to examine objectively the company's accounts, together with the underlying accounting information and related records, to enable an opinion to be formed upon the financial statements.

The auditor's relationship with a limited company needs briefly to be examined if the context of the relationship is to be fully understood. This is illustrated in Figure 3.1. The contractual relationship is between the auditor and the limited company. The limited company pays consideration to the auditor in the form of an audit fee, and in return the auditor provides an independent audit opinion on the truth and fairness of the financial statements to the shareholders. It follows that neither the shareholders nor the public nor the creditors nor the directors have any contractual relationship with the auditor and, to the annoyance of many, this was confirmed by the (1990) case of *Caparo Industries plc* v. *Dickman and Others* (1990).

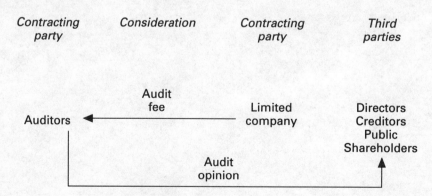

Figure 3.1 The relationship between an auditor and a limited company

Since 1844 the concept of the audit has been developed by both statute and common law precedent. The most recent legislation was the Companies Act 1989, which introduced statutory regulation of auditors. This chapter will seek to explain the management of the audit relationship and how the work of auditors is now controlled, from the initial acquisition of an audit client through to the reporting of the auditors' opinion to the shareholders.

The management of the audit relationship will be addressed both on a macro level, by explaining the measures now taken to control the profession as a whole, and on a micro level within the audit firm itself, by discussing the relevant practice quality controls that should exist.

The audit report is the only tangible evidence that any work has been performed. It is the one point of communication between auditors and users of the financial statements. The wording of the audit report and the possible form of qualification is such a major source of public criticism that the APB has issued a draft statement. This will be looked at in this chapter.

Challenges facing the profession

For today's auditor there are many challenges and pressures to face – from commerce, the public and regulatory bodies. The Companies Act 1989 brought about the final removal of self-regulation within the profession. The process began earlier in the 1980s, with the Insolvency Acts of 1985 and 1986 regulating corporate recovery work, and the Financial Services Act 1986 relating to investment business.

The profession sought to satisfy public demands for greater professional control by the implementation of various control devices (as detailed below under 'regulatory pressures'). However, these were not effective, and spectacular audit failures increased general cynicism about the profession's ability to govern itself and to take action when failures occur.

The public's expectations of the audit process steadily increased, with widespread debate about the 'expectation gap'. The expectation gap results from the apparent difference between the actual work performed by auditors and the work that the public expects auditors to perform. This expectation encompasses a variety of matters, from a review of the quality of management of the company to consideration of its future viability and to the detection of fraud.

The auditor is also under significant commercial pressure – it is sometimes forgotten that auditing is a business and that the auditor audits in order to make a profit. In the past the profit motive has not been openly discussed by the profession, and some would argue that it would seem to have been an embarrassment. However, the profit motive is a very important aspect of modern auditing and the topic needs to be addressed, particularly with regard to the audit relationship.

Auditors have two principal and conflicting motives in any audit relationship:

▶ to ensure that there is minimum risk of there being an incorrect audit opinion to the shareholders of the company
▶ to ensure that the auditing exercise is profitable for the auditor.

Auditors, therefore, strive to find a balance between the two motives, but balance is hard to achieve. There is a natural disequilibrium between the two motives – so much time would have to be spent on minimising risk that no profit would be made; maximising profit means that a thorough job could not be done and risk to the shareholders would rise to unacceptable levels – the best auditors can hope for is the stabilisation of the disequilibrium. These pressures on the audit relationship are now considered in detail.

Regulatory pressures

We have already mentioned the imbalance between the public's expectations of auditors' performance and the profession's actual performance. The profession tried to face up to the murmurings of dissatisfaction by taking various steps, such as the formation of Accounting Standards Committee in the 1970s, the Joint Disciplinary Council 1977 and the Audit Practices Committee in 1980. However, many would argue that these steps were too little and too late. In the United States the auditing profession began issuing Auditing Standards in 1940, after the case of *McKessen* v. *Robins* (1939). However, in the United Kingdom, it was not until 1961 that the Institute of Chartered Accountants of England and Wales began issuing a series of statements on auditing, and even then it stated 'That each auditor must decide for himself the nature and extent of the work which is necessary in order to enable him to discharge the responsibility he has undertaken.'

The Accounting Standards Committee was established in 1970 and has suffered frequent criticism. The Joint Disciplinary Council, which was set up in 1977 after a series of highly critical DTI reports, has often been criticised for a lack of independence, and the Audit Practices Committee, which was established in 1980 with a view to constructing a consistent and cohesive auditing framework within which audits could be performed, has not prevented the audit failures of the 1980s. Against the background of audit failure the profession could not restore the public's confidence in the manner or extent of audit work. Just some of the failures are:

▶ The Grays Building Society, where very substantial sums totalling in excess of £7 million was systematically stolen over the course of 40 years – or, as some would say, 40 audits.
▶ Johnson Matthey Bank, where a very significant under provision for doubtful debts was not detected. The large firm of auditors involved in this case made an out-of-court settlement of £50 million.
▶ Barlow Clowes, where very substantial sums of money were defrauded from investors over a period during which, in fact, there was a change of auditors from one large firm to another. In this case the auditors escaped damages, purely because the DTI allowed a writ against the firm in question to expire.
▶ Ferranti, where a fraud involving several hundreds of millions of dollars was not detected in an acquired subsidiary. In this case the large firm involved made an out-of-court settlement of £50 million, although by that time Ferranti no longer existed in a recognisable form.

In the late 1980s and early 1990s there were a number of much-publicised company failures in which the role of auditors was questioned and law suits threatened. The organisations involved include: Pollypeck; The Maxwell Group of companies; and BCCI, where a writ against the auditors was as issued for $8 billion.

It is against this background that the UK government decided to introduce the statutory regulation of auditors. The Companies Act 1989, apart from amending certain sections of the Companies Act 1985, introduced into UK company law the requirements of the European Communities 8th Directive. The act has set up a structure similar to the Financial Services Act 1986. The Act lays down provisions with:

> The purpose of securing that only persons who are properly supervised and appropriately qualified are appointed company auditors, and that audits by persons appointed are carried out properly and with integrity and with a proper degree of independence.

All auditors wishing to perform company audits must be registered with a supervisory body. A supervisory body is one that contains and enforces the requirements of the Companies Act 1989 with regard to persons eligible to seek appointments as company auditors and also with regard to the actual performance of company audit work. In the UK there are five recognised supervisory bodies:

- Chartered Association of Certified Accountants (ACCA)
- Institute of Chartered Accountants in England and Wales (ICA)
- Institute of Chartered Accountants in Ireland (ICAI)
- Institute of Chartered Accountants of Scotland (ICAS)
- Association of Authorised Public Accountants (AAPA).

The authorisation committee of each association or institute has the power to issue practising certificates to eligible individual members. There have been some transitional arrangements but from January 1996 the following requirements will apply for all eligible members of ACCA who wish to apply for a practising certificate:

- membership of the Association for not less than two years
- three and a half years' relevant practical experience in public practice under the supervision of a member holding a practice certificate
- 12 months of this experience must be post-qualification and be within five years of making the application
- the successful completion of an oral examination.

The Association also grants auditing certificates to auditing firms. To become authorised, a firm must comply with the following:

- at least one partner or director holds a practising certificate from the Association
- a majority of voting rights in whatever body manages the firm's affairs are held by persons with relevant qualifications
- each individual responsible for audit work holds a relevant qualification
- there are arrangements to prevent others influencing the conduct of audit work to the detriment of independence or integrity.

It is the Association's responsibility to ensure that its members comply with all the relevant rules such that:

- only fit and proper persons and firms are appointed as company's auditors
- audit work is conducted properly and with integrity
- technical standards are applied to the conduct of audits
- standards of competence are maintained
- compliance of regulations is monitored and enforced
- a company's auditors are able to meet claims against them arising out of audit work.

To ensure that these rules are complied with, the Association has established a monitoring unit that will carry out practice inspections within a maximum of five years. The task of the monitoring unit when inspecting a practice is to determine the awareness of Registered Auditors of their professional and legal responsibilities in relation to audits, and to see to it that proper competence is being applied to practical work with relevance to the statutory audit of financial statements. It is the function of the monitoring unit to ensure that all Registered Auditors conduct audits according to current standards. Recognised current standards are based upon APC's operational standard and it is this that the ACCA monitoring unit will apply when judging the quality of audit work.

PGA of the APC Operational Standard is reproduced here:

1 This auditing standard applies whenever an audit is carried out.

2 *Planning, controlling and recording*
The auditor should adequately plan, control and record his work.

3 *Accounting systems*

The auditor should ascertain the enterprise's system of recording and processing transactions and assess its adequacy as a basis for the preparation of financial statements.

4 *Audit evidence*

The auditor should obtain relevant and reliable audit evidence sufficient to enable him to draw reasonable conclusions therefrom.

5 *Internal controls*

If the auditor wishes to place reliance on any internal controls, he should ascertain and evaluate those controls and perform compliance tests on their operation.

6 *Review of financial statements*

The auditor should carry out such a review of the financial statements as is sufficient, in conjunction with the conclusions drawn from the other audit evidence obtained, to give him a reasonable basis for his opinion on the financial statements.

The monitoring unit will expect to find the following:

► A systematic and a coherent audit approach consistent with the nature of the client base. The audit approach by a larger practice may differ from that of a smaller practice due to the nature, size and complexity of the clients subjected to audit.

► Evidence of genuine commitment to consistent and appropriate quality controls. This will involve ensuring the practice recruits appropriate staff, encourages and carries out meaningful staff training and that relevant members of the practice are involved with continuing professional development – a mandatory requirement for all members holding practising certificates is that members must attend an average of 21 hours of structured lectures on a annual basis. The monitors will also expect evidence of regular quality control compliance reviews. These are explained in detail later in this chapter.

► Evidence that all relevant ethical guidelines are being adhered to on a consistent basis, particularly in relation to independence.

► An awareness of the need for high technical standards to be achieved and maintained throughout the practice and with all professional work.

► Continuous reviews of personnel and personnel records in relation to fit and proper criteria.

► Establishment of external consultation links where the internal resources are insufficient to satisfy the requirements. This will involve the utilisation of specialist skills necessary and also the use of continuity agreements wherever relevant.

► Adequate charging for its audit work on a realistic commercial basis. This will be difficult to judge, but it is completely unacceptable for audit work to be done at a level of fee that inhibits the quality of work.

The monitoring visit will take the form of an interview followed by a compliance or substantive review of practice systems. The interview will involve in-depth questioning to determine the competence of the practitioner and the quality standards of the practice. This will usually be followed by a review of randomly selected audit files from the practice client list to determine whether that client's audit has indeed been conducted in accordance with Auditing Standards. The monitoring approach will vary accordingly to the size and complexity of the practice, but generally it will take the form of an overall review of quality control systems.

Once the inspection of the practice is complete, any weaknesses found within the systems will be discussed with the practitioner and these will be confirmed in writing in the form of a letter of weakness. On subsequent visits the letter of weakness will to some extent determine the approach of the monitoring personnel. Practice monitoring is now a reality and its presence and the likelihood of a visit is influencing the behaviour and audit approach of all practices.

To add further credibility to the audit process the APC was replaced by the Audit Practices Board (APB) in 1991. The removal of accounting standard setting from the direct control of the profession was followed by a similar change to the APC.

The main differences between the APB and the APC are that with the APB:

► only half of the voting members are to be practising auditors, the remainder being nominated by outside bodies
► standards and guidelines will be issued in APB's own name and not be subject to approval by individual professional bodies
► additional funding will be provided for full-time professional staff and for external research.

The APB has issued the following statement of objectives:

> The APB is committed to leading the development of auditing practice in the United Kingdom and the Republic of Ireland so as to:
>
> ► establish the highest standards of auditing
> ► meet the developing needs of users of financial information, and
> ► ensure public confidence in the auditing process.
>
> To achieve these objectives, the APB intends to:
>
> ► take an active role in the development of statutes, regulations and accounting standards that affect the audit profession
> ► promote ways of increasing the value of audits and of ensuring their cost-effectiveness
> ► consult with users of financial information to ensure that the APB provides an effective and timely response to their developing needs and to issues raised by them
> ► advance the wider public's understanding of the roles and responsibilities of auditors, and
> ► establish and publish statements of the principles and procedures with which auditors are required to comply in the conduct of audits, and other explanatory material to assist their interpretation and application.

The APB's pronouncement will be Statements of Auditing Standards (SASs) supplemented by Practice Notes (PNs). One of the APB's initial tasks is to revise existing Auditing Standards and Guidelines and reissue them as SASs and PNs. It appears likely that much of the content of existing Guidelines will be upgraded to SASs.

The spectre of regulation has haunted the profession for many years. It is now a reality. The entire auditor–client relationship is now under scrutiny both from external and internal sources.

Commercial pressures

The commercial pressures facing auditors, together with the increasing public demands and greater regulatory involvement, is leading to a situation that many auditors consider to be very unhealthy for the profession as a whole. Audit assignments are becoming more risky and less profitable.

Regardless of the amount of planning and audit control, every audit assignment carries a level of risk that cannot be diluted. It will not be cost-effective or possible in the time available to eradicate the risk. There will also be a minimum amount of work that the auditor will need to perform in order to carry out an audit in accordance with the Auditing Standards. If these two assertions are accepted it follows that there is a theoretical minimum level of fees that should be charged for the audit of a limited company.

Before the audit can begin, the audit work must be comprehensively planned. This will involve the determination of critical audit areas that are likely to be encountered. The perceived critical audit areas will influence the audit approach. The greater the complexity of the critical audit areas, the greater will be the evidence requirement demanded by the audit planner. Therefore, if the audit planner perceives a certain degree of risk that has been caused by identifiable critical audit areas an audit approach must be designed with a view to obtaining sufficient audit evidence to counterbalance against the perception of the risk. The greater the perception of the risk, the more audit investigation will be required and this will increase the amount of time. As audit fees are based upon the amount of time spent on a particular job, the audit fee should increase likewise. In other words, there should be a direct correlation between perceived risk and the audit budget.

EXAMPLE 3.1 – An example of a going-concern audit programme

Client: Prepared by:
Year end: Date:
Title: Going Concern   Reviewed by:

AUDIT PROCEDURES   COMMENT ON OUTCOME
SCHEDULE REFERENCE

Discuss with the directors the future plans
for the company and the general future
prospects. Narrate appropriately on
relevant schedule.

Review balance sheet to consider the
financial health of the company. If the
company is insolvent examine the cause of
the insolvency and possible remedies
(capital introductions, capitalisation of
directors' current accounts etc.).

If appropriate, request letter of
postponement of directors' loan accounts.

Review cashflow and profit forecasts for
the next 12 months and form conclusions
about its future.

Review post-balance-sheet trading to
determine whether the state of the
business is improving or worsening.

Analyse any writs or County Court
judgements against the company.

Review age of creditors and analyse any
significant old creditors and determine
reason for oldness and review legal
correspondence from the suppliers.

If any negotiations with the company's
bankers are in progress, analyse the
current state of play.

Review order books or relevant contracts to check consistency of forecast levels of trade.

Review overhead forecast to determine the reasonableness of the forecast in light of historic levels and proposed changes.

Analyse all creditors who are:

1   Secured on company assets.
2   Secured on directors' guarantees.

Identify and quantify stock bought under reservation of title.

Analyse any unusual large or round-sum payments or receipts in the three months before and after the year end.

Analyse the age of preferential creditors:

VAT
PAYE

Calculate the redundancy payments due should the company cease trading.

If there is uncertainty about the going-concern ability of the company, narrate why, together with and any possible rescue plans.

However, public demands and the general economic environment, together with increasing regulatory awareness, has meant that the perception of risk is increasing. A very good example of this is the growing awareness of the need to actively review the going-concern concept. In the mid 1980s most auditors would not regard this as necessary. In the 1990s, however, a going-concern review should be considered as standard with all audits. An example of a going-concern audit program is shown in Example 3.1. This increased evidence requirement leads to an increase work requirement, which causes an increase in time, which in turn leads to an increase in the audit fees. However, audit fees are not directly proportional to the amount of work done, but are, in real terms, reducing. This means that the auditors' risk:return ratio is moving adversely against them. The public reaction may be one that lacks sympathy. However, the profession's reaction is to develop new approaches to auditing with a view to improving profitability and reducing risk. It intends to do this by:

▶ *Improved selective acquisition procedures* This will mean that a practice will be careful when accepting audit assignments. The integrity of a client, the health of the business and the adequacy of the client's fee expectation will be taken into account before accepting the appointment.
▶ *Improved planning procedures* It is generally accepted that the profitability of an audit and the auditor's risk exposure is determined by the quality of the planning process. If risk areas can properly be identified and audit attention directed towards those risk areas, the job should be profitable within an acceptable level of risk.
▶ *A greater reliance on the internal auditor* It is becoming far more common for external auditors to work closely with the internal auditors of a client company.

Internal auditors do represent a continuous management control, and substantial external audit work can be avoided if a good-quality internal audit department exists.

▶ *Increased audit automation* Auditing is a very labour-intensive function and certain aspects do lend themselves to automation. In all practices, regardless of size, software of varying degrees of complexity is now widely used. On large audits interrogation software is the norm rather than the exception.

Profit has often been regarded as a 'dirty' word when examining the nature and purpose of auditing. However, the commercial pressures currently experienced by auditors have a very real impact on the audit approach and the audit procedures applied.

Public pressures

The public pressures being brought to bear on auditors are also considerable. The stature of the audit in the early 1990s is probably at an all-time low. Audit failure, together with highly publicised professional fees, has meant that many people believe that the current audit does not represent value for money.

The expectation gap, explained earlier, represents the difference between what the public believes auditors should deliver and what the public perceives they do deliver.

In many practical situations the public or users of the financial statements demand that the audit is performed in increasingly complex environments in ever-diminishing time-scales. In large, quoted company audits the market demands the accounts be published very quickly. Multinational companies with many billions of pounds of turnover frequently publish their final results within two months of their year end. In the United States, Securities and Exchange Commission (SEC) reporting deadlines are even more stringent.

Auditors are criticised for failing to detect fraud or failing to report any uncertainties of a company's future prospects. There is no real question that auditors should accept these responsibilities within an agreed framework, but the more onerous the auditing task and the wider the range of users, the greater is the pressure that is brought to bear on the audit relationship.

If more is to be expected of the auditors it should be formalised by a significant review of current legislation, which has not substantially altered since the 1844 Joint Stock Company Act. It is also important to understand that the greater the task set for the auditors, the greater the cost. One question that is not so frequently addressed relates to the cost of bridging the expectation gap.

Quality control

The pressures on auditors have meant that audit firms of all sizes have had to examine and improve the quality controls applied to their clients. Quality control within a practice, regardless of size, is a professional and a commercial necessity. The work performed by a firm of accountants must be accurate and properly express the firm's opinion on a particular matter. It is a commercial necessity to ensure that a practice functions efficiently and profitably.

To 'install' a variety of quality controls into a practice, such as standardised working papers, file review and job planning, will not be an answer in itself. Mechanical controls will not enable a practice to achieve the commercial or professional quality objectives. Before any controls can be installed a quality culture must exist within the practice to be achieved by appropriate and consistent staff training. The quality control procedures in a professionally managed practice are really no different from those you would expect to find in any well-organised company. They are detailed below.

Personnel controls

Training must relate to all levels of staff in the practice, from junior clerks to senior partners. The training should cover both technical and ethical theory, and it should be real – in the past many practices have relied on on-the-job staff training, which, although a very important part of learning, needs to be supported by structured lectures and seminars.

As we mentioned earlier, continuing professional development is a requirement for all Registered Auditors. This means that a member of the Association who holds a practising certificate must attend an average of 21 hours of lectures a year over a three-year period, with a minimum of 14 hours in any one year. Practices also have to apply to become a Recognised Training Practice and their training procedures are monitored on a regular basis by the Association.

Staff recruitment is another area that is now monitored by the Association. The practice must recruit appropriately qualified and experienced staff. However, in accordance with the Association's rules, the practice must ensure that the staff are fit and proper to deal with audit client affairs. The practice is expected to maintain 'fit and proper' records of all staff and partners – for an example of a fit and proper questionnaire, see Example 3.2.

EXAMPLE 3.2 – An example of a fit and proper questionnaire for staff
_____

Name:

Address:

Telephone no:

Date of birth:

Past experience:

Examinations to date:

Have you ever had a significant
mental or physical illness?

Have you been found guilty of a
criminal offence?

Have you ever made an
arrangement with creditors or
been bankrupt?

Have you been subject to
disciplinary action by the
Chartered Association of
Certified Accountants?

Signature .... Date ....

Physical controls

Audit working papers are of great importance to the practice and therefore there must be proper custodial procedures in place:

► storage of working papers in a secure location
► proper recording of all files and all file movements
► restricted access to audit files
► authorisation procedures for file issues, particularly when the file is being taken out of the office.

These procedures may be straightforward in theory, but in practice the nature of auditing demands easy access to working-paper files and therefore the points listed above are frequently not implemented consistently.

Authorisation controls

There must be very strict authorisation controls applied within the practice, particularly in relation to the signing of the firm's name. In many cases reports are signed in the firm's name rather than by an individual. The signing authority must be limited to partners unless otherwise specifically delegated. If a report or letter is signed in a firm's name the practice will automatically take on any responsibility for any loss caused by reliance on the signed material.

Recording controls

The use of standardised working papers will allow the audit practice to provide direction to the work to be performed by the audit staff. Standardisation also helps to ensure a consistent level of quality of work within the audit firm.

Management controls

It is very important that the audit work is performed quickly, and Gantt charts should be used to plan the timing of audits and also the timing of stages of the work within individual audit processes. In very large audits critical path or network analysis may be necessary so that all the stages of the work may be timed in a sequential and efficient manner. A planning memorandum (see Example 3.4) should be prepared for each audit, detailing the duties and responsibilities of each member of the audit team.

Organisation controls

The audit practice procedures should be formalised in a manual, thus allowing reference for staff and consistency of quality and approach to the work.

Supervisory controls

This is an area of quality control that will be discussed further later in the chapter. All work must be reviewed by senior members of the practice before the audit report is written. A further level of review is the post-audit or cold review. This is where a random sample of completed files are reviewed by a unconnected member of the practice to identify general weaknesses in quality control. Problems that are found can then be dealt with in a structured manner by changing practice procedures and implementing the changes through staff training sessions.

Segregation of duties

It is important that the members of the practice staff are not involved in any audit work for clients for whom they have been performing accountancy work during the year, as objectivity will be difficult to maintain.

The controls exercised over the audit relationship come from the higher macro level of professional pronouncements by the APB and the relevant supervisory body. These should be adapted to the practice circumstances by the internal quality assurance procedures applied by the practice.

We will now examine how these quality assurance procedures should be applied into the audit relationship at a macro level.

Engagement procedures

The acquistion of a new audit client is always an occasion to celebrate. However, before accepting an audit assignment the auditors must consider certain ethical and professional matters. The quality of an audit relationship with a client is strongly based upon the initial acquisition procedures.

Client desirability

When approached by a new client, auditors should consider the following points.

The reason for changing auditors and the justification for that change

It may be that the client wants to change auditors because their existing firm will not compromise professional standards over some technical matter. To accept an appointment under these circumstances would be very difficult. However, it may be that the client has a genuine grievance against the existing auditors, or there may have been a communication problem between the auditors in the client that has resulted in an irreconcilable breakdown in the audit–client relationship. If this is the case, it is probably better for all concerned if the client changes auditors.

The historic background of the company and its directors

Auditors should consider whether it is the type of client that their practice wishes to be associated with. It may seem to be a rather pompous attitude, but if professional standards are to be achieved within a commercial framework, the quality of the potential client should be considered.

Adequacy of fee

It is important for auditors to ensure that the potential client's expectation of fees is in line with their own perception of the amount of work that will be necessary and therefore the cost of that work. If the auditors perceive that an audit fee may be, say, £5,000, and the client expectation of the potential fee is £1,000, there is little point in continuing the relationship. It is generally recognised that the quality of audit work should not be limited by the fee. Of course, all audits are finally a compromise between professional desirability and commercial reality, but if, for example, an auditor did not attend a stocktake because of a concern that the time costs may not be recoverd from the client, the auditor would be vulnerable to significant professional criticism from the supervisory body. If audit work cannot be performed properly to a recognised standard because of the fee constraints, the audit assignment should not be accepted in the first place.

Practice ability to perform the work

If the auditors are satisfied about the desirability of the client they should then consider the ability of the practice to act for the client company. This aspect should be divided into three main categories.

Ethical ability of the practice to act as auditor

There are strict ethical guidelines relating to the acquisition of a new client, particularly in relation to the auditor's independence:

- ▶ Auditors will not be able to act for a client if any member of the practice staff holds shares in the client company or is an officer of the company.
- ▶ It is unacceptable for an auditor to have a blood relationship with any shareholder or director of the potential client company. It would be a very difficult situation if an auditor felt it necessary to give a harsh qualification on the financial statements of her father's company.
- ▶ It is also important for auditors to consider whether acting for the client gives rise to a conflict of interest with other companies that they audit.
- ▶ Auditors must be vigilant that the fees from potential clients will not constitute an undesirably high proportion of total practice income as this may influence decision-making on audit opinions.

Technical ability to perform the work

Before the appointment is accepted the auditors must also consider the technical ability of the practice to provide the audit service to an acceptable standard. The auditors should consider whether the practice has the appropriate technical experience and technical depth relevant to the needs of the potential client. This is a very practical consideration. If the practice does not have the appropriate skill or experience it could do one of two things:

- ▶ To perform in-depth research in order to gain the knowledge. This would be very commendable, but the cost of the research may not be recovered from the client and therefore could represent a poor investment of practice resources.
- ▶ To perform the work for the client without complete research. This will increase audit risk beyond acceptable levels, which may lead to audit failure. Obviously this alternative is unprofessional and should not be considered as an option.

It is therefore important for the auditors to make a conscious decision about the potential client company needs and the practice ability to service those needs.

Logistical ability to perform the work

The final consideration is the practice's logistical ability to perform the work, that is, the adequacy of internal resources to service the potential client's needs. It is not simply the size of the client that is important in this consideration – a small company may have the same year end as a number of your other clients, which may mean you will not have adequate staff to cover, say, stocktaking at the necessary time. The practice staff resources should be adequate not simply in terms of staff numbers but also in terms of experience and qualification.

The acquisition decision-making process needs to be structured and evidenced by documentation. An sample client engagement questionnaire is shown in Example 3.3.

EXAMPLE 3.3 – An example of a client engagement questionnaire

---

CLIENT ENGAGEMENT QUESTIONNAIRE

1 Name of client

2 Year end

3 Turnover

4 Type of business

5 Source of introduction

---

6 Does this client compete directly against any other client?

7 Does any member of staff have a blood relationship with any director or shareholder of the company?

8 Will the expected fee represent an undesirably high proportion of total practice income?

9 Is the practice technically able to service the client to a correct standard?

10 Has the practice adequate staff resources to service the client properly (consider the size and year end of the client)?

11 Has any member of staff held shares in the client company?

12 Has any member of staff worked for the company? If so, in what capacity?

13 Are there any other reasons why the practice should not act for the client in the capacity requested?

Signed by Partner   Date:

The planning process

After acquiring a new client the management aspects of the audit will be addressed. Initial planning should commence almost immediately, and this will often involve a member of the audit firm visiting the client's premises to carry out a fact-finding exercise.

Planning should be regarded as a two-stage process: first determine the scope of the work and then design the audit strategy. The purpose of planning as stated by the APC's Operational Standard is to:

▶ establish the intended means of achieving the audit objective
▶ ensure that adequate attention is devoted to the identified critical audit areas
▶ ensure the work is performed expeditiously
▶ provide direction and control.

Auditors do not plan to fail, although they are often criticised for failing to plan. If an audit is to be performed profitably and to a good standard, the planning stage is probably the most important of the audit process.

Determination of the scope of work

The first audit planning stage, determining the scope of work, means gaining a full understanding of the business and the environment in which it operates. During this stage critical audit areas relevant to the client must be identified; this is usually done by the audit manager. The critical areas can be broken into general and specific.

General critical audit areas

These are risk areas inherent in the nature of business. They would include:

- specifically relevant legislation
- problems arising from the nature of the business
- specifically relevant accounting practices
- the market environment in which the company operates.

These can be identified when the new client is first acquired. A great deal of research will be necessary and the result of the research will be placed on the permanent file. Usually only slight amendment is necessary from one year to the next.

If, for example, you were to undertake a solicitor's audit, you must be fully aware of the Solicitor's Act 1974, and the Solicitors' Account Rules 1990. You must know that your responsibilities relate to the client account, and that all client accounting monies must be kept in a separate bank account with books and records totally separate from the normal business books and records.

Another example could be a restaurant. All restaurants have the following risk areas:

- completeness of income
- the treatment of tax deductions regarding tips and service charges
- the physical custody of stock
- casual labour.

All these matters must be highlighted during the initial research and must be included on the permanent file, so that future audit staff can familiarise themselves with no job quickly and efficiently. The main purpose of the permanent file is to facilitate future planning.

Specific critical audit areas

These are risk areas unique to the client and for the year under review. These are particularly important for the audit to be carried out profitably and for adequate evidence to be gathered to compensate for the risk exposure. They can be identified by:

- regular discussions with the management about the current year's trading and any problems being faced by the company
- regular review of board minutes (the auditor should be included on the regular circulation list)
- regular discussions with the internal auditors, if there are any, and perhaps a review of the internal auditors' letters of weakness
- detailed analytical review on a month-by-month basis.

However, analytical review is a planning tool can be used for all sizes of client. It is not simply ratio analysis on monthly management accounts, the APC, guidelines on analytical review, has defined it as follows:

> Audit procedures which systematically analyse and compare related figures, trends, ratios, and other data with the aim of providing evidence to support the audit opinion.

One of the main techniques that is frequently used to achieve a competent review is ratio analysis. However, this is not the sole component of analytical review. It can range from simple comparisons to complex regression analysis performed by computer audit software. Therefore, analytical review as a planning tool could relate to the simple comparison of trends.

In a small company it would involve the comparison of the gross profit ratio, monthly turnover, average age of debtors and stock turnover. All this information would be readily available even without the preparation of the monthly management accounts.

It is very important that the specific risk areas are identified well in advance of audit commencement, so that appropriate levels of staff, sample sizes and time budgets can be set.

An example of some specific critical audit areas could be:

▶ An unusually high level of expenditure on repairs and renewals.
▶ Unusual fluctuation in gross profit margins, which could indicate stock valuation difficulties or theft.
▶ Unusual monthly results from a particular branch in the company. This may mean that the branch is considered to be higher risk than other branches, and will require a specific audit visit.

While general critical audit areas will be mainly researched once (on the acquisition of a client), the specific critical audit areas will be identified on a continuous basis every single year.

Planning the strategy

Once you have determined the scope of the audit, you will be in a position to plan your strategy. Strategic planning cannot take place without adequate identification of critical audit areas. The result of the strategic planning will be included within the planning memorandum, which will be circulated to all audit staff in advance of the audit. An outline planning memorandum is shown in Example 3.4.

EXAMPLE 3.4 – An example of a planning memorandum

PLANNING MEMORANDUM
Bloggs Limited

From: Audit Manager   Date: 10 December 1993
To: All members of audit team

Scope of work
a) Perform audit of the financial statements to 31 December 1993
b) Prepare management letter to include all audit findings together with recommendations for improvement.
c) Prepare a financial evaluation report regarding the trading performance of the company during the year to 31 December 1993 and its current financial position.

Critical audit areas
1 *Stocktaking*
   In the past the quality of the company's stocktake has been well below acceptable standards. Stockcount teams have been poorly briefed and at some branches the stock lines have been omitted from the count.

2 *Returns*
   The company experiences a high level of returns after the year end of goods sold before the year end. In past years' audits this has caused cut-off problems and a great deal of audit effort.

Audit strategy
▶ Time budget and commencement date
▶ Staffing
▶ Materiality

▶ Overtime
▶ Expenses
▶ Accommodation
▶ Travelling
▶ Address, telephone number, fax number
▶ Audit approach

Stocktaking

In view of the difficulties found in previous years, greater attention has been given to the stocktaking instructions and the quality of the stockcount teams. The stocktake instructions have been appendixed to this memorandum. All branch stocktakes will be attended and the allocation of audit staff to branches is shown below.

The stocktakes must be closely observed and representative test counts performed in accordance with the attached sampling criteria.

If any variations from the instructions are discovered this must be immediately conveyed to the stocktake supervisor who should rectify the lapse. If corrective action is not taken, audit staff are instructed to call the Operations Director on 061-493 8276

Returns

[The strategy to the returns problem would be narrated in the same manner as above.]

EXAMPLE 3.5 – An example of a time analysis

TIME ANALYSIS

		Budgeted hours	Actual hours	Variance
1	Planning			
2	Fixed Assets			
3	Stock			
4	Trade debtors			
5	Sundry debtors and prepayments			
6	Cash at Bank			
7	Trade Creditors			
8	Sundry Creditors and Accruals			
9	Corporation Tax			
10	Statutory audit			
11	Sales			
12	Purchases			
13	Wages and PAYE			
14	Subcontractors			
15	VAT			
16	Petty Cash			
17	Group Companies			
18	P & L Review			
19	Accounts preparation			
20	Permanent file update			

continued

	Budgeted hours	Actual hours	Variance
Sub total b/fwd			
21 File Review			
22 Finalisation			
23 Evaluation report			
24 Letter of Weakness			
Total			

REASONS FOR VARIANCE

___

EXAMPLE 3.6 – An example of a planning brief

Client: Prepared by:
Year end: Date:
Title: Planning Brief: Reviewed by:

AUDIT PROCEDURES	COMMENT ON OUTCOME	SCHEDULE REFERENCE
Are all members of audit team familiar with likely problem areas?		
Has a time budget been established?		
Has the deadline been established?		
Have bank letters been requested?		
Has staff overtime been discussed and agreed?		
Have staff expenses been discussed and agreed?		
Has the systems file been fully reviewed and understood?		
Does a permanent file exist? If not, create one.		
Have debtors confirmation replies been followed up?		
Has materiality level been agreed as well as sample sizes?		

Interim letter of weakness must be made available to all staff.		
All management accounts must be made available to all staff.		
Does client wish abbreviated accounts to be filed at Companies House?		
How many bound sets of accounts does client wish?		
When is the approval meeting for the accounts?		
What is the budgeted audit fee?		
Has the correspondence file been reviewed?		
Has a planning meeting taken place?		
Has a planning memorandum been prepared?		

Strategy planning will involve the determination of:

▶ overall audit approach highlighting areas requiring emphasis
▶ deadlines, commencement dates, and overall time budget
▶ number and quality of staff
▶ confidence levels
▶ materiality levels.

As previously stated, planning is continuous and the results of audit testing at one stage may affect the approach and the direction at the next stage.

Control of the audit

The planning process should ensure that the audit is performed effectively and profitably. However, one of the main consequences of good audit planning is that it provides the auditor with the ability to control the audit process as it takes place.

The essence of good control is good communication. The day-to-day control of an audit will involve many of the quality controls that we have already looked at. To ensure proper control there must be good communication both up and down the practice hierarchy. This is illustrated in Figure 3.2. It is often a lack of communication within an audit that causes errors to be left undetected and for audit failure to occur.

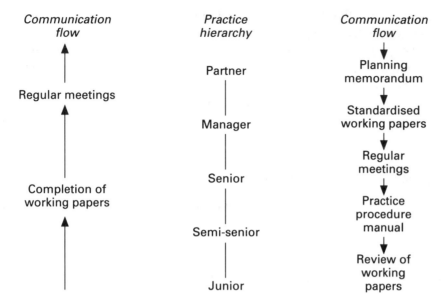

Figure 3.2 Flow diagram showing communication flow

Good control will involve detailed and regular supervision of the audit work by the hierarchy of the audit practice. This will take the form of regular meetings and frequent ongoing review of the audit working papers to ensure that the work is being performed in accordance not only with the audit planning memorandum but also with the audit strategy that had been designed in the context of the perceived critical audit areas.

The purpose of regular meetings between the audit supervisor (who may be the audit manager or assistant audit manager) and the audit staff is to make sure that if unforeseen problems do arise they are dealt with in an effective manner. On-site review of work by the audit manager or assistant manager should mean that no significant matters are left unexamined. The regular review should also ensure that the audit plan both in terms of content and timing is achieved.

The control of the audit process is an ongoing exercise that should begin with planning and conclude with the audit report. Proper ongoing control is an essential part of any audit and requires much human involvement. Standardised working papers, good timing and a coherent procedure manual all assist in the overall control, but objective review by more senior staff, particularly regarding contentious areas, must be consistently applied throughout the audit process.

Audit reports

As has already been pointed out, the audit report is usually the only evidence to the user that any audit work has been performed to justify the disclosed audit fees.

The audit report process

When you have concluded your evidence gathering and you have collated your findings within the audit file, the results will be reviewed by your manager and/or a partner. It is then necessary to consider all the findings to decide whether it is possible to provide an unqualified opinion.

To reach your final opinion, you will discuss your findings with your client's staff. You will not simply produce a qualified opinion to your client as a *fait accompli*. Your findings will be discussed so that the directors of the company can consider the implications of the audit evidence.

If you have found evidence to disagree with the truth and fairness of the financial statements, the directors may decide to make the necessary amendments in order to resolve the disagreement.

Similarly, if you have not found adequate evidence to form an opinion on a particular matter within the financial statements the directors may be able to provide further evidence to resolve the uncertainty. While striving to maintain independence, auditors must not be deliberately confrontational and, therefore, an audit qualification is usually the result of extensive discussion with the directors to ensure there is no alternative cause of action.

The structure of the audit report

There have been considerable changes to the wording of the audit report over the past years, culminating in SAS 600.

Auditors' reports on financial statements SAS 600

Statement of Auditing Standard 600, 'Auditors' Reports on Financial Statements' was the first SAS to be issued by the Auditing Practices Board, in May 1993. It applies to all financial periods ending on or after 30 September 1993.

Many aspects of previous reporting philosophy still apply, for example if an unqualified report is given the auditor continues to legally imply that:

▶ Proper accounting records have been maintained
▶ Adequate returns have been received from branches not visited (if applicable)
▶ Financial statements are in agreement with the underlying records
▶ The auditor has received adequate information and explanations necessary for the audit
▶ The Directors' Report is consistent with the financial statements.

However the standard report has been expanded to provide the user with a clearer understanding of the respective responsibilities of the directors and the auditors and also the basis of the audit opinion.

(SAS 600.1)
Auditors' reports on financial statements should contain a clear expression of opinion, based on review and assessment of the conclusions drawn from evidence obtained in the course of the audit.

It suggests that this will be achieved if the auditors' report is placed before the financial statements and, where the directors set out their responsibilities themselves, if this description is immediately before the auditors' report.

Basic elements of the auditors' report

(SAS 600.2)
Auditors' reports on financial statements should include the following matters:

a) *a title identifying the person or persons to whom the report is addressed;*
b) *an introductory paragraph identifying the financial statements audited;*
c) *separate sections, appropriately headed, dealing with*
   i) *respective responsibilities of directors (or equivalent persons) and auditors,*
   ii) *the basis of the auditors' opinion,*
   iii) *the auditors' opinion on the financial statements;*
d) *the manuscript or printed signature of the auditors; and*
e) *the date of the auditors' report.*

Title and addressee

Audit reports should now be addressed to the Shareholders, since the legal interpretation following the Caparo decision in the House of Lords 1990 now limits the auditors' duties to reporting to the shareholders. The form of wording recommended is as follows: 'Auditors' report to the Shareholders of...'

Statements of responsibility and basis of opinion

(SAS 600.3)

a) *Auditors should distinguish between their responsibilities and those of the directors by including in their report*

   i) *a statement that the financial statements are the responsibility of the reporting entity's directors;*

   ii) *a reference to a description of those responsibilities when set out elsewhere in the financial statements.*

   iii)*a statement that the auditors' responsibility is to express an opinion on the financial statements.*

b) *Where the financial statements or accompanying information (for example the directors' report) do not include an adequate description of directors' relevant responsibilities, the auditors' report should include a description of those responsibilities.*

An example of the wording of a description of the directors' repsonsiblities for inclusion in a company's financial statements would be as follows, and should preferably be included immediately before the auditors' report:

Company law requires the directors to prepare financial statements for each year which give a true and fair view of the state of affairs of the company and of the profit or loss of the company for that period. In preparing those financial statements, the directors are required to:

▶ *select suitable accounting policies and then apply them consistently;*

▶ *make judgements and estimates that are reasonable and prudent;*

▶ *state whether applicable accounting standards have been followed, subject to any material departures disclosed and explained in the financial statements (large companies only);*

▶ *prepare the financial statements on the going concern basis unless it is inappropriate to presume that the company will continue in business (if no separate statement on going concern is made by the directors).*

The directors are responsible for keeping proper accounting records which disclose with reasonable accuracy at any time the financial position of the company and to enable them to ensure that the financial statements comply with the Companies Act 1985. They are also responsible for safeguarding the assets of the company and hence for taking reasonable steps for the prevention and detection of fraud and other irregularities.

In relation to the basis of the auditors' opinion, the standard makes the following statement:

(SAS 600.4)

Auditors should explain the basis of their opinion by including in their report

a) *a statement as to their compliance or otherwise with Auditing Standards, together with the reasons for any departure therefrom;*

b) *a statement that the audit process includes*

i) *examining, on a test basis, evidence relevant to the amounts and disclosures in the financial statements,*

ii) *assessing the significant estimates and judgements made by the reporting entity's directors in preparing the financial statements,*

iii)*considering whether the accounting policies are appropriate to the reporting entity's circumstances, consistently applied and adequately disclosed;*

c) *a statement that they planned and performed the audit so as to obtain reasonable assurance that the financial statements are free from material misstatement, whether caused by fraud or other irregularity or error, and that they have evaluated the overall presentation of the financial statements.*

This generalised description of the audit process provides information as to the basis for the audit opinion which follows. The assumption is that users should be informed as to the particular set of standards which provide the bench-marks for the audit examination, the structure of the audit examination itself and the extent to which the work performed provides safeguards against material misstatements.

Expression of opinion

(SAS 600.5)
An auditors' report should contain a clear expression of opinion on the financial statements and on any further matters required by statute or other requirements applicable to the particular engagement.
The three matters that the auditor must positively express an opinion upon in the audit report are as follows:

▶ *the truth and fairness of the state of the company's affairs at the balance sheet date;*
▶ *the truth and fairness of the profit or loss for the period under review as shown in the profit and loss account, or other income statement; and*
▶ *whether the accounts have been prepared in accordance with the Companies Act 1985.*

The matters that are implied in an unqualified audit report are as stated above.

Qualified opinion

A qualified opinion is issued when either of the following circumstances exist:

a) there is a limitation on the scope of the auditors' examination (see SAS 600.7); or
b) the auditors disagree with the treatment or disclosure of a matter in the financial statements (see SAS 600.8)

and in the auditors' judgement the effect of the matter is or may be material to the financial statements and therefore those statements may not or do not give a true and fair view of the matters on which the auditors are required to report or do not comply with relevant accounting or other requirements.

Adverse opinion

An adverse opinion is issued when the effect of a disagreement is so material or pervasive that the auditors conclude that the financial statements are seriously misleading. An adverse opinion is expressed by stating that the financial statements do not give a true and fair view.
When the auditors conclude that the effect of a disagreement is not so significant as to require an adverse opinion, they express an opinion that is qualified by stating that the financial statements give a true and fair view except for the effects

of the matter giving rise to the disagreement.

Disclaimers of opinion

A disclaimer of opinion is expressed when the possible effect of a limitation on scope is so material or pervasive that the auditors have not been able to obtain sufficient evidence to support, and accordingly are unable to express, an opinion on the financial statements.

Where the auditors conclude that the possible effect of the limitation is not so significant as to require a disclaimer, they issue an opinion that is qualified by stating that the financial statements give a true and fair view except for the effects of any adjustments that might have been found necessary had the limitation not affected the evidence available to them.

The table that follows summarises the position as stated above.

	Material	Fundamental
Limitation of Scope	'Except for'	Disclaimer
Disagreement	'Except for'	Adverse

In the past auditors have been able to qualify their opinion in respect of material uncertainties by using the 'subject to' audit opinion, where the uncertainty was caused by either a limitation of scope, or an inherent uncertainty. Under the new APB approach auditors will no longer issue qualified reports solely as a result of uncertainties which cannot be resolved at the date the financial statements are approved ('inherent uncertainties'). In these circumstances they will express an unqualified opinion on the financial statements, taking into account the treatment of matters affected by uncertainty.

Fundamental uncertainty

(SAS 600.6)

a) *In forming their opinion on financial statements, auditors should consider whether the view given by the financial statements could be affected by inherent uncertainties which, in their opinion, are fundamental.*

b) *When an inherent uncertainty exists which*

 i) *in the auditors' opinion is fundamental, and*
 ii) *is adequately accounted for and disclosed in the financial statements,*

 the auditors should include an explanatory paragraph referring to the fundamental uncertainty in the section of their report setting out the basis of their opinion.

c) *When adding an explanatory paragraph, auditors should use words which clearly indicate that their opinion on the financial statements is not qualified in respect of its contents.*

Inherent uncertainty

An inherent uncertainty is defined in the standard as:

'an uncertainty whose resolution is dependent upon future events outside the control of the reporting entity's directors at the date the financial statements are approved'

Fundamental uncertainty

A fundamental uncertainty is defined in the standard as:
'an inherent is fundamental when the magnitude of its potential impact is so great that, without clear disclosure of the nature and implications of the uncertainty, the view given by the financial statements would be seriously misleading'

Limitation of audit scope

(SAS 600.7)
When there has been a limitation on the scope of the auditor's' work that prevents them from obtaining sufficient evidence to express an unqualified opinion

a) *the auditors' report should include a description of the factors leading to the limitation in the opinion of their report;*
b) *the auditors should issue a disclaimer of opinion when the possible effect of a limitation on scope is so material or pervasive that they are unable to express an opinion on the financial statements;*
c) *a qualified opinion should be issued when the effect of the limitation is not so material or pervasive as to require a disclaimer, and the wording of the opinion should indicate that it is qualified as to the possible adjustments to the financial statements that might have been determined to be necessary had the limitation not existed.*

Disagreement on accounting treatment or disclosure

(SAS 600.8)
Where the auditors disagree with the accounting treatment or disclosure of a matter in the financial statements, and in the auditors' opinion of that disagreement is material to the financial statements

a) *the auditors should include in the opinion section of their report*
    i) *a description of all substantive factors giving rise to the disagreement;*
    ii) *their implication for the financial statements*
    iii) *whenever practicable, a quantification of the effect on the financial statements.*
b) *when the auditors conclude that the effect of the matter giving rise to disagreement is so material or pervasive that the financial statements are seriously misleading they should issue an adverse opinion;*
c) *in the case of other material disagreements, the auditors should issue a qualified opinion indicating that it is expressed except for the matter giving rise to the disagreement.*

Date and signature of the auditors' report

(SAS 600.9)
a) *Auditors should not express an opinion on financial statements until those statements and all other financial information contained in a report of which the audited financial statements form a part have been approved by the directors, and the auditors have considered all necessary available evidence.*
b) *The date of an auditors' report on a reporting entity's financial statements is the date on which the auditors signed their report expressing an opinion on those statements.*

The report may be signed in the name of the auditors' firm, the personal name of the auditor, or both as appropriate. The signature is normally that of the firm because the firm as a whole assumes responsibilty for the audit. To assist identification, the report normally includes the location of the auditors' office. Where appropriate, their status as registered auditors is also stated.

Dating the auditors' report informs the reader that the auditors have considered the effect on the financial statements of events or transactions of which they are aware occurred up to that date.

Auditors cannot form an opinion until the financial statements have been signed and approved by the directors, and the date of the auditors' report is, therefore, the date on which, following

a) receipt of the financial statements and accompanying documents in the form approved by the directors for release; and

b) review of all documents which they are required to consider in addition to the financial statements (for example the directors' report, chairman's statement or other review of an entity's affairs which will accompany the financial statements); and

c) completion of all procedures necessary to form an opinion on the financial statements (and any other opinions required by law or regulation) including a review of post balance sheet events,

the auditors sign (in manuscript) their report expressing an opinion on the financial statements for distribution with those statements.

Illustrative examples of audit reports

Example 1   Unqualified opinion
Example 2   Unqualified opinion with explanatory paragraph describing a fundamental uncertainty
Example 3   Qualified opinion – disagreement
Example 4   Qualified opinion – limitation of scope
Example 5   Qualified opinion – disclaimer of opinion
Example 6   Qualified opinion – adverse opinion

Example 1 – unqualified opinion: company incorporated in Great Britain

Auditors' report to the shareholders of XYZ plc
We have audited the financial statements on pages... to ... which have been prepared under the historical cost convention (as modified by the revaluation of certain fixed assets) and the accounting policies set out on page...

Respective responsibilities of directors and auditors

As described on page... the company's directors are responsible for the preparation of financial statements. It is our responsibility to form an independent opinion, based on our audit, on those statements and to report our opinion to you.

Basis of opinion

We conducted our audit in accordance with Auditing Standards issued by the Auditing Practices Board. An audit includes examination, on a test basis, of evidence relevant to the amount and disclosures in the financial statements. It also includes an assessment of the significant estimates and judgements made by the directors in the preparation of the financial statements, and of whether the accounting policies are appropriate to the company's circumstances, consistently applied and adequately disclosed.

We planned and performed our audit so as to obtain all the information and explanations which we considered necessary in order to provide us with sufficient evidence to give reasonable assurance that the financial statements are free from material misstatement, whether caused by fraud or other irregularity or error. In

---

forming our opinion we also evaluated the overall adequacy of the presentation of information in the financial statements.

Opinion

In our opinion the financial statements give a true and fair view of the state of the company's affairs as at 31 December 19.. and of its profit (loss for the year then ended and have been properly prepared in accordance with the Companies Act 1985.

Registered auditors
Date   *Address*

Example 2 – unqualified opinion: with explanatory paragraph describing a fundamental uncertainty

Auditors' report to the shareholders of XYZ plc
We have audited the financial statements on pages... to ... which nave been prepared under the historical cost convention (as modified by the revaluation of certain fixed assets) and the accounting policies set out on page...

Respective responsibilities of directors and auditors

As described on page... the company's directors are responsible for the preparation of financial statements. It is our responsibility to form an independent opinion, based on our audit, on those statements and to report our opinion to you.

Basis of opinion

We conducted our audit in accordance with Auditing Standards issued by the Auditing Practices Board. An audit includes examination, on a test basis, of evidence relevant to the amount and disclosures in the financial statements. It also includes an assessment of the significant estimates and judgements made by the directors in the preparation of the financial statements, and of whether the accounting policies are appropriate to the company's circumstances, consistently applied and adequately disclosed.

We planned and performed our audit so as to obtain all the information and explanations which we considered necessary in order to provide us with sufficient evidence to give reasonable assurance that the financial statements are free from material misstatement, whether caused by fraud or other irregularity or error. In forming our opinion we also evaluated the overall adequacy of the presentation of information in the financial statements.

Fundamental uncertainty

In forming our opinion, we have considered the adequacy of the disclosures made in the financial statements concerning the possible outcome to litigation against B Limited, a subsidiary undertaking of the company, for an alleged breach of environmental regulataions. The future settlement of this litigation could result in additional liabilities and the closure of Limited's business, whose net assets included in the consolidation balance sheet total £... and whose profit before tax for the year is £... . Details of the circumstances relating to this fundamental uncertainty are described in note ... . Our opinion is not qualified in this respect.

Opinion

In our opinion the financial statements give a true and fair view of the state of the company's affairs as at 31 December 19.. and of its profit (loss) for the year then ended and have been properly prepared in accordance with the Companies Act 1985.

Registered auditors
Date   *Address*

Example 3 – qualified opinion: disagreement

Auditors' report to the shareholders of XYZ plc
We have audited the financial statements on pages... to ... which have been prepared under the historical cost convention (as modified by the revaluation of certain fixed assets) and the accounting policies set out on page...

Respective responsibilities of directors and auditors

As described on page... the company's directors are responsible for the preparation of financial statements. It is our responsibility to form an independent opinion, based on our audit, on those statements and to report our opinion to you.

Basis of opinion

We conducted our audit in accordance with Auditing Standards issued by the Auditing Practices Board. An audit includes examination, on a test basis, of evidence relevant to the amount and disclosures in the financial statements. It also includes an assessment of the significant estimates and judgements made by the directors in the preparation of the financial statements, and of whether the accounting policies are appropriate to the company's circumstances, consistently applied and adequately disclosed.

We planned and performed our audit so as to obtain all the information and explanations which we considered necessary in order to provide us with sufficient evidence to give reasonable assurance that the financial statements are free from material misstatement, whether caused by fraud or other irregularity or error. In forming our opinion we also evaluated the overall adequacy of the presentation of information in the financial statements.

Qualified opinion arising from disagreement about accounting treatment

Included in the debtors shown on the balance sheet is an amout of £Y due from a company which has ceased trading. XYZ has no security for this debt. In our opinion the company is unlikely to receive any payment and full provision of £Y should have been made, reducing profit before tax and net assets by that amount.

Except for the absence of this provision, in our opinion the financial statements give a true and fair view of the state of the company's affairs as at 31 December 19.. and of its profit (loss) for the year ended and have been properly prepared in accordance with the Companies Act 1985.

Registered auditors
Date   *Address*

Example 4 – limitation on the auditors' work

Auditors' report to the shareholders of XYZ plc
We have audited the financial statements on pages... to ... which have been prepared under the historical cost convention (as modified by the revaluation of certain fixed assets) and the accounting policies set out on page...

Respective responsibilities of directors and auditors

As described on page... the company's directors are responsible for the preparation of financial statements. It is our responsibility to form an independent opinion, based on our audit, on those statements and to report our opinion to you.

Basis of opinion

We conducted our audit in accordance with Auditing Standards issued by the Auditing Practices Board. An audit includes examination, on a test basis, of evidence relevant to the amount and disclosures in the financial statements. It also includes an assessment of the significant estimates and judgements made by the directors in the preparation of the financial statements, and of whether the accounting policies are appropriate to the company's circumstances, consistently applied and adequately disclosed.

We planned and performed our audit so as to obtain all the information and explanations which we considered necessary in order to provide us with sufficient evidence to give reasonable assurance that the financial statements are free from material misstatement, whether caused by fraud or other irregularity or error. In forming our opinion. However, the evidence available to us was limited because £... of the company's recorded turnover comprises sales, over which there was no system of control on which we could rely for the purpose of our audit. There were no other satisfactory audit procedures that we could adopt to confirm that cash sales were properly recorded.

In forming our opinion we also evaluated the overall adequacy of the presentation of information in the financial statements.

Qualified opinion arising from limitation in audit scope

Except for any adjustments that might have been found to be necessary had we been able to obtain sufficient evidence concering cash sales, in our opinion the financial statements give a true and fair view of the state of the company's affairs as at 31 December 19.. and of its profit (loss) for the year ended and have been properly prepared in accordance with the Companies Act 1985.

In respect alone of the limitation on our work relating to cash sales:
▶ we have not obtained all the information and explanations that we considered necessary for the purpose of our audit; and
▶ we were unable to determine whether proper accounting records had been maintained.

Registered auditors
Date   *Address*

Example 5 – disclaimer of opinion

Auditors' report to the shareholders of XYZ plc
We have audited the financial statements on pages... to ... which have been prepared under the historical cost convention (as modified by the revaluation of certain fixed assets) and the accounting policies set out on page...

Respective responsibilities of directors and auditors

As described on page... the company's directors are responsible for the preparation of financial statements. It is our responsibility to form an independent opinion, based on our audit, on those statements and to report our opinion to you.

Basis of opinion

We conducted our audit in accordance with Auditing Standards issued by the Auditing Practices Board except that the scope of our work was limited, as explained below.

An audit includes examination, on a test basis, of evidence relevant to the amount and disclosures in the financial statements. It also includes an assessment of the significant estimates and judgements made by the directors in the preparation of the financial statements, and of whether the accounting policies are appropriate to the company's circumstances, consistently applied and adequately disclosed.

We planned and performed our audit so as to obtain all the information and explanations which we considered necessary in order to provide us with sufficient evidence to give reasonable assurance that the financial statements are free from material misstatement, whether caused by fraud or other irregularity or error. In forming our opinion. However, the evidence available to us was limited because we were appointed auditors on (date) and in consequence we were unable to carry out auditing procedures necessary to obtain adequate assurance regarding the quantities and condition of stock and work-in-progress, appearing in the balance sheet at £ ... . Any adjustment to this figure would have a consequential significant effect on the profit for the year.

In forming our opinion we also evaluated the overall adequacy of the presentation of infomration in the financial statements.

Opinion: disclaimer on view given by financial statements

Because of the possible effect of the limitation in evidence available to us, we are unable to from an opinion as to whether the financial statements give a true and fair view of the state of the company's affairs as at 31 December 19.. or of its profit (loss) for the year then ended. In all other respects, in our opinion the financial statements have been properly prepared in accordance with the Companies Act 1985.

In respect alone of the limitation on our work relating to stock and work-in-progress:

▶ we have not obtained all the information and explanations that we considered necessary for the purpose of our audit; and

▶ we were unable to determine whether proper accounting records had been maintained.

Registered auditors
Date   *Address*

> **Example 6 – adverse opinion**
>
> *Auditors' report to the shareholders of XYZ plc*
> *We have audited the financial statements on pages... to ... which have been*
> *prepared under the historical cost convention (as modified by the revaluation*
> *of certain fixed assets) and the accounting policies set out on page...*
>
> **Respective responsibilities of directors and auditors**
>
> As described on page... the company's directors are responsible for the preparation of financial statements. It is our responsibility to form an independent opinion, based on our audit, on those statements and to report our opinion to you.
>
> **Basis of opinion**
>
> We conducted our audit in accordance with Auditing Standards issued by the Auditing Practices Board. An audit includes examination, on a test basis, of evidence relevant to the amount and disclosures in the financial statements. It also includes an assessment of the significant estimates and judgements made by the directors in the preparation of the financial statements, and of whether the accounting policies are appropriate to the company's circumstances, consistently applied and adequately disclosed.
>
> We planned and performed our audit so as to obtain all the information and explanations which we considered necessary in order to provide us with sufficient evidence to give reasonable assurance that the financial statements are free from material misstatement, whether caused by fraud or other irregularity or error. In forming our opinion we also evaluated the overall adequacy of the presentation of information in the financial statements.
>
> **Adverse opinion**
>
> As more fully explained in note ... no provision has been made for losses expected to arise on certain long-term contracts currently in progreess as the directors consider that such losses should be off-set against amounts recoverable on other long-term contracts. In our opinion, provision should be made for foreseeable losses on individual contracts as required by Statement of Standard Accounting Practice 9. If losses had been so recognised the effect would have been to reduce the profit before and after tax for the year and the contra work in progress at 31 December 19.. by £.... .
>
> In view of the effect of the failure to provide for the losses referred to above, in our opinion the financial statements do not give a true and fair view of the state of the company's affairs as at 31 December 19.. and of its profit (loss) for the year then ended. In all other respects in our opinion the financial statements have been properly prepared in accordance with the Companies Act 1985.
>
> *Registered auditors*
> *Date*   *Address*

The present position as to the APB programme

The detailed coverage of Auditing Guidelines and SASs will have been dealt with in Paper 10. This section is to update you as to the present position of the APB programme. The review and update of all existing auditing standards and guidelines will take into account the need for amendments arising from legislative and other developments and the widespread use of information technology in entities of different sizes. The proposed structure of the revised statements of auditing standards is as follows:

Proposed Structure of Statements of Auditing Standards

		Existing equivalent pronouncement[3]
Series 001/099	**Introductory matters**	
*010	The scope and authority of APB pronouncements[1]	
Series 100/199	**Responsibility**	
*100	Objective and general principles governing an audit of financial statements	3.101
*110	Fraud and error	3.418
*120	Consideration of law and regulations[2]	ED
*130	Going concern[2]	3.410
140	Engagement letters	3.406
*150	Subsequent events	3.402
*160	Other information in documents containing audited financial statements	3.411
Series 200/299	**Planning, controlling and recording**	
*200	Planning	3.201
210	Knowledge of the business	–
*220	Audit materiality	–
*230	Documentation	3.201
*240	Quality control for audit work	3.201/3.409
Series 300/399	**Accounting systems and internal control**	
*300	Audit risk assesment	3.202/3.204
310	Auditing in an information systems environment	3.407
Series 400/499	**Evidence**	
*400	Audit evidence	3.203
*410	Analytical procedures	3.417
*420	Audit of accounting estimates	–
*430	Audit sampling	–
*440	Management representations	3.404
450	Opening balances and comparatives	3.403
460	Related parties	–
*470	Overall review of financial statements	3.205
Series 500/599	**Using the work of others**	
*500	Considering the work of internal audit	3.408
*510	The relationship between principal auditors and other auditors	3.415
*520	Using the work of an expert	3.413
Series 600.699	**Reporting**	
*600	Auditors' report on financial statements[1]	
610	Reports to directors or management	3.414
620	The auditors' right and duty to report to regulators in the financial sector[2]	–
Series 700/799	**Engagements other than audits of financial statements**	
Series 800/899	**Particular industries and sectors**	
–	**Glossary of terms**	

Notes
1 These APB pronouncements have already been issued.
2 Development of these pronouncements is being undertaken by separate APB task forces, rather than as part of the revisions project.
3 Some existing pronouncements will be replaced by more than one SAS; conversely, others will be dealt with as part of a different topic.
4 Where the existing equivalent pronouncement is listed as ED, this indicates the existence of an exposure draft issued by the APB (or by its predecessor body, the Auditing Practices Committee) which has not yet been finalised.
5 In cases where there is no existing equivalent pronouncement, the subject matter may be referred to in other pronouncements (for example, by the IAPC).
* Pronouncement where an exposure draft or a statement of auditing standards has already been issued.

Summary

The relationships between auditors and their client companies will always be difficult. The users of the audited financial statements do not have a contractual relationship with auditors. While auditors' independence is held as being very important to the credibility of the audit, auditors are nevertheless dependent on the companies being audited for their fees.

Auditing is a business. The larger firms of accountants employ many thousands of people worldwide and are themselves multinational partnerships with billions of dollars of turnover. The profit motive underlying all audit is a healthy one, as the striving to improve profit will encourage the profession to improve its auditing techniques and procedures. Similarly, litigation is also an important part of the audit relationship as the penalties for poor auditing are substantial. The balance between profit and risk helps to maintain overall professionalism and good standards within the profession.

The introduction of professional regulation has had a great impact on the profession as a whole, but probably more on the smaller practices than on the larger ones, as it is in this area that there is more room for improvement. The structured and formal macro controls should ensure that the auditing and accounting framework is improved, but it is at a micro level where the audit client will experience the change.

Quality controls within practices are being monitored. After many years of 'freedom' there is now a structure in place for auditing the auditors. This practice monitoring adopted by all supervisory bodies will have the greatest impact in ensuring consistency of standards within the profession as a whole.

However, audit failures will still occur. But, then, aeroplanes will still crash. And after all, no matter how carefully the profession is monitored, someone has to ask '*Quis custodes custodiet*?'

Suggested Reading

Auditing Practice Committee
The Auditors Operational Standard 1980

Cadbury Report 1992

Auditing Practice Board

S. Turley and M. Cooper
Auditing in the United Kingdom 1991

Audit Reports
The Future of Auditing

Self test questions

1   What matters should an auditor consider before accepting an audit appointment from a new client?
2   What is the purpose of a letter of engagement?
3   What quality controls would you expect to find within a firm of auditors?
4   How can audits be controlled on a day-to-day basis?

Exam style questions

1   An auditing guideline has been issued on quality control. Although this guideline is mainly concerned with controls that can be exercised within the practising firm, it is also important to maintain the standard of the profession's work by means of external controls.

Required:
a) Briefly consider why it is important that audit firms should maintain the quality of their work.

b) List and briefly describe the procedures a professional firm of auditors should initiate or set up internally to maintain the quality of its audit work.

c) Describe the main procedures that the ACCA, together with other accounting bodies, have initiated in the past ten years to maintain and improve the quality of their members' audit work.

d) Briefly consider the implications of implementing peer reviews, whereby one audit firm checks the work of another. Your answer should include consideration of whether peer reviews would:

i) Improve the standard of work of auditors, and
ii) be acceptable to practising firms.

Your answer should include arguments to justify the conclusions you reach.

2 Consider the following statements:
The Caparo case and the requirement for auditors to have compulsory professional idemnity insurance will result in a lowering of the standards of audits of the accounts of limited liability companies.

The requirement of the Company Act 1989 for all auditors to be registered in creating a monopoly, which cannot be beneficial to people relying on audited accounts.

Note: The Caparo case is *Caparo Industries Plc v. Dickman and Other* (1990) – House of Lords judgement.

Required:
a) Consider whether the factors cited in the statements above will result in a lowering or raising of audit standards.

b) Describe other factors in the regulation of auditors and indicate the developments in accounting and auditing that you believe will increase the standards of audit work.

c) Summarise your reasons and reach a conclusion on whether you believe standards of audit work are improving or declining.

3 a) An Auditing Guideline has been issued on quality control. Assume you work for a medium-sized firm of certified accountants that has a number of offices, each with at least one partner. The senior partner has been considering ways of ensuring that the quality of audit work performed by the firm at its various offices is of a uniformly high standard.

Required:
Write a memorandum to the senior partner of your firm that outlines the quality control procedures that can be exercised internally within your firm.

b) Since 1978 all public companies in the United States of America have been required to have an audit committee as a condition of listing on the New York Stock Exchange.

Required:
i) Explain what you understand by the term 'audit committee'
ii) List and briefly describe the duties and responsibilites of audit committees.
iii) Consider their advantages and disadvantages.
iv) Do you think it would be beneficial to introduce audit committees into the UK?

All answers on pages 628–632.

Tangible Fixed Assets

In this chapter we will look at dealing with tangible fixed assets under SSAP 12 – Accounting for Depreciation. We will also look at accounting for investment properties under SSAP 19, and accounting for government grants under SSAP 4.

SSAP 12 – Accounting for Depreciation, was issued in December 1977. It constituted the first formal requirement to depreciate fixed assets. Experience subsequently highlighted certain practical problems that were not specifically addressed in the standard, including the later adoption by some companies of accounting practices that were not generally used when SSAP 12 was issued.

The Companies Act 1981, which implemented the EC 4th Directive on company accounts, introduced for the first time a legal requirement to depreciate any fixed asset that has a limited useful economic life. Thus, under the Act (later incorporated into the Companies Act 1985) a company is in breach of the specific requirements of the law if it fails to depreciate any fixed asset that has a limited useful economic life.

Despite this company law requirement, the ASC considered that an accounting standard dealing with the practical aspects of depreciation was still needed to complement the overall framework set out in the legal requirements.

As part of its programme of reviewing existing standards, the ASC set up a working party to review SSAP 12 in the early 1980s. The working party prepared a discussion paper, which the ASC published in December 1982 under the heading *A review of SSAP 12 – accounting for depreciation*. The discussion paper set out some of the problems that had arisen since SSAP 12 was introduced, and it identified what the working party believed were the main areas of difficulty in accounting for depreciation. In March 1985, the ASC issued ED 37, a proposed revision of SSAP 12. The revised SSAP 12 was published in January 1987.

The changes from the original SSAP 12 are not major. The principal provisions of the revised standard, dealt with in more detail below, may be summarised as follows (changes from the original standard are indicated in italics):

▶ Provision for depreciation of fixed assets having a finite useful economic life should be made by allocating the cost (or revalued amount) less estimated residual value as fairly as possible to the periods expected to benefit from their use.
▶ *The accounting treatment in the profit and loss account should be consistent with that used in the balance sheet.*
▶ Useful economic lives of assets should be reviewed regularly and, when necessary, revised. The net book amount should be written off over the remaining useful economic life *and, usually, this will cause no material distortion of future results or financial position. However, where future results would be materially distorted, the accumulated depreciation should be recalculated on the basis of the revised asset life, and the adjustment should be recognised as an exceptional item in the year of change.*
▶ If there is a permanent diminution in the value of an asset and the net book amount is considered not to be recoverable in full, it should be written down immediately to the estimated recoverable amount. *In the case of an asset that has not been revalued, such provision should be charged to the profit and loss account.*

▶ *Depreciation charged prior to a revaluation should not be written back to the profit and loss account (with exceptions).*

▶ Freehold land does not normally require a provision for depreciation. Buildings, however, should be depreciated having regard to the same criteria as apply to other assets.

The revised SSAP 12 resolved some of the practical problems arising under the original depreciation standard, but it did not deal with other practical problem areas, such as:

▶ the accounting problems arising from revaluation
▶ the capitalisation of borrowing costs.

These problem areas were addressed by the ASC in ED 51, which was issued in 1990.

SSAP 19 was issued in November 1981 and is applicable to financial statements relating to accounting periods starting on or after 1 July 1981. SSAP 12 (Revised) – Accounting for Depreciation, specifically excludes investment properties. Thus, under the accounting requirements of SSAP 12 (Revised) fixed assets are generally subject to annual depreciation charges. These reflect, on a systematic basis, the wearing out, consumption and other loss of value, whether arising from use, effluxion of time, or obsolescence through technology and market changes. Under these requirements it is also accepted that an increase in value of a fixed asset does not generally remove the necessity to charge depreciation to reflect, on a systematic basis, the consumption of the asset.

A different treatment is required where a significant proportion of the fixed assets are held not for consumption in the business operations but as investments, the disposal of which would not materially affect any manufacturing or trading operations of the enterprise. In such a case, the current value of these investments, and changes in that current value, are the prime importance, rather than a calculation of systematic annual depreciation. Consequently, for the proper appreciation of the financial position, a different accounting treatment is considered appropriate for fixed assets held as investments.

Investment properties may be held by a company that holds investments as part of its business, such as an investment trust or property investment company. Investment properties may also be held by a company whose main business is not the holding of investments.

The original SSAP 4 was issued in 1974. It concentrated on accounting for the receipt by companies of capital-based grants and actually stated that revenue grants received by companies did not produce accounting problems. The standard did not deal with the issue of when grants should be recognised as income. This problem was first addressed in ED 43 issued in 1988, and is now dealt with in SSAP 4 (Revised), which was issued in 1990.

In dealing with tangible fixed assets it is necessary to bear in mind the ASB definition in its statement of principles. These principles are outlined in Chapter 1. Thus, assets are defined as rights to future economic benefits controlled by an entity as a result of past transactions or events, that is, legal ownership is no longer a necessary factor in determining whether an asset exists.

Definitions under the accounting standard

The original SSAP 12 defined depreciation as 'the measure of the wearing out, consumption or other loss of value of a fixed asset whether arising from use, effluxion of time or obsolescence through technology and market changes'.

This definition attracted some criticism as it dealt with both depreciation as a measure of allocating cost or value (focusing on the measurement of income) and as a measure of a loss of value (where the focus is more on asset valuation). The revised standard amended the original definition to read as 'the measure of the wearing out, consumption or other reduction in the useful economic life of a fixed asset whether arising from use, effluxion of time or obsolescence through technological or market changes'.

The ASC now considers that provisions for depreciation are allocations of cost rather than reflections of loss of value.

The revised standard provides definitions of three terms that were not defined in the original standard:

▶ The useful economic life of an asset is the period over which the *present owner* will derive economic benefits from its use.
▶ The residual value is the realisable value of an asset at the end of its useful economic life. Realisation costs should be deducted when calculating residual value. The effect of future inflation should not be taken into account when calculating the asset's residual value, that is, residual value should be based on prices prevailing at the date of acquisition (or subsequent revaluation).
▶ The recoverable amount of an asset is the greater of its net realisable value and, where appropriate, the amount recoverable from its further use.

Legal requirements

Schedule 4 to the Companies Act 1985 requires that fixed assets be shown in the balance sheet under the headings of 'intangible assets', 'tangible assets' and 'investments'.

The initial carrying value of any fixed asset must be its purchase price or production cost. A company may, however, avail itself of the alternative valuation rules under which intangible fixed assets (except goodwill) may be included at their current cost and tangible fixed assets may be included at market value or at their current cost.

Where a fixed asset has a limited useful economic life, its cost less estimated residual value should be reduced by provisions for depreciation so as to write it off systematically over its useful economic life. If the alternative valuation rules are followed, the starting point for calculating depreciation is the current cost or market value.

Provision must be made for any permanent diminution in the value of a fixed asset. If such a provision is no longer considered to be necessary, it must be written back. Disclosure must be made of the depreciation charge and any charge or credit in respect of provisions for permanent diminution in value.

The following additional information must be disclosed:

▶ For each fixed asset balance sheet heading:
  – the cost or revalued amount at the beginning and end of the year
  – movements in respect of revaluations, acquisitions, disposals and transfers
  – the accumulated depreciation at the beginning and end of the period and movements in respect of the depreciation charge for the year, disposals of fixed assets and any other adjustments.
▶ Where fixed assets are accounted for using the alternative accounting rules the schedule requires disclosure of the comparable amounts determined under the historical cost accounting rules or the difference between these amounts and those shown in the balance sheet.
▶ Where fixed assets are carried at revalued amounts the schedule requires disclosure of the years of the valuations, the values given in those years and, for assets valued during the financial year, the names or qualifications of the valuers and the valuation bases used.

The revaluation problem

The practice of revaluing fixed assets to bring the book figures more into line with current values is being increasingly adopted and is particularly evident in the case of property.

The original standard stated that where assets are revalued and effect is given to the revaluation in financial statements, the charge for depreciation *thereafter* should be based on the revalued amount, and in the year of change there should be disclosed by way of note to the financial statements the subdivision of the charge between that applicable to original cost and that applicable to the change in value on the current revaluation, if material. The standard argued that it would not be appropriate to omit charging depreciation of a fixed asset on the grounds that its market value is greater than its net book value. If account is taken of such increased value, an increased depreciation charge will become necessary.

The revised standard asserts that incorporating revaluations into accounts gives useful and relevant information to users of accounts. It does not prescribe how frequently assets should be revalued, although it does state that valuations should be kept up to date. The practice of selective revaluation – that is, modified historical cost accounts – is not comprehensively dealt with in the revised standard. Despite this, it introduced a limited number of comments relating to revaluations and these are dealt with in turn below.

Consistency and articulation

One of the problems arising where companies produce modified historical cost accounts is a loss of comparability where other companies continue to produce strict historical cost accounts. Differences arise in terms of balance sheet values, profit and loss account charges for depreciation and also on the gain or loss arising on the disposal of a fixed asset.

ED 37 proposed, and the revised standard reiterated, that the depreciation charge in the profit and loss account for the period should be based on the carrying amount of the asset in the balance sheet. This is sometimes referred to as 'articulation' of the two statements. This requirement has the consequence of banning split depreciation and supplementary depreciation.

Split depreciation is the name given in practice, in respect of a revalued asset, of charging the depreciation based on the revaluation surplus to the revaluation reserve. Where the original standard required any provision for depreciation to be based on the revalued amount, it was not explicit as to where the depreciation should be charged.

The new standard states explicitly that it should be charged to the profit and loss account.

Some people argue that the Companies Act 1985 appears to permit split depreciation, and that a requirement to charge against profit the whole of the depreciation after revaluation results in a loss of comparability between those companies that revalue assets and those that do not. They say that a split depreciation charge results in the following:

▶ In practice, only some fixed assets are revalued and then on a selective basis.
▶ Such revaluations take place spasmodically, very often with very many years in between.
▶ The amount and trend of eps (earnings per share) are artificially affected when assets are selectively and periodically revalued.
▶ Extra depreciation depresses eps at the same time as the unrealised revaluation surpluses increase reserves.
▶ The revaluation gain, when realised, is taken partly or wholly to the profit and loss account increasing the variability in eps.

▶ Legally, an amount equal to the additional depreciation on the revaluation surplus is treated as realised profit for the purposes of a distribution. As it is only the historic cost depreciation that reduces the distributable profits of a company, there is no reason for any additional depreciation being charged against profit and loss account.

The problem as to where to debit the depreciation charge would not arise if the convention of permitting either only historical cost or only modified accounts were changed, so that profit and loss accounts were prepared solely on the basis of historical costs and balance sheets were prepared on the basis of modified historical cost to include revaluation of material fixed assets.

If such a basis were to be adopted, it would allow depreciation on fixed assets to be split as has been done by, for example, Woolworth; earnings would remain unaffected by the revaluations; additional depreciation would be charged against the revaluation surplus; the whole of the surplus remaining on realisation of the asset would be credited to the profit and loss account. Moreover, such a treatment would have the benefit of closing the earnings gap that is arbitrarily created by the different treatment of property assets under SSAPs 12 (Revised) and 19.

The ASC, however, believes that the accounting treatment in the profit and loss account should be consistent with that in the balance sheet. The ASC feel that the provisions of the Companies Act are ambiguous in this regard and that even if the splitting of the depreciation charge were permitted by company law it is undersirable and is accordingly not permitted by the revised standard on the grounds that:

▶ While such treatment is not forbidden under either FRS 3 or SSAP 12 (Revised) and is (implicitly) allowed by Schedule 4 of the 1985 Act, it is doubtful whether the resulting 'hybrid' accounts show a true and fair view as required by the Act.
▶ The treatment does not solve any of the problems caused by mixing historical costs and current costs. It can be nothing but confusing for users to be told that fixed assets are valued in different ways for balance sheet and profit and loss account purposes.
▶ There is some doubt as to whether such treatment would be legal under the Act – an 'it depends on what you mean by . . .' situation.
▶ It is a fundamental principle that depreciation should be related to the carrying amount of the asset in the balance sheet, and that the charge for depreciation should be based on this amount whether historical cost, modified historical cost or current cost.

Applying the same principles, supplementary depreciation – that is, an amount charged in the profit and loss account in excess of historical cost depreciation where the asset has not been revalued in the balance sheet – is also prohibited in the revised standard. However, neither company law nor the revised standard precludes a company from setting aside, as on appropriation of profits, an amount for the increased cost of replacement of fixed assets.

Depreciation prior to revaluation

When companies revalue fixed assets the more common bookkeeping approach is to reflect, in the revaluation reserve, the difference between the asset's net book amount (say cost of £100 less depreciation of £70, that is net of £30) and that shown by the latest valuation (say £140). In the fixed assets movements note, the gross amount of the asset would be increased to the revalued amount – to £140 by an adjustment of £40 – and the accumulated depreciation of £70 would be extinguished. The sum of these two adjustments – £40 + £70 – would equate to the £110 credited to the revaluation reserve.

The revised standard introduces a prohibition on crediting to the profit and loss account any depreciation charged prior to a revaluation. However, it does not specify whether the prior depreciation that is credited to the revaluation reserve represents a realised or an unrealised profit. The CCAB guidance statement, issued in 1982, on the determination of distributable profits considered the issue but, given divided opinion, stated that it was inappropriate to offer guidance on the question in that statement. As a result, if a company is relying on such a profit being realised in order to make a distribution, then it may be appropriate for the directors to seek legal advice

Provisions for permanent diminution in value

The need to write down an asset where a permanent diminution in value has occurred, as required by the original SSAP 12, is not a matter for dispute. However, in finalising the revised standard the ASC sought to specify where the write down should be charged.

At one stage, the ASC was proposing that the write down should be charged to the profit and loss account in respect of permanent diminutions in value of all assets, whether revalued or not. Some commentators took the view that while this was an appropriate accounting treatment for assets accounted for on historic cost principles, it was not necessarily appropriate for assets that have been revalued. Paragraph 20 of the revised standard notes that it does not discuss the treatment of permanent diminutions in value in the case of previously revalued assets. For the time being, therefore, the question of where to charge provisions for permanent diminutions in value of revalued assets is not dealt with in accounting standards and remains a practical problem.

The ASC – in TR 648, issued on the publication of the revised standard – recognised the problems caused by incorporating assets at revalued amounts in historical cost accounts, but stated that these aspects of revaluations are outside the scope of a standard on depreciation and that it had added a new project on fixed assets and revaluations to its work programme.

While nearly all enterprises in the United Kingdom currently prepare their financial statements under the historical cost convention, they are encouraged – see Chapter 14 on accounting for the effects of price changes – to provide valuation-based information.

There is also, of course, modified historical cost accounting in which selected fixed assets are periodically revalued. ED 51 permits fixed assets to be carried at a valuation in balance sheets prepared under the historical cost convention but only provided that the valuations are kept up to date and carried out within the framework laid down.

There have been those in the past who have favoured revaluation given:

▶ it provides useful information to users, and
▶ recognition of the valuations in the balance sheet enables performance ratios, measuring the effectiveness with which capital has been employed, to be calculated more satisfactorily.

There are also those who argue that fixed assets should be carried only at historical cost on the basis that:

▶ selective revaluation undermines the integrity of the historical cost system, and
▶ the reporting enterprise is allowed too much discretion over reported results and financial position, and
▶ if it is necessary to provide information on the market value of particular fixed assets this is best done by including relevant information in the notes to the accounts.

ED 51 – Accounting for Fixed Assets and Revaluations, states that as financial statements are conventionally prepared on the historical cost basis, it is not considered appropriate to require the carrying of some or all of an enterprise's fixed assets at a valuation in historical cost accounts, *but* at the same time it is regarded as impractical to seek to prohibit the carrying of any fixed assets at a valuation. Hence, it is proposed that fixed assets should continue to be permitted to be carried at a valuation.

The specific proposals of ED 51 regarding revaluation are designed to:

▶ improve comparability in the way enterprises undertake revaluations
▶ provide information so that enterprises that do carry fixed assets at valuation can be reliably compared with enterprises that carry all their fixed assets at cost.

Specific proposals as to valuations

The specific propsals of ED 51 as to valuations are:

▶ For each *class* of fixed assets, the directors should determine whether it is their accounting policy to carry that class at cost or at a valuation.
▶ If carried at valuation, the carrying amount should represent the *open market value* of the fixed asset except in circumstances where this value cannot be determined, in which case the *depreciated net replacement cost* of the fixed asset should be used in the valuation.
▶ A fixed asset should not be included in the balance sheet at a valuation undertaken more than five years previously (unless the directors believe that the value of such fixed assets at the balance sheet date is not materially different from that shown in the financial statements).
▶ The results of a valuation should initially be reflected in the financial statements of the period to which it relates.
▶ Subject to the five-year rule, fixed assets in a particular class may be revalued on a rolling basis in a systematic and rational manner.
▶ When land and buildings are revalued the carrying amount should be based on a valuation by an external valuer unless the enterprise has an internal property department, but even then the basis of valuation by the internal valuer must be subject to review by an external valuer.
▶ For fixed assets other than land or buildings valuation may be by either internal or external valuers.

These various proposals do not apply to investment properties.

The revaluation reserve

The problem as to what the surplus on revaluation is was briefly dealt with earlier in the chapter. Under ED 51:

▶ The balance on the revaluation reserve relating to fixed assets should equal not more than the sum of the unrealised and uncapitalised amounts arising from the revaluation of fixed assets that are still being used by the enterprise.
▶ Transfers made from revaluation reserve to profit and loss account reserve should clearly be identified. The transfer should include an amount in respect of the difference between depreciation calculated on historical cost of revalued fixed assets and depreciation based on their revalued amounts. This is in order to enable users to determine what the profit for the period would have been if the enterprise had carried all its fixed assets at historical cost.
▶ When a permanent diminution in the carrying amount of a fixed asset carried at valuation occurs, a transfer of any amount in the revaluation reserve relating to that asset should be made to the profit and loss account reserve up to the amount of the permanent diminution.

- Revaluation surpluses and deficits arising within a class of fixed assets should be netted off within the revaluation reserve. If this results in a deficit on the reserve at the end of the accounting period, the deficit should, on the grounds of prudence, be eliminated by means of a charge to the profit and loss account for the period. This should be treated as additional depreciation.
- On the disposal of a revalued fixed asset, any amount remaining in the revaluation reserve relating to that asset should be transferred to profit and loss account reserves. In normal circumstances this will be the difference between the disposal gain based on depreciated historical cost and that based on the net revalued amount. This will not always be the case; part of the revaluation reserve may have been capitalised.
- In the rare circumstances of a reversal of a permanent diminution in value of a fixed asset carried at valuation, an amount equal to the increase in the carrying amount should be credited to the revaluation reserve. A similar amount (not exceeding the amount previously charged to the profit and loss account) should then be transferred from the revaluation reserve to the profit and loss account for the period.
- When a fixed asset is valued, the difference between the revalued amount and the depreciated carrying amount immediately prior to the valuation should be credited or debited to the revaluation reserve and should not be taken to the profit and loss account for the period.

Example 4.1, in the next subsection, illustrates the application of some of these proposals.

Problems of accounting for disposal of a previously revalued fixed asset

There problems of accounting for the disposal of a previously revalued fixed asset:

- How should the gain or loss on disposal be classified?
- What is the amount of the gain or loss to be included in the profit and loss account?

Where a company sells a depreciated (operating) fixed asset, the profit or loss on sale arises from either over depreciation or under depreciation in previous years. It is, therefore, appropriate to include such profit or loss, in arriving at ordinary results, as a part of depreciation for the year. Where such amounts are material, they should be separately disclosed as exceptional.

Profits or losses on the disposal of non-depreciated (non-operating) fixed assets – for example, investment properties and fixed asset investments – do not result from over or under depreciation in previous years. They arise from events the nature of which are usually extraordinary, and should, accordingly, usually be treated as extraordinary items. This would have been the treatment under SSAP 6. Under FRS 3 (see Chapter 11), all profits and losses on disposal of fixed assets will be dealt with above the line.

Where there is little problem in answering the question as to classification of such profits or losses, as above, several approaches are possible when it comes to deciding on the amount of profit or loss to be included in the profit and loss account of the year of disposal.

If a fixed asset disposed of has not previously been revalued there is no problem. The profit or loss is simply the difference between the proceeds of sale and the net book value on the date of sale.

If, however, the disposed of fixed asset had previously been revalued, the profit or loss on the disposal consists of two elements:

▶ proceeds of sale less net book value (based on revalued amount) on the date of sale, plus

▶ the whole of the revaluation surplus *on the date of the revaluation.*

The original SSAP 6 did not deal with the problem of accounting for profits or losses on disposal of previously revalued fixed assets. ED 16, which was issued as a supplement to SSAP 6, proposed that only the first element of the gain should be included in the profit and loss account and the second retained by the company within reserves.

In ED 36, the ASC proposed that the profit or loss to be included in the reported profit of the year of disposal should include *both* the above elements of the profit or loss.

The revised SSAP 6 contained no requirements on accounting for such amounts. Thus, a company may have included in the profit and loss account of the year of disposal:

▶ *either* only the difference between sale proceeds and NBV

▶ *or* the difference between sale proceeds and NBV plus the revaluation surplus on the date of the revaluation,

but consistently for all such disposals, as a matter of accounting policy.

The problem arises given modified historical cost accounts. The problem remained in the revised SSAP 6 because there is, as yet, no requirement that companies either revalue all their assets or revalue none of them. Modified historical cost accounts gives rise to distortions of profit following the revaluation of an asset. A simple example illustrates the distorting effects of a revaluation of fixed assets (see Example 4.1).

EXAMPLE 4.1

	Historical cost £	Modified historical cost £
Cost 1/1/87	1,000	1,000
Depreciation to 1/1/91 (4/10)	(400)	(400)
	600	600
Revaluation surplus		300
Revaluation at 1/1/91		900
Depreciation for 1991		
600/6 years	(100)	
900/6 years		(150)
Net book value 31/12/91	500	750

The asset was sold at the beginning of 1992 for £975.

Looking at Example 4.1 we can see that:

▶ If the asset had not been revalued, the profit on disposal, recognised in 1992 in the profit and loss account as part of what FRS 3 would label as profit on ordinary activities before interest, would be (975 − 500) = £475.

▶ Given revaluation, *prior* to ED 36, the profit on disposal would be the sale proceeds less the NBV based on the revalued amount on the date of sale (975 − 750) = £225. This would be included in the 1992 profit and loss account as part of the profit on ordinary operations. The balance on the revaluation reserve – £300 – now wholly realised on sale would not be included in the profit and loss account for the year but may be transferred to realised reserves as a movement on reserves.

▶ Given revaluation per ED 36, the whole of the gain – that is, proceeds less net book value (£225) plus the revaluation surplus on the date of the revaluation (£300), £525 – would have been in the 1992 profit and loss account as part of the profit on ordinary operations. This achieves the same result that would have been obtained if the asset had not been revalued, that is a gain of £475 plus the reinstatement in the profit and loss account of the additional depreciation charged in 1991 because of the revaluation (150 – 100) £50.

▶ Profit and loss accounts of the company compared:

	Company does not revalue			Company does revalue		
	1991	1992	Aggre-gated	1991	1992	Aggre-gated
	£	£	£	£	£	£
Profit before depreciation (say)	3,500	4,000	7,500	3,500	4,000	7,500
Depreciation	(100)	–	(100)	(150)	–	(150)
Gain on sale	–	475	475	–	525	525
	3,400	4,475	7,875	3,350	4,525	7,875

▶ It is important to appreciate that, in accounting for the disposal per ED 36, the 1992 reported profit is not the same as it would have been had the asset not been revalued. The 1992 profit is £4,525 with revaluation, and £4,475 without revaluation. The 1991 reported profit given the revaluation in 1991, is also different. The 1991 profit with revaluation is £3,350 and without £3,400. The important thing is that the *total* reported profits, the aggregated column – the amounts which would be included in the FRS 3 profit on ordinary activities before interest – are the same. This is what ED 36 sought to achieve in this regard.

▶ The bookkeeping for the revaluation and the disposal would be as follows:

Asset – Cost

1/1/87	1,000	Revaluation reserve 1/1/91	1,000
At valuation – revaluation reserve	900	Disposal account	900

Asset – Depreciation

Revaluation reserve	400	1/1/91	400
(at 1/1/91)		Profit and loss account	
Disposal account	150	for y/e 31/12/91	150

Revaluation reserve

Cost	1,000	Depreciation	400
c/d	300	At valuation	900
Profit and loss account 1992	300	At 1/1/91 b/f	300

Disposal account

At valuation	900	Accumulated depreciation	150
Profit and loss account 1992	225	Sale proceeds	975

The profit and loss account for 1992 would include, as part of the depreciation charge for 1992, the profit on disposal of a depreciated fixed asset of (300 + 225) £525.

▶ One further problem arises if you are to account for such a disposal in accordance with ED 36. The ED required that the whole of the revaluation surplus on the date of the revaluation should be included as part of the profit on disposal in the profit and loss account of the year of disposal.

This amount, on revaluation, will be taken to the revaluation reserve. The amount in revaluation reserve may, however, have diminished on the date of sale of the asset. First, having revalued the asset, the company will have charged additional depreciation. This additional depreciation charged is the realised extent of the unrealised revaluation surplus and may have been transferred to realised reserves as a movement on reserves. If such a transfer had been made, then ED 36 proposed that it be reversed in the year of disposal so that the whole of the revaluation surplus on the date of the revaluation could be transferred to the profit and loss account of the year of disposal. Assume that the company did transfer the additional depreciation charged in 1991 of £50 from revaluation reserves to realised reserves.

The 1991 profit and loss account would disclose:

Retained profit for the year £3,350

| | | Movement on reserves | |
	Revaluation reserve	Profit and loss account	Total
	£	£	£
At 1/1/91	–	x	x
For year	300	3,350	3,650
Transfer	(50)	50	–
At 31/12/91	250	3,400	3,650

(See Chapter 13, on distributable profits. Note that the revaluation has an effect on the reported profits after the revaluation but not on the legally distributable profits of the company, which remain what they would have been, £3,400, if the company had not revalued the asset.)

The 1992 profit and loss account would disclose:

Retained profit for the year £4,525

| | | Movement on reserves | |
	Revaluation reserve	Profit and loss account	Total
	£	£	£
At 1/1/92	250	3,400	3,650
Transfer	50	(50)	–
		3,350	
Profit for the year		4,225	4,225
Transfer	(300)	300	
At 31/12/92	–	7,875	7,875

Secondly, the revaluation reserve may also have been utilised for the making of a bonus issue of shares. If this had been the case then, on the date of the disposal, an amount needs to be transferred to the revaluation reserve from the profit and loss account as a movement on reserves in order that the whole of the revaluation surplus on the date of the revaluation can be transferred to the profit and loss account of the year of disposal.

It is not difficult to appreciate why the ED 36 proposals in this regard were not adopted as standard by the revised SSAP 6. Distortions in the reported profits of each year are not eliminated following a revaluation of fixed assets. The fact that the total reported profits of the company after the revaluation remains the same taking all years from revaluation to sale is hardly a meaningful solution of the problem. Until the wider problems of accounting for the revaluation of fixed assets is resolved, there can be no universally accepted answer to the problem of accounting for disposals of previously revalued fixed assets. The issue has, however, been addressed in FRS 3 which now recognises that the profit or loss on sale of such assets to be reported in profit on ordinary activities before interest should be the difference between sale proceeds and NBV on the date of sale only.

ED 51 now proposes that the gain or loss on sale to be reported in the profit and loss account of the year of sale be the difference between the sale proceeds and the NBV of the asset on the date of disposal. The revaluation surplus, in revaluation reserve, now becomes wholly realised on sale and should be transferred to realised reserves as a movement within reserves.

Where the ED 36 approach may be described as an income approach the ED 51 approach is best described as a value approach to reporting disposal gains. Under ED 36 the revaluation surplus *does* pass through reported profits when the asset is sold; under ED 51 the revaluation surplus never passes through reported profits and is dealt with wholly within reserve movements.

It is important to appreciate that where there will be an earnings effect depending on the approach adopted, there will be no effect on total legally distributable profit.

It is interesting to observe that the ED 51 proposals as to accounting for revaluations and the disposal of previously revalued fixed assets is now standard accounting practice under FRS 3 (see Chapter 11) given the divergence of views prior to the issue of FRS 3 as to accounting for such transactions. The reasons are:

▶ Prior to FRS 3, when the whole emphasis of reporting financial performance was on the profit and loss account, it was important to establish whether the revaluation surplus should be reported as income in the profit and loss account. The income approach argued in the affirmative, while the value approach argued that this part of the disposal gain should be dealt with within reserves. No consensus view emerged in SSAP 6 (Revised).
▶ Under FRS 3, where the emphasis of reporting financial performance moves away from the profit and loss account to a more full information set, whether the revaluation surplus is dealt with in the profit and loss account or within reserves is no longer such a crucial issue.

The useful life problem

An asset's useful economic life may be:

▶ pre-determined, as in the case of a lease
▶ directly governed by extraction or consumption, as in the case of a mine
▶ dependent on its physical deterioration through use or effluxion of time
▶ reduced by economic or technological obsolescence.

The revised standard requires that the useful economic lives of assets should be reviewed regularly, and, when necessary, revised. Such a review would normally be undertaken at least every five years, and more frequently where circumstances warrant it.

The revised standard also requires that identical asset lives be used for depreciation on a historical cost basis and on any basis that reflects the effects of changing prices.

In the late 1970s, some companies developed the practice of estimating an asset's useful economic life but using a shorter period in historical cost accounts as a crude method of allowing for the effects of inflation. Some of those companies then prepared current cost accounts under SSAP 16 using realistic (that is, unshortened) useful economic lives. The revised standard requires the same, realistic lives to be used under both cost conventions, as shortening useful economic lives is not a reliable way of reflecting the effects of changing prices. Companies may therefore need to consider lengthening the useful economic lives used in their historical cost accounts.

Change in estimate of asset life

The original standard required that where there is a revision of the estimated useful life of an asset, the unamortised cost should be charged over the revised remaining useful life.

ED 37 proposed that this rule be continued given that, if asset lives were regularly reviewed, the effect of the change on the depreciation charge in future years would be relatively small and that the method ensures that the total cost of a fixed asset is charged to profit and loss account taking the life of the asset as a whole.

Some authorities, however, suggested that there might be occasions when a revision would result in distortions to the charges for depreciation in future periods. The revised standard took note of these comments and requires:

▶ Regular review of asset lives.
▶ When necessary, revision of lives.
▶ As, usually, there will be no material distortion of future results or financial position, the net book amount should be written off the revised remaining life.
▶ If, however, future results would be materially distorted, the adjustment to accumulated depreciation should be recognised in the accounts in accordance with what is now FRS 3; the adjustment will usually be dealt with in arriving at profit on ordinary activities before interest.
▶ It would be rare for a change in asset life to be so serious as to constitute a fundamental error and a prior year adjustment would not, normally, be appropriate.

EXAMPLE 4.2

	£
Asset cost 1/1/85	2,000
(useful life 10 years)	
Depreciation to 1/1/91 (6/10)	(1,200)
Net book value 1/1/91	800
Effect of revision of life	(300)
Revised net book value based on remaining life estimated at 2 years as opposed to 4 years on 1/1/91	
2/8 x 2,000	500
Depreciation 1991 500/2 years	(250)
Net book value 31/12/91	250

The total charge for depreciation in the 1991 accounts would be £550: £300 (if material) disclosed as an exceptional item, plus £250.

Reinstatement of fully depreciated assets

ED 37 proposed that where assets are fully depreciated and the omission of depreciation on such assets would result in a failure to give a true and fair view, the assets should be reinstated, with the amount at which they were reinstated being credited to reserves. The proposal was dropped and does not appear in the revised SSAP 12. The reasons for this are:

▶ It assumes that another requirement of the standard (that asset lives should be estimated realistically and reviewed regularly) has not been followed.
▶ In any case, there would be few instances where omission would impair a true and fair view.

The non-depreciation of certain assets problem

ED 37 proposed that depreciation need not be charged on what would normally be a depreciable fixed asset if the asset was maintained to such a standard that:

▶ the estimated residual value is equal to or greater than its net book amount, or
▶ its estimated useful economic life is either infinite or such that any depreciation charge would be insignificant.

ED 37 noted that 'for an asset to be treated in this way maintenance should be undertaken on a regular basis and the cost charged in the profit and loss account. In assessing whether any depreciation should be charged, regard should be had not only to the physical condition of the asset but also to the risk of obsolescence.'

The proposal, although expressed in terms of 'assets', is generally discussed in the context of buildings. For example, some brewers do not depreciate their tied properties and the practice is also sometimes applied to other assets such as hotels and various retail premises.

Commentators on ED 37 made two principal criticisms of the proposal. First, the proposal could be open to misinterpretation and abuse and companies might seek to use it beyond the circumstances for which it was intended. Second, there was concern that too much emphasis was placed on maintenance. As some commentators pointed out, expenditure on maintenance is only one of the factors that affect the value of an asset: a well-maintained asset may still be subject to depreciation through the results of obsolescence from technological and market changes. In the case of a building, its location may be at least as relevant as its state of repair. As a result of these criticisms, the proposal is not mentioned in the revised standard. However, the matter is referred to in the accompanying TR 648 (paragraph 10), where the ASC refers to the general principle of SSAP 12 – that where a fixed asset has a finite useful economic life, its cost (or revalued amount) less residual value should be depreciated over that life – and acknowledges that there may be circumstances where following this principle renders any depreciation charge unnecessary.

Alternative methods of depreciation

The revised standard, like the original standard, does not specify a method for depreciation. The revised standard simply states that there is a range of acceptable depreciation methods.

Management should select the method regarded as most appropriate to the type of asset and its use in the business so as to allocate depreciation as fairly as possible to the periods expected to benefit from the asset's use. Although the straight-line method is the simplest to apply, it may not always be the most appropriate.

Straight-line method

This is the most common method used in practice. The cost (or value) less the estimated residual value is allocated over the useful economic life so as to charge each accounting period with the same amount.

Reducing balance method

This method results in higher charges for depreciation in the earlier years of an asset's use. Given, normally, higher charges for repairs and maintenance in later years, early years bear high depreciation and low maintenance and later years low depreciation and high maintenance, the overall effect being to produce an approximately constant charge taking the two costs together.

Sum of the digits method

If an asset is expected to last 12 periods, digits 1 to 12 are allocated to each period from the last to the first. The digits are added together, here 78, and the first period charged 12/78, the second 11/78 . . . the last 1/78.

The method is similar in its effect to the reducing balance method.

Annuity method

The objective under this method is to produce an approximately constant charge for the total of depreciation and cost of capital. Depreciation is calculated so as to give a low charge in earlier years when interest costs are high, and a high charge in later years when interest costs are low.

Unit of production methods

Under these methods depreciation is related to the estimated production capability of an asset. These methods are appropriate when the use of an asset varies from period to period. The rate of depreciation per hour or unit is arrived at by dividing the depreciable amount by the estimated total hours or units.

A change from one method to another may be justified only on the ground that the new method will give a fairer presentation of the company's results and financial position – where the method is changed, the unamortised cost on the date of the change should be written off under the new method, that is, a change in method is not a change of accounting policy.

Disclosure

The 1985 Act sets out the following four categories of tangible fixed assets:

▶ land and buildings
▶ plant and machinery
▶ fixtures, fittings, tools and equipment
▶ payments on account and assets in course of construction.

Motor vehicles involved in the manufacturing process would be included in plant and machinery, whilst motor vehicles not so involved would be included in fixtures, fittings, tools and equipment.

Note that the 1985 Act requires that companies follow the strict wording of the formats and not deviate from this requirement although it does allow a company to show any item in greater detail than the format it adopts requires. (See Example 4.3.)

EXAMPLE 4.3

Note: Tangible fixed assets

	Investment properties	Land and buildings	Plant and machinery	Fixtures, fittings, tools and equipment	Assets in course of con- struction	Total
(Where relevant, this note would be required separately for the Group and for the Parent company.)						
	£	£	£	£	£	£
Cost or valuation						
At 1 January 1991						
Note 1, Note 2	x	x	x	x	x	x
Exchange differences						
Note 3	x	x	x	x	x	x
Arising on revaluation						
Note 4	x	x	x	x	x	x
Additions	x	x	x	x	x	x
Arising in respect of						
new subsidiary Note 5	x	x	x		x	x
Disposals	(x)	(x)	(x)	(x)	(x)	(x)
At 31 December 1991	x	x	x	x	x	x
Depreciation						
At 1 January 1991	(x)	(x)	(x)	(x)	(x)	(x)
Exchange differences						
Note 3	(x)	(x)	(x)	(x)	(x)	(x)
Eliminated on revaluation						
Note 4	x	x	x	x	x	x
Arising in respect of						
new subsidiary Note 5	(x)	(x)	(x)	(x)	(x)	(x)
Charge for year	(x)	(x)	(x)	(x)	(x)	(x)
Disposals	x	x	x	x	x	x
At 31 December 1991	(x)	(x)	(x)	(x)	(x)	(x)
Net Book Value						
At 1 January 1991	x	x	x	x	x	x
At 31 December 1991	x	x	x	x	x	x
Cost or valuation represents						
Valuation in 1985	x	x	x	x	x	x
Valuation in 1991	x	x	x	x	x	x
Cost	x	x	x	x	x	x
	x	x	x	x	x	x

In accordance with SSAP 19 investment properties are revalued annually and any surplus or deficit arising is taken to an investment property revaluation reserve. No depreciation is charged or provided on such properties unless they comprise leasehold properties where the unexpired term of the lease is less than 20 years. Depreciation is one of many factors involved in the annual valuation and cannot separately be identified. The directors consider that this accounting policy results in the accounts giving a true and fair view. Investment properties were revalued at their open market value at 31 December 1991 by [name of valuers].

Land and buildings are revalued on the basis of existing use/alternative use at 31 December 1991 by [name of valuer].

Had the investment properties and land and buildings not been revalued they would have been included at the following amounts:

	Investment properties		Land and buildings	
	1991	1990	1991	1990
	£x	£x	£x	£x
Cost	£x	£x	£x	£x
Aggregate depreciation	£x	£x	£x	£x

Investment properties and land and buildings at net book value comprise:

	Investment properties		Land and buildings	
	1991	1990	1991	1990
	£	£	£	£
Freeholds	x	x	x	x
Long leaseholds	x	x	x	x
Short leaseholds	x	x	x	x
	x	x	x	x

Problem areas

Some problem areas of disclosure are (the numbers correspond to the note numbers given in Example 4.3):

1   *Interest on capital borrowed* This may be included in 'cost or valuation' and, if so, must be disclosed. Listed companies must state the amount and the treatment of the related relief. Interest may be capitalised only during the period of production. This area is dealt with in further detail below.

2   *Government grants* This area is also dealt with in further detail below. The revised SSAP 4 permits the grants to be treated as either reducing the cost of the acquisition of the fixed assets or to be shown as a deferred credit. In Counsel's opinion the former approach would infringe the rule as to no netting off of items and should, accordingly, be followed only by entities that are not subject to the requirements of Schedule 4.

3   *Exchange differences* These would arise only in the disclosure notes in a group balance sheet, given that there are overseas subsidiaries within the group. The differences would arise on the fixed assets of the overseas subsidiary, at the beginning of the year translated at last year's closing rate and re-translated at this year's closing rate. (No exchange differences would arise if the temporal method were to be used.) Both cost or valuation and depreciation brought forward need to be re-translated.

4   *On a revaluation you should adopt the following procedure so as to comply with the proposals of ED 51*
    – Revalued amount less cost, is the adjustment to 'cost or valuation'.
    – Accumulated depreciation up to the date of revaluation is to be eliminated from 'depreciation'.
    – The charge for depreciation for the year should include a charge on the revalued amount *after* the revaluation to comply with SSAP 12.

5   *Arising in respect of new subsidiary* These amounts will arise where there has been an acquisition of a subsidiary during the year. The fixed assets of the subsidiary should not be included with 'additions' in the note, but dealt with separately both in 'cost or valuation' and in 'depreciation'.

6   *Permanent diminution in value of fixed assets* In accordance with the 1985 Act, provision must be made for such a diminution in value as no asset may be stated

at a value in excess of its estimated recoverable amount. If the reasons for the permanent diminution in value no longer apply in a subsequent year the provision must be written back in the subsequent year to the extent that it is no longer necessary.

The ED 51 proposals

The chapter so far has dealt with depreciation under SSAP 12 (Revised). Some of the issues arising under the original standard were dealt with in the revised standard. Others, notably the problems arising from revaluation, were not dealt with in the revised standard. The ED 51 proposals as to revaluations have been dealt with above. This section deals with the proposals of the ED including those relating to the capitalisation of borrowing costs, an area on which there is, as yet, no standard accounting practice in the UK.

Some introductory points

The ED defines a fixed asset as an asset that:

▶ is held by an enterprise for use in the production or supply of goods and services, for rental to others or for administrative purposes and may include items held for the maintenance or repair of such assets, and
▶ has been acquired or constructed with the intention of being used on a continuing basis, and
▶ is not intended for sale in the ordinary course of business.

ED 51 provides a general framework within which enterprises should account for their fixed assets. It applies to all fixed assets except investments (which are intended to be the subject of a separate statement), development expenditure and goodwill. However, the statement contains exemptions from particular requirements in relation to investment properties, leases and hire purchase contracts accounted for as fixed assets, and intangible fixed assets. The following are among the issues dealt with by ED 51:

▶ the recognition of fixed assets.
▶ determining the cost of fixed assets
▶ the capitalisation of borrowing costs
▶ enhancement costs
▶ permanent diminution in value
▶ the disposal of fixed assets (see above)
▶ the carrying value of fixed assets at a valuation (see above)
▶ the application of the revaluation reserve (see above).

The recognition of fixed assets

The IASC Framework for the Preparation and Presentation of Financial Statements was recognised by the ASC as a set of guidelines to assist it in its work of developing and revising accounting standards. The framework defines an asset as a resource controlled by the enterprise as a result of past events and from which future economic benefits are expected to flow to the enterprise. More recently, the ASB has issued its own statement of principles and its definition of assets in Chapter 3 of the statement of principles – the elements that make up financial statements – and referred to in the introduction to this chapter, is also relevant here. Under ED 51 an item that meets the definition of an asset should be recognised when:

▶ it is probable that any future economic benefits associated with the asset will flow to or from the enterprise, and

▶ the asset has a cost, and, where carried at a valuation, a value that can be measured with reliability.

Just as it is important that all fixed assets that qualify for recognition should be in the balance sheet, so it is equally important to users that fixed assets should be included only when they do so qualify.

The cost of fixed assets

Under the historical cost convention, the cost of a fixed asset is its purchase price or production cost with, in either case, the expenditure incurred in bringing the fixed asset to working condition for its intended use and location. A list of expenditures frequently included in purchase price or production cost is included in an appendix to the ED.

Capitalisation of borrowing costs

Arguments can be put forward both for and against the capitalisation of borrowing costs.

Arguments in favour:

▶ They form part of the total costs incurred in bringing a fixed asset into use for its intended purpose.

▶ Failure to capitalise such costs will result in an enterprise's results being different depending on whether it has constructed fixed assets during the period (and borrowed to finance production) or has acquired similar ones.

▶ Capitalisation leads to similar fixed assets being accounted for in a like way in the balance sheet. This results in a greater degree of comparability between the cost of self-constructed fixed assets and those of acquired ones. In the latter case, the purchase price will normally reflect the borrowing costs incurred by the enterprise that has constructed it.

Arguments against:

▶ It is illogical to treat finance costs as a direct cost of an asset during its period of production.

▶ Borrowing costs are usually incurred to support the whole of the activities of the enterprise. An attempt to associate borrowing costs with a particular fixed asset will often be arbitrary.

▶ Capitalisation of borrowing costs results in similar fixed assets having different carrying amounts depending on the method of financing adopted by the enterprise concerned.

Given that the arguments for and against are finely balanced, ED 51 proposes that:

▶ An enterprise may or may not capitalise borrowing costs on fixed assets that take a substantial amount of time to bring into service.

▶ If an enterprise does capitalise borrowing costs, it must adopt a consistent capitalisation policy within the enterprise.

▶ Through disclosure, to make clear the impact of capitalisation on the results and financial positions of the enterprise.

▶ There should be comparability between enterprises capitalising borrowing costs.

The ED 51 proposals follow from differing views as to the most appropriate treatment of accounting for such costs. The Act permits both the view that such costs form a part of the cost of the asset and the view that such costs are essentially period costs to be expensed as incurred.

The Chartered Association of Certified Accountants published a paper on this topic in 1983, which argued:

▶ the period allowed for capitalisation would be the time over which the activity on the asset continues
▶ the book value of the asset should not exceed its recoverable amount.

One shortcoming of the paper was that it did not deal with the interest rate to be used for capitalisation, an amount that is not so easily determined. Nevertheless, the paper was an indication of generally accepted accounting practice at the time.

The IASC issued IAS 23, capitalisation of borrowing costs, in 1984 and, like the ACCA paper, the IAS does not positively require inclusion or exclusion of borrowing costs from the carrying value of the asset. It merely states how the directors should determine borrowing costs in the event that they wish to capitalise such costs. Thus, the IAS states that the directors should calculate a 'capitalisation rate' for each period and to apply this rate to the expenditure incurred on the acquisition or construction or production of the relevant asset. One way of calculating this rate is to relate the borrowing cost that the company incurs during the period to the borrowings outstanding during that period.

If amounts are capitalised there is the further problem arising as to whether to capitalise the borrowing cost gross or net of tax relief. Given no specific requirements in this area in the UK, it would appear that companies may use either basis but they must do so consistently and so long as the policy adopted is clearly disclosed.

One last point in this area: the Stock Exchange requires that all listed companies (including USM) should disclose in their financial statements both the amount of interest capitalised and the amount and treatment of any related tax relief.

Enhancement costs

Expenditure on improvements to a fixed asset should be capitalised and added to the gross carrying amount of the asset. It should be distinguished from expenditure on repairs that should be charged to the profit and loss account. Expenditure should be capitalised only if it increases the expected future benefits from the existing fixed asset beyond its previously assessed performance. Examples of such future benefits include:

▶ a prolongation of the asset's life beyond that conferred by repairs and maintenance
▶ an increase in capacity
▶ an improvement in the quality of output
▶ a reduction in previously assessed operating costs
▶ a substantial increase in the open market value of the fixed asset.

Permanent diminution

A fixed asset should not be carried in the balance sheet at more than its recoverable amount unless the diminution in the recoverable amount to below its carrying amount will reverse in the foreseeable future. Given that in the past there has been some confusion as to where such write-downs should be charged – profit and loss account or revaluation reserve – ED 51 now proposes:

▶ If there has been a permanent diminution, the amount should be charged to the profit and loss account in the period in which the diminution occurs or is first perceived. If there is a diminution on a revalued asset, amounts should be transferred to the profit and loss account from revaluation reserve up to the amount of the permanent diminution.

- ► To avoid a permanent diminution being absorbed into a revaluation surplus or deficit and hence debited to the revaluation reserve, a permanent diminution should be deemed to have occurred before any downwards revaluations during the period.
- ► A permanent diminution is caused by an irreversible change in circumstances including:
  - significant technological developments
  - physical damage
  - structural changes in external economic conditions leading to reduced demand for the output produced by the fixed asset
  - a change in the law or the environment relating to the fixed asset.
- ► When considering the effects of events giving rise to permanent diminutions it may also be necessary to have regard to the impact on the depreciation of the asset concerned.

Investment properties and the FRED 9 amendment

In dealing with tangible fixed assets it is necessary to look separately at what are called investment properties. These are different from other tangible fixed assets and need, therefore, to be accounted for differently.

Definition of an investment property

An investment property is an interest in land and/or buildings:

- ► in respect of which construction work and development have been completed, and
- ► which is held for its investment potential, any rental income being negotiated at arm's length.

The following are exceptions from the definition:

- ► A property that is owned and occupied by a company for its own purposes is not an investment property.
- ► A property let to and occupied by another group company is not an investment property for the purposes of its own accounts or the group accounts.

Accounting for investment properties

Investment properties should not be subject to periodic charges for depreciation on the basis set out in SSAP 12 (Revised), except for properties held on lease, which should be depreciated on the basis set out in SSAP 12 (Revised) at least over the period when the unexpired lease is 20 years or less.

Investment properties should be included in the balance sheet at their open market value.

The names of the persons making the valuations, or particulars of their qualifications, should be disclosed together with the bases of valuation used by them. If a person making a valuation is an employee or officer of the company or group that owns the property this fact should be disclosed.

Changes in the value of investment properties should not be taken to profit and loss account but should be disclosed as a movement on an investment revaluation reserve, unless the total of the investment revaluation reserve is insufficient to cover a deficit, in which case the amount by which the deficit exceeds the amount in the investment revaluation reserve should be charged in the profit and loss account.

The carrying value of investment properties and the investment revaluation reserve should be displayed prominently in the financial statements.

As to disposals of investment properties, any profit or loss on sale should be dealt with as ordinary and, where material, as exceptional, so as to comply with FRS 3. The profit or loss on sale for inclusion in the profit and loss account should be determined by comparing sale proceeds with the net book value on the date of sale. The balance on the investment revaluation reserve, now realised on sale, should be dealt with within reserves.

Disclosure

Accounting for investment properties as set out above is justified on the grounds that an investment property is held not for consumption but as an investment. However, the specific requirement of the law, inserted for the first time in the UK in the Companies Act 1981, to provide depreciation on any fixed asset that has a limited useful economic life results, given that no depreciation is charged on investment properties, in a departure from the requirements of what is now the Companies Act 1985. In this circumstance there will need to be given in the notes to the accounts 'particulars of that departure, the reasons for it, and its effect'. It is generally considered that there is no need to quantify the amount of depreciation not provided on investment properties and that an acceptable form of disclosure to deal with the departure from the Act could read as follows:

> In accordance with SSAP 19 investment properties are revalued annually and any surplus or deficit arising is taken to an investment property revaluation reserve. No depreciation is charged or provided on such properties unless they comprise leasehold properties where the unexpired term of the lease is less than 20 years. Depreciation is one of many factors involved in the annual valuation and cannot separately be identified. The directors consider that this accounting policy results in the accounts giving a true and fair view. Investment properties are revalued at their open market value at 31 December 199X by [name of valuers].
>
> Land and buildings are revalued on the basis of existing use/alternative use at 31 December 199X by [name of valuer].
>
> Had the investment properties and land and buildings not been revalued they would have been included at the following amounts:

	Investment properties		Land and buildings	
	1991	1990	1991	1990
Cost	£x	£x	£x	£x
Aggregate depreciation	£x	£x	£x	£x

Investment properties and land and buildings at net book value comprise:

	Investment properties		Land and buildings	
	1991	1990	1991	1990
Freeholds	x	x	x	x
Long leaseholds	x	x	x	x
Short leaseholds	x	x	x	x
	£x	£x	£x	£x

FRED 9 and an amendment to SSAP 19

FRED 9 is concerned with a limited amendment of SSAP 19 to change the requirements as to the treatment of deficits that run counter to the spirit of FRS 3 on reporting financial performance. Note the following points:

▶ The statement of recognised gains and losses (SORG) introduced by FRS 3 is intended to deal with all recognised gains and losses over a period and must include valuation surpluses and deficits on investment property assets.

▶ SSAP 19, as noted above, requires the amount by which an aggregate deficit exceeds the amount in the investment revaluation reserve to be charged in the profit and loss account. This is irrespective of whether the deficit is expected to be temporary or permanent.

▶ Companies legislation recognises a charge to the profit and loss account only in respect of write-downs of fixed assets expected to be permanent.

▶ FRED 9 amends the part of SSAP 19 that deals with the situation where a charge should be made to the profit and loss account as follows:
  – deficits on individual investment properties that are expected to be permanent should be charged in the profit and loss account as required by companies legislation; and
  – all other valuation movements in investment properties should be shown in the SORG as movements on the investment revaluation reserve.

The further problem of government grants

The original SSAP 4 was concerned, essentially, with capital grants that were to be credited to the profit and loss account over the life of the related asset. This was achieved by:

▶ *either* crediting the grant against the cost of the asset and depreciating the net amount

▶ *or* crediting the grant to a deferred credit in the balance sheet and releasing the credit to the profit and loss account over the life of the related asset, effectively offsetting the gross cost-based depreciation charge.

The basic principle behind such accounting was that the grant should be recognised as income so as to be matched with the expenditure that it was intended to subsidise.

The revised SSAP 4 retains the options above as to capital grants, but does point out that in Counsel's opinion the former approach (netting) would be illegal for the majority of enterprises, that is, those governed by Schedule 4 to the 1985 Act. Effectively, therefore, standard treatment is now the deferred credit approach.

Revenue grants

Under SSAP 4 (Revised) the rules as to such grants are as follows:

▶ recognise so as to match with expenditure towards which the grant contributes

▶ if the expenditure has already been incurred include the grant in the profit and loss account as soon as it may appropriately be recognised

▶ if the grant is received in advance of costs being incurred, the grant should be deferred so as to match it with such costs when incurred.

Generally:

▶ do not recognise grants until the conditions for their receipt have been complied with

▶ if a grant becomes repayable it should be set off against any unamortised deferred credit; if there is any excess it must be charged to the profit and loss account

▶ if a grant is received in order to finance activities over a stated period, or to compensate for losses of current or future income, it should be recognised in the profit and loss account of the period in which it is paid

▶ the effect of government grants on the results of a period should be disclosed.

Application

EXAMPLE 4.4

The following information relates to government grants received and receivable by Grant plc.

Employment grant A
This is a grant of £3,000 towards employment costs incurred during 1991. The grant has not yet been received but the conditions for receipt have been met.

Solution
Employment grant B
This is a grant of £70,000 received during 1991 and given on the condition that 70 new jobs are created in Manchester and maintained for a minimum period of three years. A new factory employing the 70 employees was opened in Manchester on 1 August 1991. It is hoped that the factory will break even in its first 12 months and then make profits of £20,000 in year 2 and £30,000 in year 3.

Capital grant A
A grant of £60,000 was receivable in 1991 to help finance the acquisition of new plant and machinery costing £200,000. The machinery was acquired on 31 March 1991 and is expected to last for ten years, after which it will have a residual value of £20,000. Straight-line depreciation is to be charged from the date of acquisition. The grant was received on 30 September 1991 and used to repay Grant plc's temporary overdraft. The grant is treated as income in 1991 for taxation purposes. Corporation tax to be taken as 35%.

Capital grant B
A grant of £80,000 was received in 1991 towards the cost of the new factory in Manchester. The factory cost £200,000 and is to be written off completely over 50 years on a straight-line basis. It was a condition of the grant that it be treated as share capital. The grant was credited to a suspense account on its receipt.

State how each of these grants should be accounted for in accordance with SSAP 4 (Revised) – The Accounting Treatment of Government Grants, in the financial statements for the year ended 31 December 1991, and give the reasons for adopting this treatment in each case.

Employment grant A
Since the conditions for receipt have been met the £3,000 should be debited to prepayments and accrued income and credited to the profit and loss account. This applies the matching concept by setting off the grant against the costs to which it relates.

Employment grant B
SSAP 4 (Revised) suggests that where a grant is given on condition that jobs are created and maintained for a period of years, the grant should be matched with the cost of providing jobs for that period; but that account should be taken of any extra income which is generated by the new jobs. In this example the grant should be apportioned as follows:

	Profit before grant	Grant	Profit after grant
	£	£	£
Year 1	—	40,000	40,000
Year 2	20,000	20,000	40,000
Year 3	30,000	10,000	40,000

Five months of the first year have elapsed as at 31 December 1991 and so it would seem reasonable to credit 5/12 × £40,000 = £16,667 to profit and loss account and to credit the remaining £53,333 to accruals and deferred income.

Capital grant A

On receipt the grant would be credited to accruals and deferred income. It should be released to the profit and loss account over a ten-year period from 31 March 1991. As at 31 December 1991 £4,500 should have been released to the profit and loss account (being £60,000 ÷ 10 × 9/12). Since there will be a corporation tax charge of £60,000 × 35% = £21,000, a deferred tax credit and balance sheet asset should be set up to 'cancel out' this charge. The deferred tax asset would be released to the profit and loss account over ten years. £1,575 will have been released by the year end (being £21,000 ÷ 10 × 9/12).

Capital grant B

The grant should be credited to a nondistributable reserve for subsequent application to paying up new share capital.

Summary

1   An accounting policy note would be required.
2   The amount of grants included in accruals and deferred income should be disclosed, that is, £53,333 + £55,500 = £108,833.
3   The total amount credited to the profit and loss account should be disclosed, that is, £3,000 + £16,667 + £4,500 = £24,167.
4   The potential liability to repay the employment grant B should be considered, but disclosed only if it is felt to be a possibility.

Summary

▶ This chapter has dealt with tangible fixed assets, mainly in the context of depreciation, and has also dealt with investment properties and accounting for government grants.

▶ In dealing with SSAPs 4, 12 and 19 and the revision of SSAPs 4 and 12 and EDs 36, 37 and 51, the chapter serves to remind you of the constantly evolving nature of the financial reporting environment, so clearly evidenced by the issue of FRS 3 which has substantially altered the emphasis as to reporting financial performance.

▶ A large part of the chapter dealt with accounting for revaluations of fixed assets and the related further problem of accounting for the profit or loss arising on the disposal of such fixed assets. You should now be able to distinguish between the 'income' and 'value' approaches in respect of disposal losses or gains and to demonstrate that, whichever approach is adopted, the reported gain of the year of disposal will have an impact on the earnings of this year but not on legally available distributable profits.

▶ The chapter also covers the area of capitalisation of borrowing costs, which is dealt with in company law, and in international accounting standards, but not as yet in a UK accounting standard.

Suggested reading

Depreciation problems in the context of historical cost accounting (Deloitte Haskins & Sells 1984)

Financial Reporting 1989–1990, A survey of UK published accounts (Skerratt and Tonkin 1990)

Depreciation (Baxter 1971)

UK GAAP (Ernst & Young 1990)

Accountants Digest (Loveday 1987)

Self test questions

1   Why is there a need for an accounting standard on depreciation?

2   What is split depreciation, and why is it not permitted under SSAP 12?

3   Quentin Ltd purchases a fixed asset on 1 January 1991 for £2,400. The estimated useful life is ten years and the asset has a scrap value of £400. On 1 January 1994 the estimated useful life is shortened to a total of eight years. Calculate the depreciation charge for 1994.

4   You are provided with the costs and market values of the buildings of Justin plc as on 31 March 1995 and the depreciation charges for the year then ended as follows:

	Cost	Market value	Depreciation charge
	£000	£000	£000
Main office accommodation	1,500	1,500	15
Freehold office accommodation rented to subsidiary companies	2,500	2,500	25
Company buildings held as investments			
Freehold	4,500	6,500	45
Leasehold (more than 20 years)	3,500	5,100	35
Leasehold (less than 20 years)	1,500	2,900	15

Ascertain the value of investment properties in the balance sheet of Justin plc as on 31 March 1995.

5   Using the data in question 4, calculate the depreciation charge on buildings for the year ended 31 March 1995.

Exam style question

1   *Jupiter Ltd*
You are the financial accountant of Jupiter Ltd, a company in the electronics industry, whose accounting reference date is 31 October, and you have been provided with the following information in respect of its fixed assets:

On 1 November 1990:

	Cost	Accumulated depreciation	Total depreciable life (years)
	£000	£000	
Land	60	NIL	
Freehold buildings			
Factory	150	30	50
Salesroom	180	30	45
Plant and machinery	475	365	10
Computer equipment	295	85	4
Furniture and fittings	100	40	5
Motor vehicles	50	35	4

None of these assets will be fully depreciated by 31 October 1991.

During the year, C. Star, a chartered surveyor, was engaged to value the properties at an open market value for existing use. His valuations as on 1 November 1990 were as follows:

	£000
Land	400
Factory	240
Salesroom	150

Additions during the year were:

Plant	100
Computer	8
Motor vehicles	28

The only disposals were cars which cost £6,000 and which had accumulated depreciation at 1 November 1990 of £5,000.

All purchases and disposals took place on 1 May 1991. All depreciation is charged on a straight-line basis from the date of acquisition to the date of sale.

Required:
a) Present the detailed notes in relation to tangible fixed assets for the statutory accounts of Jupiter Ltd at 31 October 1991. The accounting policy note is not required.
b) Discuss the arguments for and against including tangible fixed assets at revalued amounts in historical cost accounts and evaluate the alternative methods of accounting for their depreciation and sale.

Note: Ignore taxation.

All answers on pages 632 –635.

Intangible Fixed Assets

This chapter deals with accounting for intangible fixed assets. It covers the regulatory framework as to and the application of accounting principles to the accounting treatment of goodwill, brand names and other related assets and research and development expenditure.

The main issues involved are:

- ▶ the measurement of cost or valuation
- ▶ the case or otherwise for capitalisation
- ▶ where there is capitalisation, the case or otherwise for amortisation.

Schedule 4 to the Act specifically permits the recognition of intangible assets in company balance sheets and permits their capitalisation where:

- ▶ *either* they were acquired for valuable consideration in circumstances that do not qualify them to be shown as goodwill
- ▶ *or* they were created by the company itself.

The ASC issued TR 780 in 1990. The release sets out the provisions as to accounting for intangible fixed assets and its proposals serve as a useful introduction to this chapter. Thus:

- ▶ intangible assets give rise to particular problems when it comes to their recognition, carrying value and useful economic lives
- ▶ they should be recognised only if:
  - – historical costs can be readily ascertained
  - – their characteristics are clearly distinguishable from goodwill
  - – their cost can be measured independently of goodwill, other assets and the earnings of the business
- ▶ where recognised the asset should be carried at its historical cost less provisions for depreciation and, if appropriate, permanent diminution in value
- ▶ the asset should be carried at valuation only if:
  - – the carrying amount is based on depreciated replacement cost and
  - – the depreciated replacement cost represents the current cost of the asset
- ▶ they should be deemed to have a maximim economic useful life of 20 years unless it can be demonstrated that a longer life is more appropriate.

There is no accounting standard in the UK which deals collectively with intangible assets. SSAP 13 (Revised) addresses the problems arising in accounting for research and development costs and SSAP 22 (Revised) deals with goodwill. There is as yet no accounting standard as to intangibles such as brand names and no accounting standard as to revaluation. Bear in mind while reading this chapter that the issues of whether or not to capitalise, and if capitalised whether or not and if whether how much to, amortise will affect the net worth and earnings of an enterprise and that it is in this context that we need accounting standards to enable uniform reporting of intangible assets.

Accounting for goodwill

It has been suggested that as we cannot observe an intangible asset, there is no concrete evidence to establish the fact that it exists. It has also been suggested that the future usefulness or value of such an asset is so nebulous that any attempt to capitalise and amortise the cost is futile.

Goodwill has been considered at some length by the ASC. In June 1980, it issued a discussion paper that dealt with the possible accounting treatments of goodwill and concluded that purchased goodwill should be eliminated by amortisation through the profit and loss account. Practice in the 1970s conflicted with the conclusion of the discussion paper. In the 1980–81 Survey of Published Accounts (ICAEW 1980–81), 195 companies were observed to have written goodwill off in the year of acquisition and only 30 to have adopted the amortisation procedure; 29 companies included goodwill at cost without amortisation.

In October 1982, the ASC published ED 30, which took into account the views expressed in the response to the discussion paper, which were evenly split between preferring the immediate write-off method and the amortisation method. Not for the first time, the ASC, in ED 30, allowed companies an option. Companies could have, had the ED proceeded in its published form to standard, selected either the immediate write-off method or the amortisation method and followed the selected policy for all acquisitions. Seventy-six letters of comment were written to the ASC on the ED and its proposals. In July 1983, the ASC issued a statement of intent to say that it had decided to authorise the development of a standard that would require companies to eliminate goodwill from their balance sheets and that the standard would indicate a preference for the immediate write-off method, but would allow the alternative of amortisation. Clearly, it was found that it was not possible to be all things to all people for all of the time. In this the ASC was not alone.

On 28 March 1984, the ASC approved in principle the text of a proposed accounting standard on accounting for goodwill. In December 1984, the standard was issued as SSAP 22 – Accounting for Goodwill. It is to be regarded as standard accounting practice in respect of financial statements relating to accounting periods beginning on or after 1 January 1985.

In terms of examination emphasis, in addition to being examinable as a topic on its own, goodwill is always relevant to consolidated accounts where the acquisition method is used. Accounting for goodwill also has a bearing on the maximum legally distributable profits of the company (see Chapter 13).

The 1984 version of standard accounting for goodwill gave no detailed guidance on how goodwill should be calculated. As a result, the practical application of that accounting standard gave rise to many anomalies, which were exploited to their advantage by companies issuing accounts in which the treatment of goodwill had a critical impact on disclosed results. Companies felt encouraged to select as the accounting treatment for goodwill that which gave the most favourable results. These various abuses have been well documented in the financial press and include:

▶ obtaining the Court's permission to write off goodwill against share premium account
▶ writing off goodwill to a specially created reserve, which could dangle indefinitely within reserves leaving earnings and other reserves intact
▶ writing off goodwill against revaluation reserve, now specifically prohibited under the Companies Act 1985 as amended
▶ taking advantage of merger relief under the Companies Act 1985 in conjuction with using acquisition accounting on consolidation
▶ inflating goodwill with provisions for reorganisation costs, writing off the costs against the provision and writing back any part of the provision not required to the profit and loss account of subsequent years

► inflating earnings by assigning low values to acquired assets with a correspondingly high value to goodwill and writing off this goodwill to reserves while enjoying low future depreciation charges on acquired assets.

These various games that companies have played in order to bypass the intentions of the ASC in the original goodwill standard forced a major reassessment of the nature of goodwill and, therefore, of the most appropriate way to account for it.

SSAP 22 (Revised) – Accounting for Goodwill, was issued in July 1989 and retains the requirements of SSAP 22 as issued in December 1984, but with additional disclosure requirements. Apart from these additional disclosure requirements the requirements of the original standard on goodwill remain unchanged. Thus SSAP 22 (Revised) is a limited revision and is not intended to change, for the present, the accounting treatments as to goodwill required by the original standard. These treatments were the subject of fundamental review by the ASC in its work on fair value and business combinations. In the interim, while SSAP 22 and SSAP 23 were undergoing this review, it was felt that the additional disclosures now required by SSAP 22 (Revised) will assist users of financial statements in gaining a better appreciation of the financial position and changes in the financial position of a reporting company that makes a business acquisition or disposal.

This chapter is concerned with the various problems arising under the original standard and how these are dealt with in the revised standard and, in passing, with some of the issues raised by ED 53, fair valuing in the context of acquisition accounting.

In dealing with these various goodwill problems this chapter also covers the proposals put forward in ED 47.

Definitions

Goodwill

This is the difference between the value of a business as a whole and the aggregate of the fair values of its separable net assets. The difference may be positive or negative.

Following from the above definition it is clear that goodwill cannot be realised separately from the business as a whole; it can be acquired or sold only as part of the process of acquiring or selling a business as a whole.

Separable net assets

These are stated to be those assets and liabilities that can be identified and either sold or discharged separately without necessarily disposing of the business as a whole. They include identifiable intangibles such as concessions, patents, licences, trade marks, publishing titles, franchise rights and customer lists.

Purchased goodwill

This is goodwill that is established as a result of the purchase of a business accounted for as an acquisition.

Consolidation goodwill

This is one form of purchased goodwill.

Non-purchased goodwill

This is any goodwill other than purchased goodwill.

While there is no difference in character between purchased goodwill and non-purchased goodwill, the value of purchased goodwill is established as a fact at a particular time by a market transaction. This is not true of non-purchased goodwill. Companies or groups should not attribute any amount to non-purchased goodwill in their balance sheets.

The main characteristics of goodwill

The fact that goodwill cannot be realised separately from the business as a whole distinguishes goodwill from all other items in the financial statements. The other characteristics of goodwill may be summarised as follows:

▶ The value of goodwill has no reliable or predictable relationship to any costs that the company may have incurred.
▶ It is impossible to value intangible factors that may contribute to goodwill.
▶ The value of goodwill may fluctuate widely, depending on internal and external circumstances over short periods of time.
▶ Any assessment of the value of goodwill is highly subjective.

As a result, any amount attributed to goodwill is unique to the valuer and to the specific date of measurement and is valid only at that time and in the circumstances then prevailing.

The situations in which purchased goodwill may arise

The standard applies to purchased goodwill including consolidation goodwill. To appreciate the difference between the two, it is important to differentiate between goodwill in the accounts of an individual entity and consolidated accounts.

As dealt with above, goodwill (purchased and consolidation) can arise only on the purchase or the sale of a business. There are two ways in which one business may acquire another. Either the acquiring company purchases the net assets of the business acquired or it purchases the share capital of the business acquired.

Where the acquiring company purchases the net assets of a business

In such a situation the acquiring company would record, in its own accounts, the fair value of the net assets acquired and the fair value of the consideration paid. Any difference arising would be recorded as purchased goodwill. The business acquired would be liquidated, no group or consolidated accounts would need to be prepared arising from the purchase and there would, therefore, be no consolidation goodwill.

EXAMPLE 5.1

Co. A purchases the business of Co. B by means of acquiring the net assets of the latter company. The fair value of the consideration amounts to £1,000 and is settled entirely in the form of cash. The fair value of the net tangible assets and the net identifiable intangible assets of Co. B on the date of the acquisition amounts to £700.

Co. A, in purchasing the separable net assets of the business of Co. B, is identified as an *individual entity*. Co. B would be liquidated after the purchase. Co. A does not in this situation have a subsidiary and does not therefore have to prepare consolidated accounts. The purchase of the business would be recorded in the books of Co. A, the individual entity, as follows:

	£	£
DR/CR Sundry net assets	700	
CR Cash		1,000
DR Purchased goodwill	300	

being the fair value of the separable net assets acquired, the consideration paid and the purchased goodwill arising on the acquisition of the business of Co. B.

As no consolidated accounts need to be prepared in this situation there can be no consolidation goodwill.

Where the acquiring company purchases the share capital of a business

In such a situation the acquired company becomes a subsidiary and we are concerned, from the viewpoint of the acquiring company, with both its accounts as an individual entity and with its consolidated accounts. This is illustrated in Example 5.2.

EXAMPLE 5.2

Facts as in Example 5.1 above, except that Co. A purchases the share capital of Co. B.

Co. A, in purchasing the share capital of the business of Co. B is now, having acquired a subsidiary company, identified as a *parent undertaking*. Co. B continues in existence and Co. A as a parent undertaking would be required to prepare consolidated accounts in addition to its own accounts.

Where one company acquires the shares of another company, and it does not use merger accounting, it will include in its own separate balance sheet the cost of the shares in the acquired company based on the fair value of the consideration given. From the viewpoint of the parent undertaking, the separable net assets will be the shares in the acquired company, not the individual assets and liabilities of the acquired company. In this situation the fair value of the consideration given will always equal the fair value to the acquiring company of the shares acquired. Therefore purchased goodwill will never arise in the accounts of the parent undertaking on a purchase of a business through the purchase of the shares of that business.

The purchase of the business would be recorded in the books of Co. A, the parent undertaking, as follows:

	£	£
DR Investment in Co. B at cost	1,000	
CR Cash		1,000

being the fair value of the investment acquired and the consideration paid.

No purchased goodwill is recorded in the books of Co. A as a separate item. (It is in fact included in the cost of the investment in Co. B.)

As Co. A is a parent undertaking it must also prepare consolidated accounts. In these accounts, given an acquisition, goodwill will arise on consolidation. This is ascertained as:

	£
Fair value of consideration given	1,000
Fair value of the separable net assets	700
Difference = consolidation goodwill	300

The standard does not require an adjustment to be made, in the parent undertaking's accounts, to the carrying value of the shares in the acquired company in respect of any consolidation goodwill written off in the group accounts. Thus Co. A will continue to carry, in its own separate balance sheet, its investment in Co. B at £1,000, even though the consolidated balance sheet incorporates only £700 of separable net assets of Co. B. The only situation which would warrant a write-down of the carrying value of the investment in the Co. A balance sheet is a permanent diminution in value of the investment.

One further problem

The standard specifically states that the amount that the acquiring company attributes to purchased goodwill should not include any value for separable (identifiable) intangibles. The acquiring company should include such amounts under the appropriate heading within intangible assets in its own balance sheet. The requirement would apply equally to an acquiring group and to consolidation goodwill. The problem is illustrated in Example 5.3.

EXAMPLE 5.3

Co. A acquires the business of Co. B. The fair value of the consideration given for the acquisition (not merger) is £5,000. The balance sheet (fair values) of Co. B on the date of the acquisition are:

	(i) £	(ii) £	(iii) £
Intangible fixed assets			
goodwill	–	–	1,000
patents etc.	–	1,000	–
Other net tangible assets	2,500	1,500	1,500
Share capital and reserves	2,500	2,500	2,500

Situation 1: Co. A acquires the separable net assets of Co. B.
Situation 2: Co. A acquires the equity of Co. B.

Situation 1: Co. A acquires the separable net assets of Co. B

(i)	£
Fair value of consideration	5,000
Fair value of separable net assets	(2,500)
Purchased goodwill	2,500

The balance sheet of the individual entity, Co. A, would include:

	£
Purchased goodwill	2,500
Tangible net assets	2,500
	5,000

(ii)	£	£
Fair value of consideration		5,000
Fair value of separable net assets		
net tangible	1,500	
identifiable intangible assets	1,000	
		(2,500)
Purchased goodwill		2,500

Note: Separable net assets include identifiable intangibles. Had these intangibles (patents etc.) been excluded from the calculation above, purchased goodwill would have been £3,500, because it would include the value of the separable identifiable intangible assets. The standard specifically states that purchased goodwill should exclude any value for separable (identifiable) intangibles. These should be separately stated in the balance sheet of the acquiring company.

The balance sheet of the individual entity, Co. A, would include:

	£
Purchased goodwill	2,500
Patents etc.	1,000
Tangible net assets	1,500
	5,000

(iii)	£	£
Fair value of consideration		5,000
Fair value of separable net assets		
net tangible	1,500	
identifiable intangibles	–	
		(1,500)
		3,500

Note: The unidentifiable intangible – goodwill – is specifically excluded from the calculation to arrive at purchased goodwill. In being excluded from the calculation it is effectively included in the figure of purchased goodwill. Had the goodwill of £1,000 been included as a separable net asset, purchased goodwill on the acquisition would have been 5,000 – (1,500 + 1,000) = £2,500. This is incorrect. The balance sheet of the individual entity, Co. A, would include under intangible fixed assets, a single figure of purchased goodwill of £3,500.

	£
1 Purchased goodwill	3,500
2 Patents etc.	–
	£3,500

The balance sheet of the individual entity, Co. A. would include:

	£
Purchased goodwill	3,500
Tangible net assets	1,500
	5,000

As Co. A is an individual entity it would not produce group accounts and therefore consolidation goodwill would not arise in any of the three circumstances above.

Situation 2: Co. A acquires the equity of Co. B

As Co. A would, in this situation, be a parent undertaking no purchased goodwill would be recorded in the separate accounts of Co. A, which would include, as an asset, the investment in Co. B at a cost of £5,000. In the group accounts, however, consolidation goodwill would be calculated as follows:

(i)	£
Fair value of consideration	5,000
Fair value of underlying separable net assets	(2,500)
Consolidation goodwill	2,500

(ii)	£	£
Fair value of consideration		5,000
Fair value of underlying separable net assets		
net tangible	1,500	
identifiable intangibles	1,000	
		(2,500)
Consolidation goodwill		2,500

Note: The consolidated balance sheet would also include patents etc. of £1,000.

(iii)	£	£
Fair value of consideration		5,000
Fair value of underlying separable net assets		
net tangible	1,500	
identifiable intangibles	–	
		(1,500)
Consolidation goodwill		3,500

Note: Consolidation goodwill includes the separate goodwill of Co. B.

Alternative methods of eliminating positive purchased goodwill

Whether purchased goodwill arises in the accounts of an individual entity or consolidation goodwill arises in the consolidated accounts, the standard requires that a company or a group should not carry purchased goodwill or consolidation goodwill in its balance sheet as a permanent item. A company or a group must eliminate goodwill using either the immediate write-off method or the amortisation method.

The immediate write-off method

Companies or groups should, normally, eliminate goodwill (other than negative goodwill – see below) immediately on acquisition against reserves and not as a charge in the profit and loss account of the year of acquisition. Two reasons are stated in the standard to justify this treatment:

▶ Purchased and consolidation goodwill is written off as a matter of accounting policy, in order to achieve consistency with non-purchased goodwill which is not included in the accounts.
▶ The write-off is not related to the results of the year in which the acquisition is made.

The amortisation or systematic write-off method

The standard describes the immediate write-off method as the 'preferred treatment' and states that companies and groups should, normally, adopt that method. However, the standard recognises that there is an alternative method. This alternative method is based on the view that, although goodwill is intangible it nevertheless exists, resources have been expended in acquiring it, and it should therefore be recognised as an asset and treated in the same way as any other asset. The standard therefore allows a company or a group to carry purchased goodwill or consolidation goodwill as an asset and to amortise it, through the profit and loss account, on a systematic basis over its useful economic life. The amortisation charge should be included in arriving at profit or loss on ordinary activities.

Accounting

There may, however, be cases where an individual company's circumstances require that it adopt different policies in relation to the goodwill that arises on different acquisitions. A company should, in general, wish to follow the preferred policy of immediate write-off. However, it may need to adopt the policy of amortisation on an acquisition that gives rise to substantial amounts of purchased goodwill because of the effect that immediate write-off would have on its reserves. Thus, a company may use the immediate write-off method for the goodwill that arises on one acquisition and the amortisation method for the goodwill that arises from another. However, once a company has chosen an accounting policy for the goodwill arising from a particular acquisition, it should apply that policy consistently to that goodwill; a company should not amortise the goodwill from a particular acquisition for several years and then write off the balance direct to reserves. It would seem that this choice also applies to consolidation goodwill in consolidated accounts.

The immediate write-off of purchased goodwill against reserves in the accounts of an individual entity

As mentioned above, companies should normally eliminate goodwill, on acquisition, against reserves. A company that does so has two options:

▶ To write off the goodwill immediately to realised reserves.
▶ To write off the goodwill immediately to a 'suitable' unrealised reserve and then transfer the amount written off from unrealised reserves to realised reserves on a systematic basis over the useful economic life of the goodwill. This option will have the same effect on distributable profits of the company as the amortisation method permitted by the standard. Under this option, although there is no immediate reduction of realised reserves, the elimination of purchased goodwill must ultimately result in a realised loss as purchased goodwill has a limited useful life. It is because of this that a systematic transfer must be made from unrealised to realised reserves each year over the economic useful life of goodwill. (For the sake of simplicity in applying this option, assume that all acquisitions take place on the first day of the period and make a full year's transfer from unrealised to realised reserves in the year of acquisition even though the acquisition did not actually take place on the first day of the period.)

Appendix 2 of the standard gives an example of when it might be appropriate to write off goodwill, initially, to an unrealised reserve. A company may do so where it has insufficient distributable reserves to cover the purchase cost of goodwill.

Strangely, the standard is silent on exactly what constitutes a 'suitable' unrealised reserve. Neither a share premium account nor a capital redemption reserve can (legally) be utilised for this purpose. The most obvious unrealised reserve is the revaluation reserve, but the 1985 Act limits the uses that a company may make of the revaluation reserve. Thus:

> an amount may only be transferred from the reserve to the profit and loss account if either:
> (i) the amount in question was previously charged to that account; or
> (ii) it represents realised profit,

and, in this light, the revaluation reserve is not a 'suitable' reserve, as a company that writes off goodwill to revaluation reserve will not be able to transfer it subsequently to realised reserve.

Appendix 2 of the standard suggests that a suitable unrealised reserve would be the reserve that arises when negative goodwill is credited to reserves (see below). However, a company may not have such an unrealised reserve. This seems to leave us with 'other reserves' as specified in the statutory balance sheet, which are unrealised.

A company that has no suitable unrealised reserves has two options:

▶ *either* the goodwill can be written off immediately against realised reserves
▶ *or* the company can adopt the amortisation method.

The second option is the more likely choice, as an immediate write-off to realised reserves will adversely affect distributable reserves.

The above discussion as to the write off of purchased goodwill against realised and unrealised reserves is in the context of an individual company only. In the case of consolidation goodwill, the distinction between realised and unrealised reserves is not relevant. Chapter 13 makes it clear that it is individual companies, not groups, that make distributions. Three related questions are therefore raised in respect of a group that writes off consolidation goodwill immediately to reserves (see below).

The immediate write-off of consolidation goodwill against consolidated reserves

The three questions are:

Q.1 Should the group write off consolidation goodwill to consolidated realised or unrealised reserves?

A. If a group writes off goodwill immediately to reserves, the write-off will not affect the distributable profits of any individual company and does not affect the total distributable profits of the group. There is no meaningful distinction between realised and unrealised reserves in consolidated accounts.

Q.2 If the group writes off consolidation goodwill to 'unrealised' reserves, should it transfer the amount written off to 'realised' reserves on a systematic basis in the same way as a company?

A. As the write-off does not affect the distributable profits of the holding company or the group such a transfer is not necessary.

Q.3. Is the consolidated revaluation reserve a 'suitable' reserve for the purpose of immediate write-off of consolidation goodwill?

A. The 1985 Act restriction regarding the use of the revaluation reserve will also apply to groups and therefore to goodwill on consolidation.

Consolidation goodwill may not be written off against consolidated share premium, capital redemption or revaluation reserves. It may be written off against consolidated other reserves or profit and loss account reserves. If it is written off against consolidated other reserves there is no need for an annual transfer of the goodwill written off to consolidated profit and loss reserves over the economic useful life.

Negative purchased goodwill

The standard requires that companies and groups should credit negative goodwill direct to reserves. Negative goodwill is the mirror image of positive goodwill. It is defined as the excess of the fair values of the separable net assets acquired over the fair value of the consideration given. The standard does not require a company or group to set up a separate reserve for negative goodwill.

Where a company writes off positive goodwill initially to unrealised reserves it must transfer the amount written off to realised reserves on a systematic basis. Negative goodwill, credited to unrealised reserves, may be transferred to realised reserves in line with the depreciation or realisation of the assets acquired in the business combination that gave rise to the goodwill.

Determining the useful economic life of purchased goodwill

The Companies Act 1985 states that only goodwill that is acquired for valuable consideration – purchased rather than internally generated goodwill – may be carried as an asset. If goodwill is carried as an asset it must be systematically written off over a period that does not exceed its useful economic life. The period over which it is being written off and the reasons for choosing that period must be disclosed in a note to the accounts. The Act does not prescribe an absolute maximum period for write-off, the British legislature having availed itself of a derogation allowed by the 4th Directive, which would otherwise require goodwill to be written off over not more than five years.

The discussion paper on goodwill, ED 30, and SSAP 22 dealt with the question of determining the useful economic life of purchased goodwill in different ways. The discussion paper suggested a maximum period of 2.5 times the p/e ratio where p was the fair value of the business acquired and e the best estimate of the annual distributable earnings of the acquired business. ED 30 proposed a maximum period of 20 years. The standard does not specify a minimum or maximum amortisation period. Also, the standard does not require companies to select the same useful economic life for goodwill arising on different acquisitions on the basis that the factors that affect the estimates of the useful economic life of purchased goodwill are likely to vary according to the different circumstances of different acquisitions. Appendix 1 of SSAP 22 deals with these factors.

The useful economic life of goodwill in respect of each acquisition needs to be determined where a company employs the amortisation treatment. It also needs to be determined where a company writes off goodwill immediately against unrealised reserves in that goodwill so written off must be transferred to realised reserves over its useful economic life.

The useful economic life of goodwill is defined as the period over which benefits may reasonably be expected to accrue from that goodwill in the acquired company, which existed and was identified at the time of the acquisition. Factors that are relevant to determining the useful economic life of purchased goodwill include:

▶ expected changes in products or markets or technology
▶ the expected period of future service of certain employees
▶ expected future demand or competition or other economic factors that may affect current advantages.

A company or group, when determining the useful economic life of purchased goodwill, should not take into account any actions, expenditure, or circumstances after the date of acquisition as these subsequent events create non-purchased goodwill, which is not included in accounts.

The purchased goodwill, the useful life of which is being determined, is only that which existed and was recognised at the time of acquisition.

The period of time during which returns can reasonably be anticipated from an investment would set an upper limit on the amortisation period.

It is inappropriate to indicate any maximum period in numerical terms. It is likely that different useful economic lives will be selected for the goodwill arising on different acquisitions.

A company or group should not revalue purchased goodwill. If there is a permanent diminution in value the company or group should write down the carrying value of purchased goodwill immediately to its estimated recoverable amount. A company or group may shorten, but may not increase, the estimated useful economic life over which it is amortising purchased goodwill.

Some past examples of the application of the requirements of SSAP 22

As stated in the Accounting Issues section of *Accountancy*, for many companies the basis of selecting which policy to adopt, per SSAP 22, in the writing off of goodwill, has been the maintenance of reserves. Individual companies carrying goodwill have been keen to protect distributable profits, whereas groups have not wished to affect adversely the presentation of their reserves or, indeed, burden the profit and loss account with an annual charge above the line.

The magazine reported in 1989/90 the following instances of the methods adopted by various companies in coping with the requirements of SSAP 22:

► For some companies/groups the write-off of goodwill arising on current acquisitions has had little impact on reserves. Thus ICI wrote off £488 million of goodwill arising during 1986 against reserves, which stood at £2.8 billion in the 1985 accounts.

► For some companies/groups, the impact of the immediate write-off of goodwill has been cushioned given the advantage taken of merger relief – see Chapter 19 – in Section 131 of the Companies Act 1985. Briefly, merger relief gives rise to the setting up of a merger reserve, rather than share premium account, on the premium element of shares issued as consideration for an acquisition of shares in a subsidiary company. The merger reserve is available for the immediate write-off of goodwill. Thus, Guinness, with genius, absorbed £220 million of goodwill on its acquisition of Bells against a merger reserve of £273 million created by the issue of 110 million shares with a nominal value of £27 million and a market value of £300 million. Burton, with its acquisition of Debenham, and Dixon with its acquisition of Curry, both also took similar advantage of merger reserves set up given the merger relief in Section 131 of the Act.

► Some companies/groups eliminate goodwill through other reserves, creating a debit balance on such reserves. Such a treatment is similar to the 'dangling debit' treatment in pre-SSAP 22 days. The Act does not permit goodwill to be carried in the balance sheet in this way. Nevertheless, the treatment is legally permissible as the amount is carried as a reserve and not as goodwill. Thus, Automated Securities Holdings disclosed in its November 1985 accounts:

	Group £000	Company £000
Merger reserve		
Arising on acquisition of Security Centres	20,828	20,828
Less: Goodwill on acquisition written off	20,828	–
	–	20,828
Other reserves		
Goodwill on acquisition 1 December 1984	3,655	542
Additions during year	28,217	1,680
	31,872	2,222
Less: Written off merger reserve	20,828	–
At 30 November 1985	11,044	2,222

Other reserves at 30 November 1985 were negative.

► Some companies/groups – Hogg Robinson, Saatchi & Saatchi, Henry Ansbacher – have sought Court approval (re capital reduction) to write off existing goodwill against their share premium accounts.

► In 19XX Mills & Allen International reported unaudited interim results, carrying this statement from the Chairman as follows: 'The group has decided after consultation with its auditors to write off goodwill as an extraordinary item through the profit and loss account over a period of up to 20 years.' This appears to be in conflict with both SSAP 22, which requires goodwill, systematically written off, to be charged above the line, and the then effective SSAP 6, which stated that extraordinary items should not recur frequently or regularly. In any event, now that SSAP 6 has been superseded by FRS 3, all items must be taken above the line.

The standard may allow only two treatments but as the examples above demonstrate, practice has shown several variations. As asked by Richard Hickinbotham, FCA, of Hoare Govett, 'Is that really what we mean to cause by a standard?' It is for this reason that the standard, having been issued, became due for revision.

Problems arising under the original standard and how these are resolved under the revised standard

Standard accounting practice cannot follow from an accounting standard that permits options when accounting for the effects of an acquisition. As already stated in the introduction, the options permitted in the original standard on goodwill – preferably immediate write-off but, possibly, as an alternative, systematic amortisation – continue to be permitted under the revised standard, which simply calls for additional disclosure to be made in respect of goodwill to enable a better appreciation of the effects of acquisitions. These additional disclosures are dealt with in turn below.

Earnings per share (eps)

If goodwill is written off wholly and immediately to reserves there is no earnings effect; if it is written off systematically over economic useful life, with an annual charge for amortisation, there is an earnings effect. Given that, under the standard, some companies may adopt the former approach and others the latter, there is a loss of comparability in eps.

Accordingly, ASC considers that it would be helpful if users of financial statements could see at a glance the eps before amortisation of goodwill of all companies selecting the amortisation treatment. This is in order that their results, and eps, may be compared on a similar basis to those of companies writing purchased goodwill off immediately to reserves. Therefore, companies that do select the amortisation treatment should disclose eps both before and after the amortisation of goodwill. Companies that follow the amortisation treatment are encouraged (but not required) to disclose eps per SSAP 3 and eps before the amortisation of goodwill under the revised standard. SSAP 3 has now been amended by FRS 3, which does allow disclosure of eps under different alternatives.

S.131 (merger relief) used in conjunction with acquisition accounting – the phenomenon of 'lost' goodwill

S.131 was introduced to give relief from the requirement to record share premium arising on an issue of shares at a premium. The section made it possible to ignore the premium element on shares issued on a merger, which was accounted for as such on consolidation. This relief is dealt with in Chapter 19.

However, creative use of the relief permitted – 'merger relief' – has been made by companies in acquisition situations, that is, where the acquisition method must be used on a business combination and where, given that goodwill arises in the consolidated accounts, fair values of both consideration paid and assets acquired are relevant.

Using the merger relief provisions of S.131 in conjunction with acquisition accounting on consolidation gives rise to the phenomenon of 'lost' goodwill. Thus:

▶ The parent company records the cost of the subsidiary at the nominal value of the shares issued as consideration.
▶ The premium on any shares issued as consideration is not recorded as S.131, relief from the requirement to record share premium, applies.

- On consolidation, fair values are required for the calculation of goodwill and consolidation adjustments would be required. The cost of the subsidiary would, as a consolidation journal, be increased so as to include the premium on the shares issued as consideration, and an equivalent amount would be credited to consolidated reserves (a S.131 reserve).
- Goodwill arising on consolidation is written off against this reserve.
- Effectively the goodwill is written off against share premium account.
- If no disclosure is made of the reserve arising on consolidation and the consolidation goodwill written off against it, the goodwill is 'lost' to the reader of such accounts.

The parent company may be able to arrange the acquisition in such a way that cash is paid to the vendor, but the company itself issues new shares (vendor placing or vendor rights arrangements). Where the S.131 reserve is used for such shares issued by the parent, it is, given the sequence of recording as noted above, possible for significant amounts paid for goodwill in a year of acquisition not to be reflected in the accounts as it is offset against the 'share premium' on shares issued.

SSAP 23 does *not* deal with the implications of recording the cost of a subsidiary in the separate accounts of the parent company. However, given the impact of S.131 in the parent company's accounts when used in conjunction with the acquisition method on consolidation, guidance is given in an appendix to the standard suggesting that the parent should record the fair value of shares issued as consideration and take the premium arising to a separate S.131 reserve. This reserve would flow through into consolidated reserves, and any goodwill written off against such a reserve would have to be disclosed as a movement on reserves.

The revised SSAP 22 requires that where there is any difference between the amount of purchased goodwill and that recognised in the accounts, the extent of the difference and the reasons for it should be disclosed. The revised standard requires disclosure of the fair value of the consideration and the amount of purchased goodwill arising. The disclosure should identify the method of dealing with goodwill arising and whether it has been set off against merger reserve or other reserves or has been carried forward as an intangible.

Ascribing fair values to separable net assets at the time of the acquisition

Both FRS 2 and SSAP 23 require that fair values be assigned to a subsidiary's net assets on the date of the acquisition for the purpose of the consolidated financial statements in situations when acquisition accounting must be used. Where such requirements were traditionally considered a disadvantage of acquisition accounting, in that upward revaluations of a subsidiary's fixed assets would give rise to additional depreciation in the consolidated profit and loss account, they have been put to advantageous use in the making of provisions in the subsidiary on the date of acquisition.

Thus, in a number of acquisitions, provisions have been made for reorganisation and other costs. In some, the amounts provided have subsequently proved more than needed so that excess provisions are then written back to income in a later accounting period.

As the provisions, when made, are charged against reserves of the subsidiary at the date of acquisition, these are reduced, and goodwill, required to be calculated as the difference between the fair value of consideration paid and the fair value of separable net assets acquired, is increased. This goodwill is normally eliminated on acquisition directly against reserves. The provisions are effectively dealt with, therefore, directly against reserves as opposed to earnings.

The larger the provisions, the larger the goodwill set off against reserves. If the write-back of provisions to profit and loss account in subsequent accounting periods is significant, and the disclosure is less than clear, post-acquisition earnings are distorted.

Similar problems can arise where stocks of the acquired company are written down to fair value and the write-down subsequently proves to be excessive.

To get around this problem the revised SSAP 22 calls for extensive disclosure for each acquisition. These include:

▶ a comparison of book amounts recorded in the subsidiary company with fair values ascribed to each major category of asset acquired
▶ an analysis of consolidation adjustments to bring the accounting policies of the subsidiary into line with those of the group
▶ revaluations
▶ reorganisation provisions
▶ provisions for future trading losses.

Most importantly, SSAP 22 calls for disclosure of movements on provisions relating to the acquisition. An example of such disclosure is shown in Example 5.4.

EXAMPLE 5.4

Fair Value Table: Acquisition: XYZ Ltd Date: 19/2/89
Consideration: 100,000 £1 ordinary shares were issued to acquire the following assets. The fair value of the consideration, using the mid-market price on 19/2/89 of £3.06, was £306,000 giving rise to goodwill of £100,000.

	Book value	Revaluation	Provisions for trading losses	Other provisions	Accounting policy alignment	Other major items	Fair value to the group
Fixed Assets	£000	£000	£000	£000	£000	£000	£000
Intangible	–	–	–	–	–	80[f]	80
Tangible	160	20[a]	–	–	–	–	180
Investments	20	5[b]	–	–	–	–	25
Current Assets							
Stock	40	–	(4)[c]	(5)[d]	(2)[e]	–	29
Debtors	35	–	–	–	–	–	35
Investments	10	–	–	–	–	–	10
Cash at bank	12	–	–	–	–	–	12
Total Assets	277	25	(4)	(5)	(2)	80	371
Liabilities							
Provisions:							
Pensions	30	–	–	–	–	–	30
Taxation	45	–	–	–	–	10[g]	55
Other	10	–	8[c]	–	–	–	18
Creditors							
Debenture	2	–	–	–	–	–	2
Bank loans	15	–	–	–	–	–	15
Trade creditor	30	–	–	–	–	–	30
Other creditors	10	–	–	–	–	–	10
Accruals	5	–	–	–	–	–	5
Total liabilities	147	–	8	–	–	10	165
Net assets	130	25	(12)	(5)	(2)	70	206

Adjustments	Explanations
Note a.	Increase in value of freehold properties since last revaluation in 1981.
Note b.	Increase in value of shares of USM investment since purchase in 1983.
Note c.	Losses expected to be incurred prior to closing down small tools division.
Note d.	Write down following reassessment of realisable value of stock which is more than one year old.
Note e.	Change of stock valuation from weighted average cost to FIFO which is used by the group.
Note f.	Recognition of intangibles – relating to publishing titles and brands acquired.
Note g.	Adjustment to deferred tax arising from the incorporation of fair values.

Movements on provisions should be disclosed and analysed between amounts used and amounts released unused.

The problem of accounting for the gain or loss on disposal of a subsidiary

SSAP 14 required, in the group accounts, that the profit or loss on disposal of a subsidiary be calculated as follows:

		£
(a)	Sales proceeds	x
(b)	*Less:* Net assets, relating to the shares sold, disposed of	(x)
(c)	*Less:* Goodwill paid on the original acquisition of the shares sold	(x)
(d)	*Add:* Any of the goodwill in (c) written off since acquisition	x
		x

The effect of (d) was to increase the reported gain (reduce the loss) on disposal.

The goodwill paid on the original acquisition of the shares sold, if previously written off *to reserves*, is more appropriately accounted for on disposal not as part of the reported gain on disposal but as a movement on reserves.

The revised SSAP 22, while it does not propose that this be adopted as the accounting procedure on disposal of shares, does require that, for each disposal there should be disclosure of:

▶ the profit or loss on disposal; and
▶ the amount of goodwill involved and how it has been treated in determining the profit or loss on disposal.

Chapter 18 deals with the FRS 2 treatment of accounting for the gain on the disposal of a subsidiary. Under FRS 2, the add back under (d) above would apply only if the goodwill paid on acquisition was systematically amortised against profits following acquisition. The add back would *not* apply if goodwill was written off against reserves immediately on acquisition.

Some additional points as to fair values – ED 53

The ED argues that the principles of fair valuing are not sufficiently well defined to ensure that the treatment of assets and liabilities in acquisition accounts is consistent and correct. The draft offers guidance on:

Fair value of the consideration

The basic principle is that the fair value of ordinary shares should be based on the value at which they could have been issued for cash. For listed securities, their fair value should be the average price (marked bid price) in the period immediately prior to the commencement of the bid. Acquisition costs should be included in the cost of the investment, unless they have been set against the share premium amount.

Deferred consideration

Deferred consideration payable in cash should be the amount of the cash payable (and that amount may need to be discounted to present value). The value of deferred consideration in a form other than cash should be based on circumstances at the date the bid was announced (and, again, discounting may be necessary). Thus:

▶ the value of the deferred consideration is fixed at the date of acquisition
▶ the number of shares to be issued to satisfy that consideration will vary
▶ according to the market value of the shares at the date the consideration is paid.

Deferred consideration, where it is certain to be paid, should be provided for at the date of acquisition. Thus, it will give rise to an immediate impact on goodwill.

Contingent consideration

Contingent consideration usually arises where the acquirer agrees to pay additional consideration only if the acquired company achieves a certain level of performance (an 'earn out').

Present practice is generally to accrue the amount that will probably become payable where this is known. However, in many instances, even the probable amount is difficult to estimate. Where it is not possible to be reasonably certain as to the amount that will become payable, companies normally give details of the contingency in a note, together with a range of possibilities in some cases.

Where contingent consideration is not provided for it will have an effect on goodwill only if, and when, paid.

Fair value of separable net assets

The paper states that the fair values of separable net assets should represent estimates of the amounts that it would have cost the acquiring company to acquire the assets directly.

The fair values may be adjusted for a period of time after the date of acquisition.

Assets and liabilities may include items not recognised by the acquired company, for example, brands, and may exclude items that were recognised by the acquired company. Fair values of non-monetary assets should be based on the replacement cost of assets acquired.

Contingencies and provisions

Contingent liabilities should be treated as in SSAP 18. Contingent assets should be treated in the same way as SSAP 18 requires contingent liabilities to be treated.

Provisions for losses on continuing businesses should not be set up in the fair value exercise. Only provisions for reorganisation costs and for losses arising in the process of running down a business segment should be made.

Change of stake

If a company increases its stake it should carry out a full fair-value exercise. Only part of the uplift in value should be treated as cost to the acquirer with the remainder being treated as a revaluation. See Example 5.5.

EXAMPLE 5.5

Event	Total value of investee
10% acquired	£10m
increased to 30%	£13m
increased to 51%	£15m
increased to 80%	£20m

It is generally accepted that:

▶ on acquiring the 10%, no fair-value exercise should be undertaken
▶ on increasing the holding to 30%, the acquirer will normally need to start treating the acquired company as an associate; this should involve determining fair values of separable net assets, although the exercise is often not carried out
▶ on increasing the holding to 51%, there is now a subsidiary, the fair-value exercise must be undertaken and the net assets of the subsidiary will be ascribed a value of £15m in the consolidated financial statements
▶ what is not clear is how the increase in stake to 80% should be treated.

The various approaches are as follows:

1   Ascribe fair values of £20m to the net assets in the consolidated accounts.
    Advantage: Regardless of whether control is acquired in one acquisition or piecemeal, the consolidated accounts, once the acquisition is complete, will be identical.
    Disadvantage: While part of the uplift will have arisen from the change in stake, part will not – this part is in fact a revaluation; the accounting convention used is therefore a mixture of cost and valuation.
2   Ignore the increase in value to £20m and retain the value of £15m which was ascribed when the company first became a subsidiary.
    Disadvantage: Goodwill and post-acquisition reserves will be overstated and asset values understated.
    Advantage: The method is simple and should be used if changes in value are insignificant or changes in stake are small.
3   Ascribe fair values to the net assets by stating a proportion of them at a fair value of £15m and the remainder at a fair value based on £20m.
        This approach ensures that net assets are carried at cost to the group but it is difficult to see what the cost actually represents. In fact, this cost is a 'mixed cost' and would be made up as follows:

	£m
At 51% acquisition	15.00
re 29% acquisition	
29% (£20m – 15m)	1.45
	16.45
Less: MI	
20% × £15m	(3.00)
	13.45

Further, there will be difficulties in interpreting post-acquisition results.

None of the approaches is ideal. (1) involves revaluation, (2) may result in serious mis-statement, and (3) may involve complex calculations and result in information that is difficult to interpret. (1) is probably best as it splits the uplift between recording a revaluation in terms of the percentage already owned and an assigning of fair values to the percentage acquired.

This area is discussed in further detail in Chapter 18 in the context of 'form' under the rules of Schedule 4 (A) paragraph (9) and 'substance' under FRS 2 and its interpretation of the legal rules in terms of the overriding obligation to present a true and fair view.

The proposed re-revision of SSAP 22

ED 47 proposes fundamental changes to SSAP 22. Where both the original and the revised SSAP 22 allowed two treatments of goodwill arising on acquisition, these are reduced to one in the proposed new standard. The treatment of immediate write-off which was the preferred treatment in the original statement is the option that has been discarded in ED 47. The reasons for choosing systematic amortisation as the only permitted treatment for goodwill are as follows:

▶ Goodwill is an asset and should be recorded in the balance sheet. In order to decide whether any item is an asset reference needs to be made to some definition of an asset. The IASC Framework for the Preparation and Presentation of Financial Statements defines an asset as 'a resource controlled by the enterprise as a result of past events and from which future economic benefits are expected to flow'. Goodwill is considered by the ASC, in the light of this definition, to have the characteristics of an asset.

▶ Those who consider that goodwill is an asset can come to this view from two different perspectives. One group sees goodwill as an asset that can be described in terms of both cause and effect while the other sees goodwill as an asset only in terms of its effects. In terms of causes, goodwill can be seen as a collection of favourable attributes enjoyed by an enterprise, which are describable but not individually identifiable. As an effect, it promises economic benefits over and above those that would normally be expected for the combination of net identifiable assets employed in the enterprise. Some examples of favourable attributes that are commonly identified as causing these higher economic benefits are:
  – advantage of location
  – quality of the workforce
  – specific market circumstances such as high costs of entry.

▶ The view that sees goodwill as an asset only in terms of its effects (the higher economic benefits) perceives the economic effects as higher than expected not because of any special describable attributes but because of the different measuring conventions used in valuing an enterprise as a whole and in valuing the individual assets and liabilities.

(Under both the above perspectives goodwill has the general characteristics of an asset. The ASC inclines to the view that goodwill is both a cause and an effect and it is this view which underlies the requirement in the proposed standard to disclose the main factors that give rise to goodwill where an amortisation period in excess of 20 years is considered justified (see below).)

▶ The IASC Framework states that an asset should be recognised 'if (i) it is probable that any future economic benefits associated with the item will flow to or from the enterprise and (ii) the item has a cost or value that can be measured with reliability'. The ASC considers that the cost of purchased goodwill can be measured with reliability and that purchased goodwill should be recognised and recorded in the balance sheet.

▶ The immediate write-off option does not recognise purchased goodwill in the balance sheet to ensure consistency of treatment between purchased and non-purchased goodwill. This treats goodwill as an asset that is so unique that general asset recognition criteria should not apply to it. The proposed standard treats goodwill similarly to other assets and uses similar recognition criteria to determine its treatment in any set of circumstances. One major change from the existing standard is that ASC now regards it as more important that purchased goodwill be treated consistently with other purchased intangible and tangible fixed assets than that purchased and non-purchased goodwill should be treated consistently.

Proposed standard accounting practice

ED 47 proposes that:

► No amount should be attributed to non-purchased goodwill in a balance sheet.
► Purchased goodwill should be recognised as a fixed asset and recorded in a balance sheet.
► The amount attributed to purchased goodwill should not include any value for identifiable intangible assets. The amount of these should be included under the appropriate heading within intangible fixed assets in a balance sheet.
► Purchased goodwill should not be treated as a permanent item in a balance sheet. It should be amortised through the profit and loss account as a charge against ordinary profits before tax. The charge should be calculated using the straight-line basis or any other systematic basis that is more conservative and considered to give a more realistic allocation.
► Purchased goodwill should be amortised over its useful economic life, which should initially be estimated at the date of acquisition. The period should be determined by identifying and evaluating the factors that gave rise to the goodwill. These factors should be reviewed annually to determine whether the amortisation period remains appropriate. The period should be changed subsequent to the acquisition if the original estimate of the life is seen to be incorrect. Note, however, that the life should be extended only if the reasons for extension relate to components of goodwill that were present at the date of acquisition.
► The useful economic life should not exceed 20 years except in the rare circumstances where it can be demonstrated by reference to the circumstances giving rise to the goodwill that a period in excess of 20 years would be more appropriate. In all cases purchased goodwill should be written off over a period that does not exceed 40 years from its date of acquisition.
► Goodwill recorded on a balance sheet should be reviewed annually to determine whether the carrying value is excessive.
► If there is a permanent diminution in value of purchased goodwill it should be written down immediately through the profit and loss account. Purchased goodwill should not be revalued upwards.
► Negative goodwill should be treated as the converse of positive goodwill. It should be shown on the credit side of the balance sheet either as deferred income or as a provision, depending on whether it arose from a bargain purchase or from general disadvantages associated with the business. A negative goodwill balance should be credited systematically to the profit and loss account over a suitable period decided in relation to the particular circumstances that gave rise to the negative goodwill. In many circumstances, the average life of the fixed assets may provide a suitable period over which credit should be taken.
► For each material disposal of a previously acquired business, if there is an amount of purchased goodwill attributable to it in the balance sheet, that amount less amortisation should be written off against the proceeds of disposal. Any adjustment for goodwill that relates to a disposal should be taken through the profit and loss account.
► Notwithstanding the requirements of FRS 3 in relation to changes in accounting policy, purchased goodwill that has been written off to reserves immediately on acquisition in accordance with standard accounting practice on that date, need not be reinstated in the balance sheet on the introduction of the proposed new standard. If such purchased goodwill is reinstated, it should be at an amount calculated as if the proposed standard had been in force at the date of its acquisition.

The Companies Act 1989

The acquisition method of accounting and the calculation of goodwill are described in the new Act. The acquisition cost is any cash consideration and the fair value of any other consideration together with any fees or other expenses of the acquisition as the company may determine. The Act provides that goodwill is only to be included in the balance sheet to the extent that it was acquired for valuable consideration. Thus, non-purchased goodwill is prohibited by law from recognition in the balance sheet.

Some further points as to amortisation

The most difficult area of controversy in accounting for purchased goodwill is whether it has a limited life and therefore should be written down systematically by an amortisation charge. ED 47, in an appendix, sets out the arguments for amortisation as follows:

▶ The purchased goodwill that exists at a particular point of time – the date of acquisition – is different from the goodwill that may exist later in the business, and does not have an indefinite life. If goodwill is a favourable conjunction of circumstances that exist at a particular point in time, it is in the nature of the changing world that any particular favourable conjunction of circumstance will not continue forever. On this premise, the purchased goodwill established in a transaction on a specific date will eventually decay and so should be expensed, over its economic useful life, against profits. The ASC considers that the vast majority of possible causal factors for goodwill acquired at any point of time will cease to generate attributable economic benefits within 20 years of the date of their acquisition.

▶ The concept of prudence suggests that an asset such as goodwill that is both unidentifiable and intangible should be allocated to the periods that benefit from it by a regular charge, because it will be difficult to tell when it has been completely eroded or fallen in value. If purchased goodwill is written down only on the occurrence of a permanent diminution it may either be carried permanently or any necessary provisions for diminution may be made later than the diminution truly occurs.

▶ The consideration given to acquire a business is normally determined having regard to the evaluation of the timing of the future economic benefits that the acquired business may be expected to generate. In evaluating such benefits, less weight is attributed to benefits expected in the more distant future than those expected sooner. The payment for goodwill, as a payment for future cash flows should, therefore, under the principles of the matching concept, be amortised against the benefits that were anticipated in setting the price paid for it. Weighting for the time value of money suggests a treatment that charges the cost of purchased goodwill against the earlier benefits generated by the business acquired.

There is an opposing view that no systematic amortisation charge should be made. There are those that consider that purchased goodwill should be recorded as an asset in the balance sheet and written down only where a permanent diminution in its value occurs. The ASC, as stated in the appendix to ED 47, does not find these arguments convincing. Those that argue against amortisation argue as follows:

▶ Purchased goodwill does not wear out, so no charge should be made either as a measure of goodwill being used up in the business or to provide for its replacement. It is argued that purchased goodwill can be seen as an asset analogous to land. As it is intangible, goodwill does not suffer wear and tear so there is no logical necessity that over time it should either diminish or wear out. Permanent diminutions in the value of goodwill should be charged against profits just as any permanent diminution in the value of land, for example, by erosion, should be recognised.

► Purchased goodwill may also be considered in terms of an investment. No amortisation or depreciation charge is made against an investment unless there is evidence that the investment has suffered a permanent diminution in value. In the case of goodwill, such a decline in value would be evidenced by a fall in the value of the business or a fall in the cash flows generated by it.

The ASC does not accept the analogy of purchased goodwill with land or with an investment. Unlike land, the goodwill purchased at the date of acquisition does not have an indefinite life.

► The residual value of purchased goodwill may be greater or equal to its original cost. Where a business increases in value by trading successfully, it is likely that the value of goodwill in it is increasing.

ASC argues that while this may well be the case, the total of this increased or maintained value for goodwill includes both purchased goodwill and internally generated goodwill and does not distinguish between them. In the acquired business, internally generated goodwill may be developed that replaces purchased goodwill; but the ASC considers that the original purchased goodwill will disappear over time and that internally generated goodwill should not be included in a balance sheet. On this premise, the original purchased goodwill has a residual value of zero as, eventually, it will all have been eroded.

► It is double counting to make an amortisation charge for purchased goodwill in the profit and loss account at the same time as the continuing costs of maintenance and enhancement of the goodwill are also being charged.

The ASC argues that the expenditure to develop or maintain goodwill is not distinguishable from the expenditure incurred in the continuing operations of a business to attain other direct benefits. The maintenance and development of goodwill can thus be seen as a free by-product and therefore as having no cost. There is thus no double counting as the amortisation charge is the only cost for goodwill.

► The systematic amortisation of purchased goodwill does not represent a real economic event. It therefore does not give information that is either useful or relevant to users of accounts. It has been argued that a systematic charge for goodwill fails to distinguish between companies that have maintained acquired goodwill and those that have not.

ASC would, however, argue that it is because goodwill is an asset involved in the earning of profits over time and the profit figure itself, both before and after the amortisation charge, will distinguish between a company that has been maintaining or enhancing its goodwill and one that has not.

Some further points in favour of systematic amortisation

A major practical argument against immediate write-off to reserves of acquired goodwill is that this treatment has acted to reduce the balance sheet totals of acquisitive groups so that they show negligible or even negative amounts of shareholders' funds at a time when the group has made acquisitions of real value to the shareholders and is flourishing and making profits. Recognition of this anomalous effect was one of the main reasons why the ASC believed the present standard should be amended.

Against this, it is argued that if the market is efficient then accounting information is correctly evaluated by the market in setting a value for any business so that different accounting treatments in similar companies do not distort their comparative values.

If the market is not efficient, alternative accounting treatments have real economic consequences for the businesses reporting under them. In this case it becomes relevant to consider whether an accounting treatment gives one set of enterprises an advantage over another that is not permitted to use that treatment. It is argued that if capitalisation and amortisation of consolidated goodwill against profits is required, there will be adverse consequences for acquisitive British companies in that:

▶ they will lose a competitive advantage over foreign acquirers who are permitted to write off goodwill directly to reserves
▶ their earnings, eps and market rating will be adversely affected
▶ their capacity to pay dividends may be impaired.

ASC argues as follows.

Competitive advantage

While it is arguable whether the existing SSAP 22 confers any real advantage on British acquirers over foreign competitors, there is no doubt that many British business people and accountants believe that it does. In the ASC's view, the arguments about the economic consequences of the accounting treatment of goodwill are unproven either way. It has reached the conclusion that goodwill arising on purchase should be capitalised and amortised on the merits of the accounting requirements. These are:

▶ Amortisation is the method that best accords with accepted accounting principles, the historical cost convention and the concept of prudence.
▶ It provides more useful financial information to the user.
▶ It gives some recognition to the fact that the issue of equity in consideration for an acquisition involves a real cost to the shareholders of the acquiring company.
▶ While the treatment is admittedly not perfect, on balance it seems to offer the best solution available.

Impact on reported results and market rating

The amortisation charge will plainly reduce reported earnings but, because it does not change cash flows or the ability to make distributions, it is by no means clear why it should adversely affect market ratings.

Dividends

The legal rules relating to distributions apply to the accounts of the holding company not the group accounts, and amortisation of consolidation goodwill does not affect individual company accounts.

Nevertheless, the alternative effects of treatments of goodwill on performance ratios remain. If goodwill is systematically amortised it is treated as a recognised loss; if it is written off immediately, it is not (see also FRS 3 in Chapter 11). Earnings are obviously enhanced under the immediate write-off treatment. Where this would have had some considerable impact on general interpretation pre-FRS 3, the effect of the alternatives is diminished under FRS 3 and the shift away from a narrow focus on eps. Given the much more substantial disclosure required under FRS 3, users should now be able to make a more informed judgement as to performance, regardless of alternative treatments adopted.

Accounting for brand names

Brands affect the price that acquisitive companies are prepared to pay for target companies. The value of well-known brands, unrecognised on the balance sheet, can be used (unsuccessfully in some cases) to attempt to prevent a takeover.

The issues involved

There are two issues:

▶ The problems of accounting for goodwill and for the tangible and intangible assets obtained on acquisition of another company – acquired brands.

▶ The desire of some companies to reflect in their balance sheets the value, as opposed to the cost, of their assets – internally created brands.

Until recently, goodwill has been an umbrella concept embracing several features of a company's activities that could lead to superior earning power, for example, outstanding workforce, excellent management, effective advertisement, market penetration. None of these has been recognised as an asset in the balance sheet as each of them is difficult to identify and impossible to sell separately.

However, some assets, which traditionally have been included within the all embracing umbrella of goodwill, *can* be individually identified and *are* separable from the company, for example, patents, licences, newspaper titles, copyrights, trademarks and brands. All of these, to use the terminology of ED 42 and ED 49 and, more recently, FRED 4, may grant their owner rights to future benefits.

The UK accounting profession, so far, has been reluctant to recognise acquired intangible assets on the balance sheet, preferring instead to deal with intangibles in aggregate as goodwill.

The existing standard on goodwill prefers the immediate write-off of goodwill to reserves but permits amortisation over economic useful life through the profit and loss account. Before the revised SSAP 22, the most popular policy was to write off goodwill immediately, given the earnings effect of annual amortisation.

Even though SSAP 22 clearly states that write-off of goodwill to reserves does not imply an equivalent loss of value, acquisitive companies, initially in favour of immediate write-off, became increasingly concerned as the group's net worth decreased and ill-formed criticism abounded about high gearing ratios and the apparent lack of reserves. Such companies have also had problems with restrictive covenants, based on reported net worth, when looking for increased borrowings to finance further acquisitions.

As a result, companies have been looking more closely at the separable assets acquired in a business combination. Indeed, SSAP 22 clearly emphasises that goodwill comprises of *unidentifiable* intangible assets and should not include those assets, including intangible assets, that are capable of individual identification and of being sold separately without disposing of the business as a whole.

Thus, identifiable intangibles such as concessions, patents, licences, trade marks and similar rights and assets (including brands) should form part of the separable net assets that are recorded in an acquiring company's accounts at fair value, even if they were not recorded in the acquired company's accounts.

It is in this context that companies such as News International have capitalised publishing rights and newspaper titles; Reckitt & Colman has shown acquired trademarks as an intangible asset on the balance sheet, and companies such as Grand Metropolitan and Rank Hovis McDougall have included brands as assets in their balance sheets.

The points made above in the main relate to the problems and issues as to acquired separable intangibles. It is necessary to distinguish between these and internally created separable intangibles. The issues raised in accounting for internally created brands are very similar to those relating to internally generated goodwill:

▶ It may be argued that there is no fundamental difference in nature between internally generated and purchased goodwill. Thus, the argument runs, both kinds of goodwill could be included in the balance sheet (assuming no write-off of purchased goodwill) to ensure comparable financial statements between acquisitive companies and companies preferring organic growth. So, too, with internally created brands

▶ It may also be argued (SSAP 22) that although it is true that no difference exists between the two types of goodwill, only purchased goodwill should be recognised in the context of historical cost accounting. This is because it results from a market transaction that crystallises its value at one point of time and because the historical cost balance sheet does not purport to represent the total value of a business as a whole. Accordingly, SSAP 22 prohibits the capitalisation of internally created goodwill. So, too, it is argued that internally created brands should not be capitalised.

The policy of valuing internally created brands has not yet been widely practised in the UK.

However, companies that fear predators and that possess highly visible, saleable, home-grown brands may be tempted to consider whether such brands should be brought on to the balance sheet. This is given that many take-over bids that seem, initially, to be at a premium in relation to a target's tangible assets could well be at an economic discount if the value of the target's undisclosed brands were to be taken into account.

To summarise:

▶ any company showing only acquired brands in its balance sheet, is within the bounds of SSAP 22

▶ moving towards recognition of internally generated intangibles (or revaluing acquired brands) is a major step towards a value-based balance sheet and raises the question of the objectives of financial statements in general and, in particular, of the function of the balance sheet.

It is permissible in law to recognise internally created brands and to revalue acquired brands under the alternative valuation rules.

It has also been argued that there is a certain logic in showing all brands at their value, even though it is much more difficult to deal with valuation where there is no market transaction involved.

The problems are these:

▶ If a company purchases a brand in isolation, its cost is obvious.

▶ If, however, a company purchases another, and in doing so purchases a parcel of assets, including brands, how is cost to be apportioned to the separable intangibles represented by brands?

▶ How is a company to value an internally created brand?

Techniques used include external valuation and, for franchised brands, the application of a multiple to royalties. In the USA and Australia, the normal method would be to apply a multiple to the sustainable contribution from the brand. The key to the valuation is the multiple.

In business combinations, the difference between the purchase consideration and the fair value of the tangible assets would normally place a ceiling on the cost of a brand. Like other assets, intangible assets such as brands may decline in value and would have to be written off to the profit and loss account as the benefit accruing to their owner diminished over their finite lives.

It is difficult to argue the case for the elimination of an intangible over an arbitrary period rather than its useful life. Further, it may be a company's policy to preserve the value and life of its brands in the same way as it maintains valuable properties so that their lives are extended indefinitely. Current thinking as to accounting for brands seems to be born out of a recognition that present accounting practice for intangible assets may be failing to reflect adequately the economic reality of a company's financial position.

Tangibility is not the issue. What is being measured is the right to a particular benefit – a trend that began with accounting for finance leases and which has appeared more recently in the definitions of an asset in ED 42, ED 49 and FRED 4. This is moving into conceptual framework territory.

One way to avoid the difficult problem of breaking down goodwill into its component parts is to revert to the method used before SSAP 22 intervened: to carry forward goodwill until it diminishes in value. This could resolve the problem of accounting for acquired brands but does not address the problem of accounting for internally created brands, unless one were to argue that internally generated goodwill should be brought on to the balance sheet as well.

It was stated, as long ago as 1929, that the most striking characteristic of the immense amount of writing on goodwill was the number and variety of disagreements reached. Nothing has changed.

ASC statements on accounting for brands

The ASC issued ED 52 – Accounting for Intangible Fixed Assets, in May 1990. The ED replaces TR 780, which dealt with the same subject. The purpose of ED 52 is to propose standard accounting practice for certain issues relating to intangible fixed assets which, taken together with ED 51 – Accounting for Fixed Assets and Revaluations, and SSAP 12 (Revised) – Depreciation, would provide a general framework for accounting for intangible fixed assets. ED 51 is discussed in detail in this textbook. Here we deal specifically with the issue of accounting for brands as dealt with in ED 52.

You should refer to Chapters 1 and 4 for the criteria for the recognition of intangible fixed assets. This section deals with the application of those criteria to accounting for brands.

There can be little doubt that brands and branding under skilful management can add significant value to commercial operations and are a major force in modern business. One aim of ED 52 is to establish the most appropriate method of accounting for them for the purpose of external financial reporting.

What is a brand?

The term 'brand', undefined as it is, is generally used with a meaning significantly different from, and wider than, a trade name. While every recognised brand has a trade name, the name is not synonymous with the brand.

Branding connotes a continuous process of assembling, developing and exploiting all the tangible and intangible elements of the product to achieve commercial advantage over competitors. The term 'brand' is thus generally used to mean a conjunction of characteristics which, operated in combination, offer the expectation of a stream of future benefits exceeding in aggregate what the constituent items could produce separately or without brand identification.

While it is not practicable to identify or list all the typical constituents of a brand, they normally include some or all of the following:

- ▶ a recognised name
- ▶ a product or range of products
- ▶ an established operation and market position

- marketing and other specialist know-how
- trading connections.

These characteristics are expected to enhance future earnings.

In practice, brands are seldom sold and acquired as bare rights to trade names. If they were, their correct description would be 'trade names' or 'trade marks'. Brand acquisitions normally involve all or part of the integrated set of supporting functions discussed above.

In all these senses, the term 'brand' is used to describe what is generally regarded for accounting purposes as goodwill, that is, a combination of factors that is expected to produce enhanced earnings in the future. This interpretation is confirmed by the fact that the most commonly used methods of evaluating both goodwill and brands involve the use of multiples or present values of projected future earnings.

It is therefore concluded in ED 52 that, for accounting purposes, brands are subsumed within goodwill and should be accounted for accordingly. It follows that internally created brands should not be included in the balance while acquired brands would simply be included in the value of purchased goodwill in the balance sheet.

This does not mean that financial information about brands is not important to the users of financial information. It is, and reporting entities are encouraged to provide relevant information about brands that will help users to evaluate them.

Some enterprises may wish to indicate, probably in a note to the financial statements, the amount of purchased goodwill being carried in the balance sheet that they consider is attributable to brand names.

While ED 52 proposes that brands should be treated as part of goodwill and not carried in the balance sheet as independent intangible fixed assets, the amounts concerned will often, in the case of brands acquired through business combinations, be eligible to be treated as purchased goodwill and capitalised and amortised in accordance with the proposals of ED 47.

The way forward in accounting for intangibles

Comment on ED 47 has been mostly critical. Finance directors, major professional firms, the CBI and even ASC members have criticised the draft. There really is nothing exceptional in the proposed standard seeking to provide a uniform treatment for purchased goodwill by requiring its systematic amortisation against earnings through the profit and loss account. After all, the rest of the world mostly writes off goodwill in this way. The USA has been doing it since 1970, the IASC recommends it, the EC approves, and they're even planning something similar in Australia. So why all the fuss?

It is about the effect on eps. The immediate write-off option of the existing standard has substantial support. Many business people find it more convenient to weaken the balance sheet than to damage the all-important eps figure. The trouble, however, is that some balance sheets have become too weak altogether and enterprises have invented new devices, including the valuation and inclusion of brands, to avoid the embarrassment of negligible net assets. ED 47 makes these artificial stratagems unnecessary. The approach is a simple one: treat purchased goodwill like other long-lived assets – they are depreciated against profits and therefore so should goodwill be.

Some people argue that if home-grown R & D projects are permitted by accounting standards to be capitalised, then so too should home-grown goodwill. Nothing so radical is proposed by ED 47; the costs of home-grown goodwill must be written off in the year concerned. The reasons for the distinction between purchased and non-purchased goodwill are both logical and clearly stated in ED 47.

Some critics have argued that, although the immediate write-off treatment is flawed, a better treatment would involve leaving purchased goodwill at original cost, unamortised, but subject to the annual review proposed by ED 47. This approach has the practical benefit of leaving reported earnings unscathed by amortisation but little conceptual merit and concepts, under the new regime, are what it is all about. The appendix to ED 47 explains that if this treatment is adopted, an arbitrary portion of non-purchased goodwill will find its way into the balance sheet.

The expected behaviour of analysts and market makers in response to a change of treatment has been used as ammunition by all sides. For those who prefer immediate write-off, the analyst's supposed disregard of balance sheet goodwill figures is adduced to support its painless amortisation. For those concerned about amortisation's effects on eps and consequently share prices, the anlayst is expected to mark shares down to reflect lower reported earnings.

Although views differ as to the market's sophistication in rejigging accounting data to reach a 'right' conclusion, it seems likely that, armed with new post-amortisation eps figures and with details of actual amortisation charged, the analyst will have no cause to alter the rating of a security simply because of a change in accounting method.

The future of an accounting standard on goodwill is also affected by the current debate as to accounting for brands, which shows no signs of abating. The group chief accountant of Rank, Hovis McDougall has called for standard-setters to wake up to the real world: 'Like it or not, in the eyes of some accountants, the "brands debate" is inextricably linked with "the goodwill debate". They hope that if the UK accounting profession puts brands on its "too difficult pile" by requiring them to be called goodwill and then requiring goodwill to be capitalised (and amortised), the brands debate will go away. I have news for them – it won't.' The debate is by no means at an end. There are those who have vociferously called for brands to be capitalised as such on the basis that putting brands on the balance sheet forces a company to look to their value as well as to profits.

The story of the ASC and goodwill has been a sorry one, comparable in some ways to the long-running saga of inflation accounting. As from 1 August 1990 the mantle of standard-setting passed to the newly formed Accounting Standards Board (ASB). Will they abandon ED 47 and frustrate an important move towards global harmonisation? Certainly, it has hard times ahead.

The ASB has issued several statements. FRS 3, which is dealt with in Chapter 11, now shifts the emphasis away from a headline number such as eps. As previously mentioned, whatever the approach adopted re intangibles full disclosure now enables better judgements to be made. The 1994 pronouncements of the ASB as to goodwill and other intangibles are dealt with in Chapter 20.

Accounting for research and development expenditure

Intangible assets, like tangible assets, have a value because they are expected to generate future benefits for an organisation. It follows therefore that, in principle, the same accounting treatment should be applied to both intangible and tangible assets. Thus the accruals concept would require the capitalisation of intangible assets and subsequent depreciation or amortisation. Intangible assets, however, are characterised by a high degree of uncertainty as to future benefits and the prudence concept would therefore require the expenditure on such assets to be immediately written off. The conflict between the accruals concept and the prudence concept, and the concept that research and development expenditure should be treated as an investment, underlie the whole of the argument concerning the accounting treatment of research and development expenditure. An accounting standard, SSAP 13 – Accounting for Research and Development, was issued in December 1977 and became standard accounting practice for accounting periods starting on or after 1 January 1978. ED 41, the proposed revision to the standard, was issued in June 1987 and SSAP 13 (Revised) in January 1989.

The questions which SSAP 13 attempts to resolve are:

▶ Which activities should be described as research and development in accounts?
▶ Should research and development costs be deferred?
▶ How should deferred costs be amortised?
▶ What is the disclosure required in respect of research and development?

The definitions used in the standard are those used by the Organisation for Economic Co-operation and Development (OECD) in the report entitled *Measurement of Scientific and Technical Activities* (referred to in SSAP 13). Although in many instances the dividing line will be indistinct, three similar but distinguishable types of operation are envisaged: pure research, applied research and development.

Pure research

This refers to original investigation that is undertaken simply to gain new knowledge or deeper understanding, whether it be scientific or technical. It is not undertaken with any specific practical application in mind although it may result in practical benefits.

Applied research

This differs from pure research in that it is aimed at achieving a particular objective. Thus there is a specific purpose for the work, for example, the development of a particular process.

Development

Development is defined as the use of knowledge acquired through research, in order to produce new or substantially improved materials, devices, products, processes, systems or services prior to starting commercial production. Development is that work that is performed from the time that a new or improved entity is designed or planned to the time that it is ready to be manufactured on a commercial basis. It will often be difficult to draw a line between development and production.

SSAP 13 does not lay down any guidelines as to which costs can appropriately be regarded as research and development costs. However, the International Accounting Standard, IAS 9, on the subject lays down that costs of activities that can be appropriately regarded as incurred for research and development purposes include:

▶ salaries, wages and related costs of personnel
▶ the cost of materials and services consumed
▶ the depreciation of equipment and facilities
▶ a reasonable allocation of overhead costs
▶ other related costs such as the amortisation of patents and licences

Costs incurred on market research are specifically excluded from the OECD's definition of research and development expenditure. Such costs should, however, be included in development costs under the standard.

SSAP 13 – accounting

Although SSAP 13 distinguishes between pure and applied research, the accounting treatment laid down is the same for both types of research, which are considered to be part of the normal ongoing activities of the company. Neither pure nor applied research is expected to produce benefits in any particular period, they are simply required to maintain a company's business and competitive position. For this reason, there is no justification for deferring the expenditure on either pure or applied research and the standard requires that such costs must be written off as they are incurred.

Expenditure on development, however, is generally undertaken when there is a reasonable expectation that specific commercial success and future benefits will accrue from the work. In such circumstances, it is considered reasonable to defer such expenditure to future periods. SSAP 13 lays down the general rule that development expenditure should be written off in the year in which it is incurred. As an exception, if the directors so wish, a company may defer such expenditure and match it against related revenue of future periods, but only if the following conditions are satisfied:

► there must be a clearly defined project
► the expenditure relating to the project must be separately identifiable
► the project must be technically feasible
► the project must be commercially viable
► future development costs to be incurred on the project together with related costs of production, selling and administration must reasonably be expected to be more than covered by related future revenues
► the company must have adequate resources to carry the project through to completion.

Where conditions for deferring development costs are satisfied, and a decision to defer is made, two further questions arise. First, at what point should amortisation commence and, second, over what period and on what basis should the expenditure be amortised?

To determine when amorisation should commence it is necessary to differentiate between the process of development and the process of commercial production. The development process means the stages involved in turning a specific idea into a commerically viable proposition. It is the costs that are incurred in these stages that may be deferred. Development costs therefore can begin to arise only once commercial possibilities have been identified. The production process is the process, after a product has been developed, of manufacture with a view to sale on a commercial basis. The costs involved in this process are separate and distinct from development costs and should be accounted for by inclusion in the value of stock.

The standard assumes, for the sake of simplicity, that the expected future benefits of the deferred development expenditure begin to arise on commencement of the production process. It lays down that the amortisation of development costs should commence at the same time.

As to the period of amortisation, the standard states that development costs must be allocated, on a systematic basis, to each accounting period by reference to:

► the sale or use of the product or process, or
► the period over which the product or process is expected to be sold or used.

This will require a commerical assessment of the product and of the pattern of its use. This involves predictions and gives rise to areas of potential uncertainty. One acceptable method is to write off deferred development costs over a number of years based on market forecasts of sales on a straight-line or weighted average basis. An alternative method, applicable where units involved are high in value and low in number, for example, aircraft, is to write off the deferred development costs as each unit is sold based on market forecasts of the likely number that will be sold.

Given that the considerations involved in deciding on a deferral of development costs involve considerable speculation into the future, the standard requires that deferred development expenditure should be reviewed at the end of each accounting period. Where the circumstances that originally justified deferring the costs no longer apply, the costs must be written off to the extent considered irrecoverable through the profit and loss account as part of profit on ordinary operations. Once written off, the old standard specifically stated that the costs should not be reinstated. The revised standard does not specifically prohibit such a write-back.

Some problem areas

Fixed assets

Fixed assets used on development projects should be capitalised and written off over their useful life. The depreciation that is written off should be included as part of the deferred development costs. The amount so dealt with should also be disclosed as part of the depreciation disclosure in the profit and loss account.

Market research

Market research should receive similar accounting treatment to the forms of research and development expenditure that are included in the OECD definitions. The standard requires, as a general rule, that market research costs should be written off as they are incurred. They may, however, as an exception, be carried forward when two conditions are satisfied. First, they must be incurred in order to ascertain the commercial viability of a project, and second, the project itself must satisfy all the other conditions for carry forward set out in the standard. Where, as a result, expenditure on market research costs are deferred, they must be disclosed separately.

The aerospace industry

One of the main problems in relation to the aircraft industry is that it is very difficult to forecast future sales. For aircraft of a military nature, development costs are generally recoverable under a contract. For civil aircraft the company will not know whether it will sell successfully until the project is completed. In this case there are two possible treatments. Either the costs should be written off as incurred or the proportion of the expenditure that is covered by minimum sales can be deferred, the remainder being written off immediately.

The computer industry

The work of these companies involves research and development expenditure of an ongoing nature, incurred in the process of continuously updating and improving hardware and software product ranges. Prior to publication of the standard some manufacturers adopted the practice of adding such expenditure to the cost of stocks. The standard indicates that such expenditure should be written off as it is incurred.

The leisure industry

Companies in this industry have problems implementing the standard, as it is difficult in the initial stages to determine whether a project will be successful. Some companies defer development expenditure but write it off either over two years or at the time when it proves abortive, whichever is earlier. This policy represents a compromise between prudence and matching, but it does not comply with the standard.

Fixed price contract work

Where development costs are incurred as a result of a contract that provides either for full reimbursement of development costs, or for payment at an agreed price covering costs of development and manufacture, development costs should be included in work-in-progress to the extent that it has not been reimbursed at the balance sheet date.

Disclosure

The accounting policy that a company has adopted in its treatment of research and development expenditure must be clearly stated. Where development costs have been deferred, they must be shown as a separate item in the balance sheet and not included as a part of current assets. In any such case the notes must show the movement of the deferred development expenditure, included as an intangible fixed asset, during the accounting period.

	£	£
Deferred development expenditure at 1 January		x
Development expenditure in year	x	
Development expenditure amortised in year	(x)	
		x
Deferred development expenditure at 31 December		x

The standard and the Companies Act 1985

The 1985 Act requires development costs to be shown separately under fixed assets, intangible assets. Such costs may be included as an asset only if there are 'special circumstances' and, if so, disclosure is required of:

▶ the period over which the amount of these costs is written off, and
▶ the reasons for capitalising the costs, that is, the 'special circumstances'.

'Special circumstances' may reasonably be taken to be compliance with the SSAP 13 criteria for deferral of development costs. The Act specifically requires the write-down of an asset in an accounting period of permanent diminution in value and subsequent write-back in a subsequent accounting period where the circumstances that gave rise to the permanent diminution in value no longer apply. This is why, presumably, there is no prohibition in the revised standard as to reinstating development costs previously written down.

SSAP 13 (Revised) has nothing to say as to accounting for development costs in the context of ascertaining the legally distributable profits of the company. The Act requires that development costs are to be treated as a realised loss in this regard *unless* there are 'special circumstances' that justify the directors in deciding otherwise. In this event the notes to the accounts must state that development costs are not treated as realised losses and explain the circumstances relied upon to justify the decision of the directors to that effect. Such a note may be prepared as follows: 'Such costs have been capitalised in accordance with SSAP 13 and are therefore not treated, for dividend purposes, as a realised loss.'

The revised standard

SSAP 13 was revised in 1989. The changes were introduced in the preceeding ED 41. The principal change proposed was a requirement for companies to disclose the research and development costs charged as an expense in the current year, including the amount of any development costs amortised. This is required by International Accounting Standard 9 and it is believed that this disclosure would provide useful information to users of accounts. The proposed revision did not make any change to the rules regarding the treatment of research and development expenditure, that is, the circumstances in which the expenditure should be written off as incurred or may be deferred to future periods.

Usefully, ED 41 included lists of examples of activities that should be included and excluded from research and development.

Examples of activities that could be included in research and development are:

- experimental or theoretical work aimed at discovery of new knowledge
- searching for applications of such work or other knowledge
- formulation and design of possible applications for such work
- testing in search for, or evaluation of, product or process alternatives
- design, construction and testing of pre-production prototypes and models
- design of products, processes, systems or services involving new technology or substantially improving those already produced or installed.

Examples of activities typically excluded from research and development include:

- routine design, testing and analysis of equipment or products for purposes of quality or quantity control
- routine or periodic alterations to existing products or processes even though these may represent improvement
- operational research
- troubleshooting in connection with break-downs during commercial production
- legal and administrative work in connection with patent applications, records and litigation and the sale or licensing or patents
- activity, including design and construction engineering, relating to the construction, relocation, rearrangement or start-up of facilities or equipment other than facilities or equipment whose sole use is for a particular research and development project.

ED 41 stated that there was a case for considerable disclosure including, for example, the nature status and costs of individual projects, whether or not written off. Such detailed disclosure causes considerable problems of definition and the proposed disclosure requirements of the ED were therefore limited to:

- accounting policy required by SSAP 2
- a disclosure of the total research and development expenditure in the year as a separate item distinguishing between expenditure written off and amortised and any development expenditure capitalised
- the movements on deferred development expenditure during the year.

In conclusion, both the Companies Act 1985 and the old accounting standard encourage immediate write-off, although development costs may be carried forward if a number of hurdles are cleared.

Unfortunately, ED 41 re-established this bias. The requirement is not that in the prescribed circumstances the expenditure should be carried forward, but that it may be. In other words, companies may continue to account for successful development expenditure as though it were unsuccessful. As a member of the ASC pointed out:

> The argument in favour of not recognising research and development expenditure as an asset is that immediate write-off is more prudent. While recognising that much research by its nature cannot result in an identifiable asset and should be written off immediately, it is doubtful that it is in the investment community's interests that the outcome of successful development should be tucked away in past years' results with no requirement for the directors to answer in due course for its success (or otherwise).

The revised standard followed, essentially, the line of ED 41. The main changes were:

- although the revised standard requires the amount of research and development costs charged to the profit and loss account to be disclosed, certain enterprises are exempt from this disclosure
- the proposal that development costs once written off should not be reinstated was not included in the revised standard, presumably given the rules as to diminution of value under the Act.

Exploration costs

Companies in the mining and oil industries have continually to be exploring for new reserves. The expenditure incurred on such exploration is material. A problem arises in accounting for such expenditure because some of the explorations are successful and others are not, some lead to future benefits and others do not. There is no accounting standard on this subject in the UK; exploration costs are specifically excluded from the requirements of SSAP 13. The matching principle would suggest that, as with research and development costs, such costs should be deferred to those periods when the subsequent benefits of incurring the expenditure are realised. However, one criterion that must be satisfied to justify such deferral is that the outcome of a project has been assessed with reasonable certainty. This is difficult in the extractive industries.

This section deals with some of the alternative ways in which exploration costs may be accounted for.

Successful efforts

Essentially, exploration costs that turn out to be successful are carried forward and costs that turn out to be unsuccessful are written off in the year in which they are incurred. An accounting policy to illustrate this method may read: 'Exploration costs are charged to income currently with the exception of exploratory drilling costs, which are initially included in property, plant and equipment pending determination of commercial reserves discovery; should the efforts be determined unsuccessful, they are charged to income.'

Full cost

Under this method the total costs of exploration are capitalised, regardless of whether or not the project is successful. Advocates of this approach argue that finding a number of dry holes is part of the process of striking a hole in which there is oil or gas. The total cost of finding an income-producing hole should, therefore, it is argued, include the costs of unsuccessful operations as to dry holes.

The alternative accounting treatments can have a substantial effect on the profits reported for a particular period, and in the USA there have been several Statements and Opinions issued by the Financial Accounting Standards Board (FASB) on the subject. Thus FAS 19 states that:

> The cost of drilling exploratory wells and the costs of drilling exploratory type stratigraphic test wells shall be capitalised as part of the enterprise's uncompleted wells, equipment and facilities pending determination of whether the well has found proved reserves. If the well has found proved reserves, the capitalised costs of drilling the well shall become part of the enterprise's wells and related equipment and facilities; if, however, the well has not found proved reserves, the capitalised costs of drilling the well, net of any salvage value, shall be charged to expense.

The standard describes a preferable, but not required, form of the successful efforts method of accounting. The debate as to the most appropriate way of accounting for exploration costs is by no means concluded.

International comparisons *re* treatment of research and development expenditure

The US standard equivalent to SSAP 13, SFAS 2, makes no distinction between pure and applied research, simply distinguishing between research on the one hand and development on the other. SFAS 2 is also different from SSAP 13 in that it requires all research and development costs to be charged to income as and when incurred, given:

▶ uncertainty of future benefits
▶ difficulty of matching current expense with (possible) future benefit
▶ the capitalisation of such costs is not useful in assessing the earnings potential of an entity.

SFAS 2 covers research and development costs incurred in creating software products and requires all companies to disclose the total research and development costs expensed in a period, whereas SSAP 13 exempts some companies from this disclosure requirement.

The international standard, IAS 9, is similar to SSAP 13 except that it specifically states that development costs once written off should not be reinstated, even though the uncertainties that led to their being written off no longer exist. In the UK this presents a problem in connection with legal rules as mentioned above. The IASC has proposed that the option of writing off development costs which meet the criteria for deferral should be eliminated, that is, that such costs must be capitalised if the capitalisation criteria are met.

Audit implications

Chapter 4 dealt with tangible fixed assets and this chapter examines the issues involved in the recognition or otherwise and disclosure attached to intangible fixed assets.

Summary

▶ This chapter deals with the accounting problems of the valuation and capitalisation or otherwise of intangible assets. The principal issue is whether such costs meet the criteria of an asset and should be recognised as such or whether they do not, in which case they should be expensed as incurred through the profit and loss account.
▶ Whether accounting for goodwill, for other intangibles such as brands, or for development costs you should consider the impact of the alternatives above in assessing earnings on the one hand and balance sheet net worth on the other, and be prepared to comment on the advantages and disadvantages of applying each of the alternative treatments currently permitted under UK accounting standards.

Suggested reading

Accountancy (August 1987)
Articles by P. Rutteman: 'Where has all
the goodwill gone?' and E. Woolf:
'Goodwill: SSAP 22 is the best answer'.

UK GAAP (Ernst & Young 1990)

*Manual of Accounting – Companies
(Coopers & Lybrand Deloitte 1990)*

*Brand Valuation: Establishing a True
and Fair View (Murphy 1989)*

*Financial Reporting 1989–90: A Survey
of UK Reporting Practice (Skerratt and
Tankin 1989)*

Self test questions

1   Kiwi plc purchased the net assets of a business. The consideration for the
purchase was settled by the issue of 200,000 £1 ordinary shares of Kiwi plc with a
market value of £1.10 each. On the date of its purchase the books of the acquired
business showed the following assets:

	£	
Goodwill	5,000	
Separate net assets		
Patents	14,000	(fair value £20,000)
Plant	120,000	(fair value £138,000)
Net current assets	30,000	

Calculate the goodwill arising on the purchase so as to comply with SSAP 22.

2   State the factors that should be taken into account in determining the
amortisation period for goodwill under ED 47.

3   Summarise the advantages and disadvantages attaching to each of the two
alternative treatments permitted under SSAP 22 as to goodwill.

4   Is goodwill an asset, or not, and should it be capitalised and systematically
amortised or eliminated on acquisition against reserves?

5   Are brands valuable assets, and should you put them on the balance sheet?

Exam style questions

1   *Scotty plc*
You are the group accountant of Scotty plc and you need to make adjustments to
the draft accounts for the year ended 30 June 1990 to reflect the acquisition of a
subsidiary, and to calculate the earnings per share.

Information in respect of the new subsidiary is as follows:

▶ On 1 October 1989, Scotty plc acquired a 90% interest in Sulu Inc., a US
corporation. The consideration of £2,450,000 comprised £1,500,000, satisfied
by the issue of 5,000,000 25p ordinary shares in Scotty plc to the vendors and
£950,000 cash payable as to £750,000 at completion and £200,000 on
1 October 1990.

▶ The financial statements of Sulu Inc. at 30 September 1989 showed net assets of $4,370,000, before deducting costs totalling $380,000 in respect of redundancies, which were identified at acquisition and subsequently paid.

▶ At a board meeting to approve the acquisition, the directors of Scotty plc were informed that an investment in plant and machinery would be required in Sulu Inc. of $300,000 in the period to 30 June 1990.

▶ Professional fees for advice in respect of the acquisition amounted to £30,000 and your finance director has estimated that the time and expenses incurred by the directors of Scotty plc in negotiating and completing the deal amounted to £20,000.

▶ Sulu Inc. valued stocks on the LIFO (last in first out) method in its financial statements. On 30 September 1989, the value of stocks held by Sulu Inc. would have been $150,000 greater if valued on the FIFO method consistent with that used by Scotty plc.

▶ The share capital of Scotty plc at 1 July 1989 comprised 47,500,000 ordinary shares of 25p each. Except for the transaction described above, there were no other movements in share capital during the ensuing year.

▶ The exchange rate at 1 October 1989 was £1 = $1.8

▶ Scotty plc amortises goodwill arising on consolidation over a three-year period.

Additional information in respect of earnings per share is as follows:

▶ The draft group profit after taxation and after any impact arising from the above matters is £1,614,000. However, the tax charge includes £200,000 of irrecoverable ACT arising on the proposed dividend and there are 3,250,000 outstanding share options exercisable in 1993 at 18p.

▶ The price of 2.5% Consolidated Stock at 30 June 1989 was 27xd.

▶ A corporation tax rate of 35% should be assumed.

Required:
a) Calculate the fair value of Sulu Inc. at 1 October 1989 giving justification for your treatment of:
   (i)   redundancy costs
   (ii)   investment in plant and machinery
   (iii) professional fees and directors' time and expenses
   (iv)   stocks.

(8 marks)

b) Calculate the goodwill arising in the consolidated balance sheet of Scotty plc that would be carried forward at 30 June 1990.

(5 marks)

c) Draft the note to the accounts relating to earnings per share and calculate the amounts to be included therein.

(7 marks)
(Total 20 marks)

Note: Ignore deferred tax.

ICAEW PE II exam question 1989

2   *Casscadura plc*
Casscadura plc is a pharmaceutical company. You are provided with the following information as to its research and development activities.

a) During the year ended 30 June 1991, the company incurred £750,000 of expenditure on a new project to develop a drug for the treatment of cancer. On 30 June 1991, it is expected that it would be at least another three years before the company would be able to establish whether the drug would be effective, and, if it were, at least another two years after that to produce a marketable product.

(6 marks)

b) As on 30 June 1990, the company had incurred expenditure of £3,000,000 on the development of a new tranquilliser and had carried this expenditure forward as an intangible fixed asset in its balance sheet as on this date. During the year ended 30 June 1991, the project was completed at a further cost of £600,000 and the drug was launched on the market on 1 January 1991. Sales in the six-month period to 30 June 1991 amounted to £2,250,000. The company anticpates that the new drug will be a market leader for two years from the launch date, that a successful competing product should be available thereafter and that total sales during this period will amount to £15,000,000. It is further anticipated that the drug will remain marketable for another two years after the appearance of the competing product and that further sales of the drug, during this period, will amount to £7,500,000 before the drug is withdrawn from the market. Profits on the new drug are forecast at £12,000,000 for the first two years with £1,500,000 of this amount arising in the six months to 30 June 1991. Further profits of £3,000,000 are forecast for the two years ending 1 January 1995. These profits are, in all years, exclusive of development costs.

(9 marks)

c) As on 30 June 1990, the company had incurred and carried forward as an intangible fixed asset on this date, expenditure of £15,000,000 on the development of a cure for influenza. During the year ended 30 June 1991, it was decided to terminate the project as test results proved adverse.

(5 marks)

Required:
In the context of SSAP 13 (Revised) on accounting for research and development, state with reasons how Casscadura plc should deal with, and disclose, research and development expenditure in its financial statements for the year ended and as on 30 June 1991.

(20 marks)

Based on ACCA AFA exam question on paper 3.1 June 1986

All answers on pages 635–639.

Stocks and Long-term Contracts

ED 40 was issued in 1986 and contained proposals for the revision of SSAP 9 – Stocks and Work in Progress, which was originally issued in 1975. The revised SSAP 9 was issued in 1988.

Until the original SSAP 9 was issued, companies adopted a wide variety of methods to value stocks and work in progress. The introduction of the standard caused a considerable amount of debate at the time, particularly in the construction industry, because it proposed radical changes in accounting for long-term contracts. Following the introduction of the Companies Act 1981 SSAP 9 once again became the focus of attention. This Act, now consolidated into the Companies Act 1985, required that current assets should be included in the balance sheet at the lower of their purchase price or production cost and their net realisable value. In respect of work in progress, this requirement was in total conflict with SSAP 9, which states that 'the amount at which long-term contract work in progress is stated in periodic financial statements should be cost plus any attributable profit ...'.

This chapter is important from an examination point of view in that it deals with an old accounting standard that was in conflict with the rules of the Act and has, therefore, been revised.

Principles of valuation and the valuation rules of the Act

The determination of profit for an accounting year requires the matching of costs with related revenues. The cost of unsold or unconsumed stocks will have been incurred in the expectation of future revenue; when the revenue will be accounted for in a later year, it is appropriate to carry forward the cost to be matched with the revenue when it arises. The applicable concept is the matching of cost and revenue in the year in which the revenue arises rather than in the year in which the cost is incurred. If there is no reasonable expectation of sufficient future revenue to cover cost incurred (for example, as a result of deterioration, obsolescence or a change in demand) the irrecoverable cost should be charged to revenue in the year under review. Thus, stocks normally need to be stated at cost or, if lower, at net realisable value.

Net realisable value is the amount at which it is expected that items of stocks can be disposed of without creating either profit or loss at the time of sale, that is, the estimated proceeds of sale less all further costs to completion and less all costs to be incurred in marketing, selling and distributing directly related to the items in question.

The comparison of cost and net realisable value needs to be made in respect of each separate item of stock. Where this is impracticable, groups or categories of stock items that are similar will need to be taken together. To compare the total realisable value of stocks with the total cost could result in an unacceptable setting off of foreseeable losses against unrealised profits.

In order to match costs and revenue, 'costs' of stocks should comprise the expenditure that has been incurred in the normal course of business in bringing the product or service to its present location and condition. Such costs will include all related production overheads, even though these may accrue on a time basis.

The methods used in allocating costs to stocks need to be selected with a view to providing the fairest possible approximation to the expenditure actually incurred in bringing the product to its present location and condition. For example, in the case of retail stores holding a large number of rapidly changing individual items, stock on the shelves has often been stated at current selling prices less the normal gross profit margin. In these particular circumstances this may be acceptable as being the only practical method of arriving at a figure that approximates cost.

The valuation rules of the 1985 Act in respect of stocks

Current assets are required to be stated by the 1985 Act at the lower of their purchase price or production cost and their net realisable value. The purchase price of an asset is the actual price paid plus any expenses incidental to its acquisition. The production cost of an asset is determined by adding direct costs of production to the purchase price.

A reasonable proportion of indirect production costs and the interest on capital borrowed to finance the production of an asset may also be included, but only in so far as they relate to the period of production. If such interest costs are included, the fact and the amount included must be disclosed in a note.

Distribution costs may not be included in the production costs of current assets. Under SSAP 9, cost is defined as 'that expenditure which has been incurred in the normal course of business in bringing the product or service into its present location and condition'. Cost is identified as comprising 'costs of purchase' and 'costs of conversion'. The latter would include overheads attributable to bringing stock to its present location and condition. Thus, under SSAP 9, costs such as transportation costs from factories to retail or distribution centres are included in the costs of stocks.

The permitted methods of valuation under the 1985 Act include LIFO and the base stock method. The latter may be used where raw materials and consumables are constantly being replaced. Where their overall value is not material and there are no material fluctuations in quantity held, such items may be included at a fixed quantity and value.

A summary of the differences between statutory requirements and 'old' standard accounting practice in respect of the valuation of stocks is shown in Table 6.1.

Contract work in progress

The Act makes no distinction between work in progress and long-term contract work in progress and requires all current assets to be included at the lower of their cost and net realisable value. SSAP 9 emphasised the need to give special consideration to work in progress arising from long-term contracts. The standard argued that, owing to the length of time taken to complete such contracts, to defer recognition of profit until completion may result in the profit and loss account reflecting not so much a fair view of the activities of the company during the year but rather the results relating to contracts that have been completed during the year. Accordingly, the standard required, subject to certain limitations, companies to take credit for profit on such contracts, not on their completion, but over the duration of the contract.

The 1981 Act required that only realised items be included in the profit and loss account. This requirement gave rise to some initial doubt as to whether attributable profit on long-term contracts, recognised in the profit and loss account, constituted a departure from the requirements of the Act. Such doubts were resolved by guidance from the accountancy bodies in TR 481, which categorically stated that such profit was realised (in accordance with principles generally accepted) and that there was no conflict with the Act in including it in the profit and loss account.

However, companies that included attributable profit in long-term contracts did have a problem with the valuation rule for current assets in the balance sheet, that is, the lower of cost and net realisable value rule for all current assets.

Table 6.1 Summary of the differences between Companies Act 1985 and SSAP 9 in accounting for valuation of stock

	Companies Act 1985	Original SSAP 9
Distribution costs	Must be excluded.	The standard includes in cost 'other' overheads indirectly attributable to bringing a product to its present location and condition. It has, under the standard, been customary to include the cost of transporting goods from factory to a company's own distribution centre.
Interest costs	May be included in cost to the extent that it accrues in respect of the period of production.	The standard, in the appendix, states, re work in progress, that it is not normal to include interest in cost unless the borrowings to which it relates can be identified as financing specific contracts.
Valuation methods	▶ FIFO ▶ LIFO ▶ Weighted average ▶ Any similar method ▶ Base stock, provided certain conditions are met	The LIFO and base stock methods are not usually considered to bear a relationship to actual cost.
Appropriate indirect overheads	May be included.	Must be included.

Disclosure requirements under the 'old' standard

The note to the balance sheet dealing with stocks and long-term contracts would have needed to disclose:

Note: Stocks and long-term contracts

	Group		Parent company	
	1988 £	1987 £	1988 £	1987 £
Stock comprises:				
Raw material and consumables	x	x	x	x
Work in progress	x	x	x	x
Finished goods and goods for resale	x	x	x	x
Payments on account	x	x	x	x
(Note that these are payments made by the company.)	—	—	—	—
	x̲	x̲	x̲	x̲
Long-term contracts comprise:				
Cost plus attributable profit less foreseeable losses	x	x	x	x
Less: Progress payments received and receivable	x̲	x̲	x̲	x̲
	x̲	x̲	x̲	x̲
	x̳	x̳	x̳	x̳

In accordance with SSAP 9 attributable profit amounting to £x (1987 £x) has been included in the value of long-term contracts. The inclusion of such profit results in a departure from statutory valuation rules for current assets but is considered necessary by the directors in order that the accounts give a true and fair view.

The cost of long-term contracts includes interest on capital borrowed to finance production of £x (1987 £x).

Where progress payments received on account exceed the value of the work completed on a contract, the excess is included under creditors. If such an excess arises on a loss-making contract the excess is included under provisions.

The replacement cost of raw materials and consumables and work in progress (dealt with separately) is greater than the balance sheet value by £x (1987 £x).

(Further disclosure should be made where (material) stocks are purchased subject to reservation of title. If the liability to the supplier is secured the extent and nature of the security should also be noted.)

The reasons for the revision of SSAP 9

ED 40 was issued primarily to provide an integrated financial statement presentation of long-term contracting activity that accords with international practice. The proposals had the further advantage of removing the conflict between SSAP 9 and the Companies Act 1985. The proposals, after some amendments have now been adopted as standard in the revised SSAP 9. The revision of SSAP 9 was necessary for the following reasons.

The conflict with the Act

The difference between the legal requirements and the requirements of SSAP 9 was that under the latter, 'attributable profit' had to be included in the carrying value of long-term contract work in progress, subject to certain limitations, whereas the former permits only attributable profit to be included in special circumstances. This conflict affected both the profit and loss account and the balance sheet.

Given the guidance in TR 481 – 'the relevant principles of recognising profits in SSAP 9 are based on the concept of "reasonable certainty" as to the eventual outcome and are not in conflict with the statutory accounting principles' – both accountants and the DTI agreed that there was no conflict in including attributable profit on long-term contracts in the profit and loss account. However, the controversy surrounding the balance sheet presentation proved more difficult to overcome.

As dealt with previously, including attributable profit in contract balances in the balance sheet is a departure from the valuation rules of the Act. However, it is permissible to include attributable profit in the balance sheet value if it is argued that it is necessary in order to show a true and fair view, as recognised by the Act. In this case it is necessary that particulars of the departure, the reasons for it, and its effect be given in a note to the accounts.

Where it was reasonably simple for companies accounting under SSAP 9 to disclose particulars of the departure and their reasons for it, there was considerable debate as to what should be disclosed as to 'effect'.

The construction industry believed that the disclosure could apply only to the figure of long-term contract work in progress after the deduction of progress payments, what may be termed the net contract value in the balance sheet. To ascertain the effect of the departure from the valuation rule applied to this value was, argued some companies, artificial, resulting in a meaningless figure. On these grounds, no disclosure as to the effect of the departure was made in the notes to the accounts.

> EXTRACT – Cable and Wireless in its 1984 accounts
> Attributable profit has been included in long-term contract work-in-progress in accordance with SSAP 9. This enables the financial statements to give a true and fair view as required by section 149 (3) of the Companies Act 1948, but constitutes a departure from the statutory valuation rules. Progress payments cannot meaningfully be allocated between cost and profit so as to determine the effect of the departure or whether it is material.

This approach, however, was not acceptable, as Counsel advised, and the DTI agreed, that the 'effect' of the departure to be disclosed should be the whole amount of attributable profit added to the cost of work in progress before the deduction of progress payments – the valuation rule applied to what may be termed the gross contract value in the balance sheet.

Because of this controversy, the DTI sought to resolve the dilemma with the ASC. The ASC issued ED 40, which proposed that the balance sheet value of work in progress should not include any attributable profit, thus eliminating the problem of departure from the Act and disclosure as to its effect. Thus, the revised SSAP 9 removes the conflict with the Act that arose under SSAP 9.

Presentation of information in the profit and loss account

The method of accounting for long-term contracts specified in SSAP 9 required that attributable profits, if any, should be recognised in the profit and loss account and added to the cumulative cost of long-term contracts in the balance sheet. SSAP 9 did not address how contract turnover and related costs should be recorded in the profit and loss account. In practice, a variety of methods were used to determine the turnover disclosed in each accounting period. However, in many cases, this had not been derived from a formal integration of turnover, cost and balance sheet accounting. The balance sheet presentation of long-term contracts continued to reflect, on a contract-by-contract basis, cumulative volumes of costs incurred and attributable profits, less payments on account, with eventual elimination of the components relating to a particular contract at the time when the contract is determined to have been completed.

ED 40 proposed that turnover and associated costs should be recorded in the profit and loss account as contract activity progresses. Therefore, the results for long-term contracts that are reported in the profit and loss account are attributable to the proportion of work completed. The ED, however, did not define the precise amount of turnover to be recognised in the profit and loss account. Paragraph 9 stated that turnover should be 'an appropriate proportion of total contract value'. This would suggest the application of a fraction, either percentage complete in terms of value or percentage complete in terms of costs, of the total contract price. Appendix 3, however, stated that turnover is 'the value of work done'. This suggested a 'work certified figure', which may well be different from an appropriate proportion of total contract value in terms of sales value or costs. Regardless of the problem of what to include as turnover, the revised SSAP 9 ensures a more integrated approach to accounting for contracts and is in line with the IAS on the topic.

Short-term contracts

One further problem with SSAP 9 was that short-term contracts had to be included in the balance sheet at the lower of cost and net realisable value. This caused problems where such a contract was substantially complete at the year end. SSAP 9 would not permit a company to recognise profit on the contract until the following year even though the contract's outcome could be foreseen with certainty at the year end. Thus, SSAP 9 was criticised by companies involved in short-term work that had the same characteristics as long-term work. The proposals of ED 40 went some way to resolving this matter. The ED proposed a new definition of long-term contracts to include some short-term contracts. Thus, in the new definition, the specific duration of performance may not be the sole distinguishing feature of a contract. Where the company is substantially engaged in contracts that extend for more than one year, the proposals suggested that it may not be appropriate to adopt a separate accounting policy for shorter-term contracts, that is, all contracts may be accounted for on a percentage of completion basis. The problem of a too-prudent approach to short-term contracts is, therefore, resolved in the revised SSAP 9.

The revised SSAP 9

New definitions

Changes from the old definitions are in italics.

(a) Long-term contracts
A contract entered into for the *design*, manufacture or construction of a single substantial asset or the provision of a service (*or of a combination of assets or services which together constitute a single project*) where the time taken substantially to complete the contract is such that the contract activity falls into different accounting periods. *A contract that is required to be accounted for as long term by this accounting standard will usually extend for a period exceeding one year. However, a duration exceeding one year is not an essential feature of a long-term contract. Some contracts with a shorter duration than one year should be accounted for as long-term contracts if they are sufficiently material to the activity of the period that not to record turnover and attributable profit would lead to a distortion of the period's turnover and results such that the financial statements would give a true and fair view, provided that the policy is applied consistently within the reporting entity and from year to year.*

(b) Payments on account
All amounts received and receivable at the accounting date in respect of contracts in progress.

(c) Attributable profit

The definition has been widened. The amount should be calculated, specifically, after estimating remedial and maintenance costs. These will include, for example, clauses covering completion of the finishing touches to a building and provisions for costs incurred under a guarantee period for maintenance that is part of the original contract.

Accounting

▶ First ascertain the total estimated profit or loss on a contract (as under SSAP 9).

▶ Ascertain attributable profit on the basis that it is prudent to recognise such profit. Given a choice, work on the cost basis: cost to date/total cost × total estimated profit. (You may be asked to work on a sales basis or other alternative basis.)

▶ The standard does not prescribe a method of calculating turnover. Recognise as turnover the same proportion of the total contract value as applied to the total estimated profit for ascertaining attributable profit to date.

▶ Associated costs of achieving the turnover recognised should be deducted from total costs to date in the contract account and charged in the profit and loss account as cost of sales to give, as gross profit, the attributable profit or foreseeable loss on a contract as calculated.

▶ Essentially, you will be given information to calculate attributable profit or foreseeable loss. You will also be given a basis for recognising either turnover or cost of sales. Given the basis for turnover, take cost of sales as the balancing item. Given the basis for cost of sales, take turnover as the balancing item.

▶ Further provisions for foreseeable losses should be included in cost of sales.

▶ When, in the early stages of a contract, it is not possible to foresee its outcome with reasonable certainty, turnover will equal the costs that are charged to cost of sales. Therefore no profit from the contract will be recognised in the profit and loss account. However, when in the later stages of the contract the outcome can be assessed with reasonable certainty, turnover should include profit prudently recognised as earned at that stage of completion.

▶ Long-term contracts in the balance sheet will comprise:

	£
Total costs to date	x
Less: Amounts transferred to cost of sales in respect of work carried out to date	(x)
Net costs	x
Less: Any foreseeable losses (if costs remaining need to be further written down)	(x)
Less: Any applicable payments on account	(x)
	x

▶ Debtors: amounts recoverable on contracts will arise where turnover recognised is greater than payments on account received and receivable.

▶ Where payments on account received and receivable are greater than turnover recognised, the excess should first be applied against any net costs remaining in the contract account. Any further excess should be classified as 'payments on account' and separately disclosed in 'creditors'.

▶ When foreseeable losses exceed net costs, the excess should be included in the balance sheet in either 'accruals' or 'provisions'.

The main difference between SSAP 9 and the revised SSAP 9 as to accounting for contracts are shown in Table 6.2 Examples 6.3, 6.4 and 6.5 further explain accounting for contracts.

In the main, the revised SSAP 9 reclassifies contract balances, under stocks per SSAP 9, as debtors in the balance sheet, thus avoiding any conflict with statutory valuation rules. The ASC justifies this treatment on the basis that, having asked Counsel to consider the matter, there is nothing in the Act to prevent such treatment and no necessity to disclose any further details regarding these amounts in the notes to the accounts.

Table 6.2 SSAP 9 compared with the revised SSAP 9

SSAP 9		Revised SSAP 9	
Balance sheet values			
Contracts	£		£
Cost plus attributable profits less foreseeable losses	x	Costs to date	x
		Amounts transferred to the profit and loss account	(x)
Payments on account received and receivable	(x)	Net costs	x
		Foreseeable losses	(x)
		Applicable payments on account	(x)
	x		x
Trade debtors			
Amounts invoiced less received	x		x
Debtors: Amounts recoverable on contracts			
	N/A	Turnover recognised less payments on account	x
Creditors: Payments on account			
Excess payments on account on profitable contracts	(x)	Payments on account less (turnover recognised plus applicable payments on account credited to the contract)	(x)
Provisions		Further provision to arrive at foreseeable loss	(x)
Excess payments on account	(x)		
Profit and loss account			
No specified treatment of items		Turnover – appropriate %	x
		Cost of sales – appropriate %	(x)
		Possible provision	(x)
		Attributable profit/	
		Foreseeable loss	x/(x)

The net effect of all these items taken together will be the same under both SSAP 9 and the revised standard.

Examples

EXAMPLE 6.1 – Where turnover recognised is greater than payments on account

	£
Contract value	1,000
Costs to date	(200)
Further costs to complete	(600)
Estimated profit	200
Attributable profit, cost basis 200/800 = 25% × 200	50
Payments on account – received	70
Payments on account – receivable	30
	100

Per SSAP 9	£
Costs to date	200
Attributable profit	50
	250
Payments on account	(100)
Contract balance	150
Trade debtor (100 – 70)	30

Per revised SSAP 9	£
Costs to date	200
Transferred 25% × 800	(200)
Contract balance	–
Trade debtor (100 – 70)	30
Debtor: recoverable on contract (25% x 1,000) less 100	150
Profit and loss account Turnover 25% × 1,000	250
Cost of sales	(200)
Gross profit	50

EXAMPLE 6.2 – Where turnover recognised is less than payments on account

	£
Contract value	2,000
Costs to date (excluding 50 below)	(500)
Costs allocated but not yet associated with work completed	(50)
Further costs to complete	(250)
Estimated profit	1,200
Attributable profit, cost basis 500/800 = 62.5% × 1,200	750
Payments on account – received	1,200
Payments on account – receivable	280
	1,480

Per SSAP 9	£
Costs to date:	550
Attributable profit	750
	1,300
Payments on account – restricted	(1,300)
Contract balance	–
Trade debtor (1,480 – 1,200)	280
Creditors: payments on account (1,480 – 1,300)	(180)

Per revised SSAP 9	£
Costs to date	550
Transferred 62.5% × 800	(500)
Net cost	50
Applicable payments on account	(50)
Contract balance	–
Trade debtor (1,480 – 1,200)	280
Creditors: payments on account 1,480 – (62.5% × 2,000 plus 50)	(180)
Profit and loss account Turnover 62.5% × 2,000	1,250
Cost of sales	(500)
Gross profit	750

EXAMPLE 6.3 – Where a provision for foreseeable losses is required

	£
Contract value	400
Costs to date	(150)
Further costs to complete	(390)
Estimated loss	(140)
Percentage complete, cost basis	
150/540 = 28%	
Payments on account, all received	150

Per SSAP 9	£
Costs to date	150
Less: foreseeable losses	(140)
	10
Payments on account – restricted	(10)
Contract balance	–
Provision: (150 – 10)	(140)

Per revised SSAP 9	£
Costs to date	150
Transferred 28% × 540	(150)
Contract balance	–
Profit and loss account	
Turnover 28% × 400	112
Cost of sales – transferred	(150)
– provision required	(102)
Gross loss	(140)
Creditors: payments on account less turnover, less credited to contract account (150 – 112)	(38)
Provision	(102)

NOTE: In examples 6.1–6.3, attributable profit is ascertained on a 'cost basis'. It follows that under SSAP 9 (Revised), turnover, cost of sales, and gross profit (on profitable contracts) will be the proportion of costs to date/total costs of contract value, total cost and total anticipated profit respectively.

As to loss-making contracts, as in Example 6.5, the further amount charged to cost of sales in order to immediately reflect the foreseeable loss in gross profit in the profit and loss account will usually be credited to the balance sheet under provisions. It may, however, be that there are net costs left on the contract account after the transfer to cost of sales. In this case any further provision for losses debited to cost of sales should be credited to the contract account to reduce it to the lower of cost and net realisable value.

Conclusion

The revised standard is an improvement on SSAP 9 in that it achieves standard practice in reporting contract activity in the profit and loss account and removes any conflict with the valuation rule of the Act. Where previously companies simply stated that turnover represented the invoiced value of sales making no mention of contract activity, this would no longer be acceptable under the revised standard. Accounting policies to satisfy the revised standard in respect of contract activity should read as follows.

Turnover

Turnover, which is stated net of value added tax, represents amounts invoiced to third parties, except in respect of long-term contracts where turnover represents the sales value of work done in the year, including estimates in respect of amounts not invoiced.

Long-term contracts

Profit on long-term contracts is taken as the work is carried out if the final outcome can be assessed with reasonable certainty. The profit included is calculated on a prudent basis to reflect the proportion of the work carried out at the year end, by recording turnover and related costs (as defined in stocks policy) as contract activity progresses. Turnover is calculated as that proportion of total contract value that costs incurred to date bear to total expected costs for that contract. Revenues derived from variations on contracts are recognised only when they have been accepted by the customer. Full provision is made for losses on all contracts in the year in which they are first foreseen.

Where the revised standard has been criticised in that it simply spreads out balances relating to contracts over stocks, debtors, creditors and provisions in the balance sheet there can be little doubt that it results in more informative disclosure than before and, therefore, represents a step forward in financial reporting.

Audit implications

You will have covered the audit implications as to stocks and work in progress in some detail in your studies of Papers 6 and 10. This section is intended to remind you of the audit problems arising in this area and to focus on the examination impact of these problems in a question on stocks and work in progress in the Financial Reporting Environment paper.

You should be aware of the audit implications as to this current asset item as:

▶ the value of stock is subjective and may therefore involve reliance on management representations
▶ the value of stock is therefore vulnerable to management manipulation
▶ stock is usually material in value
▶ an error in the valuation of stock will have a corresponding effect on profit.

You will be aware from your previous studies of many law cases involving auditors and stock – McKesson and Robbins, The Great Salad Oil Swindle and Thomas Gerrard – and of the APC Auditing Guideline as to attendance at a stock take. However, where SSAP 9 as dealt with in the earlier parts of this chapter, does deal with some of the technical aspects of stock valuation, there is no Auditing Guideline covering this area.

The three main areas that concern the auditor as to stock are:

▶ quantities
▶ ownership
▶ valuation.

Quantities of stock can be determined by either physical stock counts at or near the year end or by the extraction of balances from continuous records or from a sample count and extrapolation of results on the whole population. Ownership can be established by carrying out cut-off tests and by ascertaining stocks that are held by or on behalf of third parties.

Valuation follows the requirements of SSAP 9 and particular regard will need to be paid in this area to the possible need for any provisions for obsolescence in order to establish whether net realisable value is lower than stock.

The questions and answers at the end of the chapter deal with all of the above and also with some of the audit problems arising in respect of work in progress.

Summary

This chapter deals mainly with the reasons for the revision of SSAP 9 and accounting for contracts under the revised SSAP 9.

The main reasons for the revision of the original stocks and work-in-progress accounting standard were:

▶ conflict with the valuation rule of the Act
▶ no standard treatment of reporting contract activity in the profit and loss account
▶ a need for a change in definitions so that profit on what were described as short-term contracts could be recognised over duration as opposed to on completion.

The chapter deals with the differences between the old and revised accounting standards in accounting for contracts and illustrates how the main problems arising under the original standard are overcome in the revised standard. The latter part of the chapter serves to remind you of the audit implications arising in this area.

Suggested reading

Accountants Digest No. 158 (1984)

ED 40 – What about the balancing figure? (Loveday 1987)

UK GAAP (Ernst & Young 1990)

Manual of Accounting – Companies (Coopers & Lybrand Deloitte 1990)

Financial Reporting 1985–86: A Survey of UK Published Accounts (Skerratt and Tonkin 1986)

Self test questions

1 Why is stock considered to be a high risk audit area?
2 What should auditors do before a stocktake?
3 What matters should auditors consider when planning attendance at a stocktake?
4 What is the primary purpose of auditors when attending a stocktake?
5 What do auditors do when they attend a stocktake?
6 Why do auditors need to attend a stocktake?
7 Explain what you understand by the term 'cut-off procedures'?
8 What work will auditors perform after the stocktake with regards to the existence of stock?
9 Define costs in accordance with SSAP 9.
10 Define NRV in accordance with SSAP 9.
11 How would auditors verify the cost of raw materials in a manufacturing company?
12 How would auditors verify NRV of raw materials in a manufacturing company?
13 How would auditors verify the NRV of a finished product in a manufacturing company?
14 How should auditors check the accuracy of the purchase cut-off procedures?

15 If goods are returned after the year end during the post-balance sheet period, would this have any effect on the year end stock and if so what would the effect be?

16 Explain how stock included in the balance sheet as standard cost should be adjusted to actual costs?

17 How could auditors verify a standard cost?

18 What main matters must auditors consider when verifying the attributable overheads included within the stock valuation?

19 What is a long-term contract?

20 How should auditors verify long-term contract work in progress?

Exam style question

1   *Athos Ltd*

Athos Ltd is a civil engineering company, which at 31 July 1991 had three construction contracts in progress, information about which is as follows:

	Contract		
	A	B	C
Costs to date	£910,000	£1,500,000	£222,000
Future costs to complete	£545,000	£495,000	£666,000
Project started	1 October 1990	1 October 1990	1 October 1990
Likely completion	31 January 1992	15 April 1992	30 November 1991
Progress payments received	£757,000	£1,600,000	£200,000
Progress payments due but not paid	–	£50,000	–
Tender value	£1,700,000	£2,100,000	£875,000

Required

a) Determine the resulting balance sheet amounts that would be disclosed in the financial statements of Athos Ltd for the year ended 31 July 1991 under the provisions of SSAP 9, stating any assumptions you have made.

b) Determine the profit and loss and balance sheet amounts that would be disclosed in the financial statements of Athos Ltd for the year ended 31 July 1991 under the provisions of the revised SSAP 9.

c) Discuss and explain the background to the development of the revised SSAP 9 and the likely practical advantages and disadvantages of its provisions to preparers and to users of financial statements.

(20 marks)

Based on an ICAEW PEII examination question 1987

All answers on pages 639–644.

Tax in Company Accounts

If the tax on business profits was based on the actual reported profits of a business there would be no need for deferred tax accounting. This, however, is not the case. While reported profits are based on generally accepted accounting principles, taxable profits are ascertained on the basis of fiscal rules and regulations. Thus, for example, given incentives to invest by means of various forms of accelerated tax allowances, companies whose capital expenditure was habitually greater than the depreciation charge found that their actual tax liability was substantially lower than tax at the going rate on their reported profits.

It was recognised as best accounting practice, as long ago as 1958, to have regard in the financial statements to the deferral of tax as a result of capital allowances received. Recommendation N19, issued in 1958, stated that:

> if material, the amount of tax deferred by capital allowances should preferably be set aside and shown in the balance sheet, with appropriate description, as a separate item which may be grouped with 'future' tax. An amount so set aside should represent tax at current rates on the excess of
>
> (a) the net amount at which the relevant fixed assets are stated in the balance sheet over
> (b) the written down value of those assets for capital allowances purposes.

In 1968, Recommendation N19 was superseded by recommendation N27, which used the term 'deferred tax' and recognised that a deferred tax account should be established and maintained at current rates of taxation wherever there exist material taxation liabilities that may crystallise at some future date on profits and surpluses already brought into account. Companies in the meanwhile adopted a variety of different ways of calculating and presenting deferred tax information. It was inevitable that when the Accounting Standards Steering Committee was created in 1969, deferred tax would feature in its list of topics for action. It was to be some years before a standard on the subject was first issued only to be subsequently withdrawn, then reissued and eventually revised.

Deferred tax, like accounting for leasing and overseas transactions, is one of the technical areas of the syllabus and, traditionally, has been considered to be one of the more difficult areas of financial accounting. While it has not featured regularly in the old AFA examination, it may well feature in the particular Financial Reporting Environment paper that you are sitting for. It is important, therefore, that you approach the subject systematically and spend some time on the procedures involved in arriving at a provision for deferred tax.

In dealing, in the main, with deferred tax, it is also necessary to consider tax as a whole in the financial statements and its impact on both the profit and loss account and balance sheet of a company. Thus, it is useful to remember, from Paper 10, that SSAP 8 requires that the following items be included in the tax charge in the profit and loss account and, where material, should be separately disclosed:

▶ the amount of UK corporation tax, specifying:
  – the charge for corporation tax on the profits of the year
  – transfers between the deferred tax account and the profit and loss account
  – tax attributable to franked investment income
  – irrecoverable ACT
  – relief for overseas tax
▶ the total of overseas taxation, relieved and unrelieved.

Some of these areas are dealt with in the section dealing with tax in financial statements. This chapter also deals with FRED 2, issued in November 1992, which deals with a limited amendment to SSAP 15 arising from the interaction between SSAP 15 on the one hand and SSAP 24 on pension costs on the other hand taken together with UITF Abstract 6 dealing with accounting for post-retirement benefits other than pensions.

The interrelationship between SSAPs 3, 8 and 15

Tax in financial statements may alternatively be regarded as either an expense of the company or an appropriation of its profits. The latter view is not adopted in practice and tax, for most purposes, is treated as an expense. In this connection accounting for tax has a direct impact on earnings per share (see Chapter 28). Looking back to the elements of the tax charge in a profit and loss account as dealt with in the introduction to this chapter, you should be aware that some of those elements are 'variable' and some 'non-variable' in respect of the amount of profit paid out as dividend. Thus, corporation tax, tax attributable to franked investment income, unrelieved overseas tax as a result of the overseas tax rate being in excess of that in the UK do *not* vary given a level of dividend payments. However, irrecoverable ACT will vary depending on the level of dividends paid.

Given these variable and non-variable elements of the tax charge, SSAP 3 covers two bases of computing earnings per share:

▶ The net basis (the required basis under SSAP 3) takes account of all the elements of the tax charge in arriving at earnings for the eps calculation.
▶ The nil basis (additional disclosure under SSAP 3) takes account of only those elements of the tax charge that do not vary with the level of dividend payments and will not therefore treat irrecoverable ACT as an expense for eps purposes.

The arguments as to the relative merits of each basis are more fully explored in Chapter 28. For the purposes of this chapter, bear in mind that irrecoverable ACT, included in the tax charge under SSAP 8 has a bearing on eps under SSAP 3.

ACT also has an impact on accounting for deferred taxation under SSAP 15. In this context SSAP 8 states that ACT recoverable can be carried forward as an asset only if it is expected to be recoverable, normally, in the next accounting period. This is not quite the situation under SSAP 15, which effectively treats ACT as a timing difference in stating that ACT relating to dividends from prior periods should be:

▶ written off unless their recovery is assured beyond reasonable doubt
▶ such recovery will normally be assured only where the debit balances are recoverable out of the corporation tax arising on profits of the succeeding accounting period, *without replacement by equivalent debit balances.*

In looking at the link between these three accounting standards. Deferred tax is a component of the tax charge in the profit and loss account. As such it has an impact on earnings for eps. Deferred tax, as dealt with later in this chapter, can be arrived at on a full provision or partial provision basis. The basis adopted will obviously affect the deferred tax provided and, in turn, the tax charge, earnings and eps. Interpreting the requirements of the current SSAP 15 can lead to alternative provisions of deferred tax with a corresponding impact on performance in terms of eps which, despite FRS 3, will probably remain a measure of some influence in the analysis of a company's performance. The situation is further exacerbated by the interrelationship between SSAP 15 and SSAP 24 and the points made in FRED 2 that in respect of long-term provisions for pensions we may have to reconsider whether the partial provision approach is the most appropriate for accounting for deferred taxation.

Tax in financial statements

This section is intended to serve as a brief reminder of the points arising in accounting for tax, which you will have covered in some detail in your earlier studies of Paper 10.

Companies may and do account for income tax, corporation tax, advance corporation tax, social security and PAYE and overseas tax. Charges for taxation are made against profit and liabilities/recoverabilities as to taxation recognised in the balance sheet.

Dividends and interest as income are received by a company net of related taxation. Dividends and interest paid by a company are paid net of related taxation. A company accounts for the tax payable on dividends and interest (and so on) paid and the tax recoverable on dividends and interest (and so on) received using quarterly accounting. Dividends as income are required to be included gross of related taxation in the profit and loss account, as is interest received and paid. Dividends paid are included in the profit and loss account net of related taxation. The entries below illustrate the bookkeeping involved.

Journal entries illustrating the bookkeeping involved

DR Cash
CR FII in the profit and loss account

with the net amount of dividends received.

Such dividends are required by SSAP 8 to be included gross as income and the related tax as part of the tax charge. Therefore: DR Tax on ordinary profits in the profit and loss account CR FII in the profit and loss account with the tax suffered on FII.

DR Cash
CR UFII

with the net amount of interest (and so on) received.

Such interest (and so on) is required to be included gross as income. As the company is entitled to recover the tax suffered:

DR Tax recoverable in the balance sheet
CR UFII in the profit and loss account

with the tax suffered on UFII.

DR Unfranked payments in the profit and loss account
CR Cash

with the net amount of interest (and so on) paid.

Such interest is required to be included gross as expense. As the company is liable for the tax withheld, it must recognise the liability in the balance sheet:

DR Unfranked payments in the profit and loss account
CR Taxation payable in the balance sheet

with the tax payable on unfranked payments.

DR Dividends paid in the profit and loss account
CR Cash

with the net dividend paid.

DR Dividends proposed in the profit and loss account
CR Current liabilities in the balance sheet

with the net dividend proposed.

DR ACT recoverable in the balance sheet
CR ACT payable in the balance sheet

with the tax on the proposed dividends which is, first, payable when the dividend is paid, and secondly, when paid, recoverable out of the corporation tax liability of the accounting period when paid.

DR Tax on ordinary profits in the profit and loss account
CR Tax liability in the balance sheet

with, per the tax computation, the corporation tax liability for the year.

DR or CR Tax on ordinary profits in the profit and loss account
CR or DR Deferred tax in the balance sheet

with deferred tax arising for the period, payable or recoverable.

Memorandum calculations would be required as to ACT payable/recoverable on dividends paid and dividends received. ACT payable on any excess of tax payable on dividends paid over tax recoverable on dividends received is, when paid, an advanced payment of the corporation tax liability of the year and is therefore a reduction of such liability.

DR Balance sheet tax payable
CR Cash

with ACT, when paid.

If tax suffered on dividends received is in excess of tax payable on dividends paid, the tax recoverable is recoverable only against tax payable on future dividends to be paid and, accordingly, is not recognised as an asset in the accounts.

ACT recoverable arises on dividends payable and on any ACT paid in the year which, given restrictions, may not be offset against corporation tax liabilities to date. Both are recoverable against future corporation tax liabilities. If, however, such tax is not recoverable in the next accounting period, it is deemed to be irrecoverable and written off as part of the tax on ordinary profits of the current year. Thus, ACT on dividends payable may be:

DR Tax on ordinary profits in the profit and loss account
CR ACT recoverable in the balance sheet

and ACT paid in the year, to the extent that it is not recovered against corporation tax liabilities to date, may either be carried forward as recoverable in the balance sheet or, if not considered recoverable in the next accounting period, written off as part of the tax on ordinary profits for the current year, as above.

The Companies Act 1985

The 1985 Act requires the following particulars of tax to be stated as information supplementing the profit and loss account:

▶ The basis on which the charge for United Kingdom corporation tax and United Kingdom income tax is computed.
▶ Particulars of any special circumstances that affect liability in respect of profits, income or capital gains for the financial year or liability in respect of taxation of profits, income or capital gains for succeeding financial years.
  – The amount of the charge for United Kingdom corporation tax.
  – Whether the amount would have been greater but for relief from double taxation and the amount which it would have been but for such relief.
  – The amount of the charge for United Kingdom income tax.
  – The amount of the charge for taxation imposed outside the United Kingdom on profits, income and (so far as charged to revenue) capital gain.

These requirements are reiterated by SSAP 8 and the deferred tax impact on corporation tax is dealt with in SSAP 15 revised.

Disclosure in the notes to the profit and loss account

The note for taxation in the profit and loss account should disclose:

Tax on profit on ordinary activities:		
Group:	£	
UK corporation tax at x%		
current	x	
deferred	x	(SSAP 15 (Revised))
Double tax relief	(x)	
Overseas taxation	x	
Irrecoverable advance corporation tax	x	(SSAP 8)
Under/(Over) provisions in previous years	x	
Tax credits on franked investment income	x	(SSAP 8)
	x	
Associates: (share of taxation only)	x	(SSAP 1)
	x	

Had the group been providing the full amount of potential deferred taxation, the charge for the year would have been increased/reduced by £x.

Taxation, excluding deferred tax, in the balance sheet

The tax liability in the balance sheet would be arrived at after dealing with:

	£		£
Cash – tax paid	x	Balance brought forward	x
Overprovision in p/y	x	Under provision in p/y	x
Tax recoverable on UFII	x	CI for year, less DTR	x
Cash – ACT paid in year		Overseas tax	x
(subject to maximum offset)	x	Tax payable on	
		unfranked payments	x
Balance carried forward	x		–

What is deferred tax?

The difference between reported profits and taxable profits of a business derive from two main sources:

▶ tax-free income and disallowable expenditure giving rise to 'permanent differences'
▶ items that are dealt with for taxation in accounting periods different from those in which they are recognised in reported profits giving rise to 'timing differences'.

Permanent differences do not give rise to an accounting problem. The tax charge may appear either high in relation to reported profits given, for example, disallowable expenditure, or low given, for example, tax-free income. No accounting entries are necessary although, if the effect on the tax charge is material, the accounts should explain the circumstances that cause the distortion.

Timing differences, however, do represent an accounting problem and one that has taxed the ASC for some considerable time. These differences originate in one period and are capable of reversal in one or more subsequent periods. Accordingly they have a tax effect on the tax liability of a current year, increasing or reducing such liability, *and* a tax effect on the tax liability of a subsequent year(s) reducing or increasing such liability. A list of timing differences is included below.

Deferred taxation is simply defined as the taxation attributable to timing differences. The problem is whether the tax effects of timing differences should be recorded in the accounts in which the transactions causing the timing differences are recorded or not, and, if so, how and to what extent.

Three bases for computing deferred tax

There are, as stated in SSAP 15 (Revised), three principal bases for computing deferred tax:

1   The nil provision or flow through approach, which is based on the principle that only the tax payable in respect of a period should be charged in that period. Those who hold this view argue that any tax liability arises on taxable profits and not reported profits, and therefore it is necessary to provide only for tax on taxable profits. No provision for deferred tax would therefore be made.
2   The full provision or comprehensive allocation approach is based on the principle that financial statements for a period should recognise the tax effects, whether current or deferred, of all transactions occurring in that period. Full provision should be made for the tax effects of all timing differences.
3   The partial provision approach is based on the view that deferred tax should be accounted for in respect of the net amount by which it is probable that any payment of tax will temporarily be deferred or accelerated by the operation of timing differences, which will reverse in the foreseeable future without being replaced. On this basis, deferred tax has to be provided only where it is probable that tax will become payable as a result of the reversal of timing differences.

The approach dealt with in (1) above is inconsistent with accounting principles. The approach dealt with in (2) above was that advocated by SSAP 11. The approach dealt with in (3) above was first put forward in ED 19, then incorporated in SSAP 15 and is now the cornerstone of SSAP 15 (Revised).

The various pronouncements of ASC dealing with deferred tax

An exposure draft on deferred tax was published in May 1973. SSAP 11, based on this exposure draft was issued in August 1975. The standard required that deferred tax should be accounted for on *all* material timing differences. When SSAP 11 was issued inflation was very high. Given the pressures on companies and in order to encourage investment, stock appreciation relief was introduced in 1974 and most expenditure on plant attracted 100% capital allowances in the first year of use. Tax liabilities of companies were accordingly substantially reduced. The requirement of SSAP 11 as to full provision of the tax effects of all timing differences, however, had the effect of increasing the tax charge in the profit and loss account. It was argued that accounting for the full deferral of tax, especially regarding accelerated capital allowances, could amount to accounting for remote contingencies in that, with continuing inflation together with 100% first-year allowances, and given that tax relief is given on money values, most businesses found at least a part of their tax liabilities permanently deferred. Large deferred tax provisions were established in the balance sheet while the likelihood of payment became remote. Many argued that both management and investors were misled by the understatement of profits and capital employed, that a company's borrowing powers could be unjustifiably affected, and that potential lenders would think that companies were more highly geared than they actually were.

Such arguments led the ASC to reconsider the principles of SSAP 11, leading first to its deferment and finally in October 1978 to its withdrawal and, via ED 19, its replacement by SSAP 15.

Given the problems associated with SSAP 11, ED 19 took the view that there was no need to provide for the tax effects of a timing difference if the directors of the company could demonstrate with reasonable probability that the tax effects of a timing difference would not reverse in the foreseeable future. ED 19 was not the most clear of ASC statements; it did not state how the directors were to so demonstrate, it did not quantify 'reasonable probability' and what, several asked, did they mean by the foreseeable future? The ED did, however, establish the important point of principle that it was inappropriate to account for the tax effects of some timing differences where such tax effects were to all intents and purposes permanently deferred. This was the principle adopted by SSAP 15 and the main requirements of the original standard are listed below:

▶ Short-term timing differences must be provided for.
▶ In many businesses capital allowances are of a recurring nature and reversing timing differences would be more than offset by originating timing differences. This gives rise to an indefinite postponement of the tax liability. A tax liability will not arise, and therefore no provision need be made, if the company is a going concern and the directors are able to foresee, on reasonable evidence, that no liability is likely to arise through a reversal of the timing difference for a considerable, at least three-year, period and there is no indication that the liability will crystallise thereafter.
▶ The criteria above may be fully satisfied and any provision relating to such timing differences can be eliminated. The position should be reviewed each year. Regard should be had to the past pattern of capital expenditure and whether previous forecasts have proved reliable.
▶ If the criteria are not satisfied, deferred tax should be provided for.

- If the criteria are only partly satisfied, it may be appropriate to provide only part of the full potential deferred taxation. The partial amount should be based on substantiated calculations and assumptions, which should be explained in the notes to the accounts.
- Debit balances should be carried forward only if there is reasonable certainty as to their recovery.
- Potential deferred taxation for all timing differences should be disclosed, distinguishing between the principal categories and showing for each category the amount that has been provided for in the accounts.
- Deferred tax dealt with in the profit and loss account should be shown separately as a part of the tax charge
- A note is required as to the extent the tax charge is reduced by nil or partial provision for some timing differences.
- Adjustments to deferred taxation as a result of a change in the rate of taxation should be included and separately disclosed as part of the taxation charge for the period. A change in the rate associated with a fundamental change in the basis of taxation should be treated as an extraordinary item.
- Deferred taxation in the balance sheet is not a part of shareholders' funds.
- Tax implications of revalued assets if assets were to be sold at their revalued amounts should be disclosed.
- Tax effects of trading losses should not be recognised through deferred taxation as there is no certainty that future profits will be earned to absorb them. Credit for the tax effect of a trading loss should be taken only when the loss is utilised for tax purposes unless there is a credit balance on deferred taxation at the time the loss carry-forward arises. In this case, deferred taxation may be released to the profit and loss account but only to the extent of tax on income that can be offset against the loss for tax purposes.

ED 33 was issued in June 1983. It dealt with a proposed revision of SSAP 15 and was eventually issued, with some modification, as SSAP 15 (Revised). The revision followed from the criticism made of the original standard that it merely permitted (as opposed to required) a partial provision for deferred tax where it was considered appropriate to make such a provision.

The revised SSAP 15

SSAP 15 (Revised) applies to all financial statements covering accounting periods that start on or after 1 April 1985. The standard is based on the 'partial provision' approach. This basis is preferred to other bases of accounting for deferred tax in that it is based on an assessment of what will actually be the position as to crystallisation of such tax.

The method of computation to be used by the standard is the liability as opposed to the deferral method. Under the liability method deferred tax provisions are calculated at the rate at which it is estimated that tax will be paid or recovered on reversal of timing differences. As a result deferred tax provisions are revised to reflect changes in tax rates. Thus the tax charge or credit for the period may include adjustments of accounting estimates relating to prior periods. This method is held to be consistent with the aim of partial provision, which is to provide the deferred tax that it is probable will be payable or recoverable.

The standard followed on from ED 33 in that it requires that deferred tax should be accounted for to the extent that a liability or asset will crystallise and that it should not be accounted for to the extent that a liability or asset will not crystallise.

An assessment of whether deferred tax liabilities or assets will or will not crystallise should be based on reasonable assumptions. These should take into account all relevant information up to the date on which the financial statements are approved by the directors and also the intentions of management. This information includes financial plans or projections covering a period of years sufficient to enable an assessment to be made of the likely pattern of future tax liabilities. A prudent view should be taken in the assessment of whether a tax liability will crystallise.

Some important points

- ▶ A provision for a deferred tax liability should be reduced by any deferred tax debit balances arising from separate categories of timing differences and any ACT which is available for offset against those liabilities.
- ▶ Net debit balances on deferred tax should not be carried forward as assets except to the extent that they are expected to be recoverable without replacement by equivalent debit balances.
- ▶ ACT recoverable on proposed dividends should be carried forward if it is foreseen that sufficient corporation tax will be assessed on the profits of the succeeding accounting period, against which the ACT is available for offset.
- ▶ Other ACT recoverable should be written off unless its recovery is assured beyond reasonable doubt: out of the corporation tax on profits of the succeeding period without replacement by equivalent debit balances.

Disclosure

Profit and loss account
- ▶ Deferred tax on ordinary and extraordinary activities should be shown separately as part of the tax on ordinary and extraordinary profits.
- ▶ The amount of any unprovided deferred tax, for the period, analysed into its major components should be disclosed in a note.
- ▶ Adjustments to deferred tax arising from tax rate and tax allowance changes should be disclosed separately as part of the tax charge for the period as currently required by FRS 3 on reporting financial performance.

Balance sheet
- ▶ The major components of the deferred tax balance.
- ▶ The movements on deferred tax during the year including, specifically, the tax on anticipated disposal of a revalued asset taken directly to revaluation reserve.
- ▶ The total amount of any unprovided deferred tax analysed into its major components.
- ▶ If an asset is revalued but it is not anticipated that it will be sold, the revaluation does not constitute a timing difference. The fact that it does not and that tax has therefore not been quantified should be stated.
- ▶ If the value of an asset is shown in a note (or in the directors' report) because it differs materially from its book amount, the note should also show the tax effects, if any, that would arise if the asset were realised at the balance sheet date at the noted value.

It was not anticipated that the revised standard would substantially alter the way in which most large companies account for deferred tax.

Some comments on the revised SSAP 15

The principal difference between the original and revised SSAP 15 was a change in emphasis from 'do provide unless . . .' to 'provide to the extent that it is probable that a liability will crystallise and do not provide to the extent that it is probable that a liability will not crystallise'.

The original SSAP 15 required accounting for deferred tax on all short-term timing differences. Given the change of emphasis noted above, this requirement was dropped in the revised SSAP 15. Commentators suggested that this was inconsistent with the accruals concept. ASC, however, considers that there is a significant difference between items such as debtors and creditors that will result in a cash receipt or payment and items such as timing differences that may not. Accordingly, all timing differences should be considered together in attempting to assess whether a tax liability will crystallise.

Some commentators expressed concern that the ED 33 approach to partial provision was imprudent and created difficulties for companies without fully developed financial plans or projections. The need to take a prudent view in assessing whether a tax liability will crystallise has therefore been emphasised in the standard. Uncertainty in relation to deferred tax should be treated like uncertainty regarding any other contingency.

As to disclosure:

▶ The original SSAP 15 required disclosure of the potential amount of deferred tax for all timing differences, distinguishing between the various principal categories of deferred tax and showing for each the amount provided in the accounts.

▶ ED 33 proposed that instead of showing the principal categories of deferred tax liability provided in the financial statements a note should indicate the period(s) of time within which it is likely to crystallise.

▶ A majority of commentators were against showing this period of time and therefore, the revised standard retains the requirement to show the amount of deferred tax by category. The standard also continues to require the unprovided element of the full potential deferred tax liability to be shown analysed into its major components. This is consistent with both the Companies Act 1985 and SSAP 18 – Accounting for Contingencies. It also enables a better comparison to be made with overseas companies that prepare accounts on the basis of full provision for deferred tax.

In contrast to SSAP 15, ED 33 proposed that companies should assess the likelihood of any liability crystallising in the light of their own particular circumstances rather than by reference to a minimum period of three years. The revised standard indicates that the period of assessment may be relatively short – three to five years – where the pattern of timing differences is expected to be regular. It may need to be longer for a company with an irregular pattern of timing differences. The length of lives of the relevant assets and the enterprise's assumptions on growth in capital expenditure also affect the length of the period that needs to be considered.

The ED 33 proposal that deferred tax debit balances should not be carried forward so as to give rise to a deferred tax asset except to the extent that recovery without replacement by equivalent debit balances is assured beyond reasonable doubt is retained in the revised standard. Logically, there is no case for recognising an asset if its realisation is, effectively, permanently deferred and the proposal is now standard in SSAP 15 (Revised).

There was agreement that unremitted overseas earnings give rise to a timing difference if there is an intention to remit. If there are no plans to remit the standard does not require disclosure of the tax effects of remittance or of the directors' intentions. It does, however, require a statement that deferred tax has not been provided on these earnings.

A change does arise in the revised standard in respect of revaluations. If the gain on revaluation is permanently deferred the revaluation may be seen as a permanent difference. A statement is nevertheless required disclosing the fact that any potential deferred tax has not been quantified.

Timing differences and accounting for deferred tax

Accounting for deferred tax, as has already been stated, is accounting for the tax effects of timing differences. Thus, because of timing differences, a company will either pay more tax or less tax in future accounting periods. The purpose of the revised SSAP 15 is to provide now for that tax which, as a result of current timing differences, will crystallise in future accounting periods.

A list of timing differences

A number of timing differences arise from the use of the receipts and payments basis for tax purposes and the accounts basis in financial statements. Examples of these and other timing differences are:

▶ interest receivable accrued in the accounting period, but taxed when received
▶ dividends from foreign subsidiaries accrued in a period prior to that in which they arise for tax purposes
▶ intra-group profits in stock deferred upon consolidation until realisation to third parties
▶ interest or royalties payable accrued in the accounting period, but allowed when paid
▶ pension costs accrued in the financial statements but allowed for tax purposes when paid or contributed at some later date
▶ provisions for repairs and maintenance made in the financial statements but not allowed for tax purposes until the expenditure is incurred
▶ bad debt provisions not allowed for tax purposes unless and until they become 'specific'
▶ provisions for revenue losses on closing down plants or for costs of reorganisation upon which tax relief is not obtained until the costs or losses are incurred
▶ revenue expenditure deferred in the financial statements, such as development or advertising, if it is allowed for tax purposes as it is incurred.

A number of these differences are 'short term' timing differences in that they can be identified with specific transactions and normally reverse in the accounting period following that in which they originated. Short-term and other timing differences need to be considered together when attempting to assess whether a tax liability will crystallise.

Accelerated capital allowances are timing differences that arise from the availability of capital allowances in tax computations that are in excess of the related depreciation charges in financial statements. The reverse may also occur, whereby the depreciation charges in financial statements exceed the capital allowances available in tax computations.

In many businesses, timing differences arising from accelerated capital allowances are of a recurring nature and reversing differences are themselves offset, wholly or partially, or are exceeded, by new originating differences, thereby giving rise to continuing tax reductions or the indefinite postponement of any liability attributable to the tax benefits received. Thus an enterprise having a relatively stable or growing investment in depreciable assets can take tax relief year by year on capital expenditure. This tax relief may equal or exceed the additional tax that would otherwise have been payable in consequence of the reversal of the original timing differences through depreciation. Where for economic or other reasons a spasmodic or highly irregular pattern of capital allowances is forecast, a substantial period of time will need to be considered in attempting to assess whether a tax liability will crystallise. Where there is a declining availability of capital allowances, any originating timing differences will usually reverse, and deferred tax should be provided unless it is probable for other reasons that no tax liability will crystallise.

When a fixed asset is revalued above cost a timing difference potentially arises in that, in the absence of roll-over relief, tax on a chargeable gain may be payable if and when the asset is disposed of at its revalued amount. Where it is possible that a liability will crystallise, provision for the tax payable on disposal is required to be made out of the revaluation surplus, based on the value at which the fixed asset is carried in the balance sheet. Whether or not a liability will crystallise can usually be determined, in the absence of roll-over relief, at the time the enterprise decides to dispose of the asset.

Paragraph 42 of the standard requires that, where the value of an asset is not incorporated in the balance sheet but is given elsewhere such as in a note, the tax effects, if any, that would arise if the asset were realised at the noted value should also be shown. This also applies where the value is given in the directors' report instead of in the notes.

Roll-over relief has the effect of deferring the reversal of the timing difference arising on the revaluation of an asset beyond the date of sale, or of creating a timing difference on the sale of an asset that has not been revalued, or a combination of the two. Where roll-over relief has been obtained on the sale of an asset, with the 'base cost' of the replacement asset for tax purposes thereby being reduced, and the potential deferred tax has not been disclosed, the standard requires disclosure of the fact that the revaluation does not constitute a timing difference and that tax has therefore not been quantified, as it will not otherwise be evident from the accounts.

Translation of the financial statements of overseas subsidiaries or associated companies is not regarded as creating a timing difference. Gains and losses arising on translation of an enterprise's own assets (including investments in subsidiaries and associated companies) and liabilities may give rise to timing differences depending on whether or not the gains or losses have a tax effect.

Paragraph 30 of the standard requires that deferred assets, including those arising from losses, should be recognised only when they are expected to be recoverable without replacement by equivalent debit balances. Recovery may be affected, among other things, by the period of time for which losses are available to be carried forward for tax purposes.

Deferred tax relating to current trading losses may be treated as recoverable when:

▶ the loss results from an identifiable and non-recurring cause, and
▶ the enterprise, or predecessor enterprise, has been constantly profitable over a considerable period, with any past losses being more than offset by income in subsequent periods, and
▶ it is assured beyond reasonable doubt that future taxable profits will be sufficient to offset the current loss during the carry-forward period prescribed by tax legislation.

Deferred tax relating to capital losses may be treated as recoverable when:

▶ a potential chargeable gain not expected to be covered by roll-over relief is present in assets that have not been revalued in the financial statements to reflect that gain and that are not essential to the future operations of the enterprise as under the Taxation of Chargeable Gains Act 1992, and
▶ the enterprise has decided to dispose of these assets and thus realise the potential chargeable gain, and
▶ the unrealised chargeable gain (after allowing for any possible loss in value before disposal) is sufficient to offset the loss in question, such that it is assured beyond reasonable doubt that a tax liability on the relevant portion of the chargeable gain will not crystallise.

Advance corporation taxation (ACT)

The minimum tax charge in the profit and loss account in any accounting period will normally be the amount payable as ACT (net of any recovery) plus any amounts charged in respect of overseas tax. As noted in paragraph 7 of SSAP 8 – The

Treatment of Tax Under the Imputation System in the Accounts of Companies, ACT that cannot be recovered out of the corporation tax liability on the income of the year but which is carried forward to be recovered out of the corporation tax liability on the income of future periods may, subject to certain limitations, be deducted from the deferred tax account. Where there is no balance on the deferred tax account or to the extent that the balance is insufficient for this purpose, consideration will need to be given as to whether the ACT is recoverable out of the corporation tax liability on the income of future periods.

It may be incorrect to carry forward an amount of ACT to offset an equal credit amount of deferred tax. This is because ACT may be carried forward only at the basic rate of income tax on the gross amount of any distribution, to be set off against corporation tax at the full or small companies rates on the same gross amount of taxable income, excluding chargeable gains.

Aspects of examination

Examination questions on deferred tax would usually be concerned with one or other of the following: the opening deferred tax provision; the closing deferred tax provision; the credit or debit in respect of deferred tax in the tax charge or credit for the year, disclosure notes and various discussion aspects of the standard. Audit implications would probably be included as a part of the requirement to a question on this area.

Dealing with the numbers

The examples below are intended to make you familiar with the mechanics of accounting for deferred taxation so as to comply with the standard.

EXAMPLE 7.1 – One timing difference only

Partial plc was a company that manufactured replacement keys. It had started with the manufacture of metal keys for antique boxes where the original keys had been lost and had become recognised as specialists within this field. Their expertise has since extended to the provision of electronic, as well as mechanical, entry devices. This has resulted in the need for an ongoing capital asset investment programme. The draft profit and loss account for the year ended 30 November 1990 showed a pre-tax profit of £375,000 and it was forecast that the profit for 1991 would increase by 20% to £450,000.

The following information was available concerning the company's fixed assets as at 30 November 1990:

	£
Gross cost of fixed assets	1,000,000
Accumulated depreciation	400,000
Capital allowances	525,000

The following forecast information was available as at 30 November 1990 relating to depreciation charges and capital allowances for the next five years based on the assumption that they go ahead with the capital investment programme.

Year ending	Depreciation charge	Capital allowances
	£	£
30/11/91	234,000	265,000
30/11/92	253,000	303,000
30/11/93	276,000	193,000
30/11/94	278,000	192,000
30/11/95	248,000	262,000

The forecast depreciation charge of £234,000 and capital allowance of £265,000 were amended in the accounts prepared for the year ended 30 November 1991 to £250,000 and £289,000 respectively.

The following forecast information was available as at 30 November 1991 relating to depreciation charges and capital allowances for the next five years:

Year ending	Depreciation charge	Capital allowances
	£	£
30/11/92	250,000	289,000
30/11/93	278,000	197,000
30/11/94	275,000	193,000
30/11/95	253,000	265,000
30/11/96	254,000	278,000

Assume a corporation tax rate of 35%.

(i) Prepare the balance sheet entry for Partial plc as at 30 November 1990 for deferred tax to comply with the provisions of SSAP 15 – Accounting for Deferred Tax (Revised).

(ii) Prepare the profit and loss account and balance sheet entries for deferred taxation for Partial plc for the year ended 30 November 1991 to comply with the provisions of SSAP 15 – Accounting for Deferred Tax (Revised).

Workings (in £000s)

(i) The balance sheet entry as at 30 November 1990.
First, ascertain the full potential liability to deferred tax:

	NBV for accounts		WDV for tax	
	£		£	
Cost	1,000		1,000	
Depreciation	(400)			
Capital allowances			(525)	
	600	less	475	= £125 @ 35% = £43.75

Second, ascertain the provision required at 30 November 1990 based on forecasts of the crystallisation of the future tax effects of the timing difference.

Forecast Y/E	Capital allowances	Depreciation	Timing difference originating/ (reversing)	Cumulative timing difference
	£	£	£	£
30/11/91	265	(234)	31	31
30/11/92	303	(253)	50	81
30/11/93	193	(276)	(83)	(2)
30/11/94	192	(278)	(86)	(88)
30/11/95	262	(248)	14	(74)

Based on the maximum cumulative reversal of the timing differences foreseen, the deferred tax provision required at 30 November 1990 is 35% × 88 = £30.8. The disclosure note in the balance sheet at this date, in respect of deferred tax, would now read as follows:

Principal category of timing difference	Full potential liability	Provision made	Provision not made
	£	£	£
Accelerated capital allowances	43.75	30.80	12.95

(ii) Profit and loss account and balance sheet entries for the year ended and as at 30 November 1991.

Having ascertained the provision required at 30 November 1990, before ascertaining the amount of deferred tax to be passed through the profit and loss account for the year ended 30 November 1991, first ascertain the full potential liability to deferred tax at 30 November 1991:

	£
Capital allowances > Depreciation at 30/11/90	125
Capital allowances > Depreciation y/e 30/11/91 (289 – 250)	39
	164 @ 35% = £57.4

Second, ascertain the provision required at 30 November 1991 based on forecasts of the crystallisation of the future tax effects of the timing difference.

Forecast Y/E	Capital allowances £	Depreciation £	Timing difference originating/ (reversing) £	Cumulative timing difference £
30/11/92	289	(250)	39	39
30/11/93	197	(278)	(81)	(42)
30/11/94	193	(275)	(82)	(124)
30/11/95	265	(253)	12	(112)
30/11/96	278	(254)	24	(88)

Based on the maximum cumulative reversal of the timing differences foreseen, the deferred tax provision required at 30 November 1991 is 35% x 124 = £43.4.

Third, the deferred tax to be provided for the year to 30/11/91 can now simply be derived as the difference between the closing and opening provisions, that is, 43.4 less 30.8 = £12.6. The disclosure note in the balance sheet at 30 November 1991, including comparatives, would now read as follows:

Principal category of timing difference	Full potential liability		Provision made		Provision not made	
	1991 £	1990 £	1991 £	1990 £	1991 £	1990 £
Accelerated capital allowances	57.40	43.75	43.40	30.80	14.00	12.95

EXAMPLE 7.2 – Several timing differences

Dreadlock Ltd provides for deferred taxation, in accordance with SSAP 15 (Revised), using the liability method and providing for the tax effects of only those timing differences the tax effects of which will crystallise. You are informed that:

1   As on 30 June 1991, the draft accounts and supporting schedules of Dreadlock Ltd disclosed the following timing differences:

	£000
Development costs capitalised	142
Provision for deferred repairs	43
Interest receivable (credit taken in the accounts, but not yet received)	18

Excess of capital allowances over depreciation 674
Interest payable (debited in the accounts but not yet paid) 37
Revaluation surplus, giving rise to a chargeable gain,
after indexation allowances, of 115
Provision for general bad debts 39
The revalued asset will be disposed of in 1992.

2　The company accountant has forecast the following originating and reversing timing differences in the five years to 30 June 1996:

	1992 £000	1993 £000	1994 £000	1995 £000	1996 £000
Development costs:					
amortised	45	54	42	34	102
capitalised		114	21		
Provision for deferred repairs:					
expenses incurred	20	15	8		
Capital allowances:	672	475	805	642	800
Depreciation:	715	742	750	800	850
Interest:					
Payable	37	60	60	60	
Paid	37	37	60	60	60
Receivable	18	18	45	50	50
Received	18	18	18	45	50
Provision for general bad debts:					
Increased by	20	18			14
Reduced by			30	12	

The rate of corporation tax is currently 35% and is expected to remain at this rate in future years.

3　Dreadlock Ltd proposed an ordinary dividend of £213,000 for the year ended 30 June 1991. Basic rate of income tax is 29%. The company considers that the ACT on the dividends will be recovered, without replacement, in the following year.

Calculate the amount to be included as a deferred tax provision in the balance sheet of Dreadlock Ltd as on 30 June 1991 and prepare, in so far as the information above will allow, the notes to the accounts to support the amount included in the balance sheet.

Workings

In deferred tax, as in so many other areas of financial accounting, there are alternative approaches to getting to the requirements of a number-based question, each of which will give you a different answer as opposed to an incorrect one.

One approach to dealing with deferred tax where there are several timing differences involved is to take each timing difference separately and ascertain, as in Example 7.1, the maximum cumulative reversal foreseen and provide for deferred tax arising on such a reversal. The total deferred tax provision will be the sum of the provisions ascertained for each timing difference.

An alternative approach, as adopted below, is to look at the net effect in each forecast year of all the timing differences taken together. Some will give rise to tax payable, others to tax recoverable. The deferred tax provision required would be based on the cumulative net reversals foreseen.

(All amounts in £000s.)

First, ascertain the full potential deferred tax:

			£
Development costs capitalised	142 @ 35%	payable	50
Provision for deferred repairs	43 @ 35%	recoverable	(15)
Interest receivable	18 @ 35%	payable	6
Capital allowances > Depreciation	674 @ 35%	payable	236
Interest payable	37 @ 35%	recoverable	(13)
Provision for bad debts	39 @ 35%	recoverable	(14)
Re trading items			250
Revaluation surplus	115 @ 35%	payable	40
			290

Second, because of the separate disclosure required as to Capital allowances > Depreciation, deal with this timing difference separately and ascertain, for this one timing difference, the deferred tax provision required.

Forecast Y/E	Capital allowances £	Depreciation £	Timing difference originating/ (reversing) £	Cumulative timing difference £
30/6/92	672	(715)	(43)	(43)
30/6/93	475	(742)	(267)	(310)
30/6/94	805	(750)	55	(255)
30/6/95	642	(800)	(158)	(413)
30/6/96	800	(850)	(50)	(463)

The provision required, in respect of this timing difference, based on the maximum cumulative reversal foreseen, and assuming that capital allowances will exceed depreciation after 1996, is therefore, 463 @ 35% = £162.

Third, calculate the deferred tax provision required at 30 June 1991, based on the net effect of all (revenue) timing differences taken together.

(*Note*: Non-revenue timing differences such as revaluation surpluses should be dealt with separately. Provide for deferred tax if there is an intention to sell and there is to be no roll-over of the gain; do not provide for deferred tax if there is no intention to sell or if there is a sale and roll-over of any gain. If provision is made remember that the debit is to revaluation reserve and not to the profit and loss account tax charge as part of deferred tax for the year therein.)

		1992 £	1993 £	1994 £	1995 £	1996 £
(i)	Capital allowances > Depreciation, as in 2	(43)	(267)	55	(158)	(50)
(ii)	Development costs:					
	capitalised, benefit		114	21		
	amortised, expense	(45)	(54)	(42)	(34)	(102)
(iii)	Deferred repairs:					
	expensed, benefit	20	15	8		
(iv)	Interest:					
	payable, expense	(37)	(60)	(60)	(60)	
	paid, benefit	37	37	60	60	60
	receivable, benefit	18	18	45	50	50
	received, expense	(18)	(18)	(18)	(45)	(50)
(v)	General provision for debts:					
	increase, expense	(20)	(18)			(14)
	decrease, benefit			30	12	
Net effect in each year		(88)	(233)	99	(175)	(106)
Cumulative effect		(88)	(321)	(222)	(397)	(503)

The deferred tax provision required, as on 30 June 1991, on trading items, based on the maximum cumulative reversal foreseen, and assuming that the future situation will not worsen, is therefore, 503 @ 35% = £176.

Fourth, you are now in a position to produce the balance sheet note disclosure required as follows:

Principal category of timing difference	Full potential liability/ (recoverability) £000	Provision made £000	Provision not made £000
Accelerated capital allowances	236	162	74
Other	14	14	
	250	176	74
Revaluation surplus	40	40	
	290	216	74
ACT recoverable		(87)	
		129	

↓	↓
See 'first' above.	See 'second' above re accelerated capital allowances and 'third' above re the total provision made.

Alternative methods of accounting for deferred tax

You should be familiar with two alternative methods of accounting for deferred tax: the liability method as currently required in the UK, and the deferral method as practised in the USA. These are dealt with below.

The different methods are based on different views of the nature of deferred tax. Under the liability method we take an essentially balance sheet viewpoint and consider deferred tax to be either an asset or a liability. Under the deferral method we take an essentially profit and loss account viewpoint and consider deferred tax to be either income (tax benefit) or expense (adverse tax). The former is consistent with the partial provision basis, the latter is consistent with a full provision basis of accounting for deferred tax. There is no difference in the numbers arising under each method if there is no change in the rate of tax. When, however, there is a change in the rate of tax, you will have to follow the procedures as outlined in Table 7.1 for each method. Note again that the liability method is the required method under SSAP 15 (Revised).

Table 7.1 Procedures for accounting for deferred tax using the liability method and the deferral method when there is a change in the rate of tax

	Liability method	Deferral method
1	*The deferred tax provision brought forward* Restate the opening provision at the current, changed rate of tax.	No re-statement.
2	*Deferred tax provided for the year* Provide for the net effect of all revenue timing differences taken together at the current rate of tax.	Distinguish between originating and reversing timing differences. Taking each timing difference separately: IF originating: provide at the current rate of tax IF reversing: write back at the same rate of tax at which originally provided.
3	*Deferred tax provision carried forward* The provision represents timing differences provided for at the current rate of tax, that is, the best estimate of the tax effect that will crystallise in future years.	The provision carried forward is for different timing differences at different rates of tax.

EXAMPLE 7.3 – A simple approach illustrating the principal differences between the liability and deferral methods

Company A has only one fixed asset, purchased on 1 January 1993 for a cost of £10,000. Depreciation is provided at the rate of 10% per annum and a writing down allowance of 25% is claimed each year. The year end of Company A is 31 December. The corporation tax rate is taken as 30% in 1993 and 35% in 1994. The movements in the deferred tax provision would be as follows under the deferral and liability methods respectively:

(Deferred tax is fully provided as the whole of the originating timing differences will reverse in full at the end of the ten year depreciable period.)

	Deferral	Liability
	£	£
At 1/1/94 (Capital allowances > Depreciation)		
(2,500 > 1,000) × 30%	450	450
Increase dealt with as a separate item, in the 1994 tax charge in the profit and loss account		75
Restated 1/1/94 1,500 × 35%		525
Deferred tax for 1994 (Capital allowances > Depreciation)		
(1,875 > 1,000) × 35%	306	306
At 31/12/94	756	831

When the timing difference begins to reverse (in year 5) the deferred tax provided when it originated will be written back to the profit and loss account. Under the deferral method the first £1,500 reversing would be written back at 30%, the second £1,500 reversing at 35%, and then at whatever rates the timing differences had originally been provided at. Under the liability method all reversals would be accounted for at the rate of tax then ruling.

The impact of FRED 2 on SSAP 15 (Revised)

FRED 2 was issued in November 1992 and deals with an amendment to SSAP 15. This arises from the interaction between SSAP 15, SSAP 24 on pension costs (see Chapter 8) and UITF Abstract 6 on post-retirement benefits other than pensions (see Chapter 8). Following from the accounting as standard practice for pension costs and other post-retirement benefits, which is on a full provision basis, FRED 2 argues that it is difficult to justify a prohibition on the related deferred tax under SSAP 15, which requires a partial provision basis.

Accordingly, FRED 2, subject to normal rules as to recoverability in SSAP 2, permits either the full provision or the partial provision basis to be used in accounting for the deferred tax implications (essentially tax recoverable) of pensions and other post-retirement benefits accounted for in accordance with SSAP 24 and UITF 6. This aspect of deferred tax is explored further, in context, in Chapter 8.

Practical problems of accounting for deferred taxation

We give here an outline of the practical problems and some audit implications associated with accounting for deferred taxation and their particular relevance to the recognition of deferred tax debit balances.

SSAP 15 requires that deferred tax should be accounted for to the extent that it is probable that tax effects of timing differences will crystallise. It is this fundamental principle that applies in determining whether a deferred tax balance should be carried forward in the balance sheet. Practical problems arise in the difficulties of judgement as to evidence required and reliability of financial plans. The standard does not prescribe the time period that the projections should cover on the basis that companies should make the assessment in the light of their own particular circumstances. In practice, it is normally to be expected that financial plans in any detail may be available for only one or two years ahead, and further consideration will need to be given to the reliability of the plans and other information on which they are based.

Practical problems also arise in that there may be:

▶ changes in legislation, giving rise to changes in tax rates or capital allowances
▶ management may exercise the option to lease rather than buy assets
▶ a changing pattern of capital investment making it difficult to forecast future depreciation and capital allowances.

Under the partial provision method, which follows from the requirements of the revised standard, it is necessary to create a deferred tax provision to the extent of any net reversing timing differences. The standard recognises the symmetry of that argument, which is that deferred tax net debit balances should not be carried forward as assets except to the extent that they are expected to be recoverable without replacement by equivalent debit balances. If there is such replacement, the realisation of the asset is permanently deferred.

Many short-term timing differences resulting in deferred tax balances, for example, debit balances arising from temporarily disallowable accruals and general bad debt provisions that continually recur and are replaced, fall into this category. Such deferred tax assets should not be recognised or disclosed in the accounts of companies because they are not expected to be recoverable.

The standard does, however, permit the provision for deferred tax liabilities to be reduced by any deferred tax balances arising from separate categories of timing differences. The use of the phrase 'separate categories of timing differences' highlights an important prerequisite, which is that these balances must be capable of being offset for tax purposes. Care should also be taken where debits and credits arising in different trades are involved because these items may not be capable of being offset when the assets and liabilities crystallise.

It is important to note that, just as deferred tax liabilities should not be created unless it is probable that a liability will crystallise, so deferred tax liabilities should not be reduced by deferred tax debit balances that will not crystallise because recovery of the tax is continually deferred. For example, deferred tax liabilities should not be reduced by deferred tax debit balances arising from timing differences on recurring general bad debt provisions.

The standard lays down several conditions that need to be satisfied for trading or capital losses to be treated as recoverable – essentially, that it is assured beyond reasonable doubt that future taxable profits will be sufficient to offset the loss during the carry forward period prescribed by tax legislation.

Under the standard, deferred tax liabilities should also be reduced by ACT which is available for offset against those liabilities. If there is insufficient deferred tax to cover the ACT, and it is proposed to carry forward ACT as a debit balance, some complex considerations apply. In determining the appropriate amount of set-off between unrelieved ACT credits and the balance in the deferred taxation account, it will be necessary to take into account the normal ACT credit limitation. It is not correct merely to set an amount of ACT credit against an equal amount in the deferred taxation account. In any event, deferred tax may be carried forward as an asset only if it is recoverable, in the next accounting period, against the corporation tax liability of that period. Thus, a company would need to forecast the corporation tax liability for the next accounting period, the amount of ACT recoverable brought forward that may be set off against that liability, and the ACT arising in the next accounting period that may be set off against that tax liability. Only when ACT is forecast to be recovered without replacement by further amounts arising as recoverable should it be considered as recoverable at any one year end and treated as an asset at that year end. If not, the ACT should be deemed irrecoverable and written off as a part of the tax on ordinary activities.

Summary

▶ This chapter deals with an area, accounting for deferred tax, that most students consider as being difficult, but which in reality is relatively straightforward.
▶ Questions on this topic may well include 'written' requirements. You must, therefore, be prepared to comment on and describe:

 – what deferred tax is
 – the different bases of providing for deferred tax – nil, full, partial
 – the development of the current standard.

▶ The chapter also deals with the number-crunching aspects of deferred tax and Examples 7.1 and 7.2 take you through the procedures to be followed.
▶ You should be aware of the differences arising under the liability and deferral methods of accounting for deferred tax and of the amendment to SSAP 15 introduced by FRED 2, which may well be the start of a process to take us back, full circle, to the first standard on deferred tax, SSAP 11, and a full provision basis of accounting for deferred tax.

Suggested reading

Deferred Tax Accounting (IPA STITT 1985)

Accountants Digest 174: A Guide to Accounting Standards – Deferred Tax (ICAEW 19..)

UK GAAP (Ernst & Young 1990)

Deferred Taxation (Munson 1986)

Self test questions

1   Why does accounting for taxation under relevant UK standards result in an effective rate of tax that differs from the corporation tax rate?

2   Briefly explain the impact of 'permanent' and 'timing' differences in arriving at profit for tax purposes in a current and subsequent year.

3   Briefly examine the impact of the three possible approaches to accounting for deferred tax on the effective rate of tax being different from the actual corporation tax rate.

4   Distinguish between the 'flow through', 'comprehensive allocation' and 'partial provision' approaches in respect of deferred tax.

5   Which one timing difference gives rise to a problem in accounting for deferred tax under the revised SSAP 15 and why?

Exam style question

1   *Deftax Ltd*
The assistant accountant of Deftax Ltd has been assigned the task of ascertaining:

(a) the deferred tax provision to be made by the company at 30 June 1990 and 30 June 1991, and
(b) the deferred tax to be included in the tax on the profit on ordinary activities of the company for the year ended 30 June 1991.

Having worked overtime, unpaid, last week, the assistant accountant has prepared working papers which disclose the following:

A   Timing differences as at 30 June 1990 were as follows:

	£ 000
Accelerated capital allowances	350
Provision for deferred repairs	60

B   Timing differences arising in the year to 30 June 1991 were as follows:

	£000	£000
Excess of depreciation over capital allowances		67
Further provision for deferred repairs	22	
Amount spent and charged against the deferred repairs provision	12	10
Interest accrued on loan stock issued during the year		6

C   Forecast information for the next four years discloses:

Year to:	Accelerated capital allowances CA > Depn / (Depn > CA) Foreseen at 30/6/90 £000	30/6/91 £000	Increase/(Decrease) in deferred repairs provision Foreseen at 30/6/90 and 30/6/91 £000
30 June 1992	170	(90)	(16)
30 June 1993	(92)	(70)	(12)
30 June 1994	(73)	(68)	15
30 June 1995	(60)	140	(6)

Forecast information for the year to 30 June 1991 was no different from the actual information for this year as disclosed in (B) above.

D   Further information is provided as follows:
   a) The financial director's long-term plans show that capital allowances will exceed depreciation every year after 1995.
   b) The deferred repairs provision is expected to increase by immaterial amounts after 1995.
   c) The interest accrued is at a fixed rate of interest in respect of undated loan stock.
   d) The rate of corporation tax applicable to the company for the year ended 30 June 1990 was 35%. The rate applicable for the year ended 30 June 1991 is 30%. The change in rate is not as a result of a fundamental change in the basis of taxation, and the change in rate was not anticipated as at 30 June 1990.

The assistant accountant, exhausted as the result of the time spent extracting the information above, is unable to proceed further having forgotten all that he ever knew (not a lot) about deferred tax. He knows that you are attending a revision course and that you are, therefore, an expert on the topic. Accordingly, he has turned to you for help and advice.

Required:
a) Calculate the deferred tax provision for Deftax Ltd to be included in its financial statements as at 30 June 1990 and 1991, and the deferred tax to be included in the tax on profit on ordinary activities for the year ended 30 June 1991 so as to comply with the requirements of SSAP 15 (Revised) on accounting for deferred taxation.

(13 marks)

b) Prepare the disclosure notes to be included as a part of the financial statements to support the amounts included in respect of deferred taxation as at 30 June 1991, together with, where possible, comparative information for 1990, so as to comply with the Accounting Standard on deferred tax.

(7 marks)
(20 marks)

All answers on pages 644–647.

Accounting for Pension Costs

> Everywhere a good deal is done for old servants. Their care is a recognised charge
> on all industrial and commercial undertakings of character and long standing . . .
> There are many old people in the receipt of industrial superannuation allowances
> more or less charitable in their character, though very often given as an
> acknowledgement and recognition of past services. (Booth, 1889)

There is a long and varied history to the provision of income for retirement. The
granting of land in *coloniae* to retired Roman soldiers by their generals may be
regarded as the forerunner of today's pension arrangements. In the UK while there
may have been various ad hoc forms of pension provision going back in some cases to
medieval times, the earliest occupational pension scheme recognisable in today's
terms was probably that of the Metropolitan Police set up in 1829.

In 1834, Civil Service pensions were regulated through a superannuation Act,
which still influences the form of pension provision today. The original Civil Service
pension scheme provided a pension equal to two-thirds of salary from a retirement
age of 65 after 45 years' service. All good things come to those who wait. The lead of
the Civil Service in this area was soon followed by commercial enterprises.

In the beginning the attitude of employers was, in general, one of enlightened
self-interest. The promise of security in retirement was observed to encourage loyalty
in the workforce. The pensions were usually paid out of the employer's current
income. State retirement pensions, even today, are accounted for on this principle in
that they are paid for out of current taxation. It was only in the late 19th century that
several factors coincided to encourage the development of systematic pension
provision, not least of which was a marked improvement in life expectancy during
that period. This period saw the development of trust funds for the payment of
pensions to which both the employer and the employee might contribute during the
working life of the employee. As pension funds became more sophisticated they
provided a greater range of benefits: widow's pensions, death in service etc. In
addition to pension funds, insured pension schemes, developed in the United States,
were introduced in the UK in about 1928.

The very earliest pension schemes were of the 'money purchase' form. The
pension to be paid was contingent upon the amounts contributed to the scheme by the
employee, on the employee's behalf by the employer, and the interest earned by
investing the contributions. The advantage of such a scheme was that it had a
predetermined cost, what today would be called a defined contribution-based scheme,
and contributions could be expressed in fixed monetary terms per accounting period.
The disadvantage of such a scheme was that it did not always take into account an
employee's salary progression and it tended to give the same contribution and benefit
level for employees with different salaries, in the same company.

Modifications were required to be made to flat rate money purchase schemes,
and these came in the form of 'average salary schemes'. These allocated increasing
levels of pension benefit to a progression of salary grades. As an employee progressed,
he or she would accumulate various units of pension, which represented a constant
percentage of increasing salary; usually the employee paid a fixed contribution and
the employer made up the balance of the cost. The main deficiency of this sort of

scheme was that, being based on employees' incomes throughout their working lives, the retirement pension received would not make it possible to maintain living standards consistent with those immediately before retirement. Thus the widespread introduction of 'final salary schemes'. Despite the high cost of such schemes, and the open-ended nature of the employer's commitment – given defined benefits as opposed to defined contributions – it was recognised that only pensions based on salaries at or near to retirement met employees' needs. In such a scheme, employees would generally contribute a fixed percentage of salary, though the employee sometimes did not contribute at all, leaving the balance of contributions to be paid by the employer.

The principal types of pension scheme that may be found in the UK are:

▶ Final or final average salary schemes, in which the pension is calculated as a fraction of the retiring employee's pensionable earnings at or near to retirement or averaged over the last few years of service.
▶ Career average salary schemes, in which the amount of pension is calculated as a fraction of the total salary earned while a member of the scheme.
▶ Salary grade schemes, in which the amount of pension accrued in any one year of service is dictated by the range in which an employee's salary for that year falls.
▶ Flat rate schemes, in which the pension benefit at retirement is stated to be a fixed monetary amount independent of salary.
▶ Money purchase schemes, in which the pension benefit is equivalent to the annuity, which can be purchased with the accumulated contributions of employer and employee, together with interest earned.

This chapter deals with the problems of accounting for pension costs by an employer company and, by way of an appendix, accounting by pension schemes.

Statutory requirements

The Companies Act 1985 requires companies to disclose any provision for pensions in the balance sheet under the heading of 'Provisions for liabilities and charges'. The Act specifies that details should be given of any pension commitments, whether provision is made in the balance sheet or not.

The Act requires companies to disclose their aggregate staff costs, broken down into wages and salaries; social security costs and other pension costs. 'Pension costs' are defined in the Act as including 'any other contributions by the company for the purpose of providing pensions for persons employed by the company, any sums set aside for that purpose and any amounts paid by the company in respect of pensions without first being so set aside'. The Act also requires detailed disclosure requirements concerning directors' pensions.

The pro forma of the disclosure required regarding 'staff costs', including directors' remuneration, in the profit and loss account is:

	1994 £	1993 £
Staff costs:		
Staff costs during the year, including directors, amounted to:		
Wages and salaries	x	x
Social security costs	x	x
Other pension costs	x	x
	x	x

Note that other pension costs include contributions by the company for providing pensions for employees.

The average weekly number of persons employed by the company/group during the year was as follows:

	1994	1993
By category: production, distribution etc.	[number]	[number]

Additional disclosure as to part-time staff may be necessary in order to present a true and fair view, that is, number employed, purpose of employment, total remuneration.

Note that the average number is to be determined by dividing the relevant annual number by the number of weeks in the financial year. The relevant annual number is to be determined by ascertaining for each week in the financial year, the number of persons employed under contracts of service by the company in that week, and adding together all the weekly numbers.

Directors' remuneration:

Staff costs shown above include the following remuneration in respect of directors of the company:

(Note that in a consolidated profit and loss account, this disclosure is only in respect of directors of the holding company; directors of subsidiary companies are included only if they are also directors of the holding company.)

	1994 £	1993 £
Fees as directors	x	x
Other emoluments	x	x
Pensions paid to former directors	x	x
Compensation for loss of office	x	x
	x	x

(Note that other emoluments include salaries, pension contributions paid by the company and benefits in kind.)

The directors' remuneration shown above (excluding pensions and pension contributions paid by the company) included:

	1994	1993
Chair	£	£ ....
Highest paid director	£	£ ....

Other directors, including those above, received emoluments (excluding pensions and pension contributions paid by the company) in the following ranges:

	1994	1993
£0 to £5,000	[number]	[number]
£5,001 – £10,000	[number]	[number]
£10,001 – £15,000	[number]	[number]
£20,001 – £25,000	[number]	[number]
£35,001 – £40,000	[number]	[number]

Emoluments amounting to £x (1993 £x) have been waived by x number (1993 x number) of directors.

(Note that the remuneration of the highest paid director, other than any directors who discharged duties wholly or mainly outside the UK, must be disclosed. If the highest paid director is the Chair, then only the Chair's remuneration is disclosed. If not, then in addition to the Chair's remuneration, that of the highest paid director must also be disclosed. 'Banding' is required for all directors, but excluding those who perform their duties wholly or mainly outside the UK.)

The accounting problem

In a business where the granting of pensions to retired employees is purely a matter of grace and favour on the part of the owners, it is reasonable to adopt the 'pay as you go' method of accounting for pension costs, simply charging the pension costs to profit and loss account in the year when they are paid. Today, however, most contracts of employment require an employee to join a company's pension scheme and guarantee the employee a pension on retirement. Some schemes may be non-contributory (where the employer bears the whole burden of financing the scheme) while others are contributory (where the employer's contribution is supplemented by employees' contributions, deducted from salary and generally as a fixed percentage thereof). The employees' contribution is included in gross salary and charged to the profit and loss account. In such a scheme, given the commitment of the employer to the payment of retirement benefits, 'pay as you go' as a method of accounting for the pension cost is not acceptable. It is rejected, firstly, on the ground that it fails to comply with the matching concept. Pension benefits are seen as deferred remuneration for employees, paid following retirement, but earned by employees during their period of service. The cost of remuneration should therefore be recognised by the company in the periods of service of employees. Second, if a company were to account for pensions in such a scheme simply when paid, there is a problem of lack of assurance to employees that funds will be available to meet the pension commitment as and when the pension liability falls due.

With a compulsory pension scheme the normal method of providing for pensions is through 'funding', which means the employer, and often employees as well, make regular contributions to a pension scheme, which is legally separate from the employer and usually administered by trustees. Pension schemes and their quite separate accounts are dealt with in an appendix to this chapter. Both employees' and employer's contributions are paid out of the company to the fund, and the most obvious accounting treatment for the company is to write off the employer's contribution to profit and loss account in the same period.

In adopting this treatment, the basic assumption made is that the contribution made by the employer represents the cost to the company for the year of providing the benefits earned by employees in that year, less the amounts paid for by employees' deductions from salary. Having made this assumption, the company would then rely on the trustees of the fund (or insurance company if contributions are paid to such a company) to make good the scheme's obligations to employees, and would not carry a liability in the balance sheet in respect of these obligations.

The validity of this assumption rests upon the method adopted by the company in respect of funding. The assumption is invalid if the company adopts as to funding either the initial funding method or the terminal funding method or the discontinuance method.

Under initial funding, the contribution for the year is the estimated amount needed to provide future benefits for all employees joining the scheme in that year. Under terminal funding, the year's contribution is the estimated amount needed to provide benefits for all employees retiring during the year. Under the discontinuance method, each year's contribution is designed to secure pension rights accruing to employees during the year such that at any time the fund is actuarially solvent, that is, it is able to provide deferred pensions to all existing employees on the basis of their current salaries even if the fund were to be discontinued at a later date.

Under each of the above methods of funding, the contributions paid in the year, if recognised as the pension cost for the year, will not be the accrued cost to the company of providing the additional benefits earned by employees in the year as a deferred portion of their remuneration.

In the initial funding method and in the terminal funding method there is no relationship at all between the cost of pension provision in any one year and the benefit of the services of all employees in that year. The accruals concept is violated. In the discontinuance method of funding there is, admittedly, some relationship between current services of employees and immediately earned benefits. However, no account is taken of benefits based on future probabilities such as years of service to retirement salary levels in the last years of service and the fact that some employees will leave the company or die before retiring age.

Thus, under the discontinuance method of funding, if the contributions paid are what is recognised as pension cost of the company in any one year, then though the accruals concept is followed up to a point in fixing contribution levels, the going concern concept is ignored.

The assumption that contributions paid will equal the actuarial cost of providing for pensions in any one year would be valid only if either an accrued benefits method or a level contribution method is adopted as the basis for funding policy.

Under an accrued benefits method, distinct units of benefits are associated with each year of service of each employee, taking into account future probabilities associated with the employee. This may be done by computing the actuarial value of expected future retirement benefits, and dividing such amount by the total number of years' service to retiring age, so as to give the charge for each employee for the year.

Under level contribution methods, annual contributions are set at a fixed amount per employee, usually as a fixed percentage of each employee's salary, such that the actuarial solvency of the fund is guaranteed until the next review by the actuaries.

Both these last two methods are believed to give good approximations of the accrued cost of pension benefits earned by employees during the year. They comply with the accruals concept and justify simple expensing of the employer's contributions to the fund. The first three methods dealt with do not guarantee any such approximation between contributions and accrued costs, and may require an annual charge to profit and loss account of more, or less, than the contribution paid, with the difference being credited or debited to a deferred liability or asset on the balance sheet.

To summarise, given an estimate of the expected pension benefits in a defined benefits scheme (there is no problem as to recognition of pension cost in a defined contribution scheme), there are several methods recognised by actuaries for determining the pattern of normal contributions to the employer's pension scheme so as to accumulate a sufficient amount to meet the expected benefits when they fall due. Employers usually measure the cost of the pension provision in any period in terms of the contributions that they make to their pension scheme in that period. Because of the range of methods for determining their contribution, it is not always obvious that the amount contributed is the most appropriate measure, within an accrual accounting framework, of the cost of pension provision.

The accounting problem, therefore, involves:

▶ the problem of income measurement (what should be recognised as cost in the profit and loss account?)
▶ the problem of liability disclosure (what should be disclosed in the balance sheet?).

It is further complicated by other issues such as situations where the current value of the pension scheme's assets is less than that projected when the pattern of contributions was determined, and when the actuary's assumptions determining the level of the employer's normal contributions have to be changed. In both these situations additional contributions may need to be made. Pension cost, whether represented by normal or special contributions, is a material component of an employer's total cost and is subject to particular problems of measurement and uncertainty. Company law now requires most companies to disclose pension costs and commitments in their final statements.

ASC statements regarding accounting for pension costs

Prior to the publication of ED 32 – Disclosure of Pension Information in Company Accounts, the main official pronouncement of the disclosure of pension information by employers was Accounting Recommendation No. 21 – Retirement Benefits, issued by the ICAEW in 1960. The main recommendation covered disclosure in the employer's financial statements of any special contributions in respect of past service credits or to make good a deficiency. Routine disclosure of normal pension costs and commitments was not specifically recommended.

ED 32, by contrast, proposed that disclosure should be made in the financial statements of sufficient information concerning pension arrangements to enable users of the statements to gain a broad understanding of the significance of pension costs in the accounting period and of actual and contingent liabilities and commitments at the balance sheet date. The exposure draft listed several specific disclosures, which were subsequently dealt with in greater detail in ED 39.

An international standard was issued in 1983 and, while it requires much the same disclosure as that proposed by ED 32, it goes further than the exposure draft in covering accounting methods. It requires that normal pension costs should be charged to profit and loss account systematically over the expected working lives of employees in the pension scheme. It also requires that past service costs be charged as they arise or be allocated systematically over a period not exceeding the expected remaining working lives of the employees affected. Further, it limits the actuarial methods that may be used for determining cost by excluding the pay as you go and terminal funding methods.

Following ED 32, the ASC published a statement of intent on accounting for pension costs by companies. It set out the accounting objective that companies should comply with in accounting for such costs and made various proposals as to accounting for variations from the normal pension cost of a company. The points made in the statement were expanded upon and dealt with in ED 39.

SSAP 24, issued in 1988, was the end-product of this long process of consultation.

SSAP 24 definitions

The main principles to be followed when accounting for pension costs have already been stated above. Before looking at the requirements of the accounting standard we re-define several of the terms used above as they are used in the standard:

► A **defined benefit scheme** is one in which the rules specify the benefits to be paid and the scheme is financed accordingly.
► A **defined contribution scheme** is one in which the benefits are directly determined by the value of contributions paid in respect of each member. The rate of contribution is normally specified in the rules.
► **Accrued benefits** are the benefits for service up to a given point in time, whether the rights to the benefits are vested or not. They may be calculated in accordance with current or projected earnings.

- ▶ An **accrued benefits method** of actuarial valuation method is one in which the actuarial value of liabilities relate at a given date to:
  - – benefits for current pensioners
  - – benefits that members assumed to be in service on the given date will receive for service up to that date only.

  The given date may be a current or future date. The further into the future the adopted date lies, the closer the results will be to those of a prospective benefits valuation method.

- ▶ A **funding plan** is the timing of payments in an orderly fashion to meet the future cost of a given set of benefits.

- ▶ A **funded scheme** is where the future liabilities for benefits are provided for by the accumulation of assets held externally to the employer company's business.

- ▶ The **level of funding** is the proportion at a given date of the actuarial value of the liabilities for pension benefits that is covered by the actuarial value of the assets.

- ▶ A **current funding level valuation** considers whether the assets would have been sufficient at the valuation date to cover liabilities in respect of:
  - – pensions in payment
  - – preserved benefits for members whose pensionable service has ceased
  - – accrued benefits for members in service.

- ▶ An **experience surplus or deficiency** is that part of the excess or deficiency of the actuarial value of assets over liabilities that arises because events have not coincided with previous actuarial assumptions made.

- ▶ The **average remaining service life** is a weighted average of the expected future service of the current members up to their normal retirement or death in service dates.

- ▶ **Regular cost** is the consistent ongoing cost recognised under the actuarial method used.

SSAP 24 – the accounting rules

The accounting rules of SSAP 24 are designed to ensure that companies meet the standard's accounting objective, both in terms of regular cost and variations from this regular cost.

The accounting objective of SSAP 24

The accounting objectives of SSAP 24 are:

- ▶ Because the cost of providing pensions is part of the remuneration of employees, the cost should be allocated as fairly as possible so as to match the benefit derived from the services of employees.

- ▶ Accordingly, the accounting objective of the standard is stated to be that the employer should recognise the expected cost of providing pensions on a systematic and rational basis over the period during which benefit is derived from employees' services.

- ▶ Valuation methods adopted should provide a recommended level of contributions representing a stable percentage of payroll cost.

Accounting for variations from regular cost

The different situations in which variations may occur are:

- ▶ experience surpluses or deficiencies arising from actuarial valuations
- ▶ changes in actuarial methods or assumptions
- ▶ improvements in benefits or changes in conditions for membership
- ▶ increase to pensions in payments or to deferred pensions for which provision has not previously been made.

Experience surpluses or deficiencies
The general rule is that variations from regular cost caused by experience surpluses or deficiencies should be spread forward over the expected remaining service lives of current employees in the scheme.

Variations from regular cost would be reflected in the form of one or more of:

▶ contribution holidays
▶ a period of reduced contributions
▶ cash refunds to employers
▶ additional lump sum contributions; a period of increased contributions.

The general rule above represents a departure from the widespread practice of recognising such variations as they arise.

The standard does not specify how the variations should be allocated. The appendix to ED 39, not included in SSAP 24, suggested that the surplus to be reduced or the deficiency to be funded could be allocated on a straight-line basis so that the annual pension cost charge would be: regular cost less surplus/average remaining service lives; or regular cost plus deficiency/average remaining service lives. This is not the only possible approach.

Approached as in ED 39, the difference between the profit and loss charge and the actual contributions paid will be carried forward in the balance sheet as either prepayments or provisions. There are three exceptions to the spread forward rule:

▶ Where a surplus that causes a 'significant change' in the level of contributions has resulted from a significant reduction in the number of employees – in this case the profit and loss account should reflect the reduced level of contributions as it occurs, for example, following a major redundancy programme. (See, however, extraordinary items below.)
▶ Where the company takes a cash refund under the provisions of the Finance Act 1986, it *may* depart from the spreading principle and credit the refund to income in the period in which it occurs.
▶ Where prudence required it, a material deficiency should be recognised over a shorter period. In this case the deficiency must have been caused by a major event outside the scope of actuarial assumptions and must have resulted in significant additional contributions being paid into the scheme.

Where a material surplus or deficiency is caused directly by an extraordinary event, SSAP 6 would, prior to the issue of FRS 3, have overridden the provisions above. Individual elements of income and expenditure (including pension cost variations) that derive from a single extraordinary event would have been aggregated and would normally have been recognised in the profit and loss account in the same period. This aspect of SSAP 24 will obviously have to be reconsidered in terms of FRS 3 – see Chapter 11. Under FRS 3, to the extent that variations are recognised immediately, for example, on the discontinuance of an operation, the cost arising would be dealt with as an exceptional item. Thus, on the closure of an operation, any deficiency arising as to pensions would be treated as part of the direct costs of closure and included with closure cost in the FRS 3 profit and loss account.

Disclosure requirements

The standard requires sufficient information to be disclosed to give a user a proper understanding of the impact of the pension arrangements on a company's financial statements. Company law contains very limited disclosure requirements in respect of pensions: the pension cost charged and commitments whether or not provided for.

SSAP 24 requires much more detailed disclosure as follows.

Defined contribution schemes

- ▶ the nature of the scheme
- ▶ the accounting policy
- ▶ the charge for the period
- ▶ any outstanding or prepaid contributions at the balance sheet date

Defined benefit schemes

- ▶ whether the cost is assessed in accordance with the advice of an actuary
- ▶ if the actuary is an employee or officer of the company
- ▶ the date of the most recent formal valuation
- ▶ the amount of any deficiency on a current funding level basis – discontinuance valuation – and action taken to rectify it (no requirement to disclose a surplus on this basis)
- ▶ outline of the most recent actuarial valuation on an ongoing basis
- ▶ actuarial method used and main assumptions
- ▶ assumption regarding new entrants
- ▶ effect of any change in actuarial method
- ▶ market value of the assets of the scheme
- ▶ level of funding expressed in percentage terms and comments on any material surpluses or deficits revealed by this

Some further points as to accounting for variations from regular cost

The standard states that variations should normally be spread over the remaining service lives of employees currently in the scheme. The exceptions to this normal rule were dealt with above. The normal rule needs to be looked at in the context of the standard's overall approach, which is oriented more towards the profit and loss account than the balance sheet.

If the variations were recognised in full in the year of an actuarial valuation there could be a very significant effect on the reported earnings of that year. It is to prevent such volatility in the earnings pattern and to ensure a more smooth pattern of earnings given pension cost variations that the standard requires, normally, a spread forward approach.

With a surplus that causes a 'significant change' in the level of contributions that has resulted from a significant reduction in the number of employees, the effect of the variation should be recognised as the change in contributions occurs. The rationale for this exception to the spreading rule is that it would make little sense to spread this effect over the working lives of those who remain when it arises from those who have left. However, although this exception is expressed as being mandatory, it becomes so only when it has been determined that the reduction in employees should be regarded as 'significant', and this term is not further defined.

Regarding cash refunds, the standard provides that the company is allowed (but not required) to credit the refund to income in the year of receipt as opposed to spreading the effects forward. It is difficult to see any conceptual merit in this exception to the spreading rule.

Application of SSAP 24 – dealing with the numbers

Having been through the SSAP 24 requirements above it would be useful at this stage of the chapter to apply the rules to a given situation (Example 8.1) and to arrive at the numbers for the accounts so as to comply with the accounting standard.

EXAMPLE 8.1 – Application of SSAP 24 – a number-based example

The directors of Richelieu plc have received a report from their actuaries dealing with each of the company's two non-contributory pension schemes, based upon data at 1 January 1991.

Extracts from the report are as follows:

Works Scheme

The closure of the Buckingham division (a material business segment) in June 1991 will require an immediate contribution of £2 million to ensure that the assets of the scheme are sufficient to cover the liabilities in respect of the accrued benefits of the former employees at that location.

Other assets of the Scheme were insufficient to cover the liabilities in respect of the prospective benefits for continuing employees. The extent of the deficiency was some £5.5 million. It is recommended that one lump sum payment of £3 million be made on 31 December 1991 followed by a payment of £2.7 million on 31 December 1992, and that contributions thereafter be at the rate of £1 million per annum until 31 December 1999 and £800,000 thereafter.

The average age of the continuing employees is 50 years, their average retirement age is 61 years and benefits are determined by pensionable salary at date of retirement.

Staff Scheme

A surplus in respect of prospective benefits of £2.2 million has been disclosed by the valuation, partly due to changes in the actuarial assumptions. It is recommended that a contribution holiday be taken in 1991 and 1992 and thereafter that contributions be £400,000 per annum to 31 December 1994 and £750,000 per annum thereafter. The age profile of this Scheme is similar to that of the Works Scheme. Benefits are determined by pensionable salary at date of retirement.

On the assumption that the actuaries' recommendations are accepted, calculate the amounts to be included with respect to the pension schemes in the profit and loss account and balance sheet of Richelieu plc for the year ending 31 December 1991, complying with the provisions of SSAP 24 and drafting appropriate notes.

Workings

Amounts to be included with respect to the pension schemes in the profit and loss account and balance sheet for the year ending 31 December 1991 so as to comply with the provisions of SSAP 24 and all appropriate notes thereto are as follows.

Works Scheme

(i) The closure of the Buckingham division would under SSAP 6 have fallen to be treated as an extraordinary item. The cost of the additional amounts required to cover the deficiency in respect of the accrued pension benefits of former employees at that location would have been included as part of the extraordinary item resulting from the decision to terminate significant activities. This would under FRS 3 now be treated as exceptional and dealt with under discontinued operations as part of closure cost.

(ii) The deficiency of £5.5 million should, in accordance with SSAP 24, be spread over the average remaining service lives of continuing employees, that is, 11 years. The annual pension cost of the company, charged against profit on ordinary operations and included as a part of staff costs, is calculated as follows:

Taking the normal or regular cost of the company to be £800,000 per annum, £800,000 + (£5.5 million/11 years) = £1.3 million per annum for 11 years and £800,000 per annum therafter.

(Note: you could have arrived at the same result by adding the total contributions to be paid over 11 years: £14.3 million and dividing by 11 years to give a constant charge of £1.3 million per annum over those 11 years and £800,000 per annum thereafter.)

For the year ended 31 December 1991, the charge against ordinary profits would therefore be £1.3 million and at 31 December 1991 the balance sheet would include, as a prepayment (£3 million the contribution paid in 1991 less £1.3 million the cost recognised in the profit and loss account) £1.7 million. The prepayment would increase in the balance sheet in 1992 and reduce in each year thereafter, when the profit and loss account charge is greater than the contribution paid, reducing to nil at the end of the 11th year.

Staff Scheme

The variation of £2.2 million should, in accordance with SSAP 24, be spread over the average remaining service lives of continuing employees, that is, 11 years. The annual pension cost of the company, charged against profit on ordinary operations would be, taking £750,000 per annum as the normal or regular pension cost, £750,000 − (£2.2 million/11 years) = £550,000 per annum for 11 years and £750,000 per annum thereafter. (The same result would be obtained by adding the contributions over the 11 year period, that is, £6.05 million and dividing by 11 years.)

For the year ended 31 December 1991, the charge against ordinary profits would be £550,000 and at 31 December 1991 the balance sheet would include, as a provision (£550,000 the cost recognised in the profit and loss account less the nil contribution paid in 1991) £550,000. The provision would increase in the balance sheet for each of the next three years when the profit and loss account charge is greater than the contributions paid, and reduce in each of the next seven years when the profit and loss account charge is less than the contributions paid, reducing to nil at the end of the 11th year.

The summary of amounts dealt with in the profit and loss account and balance sheet of the company for the year ended and at 31 December 1991 is as follows:

Profit and loss account

	£000
Pension cost included as a part of staff costs and charged in arriving at profit on ordinary activities	
Works Scheme	1,300
Staff Scheme	550
Exceptional item – included as part of the cost of closure of a material business segment	2,000

Balance sheet

Prepayment arising as a result of accounting for the deficiency arising in the Works Scheme	DR 1,700
Provision arising as a result of accounting for the surplus arising in the Staff Scheme	CR 550

Appropriate notes to the accounts are:

Accounting policies: pension costs

The normal or regular pension cost of the company is equal to the employer's contributions recommended by the actuaries of the company's pension schemes using the (attained age normal method), which determines future normal contributions as a level percentage of salaries.

The actuaries periodically carry out formal actuarial valuations. The date of the most recent such valuation was 1 January 1991.

Actuarial experience surpluses and deficiencies are accounted for by spreading such amounts over the average remaining service lives of continuing employees, which is 11 years.

Variations from normal pension cost are treated as exceptional items where material.

Pension cost

Pension cost for the year amounts to £1.85 million. This is after taking account of experience surpluses and deficiencies arising from an actuarial valuation in the year. The normal or regular pension cost of the company is £1.55 million per annum.

Pension provision
Provision for pension liability amounts to £550,000. This amount arose on 1 January 1991 as a result of the spreading of an actuarial surplus arising on the company's Staff Scheme over average remaining service lives of continuing employees, resulting in contributions paid during the year being less than pension cost.

Debtors: prepayments and accrued income
These include a prepayment of £1.7 million arising on the spreading of an actuarial deficiency arising on the company's Works Scheme over average remaining service lives of continuing employees resulting in contributions paid during the year being in excess of pension cost.

Pension commitments
The company has two pension funds for its employees. The benefits are determined by pensionable salary at date of retirement. The actuarial valuation at 1 January 1991 indicated that there were insufficient assets in the Works Scheme to cover the liabilities in respect of the prospective benefits for continuing employees. The group intends to fund this deficiency of £5.5 million by paying additional contributions up to 31 December 1999.

Alternative methods of accounting for actuarial surpluses and deficits

A further discussion as to the relative merits of the treatment of actuarial surpluses and deficits under SSAP 24 with alternative methods of accounting for such items follows:

There are four possible ways to treat actuarial surpluses and deficits:

► retrospectively as a prior year adjustment
► prospectively over a stated number of years
► currently as a part of profit on ordinary activities
► currently as a part of gains or losses on extraordinary activities.

In the case of deficits, the period(s) in which funding is made may be different from the period(s) in which costs are recognised. As such surpluses or deficits arise as a result of changed assumptions of actuaries, and given that they arise neither from a change of accounting policy nor as a result of fundamental error, even though they may arise from over or under funding in previous years, it would not be appropriate to deal with them as prior year adjustments in accordance with FRS 3.

The issue is, therefore, whether they be accounted for currently or prospectively. SSAP 24 latches on to the concept of a smooth profit and loss account charge, and on the basis that erratic movements in the long-term estimates may be misleading, requires that they be dealt with prospectively over the average remaining service lives of continuing employees. It has, however, been argued, in respect of deficits, that they represent an actual liability, which should be immediately recognised in the accounts, and that it is inappropriate of SSAP 24 to argue that, under the going concern concept, a company has many years to put it right and therefore need not recognise such a liability in the accounts. Indeed, a prepayment arises in this situation. See Example 8.1. When discontinuance liabilities are not covered by assets in the pension fund, there is a strong case for giving them immediate recognition in the balance sheet. The standard does, however, permit a deficiency to be recognised over a shorter period.

Where a surplus is to be utilised by taking a contribution holiday or arranging a refund of contributions, similar considerations apply. Contribution holidays are said to distort a company's results over the period of the holiday because no pension costs are being charged. Refunds are said to distort results in the year they are made because of the large credit appearing in the accounts. Hence the SSAP 24 requirement to smooth the effect by spreading the surplus propsectively. SSAP 24 is in favour of an income rather than a balance sheet approach to accounting for pension costs. A balance sheet approach would mean that large provisions would not appear in the balance sheet when there are material surpluses in a pension scheme, nor would large prepayments when there are material deficits.

There is, therefore, a difference between the SSAP 24 accounting and 'cash accounting' and the distortion that such accounting can create on the results of companies. If pension cost was recognised only when paid (pay as you go) the results of each year would reflect the effects of pensions paid in that year. The effects of the cost arising in each year, in terms of deferred remuneration currently earned by employees but subsequently received, would not be reported.

Deferred tax and pension cost accounting – FRED 2

Deferred tax, as dealt with in Chapter 7, is simply accounting for the tax effects of timing differences. In respect of pensions, tax relief is available to the company when contributions are paid rather than when they are expensed, or passed through or recognised in the profit and loss account. There may well be a difference between the two as payments are a matter of cash availability and therefore funding ability whereas cost recognised in the profit and loss account is a matter of satisfying the accounting objective of the accounting standard.

In a scheme that is not funded, that is, where no payments are made into a separate pension scheme, tax relief will be available to the company only when the employee(s) actually retire and pension(s) are actually paid. It follows, therefore, that whenever pension costs recognised under SSAP 24 are different from the actual contributions paid, the resulting pension provision or prepayment that will appear in the balance sheet represents a timing difference for deferred tax purposes.

The problem here is the long-term nature of these timing differences. SSAP 15 (Revised) may be difficult to apply as the company would now have to consider the overall pattern of timing differences originating and reversing over a much longer period than normal.

A further conflict can be identified between SSAP 24 and SSAP 15. The former follows what is essentially an 'income' approach and therefore fully recognises accruing pension obligations. The latter follows what is essentially a 'balance sheet' or 'value' approach and, accordingly, does not permit deferred tax timing differences to be recognised as assets or liabilities if reversing timing differences are replaced by equivalent new originating timing differences.

Where this is not likely to cause any particular difficulty in funded schemes, there could be a material impact arising in accounting for unfunded schemes. The problem here is that a provision for unfunded pensions may never actually decrease because any reductions arising from the payment of pensions to retiring employees would be more than matched with increases to the provision following entrants joining the pension scheme – SSAP 15 would not permit the recognition of a deferred tax asset in this situation.

FRED 2 was issued in 1992 to address these problems. It proposes an amendment to SSAP 15 in that it suggests that we use the same recognition criteria for the tax implications of pensions and other post-retirement benefits (see below) as in accounting for the obligations to provide these benefits.

Accordingly, under FRED 2, 'either the full provision basis or the partial provision basis may be used in accounting for the deferred tax implications of pensions and other post-retirement benefits accounted for in accordance with SSAP 24 . . . The policy adopted should be disclosed.'

Other post-retirement benefits

TR 756 was issued in 1989 to deal with the application of the principles of SSAP 24 to the cost of providing post-retirement benefits other than pensions, for example, the provision of post-retirement medical insurance. Such provisions are normally unfunded.

UITF Abstract 6 on accounting for post-retirement benefits other than pensions was issued in 1992. Under the UITF consensus:

▶ such benefits, in accordance with prudence and accruals under SSAP 2, should be recognised as obligations in accounts
▶ the principles of SSAP 24 are applicable to their measurement and disclosure
▶ as employers may be engaged in negotiations that may significantly affect the obligations, the UITF allows a transitional period before it becomes mandatory to apply SSAP 24 principles to these benefits
▶ disclosure is required if the SSAP 24 principles are not adopted
▶ in changing to the SSAP 24 approach the unprovided obligation on the date of change may be recognised:
  – *either* by means of a prior year adjustment
  – *or* by spreading it forward over expected remaining service lives of current employees.

As to the deferred tax implications of the provision made, the points made above under FRED 2 apply. Thus, the full provision basis may be used.

Concluding points

SSAP 24 has been criticised in that it may not achieve a high measure of standardisation between one company and another. This is because there is still a considerable amount of flexibility in the standard in terms of:

▶ choice of actuarial method
▶ setting of actuarial assumptions
▶ selection between optional accounting treatments, which the standard either explicitly or implicitly allows.

However, the standard, despite the shortcomings noted above, does represent a significant step forward in the presentation of meaningful information about pension costs in the financial statements of UK companies. Where previously the measurement of pension cost by companies was unsophisticated, the standard requires companies to make serious attempts to account for that cost on a systematic basis. It will, at least, achieve a far higher degree of consistency as earnings trends will no longer be distorted by the effects of funding decisions. In the last analysis, the standard is more of a disclosure standard than a measurement standard and it is in this sense that it has made a positive contribution to standard accounting practice.

Summary

This chapter deals with the accounting for pension costs by an employer company and the impact of the principles of SSAP 2 and SSAP 15 in this regard. You should, having worked through the chapter, be able to:

▶ describe the accounting objective of SSAP 24
▶ distinguish 'funding' from 'cost'
▶ explain how pension provisions or prepayments arise in the balance sheet
▶ account for variations from regular cost under the requirements of the standard
▶ make all relevant disclosure
▶ comment on the deferred tax implications arising as dealt with in FRED 2
▶ account for post-retirement benefits other than pensions in accordance with UITF Abstract 6.

Suggested reading

Accounting for the Cost of Pensions (Napier 1983)

Pension surpluses in company accounts (Wilkins 1987)

Accounting for Pension Costs – The Implementation of SSAP 24 (Ernst & Yang 1989)

Manual of Accounting – Companies (Coopers & Lybrand Deloitte 1990)

Appendix: SORP 1 Accounting for pension schemes

An occupational pension is frequently one of the biggest investments that many employees are likely to have and is considered by many to be part of their overall remuneration package. In the UK, there are more than 90,000 occupational pension schemes with a total membership of 11.5 million people, or over half the working population. The assets of such schemes amount to many hundreds of billions of pounds and continue to increase. As a result of the growing social and economic importance of pensions, and in response to pressure from various quarters, the importance of pensions, and in response to pressure from various quarters, the government has enacted legislation by way of the Social Security Act 1985 and the Occupational Pension Schemes (Disclosure of Information) Regualtions 1986, which regulate the disclosure of financial and other information by Occupational Pension Schemes.

The accountancy profession's guidance on current best practice on the form and content of the accounts of pension schemes is contained in Statement of Recommended Practice No. 1 – Pension Scheme Accounts (SORP 1) which was issued in May 1986. The legislation enacted by the government and referred to above, has followed the recommendation contained in a report by the Occupational Pensions Board that the contents of annual accounts would be best left to the accountancy profession. Schedule 3 of the 'Regulations' that prescribes the contents of accounts, is similar to the recommendations of SORP 1 and schemes meeting the requirements of the SORP will in most respects comply with the legislation. The Regulations require the accounts to contain a statement that they have been prepared in compliance with SORP 1 or, if they have not, an indication of material departures from the recommendations.

A description of various pension arrangements

In the UK, pension arrangements are available to all employees through the state scheme. Many employees also benefit from membership of a private, 'occupational', scheme set up by the employer.

The state scheme

This is a two-tier scheme set up by the Social Securities Pensions Act 1975. It provides for a basic pension and an additional pension related to earnings with contributions being made by the individual and his or her employer. Anyone who has a full record of National Insurance contributions is entitled to the state basic pension at retirement age. In addition, employees whose earnings are above certain thresholds, are currently required to pay contributions that entitle them to an earnings-related pension under the State Earnings Related Pension Scheme (SERPS) which began in 1978. The state scheme makes no provision for lump sum payments on death or retirement.

Occupational pension schemes

These are arrangements made between employers and employees and are designed to provide cash benefits to employees on their retirement or to their dependants on their death. The benefits can take the form of either regular pension payments or a lump sum payment and a reduced regular payment. These schemes are usually financed by setting aside funds during the working lives of employees. The funds are usually placed under the control of trustees who hold and invest the funds under the terms of a trust deed. By creating a trust fund in this way, the pension scheme becomes a legal entity which is separate from the employer's business (the company).

Occupational pension schemes sometimes allow employees to improve their retirement benefit entitlement by making Additional Voluntary Contributions (AVCs), which may be invested in the main scheme or in separate schemes set up for that purpose.

Companies that pay pensions to former employees directly out of company funds ('pay as you go' financing) operate schemes that are referred to as unfunded schemes.

Pension schemes can be divided into two basic types: defined benefit schemes and defined contribution schemes. These are dealt with in the discussion to SSAP 24 above.

Where certain conditions are satisfied, an occupational pension scheme can elect to 'contract out' of SERPS. When a scheme is contracted out, the employer and the employee become entitled to a reduction in National Insurance contributions. A member of a contracted out scheme foregoes all his or her earnings related state pension and the occupational pension scheme is obliged to ensure that the scheme pension is at least equal to a specified amount known as the guaranteed minimum pension. Most large pension schemes in the UK are contracted out.

The regulatory environment

The environment in which pension schemes operate is different from that of the environment in which commercial organisations function.

Contract law

By law a contract of employment must contain a statement as to whether the employment is contracted in or out of SERPS. This is so whether or not the employer operates a pension scheme and whether or not the employee is entitled to membership of it. If an employee is entitled to membership of a pension scheme, the employer is under an implied contractual obligation to ensure that the scheme exists and is satisfactorily administered. However, the scheme will usually contain an express right given to the employer to terminate the scheme or cease paying contributions at any time. Any contractual rights of the employee will be against the employer. Although the trustees are responsible for paying out the benefits to members of a scheme, the employee has no rights in contract against them. Rights against trustees lie in equity and not in contract and are as a beneficiary of the trust and are subject to the trust deed.

Trust law

As pension schemes are usually established under trusts, they are governed by general trust law together with the provisions of the trust deed itself. The trust fund is placed in the charge of trustees who administer the fund on behalf of the beneficiaries, that is, the members, in accordance with the trust deed. The interests of the members are protected in two respects:

▶ The trust fund exists solely to provide benefits for them (subject to specific provisions allowing for contributions to be refunded to the employer where the scheme is in surplus).

▶ The trustees are answerable to the members for any losses resulting from their negligence or breach of trust. Where losses do not result from negligence or breach of trust, and the fund's assets are insufficient to meet pension commitments, there is no obligation on the part of trustees to honour pension promises that exceed the value of the fund's assets. In a defined benefit scheme, the employer may undertake to make good any deficiency by a higher level of contribution to continue the scheme.

Social security law

There are many detailed regulations affecting occupational pension schemes, which also cover their supervision, set out in social security legislation.

The Social Security Pension Act 1975

The Act introduced the present SERPS scheme and allowed employees to be contracted out of the state scheme.

The Social Security Act 1985 and disclosure regulations

The Act gave the Secretary of State for Social Security power to make orders in relation to the provisions of information to members of occupational pension schemes. Under this enabling power The Disclosure Regulations were laid before Parliament and came into force in November 1986. The Regulations fall under six headings:

1   Disclosure of contents of trust deed or other scheme documentation.
2   Basic information about the scheme.
3   Information to be made available to individuals.
4   Audited accounts.
5   Actuarial valuation and statement.
6   Trustees' report.

Under The Regulations, the trustees of a scheme are required to make available to members, beneficiaries and other interested parties such as trade unions, copies of The Annual Report, which should contain:

▶ A copy of the audited accounts for the scheme year.
▶ A copy of the latest actuarial statement.
▶ A trustees' report and an investment report.

SORP 1

Both the SORP and the Regulations identified that the underlying objective of a pension scheme's accounts is to give a true and fair view of the financial transactions of the scheme during the scheme's year and the disposition of its assets and liabilities at the period end. The audited accounts should provide answers to the following questions:

▶ What is the size of the funds held by trustees?
▶ Where have these funds come from?
▶ Where and how effectively have they been invested?

The recommended form and content of the accounts of a pension scheme

The Annual Report of a pension scheme, as recommended by SORP 1, should contain Accounts, a Trustees' Report, an Actuaries' Statement and an Investment Report.

Accounts

The accounts should comprise:

▶ A revenue account for the scheme year, which shows additions to and withdrawals from the fund during the year.
▶ A net assets statement at the scheme year end which shows the assets and liabilities other than those for pensions falling due after the end of the year.
▶ A movement of funds statement, which reconciles the movement in net assets of the scheme to the revenue account. This reconciliation may be shown as a separate statement or it may be incorporated in the revenue account or the net assets statement.
▶ Notes to the accounts, including explanations of the accounting policies followed in dealing with items that are judged to be material or critical to accounting for or reporting on transactions and net assets.
▶ Corresponding amounts for or at the end of the previous scheme year.
▶ Such additional information as is necessary to give a true and fair view of financial transactions of the scheme and the disposition of its net assets.
▶ A statement that the accounts do not take account of liabilities to pay pension benefits in the future and that this is dealt with in the actuary's statement, which should be read in conjunction with the accounts.
▶ The amount of sales and of purchases of investments during the year.
▶ Details of any 'self-investment' that exceeds 5% of the value of the net assets of the fund. Self-investment is defined in the Regulations as being investment in the business of the employer, of the members of the scheme, or a connected company.
▶ Details of any concentration of investment of the scheme's assets. For these purposes concentration of investment arises where assets exceeding 5% of the net assets of the scheme are invested in any one company, including connected companies and persons, or any one property.
▶ Details of the overall investment policy where insurance policies form a material part of the net assets of the scheme.

The recommendations of SORP 1 are applicable to all pension schemes in the UK other than:

▶ those that have only one member at the accounting date
▶ those that are unfunded, that is, where there is no separate fund of assets out of which future pension benefits are to be paid.

Recommended form of accounts

A recommended form of accounts is:

Revenue account
1   Contributions receivable:
   1.1 from employers:
      1.1.1 normal
      1.1.2 additional
   1.2 from members:
      1.2.1 normal
      1.2.2 additional voluntary
   1.3 transfers in:
      1.3.1 group transfers in from other schemes
      1.3.2 individual transfers in from other schemes
2   Investment income:
   2.1 income from fixed interest securities
   2.2 dividends from equities
   2.3 share of profits/losses of non-investment holding subsidiary companies
   2.4 share of profits/losses of associated companies
   2.5 rents from properties
   2.6 interest on cash deposits
   2.7 share of profits/losses of trading subsidiaries and joint ventures
3   Other income:
   3.1 claims on term insurance policies
   3.2 any other category of income that does not naturally fall into the above classification, suitably described and analysed where material
4   Benefits payable:
   4.1 pensions
   4.2 commutation of pensions and lump sum retirement benefits
   4.3 death benefits
   4.4 payments to and on account of leavers
      4.4.1 refunds of contributions
      4.4.2 state scheme premiums
      4.4.3 purchase of annuities to match preserved benefits
      4.4.4 group transfers out to other schemes
      4.4.5 individual transfers out to other schemes
5   Other payments:
   5.1 premiums on term insurance policies
   5.2 any other category of expenditure that does not naturally fall into the above classification, suitably described and analysed where material
6   Administrative expenses borne by the scheme, with suitable analysis where material.
   Where the administrative expenses are borne directly by a participating employer, that fact should be disclosed as a note; it is not necessary to disclose the amount involved.

Net assets statement
7   Investment assets:
   7.1 fixed interest securities
   7.2 equities
   7.3 index-linked securities
   7.4 managed funds and unit trusts
   7.5 non-investment-holding subsidiary companies
   7.6 associated companies
   7.7 property

7.8 cash deposits

7.9 insurance policies

7.10 net debtor/creditor in respect of investment transactions where these form part of the funds available for investment within the investment portfolio

7.11 other assets/liabilities directly connected with investment transactions (Investments should be further analysed between UK and foreign and property should be further analysed between 'short leasehold' and 'other' unless this information is provided in the investment report.)

7.12 other assets/liabilities, for example, financial futures and, where applicable, tax recoverable

8 Fixed assets held primarily for reasons other than investment potential

9 Long-term borrowings:

9.1 sterling

9.2 foreign currency

10 Current assets and liabilities:

10.1 contributions due from employees

10.2 unpaid benefits

10.3 other – not directly connected with investment transactions

Reconciliation of the movement in the net assets of the scheme

11 The reconciliation of the movement in the net assets of the scheme may be incorporated into the revenue account or net assets statement, or alternatively be shown as a separate statement. Whichever method of presentation is adopted it should clearly disclose:

11.1 opening net assets of the scheme

11.2 net new money invested, per revenue account

11.3 change in market value of investments (realised and unrealised)

11.4 closing net assets of the scheme.

The accounting policies to be stated include:

► policies adopted in applying the accruals concept to significant categories of income and expenditure such as contributions, investment income, transfer values and benefits

► bases adopted for valuations of assets

► basis of foreign currency translation

► treatment of interest on property developments

► basis adopted for accounting for investments in subsidiary and associated companies.

The main problems that arise are in relation to investments, and these should be dealt with as follows:

► Securities quoted in the UK – mid point of quotations in SEDOL.

► Securities quoted overseas at middle market prices from overseas stock exchange translated at closing rates.

► Unquoted securities – trustees' valuations.

► Units – at average of bid and offer prices.

► Financial futures, options, forward currency positions – at market value or trustees' valuations.

► Freehold and leasehold property – at open market value; disclose name and qualification of valuer and whether employee of scheme or participating employer.

► Long-term insurance policies – at the 'premium valuation method'.

► Subsidiaries:

 – investment holding subsidiaries – proportional consolidation on a line by line basis

 – other subsidiaries – single line equity method.

Associates:
- joint ventures: in the same way as investments in subsidiaries
- other: market value in the Net Asset Statement.

Dividends only in the profit and loss account.

Trustees' Report and Investment Report

The information that will normally be included in the trustees' report covers two distinct aspects of the scheme.

General information

This should provide members with a commentary on:

▶ major changes in the constitution or rules of the scheme, such as changes in the conditions of membership or changes in the way contributions are calculated
▶ membership statistics
▶ changes in benefits
▶ the financial development of the scheme as shown by the audited accounts
▶ the actuarial position of the scheme as disclosed by the actuarial valuation and statement
▶ names of the persons who served as trustees, actuaries, auditors, solicitors and bankers and changes therein since the previous year end
▶ provisions of the scheme for appointing and removing trustees.

Where contributions of the scheme have not been paid in accordance with the rules of the scheme and with the recommendations of the actuary, the trustees are required to include a statement to this effect in their report, giving the reasons and stating how the discrepancy has been or will be rectified. This is a matter on which the auditors of the scheme are also required to report and the auditors will be concerned to see that the explanations given do not contradict anything included in the accounts or the audit report.

Investment information

The investment report or the trustees' report should inform members of the investment policy and performance of the scheme, including details of any delegation of investment management responsibilites by the trustees and the basis on which investment managers are remunerated. The trustees' review is an amplification of the information contained in the accounts and will provide members with a broad understanding of how the trustees are carrying out their stewardship responsibilities. The Regulations require the review to contain details of the 'nature, disposition, marketability, security and valuation of the scheme's assets'. SORP 1 envisages that this review will often include:

▶ an analysis of investments by industrial sector
▶ an analysis of investments by geographical sector
▶ details of the 10 or 20 largest investments
▶ details of investments that represent 5% or more of any class of shares of any company
▶ details of the extent to which properties are subject to rent reviews.

The totals shown in the investment report should be reconciled to the amounts shown in the accounts.

Actuarial Statement

The actuary to the scheme should provide the trustees with a statement, to be reproduced in the Annual Report, explaining the present ability of the scheme to meet the benefits that have already accrued in respect of past service and the future ability of the scheme to meet benefits as they fall due. The actuarial statement will be based on an actuarial valuation of the scheme and must state:

▶ whether the scheme's assets as at the valuation date fully cover its liabilities at that date

▶ in the event that the assets do not cover the liabilities, the extent to which the liabilities are covered and the measures which are to be taken to cover the liabilities in full

▶ whether the resources of the scheme are likely in the normal course of events to meet in full the liabilities of the scheme as they fall due (in giving this opinion, the actuary must state the contributions that are assumed will be paid into the scheme)

▶ the methods and assumptions used in making the actuarial valuation. The valuation, which must be made by an actuary with qualifications as specified in the Regulations, must meet the following requirements:

    – be framed so as to enable the expected future course of the scheme's contribution rates and funding level to be understood

    – state whether it has been prepared in accordance with the guidelines: Retirement Benefit Schemes – Actuarial Report (GN9), published by the Institute of Actuaries and the Faculty of Actuaries

    – indicate where there have been any material departures from those guidelines.

The Regulations require the trustees to obtain an actuarial valuation of the scheme's assets in relation to its liabilities at intervals of not more than three years and six months. There is no requirement for the actuarial statement to be updated in the period between valuations, but the actuary may issue a revised statement in the intervening period if the circumstances so require.

Conclusion

What then are the problem areas for pension scheme reports to members? The Discussion Paper published by the ASC in 1982 suggested that there were really two separate questions that members wished to have answered. First, what is the extent of the funds currently held by the trustees, where have they come from and how effective has the trustees' stewardship been? This question is answered in the form of an historical account, the work of an accountant. Second, how secure are their present pension rights, and will the fund be able to meet their present prospective pensions when they fall due? This question deals with projections into the future and falls into the province of the actuary.

    The fundamental problem in designing the most appropriate form of report to members of a pension fund is the problem of which profession should be the lead writer. Those who argue that accounts should include future pension liabilities believe that pure stewardship accounts are incomplete and inadequate. Those who favour limiting the accounts to a stewardship role argue that a meaningful pension scheme report must seek to convey two separate messages – the size and origin of the accumulated funds on the one hand and the adequacy of those funds and future contribution rates to meet pension obligations on the other. They believe that, in the context of reporting to members, the clearest way to convey the second message is a direct report from the expert in the field, the actuary. They recommend that there is reference in the accounts to the need for them to be used in conjunction with the separate actuary's report to obtain an overall picture of the health of the scheme as a whole.

    This fundamental issue has been debated within both professions and by the DSS and all have agreed that this division in the reporting function is appropriate. The Regulations under the Social Security Act 1985 reflected this division and required pension scheme reports to include an actuarial statement covering the present fund's ability to meet accrued pension rights and the adequacy of the future contribution rates to ensure that prospective pension obligations can be met when they become payable. This not only separates the responsibility for the past and future facets of the overall report but also recognises the important difference in asset valuation techniques used in these separate functions. The combination of the stewardship report with the actuary's report could potentially be, as far as asset values are concerned, not comparable.

The extent of disclosure outlined in the SORP follows very closely the original ASC Discussion Paper. It takes account of the comments received on that paper and is compatible with the DSS regulations. The proposals in the SORP are based on a partnership between accountants and actuaries, the separation of the stewardship function from the actuarial comment on the funding plan, and an accounting policy of using market value as the reporting currency and, in all these, point the way forward.

Self test questions

1   Leroy who is employed by Max plc, has 8% of his gross monthly salary deducted to provide for his eventual pension. When Leroy retires, Max plc will pay him a lump sum of 1.4 times his final year salary and an annual pension thereafter of 75% of his final year salary.

Leroy has asked you to indicate whether this is an example of *either* an unfunded defined benefit scheme *or* a funded defined contribution scheme *or* a funded defined benefit scheme *or* an unfunded defined contribution scheme.

2   Vernon plc has accepted the recommendation of its actuary that it should make good a deficiency of £5 million disclosed by an actuarial valuation of its pension scheme of 31 December 1994 by doubling its regular annual contribution of £2.5 million to its pension scheme for 1995 and 1996. Thereafter the annual contribution is to revert to £2.5 million. You are informed that the average remaining service lives of employees in the scheme at 31 December 1994 was ten years.

Calculate the amount to be reported by Vernon plc as pension cost for 1995 so as to comply with SSAP 24.

3   An actuarial valuation at 31 December 1994 of the pension scheme of Furtado plc showed a deficiency of £15 million. The company's actuary recomended that the deficiency be eliminated by the company making three annual payments of £5 million commencing in 1995 in addition to regular contributions of £1.5 million per annum. The company's year end is 31 December; contributions are to continue at £1.5 million per annum from 1998 onwards, and the average remaining service lives of employees in the scheme of 31 December 1994 was ten years.

Ascertain the prepayment arising for inclusion in the balance sheet of Furtado plc at 31 December 1993.

4   Bunty plc makes an annual contribution of £100 million to its employee pension scheme. An actuarial valuation at 31 December 1994 of the assets of the pension scheme showed a surplus of 600 million. It is decided to eliminate the surplus by:

(i) making no contributions to the scheme in 1994 and 1995
(ii) reducing contributions for each of the five following years to £20 million.

The average remaining service lives of employees in the scheme at 31 December 1994 was 12 years.

Ascertain, under SSAP 24, the pension cost of Bunty plc from the year ended 31 December 1994.

5   There are four different ways in which a pension fund surplus may be applied. All four ways involve the company in making the relevant disclosure but only two ways give rise to an accounting problem.

State the four ways in which a pension fund surplus may be applied. Identify the two ways that give rise to an accounting problem. Explain the SSAP 24 treatment of the variation to cost so arising.

Exam style question

1   You are chief accountant of a company with UK trading subsidiaries. Your managing director wishes to improve his understanding of the alternative ways of accounting for pension costs and the way in which they may affect the accounts for the year ending 31 December 1988.

He also wishes to understand the implications, if any, of SSAP 24 on the results for the year. The group pension scheme is a defined benefit scheme and annual cash contributions in the year to 31 December 1988 were expected to be £1,200,000. Only two quarters' contributions have been paid and charged to the profit and loss account.

An actuarial valuation at 31 December 1987 has recently been received. This showed that the scheme was overfunded to the extent of £2.4 million and that the group would be able to cease contributions for the two financial years following that date and thereafter contribute at a reduced level of £960,000 per annum for a further ten years. Thereafter the regular cost would be £1 million per annum. The average remaining service life of employees in the scheme is 12 years.

Required:
Prepare a memorandum for your managing director comparing and contrasting the effect on the results for the year ending 31 December 1988 of adopting SSAP 24 with other currently available accounting treatments for the pension costs.

(10 marks)

Based on ICAEW PEII exam question 1988

All answers on pages 647–649.

Post-Balance Sheet Events, Contingencies and Off Balance Sheet Finance and Accounting for Capital Instruments

SSAP 17 – Accounting for Post Balance Sheet Events, and SSAP 18 – Accounting for Contingencies, were issued in 1980. The two Accounting Standards cover the accounting treatment of events that occur after the balance sheet date and matters of uncertainty at the balance sheet date where the outcome may have a material effect on the results or position of companies. You should be familiar with both these areas and their impact on the financial reporting environment from your previous studies and they are dealt with, briefly, in the first part of this chapter.

The second part of this chapter deals with off balance sheet finance, which essentially self-explanatory term is applied to financing situations where corresponding liabilities are not recorded in a company's balance sheet. Two forms of off balance sheet financing are dealt with in other chapters of this textbook: Chapter 10 looks at leasing and, given the required treatment of SSAP 21 for accounting for finance leases, a reduction although (as dealt with below) not elimination of the scope to use such vehicles for off balance sheet finance. Chapter 15 on legal requirements affecting consolidated accounts looks at the situation of the changed definition of a subsidiary resulting in the consolidation and corresponding recognition of assets and liabilities of investments not previously treated as subsidiaries. Despite the current definition of a subsidiary, it remains possible for quasi subsidiary relationships to arise and these too are dealt with below.

The problem of off balance sheet finance was addressed by the ICAEW in 1985 in TR 603, Off Balance Sheet Financing and Window Dressing. The TR made these points:

▶ Financial statements are required to give a true and fair view.
▶ An accounting solution to the case of a company entering into an arrangement that is equivalent to a borrowing is to record in its balance sheet its obligations under that arrangement.
▶ The company's interest in the use of the assets so financed would also be recorded despite the fact that the legal ownership of the asset might rest with another company or vehicle.
▶ Such accounting would reflect the economic substance of the transaction rather than its legal form.

TR 603 also indicated that the responsibility for identifying off balance sheet financing lay not only with preparers of accounts but also with auditors. Thus, under TR 603, the auditors should:

▶ consider information in accounts to ensure that users' conclusions would be justified and consistent with the circumstance of the business of the company
▶ bear in mind the need for accounts to reflect the substance of underlying transactions and balances and not merely their form
▶ consider whether the presentation adopted in the accounts may have been influenced by the desire of management to present facts in a favourable or unfavourable light.

ED 42 – Accounting for Special Purpose Transactions, was subsequently issued by the ASC. This was concerned with the problem of determining the correct method of accounting for types of complex transactions whose true intention and commercial effect may not be immediately obvious but will significantly affect the financial position and prospects of the reporting enterprise – so-called special-purpose transactions.

ED 49, reflecting the substance of transactions in assets and liabilities, was issued in 1990 by the ASC. The ASB, retaining the essential thrust of the proposals of ED 49, issued FRED 4 in 1993. FRS 5 was issued in 1994.

The third part of this chapter deals with accounting for capital instruments as required by FRS 4 published in December 1993.

Accounting for post-balance sheet events

SSAP 17, the Accounting Standard that governs this area deals with definitions, accounting and examples in respect of post balance sheet events and window dressing transactions. These are dealt with in turn starting with definitions from the Standard.

Definitions

Post balance sheet events are those events, both favourable and unfavourable, which occur between the balance sheet date and the date on which the financial statements are approved by the board of directors.

Adjusting events are post balance sheet events which provide additional evidence of conditions existing at the balance sheet date. They include events which because of statutory or conventional requirements are reflected in financial statements.

Non-adjusting events are post balance sheet events which concern conditions which did not exist at the balance sheet date.

The date on which the financial statements are approved by the board of directors is the date the board of directors formally approves a set of documents as the financial statements. In respect of unincorporated enterprises, the date of approval is the corresponding date. In respect of group accounts, the date of approval is the date where the group accounts are formally approved by the board of directors of the holding company.

Accounting under the standard

The following points from SSAP 17 summarise the accounting requirements of the Standard and indicate the extent to which account should be taken of post balance sheet events, and how and whether their effects may be reflected in published accounts:

► Adjust if events after the balance sheet date provide material evidence of conditions that existed at the balance sheet date.
► Disclosure is required of other material events that provide evidence of conditions not existing at the balance sheet date.
► Disclosure would also be required of the reversal or maturity after the year end of a transaction entered into before the year end, the substance of which was primarily to alter the appearance of the company's balance sheet. (If such a transaction had an income effect, adjustment would be required, for example, sales returns.)
► Certain post balance sheet events are adjusted for because of statutory requirements to include them in the accounts; for example, proposed dividends,

amounts appropriated to reserve, effects of changes in tax and dividends receivable from subsidiary and associated companies.

Generally, a material post balance sheet event will require adjustment if it is an adjusting event and/or it indicates that the going concern assumption is no longer valid. It will require disclosure if it is necessary for a proper understanding of the accounts (including window dressing – see below).

In exceptional circumstances, to accord with the prudence concept, it may be necessary to re-classify non-adjusting events to adjusting events. In such circumstances, full disclosure is required.

The date on which the accounts are approved by the directors should be disclosed in the financial statements.

Examples of adjusting and non-adjusting events

The appendix to SSAP 17 provides illustrative examples of these events as shown in Table 9.1. Note, however, that in exceptional circumstances, to accord with the prudence concept, an adverse event that would normally be classified as non-adjusting may need to be reclassified as adjusting. In such circumstances, full disclosure of the adjustment would be required

Table 9.1 Examples of adjusting and non-adjusting events

Adjusting	Non-adjusting
1 Subsequent determination of proceeds of sale of fixed assets purchased or sold before the year end	1 Mergers/acquisitions after the year end
2 Property valuation that provides evidence of a permanent diminution in value	2 Reconstructions after the year end
3 Evidence re NRV < cost of stocks	3 Issue of shares/debentures after the year end
4 Evidence re inaccuracy of attributable profit calculations	4 Purchase/sale of fixed assets after the year end
5 Insolvency of a debtor	5 Losses re fire/flood after the year end
6 Dividends receivable	6 Extension of activities after the year end
7 Receipt of information re rates of tax	7 Significant closure if this was not anticipated at the year end (see also Chapter 11)
8 Amounts received/receivable – re insurance claims that were in the course of negotiation	8 Decline in asset values if demonstrated to be after the year end
9 Discovery of error or fraud	9 Changes in exchange rates after the year end
	10 Effect of nationalisation/strikes after the year end
	11 Augmentation of pension benefits after the year end

Window dressing

Window dressing is the term applied to the reversal after the year end of transactions entered into before the year end, the substance of which was to alter the appearance of a company's balance sheet. The Technical Release issued on the publication of SSAP 17 describes window dressing as situations where:

▶ there is the fraudulent falsification of accounts to make things appear to be more favourable than they actually are
▶ the legal arrangement of affairs over a year end to make things, at the year end, look different from the way they are.

As the first situation is unlawful and not the subject of an Accounting Standard, the term window dressing as used in SSAP 17, is confined to the second situation listed above. The Standard requires that full disclosure be made of the transactions but that no change be made to amounts to be included in the financial statements. Thus, there is no requirement under UK Accounting Standards that the balance sheet should reflect the company's typical financial position throughout the year. The balance sheet is a snapshot of the business at a single moment in time. Surveys of UK Reporting disclose insignificant disclosure of such transactions, and SSAP 17 has been criticised in that its depiction of window dressing transactions is inadequate.

Accounting for contingencies

A contingency is defined in SSAP 18 as:

> a condition which exists at the balance sheet date, where the outcome will be confirmed only on the occurrence or non-occurrence of one or more uncertain future events. A contingent gain or loss is a gain or loss dependent on a contingency.

The treatment of a contingency existing at the balance sheet date is determined by its expected outcome. Thus, contingent losses should be accrued in financial statements where it is probable that a future event will confirm a loss that can be estimated with reasonable accuracy at the date the financial statements are approved by the directors. As to contingent gains:

▶ existing conventions preclude such gains from being accrued in financial statements
▶ contingent gains should be disclosed if it is probable that they will be realised
▶ where realisation is virtually certain, the gain is no longer a contingency and accrual is appropriate.

Material contingencies that are not accounted for should be disclosed to ensure that the financial statements do not present a misleading position. Such disclosure should indicate:

▶ the nature of the contingency
▶ the uncertainties that are expected to affect the ultimate outcome
▶ a prudent estimate of the financial effect or a statement that it is not practicable to make such an estimate.

A contingency may be reduced or avoided because it is matched by a related counter-claim or claim by or against a third party. In such cases any accrual, or the amount to be disclosed in financial statements by way of notes, should be reduced by taking into account the probable outcome of the claim. However, the likelihood of success, and the probable amounts of the claim and the counter-claim, should be separately assessed, and separately disclosed where appropriate.

In disclosing the financial effect of a contingency, the amount should be stated before taking account of taxation, and the taxation implications of a contingency crystallising should be explained where necessary for a proper understanding of the financial position.

There are some contingencies where the possibility of the ultimate outcome having a material effect on the financial statements is so remote that disclosure could be misleading. SSAP 18 does not require disclosure of remote contingencies.

Accounting for contingencies may therefore be summarised as in Table 9.2.

Table 9.2 Accounting for contingencies

	Contingent gain	**Contingent loss**
Remote	No disclosure	No disclosure
Possible/Probable	No disclosure	Disclose
Highly probable	Disclose	Provide for
Virtually certain	Accrue for	Provide for

The application of the requirements of SSAPs 17 and 18

The application of SSAPs 17 and 18 requirements are illustrated by Example 9.1

EXAMPLE 9.1

The draft accounts of Wicket plc, for the year ended 31 July 1994 show a pre-tax profit of £965,000. The directors of the company have brought the following matters to your attention for consideration:

1   An export contract, commenced in May 1993 to construct a soya bean crushing plant for an emergent nation, has run into difficulties. Originally due to be completed in July 1994 it is now clear that the project will not be completed until 1995. The costs to 31 July 1994, which have all been provided for, exceed the agreed contract price.

2   A claim for £150,000 with interest by the company against a major supplier of cattlefeed, in respect of which the company had commenced legal action in 1990, had been countered with a claim of a similar amount. At 31 July 1994, the company's solicitors believed that the claim, despite the counter-claim, would be settled in full together with interest of £70,000 and that costs would amount to £30,000. On that basis the directors had brought the amount of the claim and interest into the accounts. In October 1994, following a surprise ruling in a similar case, the solicitors have now indicated their concern and have expressed doubts on the outcome of the case.

3   Stock valued at £180,000 at 31 July 1994 held in a warehouse was totally destroyed in a fire on 13 September 1994. The stock was underinsured by 25%.

4   A commodity broker who owed £34,500 to the company at 31 July 1994 went into liquidation on 7 October 1994. The statement of affairs indicated an eventual distribution to the unsecured creditors of 10p in the £1.

5   The directors have carried forward at 31 July 1994 development expenditure amounting to £102,000 incurred in the development of a new pesticide.

6   Motor vehicles with a book value of £15,500 at 31 July 1994 were sold in September 1994 for £9,000. The company's accounting policy on depreciation of such assets is to provide 20% per annum on the net book value.

An explanation of how the matters above should be dealt with in the financial statements of Wicket plc for the year ended 31 July 1994 follows.

1 Export contract

The contract, extending as it does over a duration of more than one year, is a long-term contract as defined in SSAP 9.

In accordance with the accounting standard, any foreseeable losses should be provided for, in full and immediately, so that the value of the contract in current assets in the balance sheet is carried at the lower of purchase price and production cost or net realisable value. Given that the costs to the balance sheet date have been provided for in full, a further provision is necessary for the costs that are yet to be incurred on the contract from the balance sheet date to the anticipated date of completion in 1995.

The total amount provided for foreseeable losses should be included under either work in progress or separately under Provisions and other charges in the balance sheet at 31 July 1994, and described as provision for a loss-making contract.

The company, under SSAP 9 (revised), should recognise as turnover for the period, the value of work completed in the period and as cost of sales a transfer of costs from the contract account and any further amounts to be provided for the foreseeable loss.

Material write downs should be disclosed separately as exceptional items.

2 Claim for £150,000 with interest by the company

At 31 July 1994 the balance sheet date, the claim is a contingent gain and, presumably on the basis of certainty of crystallisation, has been brought into the accounts as a receivable, together with interest of £70,000.

Given the concern and change of view of the company's solicitors since the balance sheet date and the uncertainty as to the outcome of the case, the company now faces both a contingent gain where crystallisation is not as certain as before, and a contingent loss.

Following a ruling in a similar case, it would no longer be appropriate for the company to recognise the contingent gain as an asset in the accounts at 31 July 1994. Further, consideration needs to be given to the contingent loss that may now arise and as to whether or not provision should be made for the loss in the accounts at 31 July 1994.

Given the doubts expressed by the company's solicitors the company should:

▶ not recognise the contingent gain
▶ not provide for the contingent loss
▶ provide for the costs of £30,000
▶ disclose in the note to the balance sheet dealing with contingencies the fact of the claim and the uncertainties involved as to its outcome.

This would satisfy the requirements of the Accounting Standard on contingencies, SSAP 18.

3 Stock destroyed by fire

The destruction of the stock by fire is a post balance sheet event that does not provide additional evidence of conditions existing at the balance sheet date. It is, therefore, a non-adjusting post balance sheet event. However the notes to the accounts at 31 July 1994 should disclose the fact of the fire after the balance sheet date, the total destruction of stock valued at £180,000 and the fact that, the stock was underinsured by 25%.

4 Liquidation of commodity broker

An adjusting post balance sheet event is justified in terms of the event providing additional evidence relating to conditions existing at the balance sheet date. The renegotiation of amounts owing by debtors or the insolvency of a debtor is cited in the appendix to SSAP 17, the Accounting Standard on post balance sheet events, as an example of an adjusting event.

The company should:

▶ ascertain whether any of the £34,500 has been paid by the debtor before the debtor went into liquidation on 7 October 1994 and

▶ write down the debtor of £34,500, less any amount received prior to 7 October 1994 as a specific bad debt written off. (It is prudent to provide for the whole of the amount.)

5 Carry forward of development expenditure

The Companies Act 1985 permits a company to carry forward development costs if there are 'special circumstances' justifying capitalisation and to include the costs as intangible fixed assets in the balance sheet of a company.

Give that expenditure on such development is normally undertaken with a reasonable expectation of specific commercial success and of future benefits arising from the work, it may be argued that such expenditure should be deferred to be matched against future revenues.

In the case of Wicket plc, clearly there is a defined project on which the related expenditure is separately identifiable. Before, however, carrying forward the expenditure, the company should, in accordance with the Accounting Standard on accounting for research and development, SSAP 13 (Revised):

▶ examine the technical feasibility of the project
▶ examine its ultimate viability
▶ assess whether further costs to be incurred, together with related production, selling and administration costs, will be more than covered by related future revenues
▶ examine whether resources will be available to complete the project and to provide any consequential increases in working capital.

Where the expenditure to date is judged on a prudent view of available evidence to satisfy these criteria, the costs may be carried forward, as intangible fixed assets, and subsequently amortised over the period expected to benefit.

6 Sale of motor vehicle after the balance sheet date

The asset is sold after the balance sheet date and will give rise to a loss of £6,500. The loss will arise given under depreciation of the asset in all periods up to the date of the sale. The revised Accounting Standard on depreciation, SSAP 12, requires regular review of asset lives and the adequacy of depreciation provided in order that the cost or value of the asset is fairly allocated to each period that benefits from the use of the asset.

The following is relevant in determining whether or not adjustment should be made to the asset's value at the balance sheet date:

▶ the loss arising is not material in the context of the profits of the company
▶ the appendix to SSAP 17 cites the post balance sheet event of sales of fixed asset as, normally, non-adjusting events.

The issue, however, is the recoverable amount of the asset at the balance sheet date, and as this is less than the carrying value, the asset should be written down accordingly.

The 'off balance sheet' problem and FRS 5

The financial press regularly pronounces that there is no substitute for facts and figures and that no amount of additional disclosure can make up for inappropriate accounting. This is especially so in the case of off balance sheet finance, which is more than just another accounting treatment problem in that it casts doubt on the very purpose of preparing accounts, that is, communicating a company's position and results to others. Thus ED 42 on accounting for special-purpose transactions states that:

Financial statements are intended to assist the user's understanding of an enterprise's affairs by presenting condensed, structured information on the resources, obligations and performance of the reporting enterprise. Such a presentation is useful only if the underlying classification and analysis are based on the substance of transactions and arrangements.

What is this 'substance' and why should it take precedence over 'form'?

IAS 1 states quite categorically that transactions and other events should be accounted for and presented in accordance with their substance and financial reality and not merely with their legal form. The Corporate Report (1975), was also quite clear on this point: 'corporate reports . . . should give recognition to economic substance in preference to legal and technical form.' In the USA, APB Statement 4 (1970) provided that:

> Financial accounting emphasises the economic substance of events even though the legal form may differ from the economic substance and suggest different treatment. Usually the economic substance of events to be accounted for agrees with legal form. Sometimes, however, substance and form differ. Accountants emphasise the substance of events rather than their form so that the information provided better reflects the economic activities represented.

This part of this chapter will look at transactions where the economic effect is different from the legal effect and examine the issues involved in the presentation of a true and fair view when we report such transactions in accounts.

Some preliminary points

TR 603, which was mentioned above, defines off balance sheet finance as 'the funding or refinancing of a company's operations in such a way that, under legal requirements and existing accounting conventions, some or all of the finance may not be shown on its balance sheet'.

Where transactions give rise to off balance sheet finance it usually follows that assets as well as liabilities are off the company's balance sheet, and there is also likely to be an impact on the company's profit and loss account.

Why is off balance sheet finance entered into?

Chapter 13 of *UK GAAP* (Ernst & Young, 1992) explains the arguments for using off balance sheet transactions as including:

▶ to maintain what has been, historically, a low level of gearing in the UK
▶ high levels of gearing are interpreted by the stock market as indicating that a rights issue is imminent with an adverse effect on share price
▶ while assets are being developed with no current income being generated, and on the basis that the market takes a short-term view of results, companies match borrowings relating to the assets being developed with the assets themselves and effectively remove both from the balance sheet
▶ some areas of the activities of diverse groups, such as leasing and financial services, may have high gearing ratios and, for some of the reasons above, placed off balance sheet.

Why is off balance sheet financing an issue?

As a result of the removal of both assets and liabilities from the balance sheet, users cannot fully appreciate the economic effects of transactions entered into by companies and disclosure, under current Accounting Standards and company law, is not always forthcoming. The practice of off balance sheet finance can be described as the secret tendency of business and is not easy to chronicle given the purpose of secrecy, and it would hardly be surprising if only a few instances come into the public arena.

The application of the previously mentioned principle of substance over form should, in principle, be sufficient to reverse most of the problems arising from the practice of removing or not recognising items as assets and liabilities in a balance sheet. This follows from the requirement that accounts give a true and fair view. If there is no Accounting Standard to date it is because there is as yet no consensus as to:

▶ the limit to which the principle of substance over form should be applied
▶ the detailed guidance necessary to ensure consistency of treatment between companies

and there has been a lingering reluctance to apply the principle since the 1981 DTI report on Argyll Foods which stated that 'any emphasis on substance over form must not be at the expense of compliance with the law'.

However, the fact that users of accounts may be unable to judge the impact of transactions from the disclosures that are currently made in accounts forces an accounting solution. Adverse press comment has made this solution urgent. The *Guardian* on 22 December 1987 described off balance sheet financing as 'the creative accounting trick which improves companies' balance sheets'. An Accounting Standard, six years on, has not yet been issued.

Current requirements – FRS 5

The introduction to FRS 5 states that its objective is to ensure that the substance of an entity's transactions is reported in its financial statements. Financial statements should represent faithfully the commercial effect of the transactions they purport to represent. The Standard is long, as it gives a lengthy explanation of the application of its principles, together with detailed application notes. However, the text of the proposed Standard itself is relatively brief. Before addressing the matter of the application of the principles to selected transactions such as leasing, quasi subsidiaries, consignment stock, sale and repurchase agreements, factoring, securitised assets and loan transfers, let us look at the key definitions involved and at the issues that need to be addressed in ensuring that financial statements reflect the substance of transactions.

Definitions

The following are some of the definitions included in FRS 5:

Assets Rights or other access to future economic benefits controlled by an entity as a result of past transactions or events.

Control in the context of an asset The ability to obtain future economic benefits relating to an asset and to restrict the access of others to those benefits.

Liabilities An entity's obligations to transfer economic benefits as a result of past transactions or events.

Risk Uncertainty as to the amount of benefits. The term includes both potential for gain and exposure to loss.

Recognition The process of incorporating an item into the primary financial statements within the appropriate heading. It involves depiction of the item in words and by a monetary amount and the inclusion of that amount in the statement totals.

Quasi subsidiary A quasi subsidiary of a reporting entity is a company, trust, partnership or other vehicle which, though not fulfilling the definition of a subsidiary, is directly or indirectly controlled by the reporting entity and gives rise to benefits for that entity that are in substance no different from those that would arise were the vehicle a subsidiary.

Control of another entity The ability to direct the financial and operating policies of that entity with a view to gaining economic benefit from its activities.

Subsidiary A subsidiary undertaking as defined by the companies legislation.

Reflecting the substance of transactions

Assets and liabilities have been defined above (and also in Chapter 1 where we looked at Chapter 3 and Chapter 4 of the ASB's Statement of Principles as to the elements of financial statements and the recognition of items in financial statements). To ensure that financial statements reflect the substance of the transactions that are undertaken by an entity we need to consider the question of how to determine the substance of a transaction, the issues involved in the recognition of assets and liabilities and the issue of the disclosures that should be made.

How do we determine the substance of a transaction?
One of the problems that arise when assessing the substance of a transaction is the number of options that it may involve. The Standard requires:

▶ to determine the substance of transaction it is necessary to identify whether or not it has

  – given rise to new assets or liabilities
  – increased or decreased its existing assets or liabilities

▶ assets arise where an entity has rights to benefits and this is evidenced when it bears the risks inherent in the benefits and an entity has a liability if there is some circumstance where it is unable to avoid an outflow of benefits
▶ if a transaction involves options:

  – if there is no commercial possibility that the option will be exercised, the existence of the option should be ignored
  – if there is no commercial possibility that an option will fail to be exercised, its exercise should be assumed.

Principles underlying the recognition of assets and liabilities
These are dealt with in the ASB's Statements of Principles and, in this context, where transactions have resulted in items that meet the definition of an asset or a liability it should be recognised if:

▶ there is sufficient evidence of the existence of the item and
▶ the item can be measured at a monetary amount with sufficient reliability.

Where transactions involve the transfer of an asset it should cease to be recognised only if:

▶ no significant rights or other access to material economic benefits relating to the asset are retained and
▶ any risk retained relating to the asset is immaterial in relation to the variation in benefits likely to occur in practice.

Disclosure issues
Where the principle of substance over form is applied it is appropriate that there be

separate disclosure. Thus, where goods are held with a 'subject to reservation of title' clause, there will be a need to disclose the amount of the secured liability.

Particular disclosure problems arise where the results of transactions giving rise to assets and liabilities need to be considered together, that is, where the assets and liabilities are commercially linked for example where a transaction involving an item previously recognised as an asset is in substance a financing arrangement. There are three possibilities:

▶ Show the assets and liabilities gross in the normal way.
▶ Adopt offset or netting off. To adopt this approach the entity must have the right to insist on a net settlement and, under FRED 4:

  – the two items must be of the same kind and
  – changes in the amount of benefit flowing from one will be mirrored by the changes in the amount of benefits flowing from the other.

▶ Adopt what is referred to as linked presentation, which is a new form of disclosure permitted by FRS 5. Under this the gross amount of the asset is included and the gross amount of the liability deducted from this amount. Even though the end result is the same as under netting off above, linked presentation results in the gross amount of the asset and the liability being shown on the face of the balance sheet.

Examples of off balance sheet finance

Leasing

Accounting for lease transactions is dealt with in Chapter 10. In spite of the introduction of SSAP 21, that has been the one attempt so far to standardise the principle of substance over form, leasing can still provide a means by which companies can leave what is effectively debt off their balance sheets. As Chapter 10 will explain in some detail, leases fall to be classified as either finance or operating. Finance leases are leases where the risks and rewards of ownership, though not legal ownership, are passed to the lessee. In such situations, adopting substance over form, SSAP 21 would require the lessee company to capitalise the asset and the lessor company to recognise an asset consisting of a debtor in respect of amounts receivable from the lessee company in respect of finance lease obligations.

Under the lease classification criteria of SSAP 21, the risks and rewards of ownership are assumed to be passed to the lessee when the present value of the minimum lease payments amounts to substantially all – normally 90% or more – of the fair value of the leased asset.

A problem has arisen, in practice, in this area given that the 90% test above, even if this was not the original intention, has come to be interpreted as a hard and fast rule; the form, if you like, of the Standard. If the rule is so interpreted there is scope for setting up schemes where risks and rewards of ownership do pass to the lessee company but the amount of the discounted lease payments falls below 90%, resulting in the lease being classified as an operating lease. Such leases are not recognised as assets in the accounts of a lessee company. Such lessee companies would also not recognise the corresponding lease liability in its accounts. Such artificial schemes should be subject to the principle of substance over form and, if the spirit of SSAP 21 were to be applied, such leases should be treated as finance and not operating leases. The ASB is likely to alter the current provisions of SSAP 21 in this regard.

Until such alteration is made, note the points made here when you come to a more detailed appreciation of accounting for leases in the next chapter.

Quasi subsidiaries

Controlled non-subsidiaries, as used commonly to arise prior to the changes in the Companies Act definitions of a subsidiary, are dealt with in more detail in Chapter 15. Such entities or vehicles were set up for the principal reason of removing financing from a balance sheet and, thereby, improving gearing ratios. Picture the following scenario before the current definitions of a subsidiary became a feature of UK company law:

▶ A company requires finance and has recourse to finance.
▶ The company does not wish to increase the gearing disclosed in its balance sheet.
▶ It sets up what may be termed a special-purpose vehicle in such a way that it is not legally a subsidiary but is effectively controlled so that it will fall to be treated as an associate.
▶ The company would now raise the debt and transfer both the cash obtained and the loan obligation to the special-purpose vehicle.
▶ Assets and liabilities controlled by the company would be off its balance sheet and, if group accounts were prepared, off its consolidated balance sheet.
▶ This is because associates, in consolidated accounts, are not consolidated but included as a single net figure amounting to the investors's share of its net assets which, in this case, would be immaterial.

Following the current legal definitions of subsidiary, based more on the concept of control as opposed to the fact of ownership, it is more difficult for off balance sheet finance to arise in this way. Special-purpose vehicles such as those above would now fall to be treated as subsidiaries and would have to be consolidated with the effect that assets and liabilities of the subsidiary would come *on* to the consolidated balance sheet. However, there remain ways in which non-subsidiaries can be used to facilitate off balance finance even though such situations involve a genuine sharing of control and influence. In such situations, where there is the involvement of a genuine third party in the control and ownership structure, it is only fair that this be taken into consideration when determining the accounting treatment.

FRS 5 seeks to make certain that, even if a complicated control and ownership situation is created in such a way as to avoid consolidation under the existing rules, it will not succeed. Regarding quasi subsidiaries, defined above, FRS 5 would require that:

> ... the assets, liabilities, profits, losses and cash flows of a quasi subsidiary should be included in the group accounts of the group that controls it in the same way as if they were those of a subsidiary. Where an entity has a quasi subsidiary but no subsidiaries and therefore does not prepare group accounts it should provide in its financial statements consolidated accounts of itself and the quasi subsidiary...

Consignment stocks

There is, as yet, no mandatory treatment for accounting for consignment stocks. The current accepted treatment is that they are the stock of a supplier until an event makes them the stock of the customer. Goods are considered held on consignment if:

▶ the customer has the right to return the stock to the supplier
▶ the customer does not pay for the goods until they are sold to a third party
▶ HM Customs & Excise accepts that no sale has taken place by not requiring VAT to be paid until some further event such as sale to the ultimate customer has taken place.

The ASB has addressed the problem of accounting for such stocks in the application notes to FRS 5, taking the example of a motor manufacturer and dealer. The main features of a consignment stock arrangement could be as shown in Figure 9.1.

Manufacturer		Dealer

Supply of goods

———————————————————————————➔

▶ Title does not pass on date of transfer but:

either at the expiry of an agreed period of time

or on sale to a third party

or the adoption of the goods in some other form.

▶ Until title passes the dealer can return the goods to the manufacturer or the manfacturer can ask the dealer to return the goods.

▶ The price to be paid by the dealer can be fixed:

either at the date of supply

or at the list price of the date title passes

or by reference to the period of time for which the stock has been paid.

▶ The dealer may need to pay a financing charge or place a deposit with the manufacturer.

Figure 9.1 Consignment stock arrangement

FRS 5 analyses four factors that should be used in determining which party should treat the stock as an asset, as detailed below.

Manufacturer's right of return

The relevant question here is not whether the manufacturer *can* require the return of the goods but whether it is likely that the manfucturer *will* require the return of the goods.

You should consider as evidence the previous record in this area. If there has been a high rate of return at the request of the manufacturer the dealer should not treat the goods as stock. If the rate of return has been low it is appropriate that the stock be dealt with in the accounts of the dealer.

Another consideration is to look to financial arrangements connected with the right of return. If the dealer is provided with compensation when the right to return is exercised, this suggests that the dealer is the effective owner of the stock. Where no compensation is provided it is appropriate that the stock be reported by the manufacturer rather than the dealer.

Dealer's right of return

The main source of evidence will be, again, the past record. Where the dealer has a right to return you should look at the risks associated with the stock; that is, the risk of obsolescence and the risk that the goods will be unsold. Accordingly, the stock should attach to the manufacturer if:

▶ the right of return is regularly exercised by the dealer
▶ there is a high likelihood that the right of return, even if not usually exercised, will be exercised for the goods in question
▶ the manufacturer provides a financial incentive to the dealer to deter the dealer from returning the goods.

The stock should attach to the dealer if:

▶ there is no right of the dealer to return the stock
▶ there have been few returns in the past
▶ the dealer suffers a material penalty if stock is returned.

Stock transfer price and deposits

The transfer price will affect whether or not the dealer is protected from changes in price and which party bears the risk of slow-moving stock.

Where the price is based on the manufacturer's list price at delivery the manufacturer will have lost control over pricing at delivery and the stock becomes an asset of the dealer at that date.

Where the price charged to the dealer is the list price at the date of the transfer of legal title, this indicates that the stock remains an asset of the manufacturer until legal title is transferred.

As to slow-moving stock, in a simple arrangement, where there is no deposit and stock is supplied at a fixed price payable only when legal title is transferred, the manufacturer bears the risk of slow-moving stock. If, however, the price to be paid by the dealer increases with the time the stock is held, approximating to current interest rates, it is the dealer that bears the risk of slow-moving stock.

Dealer's right to use the stock

This is not likely to be a major factor in determining whether the manufacturer or dealer should treat the stock as an asset. If, however, the dealer exercises this right it will probably cause the legal title to be transferred and should be treated as an acquisition of stock by the dealer.

Sale and repurchase agreements

This is a simple way of eliminating debt from the balance sheet:

– sell the asset
– apply proceeds to reduce borrowings
– the premium payable on repurchase of the asset will not be recorded as interest but will be absorbed into cost of sales when the asset is repurchased.

FRS 5 identifies three situations where both the assets and the liabilities should remain *on* the balance sheet:

▶ where the sale is quite clearly a financing and not a trading transaction
▶ where there is an option as opposed to a requirement to repurchase, but only if:

– the option to repurchase is virtually certain to be exercised
– the seller is given an option to purchase (call option) and the buyer is given an option to sell (put option) so that one of the parties to the transaction is virtually certain to exercise its rights under the option
– wherever the repurchase price is linked to the original sale price and not the market value of the time of repurchase, suggesting that the transaction is for financing as opposed to trading purposes.

▶ more complex considerations arise where there is only one option, to buy or to sell, and the price is not linked to the current market value:

– Situation 1 – The buyer has the option to sell, the seller loses the benefits of ownership but retains the risks of ownership as the sale will take place, that is the buyer will exercise its option, only when the current market value is below the original price. If the possibility of a fall in value is remote it is unlikely that the option will be exercised, the transaction is effectively a genuine sale and the profit on sale should be recognised by the seller. If the value is expected to be volatile, the option may be exercised and the seller should not record the sale or profit on sale as the transaction may have to be reversed.

    – Situation 2 – The seller has the option to repurchase the asset. In this situation the risks of ownership disappear while the rewards are retained as the seller will exercise its option only if the market value of the asset increases over its original price.

Thus, under FRS 5 the accounting treatment of sale and repurchase transactions could be:

▶ *either* a secured loan by showing the asset and the liability in the balance sheet
▶ *or* a sale recorded in the usual way
▶ *or* as a transaction that has changed the asset owned by the seller, in which case the new asset should be recorded at its fair value, together with any new liability arising.

Factoring

The factoring of debts is a well-established method of obtaining finance. There are different outcomes and, therefore, different proposed accounting treatments:

▶ If, even after the debts have been factored, the seller retains risks and rewards, both the debts and the proceeds received from the factor are shown on the balance sheet, the latter as an obligation.
▶ If the seller no longer retains risks and rewards associated with the debts it would be appropriate to derecognise the debts and not to show any liability for the sale proceeds received from the factor.
▶ If the seller retains risks and rewards associated with the debts but the exposure is limited to a fixed monetary amount, a linked presentation, as described above, should be made.

Securitised assets

This is best illustrated with the securitisation of mortgages, where one company sells a portfolio of mortgages to another company and where the buying company finances the purchase by issuing debt securities. The rate of interest on these debt securities will usually be linked to the rate of interest on the mortgages. Under FRS 5, such transactions can be illustrated as in Figure 9.2.

    This gives rise to two questions when applying relevant principles to determine the accounting treatment of such transactions:

▶ Does the originator have access to the benefits of the securitised assets and exposure to their inherent risks?
▶ Does the originator have a liability to repay the proceeds of the loan notes?

Derecognition of the assets in the books of the originator is appropriate only if:

▶ the transaction takes place at arm's length price for an outright sale and
▶ the transaction is for a fixed amount of consideration and there is no implicit or explicit recourse to the originator and
▶ the originator will not benefit or suffer if the securitised assets perform better or worse than expected, and this will not be the case where the originator has a right to further sums from the issuer, which vary according to the eventual value received for the securitised assets.

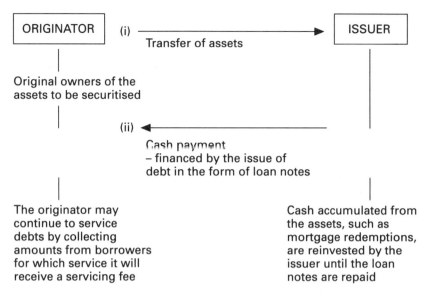

Figure 9.2 Debt securities

If it is not appropriate to derecognise you will have to consider whether the appropriate accounting treatment is separate presentation or linked presentation.

Loan transfers

These situations may be illustrated as in Figure 9.3.

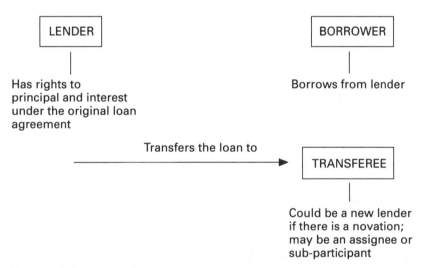

Figure 9.3 Loan transfers

Loan transfers may take place in one of three ways, as outlined below.

Assignment
This is where the rights to principal and interest are transferred to a third party, the assignee. Under a statutory assignment, notice in writing must be given to the borrower and the whole of the loan must be transferred. Under an equitable assignment no notice is required to be given and a part of the loan may be transferred.

Novation
This is where the rights and obligations under the loan agreement are cancelled and replaced by new ones, whose principal effect is to change the identity of the lender.

Sub-participation

This is where there is no legal transfer of the loan but the lender enters into a non-recourse back-to-back agreement with a third party, the sub-participant, under which the third party deposits with the lender an amount equal to the whole or part of the loan and, in return, receives from the lender a share of the cash flows arising on the loan.

The principles that apply for accounting purposes under FRS 5 are similar to those outlined above in respect of securitised mortgages.

Is FRS 5 the solution to the off balance sheet financing problem?

As FRS 5 deals with the issues raised by the practice of off balance sheet financing it raises fundamental accounting questions as to the nature of assets and liabilities and when these should be recognised in the balance sheet. Much of the Standard, apart from the proposals as to linked presentation and offset, follows the proposals of ED 49, which preceded it. The basic requirement is that the substance of an entity's transactions is reported in its financial statements and the Standard sets out general principles that are relevant to all types of transactions. Although this approach has the disadvantage of appearing abstract it has two considerable advantages in that:

▶ the principles can be applied to new types of transaction as they develop and
▶ the result will be that consistent principles will be applied over different types of transaction

and the Standard does contain detailed application notes illustrating the application of its principles to five different transaction types which, together with leasing and quasi subsidiaries are dealt with above. The Standard provides a link with the ASB's Statement of Principles in that it uses the definitions of the latter in respect of assets and liabilities and also its general recognition criteria.

The essential issue in accounting for off balance sheet finance is to determine, in terms of substance rather than form, whether an asset has been sold or the transaction is effectively one of raising finance secured perhaps on a specific asset. The Standard argues that assets should be derecognised or a sale recognised only where an entity no longer retains significant access to material benefits and where any risks it retains are immaterial. Further, the Standard deals with the issue of the quasi subsidiary and that of the disclosure of this and other transactions that used to be referred to as special-purpose transactions.

Some audit implications

The audit implications of off balance sheet finance can be summarised in terms of the impact of such omissions on the true and fair view. Practical approaches to recognition and disclosure of items have been dealt with above.

This chapter also deals with contingencies and the audit of contingencies creates special problems for auditors.

A summary of the requirements of FRS 5

The new reporting standard on off balance sheet finance, FRS 5, requires that:
▶ A reporting entity's financial statements should report the substance of the transactions into which it has entered.
▶ In determining the substance of a transaction, all its aspects and implications should be identified and greater weight given to those more likely to have a commercial effect in practice.

- ▶ Where the entity has a quasi-subsidiary, the substance of the transactions entered into by the quasi-subsidiary should be reported in consolidated financial statements.
- ▶ The standard sets out
  - how to determine the substance of a transaction;
  - whether any resulting assets and liabilities should be included in the balance sheet;
  - what disclosures are appropriate.
- ▶ Transactions requiring careful analysis will often include features such as
  - the party that gains the principal benefits generated by an item is not the legal owner of the item;
  - a transaction is linked with others in such a way that the commercial effect can be understood only by considering the series as a whole;
  - an option is included on terms that make its exercise highly likely.
- ▶ Application Notes describe the application of the reporting standard to
  - consignment stock
  - sale and repurchase agreements
  - factoring
  - securitised assets
  - loan transfers.
- ▶ Linked presentation should be used where, although the entity has significant rights to benefits and exposure to risks relating to a specific item, the item is financed in such a way that the maximum loss the entity can suffer is limited to a fixed monetary amount.
- ▶ A linked presentation shows, on the face of the balance sheet, the finance deducted from the gross amount of the item it finances.

FRS 4 and accounting for capital instruments

The development of an FRS on accounting for capital instruments followed the increasing number and variety of capital instruments that have been introduced in recent years and the different accounting treatments adopted by companies in respect of different capital instruments. The fundamental issues that needed to be addressed were:

- ▶ the criteria to be used to determine whether a capital instrument represents debt or equity, and
- ▶ the treatment of instruments such as convertible debt that may be exchanged for other instruments.

The criteria used in the FRS to determine whether a capital instrument represents a liability is whether it contains an obligation to transfer economic benefits. The FRS requires convertible debt to be reported within liabilities irrespective of the probability of future conversion.

The main requirements of the Standard

The objective of the Standard is to ensure that financial statements disclose all capital instruments issued to raise capital for a business in a clear and consistent manner, particularly as regards the classification between Debt, Non-equity shares and Equity shares. Where instruments are redeemable, that is Debt and redeemable shares, the total associated costs should be allocated to accounting periods on a fair basis which will require allocation at a constant rate over the term of the instrument. The requirements of the reporting standard include:

- ▶ If capital instruments include an obligation to transfer cash or other resources they are to be classified as liabilities.
- ▶ Convertible debt should be included in liabilities and separately disclosed. Conversion should not be anticipated. Where there is an option to redeem at a premium, the premium should be accrued over the period to the earliest date at which the option can be exercised. If and when the debt is converted no gain or loss should be recognised on conversion. The 'proceeds' for the shares issued on conversion are to be taken as the carrying amount of the convertible debt in liabilities on the date of the conversion. The proceeds will be allocated to nominal value and premium on issue in respect of the shares issued on conversion.
- ▶ Liabilities should be classified as current or non-current according to their strict contractual maturity, except where the lender is committed to refinancing the debt on the same terms.
- ▶ Liabilities should initially be recognised in the balance sheet at the amount received less any issue costs. The finance cost, made up of interest cost on dividend plus any premium payable on redemption, should be allocated to accounting periods to achieve a constant rate on the amount outstanding.
- ▶ Shareholders' funds should be analysed between amounts attributable to equity interests and non-equity interests.
- ▶ Shares should be regarded as non-equity if they have a restricted right to dividends or are redeemable.
- ▶ The amount attributed to non-equity interests should reflect the full consideration received together with any accrued premium for redemption.
- ▶ Minority interests in subsidiaries should be analysed between equity and non-equity interests.
- ▶ Gains or losses arising on the repurchase or early settlement of debt should be recognised in the profit and loss account in the period in which the repurchase or early settlement is made.
- ▶ An analysis of the maturity of debt should be presented showing amounts falling due
  - in one year or less, or on demand;
  - between one and two years;
  - between two and five years; and
  - in five years or more.
- ▶ The net proceeds from the issue of equity shares and warrants for equity shares should be credited direct to shareholders' funds. As to warrants:
  - if exercised, the amount previously recognised in respect of warrants should be included in the net proceeds of the shares issued; and
  - if they lapse unexercised, the amount previously recognised in respect of the warrants should be reported in the statement of total recognised gains and losses. Such amounts would be transferred to reserves.
- ▶ The accounting treatment for non-equity shares is the same as the treatment for debt. The company will initially record non-equity shares at the net issue proceeds and the finance costs are calculated to give a constant payment rate over the term of the shares. It is possible for the finance costs to exceed the dividend paid, in which case the difference is treated as an appropriation of profits.

Accounting for debt

To comply with the requirements of the reporting standard in this respect there are three points of procedure.

- ▶ On issue, the liability should be recorded at the net amount received after deduction of issue costs. These costs are those that are incurred directly in connection with the issue of a capital instrument and would not have been incurred had the specific instrument not been issued.

DR	Cash	X
CR	Debt	X

with the net proceeds of issue.

▶ Finance costs should be recognised over the term of the debt at a constant rate on the carrying amount. These costs should be charged in the profit and loss account. They are defined as the total amount of the payments that the issue is required to make in respect of the instrument less the net proceeds of the investment. The carrying amount of the debt should be increased by the finance cost in respect of the reporting period by

DR	Profit and loss account	X
CR	Debt	X

with the finance cost allocated to the period.

▶ Payments made in respect of the debt in each period, whether in respect of finance cost or redemption of the debt, should reduce the carrying amount of the debt by

DR	Debt	X
CR	Cash	X

with payments made in the period.

EXAMPLE 9.2

A company issues £1,000 of 10 per cent loan stock on 1 January 1995. Issue costs are £10 and the loan stock is repayable after five years at a premium of 2 per cent. The constant rate at which finance costs are allocated to periods over the term of the debt is given to you as 10.59 per cent. The loan stock would be recorded as follows:

10% Loan Stock

Cash – interest	100	1.1.1995 Cash (1,000–10)	990
(1,000 x 10%)		P/L account – interest	105
c/f 31.12 1995	995	(990 x 10.59%)	
		1.1.1996	995
Cash – interest	100	P/L account – interest	105
		(995 x 10.59%)	
c/f 31.12.1996	1,000		
		1.1.1997	1,000
Cash – interest	100	P/L account – interest	106
		(1,000 x 10.59%)	
c/f 31.12.1997	1,006		
Cash – interest	100	1.1.1998	1,006
		P/L account – interest	
c/f 31.12.1998	1,013	(1,006 x 10.59%)	107
		1.1.1999	1,013
Cash – interest	100	P/L account – interest	107
Cash – redemption	1,020	(1,113 x 10.59%)	
(1,000 x 1.02)			

Some further examples as illustrated in FRS 4

The example above showed the book keeping involved. The examples below, extracted from the standard, deal with different loans and recognition of finance costs thereon and their carrying values at the end of each period over the term of the loan.

Redeemable debt with enhanced interest

EXAMPLE 9.3

Redeemable debt is issued on 1 January 2000 for £1,000 and is redeemable at the same amount on 31 December 2014. It carries interest of £59 a year (a nominal rate of 5.9 per cent) for the first five years, after which the rate rises to £141 a year (a nominal rate of 14.1 per cent).

Finance costs should be allocated to accounting periods at the rate of 10 per cent a year. The movements on the carrying amount over the term of the debt would be as follows:

Year ending	Balance at beginning of year	Finance costs for year (10%)	Cash paid during year	Balance at end of year
	£	£	£	£
31.12.2000	1,000	100	(59)	1,041
31.12.2001	1,041	104	(59)	1,086
31.12.2002	1,086	109	(59)	1,136
31.12.2003	1,136	113	(59)	1,190
31.12.2004	1,190	119	(59)	1,250
31.12.2005	1,250	125	(141)	1,234
31.12.2006	1,234	124	(141)	1,217
31.12.2007	1,217	122	(141)	1,198
31.12.2008	1,198	120	(141)	1,177
31.12.2009	1,177	118	(141)	1,154
31.12.2010	1,154	116	(141)	1,129
31.12.2011	1,129	113	(141)	1,101
31.12.2012	1,101	110	(141)	1,070
31.12.2013	1,070	107	(141)	1,036
31.12.2014	1,036	105*	(141+1,000)	–

*rounded

Stepped interest bonds

EXAMPLE 9.4

A loan of £1,250 is entered on 1 January 2000 under which interest is payable according to the following schedule:

Year ending	Rate of interest (as a percentage of nominal amount)	Amount of interest £
31.12.2000	6.0	75
31.12.2001	8.0	100
31.12.2002	10.0	125
31.12.2003	12.0	150
31.12.2004	16.4	205

The overall effective rate is 10 per cent. The movements on the loan over its period in issue would be as follows:

Year ending	Balance at beginning of year	Finance costs for year (10%)	Cash Paid during year	Balance at end of year
	£	£	£	£
31.12.2000	1,250	125	(75)	1,300
31.12.2001	1,300	130	(100)	1,330
31.12.2002	1,330	133	(125)	1,338
31.12.2003	1,338	134	(150)	1,322
31.12.2004	1,322	133	(1,250+205)	–

Repackaged perpetual debt

EXAMPLE 9.5

On 1 January 2000 a company borrows £1,250 which is stated to be irredeemable and to carry interest of 16.275 per cent for the first ten years after which no further payments are required. The annual payments would be £203. The substance of the arrangement is that the ten payments of £203 would repay the amount borrowed and the finance charge is to be allocated using a rate of 10 per cent. The accounting would be as follows:

Year ending	Balance at beginning of year	Finance costs for year (10%)	Cash paid during year	Balance at end of year
	£	£	£	£
31.12.2000	1,250	125	(203)	1,172
31.12.2001	1,172	117	(203)	1,086
31.12.2002	1,086	108	(203)	991
31.12.2003	991	99	(203)	887
31.12.2004	887	88	(203)	772
31.12.2005	772	77	(203)	646
31.12.2006	646	64	(203)	507
31.12.2007	507	50	(203)	354
31.12.2008	354	35	(203)	186
31.12.2009	186	17*	(203)	–

*rounded

Debt issued with warrants

EXAMPLE 9.6

Debt and warrants are issued together for £1,250. The debt is redeemable at the same amount. The term of the debt is five years from 1 January 2000 and it carries interest at 4.7 per cent (£59 per year). It is determined that the fair value of the debt and the warrants are respectively £1,000 and £250.

The debt would initially be recognised at £1,000. The finance cost of the debt is the difference between the payments required by the debt which total £1,545 ((5 x £59) + (£1,250) and the deemed proceeds of £1,000, that is, £545. In order to allocate these costs over the term of the debt at a constant rate on the carrying amount (as required by paragraph 28 of the FRS) they are allocated at the rate of 10 per cent. The movements on the carrying amount of the debt over its term would be as follows:

Year ending	Balance at beginning of year	Finance costs for year (10%)	Cash paid during year	Balance at end of year
	£	£	£	£
31.12.2000	1,000	100	(59)	1,041
31.12.2001	1,041	104	(59)	1,086
31.12.2002	1,086	109	(59)	1,136
31.12.2003	1,136	113	(59)	1,190
31.12.2004	1,190	119	(1,250+59)	–

The recording of warrants has been dealt with above.

Index linked loans

EXAMPLE 9.7

A loan of £1,250 is issued on 1 January 2000 on which interest of 4 per cent (£50) is paid annually and the principal amount is repayable based on an index. The balance at the end of each year is found by multiplying the original principal amount by the index at the end of the year: the change in the amount is treated as additional finance costs. The index at 1 January 2000 is 100.

Year ending	Balance at beginning of year	Finance costs for year	Cash paid during year	Balance at end of year	Index at end of year
	£	£	£	£	£
31.12.2000	1,250	125	(50)	1,325	106
31.12.2001	1,325	100	(50)	1,375	110
31.12.2002	1,375	75	(50)	1,400	112
31.12.2003	1,400	150	(50)	1,500	120
31.12.2004	1,500	175	(1,625+50)	–	130

Note that, in this situation, the finance cost is not allocated at a constant rate but is determined, for each period, as a balancing amount. Thus, for 2003, the movement on the loan would be as follows:

4% Index linked loan

Cash – interest	50	b/f 1.1.2003	1,400
(4% x 1,250)		P/L account - interest	150
c/f 31.12 2003	1,500		(bal. item)
1,250 x 120/100			

Summary

This chapter progresses from the relative simplicities of accounting for post balance sheet events and contingencies under the relatively non-controversial SSAPs 17 and 18, to the complexities of the more profound FRS 5 based as it is on the ASB's conceptual framework as set out in its Statement of Principles.

The content and requirements of SSAPs 17 and 18 are set out here to remind you of the points to consider when deciding whether to treat events as adjusting or non-adjusting and the disclosures that should be made. The major part of the chapter, however, deals with the impact of and the solution of FRS 5 as to accounting for off balance sheet financing in reporting the substance of transactions. Thus, we looked at the questions as to what substance is and why it should take precedence over form, the reasons why off balance sheet finance is entered into, the general principles of FRS 5 and its approach to:

▶ determining the substance of transactions and
▶ applying the principles that underlie the recognition of assets and liabilities and
▶ disclosure.

The last part of this section of the chapter gave examples of transactions that could give rise to off balance sheet finance and looked at the application of the principles of FRS 5 in accounting for the substance of these transactions.

Lastly, this chapter examined the requirements of FRS 4 on accounting for capital instruments and the presentation of debt and equity in financial statements.

Suggested reading

UK GAAP (Ernst & Young 1992)

Chapter 13 gives a full account of the problems and covers the ground pre-FRS 5.

Applying GAAP 1993/94 – A Practical Guide to Financial Reporting (Chapping and Skerratt 1993)

Chapter 23 gives a short but comprehensive review of the proposals of FRED 4.

Self test questions

1   Define:

   a)   an adjusting event
   b)   a contingency.

2   Provide a definition of off balance sheet finance.

3   Give four reasons why off balance sheet finance is entered into.

4   Define a quasi subsidiary; describe how it can give rise to off balance sheet finance and state what FRS 5 requires in this regard.

5   What are the three possible ways, under FRS 5, in which sale and repurchase transactions can be reflected in the accounts of an entity?

Exam style question

Key ratios and performance measures may be affected by omission of assets and liabilities or by treatment as an associate in the consolidated accounts of an investment that has all the qualities of a subsidiary.

Required:
Outline the effect of such omission on:

▶ return on capital employed
▶ gearing
▶ working capital
▶ profit before tax.

All answers on pages 649–650

Leasing

As leasing has grown in importance as a major source of finance for industry in the UK, the question of how to account for various types of lease has itself become important.

Where a company does finance a significant amount of its capital investment through leasing, its financial statements should properly reflect the full impact of its leasing transactions. Traditional accounting practice in the UK meant that such companies did not include the obligations they have under finance leases as obligations in the balance sheet. Such obligations, and indeed the leased assets, were 'off balance sheet'. This practice has meant that those companies that financed their capital investment through leasing showed healthier balance sheet gearing ratios than those of similar companies that financed their capital investment through other sources of finance. When leasing was a minor activity in the UK this inconsistency was not important. Today, however, leasing can and does have a material effect on the financial statements of many companies. This is the principal reason behind the requirement of the standard that a lessee capitalise finance leases. Without the requirement to capitalise, users, both external and the company's own management, may be misled.

External users are aided, when finance leases are capitalised, in the making of investment or credit decisions. Divisional managers are aided in being made aware of the choice of finance for the assets under their control.

It is relevant therefore that lease transactions be accounted for on the basis of their 'substance' rather than on their strict legal 'form'. This is the view of the USA standard, FAS 13, the international standard, IAS 17, and also SSAP 21.

The difference between hire purchase contracts, credit sale agreements and leasing

Hire purchase contracts

Under a hire purchase contract goods are supplied to customers on hire until, given the fulfilment of certain conditions (usually the payment of an agreed number of instalments) the customer becomes entitled to exercise an option to purchase the asset. Until such time as this option is exercised the goods remain the property of the supplier. As the supplier retains legal title, goods supplied can be repossessed in the event of any default under the terms of the contract.

In 1964, the ICAEW issued Accounting Principle N23, which recommended that a hire purchaser account for an asset purchased on hire-purchase terms as though the asset was owned immediately with a corresponding obligation to pay instalments under the contract. The vendor company was to account for the instalments not yet received as receivables, reduced by a provision for unearned profit.

The treatment for taxation purposes followed the treatment for accounting purposes in that it was the purchaser and not the vendor that would be entitled to capital allowances.

Credit sale agreements

Under a credit sale agreement, title passes on the date of the sale to the purchaser and a binding obligation is created for the payment of the instalments, which cannot be avoided by the return of the goods. In the event of any default there is no repossession of the goods; the appropriate remedy for the vendor is to sue for the amounts still outstanding. For taxation purposes the purchaser claims the capital allowances.

Leasing

Under leasing transactions, the goods remain the property of the supplier, to whom the goods are returned at the end of the agreement. The supplier may or may not undertake to maintain the goods in working order. The supplier company claims the capital allowances.

The reasons for the growth in leasing

The Equipment Leasing Association has produced statistics to show that the cost of assets its members acquired for leasing each year had increased from £288 million in 1973 to £2,984 million in 1983. The Bank of England's figures put at 12.2% the proportion of total new investment in plant, machinery and vehicles that was financed by leasing for the third quarter of 1983 for the manufacture, construction, distribution, road transport and finance industries in the UK. Some of the reasons for this growth are detailed below.

Tax advantages

In the UK the owner of the asset, the lessor, claims capital allowances on the cost of the asset. The user, the lessee, can claim only the rental expense against trading profit for tax purposes. Thus, potential purchasers of assets who have little or no taxable profits against which the benefits of capital allowances on assets purchased may be offset, may find it more beneficial to lease rather than to buy the asset. The lessor companies, obtaining as they do the benefit of the capital allowances on purchase and the cash flow advantage of a deferral of tax, are usually able to pass on some of this benefit to lessees in the form of lower rental charges.

Interest rates

High interest rates have the effect of increasing the cash flow benefit a lessor receives from deferring tax. To maintain margins when interest rates rise, the lessor needs to increase the lease rates by a smaller proportion than the increase in interest rates. For the lessee, lease rates can be relatively more attractive during periods of high interest rates.

A combination of high interest rates, high tax rates and high rates of first year allowances resulted in all the conditions for growth in the leasing industry in the mid 1970s and early 1980s.

Source of finance

Few other sources of finance provide the same facilities as leasing. Many lease agreements effectively represent medium-term fixed rate finance. The security the lessee gives is, effectively, the leased asset itself. In comparison, bank loans could tie up the borrower's property assets as security, impose restrictions on future borrowing requirements and expose the borrower to risk from future variations in interest rates.

The Financial Act 1984

The implications of the tax changes in the FA 1984 are that much of the tax deferral aspects of leasing will disappear and that differences between lease rates and borrowing rates may well be minimal. Many countries, however, have thriving leasing industries without the stimulus of tax deferral. There are few other sources of medium-term finance that provide the same facilities as leasing does and, given that there will always be a need for medium-term fixed rate finance, the leasing industry will survive even though it may have to compete more aggressively with alternative sources of finance.

Accounting practice prior to SSAP 21

Traditional accounting practice in the UK has been for companies to treat the rental payments they make as revenue expenditure. The Companies Acts required disclosure of any items, if material, charged to revenue for the hire of plant and machinery. Rentals payable under all forms of leasing were generally included in such disclosure, though rarely with any breakdown of the total charge. Importantly, there is no statutory requirement to disclose the amount of assets leased or the obligation for future rentals payable. (The 1985 Act does, however, require disclosure of those commitments that are likely to affect the future financial requirements of a company. One obvious example for such disclosure is leasing commitments.)

Thus, prior to the standard, the majority of lessees simply wrote off rentals payable against revenue, while lessors treated finance leases sometimes as fixed assets, sometimes as receivables, and adopted a variety of methods for recognising profit over the lease term.

The distinction between operating and finance leases

The accounting treatment adopted for a lease will depend on whether the lease is a finance lease or an operating lease. The first stage in lease accounting is therefore to classify leases between finance leases and operating leases.

The standard defines a finance lease as a lease that transfers to the lessee substantially all the risks and rewards of owning an asset. That is, if, at the inception of a lease the present value of the minimum lease payments, including any initial payment, amounts to substantially all (normally 90% or more) of the fair value of the leased asset.

In essence, the present value test is simply a way of measuring whether the lessor has retained a significant investment risk (10% +) in the residual value of the asset or whether substantially all the risks (90% +) have passed to the lessee.

In the UK it is easy to identify most finance leases from their terms and conditions as most finance leasing is 100% 'full pay out' leasing, that is, the lessor recovers all investment costs, finance costs and profits during the primary (non-cancellation) period of the lease. In return, the benefit of the residual value at the end of the lease is passed to the lessee by one of two ways:

▶ *either* by selling the asset after the end of the primary period and passing the major part of the proceeds to the lessee by way of a rental rebate
▶ *or* by allowing the lessee continued use of the asset for a secondary period at a peppercorn rental.

Any lease that is not a finance lease is an operating lease.

It is usual, under a finance lease, that the lessee bears maintenance costs, the lease is (substantially) equal to the life of the asset, the lease is non-cancellable and the lessor recovers its cash investment in the lease during the lease term.

Table 10.1 shows the requirements of the lessee and the lessor under SSAP 21 for both operating leases and finance leases.

Table 10.1 The essence of the SSAP 21 requirements

		Lessee	Lessor
1 Operating leases	(i)	accural or prepayment	FA/stock in the balance sheet
	(ii)	Rental paid as expense in profit and loss account	Rental received as income in profit and loss account less depreciation/ stock value change
2 Finance leases	(i)	Tangible fixed asset in balance sheet	–
	(ii)	Obligations under finance leases in balance sheet	Receivables from finance leases in balance sheet
	(iii)	Finance charge plus depreciation as charges in profit and loss account	Finance charge as income in profit and loss account

Substantial disclosure for both lessees and lessors is required in respect of both operating and financial leases.

Accounting by lessees

Operating leases

SSAP 21 requires that rentals under operating leases be charged on a straight-line basis over the lease term unless a more systematic and more rational basis is appropriate, for example, based on flying hours for an aircraft or on mileage for a vehicle.

Finance leases

Finance leases should be recorded in the balance sheet in accordance with SSAP 21 both as an asset and as an obligation to pay future rentals. The amount of the asset and the obligation recorded at the inception of the lease will be the present value of the minimum lease payments derived by discounting those payments at the interest rate implicit in the lease. In the UK, where most leases are virtually 100% 'full pay out' leases, the fair value of the asset will normally be a sufficiently close approximation to the present value of the minimum lease payments. (The standard permits the fair value to be substituted for the present value of the lessee's minimum payments.) Exam questions often require you to ascertain the cost to be capitalised by the lessee by discounting the minimum rentals.

Assets capitalised under finance leases should be depreciated over the shorter of their useful life and the lease term, which is (a) the period for which the lessee has contracted to lease the asset plus (b) any further periods for which the lessee has the option to continue the lease and where it is reasonably certain, at the inception of the lease, that the lessee will exercise that option.

Each rental payment will need to be apportioned between finance charges and reductions in the balance of obligations for future amounts payable. The total finance charge (total rentals less capital value) should be allocated to each accounting period over the lease term in such a way that the finance charge produces either a constant periodic rate of charge on the remaining balance of the obligation or a reasonable approximation of it, that is, either the actuarial pre-tax method or the sum of the digits method which is a reasonable approximation. To ascertain the finance charges to be allocated to each period under either of these approaches, you should follow the procedures outlined in the pro formas below. Once the finance charge to be allocated has been ascertained, the bookkeeping is straightforward.

PRO FORMA 10.1 – Actuarial pre-tax method

Period	Obligation at start of period	Rental paid	Obligation during period	Finance charge at x%	Obligation at end of period
First	x	(x)	x	x	x
⋮					
Last	x	(x)	Nil	Nil	NIL
		(x)		x	

(If the rentals are in arrears, the obligation at the start of the period would be the obligation during the period, and therefore the amount on which the finance charge should be calculated.)

PRO FORMA 10.2 – Sum of digits method: procedure

	Rental in arrears	Rentals in advance
1 Ascertain total sum of digits in respect of total rentals:	$\dfrac{\text{(No. of rentals + 1)}}{2}$	$\dfrac{\text{(No. of rentals)}}{2}$
	x (No. of rentals)	x (No. of rentals less 1)
2 Allocate digit to each rental payment:		
First	No. of rentals	No. of rentals less 1
Second: Less 1	x	x
Third: Less 1	x	x
Last	1	0
Sum of as in 1 above	x	x

3 Finance charge for period

$$\text{Total finance charge} \times \frac{\text{Sum of digits re rentals in period}}{\text{Total sum of digits re all rentals}}$$

PRO FORMA 10.3 – Bookkeeping

Leased asset – leased asset capitalised

PV/Fair value	x	Depreciation – P/L account	x
		B/S NBV	x
	—		

Lease obligation

Bank – rental paid	x	PV/Fair value	x
c/f	x	Finance charge in rentals paid – P/L account	x
	—		

Profit and loss acount

Depreciation	x
Finance charge	x

In the balance sheet the lease obligation must be net of finance charges allocated to future years, that is, the net obligation, and further broken down for inclusion in creditors: amounts falling due within one year and amounts falling due after more than one year. Detailed disclosure requirements are dealt with later in the chapter.

(Note that the straight-line method of recognising finance charges may be used if it produces a result that is not materially different from that produced by the actuarial method.)

A further problem

A regular feature of examination questions dealing with finance leases in a lessee's accounts is for a question to indicate that a lease is a finance lease without indicating the cost to the lessor. In such a situation, following SSAP 21, the cost to the lessor should be determined as the present value of the minimum rental payments using the rate of interest implicit in the lease. See Example 10.1.

EXAMPLE 10.1

A lessee leases from a lessor a new machine with a useful life of five years. The lease term is five years, rentals are £3,700 per annum payable in arrears. The lease is indicated to you as a finance lease. The cost of the asset to the lessor is not known.

What is the cost of the asset to be capitalised by the lessee and what would finance charges, allocated under the actuarial pre-tax method, amount to for each of the five years of the lease term? The rate of interest implicit in the lease is 12% per annum.

12% discount factors are as follows:

The capital:

Years (t)	Present value of £1 to be received after t years	Present value of £1 per year for each of t years
1	0.893	0.893
2	0.797	1.690
3	0.712	2.402
4	0.636	3.038
5	0.567	3.605
6	0.507	4.112

Cost to be capitalised by the lessee is the present value of the minimum rental payments using the rate of interest implicit in the lease – 12%.

	Rental	Factor	PV
	£		£
1	3,700	0.893	3,304
2	3,700	0.797	2,949
3	3,700	0.712	2,634
4	3,700	0.636	2,353
5	3,700	0.567	2,098
	18,500		13,338

(Alternatively, 3,700 x 3.605 = £13,338)

Finance charges for each period (and the lease creditor outstanding at each period end) can now be determined as follows:

Period	Cash investment at beginning	Rental – –	Cash investment during	Finance charge (12%)	Cash investment at end
	£	£	£	£	£
1	13,338	–	13,338	1,601	14,939
2	14,939	(3,700)	11,239	1,349	12,588
3	12,588	(3,700)	8,888	1,066	9,954
4	9,954	(3,700)	6,254	750	7,004
5	7,004	(3,700)	3,304	396	3,700
6	3,700	(3,700)	–	–	–

Accounting by lessors

Operating leases

SSAP 21 requires that a lessor should record as fixed assets the assets it holds for leasing under operating leases, and that such assets be depreciated over their useful lives.

The lessor should recognise rental income from operating leases on a straight-line basis over the period of the lease.

Finance leases

SSAP 21 requires that income from finance leases should be allocated over the lease term in such a manner as to produce a constant periodic rate of return on the net cash investment in the lease. (Initial direct costs – for example, commissions and legal expenses – *may* be apportioned over the period of the lease on a systematic and rational basis.) This principle is referred to as the investment period principle.

Normally, a finance lessor's main expense is the cost of financing the borrowings used to finance the investment in finance leases. As a result, the lessor's finance costs for each finance lease are at their highest at the start of the lease. They then decline during the lease term as the lessor recovers the investment in the lease.

Gross earnings – the finance charges over the lease term – should be apportioned in such a way so that they emerge as a constant post-tax rate of return on each period's net cash investment in the lease. There are alternative acceptable methods of income recognition and these are dealt with in turn below.

- For hire purchase contracts:
  - *either* the sum of the digits method of allocating gross earnings
  - *or* the actuarial pre-tax method of allocating gross earnings.
- For finance leases: The major disadvantage of the sum of the digits method is that it is unsuitable for lessors. This is because it ignores the cash flows relating to the tax effects of a lease. The pattern of gross earnings that emerges under the method is not likely to match the related finance costs. The actuarial pre-tax method is unsuitable for lessors for the same reason. Given that a lessor should allocate gross earnings on the basis of its net cash investment following the investment period principle, either the investment period method (IPM) or the actuarial post-tax method may be used.

The investment period method

This method was evolved to overcome the problem of matching gross earnings with interest costs for tax-based leases. The method uses the concept that the amount of finance a lessor needs to fund an investment in the lease is the basis for the apportionment of gross earnings. This amount is referred to as the lessor's net cash investment in the lease. It represents the balance of the lessor's remaining investment in the lease after taking account of all cash flows associated with the lease.

The investment period is that period in which the lessor has a positive net cash investment in the lease. The investment period method apportions gross earnings from a lease over the investment period in proportion to each period's net cash investment in the lease.

Although it has its shortcomings, the investment period method still produces results that approximate quite closely to the more sophisticated actuarial after tax method. It also has the advantage that it is simpler to operate than the actuarial after tax method.

The actuarial post-tax method

The basis of the method is that the lessor's anticipated after tax net profit is removed from the lease cash flows in such a way that it represents a constant periodic rate of return on the lessor's net cash investment in the lease.

The difference between the result obtained by using this method and that obtained using the IPM will be insignificant where the tax effects of the lease are themselves insignificant; this is likely to be the most common situation since April 1986.

Accounting for leases by lessees and by lessors

The procedure to be adopted is now dealt with below. Example 10.2, extracted from A working guide to SSAP 21, published by the ASC illustrates the procedures to be adopted for accounting for leases by both lessee and lessor companies.

EXAMPLE 10.2

You are presented with the following cash flow summary of all cash flows, including taxation, of a lessor company arising from the leasing of an asset that has been classified as a finance lease to a lessee company.

Period (3 months)	Net cash investment at start of period	Cash flows in period (Note1)	Cash flows in period (Note 2)	Average net cash investment in period	Interest paid (Note 3)	Profit taken out of lease (Note 4)	Net cash investment at end of period
	£	£	£	£	£	£	£
1/87	–	(10,000)	650	(9,350)	(234)	(33)	(9,617)
2/87	(9,617)		650	(8,967)	(224)	(32)	(9,223)
3/87	(9,223)		650	(8,573)	(214)	(30)	(8,817)
4/87	(8,817)		650	(8,167)	(204)	(29)	(8,400)
			2,600		(876)	(124)	
1/88	(8,400)		650	(7,750)	(194)	(28)	(7,972)
2/88	(7,972)		650	(7,322)	(183)	(26)	(7,531)
3/88	(7,531)		650	(6,881)	(172)	(25)	(7,078)
4/88	(7,078)	272	650	(6,156)	(154)	(22)	(6,332)
			2,600		(703)	(101)	
1/89	(6,332)		650	(5,682)	(142)	(20)	(5,844)
2/89	(5,844)		650	(5,194)	(130)	(18)	(5,342)
3/89	(5,342)		650	(4,692)	(117)	(17)	(4,826)
4/89	(4,826)	(8)	650	(4,184)	(105)	(15)	(4,304)
			2,600		(494)	(70)	
1/90	(4,304)		650	(3,654)	(91)	(13)	(3,758)
2/90	(3,758)		650	(3,108)	(78)	(11)	(3,197)
3/90	(3,197)		650	(2,547)	(64)	(9)	(2,620)
4/90	(2,620)	(245)	650	(2,215)	(55)	(8)	(2,278)
			2,600		(288)	(41)	
1/91	(2,278)		650	(1,628)	(41)	(6)	(1,675)
2/91	(1,675)		650	(1,025)	(26)	(4)	(1,055)
3/91	(1,055)		650	(405)	(10)	(1)	(416)
4/91	(416)	(440)	650	(206)	(5)	(1)	(212)
			2,600		(82)	(12)	
1/92	(212)			(212)	(5)	(1)	(218)
2/92	(218)			(218)	(5)	(1)	(224)
3/92	(224)			(224)	(6)	(1)	(231)
4/92	(231)	226		1	(1)	–	–
		6					
		(10,000)	13,000		(17)	(3)	
		(189)			(2,460)	(351)	

Notes:

1 (a) The fair value of the asset is £10,000.

   (b) Tax is payable at the beginning of period 4 in each year. It is calculated on rentals, interest paid and capital allowances. (Interest received that arises on any cash surplus would also be taxable.) In period 4/92 the £6 is tax recoverable in 1993. The figure of £(189) is the total of tax payments less recoveries.

2 Rentals of £650 are payable in advance.

3 Interest paid is calculated at 2.5% per quarter on the average net cash investment in each period.

4 The profit taken out of the lease is calculated at 0.36% on the average net cash invested in each period until period 3/92.
5 Corporation tax is at 35%.

First, prepare, for the lessee company, the amounts to be included in the balance sheet of the company as on 4/87. Use the sum of the digits method to apportion finance charges.

Second, prepare, for the lessor company, draft profit and loss accounts for each year, 1987 to 1992, indicating:

(i) income recognised from the lease
(ii) interest
(iii) taxation, including deferred tax

using, for the recognition of income, the investment period method (IPM), *and* the actuarial method after tax.

Third, for the lessor company, based on the use of the actuarial post-tax method, ascertain the amount to be included in the balance sheet under current assets: amounts receivable under finance lease obligations at the 1987 year end.

Workings

Accounting in the books of the lessee company
The finance charge over the period of the lease amounts to the total rental payments of £13,000 less the fair value of the asset to the lessor of £10,000 = £3,000. This is to be spread over the period of the lease using the sum of the digits method. Rentals are payable by the lessee in advance.

1 Ascertain the total sum of the digits,

$$\frac{\text{Number of payments}}{2} \times (\text{Number of payments less 1})$$

$$= \frac{20}{2} \times (20 - 1) = 190$$

2 Ascertain the digits relating to the payments in the year 1987

First payment, number of payments less 1 = 19
Second payment,   less 1 = 18
Third payment,   less 1 = 17
Fourth payment,   less 1 = 16

3 Finance charge allocated to the year 1987 is

$$\frac{\text{Digits relating to payments in year}}{\text{Sum of total digits}} \times \text{Total finance charge}$$

$$\frac{19 + 18 + 17 + 16}{190} \times 3,000 = 1,105$$

4 Calculate the finance charge for the next year (1988). This iş in order to ascertain the current and non-current lease obligations at the 1987 year end. The finance charge to be allocated is:

$$\frac{\text{Digits relating to payments in year}}{\text{Sum of total digits}} \times \text{Total finance charge}$$

$$\frac{15 + 14 + 13 + 12}{190} \times 3,000 = 853$$

5 The double entry would now be as follows:

	£	£
(i) Debit: tangible fixed assets	10,000	
Credit: lease obligations		10,000
with the capital cost of the leased asset		
(ii) Debit: profit and loss account	2,000	
Credit: tangible fixed assets		2,000
with 10,000/5 years; depreciation for 87		
(iii) Debit: lease obligations	1,495	
Debit: profit and loss account	1,105	
Credit: cash		2,600

with rental paid in year split into finance charge
(debit to profit and loss account) and capital
(debit to lease obligations) elements.
(A more long-winded approach was used in Pro forma 3.)

(iv) Balance sheet amounts at year end 1987

Tangible fixed assets (10,000 – 2,000)	£8,000
Creditors: amounts falling due within one year	
Next year's rental less next year's finance charge (2,600 – 853)	£1,747
Creditors: amounts falling due after more than one year	
Rentals payable 1989 onwards less finance charges allocated to years 1989 onwards. (2,600 x 3) – (3,000 – 1,105 – 853)	£6,758

Total creditor at year end 1987 is the capital sum outstanding at this year end, i.e. (10,000 less 1,495) = £8,505 or the sum of the creditors falling due within and after one year of £1,747 + £6, 758.

The notes as to creditors as to lease obligations would disclose:

	£
Amounts outstanding in less than year	1,747
Two to five years inclusive	6,758
More than five years	–
	8,505

(v) The profit and loss account of 1987 would be debited with depreciation plus finance charges for the year, 2,000 + 1,105 = £3,105.

Accounting in the books of the lessor company

Recognition of gross earnings for the lessor company, whether on the basis of the investment period method or on the basis of the actuarial method after tax, is based on what may be termed the investment period principle.

It is necessary therefore to ascertain those accounting periods in which the lessor has a net cash investment in the lease, and it would be necessary to prepare a cash flow summary, such as that indicated in the example, to ascertain such periods.

Note carefully the form of the cash flow summary.

1 Cash flows in the period are the capital cost, rentals and taxation (payable)/recoverable. As the rentals are in advance the amounts are taken into account before ascertaining the 'Average net cash investment in period'. If the rentals were in arrears they should not be taken into account in ascertaining 'Average net cash investment' for the period. Treat a previous period's rental as being received at the beginning of the next period.

2 The basis of the calculation of interest would usually be indicated, as in the example, 2.5% per quarter on the average net cash investment in the period.

3 The column 'Profit taken out of the lease' needs some further explanation.

It is not reasonable to assume that all cash inflows arising from the lease are wholly applied to reduce the net cash investment of the lessor in the lease. Some of these inflows must be applied by the lessor towards the meeting of overheads and/or payment of dividends. The amounts required for such purposes are termed 'Profit taken out of the lease'.

There are two ways in which a question can indicate the basis of the calculation for the amount to be included in the 'Profit taken out of the lease' column for the cash flow summary:

▶ *either*, as has been done in the example above, you are told that it is to be calculated as a constant percentage on the average net cash investment in each period

▶ *or*, you could be given £ amounts to be held back for overheads and dividend payments.

If the former, you will be able to use either the actuarial post-tax method or the investment period method for the allocation of gross earnings (finance charge) over the period of the lease. If the latter, you will be able to use only the investment period method.

Under the actuarial post-tax method, the 'profit taken out' is the amount to be recognised as profit after tax each year and will represent a constant percentage of the lessor's reducing net cash investment in each period.

4 Taxation will have to be inserted into the cash flow summary in the particular period when paid (or, where there is a benefit, recovered). Note that the lessor is taxed on rentals received *not* on gross earnings recognised in the profit and loss account. Note also the relevance of capital allowances in reducing the tax of the lessor.

Thus, tax for 1987, recovered at the beginning of 4/88 is calculated as follows:

	£
Taxable income – rentals for 1987	2,600
Allowable expense – interest paid in 1987	(876)
	1,724
Less: capital allowances – 25% x 10,000	(2,500)
	(776)

At 35%, a tax benefit of £272.

Tax for 1988 *paid* at the beginning of 4/89 is calculated as follows:

	£
Taxable income – rentals for 1988	2,600
Allowable expense – interest paid in 1988	(703)
	1,897
Capital allowances – 25% (10,000 – 2,500)	(1,875)
	22

At 35%, a tax liability of £8.

5 Having completed the cash flow summary, you can now prepare draft profit and loss accounts of the lessor for all years over the lease period.

6 Note that where 'profit taken out' is indicated as a percentage the net cash investment at the end of all cash flows will reduce to nil. The percentage will have been derived to achieve this.

Draft profit and loss accounts of the lessor company using the actuarial post-tax method

	1987	1988	1989	1990	1991	1992	Total
	£	£	£	£	£	£	£
Rental	2,600	2,600	2,600	2,600	2,600	–	13,000
Less capital repayment	(1,533)	(1,742)	(1,998)	(2,249)	(2,500)	22	(10,000)
Gross earnings	1,067	858	602	351	100	22	3,000
Interest	(876)	(703)	(494)	(288)	(82)	(17)	(2,460)
Profit before tax	191	155	108	63	18	5	540
Taxation – CT	272	(8)	(245)	(440)	226	6	(189)
	463	147	(137)	(377)	244	11	351
Deferred tax	(339)	(46)	207	418	(232)	(8)	–
Net profit	124	101	70	41	12	3	351

Explanatory notes as to amounts included in the draft profit and loss accounts:

1 The first figure to be inserted into the draft profit and loss account for each year is the net profit or profit after tax for the year.
   Where the actuarial post-tax method is used for the allocation of gross earnings, the net profit for the year is the 'profit taken out of the lease' as indicated in the cash flow summary for that year – £124 for 1987 and so on.
2 Work backwards to ascertain profit before tax. With a corporation tax rate of 35%, this must be 100/65 of the profit after tax – £124 x 100/65 = £191 of profit before tax for 1987.
3 Insert for each year the interest and corporation tax for that year. These amounts are simply extracted from the cash flow summary.
4 Gross earnings and deferred taxation are now, quite simply, balancing items. Once gross earnings are known, the capital repayment is simply the rental less the gross earnings recognised for the year.

Draft profit and loss accounts of the lessor company using the investment period method

	1987	1988	1989	1990	1991	1992	Total
	£	£	£	£	£	£	£
Rental	2,600	2,600	2,600	2,600	2,600	–	13,000
Less capital repayment	(1,530)	(1,743)	(1,998)	(2,248)	(2,501)	20	(10,000)
Gross earnings	1,070	857	602	352	99	20	3,000
Interest	(876)	(703)	(494)	(288)	(82)	(17)	(2,460)
Profit before tax	194	154	108	64	17	3	540
Taxation	272	(8)	(245)	(440)	226	6	(189)
	466	146	(137)	(376)	243	9	351
Deferred tax	(340)	(46)	207	418	(232)	(7)	–
Net profit	126	100	70	42	11	2	351

Explanatory notes as to amounts included in the draft profit and loss accounts:

The procedure to be adopted where the investment period method is used as the basis of recognition of gross earnings is somewhat different from that adopted above where the actuarial post-tax method was used. Note, again, that the investment period method *may* be used where 'profit taken out of the lease' is indicated as a constant percentage of the average net cash investment in each period but that it will *have* to be used as the only basis available if the 'profit taken out of the lease' is not indicated as a constant percentage of the average net cash investment in the lease in each period so as to reduce the net cash investment to nil at the end of relevant periods.

1 Unlike the actuarial post-tax method, where gross earnings were arrived at by working backwards from net profit as a balancing item, under the investment period method it must be calculated in a working:

(i) list the net cash investment in each period from the cash flow summary
(ii) sum the total of net cash investments in all periods
(iii) gross earnings for each period =

$$\frac{\text{Net cash investment in period}}{\text{Sum of all net cash investments}} \times \text{Total finance charge}$$

Thus for 1/87, gross earnings, are $\frac{9,617}{101,170} \times 3,000 = £285$

The schedule below explains the amounts included in the draft profit and loss accounts as gross earnings in each year.

Period	Net cash investment at end of period £	Gross earnings allocation £	Total gross earnings for year £
1/87	9,617	285	
2/87	9,223	274	
3/87	8,817	262	
4/87	8,400	249	1,070
1/88	7,972	236	
2/88	7,531	223	
3/88	7,078	210	
4/88	6,332	188	857
1/89	5,844	173	
2/89	5,342	158	
3/89	4,826	143	
4/89	4,304	128	602
1/90	3,758	111	
2/90	3,197	95	
3/90	2,620	78	
4/90	2,278	68	352
1/91	1,675	50	
2/91	1,055	31	
3/91	416	12	
4/91	212	6	99
1/92	218	6	
2/92	224	7	
3/92	231	7	
4/92	–	–	20
	101,170	3,000	3,000

2 Interest is known from the cash flow summary and therefore one can ascertain the profit before tax.
3 Once profit before tax is known, net profit or profit after tax is inserted as, where the corporation tax rate is 35%, 65% of profit before tax. Thus for 1987, net profit is 65% x 194 or £126.
4 Corporation tax is known from the cash flow summary. Deferred tax is now the balancing item.

A further note as to deferred tax:

Whatever the basis adopted for recognising gross earnings, deferred tax in the draft profit and loss accounts is ascertained as a balancing item. Consider, however, why such deferred tax arises, and how the amounts included in the draft profit and loss accounts under this heading may be reconciled.

A timing difference arises in any one year given that 'finance charges' or 'gross earnings' included in the profit and loss account for any one year differs from the 'rentals received less capital allowances' for that year taken into account in ascertaining the tax payable or recoverable for that year.

Thus, using the amounts included in the draft profit and loss accounts for 1987 using the actuarial post-tax method, deferred tax for 1987 amounts to a debit in the profit and loss account of £339. This arises as a result of the timing difference arising in 1987 on the difference between, on the one hand gross earnings of £1,067, and on the other of rentals received less capital allowances of £2,600 less £2,500. The timing difference, gross earnings greater than rentals less capital allowances, is (1,067 − 100) £967. The tax effect of such a timing difference is to reduce the corporation tax liability of 1987. When the timing difference reverses in subsequent years tax will become payable in such subsequent years. Providing for the tax effect of tax payable in future years, deferred tax is provided in 1987 amounting to 35% of 967 or £339 by:

	£	£
Debit: profit and loss account tax charge	339	
Credit: deferred taxation		339

In 1988, gross earnings remain greater than rentals less capital allowances with the same tax effect arising in respect of deferred tax.

In 1989, the timing difference begins to reverse. Gross earnings are £602 and rentals less capital allowances are (2,600 − 1,406) £1,194. The timing difference gross earnings less rentals less capital allowances amounts to (1,194 − 602) £592. As a result, a greater corporation tax liability arises for the year, provided for in previous years. Release the deferred tax provision to profit and loss account, 35% x 592 = 207:

	£	£
Debit: deferred tax	207	
Credit: profit and loss account tax charge		207

Lastly, by way of illustration, consider the amounts to be included by the lessor company in its balance sheet at each year end. The capital sum receivable at the end of 1987 is the capital cost of £10,000 less the capital repayment during 1987, as disclosed by the actuarial post-tax method draft profit and loss account for 1987, £1,533, or £8,467. Amounts receivable after more than one year are this amount of £8,467 less the capital repayment for 1988 of £1,742, or £6,725.

Disclosure in financial statements

Lessee company

Balance sheet

	£
Fixed assets	
Tangible assets (include NBV of finance leases capitalised)	x
Creditors: amounts falling due within one year	
Bank loans, overdrafts and obligations under finance leases and HP contracts	(x)
Creditors: amounts falling due after more than one year	
Bank loans, overdrafts and obligations under finance leases and HP contracts	(x)

Notes to the financial statements
Accounting policies
Leased assets:

- if assets financed by leasing agreements give rights amounting to ownership, that is, finance leases, the assets are capitalised and treated as if they had been owned outright
- the amount capitalised is the present value of the minimum lease payments during the lease term
- the corresponding leasing commitments are shown as obligations under creditors
- depreciation on the capitalised assets is charged to the profit and loss account
- lease payments are treated as consisting of capital and interest elements and the interest is charged to the profit and loss account using the actuarial pre-tax method
- all other leases are operating leases and the annual rentals on such leases are charged to the profit and loss account on a straight-line basis over the lease term.

	£
Profit on ordinary operations is stated after charging:	
Depreciation on owned assets	x
Depreciation on assets held under finance leases and hire purchase contracts	x
Interest payable re loans and overdrafts repayable; finance leases and hire purchase contracts	x
Hire of plant and machinery – operating leases	x
Hire of other assets – operating leases	x

Creditors
Bank loans, overdrafts and obligations under finance leases and hire purchase contracts consist of:

	£
Bank loans and overdrafts	x
Obligations under finance leases and hire purchase contracts	<u>x</u>
	<u>x</u>

Repayable as follows:	
Under one year	x
Between two and five years	x
In over five years	<u>x</u>
	<u>x</u>

Tangible fixed assets
Either have a separate column for both cost/valuation and depreciation for finance leases and hire purchase contracts, or aggregate with other categories of fixed assets. In this latter case disclose, 'the net book value of tangible fixed assets includes an amount of £x in respect of assets held under finance leases and hire purchase contracts'.

Capital commitments
Commitments under finance leases entered into but not yet provided for in the financial statements £ x.

Commitments under operating leases

	Land and buildings	Other
At the year end the company had annual commitments under non-cancellable operating leases as follows:	£	£
Expiring within one year	x	x
Expiring within two and five years	x	x
Expiring in five years or more	x	x
	x	x

Lessor company

Balance sheet
Current assets: Debtors
Finance lease and hire purchase receivables   £ x

Notes to the financial statements

1 The amounts receivable under finance leases and hire purchase contracts comprise

	£
Finance leases	x
Hire purchase contracts	x
	x

   Included in the above amount is £x which falls due after more than one year.

2 The gross amounts and accumulated depreciation of assets held for use as operating leases should be disclosed.

3 Accounting policies
   ▶ re operating and finance leases
   ▶ depreciation policy for operating lease assets
   ▶ recognition of finance lease income; method, treatment of initial direct cost, assumption about tax rates and payment dates.

4 Contingencies; contingent rentals

5 Turnover
   operating leases – rentals receivable
   finance leases – gross earnings.

The problem of regional development grants

Regional development grants (RDGs) are normally paid to the owner of the asset for which the grant is claimed, that is, the lessor. When a lessor receives a grant on an asset that is subject to a finance lease it usually passes the benefit of that grant back to the lessee by either charging lower rentals over the lease term, or as a lump sum.

The grant received by the lessor represents two separate benefits. First there is the actual cash benefit on receipt, second there are the tax effects. The latter arises because even though the grant reduces the net cost of the asset to the lessor, the lessor is still able to claim capital allowances on the full gross cost of the asset. This latter benefit can be substantial.

It is possible that, given the passing of the benefits to the lessee, the lessor reduces the amount of rentals payable by the lessee to an amount that is below the net cost of the leased asset. In such a situation, at the end of the lease term the lessor will show a pre-tax loss but a post-tax profit.

Thus, if one were to assume a five-year finance lease commencing on 1 April 1986 the tax effects could be illustrated as follows:

	Profit and loss account			Tax at 35%
Rentals over lease term		750	Taxable income of lessor	263
Cost of asset	1,000		@ 35% Lessor claims eventual capital allowances through WDAs of 1,000 @ 35%	(350)
RDG	(220)			(87)
		(780)		
		(30)		
Taxation recoverable		87 (CR)		
Profit after tax		57		

Some lessors have preferred to eliminate this pre-tax loss and post-tax profit result of the RDG by grossing up the RDG they credit to their profit and loss account in each period for the tax benefit of the RDG and to increase the tax charge accordingly. Thus:

	Profit and loss account			Tax at 35%
Rentals over lease term		750	As above	263
Cost of asset	1,000		Capital allowances	(350)
Less RDG $220 \times \dfrac{100}{65}$	(338)		Re RDG (338 – 220)	118
		(662)		31
Profit before tax		88		
Taxation		31		
Profit after tax (as before)		57		

SSAP 21 permits a lessor to adopt either of these two alternatives but the lessor must disclose in its accounting policies the particular treatment that has been adopted and, if RDGs are grossed up in the profit and loss account, the amount by which both profit before tax and tax have increased as a result of adopting this treatment.

Leasing by manufacturers or dealers

Where the business enters into an operating lease it should not recognise a selling profit when it leases the asset. Risks and rewards of ownership will not have passed to the lessee and the business should account for the lease in the same way as any other operating lessor, that is, capitalise the asset at cost and depreciate it over its useful life. Rentals should be recognised on a straight-line basis over the period of the lease.

Where the business enters into a finance lease such a transaction gives rise to two types of income:

▶ the selling profit, which would have arisen on an outright sale of the leased asset
▶ the finance charges or gross earnings over the period of the lease.

It is possible that, in order to promote sales, the business may sometimes offer finance leasing arrangements at concessionary rates. When it does this the business should restrict the selling profit to an amount that will allow it to recognise its gross earnings at the normal commercial rate over the lease term.

Sale and leaseback transactions

Sale and leaseback transactions arise when a vendor sells an asset and immediately re-acquires the use of the asset by entering into a lease with the buyer. Before SSAP 21, it was usual for such sellers/lessees to account for any profit/loss arising on the sale as extraordinary items. Under the standard, the recognition of the profit or loss entered into will depend on (a) the type of lease entered into, and (b) whether or not the transaction was at arm's length.

Finance leasebacks

The leaseback is a financing operation; the seller/lessee does not dispose of the risks and rewards of ownership. It is inappropriate to recognise a profit or loss on such a sale wholly in the year of sale.

Normally, the book value of the asset before the sale should not be less than or more than the fair value. Adjustments to the book value should be made before determining the apparent profit or loss on the sale, which will be the selling price less the revised book value. This profit/loss should be deferred and amortised over the lease term.

A simpler way of accounting for a finance leaseback to achieve this result would be to treat the transaction not as a sale but as a source of finance. Accordingly, the seller/lessee should leave the asset in the books at its existing value and continue to depreciate this amount. On sale:

(a) DR cash
CR creditors: lease obligation
with sale proceeds
(b) DR profit and loss account
DR creditors: lease obligation
CR cash
with rental paid, apportioned between capital and finance charge.

Operating leasebacks

If the sale transaction is established at fair value any profit or loss on the sale should be recognised immediately. The seller/lessee in this case has effectively passed the risks and rewards of ownership to the lessor and it is appropriate to recognise any profit immediately. However:

▶ If sale profit is greater than fair value this excess does not represent a genuine profit and should be deferred and amortised over the shorter of the lease term and the period to the next rent review. Fair value less book value represents genuine profit and is recognised immediately.
▶ If sale profit is less than fair value a company has probably made a poor bargain and the loss should be recognised immediately.
▶ If, however, the loss is compensated by lower than market value rentals, that is, that transaction is not at arm's length, it should be deferred and amortised over the period that the reduced rentals are chargeable.

▶ If a profit arises in this situation, that is, sale profit is less than fair value but nevertheless greater than book value, the standard does not require a similar adjustment and the whole of such profit should be recognised immediately.

The effectiveness of SSAP 21 and changes under FRS 5

The main impact of SSAP 21, well before standard sottors formally addressed the problems of reporting the substance of transactions, was to require lessee companies to recognise finance leases as assets in their balance sheets and, in so doing, to also recognise the corresponding financial obligation to a lessor company. The issues relating to the recognition of assets and liabilities were addressed in EDs 42 and 49, FRED 4, and now in FRS 5.

FRS 5 states that reporting the substance of a transaction requires that the accounting treatment of the transaction should fairly reflect its commercial effect. A key step in determining the substance of a transaction is to identify its effect on the assets and liabilities of the entity. For this purpose we need to be able to apply the definitions of assets and liabilities as stated in FRS 5:

Assets: rights or other access to future economic benefits controlled by an entity as a result of past transactions or events.

Liabilities: an entity's obligations to transfer economic benefits as a result of past transactions or events.

As assets and liabilities are often founded on legal rights and obligations, these are important in determining the substance of a transaction. However, in some cases recording the legal form of a transaction may not fully indicate the commercial effect of the arrangements entered into. Such cases can, for example, include features such as the severance of the legal title to an item from the ability to enjoy the principal benefits and exposure to the principal risks associated with it. One example of this is a finance lease and it is these principles that govern the accounting treatment of such leases under SSAP 21.

Where transactions covered by FRS 5 also fall within the scope of another accounting standard, the standard containing the more specific provisions should be applied. Thus, for a sale and leaseback arrangement where there is also an option for the seller/lessee to repurchase the asset the 'Note on Application B' in FRS 5 (see also Chapter 9) should be applied.

In conclusion, the impact of SSAP 21, which deals specifically with leasing, and of FRS 5, which deals generally with reporting the substance of transactions, is mainly in relation to the practice of off balance sheet finance. Applying the principles of FRS 5 to leasing transactions would cover the following:

▶ how to determine the substance of a transaction
▶ whether any resulting assets and liabilities should be recognised in the balance sheet
▶ the disclosures that should be made.

The benefit of applying these principles to accounting for leased assets is that accounts should, as a result, be more informative and relevant.

Summary

This chapter, following on from the previous chapter, which dealt with off balance sheet finance, deals with the relevance in accounting for finance leases of 'substance' over 'form'.

The topic has been regularly examined at this level in the past and you should be fully familiar with:

▶ the conditions that distinguish a finance lease from an operating lease
▶ the capitalisation of finance leases by lessees
▶ the principles of recognising income by lessors
▶ accounting by lessors
▶ disclosure requirements
▶ accounting for sale and leaseback transactions.

Suggested reading

Manual of Accounting – Companies (Coopers & Lybrand Deloitte 1990)

UK GAAP (Ernst & Young 1990)

Financial Reporting 1987–88 – A

survey of UK Reporting Practice (Skerratt and Tonkin 1988)

Leasing: The Accounting and Taxation Implications (Wainman and Brown 1980)

Self test questions

1   Prepare an accounting policy note for leased assets in the accounts of a lessee company.

2   Motazedi plc prepares its financial statements to 31 December each year. The company is currently negotiating to lease out plant to an existing customer. You are informed that the plant will cost Motazedi plc £5 million and that the rentals are to be £800,000 per half year and that they are to be payable in advance. It is intended that the finance lease will be entered into on 1 January 1994. The profit to be taken out of the lease is indicated to you as amounting to 5.4% on the average net cash investment during each half year period. The residual value of the plant is expected to be nil at the end of the four-year lease term. Corporation tax at 35% is payable for each year, one year in arrears. Capital allowances are 25% per annum on a reducing balance basis.
    Prepare a cash flow summary for Motazedi plc.

3   Prepare summarised projected profit and loss accounts for Motazedi plc (see question 2) for the years ended 31 December 1994, 1995, 1996.

4   Indicate the amounts to be included in the balance sheet of Motazedi plc (see question 2) as amounts receivable under finance lease obligations for each of the years ending 31 December 1994, 1995, 1996.

5   State, briefly, the SSAP 21 rules as to accounting for sale and leaseback transactions.

Exam style questions

1   *Thexton M. Thexton*

Thexton M. Thexton has recently been appointed to the post of Credit Manager at a City bank and, having spent the last ten years in Tristan da Cunha, is not familiar with the more recent pronouncements of the Accounting Standards Committee and has yet to hear of the Accounting Standards Board. One of the major clients of the bank is a leasing company, which has requested the bank for an extension of its existing overdraft facility. The accounting policies of the client company include the following:

> The total gross earnings under a finance lease are allocated to accounting periods so as to give a constant periodic rate of return on the net cash investment in the lease in each period using the actuarial post-tax method.

Thexton M. Thexton is unsure as to what the accounting policy means and has written to you asking for clarification.

Your reply is to be based on the following example:

Michael plc leases equipment to a customer on 1 July 1992. The lease is classified as a finance lease. The equipment cost Michael plc £54,000 and the lease requires the lessee company to pay rentals of £9,450, half-yearly in advance, over the four-year lease term. Corporation tax is 35% in all years and writing down allowances are available at 25% per annum. The asset has a nil residual value and is sold at the end of the lease term. Profit is to be taken out of the lease at 7.87% on the average net cash investment during each period. Michael plc prepares accounts to 30 June each year and corporation tax, for each year, is payable one year after the year end.

Required:
Write a letter to Thexton M. Thexton explaining how the accounting policy of the client company of his bank referred to above, will be applied by Michael plc and including, as part of the letter:
a) a table to establish the net cash investment of Michael plc in the lease for each period of the lease
b) summary profit and loss accounts of Michael plc, indicating both profit before and after tax, arrived at using the accounting policy referred to above, for each of the years ending 30 June 1993 to 1996
c) a schedule indicating the amounts that would be included in the balance sheet of Michael plc, 'amounts receivable under finance leases', as on 30 June 1993 through to 1996.
(You are not required to explain the distinction between finance and operating leases, of which Thexton M. Thexton is fully aware.)

(20 Marks)

2 *Troon Ltd*

Troon Ltd prepares accounts to 31 December each year. On 1 January 1991, the company sold, and leased back, some of its tangible fixed assets. Details as to the cost and accumulated depreciation, sale proceeds and fair values of the assets on the date of sale and lease arrangements are provided as follows:

Item	1	2	3	4	5
	£000	£000	£000	£000	£000
Cost	1,400	600	750	975	325
Depreciation at 10% per annum 2/3/4/5/6 years respectively	(280)	(180)	(300)	(488)	(195)
NBV 1 January 1991	1,120	420	450	487	130
Sale proceeds	1,500	500	410	400	138
Fair value on date of sale	1,500	480	460	490	150
Leaseback classified as	Finance	Operating	Operating	Operating	Operating
Lease term	8 yrs				
Period to next rent review	–	2 yrs	3 yrs	2 yrs	3 yrs
Annual rental, in arrears	250	170	155	150	60

Fixed asset 3 is recognised by the company as having been sold as a bad bargain. The sale and subsequent leaseback of fixed assets 2, 4 and 5 are recognised by the company as giving rise to non-arm's-length transactions.

Required:

a) Outline the treatment required by SSAP 21 in respect of sale and leaseback transactions in respect of the sale and leaseback transactions above.

(10 marks)

b) Prepare a schedule to disclose charges and credits to the profit and loss account of Troon Ltd for the year ended 31 December 1991 dealing with, in accordance with SSAP 21 on leasing,

▶ depreciation
▶ finance charges (to be calculated using the sum of the digits method)
▶ lease rentals
▶ profit or loss recognised on sale

arising on the sale and subsequent leaseback of the five fixed assets above.

(8 marks)

c) Prepare a schedule to disclose the obligation under the finance lease to be included as a creditor in the balance sheet of Troon Ltd as at 31 December 1991.

(2 marks)

(20 marks)

All answers on pages 650–653.

Reporting Financial Performance

SSAP 6 – Extraordinary Items and Prior Year Adjustments, was issued in 1974 and, following ED 36, revised in 1986. As with leasing, deferred tax, price changes and currency translation, the treatment of extraordinary items in company accounts has proved to be controversial and problematic. In spite of the accounting standard, the issue of how best to account for such items remained unresolved until the issue of FRS 3 in 1992. In 1983 the Lex Column in the *Financial Times* commented that: 'the ambiguities in the existing standard – and the willingness of companies to exploit them – make it extremely difficult for the stock market to compare the performance of companies in related areas because of the wide discrepancies in accounting treatment.'

It is the significance that both management and users of accounts have attached to the profit derived from the ordinary activities of the business – a number that is emphasised in the statutory formats for the profit and loss acount – that has made the treatment of extraordinary items such an important issue. Per SSAP 3, prior to the issue of FRS 3, eps was calculated on earnings before extraordinary items. Accordingly, one aim of SSAP 6 was to provide guidance on disclosure and presentation so that the results of companies could be presented in a meaningful way. The main problems were:

▶ identification and the difficulty of arriving at an unequivocal definition of extraordinary items
▶ income determination and the difficulty of reaching agreement as to whether such items should be included as a part of the company's reported profit or whether they should be taken direct to reserves.

Following the formation of the ASB in 1990, there has been a sense of dissatisfaction with several accounting standards, and in particular with SSAP 6. This standard was, particularly in its application to accounting for closure costs, seen as ineffective given widespread non-compliance following the lack of clarity in its provisions.

Thus, while it was clear in SSAP 6 that reorganisation costs that related to continuing activities should be treated as part of ordinary activities, some companies that had gone in for what they called a 'fundamental restructuring' accounted for the costs arising as extraordinary. Given this lack of clear distinction between ordinary and extraordinary items, inconsistencies developed between companies and, as eps was calculated before extraordinary items, its usefulness as a performance measure was also called into question.

Disillusionment with the efficacy of SSAP 6 and the continuing incidence of 'reserve accounting', despite the requirements of the standard, gave rise to the viewpoint that extraordinary items should be eliminated altogether and that a new primary statement, the statement of total recognised gains and losses, be included as a part of the financial statements. Accordingly FRED 1 was issued in 1991 and FRS 3 in 1992. FRS 3 supersedes SSAP 6 and amends SSAP 3 on eps.

This chapter deals with, briefly, the original SSAP 6 and its revision and mainly with the requirements of FRS 3 and the way in which we now have to report financial performance.

The original standard and the reasons for its revision

There are two alternative concepts of income – current operating performance and all inclusive – and it is important to distinguish between them in order to provide a framework within which to consider the most appropriate way to account for extraordinary items.

The current operating performance concept

Advocates of this concept would argue that users of financial statements need to focus on the earnings ability associated with the company's normal activities. Such a profit amount is the most useful for the purpose of comparing the effectiveness of management, both over time and between companies, and also for making estimates as to the earning power of a company in the future. Thus, only those items relating to the 'normal' activities of a company should be included in the calculation of its profit. Items that arise from outside these 'normal' activities should be taken direct to reserves. A criticism of this concept is that it offers a great deal of flexibility to the preparers of accounts; profit amounts to what is chosen to be included in its computation.

The all inclusive concept

This concept advocates a broader view of income and argues that all movements between opening and closing revenue reserves should be included in the profit and loss account for the year. Thus, both prior year adjustments and extraordinary items should be included in the profit and loss account. A profit and loss account based on this concept is held to be more objective as there is no subjective appraisal of what should and should not be included. It was this concept that formed the basis for the requirements of SSAP 6, which argued, in its favour, that:

▶ the inclusion of non-recurring and extraordinary items enables the profit and loss account to give a better view of a company's profitability
▶ exclusion of extraordinary items is a matter of subjective judgement, leads to variations and a loss of comparability between reported results of companies
▶ exclusion could result in extraordinary items being overlooked in any consideration of a company's results over a series of years.

This concept is based on the view that one single figure of profit, operating performance, is not equally useful for all purposes and that highlighting such a figure to the exclusion of all else could lead to significant items being overlooked. The spirit of SSAP 6 was one of full disclosure.

One major objective of SSAP 6, following on from an adherence to the all inclusive concept of income, was to reduce the incidence of reserve accounting. In fact, surveys of published accounts issued by the ICAEW revealed a trend away from reserve accounting prior to the issue of the standard. Thus, in 1968/69 69% of companies surveyed dealt with profits or losses on the sale of fixed assets including investments directly in reserves, whereas by 1973/74 70% of companies surveyed dealt with such profits or losses in the profit and loss account. SSAP 6 simply reinforced an established trend. By 1982/83 only 1% of companies surveyed dealt with such profits or losses as reserve movements. In any case the prescribed formats, accounting principles and rules of the 1985 Act now eliminate the various options that companies may have previously chosen.

The standard failed in that it did not promote consistency in treatment of similar items by different companies.

Two areas that until recently, have continued to be examples of considerable diversity in practice are the treatment of foreign exchange differences, now regulated by requirements of SSAP 20, and goodwill, now dealt with in SSAP 22. As such they are no longer problem areas in the context of a standard on extraordinary items.

Yet another area that created a problem as to classification was the treatment of profits and losses arising on the sale of fixed assets. As stated previously, almost all companies included such profits and losses in the profit and loss account, but companies were equally divided on classification as exceptional or extraordinary items.

The reporting of redundancy costs was equally varied. In a 1982/83 survey, 55% of the 300 companies surveyed treated such costs as exceptional and 45% as extraordinary. Such inconsistencies followed from the broad definitions of the standard, which did not give sufficient guidance to ensure consistent treatment.

The following were identified as particular problem areas for classification of items as exceptional or extraordinary in the profit and loss account, for which further guidance was deemed necessary:

▶ profit or loss on the sale of fixed assets and, in particular, previously revalued fixed assets
▶ profit or loss on terminated activities
▶ trading results of discontinued activities prior to the decision to terminate
▶ reorganisation and rationalisation costs
▶ charges and credits resulting from a fundamental change in government legislation, for example, the changes brought about by the Finance Act 1984.

Further guidance on these areas was provided first in the discussion paper dealing with a review of SSAP 6, then in ED 36 and finally in SSAP 6 as revised.

SSAP 6 (Revised)

The revised standard, like the original standard on extraordinary items, was based on the view that, as well as profit on ordinary activities, the profit and loss account for the year should include and show separately all profits and losses, including all extraordinary items that are recognised in that year and all prior year items other than prior year adjustments, that is, following the all inclusive concept of profit.

One major problem area under the original standard – accounting for the disposal of fixed assets, including previously revalued fixed assets – has already been dealt with in Chapter 4. Under the revised standard disposal profits on operating assets would have been dealt with as ordinary and those on non-operating (non-depreciable) assets, for example, investment properties, would have been dealt with as extraordinary. Another major problem area – closure costs – is dealt with below.

The standard distinguished between programmes of reorganisation and decisions to discontinue business segments. The former, although they may involve redundancies and a reduction of the level of activities, were argued not to amount to the discontinuance of a business segment. They were seen as a normal business process and, therefore, formed part of the ordinary activities of a company. Their costs were accordingly charged in arriving at profit or loss on ordinary activities, and shown as an exceptional item if material.

The latter, however, were argued to have arisen from an event of an extraordinary nature, and, where a decision had been made to discontinue a business segment, a provision was seen as necessary for the consequences of all decisions taken up to the balance sheet date, accounted for as an extraordinary item. This would usually include some or all of the following items:

▶ redundancy costs (net of government contributions)
▶ costs of retaining key personnel during the run-down period

▶ profits or losses arising from the disposal of assets, including anticipated ongoing costs such as rents, rates and security
▶ pension costs
▶ bad and doubtful debts arising from the decision to close
▶ all debits and credits arising from trading after the commencement of implementation
▶ any losses due to penalty clauses in contracts.

Profit and losses from terminated activities arising from trading before the commencement of implementation were part of the trading results for the year and were therefore not extraordinary. However, because these results derived from a business segment that had been discontinued, they may require separate disclosure to enable the results of continuing operations to be ascertained.

What, then, was wrong with the revised SSAP, in this regard? The late 1980s and early 1990s have been an era of changing markets and technologies, competition and boom and slump. 'Restructuring' has been a recurrent and predictable feature of almost every business. As it is unusual to incur major restructuring costs without a closure of some sort or another, companies arguing shut-down of business segments have regularly charged the costs arising as extraordinary. While this was, just about, within the rules, it was widely seen as an abuse. Remember, again, that eps used to be calculated before extraordinary items. UITF Abstract 2 sought to discourage this practice and under FRS 3, given the virtual abolition of extraordinary items, the problem effectively disappears.

The ASB now believes that the performance of complex organisations cannot be summarised in a single number, such as profit before tax or eps. It is not so much the split between ordinary and extraordinary results that is important but the distinction between results from continuing and discontinued activities.

FRS 3 – the essential definitions

Ordinary activities Any activities that are undertaken by a reporting entity as part of its business and such related activities in which the reporting entity engages in furtherance of, incidental to, or arising from, these activities. Ordinary activities include the effects on the reporting entity of any event in the various environments in which it operates, including the political, regulatory, economic and geographical environments, irrespective of the frequency or unusual nature of the events.

Acquisitions Operations of the reporting entity that are acquired in the period.

Discontinued operations Operations of the reporting entity that are sold or terminated and that satisfy all the following conditions:

▶ the sale or termination is completed either in the period or before the earlier of three months after the commencement of the subsequent accounting period and the date on which the financial statements are approved
▶ if a termination, the former activities have ceased permanently
▶ the sale or termination has a material effect on the nature and focus of the reporting entity's operations and represents a material reduction in its operating facilities resulting either from its withdrawal from a particular market (whether class of business or geographical), or from a material reduction in turnover in the reporting entity's continuing markets
▶ the assets, liabilities, results of operations and activities are clearly distinguishable – physically, operationally and for financial reporting purposes.

Operations not satisfying all these conditions are classified as continuing.

Exceptional items Material items that derive from events or transactions that fall within the ordinary activities of the reporting entity and which individually or, if of a similar type, in aggregate, need to be disclosed by virtue of their size or incidence if the financial statements are to give a true and fair view.

Extraordinary items Material items possessing a high degree of abnormality, which arise from events or transactions that fall outside the ordinary activities of the reporting entity and that are not expected to recur. They do not include exceptional items nor do they include prior period items merely because they relate to a prior period.

Prior period adjustments Material adjustments applicable to prior periods arising from changes in accounting policies or from the correction of fundamental errors. They do not include normal recurring adjustments or corrections of accounting estimates made in prior periods.

Total recognised gains and losses The total of all gains and losses of the reporting entity that are recognised in a period and are attributable to shareholders.

FRS 3 – the main requirements

Reporting under FRS 3 will involve major changes in the presentation of financial performance, both in the disclosure of items in the profit and loss account and in the disclosure of items accounted for through reserves. The FRS requires several statements of performance to be disclosed which, taken together, are intended to provide best information as to the major elements of a company's performance. The principal requirements of the FRS are outlined below.

Primary statements and notes

Two primary statements of financial performance are required:

▶ the profit and loss account
▶ the statement of total recognised gains and losses.

Additional notes are also required, as follows:

▶ Where modified historical cost accounts are prepared, and there is a material difference between the result as disclosed in the profit and loss account and the result on an unmodified (strict historical cost) basis, a note of historical cost profits and losses must be prepared.
▶ A reconciliation of movements in shareholders' funds from the beginning to the end of the period (this may, alternatively, be presented as a primary financial statement).

The note on historical cost profit should be presented either immediately after the profit and loss account or after the statement of total recognised gains and losses.

The profit and loss account

The detail to be dealt with is considerably greater than before and the adjustments to be made to comparative amounts can be quite complex. The main requirements as to the profit and loss account are as follows:

Turnover and operating profit
As a minimum, the face of the profit and loss account should include an analysis of turnover and operating profit so as to show separately amounts attributable to:

▶ continuing operations
▶ acquisitions as a component of continuing operations
▶ discontinued operations.

As to the statutory format headings of all items between turnover and operating profit, the same analysis as above may be dealt with either on the face of the profit and loss account or in the notes to the financial statements.

Exceptional items

These, as defined above, should be charged or credited in arriving at profit or loss on ordinary activities. With the exception of the three items listed below, these items should be included under the statutory format headings to which they relate and should be classified, as appropriate, under results from continuing or discontinued operations. These items can be disclosed either in the notes or, if it is necessary to give a true and fair view, on the face of the profit and loss account.

The items that are to be disclosed separately on the face of the profit and loss account, after operating profit, before interest, and classified under continuing or discontinued operations as appropriate are:

▶ profits or losses on the sale or termination of an operation
▶ costs of a fundamental reorganisation or restructuring that has a material effect on the nature and focus of the reporting entity's operations
▶ profits or losses on the disposal of fixed assets.

The tax effects of exceptional items and their effects on any minority interests should be disclosed in the notes. The calculation of the attributable tax is dealt with below.

Extraordinary items

As the definition of ordinary activities is widely drawn in the standard, that is, items are ordinary irrespective of the frequency or unusual nature of events, the incidence of extraordinary items will be rare. If extraordinary items do arise they should be shown separately on the face of the profit and loss account after profit or loss on ordinary activities, after tax and minority interests but before deducting appropriations. The effects on tax and minority interests should be shown either on the face of the profit and loss account or in the notes. The calculation of the attributable tax is dealt with below.

Taxation

If there are special circumstances that affect the overall tax charge or credit for the period, adequate disclosure should be made. Thus, the effects of a fundamental change in the basis of tax (which would, under SSAP 6 and SSAP 15, have been dealt with as an extraordinary item) should be included in the ordinary tax charge or credit for the period and separately disclosed on the face of the profit and loss account.

Profits or losses on disposal of fixed assets

The reporting standard requires that this be accounted for in the profit and loss account of the year of sale as the difference between the sale proceeds and the carrying amount whether carried at cost or at valuation, that is, where there has been a revaluation, under the 'value approach' outlined in Chapter 4. This represents a change from previous accounting practice. SSAP 6 had no standard accounting practice in this regard and some companies, where there had been previous revaluations, used to use what was termed the 'income approach' as first proposed in ED 36. Under this approach, the revaluation surplus would be passed through the profit and loss account of the year of sale as part of the profit on sale. This approach, under FRS 3, will no longer be permissible.

Provisions

When an enterprise becomes demonstrably committed to a sale or termination of operations, any provisions should reflect the extent to which obligations have been incurred, but only to the extent that they are not expected to be covered by the future profits of the sold/terminated operations or the disposal of its assets.

Any such provisions should be shown after operating profit but before interest in the year in which they are made. In the following year there should be disclosure of the discontinued operation's results under statutory format headings with the utilisation of the provision being separately highlighted on the face of the profit and loss account.

Earnings per share

This must be calculated as the profit in pence attributable to each equity share, based on the profit for the year after taxation, minority interests and extraordinary items (if any) and after deducting appropriations in respect of preference shares, divided by the number of equity shares in issue and ranking for dividend in respect of the period. Given that eps is now to be calculated after extraordinary items, this represents a change from SSAP 3, which is amended accordingly by FRS 3 in this respect.

The FRS allows alternative bases for calculating eps provided that the basic eps required by the standard is given at least as much prominence as the alternative and there is a reconciliation between the two figures and the reason for showing the alternative is explained.

This aspect of FRS 3 has given rise to considerable comment and is dealt with later in this chapter. It is looked at again when we go on to 'interpretation' generally in Chapter 28.

Having dealt above with the main requirements of the reporting standard in respect of the profit and loss account, it is now necessary to introduce the other primary statements and further notes required by the standard and these are dealt with below.

Statement of recognised gains and losses

This is a new primary statement, although not quite a new idea, as something similar was put forward in the Sandilands report on current cost accounting in the late 1970s.

The statement is to include, within one statement, all the gains and losses of the year whether recognised in the profit and loss account or directly within reserves. Accordingly, this statement shows:

- the profit for the financial year
- unrealised revaluation surpluses
- exchange gains or losses on the translation of net assets of overseas subsidiaries
- other gains and losses recognised in the year.

The purpose of the statement is to show the total financial performance of an enterprise for the year.

Other statements and notes

Reconciliation of movements in shareholders' funds

The reconciliation between the opening and closing amounts of shareholders' funds may be disclosed either as a note or as a primary statement. It will include items that are not shown in the statement of total recognised gains and losses, for example:

- increases as a result of new share issues
- decreases as a result of the immediate write-off of goodwill, which, if immediately written off is not regarded as a recognised loss.

Note of historical cost profits and losses

This note will be necessary only when an enterprise follows the modified historical cost convention and there is a material difference between the result as disclosed in the profit and loss account and the result on an unmodified historical cost basis.

The note should appear immediately after the profit and loss account or after the statement of total recognised gains and losses, and it should include a reconciliation of the items that give rise to the difference between the two profit amounts.

Prior year adjustments

The rules as to prior period items under FRS 3 remain the same as they were under SSAP 6. Thus, a prior year adjustment will continue to be made, but only for:

▶ the effects of changes in accounting policies
▶ the correction of fundamental errors.

Layouts and presentation under FRS 3

The reporting standard adds considerably to the complexity of financial statements. Having dealt with the main requirements of the standard above, and a brief description of the primary financial statements and notes required by the standard, it is appropriate at this juncture to deal with layouts and presentation under the standard.

FRS 3 includes illustrative examples for general guidance on the basis that the best form of disclosure will depend on individual circumstances. Examples 11.1–11.6, taken from FRS 3, include two alternative forms of presentation in the profit and loss account, a statement of total recognised gains and losses, a note of historical cost profits and losses, a reconciliation of movements in shareholders' funds, and certain related notes.

The examples are in respect of a group of companies where:

▶ there have been both acquisitions and disposals of operations during the year under review
▶ there are no extraordinary items, though the positioning of such an item on the face of the profit and loss account is shown
▶ the profit and loss accounts have been prepared using Format 1 of the Act.

EXAMPLE 11.1 PROFIT AND LOSS ACCOUNT

	1993	1993	1992 as restated
	£ million	£ million	£ million
Turnover			
Continuing operations	550		500
Acquisitions	50		
	600		
Discontinued operations	175		190
		775	690
Cost of sales		(620)	(555)
Gross profit		155	135

Net operating expenses	(104)	(83)
Operating profit		
Continuing operations	50	40
Acquisitions	6	
	56	
Discontinued operations	(15)	12
Less 1992 provision	10	
	51	52
Profit on sale of properties in continuing operations	9	6
Provision for loss on operations to be discontinued		(30)
Loss on disposal of discontinued operations	(17)	
Less 1992 provision	20	
	3	
Profit on ordinary activities before interest	63	28
Interest payable	(18)	(15)
Profit on ordinary activities before taxation	45	13
Tax on profit on ordinary activities	(14)	(4)
Profit on ordinary activities after taxation	31	9
Minority interests	(2)	(2)
[Profit before extraordinary items]	29	7
[Extraordinary items] (included only to show positioning)	–	–
Profit for the financial year	29	7
Dividends	(8)	(1)
Retained profit for the financial year	21	6
Earnings per share	**39p**	**10p**
Adjustments	*X*p	*X*p
[to be itemised and an adequate description to be given]		
Adjusted earnings per share	*Y*p	*Y*p

[Reason for calculating the adjusted per share to be given]

Notes to the financial statements

	1993			1992 (as restated)		
	Cont.	Discont.	Total	Cont.	Discont.	Total
	£ million	£ million	£ million	£ million	£ million	£ million
Cost of sales	455	165	620	385	170	555
Net operating expenses						
Distribution costs	56	13	69	46	5	51
Administrative expenses	41	12	53	34	3	37
Other operating income	(8)	0	(8)	(5)	0	(5)
	89	25	114	75	8	83
Less 1992 provision	0	(10)	(10)			
	89	15	104			

The total figures for continuing operations in 1993 include the following amounts relating to acquisitions: cost of sales £40 million and net operating expenses £4 million (namely distribution costs £3 million, administrative expenses £3 million and other operating income £2 million).

EXAMPLE 11.2 PROFIT AND LOSS ACCOUNT

	Continuing operations Acquisitions	Discont. operations	Total	Total
	1993	1993	1993	1993	1992 as restated
	£ million	£ million	£ million	£ million	£ million
Turnover	550	50	175	775	690
Cost of sales	(415)	(40)	(165)	(620)	(555)
Gross profit	135	10	10	155	135
Net operating expenses	(85)	(4)	(25)	(114)	(83)
Less 1992 provision			10	10	
Operating profit	50	6	(5)	51	52
Profit on sale of properties	9			9	6
Provision for loss on operations to be discontinued					(30)
Loss on disposal of discontinued operations			(17)	(17)	
Less 1992 provision			20	20	
Profit on ordinary activities before interest	59	6	(2)	63	28
Interest payable				(18)	(15)
Profit on ordinary activities before taxation				45	13
Tax on profit on ordinary activities				(14)	(4)
Profit on ordinary activities after taxation				31	9
Minority interests				(2)	(2)
[Profit before extraordinary items]				29	7
[Extraordinary items] (included only to show position)				–	–
Profit for the financial year				29	7
Dividends				(8)	(1)
Retained profit for the financial year				21	6
Earnings per share				**39p**	**10p**
Adjustments				Xp	Xp
[to be itemised and an adequate description to be given]					
Adjusted earnings per share				Yp	Yp

[Reason for calculating the adjusted earnings per share to be given]

Note

	1993			1992 (as restated)		
	Cont. £ million	Discont. £ million	Total £ million	Cont. £ million	Discont. £ million	Total £ million
Turnover				500	190	690
Cost of sales				385	170	555
Net operating expenses						
Distribution costs	56	13	69	46	5	51
Administrative expenses	41	12	53	34	3	37
Other operating income	(8)	0	(8)	(5)	0	(5)
	89	25	114	75	8	83
Operating profit				40	12	52

The total figure of net operating expenses for continuing operations in 1993 includes £4 million in respect of acquisitions (namely distribution costs £3 million, administrative expenses £3 million and other operating income £2 million).

EXAMPLE 11.3 STATEMENT OF TOTAL RECOGNISED GAINS AND LOSSES

	1993 £ million	1992 as restated £ million
Profit for the financial year	29	7
Unrealised surplus on revaluation of properties	4	6
Unrealised (loss)/gain on trade investments	(3)	7
	30	20
Currency translation differences on foreign currency net investments	(2)	5
Total recognised gains and losses relating to the year	28	25
Prior year adjustment (as explained in note x)	(10)	
Total gains and losses recognised since last annual report	18	

EXAMPLE 11.4 NOTE OF HISTORICAL COST PROFITS AND LOSSES

	1993 £ million	1992 as restated £ million
Reported profit on ordinary activities before taxation	45	13
Realisation of property revaluation gains of previous years	9	10
Difference between a historical cost depreciation charge and the actual depreciation charge of the year calculated on the revalued amount	5	4
Historical cost profit on ordinary activities before taxation	59	27
Historical cost profit for the year retained after taxation, minority interests, extraordinary items and dividends	35	20

EXAMPLE 11.5 RECONCILIATION OF MOVEMENTS IN SHAREHOLDERS' FUNDS

	1993	1992 as restated
	£ million	£ million
Profit for the financial year	29	7
Dividends	(8)	(1)
	21	6
Other recognised gains and losses relating to the year (net)	(1)	18
New share capital subscribed	20	1
Goodwill written off	(25)	
Net addition to shareholders' funds	15	25
Opening shareholders' funds (originally £375 million before deducting prior year adjustment of £10 million)	365	340
Closing shareholders' funds	380	365

EXAMPLE 11.6 RESERVES

	Share premium account £ million	Revaluation reserve £ million	Profit and loss account £ million	Total £ million
At beginning of year as previously stated	44	200	120	364
Prior year adjustments			(10)	(10)
At beginning of year as restated	44	200	110	354
Premium on issue of shares (nominal value £7 million)	13			13
Goodwill written off			(25)	(25)
Transfer from profit and loss account of the year			21	21
Transfer of realised profits		(14)	14	0
Decrease in value of trade investment		(3)		(3)
Currency translation differences on foreign currency net investments			(2)	(2)
Surplus on property revaluations		4		4
At end of year	57	187	118	362

Note: Nominal share capital at end of year £18 million (1992 £11 million).

Continuing and discontinued operations

Discontinued operations have been defined above, and you should already be familiar with the point made in the standard that if operations do not satisfy all the conditions as to discontinued operations, they should be classified as continuing. This section deals with some of the further problems arising in classifying operations between continuing and discontinued for inclusion in the profit and loss account.

'Discontinued' versus 'discontinuing'

In dealing with discontinued operations it is important to distinguish such operations from those that are discontinuing. The latter may be gradually discontinued over a period of years.

The distinction between the two operations follows from the first part of the definition of discontinued operations above, that is, we have a discontinued operation if the sale or termination is completed either during the period or before the earlier of three months after the commencement of the subsequent period and the date on which the financial statements are approved.

This part of the definition effectively rules out discontinuing activities that are actually discontinued over a long period of time. These discontinuing operations should be included under continuing operations and it may be appropriate to separately disclose, within continuing operations, such discontinuing operations. See Example 11.7.

EXAMPLE 11.7 DISCONTINUING AS OPPOSED TO DISCONTINUED OPERATIONS AND SUGGESTED FURTHER DISCLOSURE

Prior to the year end a decision is taken to wind down and eventually terminate the Northern division of the enterprise. The termination is anticipated to take at least two years to complete. To reflect properly the effect of the decision in the current year, turnover and operating profit may be disclosed on the face of the profit and loss account as follows:

	1994 £000	1993 £000
Turnover:		
Continuing operations, excluding Northern division	90	80
Discontinuing operations – Northern division	35	40
Total continuing operations	125	120
(There were no acquisitions during the two years above.)		
Operating profit/(loss)		
Continuing operations, excluding Northern division	35	33
Discontinuing operations – Northern division	(11)	(18)
Total continuing operations	24	15

If necessary, a provision for the loss on closure of the Northern division would be made and disclosed as an exceptional item after operating profit in the 1994 profit and loss account.

Determining when an operation is discontinued

Returning to the definition of discontinued operations above, in addition to the timing of the sale or termination as dealt with in Example 11.7, for an operation to be discontinued it is also necessary that:

▶ activities cease in the event of a termination
▶ the sale or termination arising from:
  – *either* a withdrawal from a particular market (class of business or geographical)
  – *or* from a material reduction in turnover in the reporting entity's continuing markets

has a material effect on the nature and focus of the reporting entity's operations and represents a material reduction in its operating facilities

▶ the assets, liabilities, results of operations and activities of the discontinued operation are clearly distinguishable, physically, operationally and for financial reporting purposes.

Accordingly, the definition of discontinued operations can be taken to mean:

▶ the discontinued operation should be a separate business
▶ assets, liabilities, results and activities of the discontinued operation must be clearly distinguishable
▶ the discontinued operation must be separate from the rest of the entity's operations but it does not have to be different
▶ the discontinued operation does not have to be a business segment under SSAP 25
▶ a hotel group, for example, that sells all its hotels in South East Asia and buys hotels in Northern Europe in their place gives rise to a situation where there is a material change in 'the nature and focus of operations' and therefore to discontinued operations (and new acquisitions)
▶ a sale or termination that is undertaken for the purpose of achieving cost savings or improvements in productivity is part of an entity's continuing operations as there is no material effect on the nature and focus of operations.

EXAMPLE 11.8 IDENTIFYING OPERATIONS AS CONTINUING OR DISCONTINUED

A group's year end is 30 June 1994 and its directors have approved the accounts for the year so ended in December 1994.

1   During the year to 30 June 1994 the group decided to close a subsidiary, Tango Ltd. The closure was completed on 30 September 1994. It also decided, in May 1994, on the closure of another subsidiary, Alpha (1) Ltd, but this closure was not completed until November 1994. Also before the year end at 30 June 1994, in April 1994, the group announced a withdrawal from one of its business segments, its South American market, and that the withdrawal would be spread over the next two years.
2   During the year to 30 June 1994, the group sold one of its subsidiaries, Roger Ltd. It also closed down, in December 1993, one of its warehouses in the Isle of Dogs, the warehouse being surplus to the requirements of the group. It also, quite independently of the sale of Roger Ltd and the closure of the warehouse, achieved an 8% reduction in its workforce through both compulsory and voluntary redundancies.
3   After the year end at 30 June 1994, the group decided to sell another subsidiary, Alpha (2) Ltd, and the sale was completed on 16 August 1994.

Describe how the closures, withdrawal, reduction in workforce and sales should be dealt with in the profit and loss account of the company for the year ended 30 June 1994 under FRS 3 and explain why.

1 The decisions taken before 30 June 1994

Closure of subsidiary Tango Ltd on 30 September 1994
If we assume that the assets, liabilities, results and activities of Tango Ltd are clearly distinguishable and that the closure materially affected the nature and focus of operations and represented a material reduction in operating facilities, it should be classified as discontinued as the decision to close was taken before the balance sheet date and the closure was completed before the earlier of three months after the year end and the date of approval of the accounts by the directors.

Closure of subsidiary Alpha (1) Ltd
Even though the decision to close was taken before the year end, this closure was completed after the earlier of three months after the year end and the date of the approval of the accounts by the directors. Accordingly, it should be classified as continuing regardless of whether the closure satisfies the other conditions of discontinued activities outlined above. As the decision was taken before the year end the need for a provision should be considered. If a material provision is made it would be exceptional and disclosed, under continuing operations, after operating profit but before interest.

Withdrawal from South American market
This would have to be classified under continuing operations but could be disclosed separately within continuing operations as discontinuing, as opposed to discontinued, operations.

2 Transactions during the year ended 30 June 1994

Sale of subsidiary Roger Ltd
This is a straightforward sale during the accounting period and assuming that the other conditions of discontinued operations (see Closure of Tango Ltd above) apply, it should be classified under discontinued operations.

Closure of Isle of Dogs warehouse
Even if the assets, liabilities, results and activities of this operation are clearly distinguishable, if we argue that there is neither a material effect on the nature and focus of the group's operations nor a material reduction in its operating facilities, then the closure would be classified as continuing operations. It is this last point that applies here as the warehouse is surplus to the requirements of the group. It would, therefore, be dealt with under continuing operations.

8% reduction in workforce
If we work on the basis that no sale or closure is involved then this would be dealt with as continuing operations, exceptional if material.

3 Transaction after the year end at 30 June 1994

Sale of subsidiary Alpha (2) Ltd
As the decision to sell was taken after the year end, this should be treated as a non-adjusting post-balance sheet event and should be treated in the profit and loss account for the year ended 30 June 1994 under continuing operations. If material, disclosure should be made of the post-balance sheet event.

EXAMPLE 11.9 DISCONTINUED AND CONTINUING ACTIVITIES – A FURTHER EXAMPLE

A group has three subsidiaries of similar size all operating in the field of accountancy tuition. The group has several other subsidiaries engaged in different lines of business. One of the three accountancy tuition subsidiaries is sold/closed during the accounting period.

In the absence of any further information, indicate, by way of bullet points, how the sale/closure should be reflected in the profit and loss account for the accounting period under FRS 3.

The sale/closure should be reflected in the profit and loss account for the accounting period under FRS 3 by reference to the following:

- ▶ The sale of one of three subsidiaries all involved in accountancy tuition does not involve the sale of a segment that can be identified as the whole of the accountancy tuition operation.
- ▶ On the basis that:
  - – the sale involves a material reduction in operating facilities and
  - – involves a material reduction in turnover of the group's continuing markets and
  - – assets, liabilities, results and activities can be distinguished physically, operationally and for financial reporting purposes
  - – the sale would fall under discontinued operations under FRS 3.
- ▶ The fact that the nature of operations of the sold subsidiary is not different does not affect the classification under discontinued operations.
- ▶ If, however, there is no material effect on the nature and focus of operations, for example, the subsidiary is closed with the prime purpose of achieving cost savings for the group with its business being transferred to the remaining continuing accountancy tuition subsidiaries, the closure would, more appropriately, be dealt with as part of the continuing operations of the group.

The inclusion of discontinued operations in the profit and loss account

Discontinued operations need to be separately considered in so far as they are discontinued either by way of closure or by way of sale.

Closure

You should treat closure in the following ways:

- ▶ The results up to the date of closure should be shown as part of ordinary profits under the heading of discontinued operations.
- ▶ The profit or loss on closure should be included as an exceptional item after operating profit and before interest and shown under discontinued operations.
- ▶ Any restructuring or reorganisation of continuing operations resulting from a closure should be shown as part of continuing operations.
- ▶ The profit or loss on closure should include only revenue and costs that are directly related to the closure. FRED 1 restricted these to redundancy costs and the profit or loss arising from the sale of fixed assets. FRS 3 is not specific on this point and there would appear to be nothing in the standard that would preclude us from including other items such as penalties and the costs of retaining key personnel in the run-down period to the date of actual closure.
- ▶ Trading results from the date of the decision to close should not be included under closure costs (as they would have been under SSAP 6) but included under trading results up to the date of actual closure under discontinued activities as in the first bullet point above.

EXAMPLE 11.10 INCORPORATING DISCONTINUED OPERATIONS IN THE PROFIT AND LOSS ACCOUNT

A group prepares accounts to 31 December each year. A decision was taken, on 30 June 1994, to close one of its subsidiaries. The closure began to be implemented in September 1994 and was completed in December 1994.

Turnover, cost of sales, net operating expenses and interest payable of the subsidiary for the year ended 31 December 1993 were £10,000, £11,000, £1,000 and £250 respectively.

In the year to 31 December 1994 the subsidiary had turnover, cost of sales, net operating expenses and interest payable all up to the date of actual closure of £7,500, £9,000, £1,500 and £250 respectively.

As a result of the closure, and in addition to the trading losses indicated above, there were write-downs for stock and plant of £1,000 and £1,500 respectively, redundancy costs of £500 and penalities for breach of contract of £250.

Goodwill of £4,000 was paid on the acquisition of the subsidiary and the whole amount was written off to reserves immediately on acquisition.

There are no timing or permanent differences between accounting and taxable profit or loss and the tax rate is to be taken at 30%.

How would the closed subsidiary be included under FRS 3?

	1994	1993
	£	£
Discontinued operations:		
Turnover	7,500	10,000
Cost of sales	(9,000)	(11,000)
Gross loss	(1,500)	(1,000)
Net operating expenses	(1,500)	(1,000)
Operating loss	(3,000)	(2,000)
Loss on disclosure of discontinued operations		
(1,000 + 1,500 + 500 + 250 + 4,000)	(7,250)	–
(Note that the items below are not separated out between continuing and discontinued operations – the amounts that would be aggregated with those of the group are as follows)		
Interest payable	(250)	(250)
Loss on ordinary activities before tax	(10,500)	(2,250)
Taxation at 30%	3,150	675
	(7,350)	(1,575)
Extraordinary items	–	–
Loss for the financial year	(7,350)	(1,575)

A further problem that you may encounter when dealing with operations discontinued as a result of closure is that of setting up a provision for losses. If the decision to close is taken during the year and the closure is completed in the year, then there is no need to consider the need for a provision for losses at the year end. If, however, a decision has been taken before the year end to discontinue operations but the actual closure is completed in the next year such a provision may be necessary.

FRS 3 requires a provision to be made if a decision to close has been made and where there is a 'detailed formal plan for termination from which the reporting entity cannot realistically withdraw'. The provision should cover:

▶ the direct costs of the termination
▶ any operating losses of the operation up to the date of the termination

and, in both cases, the provision should take into account the aggregate profit if any, to be recognised in the profit and loss account from the future profits of the operation or the disposal of its assets.

The provision (for loss on closure), where material, should be included in the profit and loss account after operating profit and included under continuing operations and further analysed as discontinuing within continuing operations.

In the following accounting period:

▶ that part of last year's provision relating to trading losses should be shown in arriving at the operating result disclosed for the discontinued operation

▶ the loss on closure should be calculated and disclosed after operating profit and before interest under discontinued operations

▶ any balance of the provision should be shown against the loss on closure.

Setting up a provision for losses is illustrated in Example 11.11.

EXAMPLE 11.11 INCORPORATING PROVISIONS FOR LOSSES ON TERMINATION

A group prepares its accounts to 31 December each year and makes the decision to close a subsidiary on 30 September 1994. The actual closure is anticipated to occur on 30 June 1995.

The subsidiary had, from 1 January 1994 up to the date of the decision to close, turnover of £30,000 and operating losses of £8,000, the difference being attributable to cost of sales. The turnover and operating loss of the subsidiary, from the date of the decision to close to the year end were £6,000 and £4,000 respectively.

In the year to 31 December 1995, it is anticipated that, for the six months to 30 June 1995, the turnover and operating loss of the subsidiary are expected to be £12,000 and £6,000 respectively.

As a result of the decision to discontinue, it is further anticipated that there will be stock and fixed asset write-downs of £8,000 and £4,000 respectively.

There was no goodwill on the acquisition of the subsidiary, and tax – there are no permanent or timing differences arising between accounting and taxable profit – is taken at 30%.

Prepare the relevant extract for the 1994 profit and loss account.

	1994 £
Continuing operations	
Turnover (30,000 + 6,000)	36,000
Cost of sales	(48,000)
Operating loss (8,000 + 4,000)	(12,000)
Provision for loss on operations to be discontinued	(18,000)
(Strictly, the provision should be set up at the date of the decision and thus should include the operating results from the date of the decision to the year end. As turnover and operating profit of the subsidiary will have to be included, as above, for the full year, it would seem to be more appropriate to establish the provision at the year end. Accordingly, the provision above is made up of the anticipated operating loss to the date of actual closure as from the end of the year [6,000] plus the two write downs for assets [8,000 + 4,000 = 12,000]: 18,000 in all.)	
Loss on ordinary activities before tax	(30,000)
Taxation at 30%	9,000
Loss on ordinary activities after tax	(21,000)

The operation could be further described, within continuing operations, as discontinuing.

The 1985 actual amounts are as follows: the turnover and operating loss for the subsidiary for the six months to 30 June are £24,000 and £14,000 respectively. Further, the write-downs for stock and fixed assets are actually determined to be £10,000 in total.

Prepare the relevant extract for the 1995 profit and loss account, including comparatives

	1995 £	1994 £
Discontinued operations		
Turnover	24,000	36,000
Cost of sales	(38,000)	(48,000)
Gross loss	(14,000)	(12,000)
Less release of provision made in 1994	6,000	–
Operating loss	(8,000)	(12,000)
Provision for loss on operation to be discontinued		(18,000)
Loss on closure of discontinued operation (here restricted to the write-downs on assets)	(10,000)	
Less release of provision made in 1994 (the balance remaining of 18,000 less 6,000)	12,000	
Loss on ordinary activities before tax	(6,000)	(30,000)
Taxation at 30%	1,800	9,000
Loss on ordinary activities after tax	(4,200)	(21,000)

Observe that where the provision is dealt with in 1994 after the operating loss number, it is allocated in 1995 partly to operating loss and partly to the loss on disposal.

The provision in 1994 of £18,000 compares with the actual loss on closure of operating losses of £14,000 and asset write-downs of £10,000, that is, an additional overall pre-tax loss of £6,000.

Also note that the turnover and operating losses of the subsidiary in 1994, which were included under continuing activities in that year are now being dealt with in 1995 under discontinued activities.

Sale

Having dealt with the treatment of operations that are discontinued following closure it is necessary to deal with the different treatment of operations that are discontinued following sale. Where the discontinued activity is a sold subsidiary, the gain or loss on sale must be calculated in accordance with FRS 2 (see Chapter 18). The essential treatment of such a discontinued operation is:

▶ results up to the date of sale should be included as ordinary operations under discontinued operations
▶ the profit or loss on sale should be shown as an exceptional item after operating profit and before interest and included under discontinued operations. See Example 11.12.

EXAMPLE 11.12 TREATMENT OF OPERATIONS THAT ARE DISCONTINUED GIVEN A SALE AS OPPOSED TO THE CLOSURE OF THE OPERATION

One of the subsidiaries of a group had turnover and operating profits, for the year ended 31 December 1994, of £15,000 and £3,000 respectively. In the year ended 31 December 1995, the year in which the subsidiary is sold, the subsidiary had, from the beginning of the year to the date of sale, turnover and operating profit of £4,000 and £1,000 respectively.

Sale proceeds were £7,500.

Goodwill paid at acquisition and written off immediately to reserves on acquisition amounted to £2,000.

The net assets of the subsidiary on the date of sale amounted to £2,500. The subsidiary had borrowings and paid interest of £350 in 1994 and £100 in 1995 up to the date of its sale.

Tax is taken at 30% and there are no differences between accounting and taxable profit.

Prepare the relevant extract for the 1995 profit and loss account, including comparatives

	1995	1994
	£	£
Discontinued operations		
Turnover	4,000	15,000
Cost of sales	(3,000)	(12,000)
Operating profit	1,000	3,000
Profit on disposal of discontinued operations	3,000	–
(sale proceeds £7,500 less net assets 'sold' £2,500 less goodwill paid on acquisition £2,000)		
Interest payable	(100)	(350)
Profit on ordinary activities before tax	3,900	2,650
Tax at 30% on profit on ordinary activities	(1,170)	(795)
Profit on ordinary activities after tax	2,730	1,855
Extraordinary item	–	–
Profit for the financial year	2,730	1,855

The date of sale should be taken as the date on which a binding legal agreement for the sale of an operation is entered into.

In respect of provisioning for losses, the explanatory section of FRS 3 considers the situation where the decision to sell has been taken but there is no legally binding sale agreement. In this situation no provision should be made for the direct costs arising from the decision to sell and for future operating losses. You could adopt the view that on the ground of prudence a provision should be made. In any event, permanent diminutions in asset values arising as a consequence of the decision to sell should be recorded.

The treatment of acquisitions within a period

These should be disclosed separately in aggregate as a component of continuing operations. The minimum analysis on the face of the profit and loss account is in respect of turnover and operating profit. The other items may be analysed in the notes instead of on the face of the profit and loss account.

Where it is not possible to determine the post-acquisition results of an operation to the end of the current period, the FRS states that an indication should be given of the contribution of the acquisition to the turnover and operating profit of the continuing operations in addition to the information required by the 1985 Act.

Accounting for acquisitions gives rise to other problems such as setting up provisions for reorganisation and the effects of such provisions on goodwill and on the reported post-acquisition profits of the subsidiary. Such problems have been dealt with in Chapter 5 on goodwill and are also dealt with in Chapter 20, which deals further with the problems arising under acquisition accounting. The ASB is developing a standard on fair value accounting. FRED 7 was issued in 1993 and is dealt with in Chapter 20.

The Act requires disclosure of the profit or loss of the undertaking acquired:

▶ for the period from the beginning of the year to the date of acquisition
▶ for the previous financial year.

The usefulness of this information is that we can compare the information above with the post-acquisition results and look into any significant variations in the trend of the acquiree's results.

Exceptional items

Where the definition of these items is similar to the definition under SSAP 6, it is the broadening of the definition of ordinary activities under FRS 3 that results in what would, under SSAP 6, have been dealt with as extraordinary, now being dealt with as ordinary and exceptional instead.

There are three types of items that will not necessarily be, but usually are, exceptional items and which must be shown on the face of the profit and loss account – after operating profit and before interest – and included under continuing or discontinued operations as appropriate. These are profits or losses on the sale or termination of an operation, which we have dealt with above; costs of a fundamental reorganisation or restructuring having a material effect on the nature and focus of the entity's operations and profits or losses on the disposal of fixed assets, which are dealt with in some detail in Chapter 4.

The FRS 3 treatment as to fundamental restructurings results in the withdrawal of UITF Abstract 2 on this topic. The standard does not define what is meant by a fundamental restructuring and this may be seen as a weakness in the FRS – how, for example, would you deal with a relocation; should the costs be included in operating results or dealt with after operating results as above?

All other exceptional items should be shown under the statutory format headings to which they relate, which means that they will be shown in arriving at operating profit. Such items may be dealt with in the notes or on the face of the profit and loss account if necessary to give a true and fair view. Thus, for example, a provision for losses on contracts of a construction company could be included in cost of sales and insurance claims could be dealt with in other operating income. Reorganisation costs may, however, have to be dealt with under various headings. Losses on the expropriation of assets overseas do not have an appropriate statutory heading and may be better dealt with within one of the three items shown after operating profit.

Tax and minority interests in respect of exceptional items

The tax relating to the three items that are required to be disclosed after operating profit must be shown in a note to the profit and loss account. The related tax is required to be shown in aggregate and not in respect of each individual item. The minority interest in the items must also be calculated and disclosed in the notes.

There is no requirement to disclose tax or minority interest relating to other exceptional items.

FRS 3 requires that the tax attributable to the exceptional items disclosed after operating profit should be calculated by computing the tax on the profit or loss on ordinary activities as if the items did not exist and then comparing the notional tax charge with the tax charge on the profit or loss for the period. Any additional tax charge or credit should be attributed to the exceptional items.

How FRS 3 is new

What is new under FRS 3 is the figure of total gains and losses as disclosed in the statement of total recognised gains and losses. This statement is an innovation in UK accounting and is fundamental to the concept of 'performance' under FRS 3. Both accounting standards and the Act require items to be taken direct to reserves. Under SSAP 6 it was possible for items taken directly to reserves to be obscured as it was possible merely to make a cross-reference to the reserve movements note on the face of the profit and loss account. Under FRS 3 the statement of total gains has the same prominence as other primary statements and it is no longer possible to 'lose' items that are essential to users' understanding of an entity's results.

Note that goodwill written off directly to reserves on acquisition is not a recognised loss for this purpose and neither is goodwill written back to reserves on disposal of the business a recognised gain for this purpose.

More fundamentally, FRS 3 changes the way eps is calculated and will, therefore, affect the p/e so far regarded as the most important investment ratio. So much so that the *Financial Times* asked in 1993 whether the p/e ratio is now dead. As items formerly treated as extraordinary are now moved 'above the line' the FRS 3 eps number is likely to be much more volatile than in the past. One of the aims of the ASB in issuing FRS 3 was to reduce the importance of a single eps number, a number we know is capable of manipulation. Under FRS 3 investors are given and will be forced to look at more information on which to base their valuations of companies.

The Institute of Investment Management and Research is working on a report expected to produce a recommended method of producing a 'normalised' eps number showing what a company has earned from its continuing operations. It is possible that analysts will latch on to this 'ongoing' eps and resultant p/e.

FRS 3 will also have an effect on the way the *Financial Times* reports financial results – the policy to be adopted as to the London Share Service prices and the appropriate treatment of eps and p/e ratios is yet to be announced.

David Tweedie the chairman of the ASB has said that there is a need to develop accounting standards that non-accountants can understand. It has to be said that FRS 3 does not fall into this category. However, as, essentially, the standard deals with disclosure and presentation rather than specifying new treatments of the numbers, it must be seen as a positive contribution to financial reporting, and in encouraging analysts to move their focus away from a single performance indicator encourages them to use a wider range of measurements.

Summary

FRS 3 is a long standard and, in that it introduces a new form of presenting information as to financial performance and new statements is, to start with, daunting. With increased familiarity it becomes less so. You need to look at FRS 3 as follows:

▶ be fully familiar with the layout of the statements and notes as in Examples 11.1 to 11.6
▶ be able clearly to distinguish continuing from discontinued activities
▶ be able to deal with provisions on discontinuing activities
▶ be able to account for exceptional items under the standard
▶ be able to prepare and critically comment on the statement of recognised gains and losses and the movements on shareholders' funds
▶ be able to account for the disposal of previously revalued assets (exam style question 1, Pringle Ltd, deals with this aspect of the FRS)
▶ be able to comment on the impact of FRS 3 on eps and the change from the previous emphasis on this number.

Suggested reading

Accounting Guides – Reporting Financial Performance – A Commentary on FRS 3 (Coopers and Lybrand 1992)

Self test questions

1   Will there be any extraordinary items under FRS 3?

2   Pingo plc is the parent company of a group with several wholly owned subsidiaries. The group prepares its financial statements to 31 December each year.

On 31 October 1993 it was decided that a subsidiary company, Pongo Ltd, should withdraw from the markets in which it is operating, such markets consisting of a substantial part of the company's existing business. Employees were informed of the intended closure of Pongo Ltd in November 1993 and its operations were actually discontinued on 31 March 1994. The following information has been provided as to Pongo Ltd:

	Actual	Forecast (at 31.12.93)
	12 months to 31.12.93	3 months to 31.3.94
	£000	£000
Sales	25,500	4,000
Operating expenses	22,000	6,000
Deficiency arising on pension fund	–	300
Profit on sale of assets	–	1,100
Redundancy costs	–	1,500

A provision for closure costs was made, at 31 December 1993 based on the information above, in the 1993 accounts.

The actual data for Pongo Ltd for the three months to 31 March 1994 is now provided as follows:

	£000
Sales	4,700
Operating expenses	5,800
Redundancy costs	1,500
Deficiency arising on pension fund	350
Profit on sale of assets	900

Prepare a schedule to show how this operation would be dealt with in the FRS 3 consolidated profit and loss account of the Pingo plc group for the year ended 31 December 1994, including comparatives for the immediately preceding year.

3   Following on from the information in question 2 above, Bingo Ltd, another wholly owned subsidiary of the Pingo plc group, purchased a building for operational use on 1 January 1990 for £800,000, estimated useful life 50 years. The building was revalued on 1 January 1992 to £1,200,000. The estimated residual value of the building is nil and depreciation is provided on a straight-line basis. The building was sold in February 1994 for £2,000,000. A full year's

depreciation is provided in the year of acquisition but none in the year of sale.

Explain how the gain on sale would be reported in the FRS 3 consolidated profit and loss account for the year ended 31 December 1994. Describe the content of the FRS 3 statement of historical profits and comment critically as to its purchase in assessing financial performance.

4 The Times has reported that 'to attempt to define a single earnings figure for all purposes is bound to fail' and asserted that 'one number cannot do everything'.

Discuss this statement in the light of the ASB's belief, extolled by David Tweedie, its chairman, that the perception that accounts could be broken down into one magic earnings per share figure should itself be broken.

Exam style questions

1 *Pringle Ltd*
ED 36 was issued by the ASC as part of its general policy of reviewing existing accounting standards. It was followed by SSAP 6 (Revised), which has now been superseded by the ASB's FRS 3.

One area of difference between ED 36 and SSAP 6 (Revised) was in accounting for the profit or loss on previously revalued fixed assets. ED 36 proposed that the profit or loss on such a disposal which should be reported – that is, passed through the profit and loss account of the year of disposal – should be the difference between sale proceeds and depreciated historical cost. SSAP 6 (Revised) stated that this was not the only method of calculating the reported profit or loss on the sale of such a fixed asset. The principal alternative is to calculate the profit or loss as the difference between sale proceeds and the carrying amount of the asset on the date of sale. This alternative approach was proposed as standard accounting practice in ED 51 and is now the required basis of accounting for the gain or loss on the disposal of a previously revalued asset under FRS 3.

Pringle Ltd is a company that periodically revalues some of its fixed assets. An item of plant purchased on 1 January 1989 for £875,000, useful life ten years, was revalued on 1 January 1991 at £1,040,000 and again on 1 January 1992 at £1,200,000. The asset was sold on 1 January 1993 for £1,450,000.

The balance on profit and loss account of the company was as follows:

	£
At 31/12/90	5,678,000
For the y/e 31/12/91 – before depreciation	110,000
For the y/e 31/12/92 – before depreciation	95,000
For the y/e 31/12/93 – before the gain on sale	33,000

Required:
a) On the basis that i) there is no revaluation, that is, strict HCA
                ii) there is revaluation as above, that is, modified HCA
prepare the statement of movements on reserves for the years ended 31 December 1991 and 31 December 1992, clearly identifying 'earnings' and 'legally distributable profits'. Comment on the differences arising.

b) On the basis that i) there is strict HCA
                ii) there is modified HCA – ED 36 basis (income approach)
                iii) there is modified HCA – ED 51 and FRS 3 basis (value approach)

calculate the gain arising on disposal to be reported for the y/e 31 December 1993 and the statement of movements on reserves for the year, clearly identifying 'earnings' and 'legally distributable profits'. Comment on the differences arising.

c) Prepare, for all three years, given modified HCA, the FRS 3 note of historical profits and losses. (20 marks)

2 *Rabbit plc*

Rabbit plc sells a variety of goods by mail order through agents in the UK and through an agency in France, which accounted for 12% of the turnover during the year.

The agency in France was set up by Rabbit plc as a selling agency branch. However, subsequent to a decision, prior to 31 March 1994, to withdraw from overseas markets the agency ceased operations on 9 May 1994. The operating profit up to cessation was £280,000 after the year end. The direct closure costs of £720,000 have not yet been provided for.

The operations in France accounted for 14% of costs of sales, 15% of distribution costs and 6% of administration expenses.

Significant operations were acquired at the year end in the UK. The acquisitions were partly financed by the issue of £6 million of 12% Debenture stock at 95. The debentures are secure with a floating charge and are redeemable in 2003.

The following is a list of balances extracted from the accounting records as at 31 March 1994.

	£000
Other administrative, selling and delivery expenses	18,473
Ordinary share capital, issued and fully paid	45,000
Costs of goods sold	242,000
Bank overdraft	10,832
Salaries and wages	25,560
Profit and loss account balance, 1 April, 1993	4,050
Audit fees	34
Interest on bank overdraft	855
Provision for doubtful debts	234
Prepaid expenses	988
Trade creditors	37,980
12% Debentures Stock	5,700
Share premium account	12,700
Revaluation reserve	4,100
Interim dividend, paid November 1993	2,700
Advance corporation tax recoverable on interim dividend	900
Stocks of goods for resale	55,407
Directors' total emoluments	322
Bad debts written off	1,003
Value added tax – credit balance	1,845
Corporation tax account – debit balance	36
Deferred tax	10,350
Sales, exclusive of value added tax	337,500
Agent's commission	24,345
Hire of equipment	207
Trade debtors	77,400
Accrued expenses	225
Unclaimed dividends	002
Proceeds of the disposal of equipment and vehicles	57

Loans to employees to purchase the company's shares	600
Profit on translation of amounts due from overseas agency	200
Purchase of equipment and vehicles during the year	292
Fixed assets, net book values at 1 April 1993	19,103
Reorganisation and restructuring costs	550

Additional information:

▶ Stocks, which include goods held by agents, have been valued at the lower of purchase price and net realisable value. Of the goods sent on consignment to France 20% were unsold at the year end. Included in cost of goods sold is £4,000,000, being freight, insurance and warehousing, which can be taken as attributable to all the goods sent on consignment.

▶ Account must be taken of the following outstanding items:

   − agents' commission £855,000
   − interest on bank overdraft £22,000
   − auditors' expenses £5,000

▶ The provision for doubtful debts is to be increased to £254,000.

▶ Appropriations are to be made for:

   − a final dividend of 2.25 pence per share
   − the creation of a stock replacement reserve by transfer of £135,000.

▶ A provision of £90,000 is to be made for obsolete stock.

▶ The bank overdraft is secured on the freehold property and is not due for repayment until 1997.

▶ Corporation tax, at the rate of 33% has been estimated to be £12,600,000 based on the year's profit. £112,000 is to be transferred to the deferred tax account representing the excess of capital allowances over depreciation charges. The company provides for all timing differences, on the liability method, except for those which are not expected to reverse in the future. Tax paid in January 1994 (based on the 1993 profits) was £7,936,000, which was £36,000 more than originally estimated.

▶ Salaries and wages are to be apportioned between the administrative and distributive functions on the basis of 3:7. The amount shown in the list of balances includes:

   − Social Security costs of £4,065,000
   − contributions to works and staff pension fund of £3,375,000.

The average number of employees during the year was 3,540 of which 60% were involved in distribution.

▶ The directors' total emoluments of £322,000 include fees of £14,500, pensions to former directors £42,500 and compensation of £41,000 paid to a director who resigned during the year. The total amount is to be charged as £265,000 to administrative expenses and £57,000 to distributive expenses.

   Two non-executive directors each received £4,500. The chief executive received £46,500, the merchandise and the catalogue directors each received £29,500; the chairman £18,000; the distribution and the operations directors £28,000 each, and the computer, personnel and finance directors each received £20,000. The chairman waived emoluments of £3,000.

▶ Other administrative, selling and delivery expenses include £7,184,000 of administrative costs.

▶ The charge for bad debts is unusually high due to the substantial increase in the agency recruitment programme in the previous year and the effect on collection methods during the changeover from manual to computer operation. These two items account for £900,000.

- The hire of equipment relates to the company's computer facility, mainly used for administration.
- The equipment and vehicles disposed of were all used in the distribution of the company's goods. They had a written-down value of £90,000 and originally cost £158,000.

An analysis of the fixed assets at 1 april, 1993 revealed:

	Freehold property £	Equipment and vehicles £
Cost or valuation	17,797,000	5,738,000
Accumulative depreciation	1,822,000	2,610,000

The amounts to be charged for the year as depreciation are:

Freehold property £203,000, of which £72,000 is to be charged to administrative expenses.

Equipment and vehicles £540,000, of which £180,000 is to be charged to administrative expenses.

The freehold land included above was revalued by chartered surveyors at the year end at £1,200,000 above book value. A provision for deferred tax is not considered necessary.

No depreciation is provided on freehold land.

The depreciation based on historical cost would be £120,000 lower.

- The company has an authorised share capital of 300 million ordinary shares of £0.25 each.
- Bills of exchange discounted but which have not yet matured amounted to £420,000.

Required

From the information provided prepare a profit and loss account and a statement of total recognised gains and losses for the year ended 31 March 1994 and a balance sheet as at that date, all statements to comply, as far as possible, with the requirements of the Companies Act 1985 and with FRS 3. Assume an income tax rate of £25%.

(60 marks)

Note: Goods on consignment should be valued at 'Cost at destination', i.e. including a fair proportion of expenses incurred.

All answers on pages 654–662.

Cash Flow Statements

SSAP 10, which dealt with statements of source and application of funds, was issued by the ASC in 1975. Its requirements were almost universally complied with by companies that came within its scope, and audit reports have included specific reference to the audit of the source and application of funds statement.

The explanatory note to SSAP 10 stated that, in addition to the amount of profit made during the year (disclosed in the profit and loss account) and the disposition of resources at the beginning and end of the year (disclosed in the balance sheet), it is necessary, for a further understanding of a company's affairs, to also identify the movements in assets, liabilities and capital that have taken place during the year and the effect on net liquid funds. This information is not disclosed by a profit and loss account or balance sheet, but can be made available in the form of a statement of source and application of funds.

A source and application of funds statement showed the sources from which funds flowed into the company and the way in which they were used. It showed the funds generated as absorbed by the operations of the business and the manner in which any resulting surplus of assets was applied, or any deficiency of assets financed, distinguishing the long-term from the short-term. The statement distinguished the use of funds for the purchase of new fixed assets from funds used in increasing the working capital of a company. The purpose of the statement was to provide a link between the balance sheet at the beginning of the period, the profit and loss account for the period and the balance sheet at the end of the period.

SSAP 10 did not prescribe the form and content of the funds flow statement and its usefulness was thereby reduced in the variable accounting practice that developed as a result. Another weakness of SSAP 10 was a lack of a clear understanding and agreement about what is meant by the term 'funds'. This is a nebulous concept and the distinct lack of consensus as to what the term means was well illustrated by the variety of definitions adopted by companies in preparing source and application of funds statements. The main definitions adopted in practice were:

► net liquid funds
► working capital
► net borrowing
► total external financing.

In each case 'funds' could have included amounts that may not have resulted in the inflow or outflow of cash for months rather than days.

Another weakness of SSAP 10 was a lack of consensus as to the objectives of a funds statement. The standard failed to provide a conceptual framework for the preparation of a funds statement and did not explain the need to provide users with information to help them form views on liquidity, financial flexibility and risk. The standard described *what* the funds statement should show; it did not answer the question as to *why* it should be shown.

The need for a change from funds flow to cash flow reporting gradually began to emerge. A research study conducted by Professor T. A. Lee on behalf of ACCA disclosed that a growing number of UK companies were producing funds flow statements on a cash or near cash basis. In the USA, FASB reinforced the importance of providing cash flow information through Concepts Statement 1 on the objectives of financial reporting by stating:

> Financial reporting should provide information to help present and potential investors and creditors and other users in assessing the amounts, timing, and uncertainty of prospective cash receipts from dividends or interest and the proceeds from the sale, redemption, or maturity of securities or loans. The prospects for those cash receipts are affected by an enterprise's ability to generate enough cash to meet its obligations when due and its other cash operating needs, to reinvest in operations, and to pay cash dividends.

FASB issued SFAS 95 in 1987, which required a statement of cash flows as a part of financial statements.

The IASC was not to be left behind. Its framework for the preparation and presentation of financial statements states that:

> Information concerning changes in the financial position of an enterprise is useful in order to assess its investing, financing and operating activities during the reporting period. This information is useful in providing the user with a basis to assess the ability of the enterprise to generate cash and cash equivalents and the needs of the enterprise to utilise those cash flows.

In the UK, ASC issued ED 54 and, in 1991, the ASB issued its first financial reporting standard, FRS 1, which supersedes SSAP 10.

You will have dealt with the preparation of a cash flow statement in your studies for Paper 10. This chapter will deal with various preparation type points but will concentrate on the problems arising in reporting cash flows from, for example:

▶ the treatment of finance leases
▶ the treatment of the acquisition of a new subsidiary (and disposals)
▶ the treatment of exchange differences.

The format of a cash flow statement under FRS 1 – a reminder

You should already be familiar with illustrative example 1, provided for general guidance in FRS 1, dealing with a single company. This chapter is more concerned with application problems arising under illustrative example 2 for a group, which is reproduced in Example 12.1, and further explanation of some of the items included therein.

EXAMPLE 12.1 – FRS 1 ILLUSTRATIVE EXAMPLE 2 – GROUP

XYZ GROUP PLC
Cash flow statement for the year ended 31 March 1992

	£000	£000
Operating activities		
Cash received from customers	195,016	
Cash payments to suppliers	(109,225)	
Cash paid to and on behalf of employees	(56,434)	
Other cash payments	(12,345)	
Net cash inflow from continuing operating activities	17,012	
Net cash outflow in respect of discontinued activities and reorganisation costs	(990)	

Net cash inflow from operating activities		16,022
Returns on investments and servicing of finance		
Interest received	508	
Interest paid	(2,389)	
Interest element of finance lease rentals payments	(373)	
Dividend received from associated undertaking	15	
Dividends paid	(2,606)	
Net cash outflow from returns on investments and servicing of finance		(4,845)
Taxation		
UK corporation tax paid	(2,880)	
Overseas tax paid	(7)	
Tax paid		(2,887)
Investing activities		
Purchase of tangible fixed assets	(3,512)	
Purchase of subsidiary undertakings (net of cash and cash equivalents acquired) (See note 7)	(18,221)	
Sale of plant and machinery	1,052	
Sale of business (See note 8)	4,208	
Sale of trade investment	1,595	
Net cash outflows in respect of unsuccessful takeover bid	(3,811)	
Net cash outflow from investing activities		(18,689)
Net cash outflow before financing		(10,399)
Financing		
Issue of ordinary share capital	(49)	
New secured loan repayable in 1995	(1,091)	
New unsecured loan repayable in 1993	(1,442)	
New short-term loans	(2,006)	
Repayment of amounts borrowed	847	
Capital element of finance lease rental payments	1,342	
Net cash inflow from financing		(2,399)
Decrease in cash and cash equivalents		(8,000)
		(10,399)

Notes to the cash flow statement

1 RECONCILIATION OF OPERATING PROFIT TO NET CASH INFLOW FROM OPERATING ACTIVITIES

	£000
Operating profit	20,249
Depreciation charges	3,158
Profit on sale of tangible fixed assets	(50)
Increase in stocks	(12,263)
Increase in debtors	(3,754)
Increase in creditors	9,672
Net cash inflow from continuing operating activities	17,012
Net cash outflow in respect of discontinued activities and reorganisation costs	(990)
Net cash inflow from operating activities	16,022

2 ANALYSIS OF CHANGES IN CASH AND CASH EQUIVALENTS DURING THE YEAR

	£000
Balance at 1 April 1991	78
Net cash outflow before adjustments for the effect of foreign exchange rate changes	(8,000)
Effect of foreign exchange rate changes	(102)
Balance at 31 March 1992	(8,024)

3 ANALYSIS OF THE BALANCES OF CASH AND CASH EQUIVALENTS AS SHOWN IN THE BALANCE SHEET

	1992 £000	1991 £000	Change in year £000
Cash at bank and in hand	1,041	1,279	(238)
Bank overdrafts	(9,065)	(1,201)	(7,864)
	(8,024)	78	(8,102)

4 ANALYSIS OF CHANGES IN FINANCING DURING THE YEAR

	Share capital (including premium) £000	Loans and finance lease obligations £000
Balance at 1 April 1991	10,334	7,589
Cash inflows from financing	49	2,350
Shares issued for non-cash consideration	9,519	
Loans and finance lease obligations of subsidiary undertakings acquired during the year		3,817
Inception of finance lease contracts		2,845
Balance at 31 March 1992	19,902	16,601

[Note to preparers of financial statements

The disclosures set out below in respect of non-cash transactions may be combined with information disclosed elsewhere in the financial statements, e.g. the disclosure in respect of subsidiary undertakings acquired during the year could be combined with the disclosures required by paragraph 13(5) of Schedule 4A to the Companies Act 1985.]

5 MAJOR NON-CASH TRANSACTIONS

a During the year the group entered into finance lease arrangements in respect of assets with a total capital value at the inception of the leases of £2,845,000.
b Part of the consideration for the purchases of subsidiary undertakings and the sale of a business that occurred during the year comprised shares and loan notes respectively. Further details of the acquisitions and the disposal are set out below:

6 PURCHASE OF SUBSIDIARY UNDERTAKINGS

	£000
Net assets acquired	
Tangible fixed assets	12,194
Investments	1
Stocks	9,384
Debtors	13,856
Taxation recoverable	1,309
Cash at bank and in hand	1,439
Creditors	(21,715)
Bank overdrafts	(6,955)
Loans and finance leases	(3,817)

Deferred taxation	(165)
Minority shareholders' interests	(9)
	5,522
Goodwill	16,702
	22,224

Satisfied by

Shares allotted	9,519
Cash	12,705
	22,224

The subsidiary undertakings acquired during the year contributed £1,502,000 to the group's net operating cash flows, paid £1,308,000 in respect of net returns on investments and servicing of finance, paid £522,000 in respect of taxation and utilised £2,208,000 for investing activities.

7 ANALYSIS OF THE NET OUTFLOW OF CASH AND CASH EQUIVALENTS IN RESPECT OF THE PURCHASE OF SUBSIDIARY UNDERTAKINGS

	£000
Cash consideration	12,705
Cash at bank and in hand acquired	(1,439)
Bank overdrafts of acquired subsidiary undertakings	6,955
Net outflow of cash and cash equivalents in respect of the purchase of subsidiaries	18,221

8 SALE OF BUSINESS

	£000
Net assets disposed of	
Fixed assets	775
Stocks	5,386
Debtors	474
	6,635
Loss on disposal	(1,227)
	5,408
Satisfied by	
Loan notes	1,200
Cash	4,208
	5,408

The business sold during the year contributed £200,000 to the group's net operating cash flows, paid £252,000 in respect of net returns on investments and servicing of finance, paid £145,000 in respect of taxation and utilised £209,000 for investing activities.

Net cash flow from operating activities

This section looks at some further points regarding the net cash flow from operating activities and Note 1 to the cash flow statement (CFS) regarding reconciliation of operating profit to net cash flow from operating activities.

ED 54 proposed two different methods of reporting cash flows from operating activities, the indirect and the direct methods, or the net and gross approaches. Obviously, the net cash flow from operating activities would be the same under either method or approach; it is simply a question of reporting how we get to the net number.

Under the indirect method, the CFS would start with the net cash flow from operating activities, £16,022 in Example 12.1. This figure will have been arrived at by adjusting operating profit to remove the effects of:

▶ non-cash items
▶ changes in working capital
▶ any items relating to other categories of cash flows.

These adjustments are required to be disclosed in the notes to the CFS as in the reconciliation in Note 1 in Example 12.1.

Under the direct method, the gross operating cash receipts and payments – that is, amounts actually paid to suppliers and employees and received from customers – are reported on the face of the CFS so as to come down to the same net operating cash flow as under the indirect method. Look at the individual items under operating activities that are included in Example 12.1 in italics. The net cash flow of £16,022 is the same as under the indirect method. It is the way in which we get to the net cash flow that is different. Remember that FRS 1 requires the Note 1 disclosure (reconciliation of operating profit to the net cash flow from operating activities) even where the direct method is used.

Example 12.2 shows workings for both indirect and direct methods for cash flows from operating activities.

EXAMPLE 12.2 – INDIRECT VERSUS DIRECT METHODS FOR CASH FLOWS FROM OPERATING ACTIVITIES

Profit and loss account y/e 31.12.94

	£
Turnover	600
Cost of sales	(328)
Gross profit	272
Wages and salaries	(140)
Expenses, incl. depn	(100)
Retained for year	32

Balance sheets	31.12.94	31.12.93
	£	£
Fixed assets – cost	200	160
– depn	(132)	(96)
	68	64
Current assets		
– stock	136	80
– debtors	66	54
– bank	16	20
Current liabilities		
– creditors	(32)	(36)
	254	182
Share capital	204	164

P & l account	50		18
	254		182

There are no disposals of fixed assets during 1994. All tax, including VAT, is ignored.

Ascertain the net cash flow from operating activities under:
(i) the indirect method
(ii) the direct method.

(i) The indirect method
We need to establish the net cash flow from operating activities as the starting point for the CFS. The way in which we derive this number is by reconciling the amount of operating profit to the net cash flow from operating activities as follows:

	£
Operating profit	32
Depreciation	36
Increase in stock	(56)
Increase in debtors	(12)
Decrease in creditors	(4)
Net cash outflow from operating activities	(4)

(ii) The direct method
We need, under this method, to ascertain the gross cash flows arising from:

► payments to suppliers
► payments for expenses
► payments for wages and salaries
► receipts from customers.

These gross amounts would now be reported on the face of the CFS to give the net cash flow from operating activities – (4) – as ascertained under the indirect method above.

Regressing to our accounting infancy, using T accounts, these gross cash flows are:

Cash paid to suppliers

	£		£
Opening stock	80	Opening creditors	36
Cash paid to suppliers (balance)	388	Cost of sales per p & l account	328
Closing creditors	32	Closing stock	136
	500		500

Assuming that there are no creditors in the balance sheets in respect of expenses, the expenses of (100 – 36) = £64, excluding depreciation, can be taken as the cash paid.

Further assuming that there are no creditors in the balance sheets in respect of wages and salaries, the cash paid in this respect can be taken as £140.

Receipts from customers

	£		£
Opening debtors	54	Cash received from customers (balance)	588
Turnover per p & l account	600	Closing debtors	66
	654		654

Extract from the cash flow statement for the year ended 31 December 1994:

	(i)	(ii)
	£	£
Cash received from customers		588
Cash paid to employees		(140)
Cash paid to suppliers		(388)
Cash paid for expenses		(64)
Net cash flow from operating activities	(4)	(4)

Note to the CFS (required, under FRS 1, regardless of method or approach adopted for cash flows from operating activities):

Reconciliation of operating profit to net cash outflow from operating activities – this would be as laid out under the indirect method.

Why FRS 1 allows a choice between the two approaches

The advantages of the direct method may be stated to be as follows:

▶ it explains how the organisation uses cash in that it shows the actual sources and uses of the cash flows
▶ it can provide useful information in estimating future cash flows regarding suppliers and customers that is not apparent under the indirect method
▶ it clearly distinguishes profit from cash
▶ provided an accounting system is established to derive the information, the amounts are easily verifiable
▶ it introduces new information into the financial statements as a whole.

The advantages of the indirect method may be stated to be as follows:

▶ changes in working capital are shown (though this would, under FRS 1, have to be disclosed whichever approach is adopted)
▶ it is useful in providing information as to working capital details, which can be used to assess future cash flows by adjusting estimated profit levels (again, as FRS 1 requires such disclosure to be made regardless of approach adopted, the direct method would be no less useful in this regard).

Comment received in response to ED 54 suggested that the costs of providing the information under the direct method were not outweighed by the benefits to users of providing such information. The ASB concurred with this viewpoint and, as already indicated, does not require the direct method to be used although its use is encouraged. If the indirect method is used, in keeping with the fundamental objective that a CFS should include only actual cash flow movements, FRS 1 requires, in this case, the CFS to start with the net cash flow from operating activities.

Thus, the FRS requires the information (Note 1 in Example 12.1) given under the indirect method whichever method is used, but allows enterprises to make further disclosure, on the face of the CFS, under the direct method.

One practical point here: 'operating profit' does not appear in the Schedule 4 profit and loss account formats as a separate item (although several companies do make such disclosure). If operating profit is not separately disclosed, the reconciliation should be made between profit before interest and tax and the net cash flow from operating activities.

Some further points on operating activity cash flows

Note that Example 12.1 distinguishes between the net cash flow from continuing operating activities and that in respect of discontinued activities and reorganisation costs. This follows the FRS 3 approach to reporting financial performance (see Chapter 11).

As to whether cash flows should be reported gross or net of VAT, FRS 1 requires entities to report operating cash flows on a net basis, that is, cash flows should be reported net of VAT and other sales taxes. If, however, all or part of the VAT is irrecoverable (for example, VAT on the purchase of motor vehicles) the cash flows should be shown gross of the irrecoverable tax.

As to the net amount paid to or repaid by the tax authorities, FRS 1 requires such amounts to be allocated to cash flows from operating activities (unless a different treatment is more appropriate).

Cash flows relating to items that are classified as exceptional should be shown separately under the appropriate heading.

Returns on investments and servicing of finance

Where most of the items here are not likely to prove difficult to derive in terms of cash flows the derivation of some of the cash flows arising under this heading do require further explanation.

Interest element of finance lease rental payments

If you look at Example 12.1, you will see that the capital element of the rental payments is dealt with under cash flows from financing activities. To determine both this amount (for financing activities) and the interest element (for returns on investments and servicing of finance), reconcile the movements on the finance lease creditors from the opening to the closing balance sheet as follows:

Finance lease obligations:

	£		£
Rentals paid	x	b/f – current	x
		– non current	x
		Capitalised during the year	x
c/f – current	x	p&l account – interest allocated	
– non-current	x	to the current year	x

The interest element is separately dealt with above. The capital element is simply rentals paid less the interest allocated to the current year.

Note that amounts capitalised during the year, the capital cost of finance leases entered into during the year, which is debited to fixed assets and credited to finance lease obligations as above, represent non-cash transactions. From the viewpoint of the CFS, there is no question of such amounts appearing on the face of the CFS. These amounts are dealt with by way of further note (see Note 5 in Example 12.1).

Dividends received from associated undertakings

Income from associated undertakings is excluded from cash flows from operating activities. The dividends actually received from associates, to be included under returns on investments and servicing of finance, can be determined as follows:

Associated undertakings – equity method – consolidated accounts:

	£		£
b/f	x	Cash – dividends received	x
		Debtors – dividends receivable	x
Consolidated p&l account –		CPL Ac. – share of tax	x
share of profit before tax	x	CPL Ac. (or direct to reserves)	
		– goodwill paid, written off	
		in the current year	x
	—	c/f	x

The only cash movement in the reconciliation above is that arising from dividends actually received from associates and it is this that is included as a cash inflow in returns on investments and servicing of finance.

Dividends paid

The dividends paid by the parent are easily determined by reconciling the opening and closing dividend creditor by adjusting for the dividends passed through the consolidated profit and loss account for the year.

It is that part of the dividends of a subsidiary that is paid to the minority that requires further explanation. This amount of a subsidiary's dividend must be included as a cash outflow in returns on investments and servicing of finance. It is derived as follows.

Minority interest in the consolidated balance sheet:

	£		£
		b/f MI in share capital and reserves	x
		Dividends payable by subsidiaries to MI – in current liabilities	x
Dividends paid, by subsidiaries, to MI during the year	x	MI in the net assets of a subsidiary acquired during the year – on the date of the subsidiary's acquisition	x
		MI share of revaluation surpluses of subsidiaries, arising during the year	x
		MI share of the consolidated stage exchange difference – gain – arising during the year from overseas subsidiaries	x
		MI in subsidiaries' profits for the year	x
c/f MI in share capital and reserves	x		
Dividends payable by subsidiaries to MI – in current liabilities	x		—

The above is a full reconciliation of the movements on minority interests during the year. The dividend paid to the minority is included as an outflow in returns on investments and servicing of finance. Two items, which are looked at in more detail later in this chapter, are:

► Where a new subsidiary is acquired during the year, the minority interest in the group will increase, initially, by the minority interest's share of the new subsidiary's net assets at its acquisition date. This increase must be brought into the reconciliation above. (Equally, the minority interest will reduce on the disposal of a subsidiary that is no longer to be consolidated although it will increase following a partial disposal by the group where the subsidiary continues to be consolidated. Think about this aspect of the impact on a minority when you read through Chapter 18 on changes in the composition of a group.)

▶ Where there are overseas subsidiaries included in the consolidated accounts, that part of the consolidation stage exchange difference which (see Chapter 22) arises on the retranslation of the net assets of overseas subsidiaries at each year end and which relates to the minority interest must be credited or debited, share of gain or loss, to the minority interest in the reconciliation above.

Tax paid

FRS 1 requires all taxation cash flows arising from revenue and capital profits to be disclosed in a separate section of the CFS headed 'taxation'. Enterprises should include under this heading:

▶ cash payments for corporation tax including payments of ACT and purchases of certificates of tax deposits
▶ cash receipts from tax rebates, claims or overpayments.

Cash flows arising from employees' income taxes should not be shown under this heading. Further, if interest is paid where income tax is deducted at source, payments of such tax should be included with the net interest paid and included under returns on investments and servicing of finance. The treatment should be similar for interest received net of tax.

The tax paid to be included under this heading can be determined as follows:

	Tax paid	
	£	£
	b/f – net of all CT, ACT, and DT balances	x
Tax paid in year	x	
	Tax balances – CT, ACT, and DT in the net assets of a subsidiary acquired in the year on the date of its acquisition	x
c/f – net of all CT, ACT and DT balances	x	
	CPL Ac. – tax charge for year but excluding share of assoc. tax	x

The tax balances in the net assets at acquisition date of a subsidiary acquired during the year must be included in the reconciliation above.

Note that the share of tax of associates will already have been taken account of in arriving at the dividends received from associates and cannot again be included here. Make sure that you exclude the share of associates' tax when you bring in the tax charge from the consolidated profit and loss account.

Two further problem areas

In dealing with cash flows it is necessary to deal with two problem areas, both of which have been dealt with, in passing, in the chapter so far. These are the problem areas of subsidiaries acquired or sold/discontinued during the period and exchange differences both at the individual company and consolidation stages. We need to deal with these problem areas at this stage because they do have an impact on almost every line of the CFS and you need to be informed as to how to deal with their impact in ascertaining cash flows arising from the various activities of the enterprise.

Exchange differences

Accounting for overseas transactions is covered in Chapter 22 and you will need to have covered that chapter before considering the impact of exchange differences in a CFS.

The individual company stage

At this stage most exchange differences arise on the retranslation of monetary items at either the rate on the settlement date or at the rate on the balance sheet date if such items are still outstanding at the year end. Under SSAP 20, except where the offset procedure is used, these exchange differences are recognised in the profit and loss account. This is illustrated in Example 12.3.

If the exchange differences arise on settled transactions there will be a cash flow effect reflected in changed cash balances and there is no need for any adjustment in the CFS.

If, however, the exchange differences arise on outstanding transactions there will be no effect on the cash balances of the enterprise and this needs to be adjusted for in arriving at relevant cash flows for the CFS.

EXAMPLE 12.3 EXCHANGE DIFFERENCES AT THE INDIVIDUAL COMPANY STAGE

You are given the following information:

Summarised balance sheets:

	31 December 1994 £	1993 £
Fixed assets – cost	25,000	20,000
– depreciation	(5,000)	(4,000)
	20,000	16,000
Stock	6,000	4,500
Debtors	4,300	1,800
Cash	4,000	2,000
Creditors	(1,500)	(700)
Loans	(1,000)	–
	31,800	23,600
Share capital	10,000	10,000
Profit and loss account		
b/f 1/1/94		13,600
y/e 31/12/94	13,600	
Operating profit	10,200	
Tax, assume paid in year	(2,000)	
	31,800	27,600

No fixed assets are sold during 1994.

The company enters into overseas purchases, sales and loans and exchange differences arising, taken to profit per SSAP 20, are as follows:

	On transactions	
	settled during 1994	outstanding at 31/12/94
	£	£
Re debtors – loss	(300)	(250)
Re creditors – gain	200)	150
Re loan – gain	–	100

Prepare a CFS from the information you have available using the net or indirect approach for cash flows from operating activities.

Workings

Using the indirect approach for operating activities, first reconcile operating profit to the net cash flow from operating activities as follows:

	£
Operating profit	10,200
Depreciation (5,000 – 4,000)	1,000
Add: Losses on outstanding debtors	250
Deduct: Gains on outstanding creditors	(150)
Deduct: Gains on outstanding loans	(100)
Increase in stock (6,000 – 4,500)	(1,500)
Increase in debtors (4,300 – 1,800 + 250)	(2,750)
Increase in creditors (1,500 – 700 + 150)	950
Net cash inflow from operating activities	7,900

Summary CFS:

	£
Net cash inflow from operating activities	7,900
Returns on investment and servicing of finance	–
Taxation	(2,000)
Investing activities – purchase of fixed assets	(5,000)
Financing activities – cash received on loan (1,000 + 100)	1,100
Increase in cash and cash equivalents	2,000

Remember to adjust for exchange differences on outstanding overseas monetary amounts but *not* to adjust for exchange differences arising on overseas monetary amounts that are settled during the year.

Note, re financing activities, that the amount of the loan is the actual cash amount received as it would have been arrived at in terms of the rate on the date that the loan was entered into.

If the offset procedure is used at the individual company stage then remember that the exchange differences arising on the retranslation of overseas equity investments and overseas loans are taken direct to reserves and not to the profit and loss account for the year. Accordingly:

▶ no adjustment needs to be made to operating profit for these exchange differences as they are not included in operating profit
▶ you must, however, take the exchange differences into account in reconciling the movements on loans for the cash flows arising on loans and the movements on overseas equity investments for the cash flows arising on these.

The consolidation stage

There are (see, again, Chapter 22) two methods for translating net assets and earnings of overseas entities in consolidated accounts, that is, the closing rate/net investment method and the temporal method. Under the former there is a choice available between the closing and average rates for the year in respect of profit and loss account items.

FRS 1, oddly, requires the same rate to be used to translate the cash flows of an overseas entity as is used for the translation of the profit and loss account items for inclusion in the £ consolidated profit and loss account. We, therefore, have to consider three possible situations here, that is:

▶ closing rate/net investment method used – P/L rate, closing
▶ closing rate/net investment method used – P/L rate, average
▶ temporal method used – P/L rate, average.

The closing rate/net investment method is used and the closing rate is used for the translation of the profit and loss account items of the overseas entity

Under this method, SSAP 20 would require the group's share of the consolidation stage exchange difference arising to be taken direct to consolidated reserves. The minority would be credited or debited with its share of any gain or loss arising.

As no part of this consolidation stage exchange difference goes to the profit for the year, there is no case for any adjustment of operating profit in respect of such exchange differences.

Chapter 22 explains the nature of such a consolidation stage exchange difference in this situation. It arises on the retranslation of the opening net asset items of the overseas entity from the closing rate at the previous year end to the closing rate at this year end. As the net asset items of the overseas entity are consolidated into the consolidated accounts, it follows that the exchange differences relating to the separate assets and liabilities of the overseas entity must be taken account of in reconciling movements on consolidated balance sheet items to ascertain the group cash flows arising. This is illustrated in Example 12.4.

EXAMPLE 12.4 – TREATMENT OF THE CONSOLIDATION STAGE EXCHANGE DIFFERENCE IN THE CFS WHERE THE CLOSING RATE/NET INVESTMENT METHOD IS USED AND PROFIT AND LOSS ACCOUNT ITEMS ARE TRANSLATED AT CLOSING RATES

You are informed that the consolidation stage exchange difference for the year ended 31 December 1994 in respect of an 80% controlled overseas subsidiary amounts to a gain of £100.

You are further informed that this exchange gain arises on the separate assets and liabilities of the overseas entity, as follows:

		£
Re the overseas entity:	plant	60
	stock	20
	debtors	42
	cash	25
	creditors	(47)
		100
Minority interest therein 20%		(20)
Group's share taken direct to reserves		80

The minority must be credited with £20 in reconciling the movements on the minority interest in the consolidated balance sheet so that you can properly derive the dividends actually paid by subsidiaries to the minority for inclusion in the cash – see the pro forma for the minority in returns on investments and servicing of finance above.

Note the treatment of the other items making up the consolidated stage exchange difference below. These amounts must be included in dealing with changes in consolidated net asset items as follows:

Fixed assets

	£		£
b/f Consolidated fixed assets	x		
Exchange gain on plant of overseas subsidiary	60	Disposals – NBV	x
Additions:			
(i) for cash	x		
(ii) arising on the acquisition of new subsidiary	x		
(iii) finance leases capitalised	x	CPL Ac. – depreciation for the year	x
	—	c/f Consolidated fixed assets	x

Proceeds of the disposal would be dealt with under investing activities.

Any profit or loss on disposal would be dealt with in the operating profit reconciliation in Note 1 to the CFS as would the depreciation above.

The additions for cash would be dealt with under investing activities but the additions arising from the acquisition of a new subsidiary do not come into the CFS; neither, as already dealt with, do finance leases capitalised.

Stock

	£		£
b/c Consolidated stock	x		
Exchange gain on stock of the overseas subsidiary	20		
Increase in year for the Note 1 reconciliation	x	c/f Consolidated stock	x

The £20 does not pass through the CFS.

Exactly the same procedure would be followed for ascertaining the increase or decrease in debtors and creditors for the Note 1 reconciliation.

A further point arises in respect of Bank and Cash. To the extent that these include balances held in the overseas entity, such balances will have been retranslated at year end rates giving rise to a part of the consolidation stage exchange difference – £25 in this example. The increase or decrease in cash and cash equivalents would now be determined as follows:

Cash and cash equivalents

	£		£
b/f Consolidated cash . . .	x		
Exchange gain on cash . . . holdings of overseas subsidiary	25		
Increase in cash . . . for CFS	x	c/f Consolidated cash . . .	x

Look again at Example 12.1 and at Note 2 in the example and appreciate that the effect of foreign exchange rate changes of £(102) included in Note 2 is the equivalent of the gain of £25 arising in Example 12.4.

The closing rate/net investment method is used and the average rate is used for the translation of the profit and loss account items of the overseas entity

In this case, a further exchange difference arises at the consolidation stage on the retranslation of net assets arising during the year – that is, the profit for the year that will have been translated at average rates for the consolidated profit and loss account but at closing rates for the consolidated balance sheet. Exactly the same procedures as in the previous situation could be used for this element of the exchange difference, which does not affect group cash flows.

However, given the FRS 1 requirement that the cash flows of the overseas entity to be included in the CFS must be included on the same basis as results included in the profit and loss account we have, as the Billary advisers might put it, a problem. One interesting approach to this problem is put forward by Guy Loveday in *Accountancy* – thus, under the closing rate method where average rates are used for the profit and loss account it will not be possible to prepare the CFS from the opening and closing consolidated balance sheets as in the previous situation:

> It would appear that a group cash flow statement which complies with FRS 1 (where average rates are used) could only be produced practically by preparing cash flow statements for each overseas subsidiary, translating them using the average rate and then consolidating them into the group cash flow statement after eliminating intercompany items. This would be a difficult and time-consuming exercise. I suspect that many groups currently using average rates will switch to closing rates . . . to facilitate the preparation of their group cash flow statements . . .

The temporal method is used

The treatment of exchange differences arising in this situation are not specifically dealt with in FRS 1, which is one reason why you need this textbook.

As the consolidation stage exchange difference under this method arises only on monetary items of the overseas subsidiary, and the exchange difference is recognised in the consolidated profit and loss account, given the impact on group cash flows, we would suggest that the treatment to be followed is the same as for exchange differences at the individual company stage as dealt with above.

Subsidiaries acquired during the year

This was a problem area in funds flow under SSAP 10, such subsidiaries being included under either of two equally acceptable methods – 'line by line' or 'single line' – giving rise to considerable variation in the effects disclosed in the funds flow statement and in neither case disclosing the cash flow impact of such purchases.

The CFS is concerned only with actual cash flows. Therefore, where a subsidiary is acquired during the year the cash effect of the acquisition – inflow or outflow – based on the net of any cash paid as consideration and cash and cash equivalents of the new subsidiary taken over by the group on its acquisition, is included under investing activities.

Turn to Example 12.1 again. The amount included under investing activities – outflow of £(18,221) is explained in Note 7 to the example.

In an exam question that deals with this aspect of a CFS, the question will give you a breakdown of the separate assets and liabilities of the new subsidiary on the date of its acquisition, that is, the sort of information for you to be able to prepare Note 6 to Example 12.1. You must remember to incorporate these amounts when reconciling consolidated balance sheet items for all net asset items *except* cash and cash equivalents.

Thus, using the numbers in Note 6 and carrying on with some of the approaches already dealt with in this chapter, the fixed assets reconciliation would look like:

Fixed assets			
	£		£
b/f Consolidated fixed assets	x		
Exchange difference on fixed assets of overseas subsidiaries – gain – as above	60		
Fixed assets of new subsidiaries on date of subsidiary acquisition	12,194	Depreciation charged in consolidated p&l account	x
Purchase of fixed assets	3,512	Disposals – NBV	x
Finance leases capitalised	2,845	c/f Consolidated fixed assets	x

The CFS would include the proceeds of the disposal as an inflow and an outflow for purchases of £3,512. The Note 1 reconciliation would include the depreciation amount and any profit or loss on disposal. Note 5 would include disclosure of fixed assets capitalised.

You would follow the same approach in dealing with all other consolidated balance sheet net assets amounts *except* cash and cash equivalents.

(The treatment for disposals of subsidiaries would effectively be the reverse of the treatment for acquisition above. Look at the inflow of £4,208 under investing activities in Example 12.1 and also at Note 8, which explains how the amount is arrived at.)

The scope of FRS 1

The FRS applies to all enterprises intended to give a true and fair view *except* those that are:

▶ small entities permitted to file abbreviated financial statements (see Chapter 1)
▶ wholly owned subsidiaries of a parent undertaking that is established under the law of any EC member state – this exemption applies only if the parent draws up consolidated accounts in English including a consolidated CFS
▶ building societies
▶ mutual life insurance companies.

The revision of FRS 1

FRS 1, originally conceived by the ASC and subsequently adopted by the ASB, was two years old in 1994. As part of its programme of reviewing all major new standards after sufficient time has elapsed for their effectiveness to be judged, ASB has asked for comments on the cash flow standard and, particularly, for comments on:

▶ the definition of cash and cash equivalents and the treatment of short-term investments
▶ the format of the statement and whether it should provide a reconciliation to net debt in order to better assist understanding of cash flows
▶ the treatment of items as gross or net or both
▶ the scope of the standard.

The review and eventual revision should also reflect the treatment of forex differences, on which FRS 1 is vague, and harmonisation with FRS 3 and the reporting of cash flows from continuing and discontinued operations.

Summary

This chapter has been concerned in the main with the practicalities of the preparation of a CFS. The interpretation of the information disclosed is best left to the 'interpretation' chapters with which this textbook concludes. The only way that you can master these practicalities is to apply the procedures dealt with here to exam standard questions. Two such questions – one dealing with the acquisition of a subsidiary during the year and another with exchange differences at the consolidation stage – are included with this chapter.

Exam style questions

1   *Nero plc*
    The draft profit and loss account, balance sheets and notes of Nero plc group are as follows.

Consolidated profit and loss account for the year ended 31 December 1992:

	£000	£000
Group operating profit		253
Income from interests in associated undertakings		60
Interest payable and similar charges		46
Group profit before tax		267
Taxation – group	92	
– associated undertakings	15	(107)
Group profit after tax		160
Minority interest		(15)
		145
Extraordinary items (Note 1)		(42)
Profit for the financial year		103
Dividends		(40)
Retained profit		63

Consolidated balance sheets:

	31 Dec 1992		31 Dec 1991	
	£000	£000	£000	£000
Tangible fixed assets (Note 2)		543		350
Interests in associated undertakings		280		250
Current assets:				
Stock	370		310	
Debtors (Note 3)	295		215	
Cash in bank and in hand	32	697	10	535
Creditors: within one year:				
Obligations under finance leases	60		50	
Overdraft			65	
Trade creditors	150		135	
Corporation tax	50		40	
ACT	10		5	
Dividends	30		15	
Accruals for interest and				
finance charges	15	(315)	5	(315)

Creditors: more than one year:		
Obligations under finance leases	(195)	(30)
	1,010	790

Capital and reserves:		
Ordinary shares (Note 4)	113	100
Share premium (Note 5)	352	190
Capital redemption reserve (Note 5)	102	100
Profit and loss reserve (Note 5)	348	345
	915	735
Minority interest	95	55
	1,010	790

Notes:

1   *Extraordinary items*

Extraordinary items comprise closure costs of £40,000 less tax of £14,000 and a premium on purchase of own shares of £16,000.

2   *Tangible fixed assets*

	£000
Net book value at start of year	350
Additions	328
Net book value of disposals	(50)
Depreciation charge	(85)
Net book value at end of year	543

£245,000 of the fixed asset additions were acquired finance leases. Fixed assets disposed of comprise assets sold during the year for £25,000 cash and £5,000 trade-in allowance against new fixed assets.

3   *Debtors*

	31 Dec 1992	31 Dec 1991
	£000	£000
Trade debtors	285	215
Dividends receivable from associates	10	
	295	215

4   *Ordinary shares*

	£000
At start of year	100
Issue	15
Purchase of own shares	(2)
At end of year	113

5   *Reserves*

	Share premium £000	Capital redemption £000	Profit and loss £000
Balance at start of year	190	100	345
Premium on issue	167		
Expenses of issue	(5)		
Transfer		2	(2)
Retained profit			63
Goodwill on acquisition	___	___	(58)
Balance at end of year	352	102	348

6   *Acquisition of new subsidiary*
During the year an 80% holding in Polanski Ltd was acquired. Details of the acquisition are as follows:

	£000
Fixed assets	64
Stocks	24
Debtors	18
Cash	112
Creditors	(28)
Corporation tax	(10)
	180
Minority interest (20%)	(36)
Goodwill	58
	202
Shares issued – market value	182
Cash	20
	202

Required:
Prepare the group cash flow statement for Nero plc for the year ended 31 December 1992, in accordance with FRS 1.

(20 marks)
From Accountancy, June 1992

2 *Proserpina plc*

The draft balance sheets and profit and loss account of Proserpina plc are as follows.

Consolidated balance sheets:

	31 Oct 1992 £000	31 Oct 1991 £000
Fixed assets		
Tangible assets	10,969	7,642
Investments	2,100	2,100
Current assets		
Stock	7,245	6,100
Debtors	6,410	7,211
Cash at bank and in hand	953	165
Creditors: amounts falling due within one year:		
Trade creditors	(1,920)	(1,690)
Dividend payable by Proserpina plc	(267)	(240)
Dividend payable to minority	(75)	(60)
Corporation tax	(2,655)	(2,738)
ACT	(89)	(80)
Creditors: amounts falling due after more than one year:		
Loans	(1,002)	(1,410)
	21,669	17,000
Capital and reserves:		
Called up share capital	5,000	5,000
Share premium	3,000	3,000
Profit and loss account	11,150	7,003
	19,150	15,003
Minority interest	2,519	1,997
	21,669	17,000

There were no fixed asset disposals during the year. The depreciation charge for the year was £1,977,000. There were no fixed asset creditors at either year end.

Debtors as at 31 October 1992 include called up share capital not paid of £1,235,000 (1991: £2,746,000).

Draft consolidated profit and loss account for the year ended 31 October 1992:

	£000
Group operating profit	6,955
Income from fixed asset investments	64
Interest payable	(174)
Group profit before tax	6,845
Tax – corporation tax	(2,830)
– tax credits on dividends	(10)
Group profit after tax	3,999
Minority interest	(226)
Profit attributable to members of Proserpina plc	3,773
Dividends	(600)
Retained profit	3,173
Reserves as at 1 November 1991	7,003
Exchange gain on translation	1,356
Exchange loss on loan	(382)
Reserves as at 31 October 1992	11,150

Exchange gain:

The exchange gain on translation is made up as follows:

	£000
Fixed assets	1,228
Stocks	393
Debtors	211
Cash	39
Creditors	(63)
Minority interest	(452)
	1,356

Required:

Prepare the group cash flow statement for Proserpina plc for the year ended 31 October 1992, in accordance with FRS 1.

(20 marks)

From Accountancy, July 1992

All answers on pages 663–665.

Realised and Legally Distributable Profit

Until the Companies Act 1980, there was practically no mention of distributable profit in UK company law. Table A of the 1948 Act simply stated that no dividend shall be paid otherwise than out of profits, and case law on the subject is often contradictory and occasionally divorced from commercial reality. Thus, in *Ammonia Soda Co.* v. *Chamberlain*, it was decided that a company could make a distribution out of its current year's profits without making good previous years' losses, while in *Dimbula Valley (Ceylon) Tea Co.* v *Lawrie*, it was decided that a company could distribute its unrealised gains. This quite unsatisfactory state of affairs was resolved in the 1980 Act by the introduction of specific rules as to the reserves that different classes of company could utilise for the purpose of a distribution. The 1981 Act provided a definition of realised profits. The 1985 Act brings together the previous rules as to distribution of profits and assets.

The general rule: S. 263

A distribution means every description of distribution of a company's assets to its members, whether in cash or otherwise, except:

▶ an issue of shares as fully or partly paid bonus shares
▶ the redemption or purchase of any of the company's own shares out of capital or out of unrealised profits
▶ the reduction of share capital by extinguishing or reducing the liability of any of the members on any of the company's shares in respect of share capital not paid up, or by paying off paid up share capital
▶ a distribution of assets to members of the company on its winding up.

A company's profits available for distribution are its accumulated, realised profits, so far as not previously utilised by distribution or capitalisation, less its accumulated, realised losses, so far as not previously written off in a reduction or reorganisation of capital.

Realised profits are defined as such profits of the company as fall to be treated as realised profits in accordance with principles generally accepted with respect to the determination for accounting purposes of realised profits at the time when those accounts are prepared. Principles that are generally accepted are the principles as stated in various SSAPs and FRSs. The interaction of the law with accounting standards is therefore of fundamental importance.

The interaction of the Act with accounting standards

Where the law was previously concerned with disclosure in the context of an overall true and fair view it is now, in so far as it sets out a framework of accounting principles and rules, also concerned with accounting measurement. There is thus a closer interaction between the law, as it is currently stated, and accounting standards than existed previously, for example, the accounting principles stated in the Act correspond with the four fundamental accounting concepts of SSAP 2 and the depreciation rules stated in the Act are similar to those stated in SSAP 12.

However, some of the rules now stated in law are not dealt with in an existing SSAP or FRS, for example, the law permits capitalisation of interest on money borrowed to finance the production of an asset whereas there is no FRS, as yet, on the capitalisation of interest costs. Further, some of the rules give more flexibility than the relevant SSAP or FRS, for example, the Act permits the valuation of stocks using such methods as LIFO whereas this is specifically prohibited in SSAP 9. There are also some rules, for example, as to development costs, that are approached from a different viewpoint when compared with the relevant accounting standard. Thus the law states that development costs may be capitalised only if there are 'special circumstances', which are not defined. It is reasonable in this context to assume that the circumstances under which development costs may be capitalised under SSAP 13 will satisfy the 'special circumstances' requirement of the Act and the DTI has confirmed that this is so. In some cases there is a potential conflict between an SSAP and the Act, for example, in respect of SSAP 19 on investment properties where no depreciation is charged and SSAP 20 on foreign currency translation where unrealised gains are included in the profit and loss account.

The overriding requirement of the law is that the financial statements give a true and fair view. One of the accounting principles stated above is that only profits realised at the balance sheet date be included in the profit and loss account. The Act defines these realised profits as those that are determined by generally accepted principles, that is, those stated in various SSAPs and FRSs. The interaction of the law with accounting standards is therefore of fundamental importance.

Generally accepted principles – SSAPs and FRSs

It would be useful at this point to look to various SSAPs and FRSs – principles that are generally accepted – from the viewpoint of legally distributable profits.

Several accounting standards deal with aspects of consolidated accounts – FRS 2, SSAP 1, SSAP 20, SSAP 22 and SSAP 23. The law as to distributable profits affects only individual companies, as it is only an individual company that can make a distribution. Therefore, the accounting principles dealt with in the accounting standards above, which relate to consolidated accounts, are not relevant in ascertaining the legally distributable profits of individual companies. Where such companies have investments in subsidiary or associated undertakings it is only the dividends received and receivable from such undertakings that would count towards the legally distributable profits of an individual investor company.

Because of early difficulties of interpretation as to which items should be treated as realised and unrealised, the CCAB issued, in 1982, two guidance statements:

▶ TR 481 on the determination of realised profits
▶ TR 482 on the determination of distributable profits

and, despite their age, the main conclusions of these two statements remain relevant for the purposes of this chapter. Thus, under TR 481:

▶ Items that are required by an accounting standard to be recognised in the profit and loss account should, normally, be treated as realised unless the accounting standard specifically requires the items to be treated as unrealised. Therefore, under SSAP 9 (Revised), attributable profit (turnover recognised less attributable cost of sales) on long-term contracts is recognised in the profit and loss account and, to this extent, should be treated as realised.
▶ A profit may be recognised in the profit and loss account so as to comply with an accounting policy not covered by an accounting standard. Such profits should be treated as realised to the extent that they are consistent with the fundamental

concepts of accruals and prudence following SSAP 2.

▶ Where it is argued by a company that a true and fair view cannot be given without including unrealised profits, in the profit and loss account, the Act would require a company to include the unrealised item in its profit and loss account. Schedule 4 permits directors to include unrealised items in the profit and loss account if there are 'special reasons' for doing so. This is applicable in the context of SSAP 20 and the inclusion of net exchange gains on long-term overseas loans in the profit and loss account of an individual company. Such unrealised profits would not be legally distributable.

Summary of points to bear in mind in respect of fixed assets

In ascertaining the profits available for distribution under S. 263, you need to bear the following points in mind:

1 Except for a provision in respect of a diminution in value of a fixed asset arising on a revaluation of all the fixed assets of the company, or of all its fixed assets other than goodwill, a provision of any kind is treated as a realised loss.

2 If a fixed asset is revalued and an unrealised gain is made, such a gain is treated as realised to the extent of any additional depreciation charged against profits following the revaluation. A revaluation of a depreciable fixed asset will normally reduce reported profits of any one year through additional depreciation charges, but will have no effect on the legally distributable profits of that year.

3 For the purposes of revaluing an asset, if its cost/value is lost or unknown, its earliest known value after acquisition may be used.

4 As stated in (1), a provision in respect of a diminution in value arising on a revaluation of all the fixed assets of the company is not treated as a realised loss. The company does not have to record such revaluations; any consideration by the directors of the value at a particular time of a fixed asset is treated as a revaluation of the asset for the purposes of the exception in (1).

5 Where assets that have not actually been revalued are treated as revalued as in (4), the exception in (1) applies only if the directors are satisfied that their aggregate value at the time in question is not less than the aggregate amount at which they are for the time being stated in the company's accounts.

6 There must be a note to the accounts whenever the directors propose to take advantage of (4)/(5) as to the definition of a revaluation.

7 Development costs are to be treated as a realised loss unless there are 'special circumstances' justifying the carrying of such costs as an asset, and that the notes to the accounts state that such costs are not treated as realised losses for the purposes of distribution, and explain the circumstances relied upon to justify the decision of the directors to that effect.

The additional rule for public companies: S. 264

In addition to the rule under S. 263, a public company is not entitled to make a distribution if the result would be to reduce the value of the assets below that of the liabilities and capital. Thus, after a distribution, the net assets of a public company must amount to at least as much as the aggregate of its called up share capital and undistributable reserves.

Net assets are the aggregate of the company's assets less the aggregate of its liabilities including any provisions for liabilities or charges.

Undistributable reserves are:

- ▶ the share premium account
- ▶ the capital redemption reserve
- ▶ the amount by which the company's accumulated unrealised profits exceed its accumulated unrealised losses
- ▶ any other reserve that the company is prohibited from distributing by any enactment or by its memorandum or articles.

The effect of this additional rule is that a public company cannot distribute its net realised profits until it has first made good any excess of unrealised losses over unrealised profits.

Investment companies: S. 265 and insurance companies: S. 268

S. 265

An investment company is defined as a public company that has given notice in the prescribed form to the Registrar of Companies of its intention to carry on business as an investment company and which has complied with the specified requirements of the Act in this regard.

Such a company may make a distribution out of its accumulated realised revenue profits less its accumulated realised and unrealised revenue losses. The distribution must not, however, reduce the amount of its assets to less than one and a half times the aggregate of its liabilities.

S. 268

S. 268 deals with the distributable profits of insurance companies. It states that any amount properly transferred to the profit and loss account of the company from a surplus in the fund(s) maintained by it and any deficit in such a fund(s) are to be treated as realised profits and realised losses. Subject to this, any profit or loss arising in the business is to be left out of account for the purposes of distributable profits.

Ascertaining maximum legally distributable profits

In order to deal, effectively, with exam questions on this topic, you need to be aware of sundry accounting considerations, which are dealt with elsewhere in this book. This section attempts a suggested approach to ascertaining maximum legally distributable profits of a company and draws your attention to such accounting considerations.

Private companies

If the company to be dealt with is a private company, you need be concerned only with the S. 263 rule: the legally distributable profits of such a company are its accumulated realised profits less its accumulated realised losses. Note that no distinction is drawn between revenue and capital reserves.

Given the application of the legal requirement that only realised items be included in the profit and loss account, accumulated realised profits less accumulated realised losses must equal the accumulated balance on the profit and loss account of a company.

Problems as to legally distributable profits can, however, arise in that it is possible that:

▶ unrealised items are included in the profit and loss account

▶ realised items are excluded from the profit and loss account.

The following points should be borne in mind in deciding on whether or not an adjustment (add back or take away) is required to the amount held in profit and loss account reserves in order to derive the maximum legally distributable profits of a company:

▶ Revaluation surpluses arising on revaluations of fixed assets are unrealised gains that are taken direct to revaluation reserve. Such amounts become realised through use or on sale of the relevant fixed assets and, on becoming realised, become legally distributable. See Chapter 4 on tangible fixed assets.

▶ Revaluation deficits are deemed, in the first instance, to be realised losses. So long as such amounts have been passed through profit and loss account, no further adjustment is necessary. If such amounts have been debited to revaluation reserve, a deduction would be required from the balance on profit and loss account to this extent to ascertain the legally distributable profits of a company. There are, however, three exceptions to this general rule of deficits on revaluation of fixed assets being treated as realised losses. These are:

  – if the deficit offsets a previous gain taken to revaluation reserve, on the same asset
  – if there is a revaluation of all fixed assets, except goodwill, and there is a net surplus arising on such a revaluation.
  – if the directors 'consider' the assets not revalued and are satisfied that their aggregate value is not less than the aggregate amount at which they are stated in a company's accounts.

▶ Development costs must be treated as realised losses, unless there are 'special circumstances' justifying the capitalisation of such costs, in which case they are not treated as realised losses.

▶ Purchased goodwill written off is dealt with in detail in Chapter 5. Ultimately, such goodwill must result in a realised loss and be reflected as a debit against the balance on profit and loss account. Such amounts may, however, initially, be debited, per SSAP 22 (Revised) against a 'suitable' unrealised reserve.

▶ Attributable profit on long-term contracts included in the profit and loss account, per SSAP 9 (Revised), is treated as a realised amount and should not be excluded when ascertaining legally distributable profits.

▶ Government grants received are treated as realised as when dealt with in profit and loss account, per SSAP 4 (Revised).

▶ Net exchange gains on the retranslation of long-term overseas loans to the extent that they are included in the profit and loss account under SSAP 20 should be treated as unrealised and excluded from distributable profits.

We will now apply these points to the two problem areas above.

Unrealised items included in the profit and loss account

Such items would have to be excluded from the balance on profit and loss account to ascertain the legally distributable profits of a company. So long as a company has complied with SSAPs in arriving at its accumulated balance on profit and loss account, with one exception, no unrealised items will be included in the profit and loss account. The one exception arises in respect of some exchange differences which, per SSAP 20, would have been included in the profit and loss account. This problem area is dealt with in some detail in Chapter 22, which concludes by arguing that net exchange gains on retranslation of long-term monetary items included, per SSAP 20, in the profit and loss account, should be excluded in arriving at profits available for distribution.

Realised items, excluded from profit and loss account

Such items would have to be added back to the balance on profit and loss account in ascertaining the legally distributable profits of a company. Such items would comprise, for example, a revaluation surplus on the revaluation of fixed assets that becomes realised through use or on sale of the relevant fixed asset. As noted above, such a revaluation surplus is unrealised on the date of revaluation. It becomes realised, following revaluation through use or on the eventual sale of the revalued asset. The extent of the realised amount of the revaluation surplus is the additional depreciation charged, per SSAP 12 (Revised), following revaluation of the fixed asset. Such amounts may be transferred by a company from revaluation reserve to profit and loss account as a movement on reserves. In this case it would be included in the accumulated balance on profit and loss account, and no further adjustment is necessary in ascertaining legally distributable profits. Given, however, that there is no legal requirement for such transfers to be made, it is possible that realised amounts on revaluation reserve remain in the credit of such a reserve. In this case an adjustment, an add back to the balance on profit and loss account, would be necessary to ascertain the legally distributable profits of a company.

Any balance of revaluation surplus in revaluation reserve, following the sale of a previously revalued fixed asset, becomes wholly realised on sale and is therefore legally distributable. Accounting for such a gain is dealt with in Chapter 4.

To summarise:

▶ The reserves of a company could comprise, *inter alia*:
  - share premium account
  - revaluation reserves
  - other reserves:
    - capital redemption reserve
    - reserve for own shares
    - reserves required by the articles of association
    - negative goodwill
    - merger reserve
  - profit and loss account.
▶ The legally distributable profits of a private company are shown by the balance on the profit and loss account, adjusted, where necessary, for unrealised items that are included or realised items that are excluded therein. These adjustments could involve:
  - exclusion of net exchange gains (not losses) on long-term overseas monetary items included in the profit and loss account
  - the add back of any amounts on revaluation reserve which are realised gains, and which have not been transferred to the profit and loss account
  - the deduction of any amounts on revaluation reserve which are realised losses, and which have not been transferred to the profit and loss account.
▶ Note that it is possible, though not desirable, for a company to have a debit balance on revaluation reserve arising from deficits on revaluation of fixed assets. Normally, as mentioned above, such deficits must be treated as realised losses. In the case of a private company, however, it may be that the directors have 'considered' the value of the assets not revalued and thus do not have to treat such deficits as a realised loss.
▶ Note also that the rules as to distributable profits are relevant only in the context of individual companies and that they do not apply to groups, that is, that the distinction drawn in the rules between realised and unrealised reserves is not relevant to group accounts.
▶ Further note that the legally distributable profits of a company would be the same regardless of the accounting convention adopted – the fact that a company prepares its accounts on the basis of current cost would have no effect on the

profits that it could legally distribute, which would be exactly the same as if it had prepared its accounts on the basis of historical cost.

The question of how much a company should distribute is a quite separate issue, and is dealt with in Chapter 14 in the context of accounting for the effects of changing prices.

Public companies

If the company to be dealt with is a public company, you should comply with the S. 263 rule and with the S. 264 rule, which was stated above. The application of the S. 264 rule may or may not have an effect on the legally distributable profits of a public company. There will be an effect only if the company has a net unrealised loss.

Investment companies

Whereas the distributable profit rules dealt with in S. 263 and S. 264 make no distinction between capital and revenue reserves, the distinction is relevant in the rule in S. 265, which is applicable to investment companies. Thus, as stated above, investment companies may make a distribution out of their accumulated realised revenue profits less their realised and unrealised revenue losses. Capital profits and losses, whether realised or unrealised, are not relevant to the distributions of such companies.

The profits available for distribution by investment companies may need to be further reduced, either on the basis of the capital maintenance test (net assets after distribution must be at least equal to share capital plus non-distributable reserves) which applies to all public companies, or on the basis of an asset ratio test, where the requirement is that a distribution may not reduce the amount of the investment company's assets below 150% of the aggregate of its liabilities.

Example 13.1 should help in clarifying the application of the S. 263, S. 264 and S. 265 rules in so far as they apply to private, public and investment companies.

EXAMPLE 13.1

You are provided with details of the share capital and reserves of four different companies as follows:

Company	A	B	C	D
	£	£	£	£
Share capital	1,500	1,500	1,500	1,500
Share premium	150	150	150	150
Unrealised capital profits	900	900	900	900
Unrealised revenue profits	–	–	150	150
Unrealised capital losses	–	(1,050)	(1,050)	(1,050)
Unrealised reveue losses	–	(375)	(375)	(375)
Realised revenue profits	1,800	1,800	1,800	1,800
Realised capital profits	–	–	150	150
Realised capital losses	–	–	–	(900)
Realised revenue losses	–	–	(225)	(225)
Share capital and reserves	4,350	2,925	3,000	2,100
Total liabilities	1,950	1,950	1,950	1,950
Total assets	6,300	4,875	4,950	4,050

Calculate and state, for each of the four companies above, the maximum legally distributable profits on the basis that each of the companies are (a) investment companies, (b) non-investment public companies.

Workings

Distributable profits

(a) Investment companies: per S. 265 CA 1985

> . . . an investment company may make a distribution at any time out of its accumulated, *realised revenue* profits, so far as not previously utilised by distribution or capitalisation, less its accumulated *revenue* losses (whether realised or unrealised), so far as not previously written off in a reduction or reorganisation of capital duly made –
>
> (i) if at that time the amount of its assets is at least equal to one and a half times the aggregate of its liabilities, and
> (ii) if, and to the extent that, the distribution does not reduce that amount to less than one and a half times that aggregate.

Thus, each company may distribute the lower of its realised revenue profits less its (realised plus unrealised) revenue losses and its total assets less 1.5 times its total liabilities.

Company A
Lower of (1,800 – (Nil + Nil))   and (6,300 – (1.5 × 1,950))
         1,800   and   3,375
              i.e. £1,800

Company B
Lower of (1,800 – (Nil + 375))   and (4,875 – (1.5 × 1,950))
         1,425   and   1,950
              i.e. £1,425

Company C
Lower of (1,800 – (225 + 375))   and (4,950 – (1.5 × 1,950))
         1,200   and   2,025
              i.e. £1,200

Company D
Lower of (1,800 – (225 + 375))   and (4,050 – (1.5. × 1,950))
         1,200   and   1,125
              i.e. £1,125

(b) Public companies: per S. 264 CA 1985

The lower of total realised reserves (profits and losses) and the total of realised reserves plus unrealised reserves (not share premium or capital redemption reserve).

Company A
Lower of (1,800)   and (1,800 + 900)
         1,800   and   2,700
              i.e. £1,800

Company B
Lower of (1,800)   and (1,800 + (375) + (1,050) + 900)
         1,800   and   1,275
              i.e. £1,275

Company C
Lower of:
(1,800 + 150 + (225))   and (1,725 + (375) + (1,050) + 150 + 900)
        1,725   and   1,350
            i.e. £1,350

Company D
Lower of:
(1,800 + 150 + (900) + (225))   and (825 + (375) + (1,050) + 150 + 900)
        825   and   450
                i.e. £450

Summary

This chapter deals with the legal rules as to the profits that may, legally, be distributed by companies be they private, public, investment or insurance companies.

Under S. 263 and S. 264 of the CA 1985 the distributable profits of a company are, essentially, its net accumulated realised profits. In this context it was necessary to explain what is meant by the term 'realised' and to consider the interaction of the Act with Accounting Standards in this regard. The chapter describes the main conclusions of two statements, TR 481 and TR 482 in respect of the determination of realised profits and the determination of distributable profits.

The main problems you are likely to have to resolve in an examination question on this topic will be concerned with first, determining unrealised items that are included in the profit and loss account and, second, realised items that are excluded from the profit and loss account. The chapter provides guidance on dealing with, in the context of determining the legally distributable profits of a company:

▶ revaluation surpluses and deficits
▶ development costs capitalised
▶ the write-off of goodwill
▶ attributable profit on long-term contracts
▶ government grants received
▶ exchange differences.

Keep in mind that this topic brings together many of the areas dealt with in the other chapters of this textbook, for example, the impact of alternative treatments as to goodwill, and the treatment of exchange differences in individual companies. It is this that makes the topic so appropriate as a question for examination at this professional stage.

Suggested reading

Manual of Accounting – Companies (Coopers and Lybrand Deloitte 1990) Chapter 19 is relevant to the topic of realised and legally distributable profit.

The reporting of profits and the concept of realisation (Camsberg and Hoke 1989) This report was commissioned by the ICAEW's Research Board at the request of the ASC.

1   State, briefly, the rules as to legally distributable profits for private, public and investment companies under S. 263, S. 264 and S. 265 of the Companies Act 1985.

2   Summarise the three main conclusions of TR 481 as to determining realised profits.

3   An asset has a cost of £200 and accumulated depreciation up to 1 January 1995 of £40. It is revalued to £240 on 1 January 1995. If

i) depreciation for 1995 is to be based on a remaining useful life of eight years on 1 January 1995, and

ii) the profit available for distribution before charging depreciation in 1995, is £70

what is the amount to be transferred to the revaluation reserve?

How much of this amount becomes realised through the use of the asset?

What is the profit available for distribution after taking into account the depreciation for 1995?

4   Pingo plc, in its own separate accounts, has the following balances in its reserves at 30 June 1994:

	£
Profit and loss account	1,080
Exchange differences	280

The exchange difference reserve is made up of gains on overseas equity investments and losses on overseas loans of £640 and £360 respectively.

The profit and loss account includes attributable profit on long-term contracts of £40.

What are the maximum legally distributable profits of Pingo plc at 30 June 1994?

5   If an analysis of the reserves of Pongo plc reveals realised profits of £75, unrealised profits of £30, realised losses of £9 and unrealised losses of £6, what are the maximum legally distributable profits of Pongo plc?

Exam style question

1   *Tower plc*

Three unrelated companies, Tower plc (a public company), Book Ltd (a private company) and Holdings plc (a quoted investment company) have summarised balance sheets, as on 30 June 1991, as set out below with relevant additional information.

a) Tower plc

	£m		£m
Share capital	2.0	Fixed assets	3.3
Share premium account	0.5		
Revaluation reserves	1.0	Net current assets	2.7
Profit and loss account	2.5		–
	6.0		6.0

(i) A partial revaluation of fixed assets took place during the year with the following result:

	£m
Surplus on land	0.65
Surplus on buildings	0.35
Surplus on plant and machinery	0.10
Deficit on fixtures and fittings	(0.10)
	1.00

The directors consider that the value of the remaining fixed assets not revalued is equal to their net book amounts.

(ii)   Depreciation is provided at 2% on buildings, 15% on plant and machinery, and 20% on fixtures and fittings. All fixed assets are depreciated for the full year on the cost or revalued amounts.

(iii)   Fixed assets comprise:

	£m
Land	1.2
Buildings	0.8
Plant and machinery	0.8
Fixtures and fittings	0.3
Development costs	0.2
	3.3

(b) Book Ltd – Current cost balance sheet

	£000		£000	£000
Share capital	45	Fixed assets		50
Current cost reserve	40	Investment in Worm Ltd		40
Retained profit	55	Current assets		
		Stock	10	
		Long-term work in progress	30	
			40	
		Cash	10	50
	140			140

(i) No provision has yet been made for the losses of the subsidiary, Worm Ltd. It is estimated that the net assets of Worm Ltd in which Book Ltd has an interest of 60% are worth £50,000.

(ii) The current cost reserve comprises:

	£000
CCA adjustments passed through profit and loss account	13
Uplift of fixed assets to CCA values	27
	40

(iii) Long-term work in progress includes a profit element of £6,000 calculated in accordance with SSAP 9.

(c) Holdings plc

	£000		£000	£000
Share capital	650	Fixed assets		
Share premium	325	Tangible		20
Reserves	4,380	Investments		5,647
				5,667
		Current assets		
		Debtors	98	
		Investments	2,436	
		Cash	147	
			2,681	
		Less creditors falling due within one year	(1,793)	
				888
		Creditors falling due in more than one year		(936)
		Provisions		(264)
	5,355			5,355

Reserves consist of:

	£000
Unrealised capital losses	(48)
Unrealised revenue profits	140
Unrealised revenue losses	(17)
Realised capital profits	2,890
Realised capital losses	(1,241)
Realised revenue profits	2,666
Realised revenue losses	(10)
	4,380

Required:

a) State concisely for each of the three types of company mentioned, the principles for calculating distributable profits under the Companies Act 1985.

(5 marks)

b) Calculate for each of the three companies the maximum legally distributable profits. (7 marks)

c) Discuss the reasons why it is not normally commercially or practically desirable to make the maximum distribution. (7 marks)

(19 marks)

ICAEW PEI exam question, December 1985

All answers on pages 665–668.

Accounting for the Effects of Changing Prices

Since 1975 there have been seven published versions of current cost accounting (CCA). As the Lord Chancellor said in a debate in connection with the consolidation of the Companies Acts, 'this is really an area where we must travel, hopefully, through stations rather than imagine that we are going to arrive at a final terminus'.

Relevant dates in the development of accounting for the effects of changing prices in the UK are as follows:

N12: Rising price levels in relation to accounts	1949
N15: Accounting in relation to changes in the purchasing power of money	1952
ED 8/SSAP 7: Accounting for changes in the purchasing power of money	1974
The Sandilands Committee:	
Government decision to set up Committee	1973
Committee appointed	1973
Report signed	1975
Report published	1975
The Inflation Accounting Steering Group:	1976
ED 18: Current cost accounting	1976
ASC: Statement of intent	1977
Hyde Guidelines: Interim recommendations by ASC	1977
ED 24: Current cost accounting	1979
SSAP 16: Current cost accounting	1980
Interim report of the CCA monitoring working party	1983
Final report of the CCA monitoring working party	1983
SSAP 16: 'Current cost accounting' statement of intent by the ASC	1984
ED 35: Accounting for the effects of changing prices	1984
Capital maintenance concepts: the choice	1985
Accounting for the effects of changing prices: a handbook	1986

This chapter has been kept as brief as possible to cover the salient features of this long and continuing debate.

Capital maintenance concepts

A particularly important aspect of accounting for changing prices, inaccurately called inflation accounting, is the choice of capital maintenance concept. As the measurement of income is a central purpose of financial accounts, this implies some measurement of initial 'well-offness', opening capital, which must be maintained before revenue can be regarded as giving rise to a profit. The discussion of this aspect of price level accounting has been one of the most complex and potentially confusing areas of the long debate surrounding the issue.

The crucial capital maintenance issue is the choice between 'financial capital' and 'physical capital'. The former approach views the capital of a business as a fund of purchasing power attributable to shareholders. This is the approach associated with traditional historical cost accounting, in which capital is defined as a monetary amount. In periods of inflation, this may be modified to 'real financial capital', by adjusting money capital by a general purchasing power index, as in current purchasing power accounting, so that the capital maintained is a fund of real purchasing power. The alternative approach, physical capital maintenance, came to the fore in the report of the Sandilands Committee, and has been embodied in subsequent current cost proposals. This defines capital in terms of some physical measure, such as operating capability, and profit is recognised only after setting aside whatever funds are necessary to maintain that physical state. Financial and physical capital maintenance concepts should not be regarded as mutually exclusive. Both can be incorporated in a 'real terms' system, which reports operating profit using a physical capital maintenance concept but then adds various gains and losses to yield a final measure of total gains, which is based on real financial capital maintenance.

Historical cost accounting (HCA)

In accounting theory, a person's capital is increased by that portion of periodic income that has not been consumed. Financial accounting procedure effects this transfer by crediting net income to capital account, and if consumption (drawings) is less than that income, capital is increased by the difference. In the case of companies, dividends are analogous to drawings, and retained income is added to the total of the shareholders' equity. Capital, under this system, is seen as the money value of shareholders' funds at the beginning of a period and profit as income or the surplus remaining after maintaining the money value of such financial capital.

When, however, prices are increasing, it is difficult to argue that historical cost accounts reflect the economic reality of a company's financial performance and position. In inflationary periods, historical cost information suffers from three major deficiencies:

▶ A company's balance sheet may not reflect the current value of its assets.
▶ Profit will generally be overstated as costs of an earlier period are matched with current revenues, no distinction is drawn between 'operating' and 'holding' gains, and the need to maintain a company's capital in terms of either purchasing power of the owners' stake or operating capacity is neglected.
▶ Trend information will be distorted as rising prices affect the financial position, revenues, expenses and distribution. The money value of financial capital, and the surplus after maintaining such capital, are therefore inadequate as measures in reporting corporate position and performance when prices are changing.

In these various ways historic cost accounts can be misleading for decision-making purposes and the effectiveness of management in respect of operating results can be concealed.

Some of these shortcomings are overcome by the use of accounts prepared under the modified historical cost convention, which deals with the periodic revaluation of selected assets. If such accounts still prevail despite their remaining limitations (for example, lack of comparability) it is only because alternative accounting systems, based on alternative concepts of capital and its maintenance, as explained below, do not provide a total solution to the problems of accounting for changing prices.

Curent purchasing power (CPP) accounting

Financial capital maintenance is the concept that is most natural to the accountant and the most consistent with traditional accounting methods. There are two methods of measuring financial capital – money financial capital and real financial capital, both of which were mentioned earlier. Money financial capital is the concept that underpins historical cost accounting and its deficiencies in an inflationary period have already been noted. Real financial capital is the concept on which CPP accounting is based. It is never used in conjunction with historical cost valuation. CPP accounting involves general index adjustments of the historical cost asset values as well as the capital to be maintained. All non-monetary assets are restated by the application of the same general index which is applied to capital so that, in a period of inflation, neither a profit nor a loss is reported on such assets. Monetary items are fixed in value in terms of monetary units. Thus, the CPP method shows a loss on the holding of monetary assets and a gain on borrowings. (The MWCA and GA – monetary working capital adjustment and gearing adjustment – of SSAP 16 can be regarded as attempts to reflect aspects of the same phenomena without having to resort to general price indices.)

CPP calculations are quite objective, reflecting only changes in a general price index and avoiding the problems of 'soft' market valuations of individual assets, but they are subject to all the problems of the historical cost base. Moreover, they are quite complicated in their (P)SSAP 7 form. Its one cruel deficiency is its failure to deal with changes in the specific prices of the specific assets used and held by the firm. Further, CPP general index adjustment of historical costs may produce a grossly misleading picture of the current market values of assets when relative price changes are large.

Current cost accounting (CCA)

Under physical capital maintenance we have to consider maintaining a company's productive assets (as opposed to shareholders' funds), today's prices being more important than yesterday's. For this reason, all physical or operating capacity methods of accounting for price level changes involve the valuation of assets at their current cost. There are two concepts of operating capacity:

▶ The value concept of operating capacity considers the capacity of the company's assets to continue to produce the same value of goods and services.
▶ The volume concept of operating capacity considers the capacity of the company to produce the same volume of goods and services. It is this approach that was adopted by SSAP 16.

The benefits of adopting a physical as opposed to a financial view of capital, as well as the drawbacks, are dealt with below.

A summary

It is useful at this stage, in order that you may better appreciate the points made in the sections that follow, to summarise the various points made above as to capital, capital maintenance and income or profits in the context of changing prices as follows:

Table 14.1 Changing prices in respect of capital, capital maintenance and income on profits

	Financial capital maintenance (money values)	Financial capital maintenance (real values)	Physical or operating capital maintenance
Accounting system	HCA	CPP	CCA
Accounts reflect the effects of:	No price changes	General price changes	Specific price changes
Principal shortcoming	No account taken of any price changes	No account taken of specific price changes	No account taken of general price changes

If one were to argue, as is argued in the ASC Handbook on accounting for the effects of changing prices, that it is important that financial statements reflect the effects of all price changes, it is clear from the above that neither one system of capital maintenance nor one system – CPP or CCA – of accounting for the effects of changing prices is likely to be relevant to all companies in all circumstances. The only way forward, therefore, is to combine both financial and physical capital concepts in a system of accounting that will reflect the effects of all price changes affecting a company. Such a system is the real terms system of accounting, which is dealt with at the end of this chapter.

Some further points regarding the effects of and accounting for general inflation

One major shortcoming of historical cost accounts, as dealt with above, is that it does not take into account the effects of inflation, that is, losses arising on the holding of monetary assets and gains arising on the holding of monetary liabilities. Accounts prepared on the basis of CPP do reflect such losses and gains. Consider the simple illustration in Example 14.1.

EXAMPLE 14.1 – DISTINGUISHING BETWEEN HCA AND CPP AND DIFFERENTIATING BETWEEN THE MAINTENANCE OF FINANCIAL CAPITAL IN 'MONEY' AND IN 'REAL' TERMS

Balance sheets at 31 December:

	1993		1994	
	HCA £H	CPP £C	HCA £H	CPP £C
Fixed assets (no depreciation)	$50,000 \times \dfrac{130}{100}$	65,000	$50,000 \times \dfrac{130}{100}$	65,000
Net current assets (no stock, therefore all monetary)	$30,000 \times \dfrac{130}{120}$	32,500	45,000	45,000
Loan	$(10,000) \times \dfrac{130}{120}$	(10,833)	(10,000)	(10,000)
	70,000	86,667	85,000	100,000
Capital – shareholders' funds at 1 January	–	–	70,000	86,667
Surplus profit for the year	–	–	15,000	13,333
	70,000	86,667	85,000	100,000

One important point of difference between HCA and CPP is in respect of the unit of measurement. Where HCA numbers are in terms of money values, that is, a constant unit of measurement, CPP numbers are in terms of real values or purchasing power, that is a constantly changing unit of measurement. All values in a CPP balance sheet, at any one date, will be in terms of purchasing power at that date. If, therefore, purchasing power, as expressed by the RPI was given to you as:

At the date of acquisition of fixed assets	100
At 31/12/93	120
Average for 1994	125
At 31/12/94	130

All numbers in the 1993 CPP balance sheet would be expressed in terms of the RPI of 120. This CPP balance sheet is no longer relevant, at a later date, when there has been a change in the RPI. Accordingly, if you were to consider the 1993 CPP balance sheet in 1994, as the comparative for the 1994 CPP balance sheet, the 1993 CPP balance sheet would need restating in terms of the RPI at 31 December 1994 of 130. It is this restated balance sheet that is included in column 2. The numbers are derived as follows:

Non-monetary items $\qquad$ $HC \times \dfrac{RPI\ 31/12/94}{RPI\ at\ acquisition}$

Monetary items $\qquad$ $HC \times \dfrac{RPI\ 31/12/94}{RPI\ 31/12/93}$

The adjusted CPP values now represents the 31/12/93 balance sheet in terms of purchasing power at 31/12/94. It is this adjusted balance sheet that can now be properly compared with the 1994 CPP balance sheet, which will be arrived at in terms of purchasing power at 31 December 1994.

The CPP balance sheet at 31/12/94 as included in column 4 is arrived at by adjusting the historical cost numbers as follows:

Non monetary items $\qquad$ $HC \times \dfrac{RPI\ 31/12/94}{RPI\ at\ acquisition}$

Monetary items $\qquad$ HC – no adjustment

Two points are relevant here. First, CPP works on the assumption that non-monetary assets are not affected by inflation. Compare the £C values for fixed assets in the (restated) 1993 balance sheet and in the 1994 balance sheet. The £C value, £65,000, is the same, that is, no gain or loss is recognised on the holding of non-monetary items. Second, the £C value of monetary items at *one particular balance sheet date* is the £H value of these items at *that date*. Thus, the net current assets (excluding stock) and loans at 31 December 1994 in the CPP balance sheet date are in terms of their money values at that date.

Relating the profit or surplus for the year in the 1994 balance sheets to the discussion in the previous section:

▶ the historical cost profit of £15,000 is arrived at after maintaining the money value of shareholders' funds at the beginning of the year of £70,000
▶ the CPP profit of £13,333 is arrived at after maintaining the real value or purchasing power of shareholders' funds at the beginning of the year of £86,667.

The gains and losses arising on the holding of monetary items through the year are now identified in the 1994 profit and loss account, which is set out (by way of pro forma for all items before profit after tax) below.

Profit and loss account for the year ended 31 December 1994

	HCA £H		CPP £C
Sales	x	130/125	x
Opening stock	(x)	130/RPI date of acq.	(x)
Purchases	(x)	130/125	(x)
Closing stock	x	130/RPI date of acq.	x
Depreciation	(x)	130/RPI at FA acq.	(x)
Expenses	(x)	130/125	(x)
	15,000 × 125/130		15,600

Gains on the holding
of monetary liabilities
– loan

$10,000 \times \dfrac{(130 - 120)}{120}$	–	833
		16,433

Losses on the holding of
monetary assets

(i) At 1/1/94

$30,000 \times \dfrac{(130 - 120)}{120}$	–	(2,600)
		13,933

(ii) Arising during the year

$15,000 \times \dfrac{(130 - 125)}{125}$	–	(600)
	15,000	13,333

In this way CPP provides information as to the effects of inflation.
The numbers so provided are useful in that:

▶ they do reflect the effects of general price changes
▶ they provide a number for profit after the maintenance of the real value of financial
 capital
▶ the restated numbers each year are useful when it comes to examining trends of
 results and financial position.

They are not so useful in that:

▶ no account is taken of specific price changes and the maintenance of operating
 capability
▶ holding gains are not identified
▶ the value of fixed assets does not keep pace, exactly, with the rate of inflation
▶ the unit of measurement is not constant and this could be confusing.

It is for these various reasons that we need to consider the effects of changing prices in
a different light as in CCA systems below.

The scope of SSAP 16 and a summary of its framework

Scope
The standard applied to most listed companies and other large entities whose annual
financial statements were intended to give a true and fair view of financial position
and profit or loss. It did not apply to:

▶ unlisted entities unless they were classified as 'large companies' in company law
▶ most wholly owned subsidiaries
▶ specific types of entity on the ground that CCA may not have been wholly
 appropriate to them.

A summary of the SSAP 16 framework

The standard is based upon a concept of capital represented by the net operating
assets of a business (that is, fixed assets, stock and monetary working capital). The
fixed assets and stock are expressed in the balance sheet at their 'value to the
business', which is normally current cost (net replacement cost) but it could be a
recoverable amount (the greater of net realisable value or the amount recoverable from
further use) if a permanent diminution in value to below current cost has been
recognised. The Sandilands Report dealt with the concept of 'deprival value'. Thus
the value to the business of an asset was the lower of, on the one hand, replacement

cost and, on the other hand, the higher of net replacement value and present value or economic value. The net operating assets can be said to represent, in accounting terms, the operating capability of the business and usually will have been financed both by shareholders' capital and by borrowing.

In determining current cost profits for an accounting period the objective is achieved in two stages. In the first stage the current cost operating profit/loss is determined. This is the surplus/deficit arising from the ordinary activities of the business in the period, after allowing for the impact of price changes on the funds needed to maintain operating capability, but without taking into account the way in which the business is financed. It is calculated before interest on net borrowing and before taxation.

In the second stage, the current cost profit/loss attributable to shareholders is determined. In arriving at the net result account is taken of the way in which the business is financed. To the extent that net operating assets of the business are financed by borrowing, the full allowance for the impact of price changes on operating capability made in arriving at operating profit may not be required, because the repayment rights of lenders are fixed in monetary amounts. Current cost profit attributable to shareholders therefore reflects the surplus for the period after allowing for the impact of price changes on the funds needed to maintain the shareholders' proportion of the operating capability. It is shown after interest, taxation, extraordinary items and a gearing adjustment.

The difference between historic and current cost profit computations can be summarised broadly in terms of four adjustments to historic cost profit. The first three are:

1 A depreciation adjustment (DA) – the difference between current and historic cost charges for depreciation.
2 A cost of sales adjustment (COSA) – the difference between current and historic cost of sales.
3 A monetary working capital adjustment (MWCA) – to allow for the impact of price changes on this portion of operating capability.

These three adjustments affect operating profit computations, whereas the fourth adjustment, the gearing adjustment (GA), allows for an abatement of the first three adjustments, according to a gearing proportion (net borrowing/net borrowing plus shareholders' equity), in calculating the current cost profit attributable to shareholders.

A current cost reserve (part of shareholders' funds) is carried in current cost balance sheets, which includes, where appropriate:

▶ unrealised revaluation surpluses on fixed assets, stock and investments
▶ realised amounts to the cumulative net total of the four current cost adjustments mentioned above.

SSAP 16 suggested three types of relationship between historical cost and current cost accounts and companies did, in the past, produce one or other of the following:

1 historical cost accounts as the main accounts with supplementary current cost accounts which were prominently displayed
2 current cost accounts as the main accounts with supplementary historical cost accounts
3 current cost accounts as the only accounts accompanied by adequate historical cost information.

The current cost operating adjustments

It is important that you are able both to calculate the effects of specific price changes on the operating capability of a company and to be able to discuss the purpose of each of the current cost operating adjustments. This is because the adjustments remain relevant in the context of the proposals put forward in the Handbook on accounting for the effects of changing prices. Each of the three adjustments are dealt with in turn below.

Stock and the cost of sales adjustment (COSA)

The COSA is the adjustment required to eliminate realised holding gains arising on stock sold during the year. No single method of calculating the effect of price changes on the current replacement cost of stock can be capable of universal application. Alternative methods are:

▶ The use of indices that reflect changes in the price of goods and services used by the business in the period in conjunction with the averaging method, as shown in Pro forma 14.1.

PRO FORMA 14.1

	HC £		CC £
Closing stock	x	Average stock index for year Stock index at acquisition	x
Less: Opening stock	(x)	Average stock index for year Stock index at acquisition	(x)
Total change	x	Volume change	x

The difference between the total change and the volume change = the price change or the COSA.

▶ The use of standard costs updated for price variances applicable at the valuation date.
▶ Actual data relating to individual items; actual costs of purchase; use of price lists; application of appropriate price indices to the cost of individual items in stock. Thus, the COSA for each sale can be ascertained as the replacement cost of each item sold on the date of sale less its historical cost of purchase.
▶ A LIFO valuation of stock will result in the current cost of sales, but only so long as the volume of stock is not decreasing.

As stock is to be valued at the lower of its current replacement cost and its recoverable amount, any write-down to recoverable amount should be charged to profit and loss account. In these circumstances, the averaging calculation should be based on the recoverable amounts.

Several problem areas relating to COSA were dealt with in the Working Guide to SSAP 16. Thus, problems arise on:

▶ *Seasonal purchases* No relevant replacement cost is available at the date the stock is consumed. Moreover, if prices are volatile, it would be inappropriate to match against current revenues future costs that bear no relation to current activities. For such items you should:

- *either* calculate a COSA based on an index that corresponds with the long-term trend in replacement costs
- *or* exclude such stock from the COSA and include it in the MWCA.

▶ *Dealing stock* Replacement cost at the time of sale would be equal or close to the selling price. The COSA would therefore eliminate the whole profit/loss on the transaction. No COSA should be calculated. Such stock should be included in the MWCA.

▶ *Contract work in progress*:
- Contracts that are repetitive in nature: A COSA should be calculated in the normal way. Relevant replacement costs can be ascertained.
- Unique contracts: Work in progress, net of progress payments, may be treated as a monetary asset and be subject to MWCA. This is because relevant replacement costs cannot be ascertained.

In addition to ascertaining the realised holding gain (COSA) on stock sold in the year, it is also necessary, in ascertaining the effect of specific price changes on stocks, to ascertain the unrealised holding gain on stock still held at a year end. This may be ascertained as per Pro forma 14.2.

PRO FORMA 14.2

Unrealised stock holding gains on stock:

	HC £		CC £	Difference
Opening stock	x	$\dfrac{\text{Stock index at OP B/S date}}{\text{Stock index at acquisition}}$	x	CR/CCR
Closing stock	x	$\dfrac{\text{Stock index at CL B/S date}}{\text{Stock index at acquisition}}$	x	
	x		x	CR/DR – CCR with increase or decrease in year.

Monetary working capital and the monetary working capital adjustment (MWCA)

Monetary working capital comprises items that are used in the day-to-day operating activities of the business, that is, trade debtors and creditors (exclude creditors relating to fixed assets; cash floats; the non-fluctuating elements of bank balances or overdrafts). Stock not included in the COSA should be included in monetary working capital. In principle, the profit element in debtors should be excluded.

Where monetary working capital is a net liability greater than the historical cost value of the stock, the excess does not fund working capital and should be excluded from the monetary working capital adjustment and included in the gearing calculation as part of net borrowings.

The MWCA can be ascertained using an averaging method, as shown in Pro forma 14.3.

	HC		Adj
Closing MWC	x	Av. stock or general index for year / Index at CL B/S date	x
Less:			
Opening MWC	(x)	Av. stock or general index for year / Index at OP B/S date	(x)
Total change	x	Volume change	x

The difference between the total change and volume change is the MWCA for the year. Note that you may also use as the denominator, the stock index at the date of acquisition.

If, on average, a company holds net monetary assets in monetary working capital, the MWCA would be a charge against profits to support the operating capability tied up in (net) debtors while the costs of inputs to production are rising. If, on average, a company holds net monetary liabilities in monetary working capital, the MWCA would be a credit to profits or an abatement of the COSA to support the fact that, as stock purchases are financed by trade credit, there is no need for the whole of the COSA.

Fixed assets and the depreciation adjustment (DA)

Realised and unrealised holding gains on fixed assets may be ascertained as shown in Pro forma 14.4.

PRO FORMA 14.4

	HC (1)	CC at 1/1 (2)	CC at 31/12 (3)	Difference
NBV 1 January (excluding FA sold during year)	x uplift	x uplift	x	CR CCR
				(2-1) b/f
				(3-2) for year
Additions at cost	x	uplift	x	CR CCR for year
	x		x	
HC Depreciation	(x)	depn. on AVFA	(x)	The DA is CR to the depreciation
	x	CC values in year	x	provision account (not the CCR)
c/y backlog depreciation for year on closing CC values	x			
Less: On average CC values	(x)			
			(x)	DR CCR
	CC B/S	31 December	x	

Treatment of fixed assets disposed of in the year is shown in Pro forma 14.5.

	HC	CC on date of disposal	Difference
NBV on date of disposal	x uplift	x	DR CCR
Proceeds	(x)	(x)	
	(x)	(x)	DR P/L

The debit to the profit and loss account is a current cost operating adjustment and is applied in arriving at the current cost operating profit. It is therefore also taken into account in arriving at the gearing adjustment.

An explanation of backlog depreciation in CCA: Where assets are restated at their gross replacement cost, the depreciation provision in CCA must be based on such gross replacement cost. Backlog depreciation may be divided into previous years and current year, as explained below.

Previous years

The restatement of the depreciation brought forward from previous years into line with current replacement cost. The charge in strict replacement cost accounting would be made against revenue reserves. In CCA, as in SSAP 16, it is argued that the present operating capability of the business regarding fixed assets is maintained by charging against each year's revenue the value to the business of the assets consumed in that year. Backlog depreciation does not form part of this consumption but represents the effect of current price changes on past consumption and, therefore, is not charged against revenue in arriving at operating profit. As a result, the total CC depreciation charges (as opposed to provisions) will not equal the ultimate replacement cost of the asset consumed. SSAP 16 is not concerned with ultimate replacement and the provision of cash in this regard, which, it argues, is a matter for financial management. The backlog, therefore, is taken to the current cost reserve and netted against the gross unrealised surplus on fixed assets.

Current year

In so far as the current year's CC depreciation charge is based on average CC values during the year, there is a shortfall in the total provision required in the balance sheet, which at the year end must be in line with year end values. The difference between the depreciation charged for the year in the profit and loss account and the depreciation for the year required in the balance sheet is what is termed current year's backlog depreciation. It can be dealt with only against the current cost reserve, as a charge against revenue would distort the charge for the year on the basis of consumption during the year.

The SSAP 16 gearing adjustment (GA)

The fourth SSAP 16 current cost adjustment takes account of the probability that some of a company's operating capability may be financed by borrowing in addition to shareholders' funds. To this extent, the effects of price changes on the company's operating capability need not be borne by shareholders, and the gearing adjustment results in an abatement of the sum of the current cost operating adjustments, as dealt with above, applied against profits. In order to ascertain the amount of such abatement:

First, ascertain whether there are, on average, any net borrowings – see Pro forma 14.6.

	Opening £	Closing £
Debentures, loans	x	x
Taxation, including deferred	x	x
HP creditors, lease finance	x	x
Bank overdrafts	x	x
Bank balances	(x)	(x)
	x	x
	Average = x	

If there are no net borrowings – that is, if the company has no gearing – there is no gearing benefit and there is no justification for an abatement of the current cost operating adjustments and there is no gearing adjustment.

If there are net borrowings, do the following:

Second, ascertain the gearing proportion, as follows:

Av. net borrowings
—————————————————
Av. net operating assets (CC values)

Third, apply this proportion to the sum of the current cost operating adjustments (COSA + MWCA + DA) and release such amount from the current cost reserve (CCR) to the profit and loss account.

Preparation of current cost accounts

The workings to ascertain the current cost adjustments dealt with above, and their effect upon historical cost profit can now be illustrated in terms of an example (see Example 14.2).

EXAMPLE 14.2

The published historical cost profit and loss account of a company for the year ended 31 December 1993 were as reproduced below.

	£000	£000	£000
Net trading profit			1,000
after charging:			
Directors' emoluments		80	
Auditors' fees and expenses		20	
Depreciation (net): Buildings	34		
Plant	174		
		208	
Interest on 15% debentures (gross)			(120)
Net Profit before taxation			880
Taxation:			
Corporation tax based on profits for year	270		
Transfer to deferred taxation account	150		
	420		
Less: Overprovision for taxation in previous year	(10)		
			(410)

Net profit after taxation		470
Dividends:		
Ordinary – paid (5%)	(50)	
* – proposed (15%)	(150)	
		(200)
Retained earnings		270

Prepare a supplementary current cost profit and loss account in accordance with SSAP 16, utilising the following information:

(i) Land, buildings and plant on hand at 31 December 1991 were revalued at that date, and subsequent additions were capitalised at cost, as follows:

	Land	Buildings	Plant
31 December 1991: Valuation	£250,000	£500,000	£1,000,000
Depreciation		(100,000)	(500,000)
(All these assets were owned at 31 December 1992)			
Year 1992: cost		80,000	130,000
Year 1993: cost		100,000	150,000

Depreciation in 1992 and 1993 has been on the straight-line basis (calculated on the gross values at the year end): buildings 5% per annum; plant 15% per annum.

During 1993, plant valued at 31 December 1991 at £160,000 less £70,000 depreciation was sold for £60,000; its net book value then was £66,000.

(ii) At 31 December 1993, the market value of the land was professionally appraised at £300,000. In revaluation of the buildings for CCA purposes, the following indices of building costs were applied:

1991 (year end)	100
1992 (average)	110
1992 (year end)	125
1993 (average)	130
1993 (year end)	150

(iii) The corresponding indices of plant costs were:

1991 (year end)	100
1992 (average)	110
1992 (year end)	125
1993 (average)	135
1993 (year end)	145

(iv) The stocks (at FIFO cost) were:

31 December 1992	£750,000
31 December 1993	£900,000

In each case they represented three months' average consumption, and the relevant price indices were:

1992	October	99
	November	100
	December	101
1993	October	119
	November	120
	December	122
(mid-month in each case)		
1993	(Average)	110

(v) Monetary working capital (defined as excess of debtors over creditors) was:

31 December 1992 £160,000
31 December 1993 £200,000

Relevant buying and selling prices may be assumed to have risen by the same percentages over time, and the price indices in (iv) above are to be used.

(vi) The following items appeared in the previous year's and current year's current cost balance sheets:

	31/12/92	31/12/93
	£000	£000
Reserves	355	757
Taxation liabilities (less ACT)	299	433
Proposed dividends (net)	120	150
ACT thereon (3/7ths)	51	64
Bank balance (positive)	318	570

(vii) No securities were issued or redeemed in 1988.

Workings

First, ascertain the realised holding gains arising during the year. A realised holding gain is simply the difference between the replacement cost of an asset on the date of its consumption or sale and the historical cost of its purchase.

(i) COSA (Using the averaging method)

	£000	£000	£000
Closing stock	$900 \times 110/120$	825	
Less:			
Opening stock	$(750) \times 110/100$	(825)	
	150	NIL	COSA = 150

(ii) MWCA	£000	£000	£000
Closing MWC	$200 \times 110/120$	183	
Less:			
Opening MWC	$(160) \times 110/100$	(176)	
	40	7	MWCA = 33

(Note that year end indices may have been used as the denominators.)

(iii) DA

Buildings

	HC	HC Depreciation	CC Depreciation
	£000	£000	£000
1986	500 at 5%	$25 \times 130/100$	32.5
1987	80 at 5%	$4 \times 130/110$	4.7
1988	100 at 5%	$5 \times 130/130$	5
		34	42.2

Note: assuming assets purchased evenly during year.

Plant (still held by the company at the 1993 year end)

	£000	£000	£000
1991	1,000		
Disposal	(160)		
	840 at 15%	$126.0 \times 135/100$	170.1
1992	130 at 15%	$19.5 \times 135/110$	23.9
1993	150 at 15%	$22.5 \times 135/135$	22.5
		168.0	216.5

Plant (disposed of during year, assuming that sold evenly during the year)

	HC £000	CC £000	Difference
NBV date of disposal	66 × 135/100	89.1	23.1
Proceeds	60	60	
Loss on disposal	6	29.1	23.1

Summary:	£000
Buildings 42.2 – 34 =	8.2
Plant (1) 216.5 – 168 =	48.5
(2) 29.1 – 6 =	23.1
	79.8

Second, ascertain the gearing proportion and the gearing adjustment.

	1992 £000	1993 £000
Net borrowings:		
15% debentures (120 × 100/15)*	800	800
Taxation	299	433
ACT payable	51	64
	1,150	1,297
Less: Bank balance	(318)	(570)
	832	727

Average = 779.5

Shareholders' funds:		
Share capital (50 × 100/5)**	1,000	1,000
Reserves (current cost)	355	757
Proposed dividend	120	150
Net operating assets	2,307	2,634

Average = 2,470.5

Notes:* 15% debentures are arrived at by grossing up the interest in the profit and loss account.

** Share capital is arrived at by grossing up the dividend paid in the profit and loss account.

$$GA = \frac{779.5}{2,470.5} \times (33 + 150 + 79.8) = 82,900$$

Note that the gearing adjustment should have taken into account the DA that would have arisen had the 1986 assets not been revalued in HCA. As the original cost of these assets was not given in the question no adjustment has been made for such an amount.

Third, prepare the current cost profit and loss account.

Current cost profit and loss account for the year ended 31 December 1988:

		£000
Turnover		5,000
Historical cost profit before interest and taxation		1,000
Current cost operating adjustments		
DA	79.8	
COSA	150	
MWCA	33	(262.8)

Current cost operating profit			737.2
	GA	82.9	
	Interest	(120)	(37.1)
			700.1
Taxation			(410)
Current cost profit attributable to shareholders			290.1
Dividends			(200)
Current cost retained profit for the year			90.1

Note that only realised holding gains are dealt with against profit. Unrealised holding gains – that is, the replacement cost of an asset at the balance sheet date less the historical cost of its purchase – are taken direct to a current cost reserve.

All holding gains would be collected in the current cost reserve as shown in Pro forma 14.7.

PRO FORMA 14.7

		Current cost reserve	
		b/f	
		URS on fixed assets	x
		URS on stocks	x
		CC operating adjustments less	
		GA in previous years	x
		Increase in URS on fixed	
Backlog depreciation	x	assets in year	x
GA	x	Increase in URS on stocks in year	x
		COSA	x
c/f	x	MWCA	x(x)

Depreciation adjustments charged against profit and credited against the depreciation provision account results in the URS on fixed assets in the current cost reserve becoming realised. This follows the same reasoning as dealt with in Chapter 4, whereby, following a revaluation of a fixed asset, the revaluation surplus becomes realised to the extent of the additional depreciation charged against profit following the revaluation.

A critical appraisal of SSAP 16

When the ASC issued SSAP 16 in March 1980, it said that no change to the standard would be made for three years. This was to enable producers and users of accounts to gain experience in producing and using current cost information. Towards the end of that period, ASC commissioned various surveys and research projects to be carried out for the Consultative Committee of Accountancy Bodies into certain aspects of CCA. One research project that generated considerable publicity was a study carried out by Professor Bryan Carsberg's research team on 'The usefulness of current cost accounting'. The study concluded that current cost information was widely used by analysts, investors and government bodies and that the benefits of providing the information outweighed the costs of preparing and auditing CCA information.

The CCA monitoring working party, set up to monitor the implementation of SSAP 16 over the preliminary three-year period, reported its findings in September 1983. The report concluded that a revised standard should be produced, and that the new standard should require companies to show the effects of changing prices in their accounts when those effects were material. It also recommended that current cost information should be given in the notes to the historical cost accounts and that this information would be essential if the financial statements were to show a true and fair view.

On 29 March 1984 the ASC issued a statement of intent (SOI) on the future of SSAP 16. The proposals contained in the SOI required all public companies, regardless of size or activity, to reflect in their accounts the effects of changing prices where those effects were material. In order to encourage companies to comply with the proposed requirements the ASC stated that if companies' accounts are to show a true and fair view, they must include some form of inflation-adjusted information.

ED 35 – Accounting for the Effects of Changing Prices, was issued in July 1984. SSAP 16 was to remain in force until it was either replaced by a new standard or removed from standard accounting practice altogether. The proposed standard basically followed the proposals outlined in the SOI. It was to apply to all public companies other than value based companies and wholly owned subsidiaries. The main points dealt with in ED 35 are summarised below.

SSAP 16 was not successful. A survey of published accounts in 1983 stated that:

> The subjective impression formed on reviewing these SSAP 16 disclosures is that, with a few notable exceptions, companies presented only the minimum of details . . . The details provided appear to be largely of a ritual character, insufficient for expert assessment . . . only 32% of statements offer an explanation of their purpose . . . In conclusion, the decade of accounting for price changes has been a decade of learning; learning about the deficiencies of historical cost accounting and learning how to remedy some of the limitations.

SSAP 16 no longer has mandatory status. Before going on to consider the current set of proposals put forward by the ASC as to accounting for the effects of changing prices, it is necessary to deal with that old chestnut of an exam question, a discussion of the advantages and disadvantages of CCA as put forward by SSAP 16.

There is no doubt that, in a period of changing prices, CCA produced under SSAP 16 is a better guide to the profitability of a company, and possibly to the value of its assets, than HCA. This is because CCA makes allowances for the amount a company needs to earn to continue the existing business, that is, the operating adjustments, and for the benefit of borrowing (the gearing adjustment). CCA is of considerable benefit to management in arriving at a pricing policy and also in arriving at dividend decisions. Ratios based on CCA are far more meaningful than those based on HCA given that profits are overstated and capital employed understated in HCA. Some of the principal shortcomings of HCA dealt with at the start of this chapter are effectively overcome in CCA. Thus, profit in so far as it is arrived at after charging current costs for the cost of sales and depreciation, takes into account the effects of specific price changes on profits and, given that asset values in the balance sheet are stated at current cost, the effects of specific price changes on asset values retained at the balance sheet date are taken into account.

There were, nevertheless, several reasons for the abandonment of SSAP 16. These, the disadvantages of CCA, are dealt with in turn below.

No account taken of inflation

The principal shortcoming of CCA is that it does not adequately take into account the effects of general price changes and the effects of inflation – the loss arising on a holding of monetary assets and the gain arising on a holding of monetary liabilities. SSAP 16 did, however, recognise the importance of the 'proprietorial view' of profit and did put forward, as a voluntary disclosure requirement, the need to produce a further statement indicating the effect of inflation on shareholders' funds. A simple form of such a statement is shown in Pro forma 14.8.

	£
Current cost shareholders' funds at beginning of the period	x
Adjustment for inflation (% change in RPI in year × opening (CC) shareholders' funds)	x
	x
Surplus for the year after taking into account the effects of inflation	
Current costs shareholders' funds at the end of the period	x
	x

The effects of inflation are dealt with in the real terms systems of accounting for the effects of changing prices as dealt with below, and it is interesting to note the similarity between the SSAP 16 voluntary disclosure note and the proposed note to HCA as to the effects of changing prices as dealt with in the ASC Handbook dealing with the problem.

The problem of comparability

One of the shortcomings of HCA in a time of changing prices is that trend information is distorted. This is also one of the shortcomings of CCA. The ASC issued a discussion paper – *Corresponding amounts and 10 year summaries in CCA* – to deal with this problem and made the following useful points.

Users of financial statements are concerned with two, amongst other, questions:

▶ How does the latest year compare with the previous year?
▶ What has been the trend over a number of years?

CCA allows for the impact of specific price changes in arriving at the results for a year, but the results of a year so arrived at are not comparable with the results of a previous year arrived at applying the same CC principles. This is because the results of each year are stated in terms of the pounds of each year, and no adjustment will have been allowed for the critical influence of the changing value of money.

The discussion paper stated that the previous year's results allow a judgement to be made as to the performance of the company in the current year while comparisons over several past periods allow judgements to be made as to the long-term trends or development of the company.

Both areas of performance and development involve a change in first financial size, and second in physical size of the company. No one method can measure the change in both, year to year, or over the long term.

Two means of adjustment were discussed:

▶ the use of specific costs to adjust past figures
▶ adjustment using a general index.

The first is appropriate in arriving at the operating profit of a particular period after maintaining operating (physical) capability. If you were to adjust last year's CCA figures by applying this year's specific current costs the figures would be meaningful only if the make up of the assets and the operations of the company remained unchanged. This would be unrealistic. Moreover, it would lead to some considerable confusion.

The second would show the financial change resulting through a change in general prices and the changing value of money. The CCA of the previous year(s) would be translated into pounds of the current year. Like would then be compared to like.

The following indices could conceivably be used:

- ▶ GDP – excludes imports and taxes
- ▶ TDE – excludes exports
- ▶ TFE – includes imports and exports
- ▶ RPI – measures changes in prices regarding consumption by households.

The first three are calculated infrequently – quarterly. They are not available immediately at quarter end. They are subject to revision after publication. The RPI and the TFE have shown a similar trend over time. The ASC proposed that the RPI be the index used for the adjustment of comparative information.

By either deflating all figures to the index of a base period or by uplifting past figures to the index of the latest year, it was agreed that the distortions occasioned by changes in the value of money would be eliminated but otherwise leave the relationship of one year to another unchanged.

This shortcoming of CCA and these approaches to the solving of the problem are also dealt with in the ASC Handbook on accounting for the effects of changing prices.

The lack of universal application of CCA

Operating or physical capital concepts, on which CCA is based, are not suitable for all companies and CCA, therefore, does not have universal application in fully reflecting the effects of changing prices. Thus, this concept is less suitable as a concept for companies in which asset value increases are viewed as an alternative to trading as a means of generating gains. Financial capital concepts are more suitable for such 'value-based companies'. Such companies do not have the maintenance of their operating capital as a prime objective. Indeed, they do not have an easily identifiable operating capacity to maintain.

Indexation problems

It could be argued that broad-based specific indices may not be suitable for use in arriving at the current cost of specific assets used by different companies.

Tax

CCA as a system does not provide any part of the basis on which a company is taxed. This is not surprising, given the scope for discretion in CCA. However, unless a system of accounting is acceptable to the Inland Revenue, with capital allowances based on cost adjusted for inflation and can therefore become the only accounts a company produces, it will fail the test of universal application.

Complicated and not wholly accepted adjustments

SSAP 16 was very complicated. The ASC's step-by-step guide covered well over 100 pages. In additiion, and contributing to the lack of its universal application, there was no consensus as to the use and purpose of the SSAP 16 adjustments. Where it was generally agreed that the COSA and DA serve a useful purpose, there was no such consensus view as to the use and purpose of the MWCA and GA. Indeed, several alternative GAs were proposed. These are dealt with below.

ED 35 and alternative gearing adjustments

In the light of reports from the CCA monitoring working party, submissions from various accounting institutions, results of sponsored research studies and the reactions from business and industry in general during the first three years of operating SSAP 16, the ASC published a proposed compromise solution in July 1984: ED 35 – Accounting for the Effects of Changing Prices.

ED 35 reported widespread agreement that companies ought to reflect the effect of changing prices in their financial statements. The answering of the question as to how this may best be done remained a problem. The ED proposed a single set of accounts with information on the effect of changing prices shown in a note to the accounts where not given in the accounts themselves.

ED 35 could not progress to standard as it, prematurely, suggested that information as to the effects of changing prices was essential to a true and fair view. It was, however, interesting in that it proposed, given the criticisms made of the SSAP 16 gearing adjustment, alternative gearing adjustments, which are dealt with below.

The ED 35 note to the accounts

EXAMPLE 14.3

Note xx – Effects of changing prices

The Group

	1985 £000	1984 £000
Working capital adjustment	560	470
Depreciation adjustment	950	850
Adjustment to profit on disposal of fixed assets	155	150
Adjustment to income from associated companies	55	50
	1,720	1,520
Gearing adjustment	(310)	(300)
Amount of profit on ordinary activities after taxation required to meet current cost adjustments	1,410	1,220
Adjustment to minority interests	(170)	(120)
Adjustment to extraordinary items	80	60
Amount of profit for the financial year required to be retained to meet the effects of changing prices	1,320	1,160
Gross current cost of fixed assets	16,640	10,490
Accumulated current cost depreciation	8,110	5,990
Net current cost of fixed assets	8,530	4,500
Current cost of stocks	4,000	3,010

The alternative gearing adjustments of ED 35

Given the argument that there are various alternative valid ways in which a gearing adjustment can be calculated, the ASC gave a choice of three alternative methods for the calculation of the gearing adjustment in accordance with ED 35.

The first method explained in ED 35 is the form of gearing adjustment required by SSAP 16:

Gearing proportion × (COSA + MWCA + DA)

The method abates the current cost adjustments for depreciation, cost of sales and monetary working capital for the period to the extent that they fall on providers of loan capital rather than on providers of equity capital. The abatement is calculated by applying the average gearing ratio in the period to the aggregate of the current cost operating adjustments.

The gearing benefit so calculated is the benefit applying only to realised holding gains, the COSA, MWCA, and DA, for the period. It excludes the benefit arising from unrealised holding gains in the period, that is, the unrealised revaluation surpluses in the period on stocks and fixed assets.

The second method is based on that part of the total holding gains for the period that can be regarded as being financed by borrowings, that is, both the current cost adjustments made in the profit and loss account and the unrealised revaluation surpluses that arise on stocks and fixed assets. It is calculated:

Gearing proportion × (Closing current cost reserve before calculating
the gearing adjustment
Less the opening current cost reserve)

or, put another way,

Gearing proportion × (COSA + MWCA + the URS on FA and stocks in year)

Note that in this latter case the DA for the year is included in the URS on FA during the year.

The third method of calculating the gearing adjustment reflects the effect of general price changes on either the net borrowings of the company or the net monetary assets of the company (in both cases excluding those items included in monetary working capital). The amount derived from this calculation is added to the net charge or credit for interest paid or received during the period in money terms and shows the net interest charge or credit for the period in real terms.

Thus:

▶ Ascertain the rate of increase in general prices during the period.
▶ Apply this rate, depending on the balance sheet of the company, to either the company's net borrowings or net monetary assets. In the former case the gearing adjustment will be a benefit to the company, in the latter a negative gearing adjustment arises, a debit to profit and loss account, reflecting the loss suffered by the company on a holding of net monetary assets in a period of inflation.

This last method meets one of the criticisms made against the SSAP 16 gearing adjustment in that SSAP 16 did not consider a negative GA – that is, if a company had no gearing, there was no gearing adjustment as opposed to a further charge against profits to reflect the loss on a holding of monetary assets.

The ASC Handbook on accounting for the effects of changing prices

The introduction to the Handbook states that its objectives are to explain and discuss the methods that may be adopted by a company to reflect the effects of changing prices in its accounts, and to identify those methods that the ASC considers most appropriate. The Handbook is intended as a summary and reference work providing useful guidance to those who wish to prepare, use or audit information on the effects of changing prices.

The debate on which method to adopt when accounting for the effects of changing prices has generally been expressed in terms of a choice between two methods. In the UK, these methods are known as current cost accounting (CCA), in which adjustments are made for specific price changes, and constant or current purchasing power (CPP) accounting, in which adjustments are made for changes in the general level of prices. Although the debate has often been expressed as a straight choice between CCA and CPP, it is in fact necessary, when establishing a method of determining profit, to specify:

▶ the basis that is to be adopted for valuing assets (HC or CC)
▶ the capital maintenance concept that is to be used (financial or operating capital maintenance concept)
▶ the unit of measurement to be used (the nominal pound or the unit of constant purchasing power).

ASC considers it most appropriate for companies to disclose information about the current year's results and financial position on the basis of current cost valuation, using either the operating or financial capital maintenance concept and the nominal pound as the unit of measurement.

Information on this basis can be incorporated into a company's main accounts. If this approach is not practicable, then information on the effects of changing prices can most readily be disclosed in the notes to the accounts. This note is in the form of an 'adjusted earnings statement', and would show the difference between the earnings attributable to ordinary shareholders on the basis used in the profit and loss account and those earnings stated after maintaining the operating or real financial capital of the company; it would include the adjustments for additional depreciation (DA) and additional cost of sales (COSA) and any further adjustments consistent with the capital maintenance concept adopted. The ASC also considers it helpful for companies to disclose certain key pieces of information such as:

▶ the gross and net current cost of fixed assets
▶ the accumulated current cost depreciation
▶ the current cost of stocks.

The choice of capital maintenance concepts

Previous sections of this chapter have dealt with the financial, money values or real values, and physical or operating concepts of capital and capital maintenance. A major part of the problem in the debate on accounting for the effects of changing prices is that no one concept is appropriate to all companies in respect of all price changes. The ASC now takes the view that both concepts are useful in appropriate circumstances. Each concept has different objectives; financial capital concepts are based on a proprietorial view of profit, operating capital concepts are based on an entity view of profit. The choice of which one to use will depend in part on the nature of a company's business. Some companies may wish to provide information based on both concepts. This is achieved by adopting a 'real terms' system of accounting for the effects of price changes and is dealt with in greater detail below.

The factors to be taken into account in choosing between different capital maintenance concepts are as follows.

A company that is seeking to measure the 'real' return on its shareholders' capital will do this by comparing capital at the end of the period with opening shareholders' invested capital restated in terms of constant purchasing power.

If, however, the aim of the company is to demonstrate its capacity to continue in existence by ensuring that at the end of the accounting period it is as capable of producing a similar quantity of goods and services as it was at the beginning, profit would be regarded as the surplus remaining only after its operating capital had been maintained.

A company may determine its reporting objective based on its perception of the users of its accounts. To shareholders in general a financial capital maintenance view may seem the most natural. Managers and employees, however, may consider shareholders to be only one of the many stakeholders in a company and may consider the company's major objective as being one of perpetuating its existence in its identified market. They, therefore, could well look at a company's objectives in terms of maintaining operating or physical capital. Information on the maintenance of operating capital may also be useful to shareholders in assessing the company's current and future potential for generating distributable cash flows.

The selection of reporting method is also influenced by the nature of a company's business. Financial capital maintenance is most suitable for companies in which asset value increases are viewed as an alternative to trading as a means of generating gains. It is particularly suitable for:

▶ companies that do not have an easily definable operating capital to maintain
▶ companies that do not have the maintenance of their operating capital as an objective
▶ unique or discontinuous ventures such as those engaged in the extractive or construction industries or companies engaged in commodity trading
▶ value-based companies, such as insurers, property companies, investment trusts or other similar long-term investment entities.

The true measure of the performance of such companies in times of inflation, is their ability to produce 'real' profits above the level of those nominal profits that arise simply as a result of general inflation. The consistent measurement of such gains requires not only that opening capital be adjusted by a general index, but also that assets be valued at their current cost.

Operating capital maintenance is of fundamental relevance to other, manufacturing, companies. Thus, companies that experience large fluctuations in the price of their inputs sometimes find that results on a historical cost basis are difficult to interpret and prefer to report in current cost terms and to take decisions on that information. The operating capital approach regards only the current cost operating profit as the result for the period and treats any other gain or loss as a reserve movement. The effect is to charge against profits the current cost of consumption of assets.

As one is concerned with the effects of all price changes, general and specific, companies should provide a profit figure both on an operating capital maintenance concept and a broader figure that encompasses gains on holding assets, to the extent that these are real gains after allowing for inflation. Which of these figures is found to be most useful will depend upon both the use to which the information is being put and the nature and circumstances of the company. For example:

▶ In the case of a manufacturing company that intends to maintain its present operating capital, current cost operating profit may be an important piece of information to those wishing to estimate future earning capacity. The real gain or loss on assets held may be relatively unimportant.
▶ For a property company, in which the capital appreciation of properties may be as important a factor as rents earned, the wider concept of total gains may be considered relatively more important.

The real terms system of accounting

This system accounts for the effects of changing prices by measuring whether a company's financial capital – that is, shareholder's funds – is maintained in real terms. It involves the measurement of assets at current costs. This method is appropriate for all types of company, and is particularly suitable for value-based and other types of company that do not have a definable operating capital.

The basic approach to profit measurement under the real terms system is to:

▶ calculate the shareholders' funds at the beginning of the period based on current cost asset values

▶ restate that amount in terms of pounds at the reporting date by adjusting it by the relevant change in a general index such as the RPI

▶ compare the above with the shareholders' funds at the end of the year based on current cost asset values.

If the year end figure is greater than the restated opening figure, a real terms profit has been made.

The real terms system of accounting and the ASC Handbook proposals as to accounting for the effects of price changes

The Handbook states that information on the effects of changing prices is important for a proper appreciation of a company's results and financial position. The information may be presented as the main accounts, in the notes to the accounts, or as information supplemental to the financial statements. It is considered likely that most companies that wish to report the effects of changing prices would prefer to prepare historical cost main accounts and to disclose information on the effects of changing prices in the notes to these accounts. The rest of this section deals with such a note included as a part of the historical cost main accounts.

This note can take various forms, ranging from an abridged set of accounts to information that can be used to calculate the impact of changing prices on the company's performance and financial position.

Information on the effects of changing prices on the company's performance will usually be most appropriately given in the form of an 'earnings adjusted statement'. This should analyse the difference between the earnings attributable to ordinary shareholders on the basis used in the profit and loss account and the earnings attributable to ordinary shareholders after maintaining the operating or real financial capital of the company. It will usually show:

▶ a cost of sales adjustment
▶ a depreciation adjustment
▶ any adjustments relating to monetary items, the effect of borrowing or equity interests consistent with the capital maintenance concept adopted; these adjustments may include a monetary working capital adjustment and a gearing adjustment
▶ any other adjustments reflecting the effects of changing prices that are consistent with the capital maintenance concept adopted and which the directors consider appropriate.

A suggested layout is shown in Pro forma 14.9.

PRO FORMA 14.9

	£	£	Explanatory notes
Earnings attributable to ordinary shareholders as reported		x	1
Deduct: Cost of sales adjustment	(x)		
Depreciation adjustment	(x)		
Total current cost operating adjustments		(x)	2
Current cost operating profit		x	3
Add: Realised holding gains	x		4
Unrealised holding gains	x		5
Total holding gains		x	
		x	
Deduct: Inflation adjustments to shareholders' funds		(x)	6
Profit attributable to ordinary shareholders adjusted for the effects of price changes (total real gains)		x	

Explanatory notes

1 The earnings attributable to ordinary shareholders as reported would be the historical cost earnings as indicated in the profit and loss account of the historical cost main accounts of the company. The adjustments that follow provide an indication of the effects of changing prices on such earnings. The relevance of these adjustments is explained in terms of the shortcomings of the HCA system, as to profits, when prices change.

2 The total current cost operating adjustments: These reflect the effects of specific price changes on assets consumed by a company, that is, stocks and fixed assets. Such adjustments quantify the 'realised holding gains' made by the company during the year. These are highlighted in the statement above. The statement above includes only two of the four current cost adjustments dealt with earlier. It does not include a monetary working capital adjustment and/or a gearing adjustment. This is because it is argued that while the principles underlying charging additional depreciation and cost of sales are well established and are generally accepted in practice, the treatment of monetary working capital remains the subject of much debate. This is because some commentators do not view the allowance as being consistent with the operating capital maintenance concept. Some do not consider monetary working capital to be part of net operating assets. If it is wished to make an allowance for additional working capital, such an allowance – the MWCA – can be calculated, as explained earlier in the module, and included as a separate adjustment in the total of the current cost operating adjustment above. The operating adjustments included above (including or excluding an MWCA), do not take full account of the manner in which the company is financed. While some commentators argue that an allowance should be made in determining profit to take account of such financing arrangements, there is no agreement among them as to how this effect should be calculated. Some argue that an allowance in respect of the company's gearing – a gearing adjustment – should be made. Others argue that any allowance for the effect of such financial arrangements is inconsistent with the idea of determining profit

after maintaining operating capital and should not, therefore, form part of any operating capital maintenance concept accounting system. However, for those companies that nevertheless wish to make some form of allowance, two alternative gearing adjustments are possible. These are described in the Handbook as:

▶ *Type 1 gearing adjustment* The total amount of the current cost operating adjustments is abated in proportion to the gearing ratio unless the net borrowing is negative, in which case no adjustment is made. This type of gearing adjustment is the one that was most commonly used under SSAP 16 and is simply calculated as:

The gearing proportion × Total current cost operating adjustments

▶ *Type 2 gearing adjustment* The Type 1 gearing adjustment deals only with the operating profits earned from assets and ignores any appreciation in the value of such assets. It is sometimes argued that this is unnecessarily prudent and that, in substance, that appreciation in the value of assets is no different from the operating profits earned from them. The Type 2 gearing adjustment, sometimes referred to as the 'natural gearing adjustment' and sometimes as the 'ICI adjustment', extends the Type 1 adjustment to the appreciation in value of the assets and, therefore, treats appreciations in value and operating profits consistently. The Type 2 gearing adjustment is calculated as:

The gearing proportion × [Total current cost operating adjustments *plus* the unrealised holding gains on fixed assets and stocks arising during the year]

That is, the gearing benefit arising from both the realised and the unrealised holding gains.

If a company wished to incorporate both a MWCA and a GA into the statement above, the suggested layout would be prepared as shown in Pro forma 14.10.

PRO FORMA 14.10

	£	£
Earnings attributable to ordinary shareholders as reported		x
Deduct: Cost of sales adjustment	(x)	
Monetary working capital adjustment	x/(x)	
Depreciation adjustment	(x)	
Total current cost operating adjustments		(x)
Current cost operating profit		x
Abatement of current cost operating adjustments, the Type 1 or Type 2 gearing adjustment		(x)
		x
Add: Realised holding gains (COSA + or – MWCA + DA – GA)	x	
Unrealised holding gains	x	
Total holding gains		x
		x

The rest of the statement would be as above, in Pro forma 14.9.

3   *Current cost operating profit* This amount, highlighted in the statement above, distinguishes between holding gains and operating gains and thereby eliminates

one of the shortcomings of HCA when there are specific price changes. Some companies, manufacturing companies in particular, would regard the current cost operating figure, with or without an MWCA, as significant information in that it:

▶ excludes from profit, fluctuations in prices while assets are being held as opposed to consumed
▶ charges against income the current cost of assets consumed, thus ensuring retention of sufficient resources to allow the company to continue at the same level of operations, that is, to acquire, at current prices, the same volume of assets consumed without recourse to additional finance.

It is useful, in this explanatory note, to refer back to one of the shortcomings already noted as to CCA and the application of the operating capital maintenance concept: its lack of application to companies such as value-based companies. For such companies, attempting to quantify realised holding gains will not always be appropriate, and such price level adjustments may be excluded from the statement altogether. A suggested layout of an adjusted earnings statement for such a company could be amended to read as follows:

PRO FORMA 14.11

	£	£
Net profit for the period before dividends	x	
Realised capital surpluses less losses on disposal of investments		x
		x
Unrealised surpluses less losses on revaluation of investments	x	
Deduct: Previously recognised unrealised revaluation surpluses less losses now treated as realised (as above)	(x)	
		x
Net increase in reserves before dividends		x
Inflation adjustment to shareholders' funds (opening shareholders' funds at current cost x % change in RPI in year)	(x)	
Excess before dividend	x	
Dividends	(x)	
Excess after adjusting for the effects of price changes	x	

4 *The realised holding gains* These are the sum of the current cost operating adjustments, abated by, if applied, the gearing adjustment. The current cost operating adjustments are deducted from HC profits in order to highlight the useful, for manufacturing entities, amount of current cost operating profit. They represent the effects of specific price changes on assets consumed by the company. Given that they do represent gains, albeit gains that should be withheld, these gains are now added back in the adjusted earnings summary which is a statement of total gains arising in the year.
5 *Unrealised holding gains* are simply those arising on assets still held at the balance sheet date, that is, the difference between the current cost of fixed assets or stocks at the balance sheet date and their historical cost of purchase.

6   *The inflation adjustment to shareholders' funds* This last adjustment deducts from the total gains so far arising, a charge for general inflation and results in a figure for total real gains. Arguably, it is relevant to all companies. The adjustment takes account of one of the principal objections to CCA systems of accounting: that operating financial maintenance concepts do not take account of the effects of changes in the general price level. The allowance for these price changes is calculated by applying the following formula:

Opening shareholders' funds at current cost × The % change in RPI during the year

One objection which may be raised against the total gains concept is that, like operating capital, it relies heavily on asset valuations which may be subjective. Despite the practical problems that sometimes arise, it is argued that greater usefulness compensates for less objectivity.

Where abridged accounts reflecting the effects of price changes are not provided, and such information is provided by way of a note dealing with adjustments to earnings, as above, in the historical cost main accounts, it would also be relevant to disclose, in addition:

▶ the gross and net current cost of fixed assets
▶ the accumulated current cost depreciation
▶ the current cost of stocks.

Summary

Inflation has imposed a severe test on historical cost accounting as a reliable basis for reporting results and financial positions of companies. It is widely considered that where a company's results and financial position are materially affected by changing prices, historical cost information alone is insufficient. From an examination point of view, in preparing for (an always possible) question on this area, you should be aware of and be capable of dealing with:

▶ The various shortcomings of historical cost accounts in a period of changing prices.
▶ The two alternative remedies that were put forward by the ASC:
  – CPP accounting, which is based on the maintenance of real financial capital
  – CCA, as put forward in SSAP 16, which is based on the maintenance of operating in physical capital.
▶ The adjustments required to quantify the effects of both general and specific price changes on results and financial positions of companies.
▶ The shortcomings of the CPP and CCA approaches in reflecting and accounting for the effects of all price changes.
▶ The ASC Handbook on accounting for the effects of changing prices, which proposes a combination of the CPP and CCA approaches, the method referred to as the 'real terms systems of accounting', in best reflecting the effects of price changes.
▶ The form of the adjusted earnings statement proposed by the Handbook and its adaptation to the different circumstances of different types of companies: manufacturing type companies on the one hand, and value-based companies on the other.

The two questions that support this chapter cover most of this examinable ground.

The effects of price changes are also most relevant to the 'interpretation' aspects of the examination syllabus for this paper. Price change effects in this context are dealt with in further detail in Chapter 31 of this book.

Exam style question

1   *Muirfield Ltd*

The directors of Muirfield Ltd have sent you the draft historical cost accounts of the company, which are as follows:

Summarised balance sheets

	30 June 1991	30 June 1990
	£000	£000
Fixed asset at cost	600	600
Less: Depreciation	(360)	(270)
	240	330
Stocks	235	150
Trade debtors	160	120
Cash	120	70
Trade creditors	(80)	(90)
10% debentures	(280)	(280)
Ordinary shareholders' funds	395	300

Summarised profit and loss account for the year ended 30 June 1991

	£000
Sales	1,300
Opening stock	(150)
Purchases	(1,040)
Closing stock	235
	345
Sundry expenses	(132)
Interest	(28)
Depreciation	(90)
Profit retained for the year	95

You are informed that:

a) There was only one fixed asset, which was purchased on 1 July 1986. If the company were to have purchased the same asset new on 30 June 1990 it would have cost £812,500, and on 30 June 1991, £987,500. The 'depreciation adjustment' is to be based on year end values.

b) Stock, at each year end, was acquired three months before the year end, and price indices for stock held by the company at the end of each month, are as follows:

March 1990	115
June 1990	126
March 1991	141
June 1991	147
Average for the year ended 30 June 1991	138

(c) The 'monetary working capital adjustment' for the year ended 30 June 1991 is £8,000 (debit to operating profit) and the 'gearing adjustment' is £27,000.

(d) The retail price index has increased by 4.6% during the year ended 30 June 1991.

Required:

Write a report to the directors of Muirfield Ltd. Your report should:

a) outline the shortcomings of historical cost accounts in a period of changing prices

b) explain how the effects of changing prices may most appropriately be reflected in the company's financial statements as on 30 June 1991

c) include a statement of gains made by the company, indicating the effects of changing prices, on the lines suggested by the ASC Handbook on accounting for the effects of changing prices.

(20 marks)

All answers on pages 668– 670.

Consolidated Accounts 1 – The Companies Acts and FRS 2

This chapter deals with the definition of a subsidiary, subsidiaries to be excluded from consolidation, different concepts of a group and exemptions from the legal requirement to prepare consolidated accounts where there are subsidiary undertakings. It also deals with some of the problems arising in consolidated accounts as a direct result of the legal definition of a subsidiary under the old S. 736, especially the problem of the controlled non-subsidiary and the problem of off balance sheet finance arising wherever such investments are not consolidated.

The main motivation for the changes in the Act as to the law on groups and group accounts was the requirement for member states to implement the EC 7th Directive on consolidated accounts. The changes, however, went beyond the minimum necessary to implement the directive in that the government took advantage of the opportunity to reduce the scope for off balance sheet schemes. The main effect of this was that some companies that were not subsidiaries under the old S. 736 will now be required to be consolidated under the amended 1985 Act. Further, vehicles other than companies, certain partnerships and joint ventures, can also now come within the consolidation requirement.

The amended Act now requires group accounts to be in consolidated form. In this it reinforces SSAP 14, which has been superseded by FRS 2. The effect of this is that other forms of group accounts may be prepared only in circumstances where consolidated accounts would not give a true and fair view. It will remain possible for subsidiaries to be excluded from consolidation although the circumstances where this will be permitted are reduced. Many groups will no longer be able to exclude subsidiaries from consolidation on the ground of dissimilar activities.

Two new exemptions from preparing group accounts were introduced by the amended 1985 Act. Small and medium-sized groups are now exempt and the previous exemption for wholly owned subsidiaries has been replaced by a new, wider exemption.

This chapter also deals with FRS 2, which was issued in July 1992. Carrying on from ED 50, the FRS takes the opportunity to carry out a fundamental review of the accounting issues involved in consolidated accounts. It aligns accounting standards with the law as it now stands on consolidated accounts, gives guidance on the interpretation of the Act and includes definitions of 'actual exercise of dominant influence' and 'managed on a unified basis'. Other aspects of consolidated accounts dealt with in FRS 2 such as changes in stake, deemed disposals and provisions for unrealised profit are dealt with in the chapters that follow on the mechanics of consolidated accounts. Before we can deal with these it is essential that you fully comprehend the circumstances that give rise to a group and the need to prepare consolidated accounts.

The UK situation prior to the implementation of the EC 7th Directive

In the UK groups of companies became a significant form of business structure around the time of World War I. At that time there were no reporting requirements for consolidated accounts. The first time a company presented a consolidated balance sheet to its members was in 1920 (Nobel Industries Limited) and the first consolidated profit and loss account was published in 1933 (The Dunlop Rubber Co. Limited). The Stock Exchange made the publication of financial statements a requirement for new issuers in 1939 and the ICAEW published recommendations in 1944 that made consolidated accounts best practice for all groups.

The first legal requirement for group financial statements was introduced by the Companies Act 1947, which was subsequently consolidated into the Companies Act 1948. These requirements were consolidated into the Companies Act 1985 and remained unchanged until incorporation into UK law of the EC 7th Directive on company law, which was one of the main purposes of the Companies Act 1989.

The accounting standard on group accounts in the UK was SSAP 14, issued in 1978. It supported the then legal requirements, dealt with the form that group accounts should take, set out the circumstances in which subsidiaries should be excluded from consolidation and dealt with sundry matters concerned with the mechanics of the consolidation process. SSAP 1 on associated companies was issued in 1971. In recent years additional accounting standards have been published to deal in greater detail with accounting for business combinations. SSAP 22 on accounting for goodwill (see Chapter 5) was issued in 1984 and SSAP 23 on accounting for acquisitions and mergers (see Chapter 19) was issued in 1985.

As a result of the Companies Act 1989 SSAP 1 requires revision and SSAP 14 has been superseded. ED 50, which was issued in 1990, deals with the proposed revision of SSAP 1 and FRS 2 is the current accounting standard for subsidiary undertakings. SSAP 22 was revised in 1989 and as a result of a review of matters dealing with the treatment of goodwill the (now defunct) ASC issued two exposure drafts, EDs 47 and 48, containing new proposals to replace the requirements of SSAPs 22 and 23. In addition, ED 53, dealing with the problems of fair value in the context of acquisition accounting, was issued in 1990. FRS 2 – Accounting for Subsidiary Undertakings, was issued in 1992 following the preceding ASB interim statement on consolidated accounts.

The legal definition of a subsidiary pre the Companies Act 1989

The definition was that 'a company is deemed to be a subsidiary of another if that other either:

▶ is a member of it and controls the composition of its board of directors, or
▶ holds more than half in nominal value of its equity share capital, or
▶ the first mentioned company is a subsidiary of any company which is that other's subsidiary.' (S. 736 CA 1985 pre 1989)

Note that equity shares are any shares that are entitled to participate in a surplus in a capital distribution.

Several problems arose from this definition as to establishing the entities that comprised the group. Some of these were as follows:

▶ Rights attaching to debentures were ignored. The right to appoint directors could attach to debentures whereby a company could control the board of another without being its holding company. The new definitions *do not* exclude rights deriving from debentures held by a member of a company.
▶ Two companies could appoint equal numbers of directors resulting in no control over the board of the investee. Effective control could have rested with one company if their appointees had more votes on the board. The new definitions establish that it is the right to appoint directors having a majority of votes at board meetings that will create a parent/subsidiary relationship.
▶ As to ownership of equity shares, it was possible to have effective control without

the controlled company being a subsidiary. Equally, it was possible to have a subsidiary without effective control. With the replacement of the criterion of majority equity ownership by one of control over the majority of voting rights neither of these two situations can now occur.

▶ Special-purpose vehicles such as partnerships or joint ventures could be set up to avoid the consolidation requirement. Under the new rules such vehicles will not be 'subsidiaries' but can be 'subsidiary undertakings' and if so would have to be consolidated.

▶ Options over shares could have been used to delay consolidation. This will no longer be possible given that options come within 'participating interests' and the holding of options in an undertaking can result in it being a 'subsidiary undertaking' if, as a result, 'dominant influence' is exercised.

Rules for subsidiaries excluded from group/consolidation accounts

The rules regarding subsidiaries excluded from group/consolidation accounts under the Companies Act 1985 prior to its amendment and under SSAP 14 prior to its being superseded by FRS 2 are outlined below.

S. 229 of the 1985 Act prior to its amendment stated that a subsidiary may be excluded from group accounts if:

▶ the activities of a subsidiary are dissimilar to the rest of the group, or
▶ inclusion of the subsidiary would have a harmful or misleading effect, or
▶ inclusion of the subsidiary would be insignificant, or
▶ inclusion of the subsidiary would be impracticable, or
▶ inclusion of the subsidiary would involve disproportionate expense or delay.

SSAP 14 was more prescriptive about subsidiaries excluded from consolidation. The standard required that subsidiaries must be excluded from the consolidated accounts if:

▶ The activities of the subsidiary are dissimilar to the rest of the group. Inclusion of such a subsidiary would be misleading and information about the subsidiary would be better provided by presenting separate financial statements for such a subsidiary. Such a subsidiary would be included in the consolidated accounts using the equity method of accounting for investments. In so far as the equity method results in the carrying value of the investment in the balance sheet amounting to the investor's share of net assets of the investee, assets and liabilities of the subsidiary that are controlled by the group would effectively be off the group balance sheet.

▶ There is a lack of effective control, that is, where less than half of the voting equity is owned or where there is no control over the board of the subsidiary. Such subsidiaries would be included in the consolidated accounts under either the cost method or the equity method of accounting for investments. Such a situation can no longer arise; if there is no effective control over the undertaking it cannot be a subsidiary undertaking.

▶ There are severe restrictions imposed upon control. Profits of such a subsidiary should be consolidated up to the date of severe restrictions. No further credit should be taken for earnings of such a subsidiary in the consolidated profit and loss account unless dividends are actually received from the subsidiary. The investment should be included in the consolidated balance sheet under the equity method at the date of severe restrictions less any amounts written off for permanent diminution in value.

▶ There is only temporary control. Such subsidiaries would be dealt with in the consolidated accounts under the cost method and would be included in the consolidated balance sheet as a current asset investment.

The two main problem areas under these rules were where subsidiaries were not consolidated given dissimilar activities and where there was a lack of effective control. As the latter situation is no longer possible it is the former that remains a problem – see below for the current UK requirements as to subsidiaries with dissimilar activities.

The UK situation post-implementation of the EC 7th Directive

The question of the definition of a subsidiary is fundamental to any discussion regarding group or consolidated accounts. It is also related to the topic of off balance sheet finance and the question about whether the consolidated balance sheet should embrace the assets and liabilities of an entity that holds certain assets and liabilities that management may not wish to include in the group financial statements.

Article 1 of the EC 7th Directive sets out six sets of circumstances under which a parent/subsidiary relationship will be regarded as existing so as to require the parent to present consolidated financial statements. These have been incorporated into UK company law, the 1985 Act as amended by the 1989 Act, as detailed below.

Definition of parent and subsidiary undertakings following the Companies Act 1989

An undertaking is the parent undertaking (P) of a subsidiary undertaking (S) if:

▶ P holds a majority of the rights to vote at general meetings of S on all or substantially all matters or has the right to direct its overall policy or alter its constitution, or
▶ P is a member of S and has the right to appoint or remove directors holding a majority of voting rights at meetings of the board, or
▶ P has the right to exercise a dominant influence over S:
  – by virtue of provisions contained in S's memorandum or articles, or
  – by virtue of a written control contract, or
▶ P is a member of S and controls alone, pursuant to an agreement with other members, a majority of the voting rights in S, or
▶ P has a participating interest in S and:
  – P actually exercises a dominant influence over S, or
  – P and S are managed on a unified basis, or
▶ P is the parent of any undertaking which is S's parent.

Definition of various terms with brief commentaries

Undertaking means:

▶ a body corporate or partnership, or
▶ an unincorporated association carrying on a trade or business, with or without a view to profit.

Dominant influence and **managed on a unified basis** are not defined in the Companies Act 1985 as amended, as the legislators wished 'the ordinary spirit of the legislation' to be followed. The intention is to bring into the consolidation all undertakings that are controlled by the parent undertaking.

For the purpose of the third subsidiary undertaking situation above **dominant influence** requires that P at least has a right to give directions on the operating and financial policies of S, which its directors are obliged to follow whether or not they are for the benefit of S.

Such a control contract is not usually possible under general principles of UK law as it would conflict with directors' fiduciary duty to conduct the affairs of the company in accordance with its own best interests, and is allowed only where the memorandum and articles specifically permit it. (Such a contract is, however, a feature of German business organisations.) As a result, this part of the definition above is likely to be of relevance only where a company has a business operation in Germany or another state that adopts the German approach.

In determining whether P *actually* exercises a dominant influence re the last part of the definition above many factors will have to be considered, for example:

▶ the degree of board representation
▶ the degree of influence over the operating and policy decisions of the undertaking
▶ the degree of participation by the investing company in the risks attaching to the undertaking's business
▶ the rewards and benefits that the investing company will derive from its investment
▶ whether to exclude the undertaking from consolidation would affect the truth and fairness of the group's financial statements.

Economic dependence – principal supplier/customer – alone does not necessarily indicate 'dominant influence'. However, taken together with a 'participating interest' it may well suggest such influence. FRS 2 on subsidiary undertakings in consolidated accounts defines the actual exercise of dominant influence as the exercise of an influence that achieves the result that the operating and financial policies of the undertaking influenced are set in accordance with the wishes of the holder of the influence and for its benefit whether or not those wishes are explicit.

FRS 2 also contains the following definitions:

▶ **Control** is the ability to direct the financial and operating policies of an undertaking with a view to gaining economic benefits from its activities.
▶ **Participating interest** means an interest held by an undertaking in the shares of another undertaking that it holds on a long-term basis for the purpose of securing a contribution to its activities by the exercise of control or influence arising from or related to that interest. A holding of 20% or more shall be presumed to be a participating interest unless the contrary is shown. An interest in shares includes convertible securities and options to acquire shares.
▶ **Management on a unified basis** arises if the whole of the operations of the undertakings are integrated and they are managed as a single unit. Unified management does not arise solely by virtue of an undertaking's managing of another.

As with the old definition of a subsidiary – see S. 736 above – it is possible under the new definition for an undertaking to have two parent companies. The UK position as in FRS 2 is that only one enterprise may control another in the manner that makes consolidation the appropriate treatment. Where two investing companies disagree on a particular matter, the enterprise in which they are interested will be able to act only according to the wishes of one of them. Thus only one enterprise can actually exercise dominant influence.

The new rules as to excluded subsidiaries following the Companies Act 1989

The general rule under the 1985 Act as amended is that all subsidiary undertakings should be included in the consolidated financial statements. However, there are now five exceptions to this rule and these differ slightly from those of the Act prior to amendment. The exemptions that allow groups to exclude subsidiaries from consolidation are now very similar to the provisions in the now superseded SSAP 14 and are as follows:

- inclusion not material
- severe long-term restrictions
- disproportionate expense or undue delay
- subsequent resale
- dissimilar activities.

Under the Act a subsidiary *may* be excluded for any of the first four reasons above but *must* be excluded for the last reason. It is relevant in this context to note that there is an overriding requirement that consolidated accounts must give a true and fair view of the state of affairs and profit and loss account of the undertakings included in the consolidation as a whole so far as concerns members of the parent company.

Regarding materiality, two or more undertakings may be excluded only if they are not material taken together. As any FRS deals only with material items, this ground for exclusion is not specifically mentioned in FRS 2.

FRS 2 states that disproportionate expense or undue delay can be relevant only in the context of a non-material subsidiary. Neither expense nor delay can justify excluding from the consolidated accounts of a group a subsidiary undertaking that is material in the context of the group.

As to subsequent resale, FRS 2 states that an interest in another undertaking is held exclusively with a view to subsequent resale if the undertaking has never formed a continuing part of group activities and has not previously been included in the consolidated accounts of the parent. There must be an immediate intention to sell and the expectation of a sale within approximately one year.

Regarding dissimilar activities, FRS 2 makes the following points:

- the Act requires exclusion where inclusion would not be compatible with the obligation to give a true and fair view
- it is exceptional that the activities of a subsidiary undertaking should so differ from those of the other undertakings included in the consolidation that inclusion would be incompatible with the obligation to give a true and fair view
- unless, exceptionally, there are conclusive grounds for believing that the inclusion of a subsidiary undertaking in the consolidated accounts is incompatible with showing a true and fair view of the group, all subsidiary undertakings, whatever their activities, should be consolidated with the group.

Summarising the two main headings above, the main motivation for the changes in the Act as to the law on groups and group accounts was the requirement for member states to implement the EC 7th Company Law Directive. The changes, however, go beyond the minimum necessary to implement the directive in that the UK government took advantage of the opportunity to reduce the scope for off balance sheet schemes. The main effects of the changes are:

- some companies that were not previously subsidiaries will now be required to be consolidated as subsidiary undertakings
- vehicles other than companies can now come within the consolidation requirement
- there can no longer be a subsidiary undertaking without the exercise of effective control.

Different concepts of the group

Instead of providing a Community-wide approach to group structure and consolidation, the directive recognises varying concepts and practices applied throughout the Community and offers a choice of options. It is, therefore, possible for different member states to comply with the directive and yet apply fundamentally different concepts of grouping.

There are three major concepts of a group for which the directive caters.

The parent company concept

This concept emphasises legal control and assumes it is for the equity investors of the parent company that group accounts are prepared and to whom a true and fair view must be disclosed. This concept makes no attempt to disclose a true and fair view to minority shareholders or to other users. It assumes that a group consists of a parent company and a number of dependent or subsidiary companies that are dominated by the parent company exercising voting power vested in the ordinary shareholders. In other words, dominance is established by the existence of the power to exercise control, rather than the actual exercise of control. It is the legal form that is the rule rather than the commercial substance.

This concept would require 100% consolidation of all subsidiaries but recognises that the interest of the parent company's members is limited to the parent's shareholding in subsidiaries. Thus, minority interests are not recognised as shareholders' funds but shown separately in the consolidated balance sheet. Net assets are included in the consolidated balance sheet at the whole amount of their fair value but goodwill is calculated only from the viewpoint of the majority investor.

The entity concept

Rather than examining the *de jure* control, the entity concept emphasises *de facto* control and is based on the existence of an economic unit. The actual exercise of control is the test rather than, as above, the power to exercise control. Commercial substance takes precedence over legal form. It is founded on the principle that the group consists of a number of entities drawn together, usually by unified management, into an economic unit. Accordingly, equal importance is given to all shareholders, whether the majority or the minority. A group that consists of two equally large companies can be accommodated under this concept; and so also can a situation where a family group owns shares in two or more companies between which there is no legal connection but which can, in substance, if not in strict legal form, be regarded as an economic unit.

Under this concept 100% consolidation of all subsidiaries is required (even where less than 100% of the shares are owned), intragroup profits would be eliminated 100% and to the extent that minority interests are recognised they would be treated as a part of shareholders' funds. Goodwill is calculated by reference to the whole interest in the subsidiary and is allocated to minority interests. The concept has been used in Germany.

The proprietary concept

This concept caters for enterprises that belong to more than one group or only partially to a group. In these cases there is no single parent company, no minority interest, no legal dominance and no economic unit. This situation allows for partial consolidation either by bringing a proportionate share of the individual assets and liabilities into the consolidation (proportional consolidation) or by bringing the share of the post-acquisition retained profits into the consolidation (equity method as under

SSAP 1).

This concept is the foundation for the equity method and for proportional consolidation that is used in France. Under this concept fair values are reported in respect of the majority but not in respect of minority interests. If the net assets of the subsidiary are fully consolidated, they will therefore be carried at mixed values.

In the UK the fundamental concept used to be the parent company concept, which removed all subjectivity from the decision about the existence of a group – a parent either owned more than 50% of the equity or not. However, the UK also recognised the entity concept and included in the definition of a subsidiary a company in which at least one share is held and the board of directors is controlled. The entity concept is not, however, applied in the UK as minority interests are not shown as a part of shareholders' funds. UK accounting practice also encompasses the proprietary concept but only in situations where a majority interest is not held and where significant influence is exercised.

The view of consolidation developed in ED 50 and continued with in FRS 2 is that the parent's investors are the users for whom consolidated accounts are primarily prepared. However, they need information not only on the group as a whole but also on the distinction between what they own and what others own – what ED 50 called the control/ownership concept.

A comparison of the different concepts of the group is shown in Example 15.1.

EXAMPLE 15.1 – COMPARING DIFFERENT CONCEPTS OF THE GROUP

Basic data: Company X buys 75% of Company Z for £600 when company Z has total net assets with a fair value of £500 and a book value of £400.

The consolidated balance sheet of Company X would include Company Z as follows:

	Entity concept £	Proprietary concept £	Parent co. concept £
Net assets of Company Z	500	475	500
Consolidation goodwill	300	225	225
	800	700	725
Minority interest	(200)	(100)	(125)
Investor interest	600	600	600

Notes

Entity concept
Both the tangible net assets and goodwill are reported in the balance sheet at the full amount of their fair value as determined by the transaction involving the majority shareholder. Thus, as the majority's share of goodwill is (600 less 75% of 500) £225, the total goodwill is (225 x 100/75) £300. The total of £800 is then apportioned between the majority and minority shareholders.

The rules introduced by the 1989 Act do not permit the use of the entity concept because they require goodwill to be calculated by comparing acquisition cost with the investor's proportionate share of the investee's capital and reserves after adjusting for fair values. This approach is also ruled out by IAS 22.

Proprietary concept
Goodwill is stated as it is required to be stated under the new legal rules. However, the minority interest is left unaffected by the transaction of the majority shareholder; it is simply shown as their share of the book values of the tangible net assets (25% x 400).

Tangible net assets are carried on a mixed basis: 75% at fair values (75% x 500) and 25% at book values (25% x 400), that is, 375 + 100 = £475.

These problems would be eliminated if proportional consolidation were adopted, in which case the minority interest would be ignored and only the majority's share of the net tangible assets of the investee would be consolidated: 375 plus goodwill of 225 = £600. The 1989 Act does not permit proportional consolidation for subsidiary undertakings.

Parent company concept

This includes net tangible assets at the whole amount of their fair value, but it includes goodwill only in so far as it applies to the majority investor. Under IAS 22 the proprietary concept is the preferred approach with the parent company concept as a permitted alternative.

These different concepts are also relevant to the treatment of profit unrealised on intragroup transactions. Assume Company X sold stock to Company Z for a profit of £50 and Company Z retains this stock at the year end. Under the entity concept, as it is the parent which has made the sale, the whole write-down of stock of £50 would be charged against the group profit and loss account with no charge to minority shareholders. Under the proprietary concept, as the minority are regarded as outsiders, 25% of the profit is regarded as realised by the group. Thus, the write-down of stock would be restricted to £37.5 all of which would be charged to the group. The 1989 Act permits intercompany profit eliminations to be made at either their gross amounts or in proportion to the investor's stake in the investee. FRS 2 requires that the whole of the profit is eliminated and that the adjustment be apportioned between the majority and minority interests in proportion to their holdings in the selling company.

Exemptions from preparing consolidated accounts

The Act now allows two exemptions from the requirement for a parent company to prepare consolidated accounts:

▶ An immediate subsidiary of an EC parent need not prepare consolidated accounts provided:
  – the company is a wholly owned subsidiary, or
  – the parent holds more than 50% of the shares and a notice requiring the preparation of consolidated accounts has not been served by more than half of the remaining shares or 5% of the total.
  The company must be included in consolidated accounts of a larger group and disclose, in its own individual accounts, its exemption and details of the parent in whose accounts it is included.
▶ A small or medium-sized group will be exempt from the obligation to prepare consolidated accounts. The rules to be applied are similar to those governing exemptions of companies from the obligation to file full accounts with the Registrar of Companies.

Summary

This is the first of several chapters dealing with various aspects of consolidated accounts. Later chapters deal with the practice of consolidation in the context of different group structures, alternative consolidation methods and groups including overseas entities. This chapter deals essentially with the regulatory framework as to consolidated accounts. Before we get to practise on consolidated accounts it is first necessary to define a group. This chapter is therefore concerned with the following two questions:

▶ When does an undertaking fall to be treated as a subsidiary undertaking?
▶ even though an undertaking is a subsidiary undertaking, are there some

circumstances where such undertakings should not be consolidated into the consolidated accounts?

In dealing with these questions the chapter examines the following areas:

▶ the principal problems arising in consolidated accounts under previous legislation and standard accounting practice:
  – subsidiaries with ineffective control
  – controlled non-subsidiaries
  – the exclusion of some subsidiaries from consolidation
▶ how these problems are overcome under current legislation and standard accounting practice.

In passing, the chapter also looks briefly at alternative concepts of the group and also at the two legally available exemptions from the requirement to prepare consolidated accounts even when there are subsidiary undertakings within the group.

Consolidated Accounts 2 – Accounting for Simple Groups

Chapter 15 addressed the question of what constitutes a group and the legal requirements for consolidation. This chapter deals with the practice, given subsidiary undertakings, of preparing consolidated accounts in the context of simple group structures, that is, where there is a parent with one or more subsidiary undertakings. The further procedures involved in dealing with more complex group structures – for example, where a parent has a subsidiary undertaking that has its own subsidiary undertaking – are dealt with in Chapter 17.

The main objective of consolidated accounts is to report the results and state of affairs of the group as if the activities, assets and liabilities of the group were those of a single entity. These consolidated accounts should give the shareholders of the parent company a true and fair view of results and state of affairs of the whole group controlled by their company. In preparing consolidated accounts it is necessary to combine information from the accounts of the separate undertakings comprising the group and to make such adjustments as are necessary. These adjustments include the following:

▶ the substitution of (the fair value of) the net assets of the subsidiary for the book value (cost) in the parent company's accounts of its shareholding in the subsidiary
▶ the elimination of balances due to and by companies within the group by setting off debits against credits
▶ the elimination of profits on transactions within the group where the profit is unrealised from a group viewpoint given no final transaction between the group as a whole and a third party from outside the group.

It is the first of these adjustments that is the most significant. In acquiring a controlling interest in the shares of a subsidiary undertaking, the parent company effectively acquires control over its underlying net assets. It is these net assets that are substituted for the cost of the investment in the accounts of the parent; the cost of the investment is eliminated from the consolidation.

Given that the cost of the investment is unlikely to equal the fair value of the net assets of the subsidiary at the date of its acquisition, there will be a difference that is either positive or negative goodwill arising on consolidation. Goodwill was dealt with in Chapter 5. This chapter and subsequent chapters dealing with acquisition accounting, looks at consolidation goodwill.

In consolidating the net assets of the subsidiary into the consolidated balance sheet you must comply with the objective of showing the state of affairs or financial position of the group as a whole. To the extent to which net assets are not attributable to the parent undertaking's shareholding they are attributable to and financed by minority interests. These represent a source of finance for group activities from non-shareholders of the parent undertaking and are separately disclosed in the consolidated accounts.

The net assets of the subsidiary at any date following acquisition consist of:

▶ its net assets at acquisition, and
▶ its net assets since acquisition, financed by retained post-acquisition reserves.

The group's share of these post-acquisition reserves will be reflected in an increase in the group's own reserves with the appropriate movement for the year reflected through the consolidated profit and loss account.

FRS 2 sets out the manner in which consolidated accounts are to be prepared, the purpose of such accounts being to provide financial information about the economic activities of a group. Thus, consolidated financial statements 'are intended to present financial information about a parent undertaking and its subsidiary undertaking as a single economic entity to show the economic resources controlled by the group, the obligations of the group and the results the group achieves with its resources'.

This chapter deals, piecemeal, with the main problems arising in preparing consolidated accounts. The chapter considers:

▶ a simple example dealing with goodwill, minority interest, distinguishing pre-acquisition and post-acquisition reserves of a subsidiary, consolidated reserves – the basic approach to consolidation
▶ the fair value problem
▶ some other problems with consolidation goodwill
  – goodwill in the balance sheet of a subsidiary at its acquisition date
  – bonus issues of shares by a subsidiary
  – preference shares and debentures of a subsidiary
▶ intercompany transactions
▶ the treatment of the minority interest.

Having dealt with these various consolidation problems, all of which you will have encountered at Paper 10, we will look at the consolidation exercise in respect of simple group structures.

Definitions

You will find the following definitions from FRS 2, already dealt with in part in Chapter 15, useful when reading and working through this chapter.

> **Consolidation** The process of adjusting and combining financial information from the individual financial statements of a parent undertaking and its subsidiary undertakings to prepare consolidated financial statements that present financial information for the group as a single economic entity.

> **Control** The ability of an undertaking to direct the financial and operating policies of another undertaking with a view to gaining economic benefits from its activities.

> **Parent undertaking** and **subsidiary undertaking** An undertaking is the parent undertaking of another undertaking (a subsidiary undertaking) if any of the following apply. [*From s 258 and 10A Sch*]

> a) It holds a majority of the voting rights in the undertaking. [*From s 258(2)(a)*]
> b) It is a member of the undertaking and has the right to appoint or remove directors holding a majority of the voting rights at meetings of the board on all, or substantially all, matters. [*From s 258(2)(b) and 10A Sch 3*]
> c) It has the right to exercise a dominant influence over the undertaking: [*From s 258(2)(c) and 10A Sch 4*]
>   i) by virtue of provisions contained in the undertaking's memorandum or articles; or
>   ii) by virtue of a control contract. The control contract must be in writing and be of a kind authorised by the memorandum or articles of the controlled undertaking. It must also be permitted by the law under which that undertaking is established. [*From 10A Sch 4(2)*]

d) It is a member of the undertaking and controls alone, pursuant to an agreement with other shareholders or members, a majority of the voting rights in the undertaking. [*From s 258(2)(d)*]

e) It has a participating interest in the undertaking and: [*From s 258(4)*]

i) it actually exercises a dominant influence over the undertaking: or

ii) it and the undertaking are managed on a unified basis.

f) A parent undertaking is also treated as the parent undertaking of the subsidiary undertakings of its subsidiary undertakings. [*From s 258(5)*]

For the purpose of section 258 [parent and subsidiary undertakings] an undertaking shall be treated as a member of another undertaking: [*From s 258(3)*]

i) if any of its subsidiary undertakings is a member of that undertaking; or

ii) if any shares in that other undertaking are held by a person acting on behalf of the parent undertaking or any of its subsidiary undertakings.

Any shares held, or powers exercisable, by a subsidiary undertaking should be treated as held or exercisable by its parent undertaking.

Group A parent undertaking and its subsidiary undertakings. [*From s 262*]

Minority interest in a subsidiary undertaking The interest in a subsidiary undertaking included in the consolidation that is attributable to the shares held by or on behalf of persons other than the parent undertaking and its subsidiary undertakings. [*From 4A Sch 17*]

Equity method A method of accounting for an investment that brings into the consolidated profit and loss account the investor's share of the investment undertaking's results and that records the investment in the consolidated balance sheet at the investor's share of the investment undertaking's net assets including any goodwill arising to the extent that it has not previously been written off.

For the rest of this chapter parent undertakings and subsidiary undertakings will simply be referred to as the parent and the subsidiary respectively.

The objective and preparation of consolidated accounts

As already noted, the objective is to present financial information about a parent and its subsidiaries as a single economic activity. See Example 16.1.

EXAMPLE 16.1 PREPARATION AND OUTCOME OF CONSOLIDATED ACCOUNTS

A parent, P Ltd, acquires 80% of the shares and thereby acquires control of a subsidiary, S. Ltd, on 31 December 1994. Summary balance sheets at 31 December 1995 are:

	P Ltd £	S Ltd £
Investment in S Ltd at cost	600	
Other net assets	1,100	800
	1,700	800
Share capital	1,000	500
Reserves at 31 December 1994	450	100
Profit for the year ended 31 December 1995	250	200
	1,700	800

To consolidate, follow these procedures:

1 Eliminate the cost of the subsidiary in the parent balance sheet and the group's share of the share capital and reserves of the subsidiary at its acquisition date, any difference being goodwill. Thus goodwill arises of (600 – [80% × 600]) £120. This would be, under SSAP 22 (Revised), written off immediately on acquisition to consolidated reserves.
2 Sum the net assets of the parent and subsidiary (1,100 + 800) to give consolidated net assets of £1,900. Remember not to include the cost of the subsidiary in the parent's balance sheet.
3 Ascertain the minority interest in the net assets of the subsidiary to be included in the consolidated balance sheet (20% × 800) to give £160.
4 Share capital in the consolidated balance sheet is only that of the parent.
5 Consolidated reserves – a balancing item – consist of those of the parent plus the group's share of the post-acquisition reserves of the subsidiary less any consolidation goodwill written off against reserves: ([450 + 250] + [80% × 200] – 120) £740.
6 The consolidated balance sheet, derived from the balance sheets of the parent and subsidiary would be as follows:

At 31 December 1995	P Ltd £	S Ltd £	Consolidated £
Investment in S Ltd at cost	600		–
Other net assets	1,100	800	1,900
			1,900
Share capital			1,000
Reserves			740
Minority interest			160
			1,900

The fair value problem

In acquisition accounting we are concerned with fair values, for the consideration paid by the parent and for the net assets (effectively acquired by the parent) of the subsidiary on the date of its acquisition. This is because, in acquisition accounting, we are concerned with the premium paid on acquisition, or goodwill. The practical problems arising in determining such fair values are dealt with in ED 53 and a Discussion Paper and further exposure draft issued by the ASB, which are looked at in detail in Chapter 20. This section of this chapter addresses the problems arising in the consolidated accounts from assigning fair values to a subsidiary's net assets at its acquisition date.

When a subsidiary is acquired, FRS 2 requires that its identifiable net assets be brought into the consolidation at their fair values on the date the undertaking becomes a subsidiary. Fair values also need to be assigned on an increase of stake in the subsidiary – this aspect of the fair value problem is covered in Chapter 18.

The essential rules are these:

▶ Fair value adjustments on the date of the subsidiary's acquisition are treated as pre-acquisition or having an impact on the value of the subsidiary's net assets on the acquisition date; such adjustments will, therefore, have an impact on goodwill.
▶ Any additional depreciation arising for the consolidated accounts as a result of increases in value are treated as a charge against post-acquisition reserves of the subsidiary.
▶ The minority interest will participate in both the fair value adjustments and any subsequent additional depreciation to be charged.

How to deal with fair values is illustrated in Examples 16.2 and 16.3.

EXAMPLE 16.2 FAIR VALUE ADJUSTMENTS AT ACQUISITION DATE

A parent, P plc, purchased 80% of the ordinary shares and thereby acquired control of a subsidiary, S Ltd, on 1 June 1994 for a cost of £10,800. The summarised balance sheet of S Ltd on this date showed:

	£
Goodwill	1,000
Other (separable) net assets	8,200
	9,200
Ordinary share capital	2,000
Profit and loss account	7,200
	9,200

The fair value of the separable net assets of S Ltd exceeded their book value on this date by £300.

These amounts would be dealt with, on consolidation, as follows:

1   Consolidation goodwill would be:

	£
Cost	10,800
Less: 80% × (8,200 + 300)	(6,800)
	4,000

2   Note that you include only the subsidiary's separable or identifiable net assets at their fair values in the goodwill calculation; you do not include inseparable or unidentifiable items such as goodwill.

3   The consolidated balance sheet at this date will include other (separable) net assets at their value to the group, that is fair value at acquisition date of (8,200 + 300) £8,500.

4   The goodwill of £1,000 in the subsidiary's balance sheet on the date of its acquisition is not included in the consolidated balance sheet. The group's share of this amount is included in the consolidation goodwill arising of £4,000. It is effectively written off against pre-acquisition reserves of the subsidiary and, to the extent that it reduces total net assets at the acquisition date, it also increases the consolidation goodwill as a result.

5   Any additional depreciation following acquisition to be charged against consolidated reserves as a result of assigning fair values is a charge against the post-acquisition reserves of the subsidiary.

6   Under FRS 2, where net assets of a subsidiary are included in the consolidated balance sheet at fair values:

   ▶ those attributable to the minority interest are included on the same basis as those attributable to the group
   ▶ goodwill on consolidation is recognised only with respect to the part of the subsidiary undertaking that is attributable to the group; no goodwill is attributed to the minority interest.

EXAMPLE 16.3 FAIR VALUES ASSIGNED AT ACQUISITION DATE AND ADDITIONAL DEPRECIATION TO BE PROVIDED IN THE CONSOLIDATED ACCOUNTS

Pippa plc, the parent, acquired Simba Ltd, a subsidiary, having obtained control following the purchase of 75% of its ordinary shares on 30 June 1993.

The balance sheet of Simba Ltd at 30 June 1995 discloses fixed assets with a net book value of £63,000.

Fair values were assigned to Simba Ltd's fixed assets for the purpose of the consolidation at 30 June 1993. The fair value on this date of these fixed assets is indicated to you as £110,000.

Depreciation is at 10% per annum on the reducing balance. Simba Ltd does not record fair values in its own accounts.

Ascertain:

▶ the revaluation reserve arising on the acquisition date for the purposes of the consolidated accounts
▶ the additional depreciation to be charged/provided in the consolidated accounts.

How would these amounts be dealt with in the consolidated accounts 1993 through to 1995?

Determine relevant amounts by constructing a chart as follows:

	Book values	Fair values	Adjustments for consolidation
	£	£	£
30 June 1993	77,777	110,000	32,223
y/e 30 June 1994: depreciation (10/90 × 70,000)	(7,777)	(11,000)	(3,223)
30 June 1994	70,000	99,000	
y/e 30 June 1995: depreciation (10/90 × 63,000)	(7,000)	(9,900)	(2,900)
30 June 1995	63,000	89,100	

The revaluation reserve arising for the consolidated accounts at 30 June 1993 is £32,223; 25% of this would be allocated to minority interest and 75% would be treated as pre-acquisition by the group and included in the consolidation goodwill calculation. No part of this revaluation reserve would be included in consolidated reserves.

The additional depreciation of £3,223 in 1994 and £2,900 in 1995 would be charged, on consolidation, against the post-acquisition reserves of Simba Ltd.

The fixed assets of Simba Ltd would be incorporated into the consolidated accounts at 30 June 1995 at £89,100 and consolidation adjustments as to Simba Ltd's fixed assets would be as follows:

	£		£
Book value 30 June 1995	63,000	Profit and loss account:	
Revaluation	32,223	additional depreciation	
		1994	3,223
		1995	2,900
		c/f CBS 30 June 1995	89,100

There is much more to the problem of fair values. These are dealt with in ED 53 and the 1993 ASB Discussion Paper on fair values and are looked at in Chapter 20 of this textbook.

Intercompany adjustments

Most intercompany transactions present no problems in preparing the consolidated balance sheet and the consolidated profit and loss account; items simply cancel out on consolidation.

Simple adjustments

How to deal with simple adjustments is shown in Examples 16.4 and 16.5.

EXAMPLE 16.4

Hopalong plc has two subsidiaries, Tonto Ltd (80% owned) and Silver Ltd (75% owned). Tonto Ltd made a long-term loan of £5m to Silver Ltd. How would the loan appear in the financial statements of the Hopalong plc group?

These financial statements would consist of, first, the separate accounts of Hopalong plc in which the loan would not feature. Given subsidiaries, Hopalong plc would have to prepare, second, consolidated accounts in which the loan that would have appeared in the Tonto Ltd accounts as a debtor and in the Silver Ltd accounts as a creditor will cancel out on consolidation. Accordingly, the loan appears in neither the separate accounts of Hopalong plc nor in its consolidated accounts.

EXAMPLE 16.5

Horace plc owns 80% of the ordinary shares of Bipsum Ltd, a subsidiary given the exercise of dominant influence by Horace plc. Extracts from the accounts of the two companies are as follows:

	Horace plc	Bipsum Ltd
	£	£
Trade creditors	15,000	17,000
Amount owed to subsidiary	1,500	–
Amount owed to associates	1,200	1,100
UK taxation	1,100	1,150
Proposed dividends	1,500	1,200
Accruals and deferred income	150	170
	20,450	20,620

Ascertain the total amount of creditors to be included in the consolidated balance sheet of Horace plc.

	£
To start, the sum of 20,450 + 20,620	41,070
Less: Intercompany items:	
Amount owed to subsidiary	(1,500)
Subsidiary dividend receivable	
by parent 80% × 1,200	(960)
	38,610

Note that associates are not consolidated; they are included in the consolidated accounts under the equity method (see Chapter 21). It is for this reason that any amounts due to or from associates in the balance sheet of the parent, including dividends receivable from associates, will remain in the consolidated balance sheet.

Parent owns debentures of subsidiary

If a subsidiary has debentures, either none or some or all of these debentures may be owned by the parent. If none of the debentures are owned by the parent, the whole amount represents a group liability and will appear as such in the consolidated balance sheet. If some of the debentures are owned by the parent, cancel the cost of the debentures in the parent's books with the nominal value of the debentures owned (and treat any difference as part of consolidation goodwill); the nominal value not owned is a group liability and will appear as such in the consolidated balance sheet. If all of the debentures are owned, cancel cost in the parent's balance sheet with nominal value owned as above and no liability appears for the debenture in the consolidated balance sheet.

Adjustments for dividends

Particular problems arise in this area in the year of acquisition of a subsidiary. These problems are looked at later in this chapter when we will look separately at the situation of a subsidiary acquired during an accounting period. In this section we are concerned with dividends paid or proposed by a long-standing subsidiary that are received or receivable by the parent.

Dividends paid by the subsidiary

These will have been received by the parent to the extent of its share, cash will have been paid by the subsidiary and received by the parent (and minority interests to the extent of their share). There is nothing in the balance sheet of either company that cancels out on consolidation.

Dividends proposed by the subsidiary

Consolidation problems arise in this area as the subsidiary may or may not have accounted, in its own books, for the dividends payable and the parent may or may not have accounted, in its own books, for the dividends receivable from the subsidiary.

If the subsidiary has accounted for the payable and the parent for the receivable, there will be a creditor in the balance sheet of the subsidiary and a debtor in that of the parent. Cancelling the debtor against the creditor will leave us with a creditor for the consolidated balance sheet amounting to the dividends of the subsidiary payable to the minority interest.

If the subsidiary has accounted for the payable but the parent has not accounted for the receivable do the following:

▶ set up the debtor in the parent's accounts by:
DR Dividends receivable in debtors
CR Profit and loss account
being dividends receivable from subsidiary
▶ cancel the debtor so established against the creditor for dividends payable in the balance sheet of the subsidiary to leave, for the consolidated balance sheet, a creditor representing the dividend of the subsidiary payable to the minority interest.

If neither the subsidiary nor the parent have recorded the dividends, you will need to set up the creditor in the subsidiary and the debtor in the parent, cancel out and determine the subsidiary's dividend payable to the minority interest for inclusion as a group liability in the consolidated balance sheet.

Dividends in the consolidated profit and loss account

Appropriations for dividends in the consolidated profit and loss account are restricted to the dividends paid and proposed by the parent.

Dividends paid and/or proposed by a subsidiary do not, as such, pass through the face of the consolidated profit and loss account either as paid/payable by the subsidiary or as received/receivable by the parent. The consolidated profit and loss account is considered more fully later in the chapter. Consolidated profit before tax is the sum of the profit before tax of the parent and the subsidiary. If the parent has taken credit for dividends from the subsidiary in its own profit and loss account, such dividend receipts must be excluded from consolidated profit before tax. This is because you are including in consolidated profit before tax, the whole of the profit of the subsidiary out of which the subsidiary's dividends are paid; to also include the parent's share of the subsidiary's dividend in consolidated profit before tax would be to double count for the dividend. This is shown in Example 16.6.

EXAMPLE 16.6 DIVIDEND ADJUSTMENTS

Popple plc controls Soufflé Ltd and owns 70% of its ordinary shares. Summary profit and loss accounts of the two companies for the year ended 31 December 1994 are as follows:

	Popple plc £	Soufflé Ltd £
Profit before tax	7,500	6,000
Tax	(2,500)	(1,800)
Dividends – paid	(1,000)	(800)
– proposed	(2,000)	(1,500)
Retained	2,000	1,900

Popple plc has taken credit for the dividend received from Soufflé Ltd but not for dividends receivable.

Prepare a schedule to arrive at consolidated profit and loss account details for the year ended 31 December 1994.

	Popple plc £	Soufflé Ltd £	Consolidated p&l account £
Profit before tax	7,500		
Less: Intercompany dividend 70% × 800	(560)		
	6,940	6,000	12,940
Tax	(2,500)	(1,800)	(4,300)
	4,440	4,200	8,640
Minority interest	30%	(1,260)	(1,260)
		2,940	7,380
Intercompany dividends			
70% × 800	560	(560)	
70% × 1,500	1,050	(1,050)	
	6,050	1,330	7,380
Dividends (1,000 + 2,000)	(3,000)		(3,000)
	3,050	1,330	4,380

Intercompany sales/transfers

Such intragroup transactions may result in profits or losses being included in the book value of assets to be included in the consolidation. FRS 2 requires elimination in full of all such profits or losses, as, for the group as a whole, no profits or losses have arisen. This (full) elimination of profits or losses relating to intragroup transactions should be set against the interests held by the group and the minority interest in respective proportion to their holdings in the undertaking whose individual financial statements recorded the eliminated profits or losses.

Therefore, if the parent has made the sale and the profit, there is no charge to minority interest; if the subsidiary has made the sale and the profit, there is a charge against the minority interest. Examples 16.7 – 16.10 illustrate this.

EXAMPLE 16.7 THE PARENT MAKES THE SALE TO THE SUBSIDIARY

Dinky Ltd is the only subsidiary of Pinky plc. The net current assets of Dinky Ltd and Pinky plc at 31 December 1994 were £25,000 and £20,000 respectively. During the year ended 31 December 1994, Pinky plc sold goods that cost £3,000 to Dinky Ltd for £5,000 on credit. Dinky Ltd has recorded the purchase but has neither sold nor paid for these goods as at 31 December 1994.

How would this transaction be dealt with in the consolidated accounts at 31 December 1994?

Consolidated turnover must exclude the whole of the intercompany sale of £5,000.

Consolidated cost of sales must exclude the cost of the purchase to Dinky Ltd of £5,000.

Consolidated cost of sales must be debited with a provision for unrealised profit, in the consolidated accounts of (5,000 – 3,000) £2,000. The consolidation adjustment is:

DR Pinky plc profits   2,000
CR Stock in the CBS   2,000

being elimination of profit on intercompany sale.

If there were a minority interest in Dinky Ltd, it would not be affected.

Consolidated net current assets would be, at 31 December 1994 (25,000 + 20,000 – 2,000) £43,000.

EXAMPLE 16.8 THE SUBSIDIARY MAKES THE SALE TO THE PARENT

Bunny plc has control over its 80%-owned subsidiary, Funny Ltd. During 1994, Funny Ltd sold goods to Bunny plc for £80,000, which was the cost of the goods to Funny Ltd plus 25%. At 31 December 1994, £40,000 of these goods remained unsold.

What is the impact of this transaction in the consolidated accounts at and for the year ended 31 December 1994?

Consolidated turnover and cost of sales must each be reduced by the whole of the intercompany sale of £80,000. The whole of the unrealised profit is $25/125 \times 40,000 = £8,000$ and must be eliminated from profit and from stock value in the consolidated balance sheet. The minority interest in Funny Ltd of 20% must bear its share of this provision. The consolidation adjustment is:

DR Funny Ltd profit   8,000
CR Stock in the CBS   8,000

As Funny Ltd profits are reduced the minority interest in these profits is also reduced.

EXAMPLE 16.9 A SUBSIDIARY MAKES THE SALE TO ANOTHER SUBSIDIARY

Woody plc has two subsidiaries, Pommy Ltd and Moe Ltd in which it owns 80% and 70% of the ordinary shares respectively. Summarised profit and loss account data for the three companies for the year ended 31 December 1994 is as follows:

	Woody plc £	Pommy Ltd £	Moe Ltd £
Turnover	9,000	11,000	14,000
Cost of sales	(3,000)	(4,000)	(4,500)
	6,000	7,000	9,500
Tax	(2,000)	(3,000)	(3,500)
	4,000	4,000	6,000

During the year Pommy Ltd sells goods to Moe Ltd for £2,000 making a profit of 20% on the cost of the sales. Moe Ltd retains all of these goods in its stock at 31 December 1994.

Prepare a summarised consolidated profit and loss account for the year ended 31 December 1994.

	Woody plc £	Pommy Ltd £	Moe Ltd £		Consolidated p&l account £
Turnover	9,000	11,000	14,000	(2,000)	32,000
Cost of sales	(3,000)	(4,000)	(4,500)	2,000	(9,500)
Provision 20/120 × 2,000		(333)			(333)
	6,000	6,667	9,500		22,167
Tax	(2,000)	(3,000)	(3,500)		(8,500)
	4,000	3,667	6,000		13,667
Minority interest		20% (733)	30% (1,800)		(2,533)
	4,000	2,934	4,200		11,134

The consolidation adjustment is to eliminate the whole of the unrealised profit for the consolidated accounts. Given that it is a subsidiary that has made the profit and the sale it is necessary to allocate a part of the provision to the minority interest.

EXAMPLE 16.10 TRANSFERS OF FIXED ASSETS WITHIN THE GROUP

A parent company purchased an asset at a cost of £10,000 on 1 January 1993 – useful life ten years, net book value £8,000 on 1 January 1995. It transferred this asset to a 70%-owned subsidiary on 1 January 1995 at a transfer price of £12,800 (no change in remaining useful life). The subsidiary charges depreciation for 1995 of (12,800/8 years) £1,600. The net book value of the asset in the books of the subsidiary at 31 December 1995 is, accordingly, £11,200.

Following FRS 2, outline the consolidation adjustments required for the consolidated accounts as at and for the year ended 31 December 1995.

The basic principle is that the asset should be included in the consolidated balance sheet at 31 December 1995 at its original cost to the group: 7/10 × £10,000 = £7,000. The asset therefore needs to be written down in the consolidated accounts by (11,200 – 7,000) £4,200. A two-fold adjustment is required to achieve this:

First, eliminate the profit (12,800 – 8,000) £4,800. The consolidation adjustment would be to:

DR Parent profit   4,800
CR Asset   4,800

Second, adjust for the additional depreciation charged by the subsidiary; the depreciation in the consolidated accounts should be based on original cost to the group, that is, for 1995, 1/10 × 10,000 = £1,000. As the subsidiary has charged £1,600 an adjustment of £600 is required on consolidation as follows:

DR Asset   600
CR Subsidiary profit   600

The minority interest is not affected by the transfer except to the extent of the depreciation charged on the asset (now held by the subsidiary) in the consolidated accounts.

The preference dividend problem

A subsidiary may, in addition to ordinary shares, have preference shares in issue. A parent may own none or some or all of these preference shares and, in the consolidated accounts, we need to consider the impact of such preference shares on both the consolidated balance sheet and the consolidated profit and loss account, as shown in Examples 16.11 and 16.12.

EXAMPLE 16.11 IMPACT ON THE CONSOLIDATED BALANCE SHEET

Willy Ltd is the sole subsidiary of Billy Ltd. The balance sheet of Willy Ltd at 31 December 1994 has been summarised as follows:

	£
Total assets less current liabilities	930
10% debentures	300
Ordinary shares	150
Preference shares	300
Profit and loss account	180
	930

Billy Ltd owns 50% of the debentures, 60% of the ordinary shares and 40% of the preference shares of Willy Ltd.

What is the impact of this information on the Billy Ltd consolidated balance sheet at 31 December 1994?

The minority interest in the consolidated balance sheet would be made up as follows:

	£
Re ordinary shares 40% × (150 + 180)	132
Re preference shares 60% × 300	180
	312

The £150 of 10% debentures not owned by the group is not included in minority interests but dealt with under creditors in the consolidated balance sheet.

EXAMPLE 16.12 IMPACT ON THE CONSOLIDATED PROFIT AND LOSS ACCOUNT

Diva plc owns 60% of the ordinary share capital and 25% of the preference share capital of its subsidiary Devi Ltd.

The accountant of Devi Ltd supplies you with the following details as to the company for the year ended and at 31 December 1994:

	£
Profit after tax	200,000
Proposed ordinary dividend	80,000
10% £1 preference shares	400,000

Calculate the minority interest in the profits of Devi Ltd in the Diva plc consolidated profit and loss account for the year ended 31 December 1994.

Follow this approach:

	Diva plc	Devi Ltd	Consolidated p&l account
	£	£	£
Profit after tax	x	200,000	x
Deduct: Preference dividend of subsidiary 10% × 400,000		(40,000)	
Add: Preference dividend receivable by parent 25% × 40,000	10,000		
Deduct: Preference dividend payable to the minority interest			(30,000)
	x	160,000	x
Minority interest in earnings available for ordinary shares	40%	(64,000)	(64,000)
		96,000	x

The total minority interest in the earnings of Devi Ltd is (30,000 + 64,000) £94,000.

Subsidiaries acquired during the year

In acquisition accounting, as distinct from merger accounting (which is dealt with in Chapter 19), pre-acquisition reserves of a subsidiary are distinguished from its post-acquisition reserves; only the latter are included in consolidated reserves. The date for accounting for an undertaking becoming a subsidiary undertaking is the date on which control of that undertaking passes to its new parent undertaking. The following points are relevant in this connection:

▶ If control is transferred by a public offer, the date control is transferred is the date the offer becomes unconditional, usually as a result of a sufficient number of acceptances being received.
▶ For private treaties, the date control is transferred is generally the date an unconditional offer is accepted.
▶ If an undertaking becomes a subsidiary undertaking as a result of the issue or cancellation of shares, the date control is transferred is the date of issue or cancellation.
▶ The date on which the consideration for the transfer of control is paid is often an important indication of the date of acquisition but it is not conclusive evidence of the date of the transfer of control.
▶ The date that control passes may be indicated by the acquiring party commencing its direction of the operating and financial policies of the acquired undertaking or

by changes in the flow of economic benefits.

The effective date is important as you will need to ascertain the fair values of the subsidiary's identifiable net assets on this date for the purpose of calculating consolidation goodwill and because the earnings of the subsidiary to be consolidated are the earnings arising after this date. It is therefore important to establish, in the year of the acquisition of the subsidiary, its pre-acquisition and post-acquisition reserves. In this context reserves of the subsidiary brought forward at the beginning of the year will be wholly pre-acquisition. It is the reserves for the year that will need to be split between pre-acquisition and post-acquisition; follow the method in Pro forma 16.1.

PRO FORMA 16.1 DISTINGUISHING PRE-ACQUISITION AND POST-ACQUISITION RESERVES OF A SUBSIDIARY ACQUIRED IN THE CURRENT YEAR

	Pre-acquisition £	Post-acquisition £
Brought forward	x	
For the year:		
Profit *before* dividends (either time apportion or take amounts indicated as specifically pre-acquisition and post-acquisition in a question)	x	x
Fair value adjustments	x/(x)	
Additional depreciation on fair value adjustments	____	(x)
	x	x
Deduct dividends as follows:		
Dividends *paid before* acquisition are wholly pre-acquisition	(x)	
Dividends paid and proposed (received and receivable by the parent) after acquisition should be dealt with as follows:		
(i) allocate as much as possible to post-acquisition reserves		
(ii) only if the post-acquisition reserves of the subsidiary are insufficient to absorb all of these dividends should you allocate any part of the dividend to pre-acquisition reserves.	(x)	(x)
	x	–

In its own books, the parent will account for the dividends paid and/or proposed by the subsidiary after its acquisition date as follows:

	£	£
DR Cash/debtors	x	
CR Profit and loss account – realised amount		x
CR Cost of subsidiary – unrealised amount		x

being share of dividends paid/proposed by the subsidiary received/receivable by the parent.

The realised amount is the share of the subsidiary's dividend allocated to post-acquisition reserves; the unrealised amount is the share of that part of the dividend allocated to pre-acquisition reserves.

The treatment above is justified in that the amount of the dividend included in the parent's profit and loss account is covered by its share of pre-dividend, post-acquisition reserves of the subsidiary. It is only to the extent that post-acquisition profits do not cover the whole of the dividend that we need consider what is effectively a provision for diminution in the value of the investment in crediting the parent's share of the uncovered dividend against the cost of the subsidiary. See Example 16.13.

EXAMPLE 16.13 ACQUISITION OF SUBSIDIARY DURING THE ACCOUNTING PERIOD

Pimpernel plc owns 80% of the ordinary shares of its subsidiary, Pompadour Ltd. The shares were acquired on 30 September 1994 at a cost of £150,000. Extracts from Pompadour Ltd's accounts for the year ended 31 December 1995 are provided as follows:

	£	£
Ordinary share capital		50,000
Reserves:		
At 31 December 1993		30,000
For the year ended 31 December 1994:		
Profit after tax	65,000	
Dividend paid 30 June 1994	(15,000)	
Dividend proposed	(20,000)	30,000
		110,000

The profits of the subsidiary arise evenly during the year. Fair values exceeded the book values of the assets of Pompadour Ltd on 30 September 1994 by £70,000. Pompadour Ltd has not recorded fair values in its own accounts. Additional depreciation based on fair values for the consolidated accounts, following acquisition, amounted to £7,000.

Distinguish between pre-acquisition and post-acquisition reserves of Pompadour Ltd.

Calculate goodwill arising on consolidation.

Describe how Pimpernel plc should account for the dividends receivable from Pompadour Ltd in its own separate accounts.

	Pre-acquisition	Post-acquisition
At 31 December 1993	30,000	
y/e 31 December 1994		
9/12 × 65,000	48,750	
3/12 × 65,000		16,250
Revaluation adjustment	70,000	
Additional depreciation		(7,000)
Dividend paid 30 June 1994	(15,000)	
	133,750	9,250
Dividends proposed – 20,000	(10,750)	(9,250)
	123,000	–

Consolidation goodwill is ascertained as follows:

	£
Cost	150,000
Less: Dividend from Pompadour Ltd treated as unrealised (80% × 10,750)	(8,600)
	141,400
Less: 80% × (50,000 + 123,000)	(138,400)

$$\underline{\underline{3,000}}$$

Pimpernel plc will account for dividends receivable from Pompadour Ltd as follows:

	£	£
DR Debtors (80% × 20,000)	16,000	
CR Profit and loss account (80% × 9,250)		7,400
CR Cost of Pompadour Ltd (80% × 10,750)		8,600

In the consolidated profit and loss account of the year of acquisition of the subsidiary, in order to comply with FRS 3 and the separate disclosure required under continuing operations of acquisitions in the period, include only post-acquisition amounts for turnover, cost of sales, expenses, investment income, interest and tax for the new subsidiary.

Minority interests

Given the legal definition of a subsidiary – which is based on control rather than ownership – there is, in principle, no upper limit to the proportion of shares in a subsidiary held as a minority interest.

The amounts reported in the consolidated balance sheet and profit and loss account for the minority interest indicate the extent to which assets and liabilities and profits or losses of subsidiaries included in the consolidation are attributable to shareholders other than the parent (or its other subsidiaries, in more complex group structures).

As indicated earlier in this chapter, the net identifiable assets of a subsidiary are presented on the same basis as those attributable to group interests. This is achieved by including 100% of these assets, based on their fair values at the date of the acquisition of the subsidiary, in the consolidated balance sheet and then indicating the amount attributable to the minority interest proportion therein. This, FRS 2 argues, presents the assets and liabilities on a consistent basis for the group as a whole.

However, returning to the earlier examples in this chapter, goodwill arising on the acquisition of a subsidiary is recognised only in relation to the group's interest and no part is attributed to the minority interest. FRS 2 argues that to estimate the amount of goodwill attributable to the minority interest by extrapolation would result in recognising an amount for goodwill that is hypothetical; this is because the minority interest is not a party to the transaction by which the subsidiary is acquired by the parent or its group.

The loss-making subsidiary and minority interests therein

Under FRS2, losses must be attributed to the minority interest in a loss-making subsidiary; even if this leads to a debit balance for the minority interest in the consolidated balance sheet. The following further points are relevant in this context:

▶ Accumulated losses of subsidiaries do not necessarily require funding by the parent.
▶ Debit balances for minority interests represent net liabilities attributable to the minority as opposed to a debt due from the minority interest to the group.
▶ The group should provide for any commercial or legal obligation, whether formal or implied, to provide finance that may not be recoverable in respect of accumulated losses attributable to the minority interest.

▶ Such provisions would include minorities' share of any liability guaranteed by the group or a liability that the group is likely to settle for commercial reasons.

▶ Any provision made with respect to minority interest debit balances should be set directly against the minority interest amount in the profit and loss account and balance sheet.

The treatment of a minority interest in a loss-making subsidiary is shown in Example 16.14.

EXAMPLE 16.14

Biggleswade plc owns 60% of a loss-making subsidiary, Baroness Ltd, which discloses net liabilities. Biggleswade plc has issued a legally binding letter of support to the subsidiary.

How should Biggleswade plc treat the minority interest in Baroness Ltd in its consolidated financial statements?

Under the now superseded SSAP 14, the debit balance attributable to the minority interest would be recognised only if there was a binding obligation on minority shareholders to make good losses incurred and if such losses could be met.

FRS 2 takes a different approach. It requires recognition of a debit balance for the minority interest whether or not the minority shareholders have a binding obligation to make good the losses incurred. However, FRS 2 also states that the group should provide against the debit minority interest where there is a commercial or legal obligation to make it good.

In this situation, a letter of support does indicate such an obligation and provision should be made against the debit minority interest in the consolidated balance sheet:

DR Profit and loss account
CR Minority interest

The provision should be reversed when profits attributable to the minority interest make good the earlier losses.

Summary

This chapter deals with consolidated accounts and accounting for simple groups, that is, where there is a parent with one or more subsidiaries. You will be familiar with the process of consolidation in such situations from Paper 10. For this reason, as opposed to dealing in detail with how to consolidate in such group situations, except for the brief illustration in Example 16.1, we have concentrated on the 'small' areas that appear repetitively, as parts of longer consolidation examination questions. The explanations included in dealing with: fair values, intercompany adjustments (including dividends, provision for unrealised profit and preference shares), subsidiaries acquired during the period, and minority interests, remain relevant to the consolidation chapters that follow.

Suggested reading

Bogie on Group Accounts (Shaw, 1973)   *GAAP (Ernst & Young 1990)*

Group Accounts – The Fundamental Principles, Form and Content (Wilkins 1979) UK

Self test questions

1   State the main objective and purpose of consolidated accounts.

2   Why do fair values need to be assigned to a subsidiary's net assets at the date of its acquisition?

3   Why do we need to adjust for intragroup transactions in the consolidated accounts?

4   State the requirements of FRS 2 in respect of accounting periods and dates.

5   State, briefly the FRS 2 requirements regarding minority interests.

Exam style questions

1   *Delta Ltd*
Delta Ltd, which has an issued share capital of 230,000 ordinary shares of £1 each fully paid, has a balance brought forward on revenue reserve of £103,900 as on 1 December 1994.

You also receive the following information:

▶ On 30 April 1993 Delta Ltd acquired 81,000 ordinary shares of 50p each in Echo Ltd for £52,000 at which date Echo Ltd had an issued share capital of 180,000 ordinary shares of 50p each and a credit balance on revenue reserve of £24,800.

▶ On 30 November 1994 Echo Ltd had reserves of £31,350 and on 31 January 1995 the 50p ordinary shares were split by converting each into two 25p ordinary shares. Delta Ltd acquired 45,000 ordinary shares of 25p each in Echo Ltd on 31 August 1995 for £31,000.

▶ On 30 June 1995 Delta Ltd purchased 192,000 ordinary shares of 50p each in Foxtrot Ltd for £156,000. Foxtrot Ltd has an issued share capital of 240,000 ordinary shares of 50p each.

On 1 December 1994 the credit balances on revenue and capital reserves were £56,250 and £20,000 respectively.

Freehold property owned by Foxtrot Ltd was revalued upwards by £32,000 as on 30 May 1995 and is to be included in the 1995 accounts at valuation.

▶ Draft accounts for the year ended 30 November 1995 showed a profit for each of the three companies of: Delta Ltd, £37,300; Echo Ltd, £25,500; Foxtrot Ltd, £27,600.

Required:
Using the above information calculate the amounts to be included in the consolidated balance sheet of Delta Ltd as on 30 November 1995. Your workings should be clearly presented.

(18 marks)

ICAEW PEI exam question November 1988

2   *Bell Ltd*
The summarised profit and loss accounts of Bell Ltd, Book Ltd and Candle Ltd for the year ended 30 September 1995, and their issued share capitals as on that date were as follows:

	Bell Ltd £	Book Ltd £	Candle Ltd £
Turnover	4,865,300	1,927,500	2,981,600
Cost of sales	3,352,170	1,254,790	1,569,280
Gross profit	1,513,130	672,710	1,412,320
Administrative expenses	807,860	492,200	990,640
Operating profit	705,270	180,510	421,680
Provision for corporation tax	286,110	45,260	129,850
	419,160	135,250	291,830
Dividend paid	–	–	63,000
Retained profit	419,160	135,250	228,830
Issued share capital	362,000	275,000	210,000

You also obtain the following information:

▶ The issued share capital of each company consists of ordinary shares whose par values are respectively: Bell Ltd, £1 each; Book Ltd, 50p each; and Candle Ltd, 50p each.
▶ Bell Ltd had acquired 269,500 ordinary shares in Book Ltd on 1 January 1992 when the credit balance on profit and loss account was £49,370. Book Ltd is to be treated as an associated undertaking.
▶ On 1 July 1995 Bell Ltd acquired 264,600 ordinary shares in Candle Ltd. Bell Ltd is to be treated as a subsidiary undertaking.
▶ The credit balances on profit and loss account of Bell Ltd, Book Ltd and Candle Ltd on 1 October 1994 were £298,570, £106,430 and £86,390 respectively.
▶ The administrative expenses of Candle Ltd included a payment of £38,000 made on 31 March 1995 to a former director in respect of compensation for loss of office. This exceptional item was not connected with the investment in the company by Bell Ltd.
▶ Candle Ltd paid a dividend of 15p per share on 31 May 1995.
▶ Provision is to be made for final dividends of 105p and 20p per share in Bell Ltd and Book Ltd respectively.
▶ Corporation tax is provided at 35% on assessable profits.

Required:
Prepare the consolidated profit and loss account of Bell Ltd and its subsidiary company incorporating the results of its associated company for the year ended 30 September 1995, together with your consolidation schedules. Assume that Bell Ltd does not publish a separate profit and loss account for its own results.

NOTE: Ignore advance corporation tax.

(14 marks)

ICAEW PEI exam question November 1988

All answers on pages 670–673.

Consolidated Accounts 3 – More Complex Groups

Chapters 15 and 16 dealt with the legal requirements as to consolidated accounts and consolidation practice, under FRS2, for simple groups where the structure of the group is *horizontal,* or one where control in one or more subsidiaries is exercised directly by the parent. Such a structure, as dealt with in Chapter 16, is shown diagramatically in Figure 17.1. In such structures, there is no control exercised by one subsidiary over another.

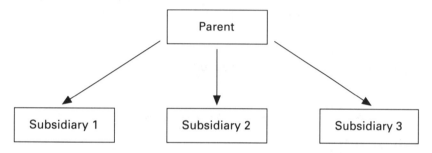

Figure 17.1 Horizontal structure of a group

In this chapter, we deal with more complex group structures where, as is often the case, a parent undertaking will control another undertaking through control exercised/shares held by one of its subsidiary undertakings. In these situations the structure of the group may be either *vertical* or *mixed* or, as examined later in the chapter, *diamond shaped.* A vertical group is shown diagrammatically in Figure 17.2.

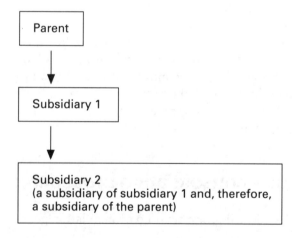

Figure 17.2 Vertical structure of a group

A mixed group is one where the parent has a direct holding in subsidiary 2 over and above its direct holding in subsidiary 1 and, through subsidiary 1, an indirect holding in subsidiary 2. Such a group is shown diagrammatically in Figure 17.3.

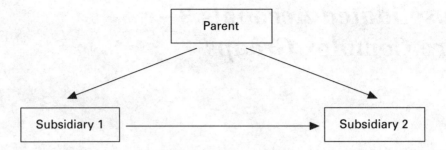

Figure 17.3 Mixed structure of a group

The diamond structure is one that was designed to give an investing company a majority interest in the equity shares of another company *without* it being treated as a subsidiary. Such schemes can result in a situation where an investing company can continue to elude the Companies Act definitions of a subsidiary as to its investments, that is, giving rise to a situation where the investing company derives the major part of the benefit from its investment but does not control it. This kind of group structure is more fully dealt with in Chapter 9 on the off balance sheet finance problem, but it is also dealt with here in the context of more complex groups.

The main emphasis of this chapter is to indicate the application of the acquisition method to consolidations that involve sub-subsidiaries.

The two alternative methods of consolidating a sub-subsidiary

Where a parent undertaking has an indirect interest in another undertaking that is a subsidiary of a subsidiary of the parent, such a sub-subsidiary can be consolidated into the consolidated accounts of the parent undertaking using:

▶ *either* the indirect method
▶ *or* the direct method.

Under the indirect method the subsidiary will first prepare its own consolidated accounts and these will then be consolidated into the parent undertaking's accounts. Under the direct method the subsidiary is consolidated directly into the parent undertaking's consolidated accounts in terms of effective ownership. Thus if P owns/controls 75% of S and S owns/controls 80% of SS, goodwill and the minority interest in SS will be calculated on the basis that the group's effective share of SS is 75% × 80% or 60%. It is this latter approach that we will use as our approach to the consolidation of sub-subsidiaries below.

Vertical groups – consolidation procedures

Example 17.1 shows a vertical group with no consolidation goodwill and acquisitions on the same date.

EXAMPLE 17.1

P plc, S Ltd and SS Ltd were all incorporated on the same date several years ago. At that time P plc subscribed for 60% of the ordinary share capital of S Ltd and S Ltd subscribed for 80% of the ordinary share capital of SS Ltd. P plc controls S Ltd and S Ltd controls SS Ltd, which is, accordingly, deemed to be controlled by P plc. The balance sheets of the three companies at 31 December 1994 are as follows:

	P plc	S Ltd	S Ltd
	£	£	£
Investments in subsidiary undertakings at cost	3,600	1,600	–
Sundry net assets	8,000	5,200	2,400
	11,600	6,800	2,400
Ordinary share capital	10,000	6,000	2,000
Profit and loss account	1,000	800	400
	11,600	6,800	2,400

There is no consolidation goodwill arising. Prepare the consolidated balance sheet and explain the amounts included under consolidated reserves and the minority interest.

The consolidated balance sheet at 31 December 1994:

	£
Sundry net assets (8,000 + 5,200 + 2,400)	15,600

	£
Ordinary share capital	10,000
Consolidated reserves	2,272
Minority interest	3,328
	15,600

	S Ltd		SS Ltd
Group interest			
direct	60%		–
indirect	–	(60% × 80%)	48%
Minority interest	40%		52%

	£
Minority interest:	
in S Ltd (40% × 5,200)	2,080
in SS Ltd (52% × 2,400)	1,248
	3,328

	£
Consolidated reserves:	
P plc	1,600
S Ltd (60% × 800)	480
SS Ltd (48% × 400)	192
	2,272

The main point arising on Example 17.1 is that the minority interest in and the group's share of the reserves of the subsidiary are calculated by reference to *effective* ownership.

Example 17.2 shows a vertical group with consolidation goodwill and acquisitions on the same date.

EXAMPLE 17.2

P plc owns 80% of the ordinary shares of S Ltd which owns 70% of the ordinary shares of SS Ltd. The balance sheets of the three companies at 31 December 1994 are summarised as follows:

	P plc £	S Ltd £	SS Ltd £
Cost of investment in S Ltd	300	–	–
Cost of investment in SS Ltd	–	60	–
Sundry net assets	2,100	180	57
	2,400	240	57
Ordinary share capital	1,500	150	45
Profit and loss account	900	90	12
	2,400	240	57

P plc acquired its holding in S Ltd and S Ltd acquired its holding in SS Ltd on 1 January 1992, when the profit and loss account of S Ltd stood at £60 and that of SS Ltd stood at £15.

All goodwill is to be written off to reserves immediately on acquisition.

Prepare the consolidated balance sheet at 31 December 1994 and explain the make-up of consolidated reserves and the minority interest included therein.

The consolidated balance sheet at 31 December 1994:

	£
Sundry net assets (2,100 + 180 + 57)	2,337
Ordinary share capital	1,500
Consolidated reserves	776
Minority interest	61
	2,337

	S Ltd	SS Ltd
Group interest		
direct	80%	–
indirect		(80% × 70%) 56%
Minority interest	20%	44%

		£
Minority interest		
in S Ltd	(20% × 180)	36
in SS Ltd	(44% × 57)	25
		61

Consolidation goodwill

	£	£
in S Ltd – Cost	300	
Less: 80% (150 + 60)	(168)	
		132
in SS Ltd		
Cost – group's share 80% × 60	48	
Less: 56% (45 + 15)	(34)	
		14
		146

Consolidated reserves:	£
P plc	900
S Ltd 80% (90 – 60)	24
SS Ltd 56% (12 – 15)	(2)
	922
Less: Write off of consolidation goodwill	(146)
	776

Over and above the main point arising from Example 17.1, the further point arising from Example 17.2 is the basis of the calculation of consolidation goodwill arising in respect of the sub-subsidiary. Note particularly that:

▶ Cost is the cost paid by the *group*. In Example 17.2, as P plc owns 80% of S Ltd the cost to the group of the amount paid by S Ltd for SS Ltd is only 80% of that cost.
▶ Share capital and reserves at the acquisition date or net assets at acquisition are brought into the calculation by reference to the group's *effective* share, through S Ltd, in SS Ltd.

Example 17.3 shows a vertical group with consolidation goodwill and acquisitions on different dates.

EXAMPLE 17.3

B Ltd purchased 75% of the ordinary shares of C Ltd on 31 March 1992 for £200, when the reserves of C Ltd were £40.

A Ltd purchased 80% of the ordinary shares of B Ltd on 31 March 1994 for £322, when the reserves of B Ltd were £100 and the reserves of C Ltd were £80.

Included in the balance sheets of the three companies at 30 June 1996 was the following information:

	A Ltd	B Ltd	C Ltd
	£	£	£
Ordinary share capital	400	200	160
Reserves	280	150	120
	680	350	280

1   Calculate the amount of consolidation goodwill arising.
2   Determine the amount of consolidated reserves, before any amortisation of consolidation goodwill, at 30 June 1996.

3   Determine the minority interest to be included in the A Ltd consolidated balance sheet at 30 June 1996.

4   Prepare the consolidated balance sheet of the A Ltd group at 30 June 1996.

In such situations it is useful, as an initial appraisal, to establish the point in time when subsidiaries become group companies and their reserves on these dates. This can be done diagrammatically as follows:

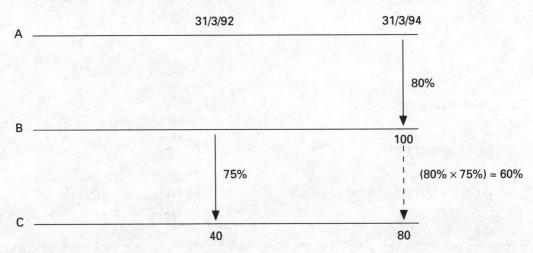

Following from the above, both B Ltd and C Ltd become group companies of the A Ltd group on 31 March 1994.

1   Consolidation goodwill

	£	£
Paid by the group re A Ltd's purchase of shares in B Ltd		
Cost	322	
Less: 80% (200+100)	(240)	82
Paid by the group re B Ltd's purchase of shares in C Ltd		
Cost (80% × 200)	160	
Less: 60% (160 + 80)	(144)	16
		98

2   Consolidated reserves at 30 June 1996, before the amortisation of any consolidation goodwill

	£
A Ltd	280
B Ltd 80% (150 – 100)	40
C Ltd 60% (120 – 80)	24
	344

3   The minority interest for inclusion in the consolidated balance sheet at 30 June 1996

	£
In B Ltd 20% × (350 – 200)	30
In C Ltd 40% × 280	112
	142

4   The consolidated balance sheet at 30 June 1996

	£
Separable net assets (680 – 322) + (350 – 200) + 280	788

Ordinary share capital		400
Consolidated reserves (344 – 98)		246
Minority interest		142
		788

The point of principle arising from Example 17.3 is to determine when each company becomes a group company. It is from that date that post-acquisition reserves are determined for the consolidated accounts.

Mixed groups – consolidation procedures

A mixed group, as already noted above, is one where, over and above an indirect holding in a subsidiary, a parent also has a direct holding in that subsidiary. The main points to be aware of in preparing consolidated accounts for such groups are essentially the same as for vertical groups, with the added point of the direct holding in the subsidiary which may, given different dates of acquisition, give rise to a piecemeal or step-by-step acquisition as dealt with in Chapter 18. Example 17.4 shows a mixed group with consolidation goodwill and acquisitions at different dates.

EXAMPLE 17.4

The individual company balance sheets of the three companies making up Border Group plc are summarised as follows at 31 December 1995:

	Border plc	Boon Ltd	Bernard Ltd
	£	£	£
Cost of investment in Boon Ltd	300	–	–
Cost of investment in Bernard Ltd	60	300	–
Sundry net assets	400	300	720
	760	600	720
Share capital	200	200	180
Reserves	560	400	540
	760	600	720

Border plc acquired its 80% interest in Boon Ltd in June 1993, when the reserves of Boon Ltd were £240.

Boon Ltd acquired its 62.5% interest in Bernard Ltd in December 1993, when the reserves of Bernard Ltd were £220.

Subsequent to Bernard Ltd becoming a subsidiary of the Border Group, Border plc acquired a 17.5% interest in Bernard Ltd in June 1994, when the reserves of Bernard Ltd were £350.

Prepare the consolidated balance sheet of the Border Group at 31 December 1995 indicating the make-up of consolidated reserves, after the write-off of consolidation goodwill, and the minority interest therein.

As in Example 17.3, establish the point in time when subsidiaries become group companies and any subsequent increases in stake and their reserves on these dates.

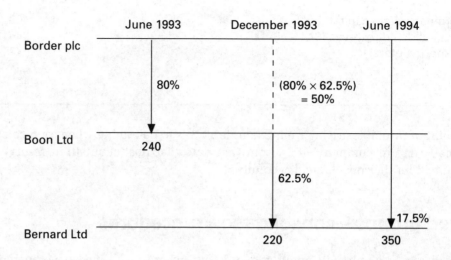

The minority interest for inclusion in the consolidated balance sheet at 31 December 1994 is:

	£
In Boon Ltd 20% × 600	120
In Bernard Ltd (100 − 50 − 17.5)=32.5% × 720	234
	354
Less: Minority interest share of cost paid by Boon Ltd for Bernard Ltd (20% × 300)	(60)
	294

Consolidated reserves for inclusion in the consolidated balance sheet at 31 December 1994 are, before dealing with consolidation goodwill:

	£
Border plc	560
Boon Ltd 80% (400 − 240)	128
Bernard Ltd	
(i) 50% (540 − 220)	160
(ii) 17.5% (540 − 350)	33
	881

Consolidation goodwill is calculated as follows:

	£	£
Boon Ltd		
Cost:	300	
Less: 80% (200 + 240)	(352)	
Negative goodwill		(52)
Bernard Ltd		
(i) Cost (80% × 300)	240	
Less: 50% (180 + 220)	(200)	
Positive goodwill		40
(ii) Cost	60	
Less: 17.5% (180 + 350)	(93)	
Negative goodwill		(33)
Net negative goodwill		(45)

The consolidated balance sheet at 31 December 1995:

	£
Sundry net assets (400 + 300 + 720)	1,420
Share capital	200
Consolidated reserves (881 + 45)	926
Minority interest	294
	1,420

Further problems arising

So far, in dealing with vertical and mixed group structures we have only looked at the preparation of the consolidated balance sheet and the procedures involved in ascertaining consolidation goodwill, consolidated reserves and the minority interest therein. Before we go on to look at such structures in the context of a consolidated profit and loss account there are two further problems to resolve:

▶ Dividends have to be dealt with in the consolidated accounts in order to ensure that only those dividends payable outside the group should be included as liabilities in the consolidated balance sheet. In vertical and mixed group structures it is important to appreciate that dividends must be allocated by reference to actual percentages involved, that is, by the direct as opposed to the indirect route.

▶ The subsidiary in which the parent has an indirect holding may have preference shares. These will have to be allocated on consolidation to the group and minority interest. This is done by reference to the relevant direct interest of the parent in the ordinary shares of the subsidiary, which is the immediate parent of the sub-subsidiary.

Example 17.5 deals with dividends and preference shares.

EXAMPLE 17.5

Summarised balance sheets of the three companies of the A Ltd group are as follows:

Balance sheets at 31 December 1993

	A Ltd £m	B Ltd £m	C Ltd £m
Cost of shares in B Ltd	182	–	–
Cost of shares in C Ltd	–	89.5	–
Sundry net assets	395.3	169.5	113
	577.3	259	113
Ordinary share capital	200	100	50
Preference share capital	–	60	20
Profit and loss account and other reserves	377.3	99	43
	577.3	259	113
Sundry net assets include creditors for dividends payable as follows:			
ordinary	(20)	(15)	(5)
preference	–	(4.2)	(1.4)

A Ltd purchased 75% of the B Ltd ordinary shares and 60% of the B Ltd preference shares on 31 December 1992 when the reserves of B Ltd were £86m. The ordinary shares cost £144m and the preference shares cost £38m.

B Ltd purchased 60% of the C Ltd ordinary shares and 80% of the C Ltd preference shares on 31 December 1990 when the reserves of C Ltd were £23m. The reserves of C Ltd on 31 December 1992, the time at which C Ltd becomes an A Ltd group company, were £40m. The ordinary shares cost £71m and the preference shares £18.5m.

A Ltd has not yet taken credit for any dividends receivable from its subsidiaries.

1   Calculate consolidation goodwill arising.
2   Determine the minority interest for inclusion in the consolidated balance sheet at 31 December 1993.
3   Determine the total of consolidated reserves, after eliminating the whole of any consolidation goodwill, for inclusion in the consolidated balance sheet at 31 December 1993.
4   Prepare the consolidated balance sheet of the A Ltd group at 31 December 1993.

Shareholdings may be summarised as follows:

	B Ltd		C Ltd	
	Ordinary	Preference	Ordinary	Preference
Group interest				
direct	75%	60%	–	–
indirect				
(through B Ltd)			(75% × 60%) 45%	
			(75% × 80%)	60%
Minority interest	25%	40%	55%	40%
Acquired by the group	31 December 1992		31 December 1992	

Note the point following on from previous examples that the indirect holdings in C Ltd are determined in accordance with the percentage of *ordinary* shares owned in B Ltd.

1   Consolidation goodwill

	£m	£m
Re B Ltd:		
Ordinary shares		
Cost	144	
Less: 75% (100 + 86)	(139.5)	
		4.5
Preference shares		
Cost	38	
Less: (60% × 60)	(36)	
		2
Re C Ltd:		
Ordinary shares		
Cost (75% × 71)	53.25	
Less: 45% (50 + 40)	(40.5)	
		12.75
Preference shares		
Cost (75% × 18.5)	13.875	
Less: (60% × 20)	(12)	
		1.875
		21.125

Note that the cost of shares is by reference to group holdings and that the percentage of net assets relating to shares acquired is by reference to the summary of shareholdings above.

Before ascertaining the minority interest and consolidated reserves, make sure that all dividends receivable have been accounted for. Reserves to be allocated will therefore need to be adjusted as follows:

	A Ltd £m	B Ltd £m	C Ltd £m
Per balance sheets	377.3	99	43
Receivable from C Ltd	–		
Ordinary (60% × 5)		3	
Preference (80% × 1.4)		1.12	
Receivable from B Ltd			
Ordinary (75% × 15)	11.25		
Preference (60% × 4.2)	2.52		
Adjusted reserves	391.07	103.12	43

Dividends payable to the minority interest are therefore (15 + 4.2 + 5 + 1.4) less (3 + 1.12 + 11.25 + 2.52) or £7.71m.

2   Minority interest

		£m	£m
Re B Ltd			
Ordinary shares (25% (100 + 103.12))		50.78	
Preference shares (40% × 60)		24.00	
		74.78	
Less: Cost of shares attributable to minority interest of B Ltd			
Ordinary shares of C Ltd			
(25% × 71)	17.75		
Preference shares of C Ltd			
(25% × 18.5)	4.625		
		(22.375)	
			52.405
Re C Ltd			
Ordinary shares			
(55% (50 + 43))		51.15	
Preference shares			
(40% × 20)		8	
			59.15
			111.555

3   Consolidated reserves

	£m
After taking account of dividends receivable	
A Ltd	391.07
B Ltd 75% (103.12 – 86)	12.84
C Ltd 45% (43 – 40)	1.35
	405.26
Less: Consolidation goodwill written off	(21.125)
	384.135

4   The consolidated balance sheet at 31 December 1993

	£m
Sundry net assets (395.3 + 169.5 + 113)	677.8
Add: Dividends payable by subsidiaries (15 + 4.2 + 5 + 1.4)	25.6
Less: Dividends payable to minority interest	(7.71)
	695.69
Ordinary share capital	200
Consolidated reserves	384.135
Minority interest	111.555
	695.69

The consolidated profit and loss account

The procedures to be followed in preparing a working schedule to arrive at the numbers for inclusion in a consolidated profit and loss account remain the same whatever the structure – horizontal, vertical or mixed – of the group.

Example 17.6 shows the consolidated profit and loss account for indirect holdings acquired during the year.

EXAMPLE 17.6

P plc acquired 80% of the ordinary shares of S Ltd when S Ltd was incorporated in 1982. S Ltd acquired 90% of the ordinary shares of SS Ltd, for cash, on 1 January 1994. Summarised profit and loss accounts for the three companies, for the year ended 31 December 1994, are provided as follows:

	P plc £m	S Ltd £m	SS Ltd £m
Turnover	700	200	200
Cost of sales	(307)	(100)	(110)
Gross profit	393	100	90
Distribution and administration costs	(97)	(13)	(14)
Operating profit	296	87	76
Dividend receivable from S Ltd	4	–	–
Dividends receivable from other fixed asset investments	3	4	–
Profit before tax	303	91	76
Tax	(82)	(30)	(21)
Profit after tax	221	61	55
Dividends proposed	(15)	(5)	–
Retained profits for the year	206	56	55
Retained profits brought forward	25	(10)	50
Retained profits carried forward	231	46	105

P plc sold assets to SS Ltd immediately following the purchase of shares in SS Ltd by S Ltd on 2 January 1994. The cost of the asset was £5m and it was sold to SS Ltd for £7m. Other intercompany sales amounted to £40m. Other than the sales to SS Ltd all other intercompany sales had been sold outside the group prior to 31 December 1994.

It is group policy to change depreciation on assets at 20% on cost with a full year's depreciation being charged in the year of acquisition and none in the year of sale.

Prepare the consolidated profit and loss account for the year ended 31 December 1994.
Assume that all depreciation is included in distribution costs.

The consolidated profit and loss account totals would be as follows for the year ended
31 December 1994:

	P plc £m	S Ltd £m	SS Ltd £m	Adj. £m	CPL Ac £m
Turnover	700	200	200	(47)	1,053
Cost of sales	(307)	(100)	(110)	17	
					(472)
Provision for unrealised profit	(2)				
Gross profit	391	100	90	–	581
Distribution and administration expenses	(97)	(13)	(14)	–	
Eliminate additional depreciation charged by SS Ltd (20% × £2m)			0.4	–	(123.6)
Operating profit	294	87	76.4	–	457.4
Income from other fixed asset investments	3	4	–	–	7
	297	91	76.4	–	464.4
Tax	(82)	(30)	(21)	–	(133)
	215	61	55.4	–	331.4
Minority interest 10% + (20% × 90%)		20% (12.2)	28%(15.5)		(27.7)
	215	48.8	39.9	–	303.7
Intercompany dividends 80% × 5	4	(4)			
	219	44.8			
Dividends proposed	(15)				(15)
Retained for the year	204	44.8	39.9	–	288.7
Brought forward	25				
(80% × (10))		(8)			
SS – all pre-acquisition			–		17
	229	36.8	39.9		305.7

Note the basis of arriving at the minority interest in SS Ltd which is 10% direct plus
(20% (through S Ltd) × 90%) indirect.

The diamond structure

An example of a diamond structure dealt with in the chapter on 'off balance sheet
finance' is shown in Example 17.7.

EXAMPLE 17.7

The example is taken from the accounts of Dixons Group plc, 28 April 1990.

Extract from notes to the accounts:

> 31 Principal subsidiary and related companies
>
> *Related companies*
> Dixons Group plc owns 50 'A' ordinary shares (100%) and 900 preference shares (100%) of Timelark Limited, Dixons Group plc owns 50 'A' ordinary shares (100%) and nil 'B' ordinary shares of Dovelamb Limited. Dovelamb Limited owns 50 'B' ordinary shares (100%) of Timelark Limited. Substantially all the economic benefit of both Timelark Limited and Dovelamb Limited is attributable to Dixons Group plc. Timelark Limited owns all the ordinary share capital of Bill Donald Investments Limited, Easedram Limited and Jayhold Limited, which are all investment companies operating in the UK. Dixons Group plc owns all the preference share capital of Bill Donald Investments Limited.

Graphically the shareholding structure looks like this:

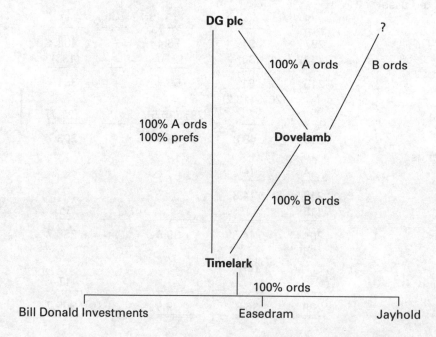

The accounts do not specify the voting and distribution rights attaching to the various shares, but it is not difficult to see how the majority of the benefits, and potentially the risks, of the investment companies could flow up to Dixons. Under the unamended Companies Act, Timelark and Dovelamb may not fall to be treated as subsidiaries because Dixons does not own directly more than 50% equity in either company. (In this case, the preference shares held by DG plc in Timelark have presumably been structured so as not to fall within the Companies Act definition of equity share capital.)

Source: D.A. Pimm 'Off balance sheet finance'. In D.J. Tonkin and L.C.L. Skerratt (eds) *Financial Reporting 1990–91 – A Survey of UK Reporting Practice*, London, ICAEW 1991

The main problem arising in Example 17.7 is not so much the actual preparation of consolidated accounts given the indirect holdings included, but whether or not an investment falls to be treated as a subsidiary to start with and, therefore, whether or not it should be consolidated. This point is of direct relevance to the whole area of 'substance' versus 'form' and is examined in greater detail in Chapter 9, which deals with the off balance sheet finance problems. Taking a slightly less complex situation than the one above, if:

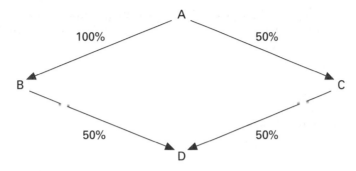

is D a subsidiary of A? To answer this you need to look beyond mere *ownership* and to establish whether or not control is exercised.

Summary

This chapter takes you beyond the mechanics of accounting for horizontal groups into the realm of more complicated group structures. The important points to remember are:

▶ For the purpose of goodwill, cost is the cost paid by the group. Thus, if an existing 70% subsidiary pays £100 for its own subsidiary, as far as the group is concerned cost is 70% × 100 or £70.
▶ The proportion of net assets attributable to the group and the minority interest is any direct holding plus (through another subsidiary) any indirect holding.
▶ Dividends must be allocated in terms of actual percentages.
▶ Preference shares in a sub-subsidiary are allocated by reference to the direct interest of the parent in the *ordinary* shares of the subsidiary which owns preference shares in a sub-subsidiary.

Suggested reading

Group Accounts (Wilkins 1979)

Group Accounts (Bogie 1973)

Both Wilkins and Bogie deal with points of procedure involved and the problems arising with indirect holdings.

Financial Reporting 1990–91 – A survey of UK reporting practice 1991 (Tonkin and Skerratt 1991)

This publication has a useful chapter on associated companies and diamond structures.

Exam style question

1   *Hellenic Ltd*
    A new company, Hellenic Ltd, which was incorporated on 1 October 1992 and commenced operations on that day, became a subsidiary of Troy Ltd on 1 April 1993, when the latter obtained 60% of the ordinary shares of Hellenic Ltd for £51,040.

    Sparta Ltd is the holding company of Troy Ltd, having purchased 80% of the Troy Ltd ordinary shares on 1 June 1992 for £107,200.

Subsequent to Hellenic Ltd becoming a member of the group, Sparta Ltd purchased 25% of the ordinary shares of Hellenic Ltd on 1 July 1993 for £24,400.

In addition, Sparta Ltd has had a long-standing holding of 38% of the ordinary shares of Athens Ltd, acquired at a cost of £45,500 when the net assets of Athens Ltd comprised:

	£
Goodwill	7,500
Patents	2,000
Tangible fixed assets	98,700
Net current assets	14,000
Long-term creditors and provisions	(12,500)
	109,700

The reserves of Athens Ltd, on the date of acquisition of 38% of the company's shares by Sparta Ltd, amounted to £20,700.

The following are the summarised separate balance sheets of the four companies on 30 September 1993:

	Hellenic Ltd £	Troy Ltd £	Sparta Ltd £	Athens Ltd £
Ordinary share capital	72,000	120,000	250,000	89,000
Profit and loss account:				
Balance on 1 October 1992	–	(18,000)	123,000	47,000
Profit/(loss) for the year to				
30 September 1993	12,800	52,000	64,000	10,400
Net assets	84,800	154,000	437,000	146,400

Troy Ltd made a loss of £36,000 for the year to 30 September 1992. The net assets of Athens Ltd on 30 September 1993 include goodwill of £7,500 and patents of £2,000. Athens Ltd is an associated company as defined in SSAP 1 – Accounting for Associated Companies, of Sparta Ltd.

Required:
Prepare a summarised consolidated balance sheet for Sparta Ltd and its subsidiaries, including its associated company, as on 30 September 1993. Present, as a part of your answer, working schedules to support amounts included for consolidation goodwill, the minority interest, the associated company and consolidated reserves.

(20 marks)

All answers on pages 674–675

Consolidated Accounts 4 – Changes in the Composition of a Group

Chapter 15 introduced the definition of a group and the consolidation requirement. Chapters 16 and 17 dealt with the practice of consolidation and the procedures involved in dealing with:

- ▶ consolidation goodwill
- ▶ assigning fair values
- ▶ intercompany balances
- ▶ profit on intercompany transactions that are unrealised from the viewpoint of the group
- ▶ dividends from subsidiaries
- ▶ minority interests in profits and net assets
- ▶ vertical and mixed groups.

Chapter 21, looking ahead, deals with associated undertakings and the equity method of accounting.

This chapter, which does deal in part with the equity method of accounting for investments, is concerned with the accounting problems arising from changes in the composition of a group. Thus, following the disposal of shares held or purchases of shares to increase an existing stake, the structure of a group may change. What were subsidiary undertakings may, for example, become associated undertakings and vice versa. This chapter considers the impact on position, profit and loss account and reserves where:

- ▶ given disposals, the remaining holding is zero, or classified as a trade investment, an associated undertaking or, given retention of control, as a subsidiary undertaking
- ▶ given acquisitions, either the acquisition results in an associated undertaking becoming a subsidiary undertaking, or, where there is an increase in stake, in an existing subsidiary undertaking
- ▶ there is a change in the internal structure of a group, for example, where the shares of a subsidiary undertaking held by the parent are transferred to another subsidiary undertaking within the group.

In dealing with changes in the composition of a group we will be concerned with some aspects of company law (Schedule 4(A) to the Act and the Act's sections dealing with group reconstructions); the major part of the chapter, however, is concerned with the requirements of FRS 2 in this regard.

Accounting for disposals of shares in subsidiary undertakings

This part of the syllabus breaks new ground in that you will not have covered this aspect of consolidated accounts in your studies for Paper 10. The following sections deal with the requirements of FRS 2 for calculating the gain or loss on disposal and the procedures involved in reporting the effects of the disposal, in various disposal situations, on the balance sheet, profit and loss account and reserves of the group.

The general rule, in so far as the consolidated profit and loss account is concerned, is to treat an investment as a subsidiary, that is, consolidate earnings for the period in which the investment is a subsidiary; treat the investment as an associate, that is equity account for the earnings for the period in which the investment is an associate; and treat the investment as a trade investment, that is, use the cost method, taking credit only for the dividends received and receivable from the investment for the period it was a trade investment. (See exam style question 1 at the end of this chapter.)

Where there is a disposal, total or partial, there will be a gain or loss arising to be dealt with in the consolidated profit and loss account of the year of sale. The accounting problems arising on the calculation and reporting of such a gain or loss are dealt with below.

The situation regarding disposals under the old SSAP 14

Under SSAP 14 there were two requirements in this area:

▶ the consolidated profit and loss account should include the subsidiary's results up to the date of the disposal
▶ the gain or loss on disposal should be the difference between the sale proceeds and the holding company's share of net assets, together with goodwill (less any amounts written off) on acquisition.

To comply with the standard, the gain or loss to be included in the consolidated profit and loss account, therefore, amounted to:

	£
Sale proceeds	x
Less: Net assets of the sold subsidiary relating to the shares sold	(x)
Less: Goodwill paid on the acquisition of the shares now sold	(x)
Add: Any of the goodwill paid on the acquisition of the shares now sold that has been written off since acquisition	x
	x
Tax (as for the parent company)	(x)
	x

Where no problem arose under the first requirement given above, an accounting problem did arise under the second in respect of the treatment of goodwill when sold.

The problem with the SSAP 14 gain on disposal

Prior to SSAP 22 on accounting for goodwill, it was usual for goodwill on acquisition to be carried, unamortised, as an asset in the consolidated balance sheet. As goodwill was not written off, the gain on disposal under SSAP 14 was simply: sale proceeds less net assets representing the shares sold less the goodwill paid on the acquisition of the shares sold.

Following the issue of SSAP 22, goodwill could no longer be carried unamortised as an asset in the balance sheet. Either goodwill was to be amortised wholly at acquisition by being written off immediately to reserves, or it was to be systematically amortised against reported profits over economic useful life. Thus, some or all of such goodwill had to be written off since acquisition and, to the extent it was written off, such goodwill would have had an impact on the SSAP 14 disposal gain. As this impact was an increase in the disposal gain reported under SSAP 14 the question then arose as to whether such an increase was appropriate. It was argued that the SSAP 14 treatment remained appropriate if the treatment following acquisition was systematic amortisation. On the basis that goodwill was debited to the profit and loss account following acquisition, it was considered appropriate that this same goodwill was credited to the profit and loss account, as part of the gain on disposal, when sold.

The SSAP 14 treatment was considered not appropriate if the treatment on acquisition was immediate write-off to reserves. On the basis that goodwill was not debited to the profit and loss account of any one year, the view was put forward that goodwill written off (to reserves) should not be added back to arrive at the gain, as was the case under SSAP 14, but that this goodwill should be left out of the gain on disposal and be dealt with instead as a write-back within reserves. On this basis the gain for the consolidated profit and loss account would be restricted to: sale proceeds less net assets representing the shares sold less goodwill paid on the acquisition of the shares now sold.

This was effectively the consensus arrived at in UITF Statement No. 3, that is, if:

- ▶ sale proceeds are (i)
- ▶ net assets representing shares sold are (ii)
- ▶ goodwill paid on the acquisition of shares sold is (iii) and
- ▶ any of such goodwill written off since since acquisition is (iv)

the disposal gain would always be (i) less (ii) less (iii), but would include only an addition for (iv) if goodwill was systematically amortised since acquisition, but not if goodwill was written off immediately on acquisition against reserves.

The situation regarding disposals under FRS 2

FRS 2 states:

> When an undertaking ceases to be a subsidiary undertaking during a period, the consolidated financial statements for that period should include the results of that subsidiary undertaking up to the date that it ceases to be a subsidiary undertaking and any gain or loss arising on that cessation, to the extent that these have not been already provided for in the consolidated financial statements.

In this regard FRS 2 is no different from SSAP 14. The difference in treatment arises in ascertaining the gain on disposal to be included in the consolidated profit and loss account of the year of sale.

Under FRS 2, where a group reduces its interest in a subsidiary undertaking:

> it should record any profit or loss arising calculated as the difference between the carrying amount of the net assets of that subsidiary undertaking attributable to the group's interest before the reduction and the carrying amount attributable to the group's interest after the reduction together with any proceeds received. The net assets compared should include any related goodwill not previously written off through the profit and loss account . . .

If goodwill has been systematically amortised since acquisition, the goodwill *will* have been written off through the profit and loss account. Thus, to comply with FRS 2, the gain on disposal to be reported through the consolidated profit and loss account will be:

			£
	(i)	Sale proceeds	x
Less:	(ii)	Net assets representing shares sold	(x)
Less:	(iii)	Goodwill paid on the acquisition of shares now sold	(x)
Add:	(iv)	That part of (iii) above amortised against profits since acquisition	x
			x
		Tax – as for the parent undertaking	(x)
			x

Expressed in a different way, this gain is equal to the sale proceeds less the net assets effectively sold together with any unamortised goodwill remaining in the consolidated balance sheet in respect of the shares now sold.

If, however, goodwill was written off immediately to reserves on acquisition, the goodwill *will not* have been written off through the profit and loss account. Thus, to comply with FRS 2, the gain on disposal to be reported through the consolidated profit and loss account will be:

			£
	(i)	Sale proceeds	x
Less:	(ii)	Net assets representing shares sold	(x)
Less:	(iii)	Goodwill paid on the acquisition of shares now sold	(x)
			x
		Tax – as for the parent undertaking	(x)
			x

This gain is effectively arrived at by first reinstating the goodwill written off to reserves (in respect of the shares now sold) as an asset and then deducting this goodwill together with the net assets of the subsidiary representing the shares sold from the sale proceeds.

Even though SSAP 14 has now been superseded it is possible that a discussion-based question will require you to consider the pre-FRS 2 basis for calculating the disposal gain in getting you to justify the basis now adopted by FRS 2. On the basis that you will not be fully able to understand the present without being aware of the past, we will compare the two approaches in Example 18.1.

EXAMPLE 18.1 – COMPARING THE OLD SSAP 14 REQUIREMENT WITH THE CURRENT FRS 2 REQUIREMENT

Summarised balance sheets at 31 December 1992:

	H	Subsidiary 1	Sudsidiary 2
	£	£	£
Fixed assets	10,000	8,000	7,000
Cost of 75% interest in Subsidiary 1	4,000		
Cost of 80% interest in Subsidiary 2	3,500		
Net current assets	6,500	7,000	5,000
	24,000	15,000	12,000

£1 ordinary shares	6,000	2,000	2,500
Reserves	18,000		
at acquisition		1,500	500
post acquisition b/f		10,000	7,000
year to 31/12/92		1,500	2,000
	24,000	15,000	12,000

Profit and loss accounts for the year ended 31 December 1992:

	H	Subsidiary 1	Subsidiary 2
	£	£	£
Profit before tax	5,000	4,000	4,500
Tax	(1,500)	(2,000)	(1,500)
	3,500	2,000	3,000
Proposed dividends	(2,000)	(500)	(1,000)
Retained for the year	1,500	1,500	2,000

Notes:

1   H has not taken credit for dividends receivable from subsidiary 1 and subsidiary 2.
2   The balance sheets and profit and loss accounts above do not reflect either the sale of shares or the sale proceeds.
3   All goodwill is written off immediately on acquisition direct to consolidated reserves.
4   Tax on the gain is to be calculated at 25%.

Total disposal – on the basis that H sells its entire interest in subsidiary 2 on 30 June 1992 for £17,000.

Under SSAP 14:

We need to calculate the following:

(i)   The SSAP 14 gain on disposal.
(ii) The consolidated balance sheet at 31 December 1992.
(iii) The consolidated profit and loss account for the year ended 31 December 1992.
(iv) Statement of movements on consolidated reserves for the year ended 31 December 1992.

(i)   The SSAP 14 gain on disposal:

	In the parent co.	In the consolidated accounts
	£	£
Sale proceeds	17,000	17,000
Less: Cost of shares sold	(3,500)	N/A
Less: Net assets representing shares sold	N/A	*(9,200)
Less: Goodwill paid on the acquisition of the shares now sold	N/A	**(1,100)
Add: Any of the goodwill above written off since acquisition	N/A	1,100
	13,500	7,800
Tax at 25%	(3,375)	(3,375)
	10,125	4,425

Notes:

* Net assets of subsidiary 2 on 30 June 1992, before dividends paid or proposed after the disposal date, are 2,500 + 500 + 7,000 + (6/12 × 3,000) = 11,500 and 80% thereof = 9,200.

** Goodwill paid on acquisition, and written off immediately against group reserves, was:

Subsidiary 1 – 4,000 less 75% × (2,000 + 1,500) = £1,375
Subsidiary 2 – 3,500 less 80% × (2,500 + 500) = £1,100

Total consolidation goodwill   £2,475

(ii) Consolidated balance sheet at 31 December 1992:

Note: Where there is a change in the composition of a group during an accounting period, the consolidated balance sheet at the end of that period must be based on the group position at the period end, that is, consolidate any subsidiaries, equity account for any associates and cost account for any trade investments.

		£
Fixed assets	10,000 + 8,000	18,000
Net current assets	6,500 + 7,000 = 13,500	
Add: Proposed dividend of subsidiary 1	500	
Less: Dividend payable to MI 25% × 500	(125)	
Add: Sale proceeds	17,000	
Less: Tax on gain on sale	(3,375)	
		27,500
		45,500
Ordinary share capital		6,000
Reserves – balancing item		35,750
MI – subsidiary 1 – 25% × 15,000		3,750
		45,500

(iii) Consolidated profit and loss account for the year ended 31 December 1992:

	H	Subsidiary 1	Subsidiary 2	Consolidated p&l account
	£	£	£	£
Profit before tax 6/12 × 4,500	5,000	4,000		
			2,250	11,250
Tax 6/12 × 1,500	(1,500)	(2,000)		
			(750)	(4,250)
	3,500	2,000	1,500	7,000
MI	–	25% (500)	20% (300)	(800)
	3,500	1,500	1,200	6,200
Transfer – realised on sale	1,200*		(1,200)	
	4,700		–	
Gain on sale	4,425*			4,425
	9,125	1,500	–	10,625
Intercompany dividends 75% × 500	375	(375)		
	9,500	1,125	–	10,625
Dividends	(2,000)			(2,000)
Retained	7,500	1,125	–	8,625

(iv) Statement of movements on consolidated reserves for the year ended 31 December 1992:

FINANCIAL REPORTING ENVIRONMENT

	Parent	Subsidiaries		Goodwill	Total
		1	2		
	£	£	£	£	£
1/1/92					
18,000 – 1,500	16,500				
75% × 10,000		7,500			
80% × 7,000			5,600		
Goodwill written off on acquisition				(2,475)	27,125
Transfer – realised on sale	5,600*		(5,600)		
Profit for the year	7,500	1,125			8,625
Goodwill adjustment**	(1,100)			1,100	
31/12/92	28,500	8,625	–	(1,375)	35,750

** Why have we included the goodwill adjustment above? The gain for the parent company as calculated above is 10,125. This is dealt with in the consolidated accounts as follows (marked * in the consolidated profit and loss account and in the movements on reserves above):

in the consolidated pre-gain profit of 6,200	1,200
the gain included in consolidated profit	4,425
in consolidated reserves b/f	5,600
	11,225

This is greater than the parent company gain of 10,125 by 1,100, that is, the goodwill paid on acquisition written off to reserves at acquisition, which was added back in arriving at the consolidated gain above. To eliminate this overstatement and also to remove the goodwill for subsidiary 2 from group reserves it is necessary to make the adjusting transfer as in the reserve movements schedule above.

The problem with the SSAP 14 gain arose where goodwill was originally written off to reserves on acquisition. In this situation the reported gain on disposal in the consolidated accounts would have been overstated and a compensating adjustment would have had to have been made within the reserve movements schedule as explained above. To eliminate these problems FRS 2 would now require the gain to be calculated without adding back goodwill previously written off direct to reserves. Note, however, that if goodwill had been systematically amortised since acquisition, and annual charges made in the consolidated profit and loss account each year, then such goodwill, so written off, *will*, under FRS 2, be added back (as in SSAP 14) in arriving at the group gain.

Under FRS 2 there would be no need for a goodwill adjustment within reserve movements as above (see below), but the goodwill initially written off to reserves will now have to be written back within reserves.

Under FRS 2:

(i) The FRS 2 gain:

	£
Sale proceeds	17,000
Less: Net assets representing the shares sold	(9,200)
Less: Goodwill paid on the acquisition of the shares now sold	(1,100)
	6,700

(Note again, as explained above, that there is no add back of the goodwill deducted above as none of this goodwill was written off through the profit and loss account. Had there been systematic amortisation following acquisition, any goodwill written off against the profit and loss account would be added back in arriving at the group gain.)

Tax on the disposal gain – note that this does not change – it remains what it was for the parent company, that is, based on sale proceeds less the cost of the shares sold	(3,375)
The FRS 2 gain	3,325

which is less than the old SSAP 14 gain to the extent of the goodwill of £1,100 previously written off direct to reserves.

(ii) The consolidated balance sheet at 31 December 1992:

This does not change and will be the same as the consolidated balance sheet at this date following SSAP 14 accounting for the gain above.

(iii) The consolidated profit and loss account for the year ended 31 December 1992:

This will be different from the consolidated profit and loss account following the SSAP 14 treatment regarding the disposal gain.

	H	Subsidiary 1	Subsidiary 2	Consolidated p&l account
	£	£	£	£
Profit after tax	3,500	2,000	1,500	7,000
MI	–	25% (500)	20% (300)	(800)
	3,500	1,500	1,200	6,200
Transfer – realised on sale	1,200		1,200	
	4,700		–	
Gain on sale	3,325			3,325
	8,025	1,500	–	9,525
Intercompany dividends 75% × 500	375	(375)		
	8,400			
Dividends	(2,000)			(2,000)
Retained	6,400	1,125	–	7,525

(iv) Statement of movements on consolidated reserves for the year ended 31 December 1992:

Note the differences within reserves compared with the movements following from the SSAP 14 treatment of the disposal gain above. Here, given that goodwill was written off immediately against reserves on acquisition and not added back in arriving at the FRS 2 gain:

▶ there is no need for a goodwill adjustment as before
▶ the goodwill previously written off now needs to be written back within reserves.

	Parent	Subsidiaries 1	2	Goodwill	Total
	£	£	£	£	£
1/1/92	16,500	7,500	5,600	(2,475)	27,125
Realised on sale					
(i) profits	5,600		(5,600)		
(ii) goodwill				1,100	1,100
Profit for the year	6,400	1,125			7,525
31/12/92	28,500	8,625	–	(1,375)	35,750

Accounting under FRS 2 – current standard accounting practice

It is important that you are aware of the old SSAP 14 treatment and the fact that, if goodwill was written off immediately on acquisition against reserves, the SSAP 14 gain on disposal would be overstated. Having established that awareness, let us now concentrate on the present and follow the FRS 2 treatment only.

In Example 18.1 we dealt with a total disposal and its impact on the gain calculation, the consolidated balance sheet at the end of the year of disposal, the consolidated profit and loss account and reserve movements for the year of disposal. We will now look at partial disposal situations.

Situation 1 – retention of control

EXAMPLE 18.2

H disposes of one quarter of its holding in subsidiary 2 on 30 September 1992 for cash proceeds of £5,000. Its holding is now 80% − 20% = 60%, that is, H retains control and subsidiary 2 remains a subsidiary.

(i)   The FRS 2 gain on sale:

In the parent company:

The gain is sale proceeds less the cost of the shares sold
   5,000 less $(1/4 \times 3,500)$ = 4,125
   Tax at 25% = 1,031

In the consolidated accounts:

	£
Sale proceeds	5,000
Less: Net assets representing shares sold	(2,450)
$20\% \times (2,500 + 500 + 7,000 + [9/12 \times 3,000])$	
Less: Goodwill paid on the shares now sold $1/4 \times 1,100$	(275)
	2,275

Note, yet again, none of the goodwill of 275, deducted above, is added back in arriving at the group gain under FRS 2. This is because all of this goodwill was written off against reserves at acquisition. If some of this goodwill had been systematically amortised since acquisition by write-off to the profit and loss account each year, then this amount of goodwill, so written off, would be added back in arriving at the group gain.

Tax – as above	(1,031)
	1,244

(ii) The consolidated balance sheet at 31 December 1992:

Note that subsidiary 2 remains a subsidiary at the year end and, therefore, is consolidated into the group at the year end.

		£
Fixed assets 10,000 + 8,000 + 7,000		25,000
Net current assets 6,500 + 7,000 + 5,000	18,500	
Add: Dividends proposed by subsidiaries 500 + 1,000	1,500	
Less: Dividends payable to MI		
25% × 500	(125)	
40% × 1,000	(400)	
Add: Sale proceeds	5,000	
Less: Tax on gain on sale	(1,031)	
		23,444
		48,444
Ordinary share capital		6,000
Reserves – balancing item		33,894
MI – Subsidiary 1 25% × 15,000		3,750
– Subsidiary 2 40% × 12,000		4,800
		48,444

(iii) The consolidated profit and loss account for the year ended 31 December 1992:

Note that as subsidiary 2 is a subsidiary for the whole year it is consolidated for the whole year.

	H	Subsidiary 1	Subsidiary 2	Consolidated p&l accounts
	£	£	£	£
Profit after tax	3,500	2,000	3,000	8,500
MI		25%(500)		
20% × 3,000 × 9/12			(450)	
40% × 3,000 × 3/12			(300)	
				(1,250)
	3,500	1,500	2,250	7,250
Transfer – realised on sale				
20% × 3,000 × 9/12	450		(450)	
	3,950		1,800	
Gain on sale	1,244			1,244
	5,194	1,500	1,800	8,494
Intercompany dividends				
75% × 500	375	(375)		
60% × 1,000	600		(600)	
Dividends	(2,000)			(2,000)
Retained	4,169	1,125	1,200	6,494

Note: For the sake of simplicity the gain is dealt with net of related tax, as a separate item above. Under FRS 3, the pre-tax gain would be disclosed as a separate item after operating profit before tax; the related tax on gain would be included in the tax change for the year.

(iv) Statement of movements on consolidated reserves for the year ended 31 December 1992:

	Parent	Subsidiaries 1	2	Goodwill	Total
	£	£	£	£	£
1/1/92	16,500	7,500	5,600	(2,475)	27,125
Realised on sale					
(i) profits					
20% × 7,000	1,400		(1,400)		
(ii) goodwill					
25% × 1,100				275	275
Profit for year	4,169	1,125	1,200		6,494
31/12/92	22,069	8,625	5,400	(2,200)	33,894

Situation 2 – loss of control but retention of significant influence

EXAMPLE 18.3

H sells one half of its holding in subsidiary 2 on 31 March 1992 for cash proceeds of £10,500. 80% – 40% = 40%: subsidiary 2 is an associate at the year end.

(i) The FRS 2 gain:

In the parent company:

The gain is sale proceeds less the cost of the shares sold
  10,500 less (1/2 × 3,500) = 8,750
  Tax at 25% = 2,188
In the consolidated accounts:

	£
Sale proceeds	10,500
Less: Net assets representing the shares sold	
40% × (2,500 + 500 + 7,000 + [3/12 × 3,000])	(4,300)
Less: Goodwill paid on the shares now sold	
1/2 × 1,100	(550)
	5,650
Tax – as above	(2,188)
	3,462

(ii) The consolidated balance sheet at 31 December 1992:

Note that subsidiary 1 is consolidated and that subsidiary 2 is included, being an associated company at the year end, under the equity method.

		£
Fixed assets – tangible 10,000 + 8,000		18,000
Fixed asset investment – associated company share of separable		
net assets + goodwill paid – goodwill written off = 40% × 12,000		4,800
Net current assets 6,500 + 7,000	13,500	
Add: Dividends payable by sub 1	500	
Less: Dividend payable to MI 25% × 500	(125)	
Add: Dividend receivable from associate (subsidiary 2) 40% × 1,000	400	
Add: Sale proceeds	10,500	
Less: Tax on gain on sale	(2,188)	
		22,587
		45,387
Ordinary share capital		6,000
Reserves – balancing item		35,637
MI (subsidiary 2) 25% × 15,000		3,750
		45,387

(iii) The consolidated profit and loss account for the year ended 31 December 1992:

	H	Subisidary 1	Subsidiary 2		Consolidated p&l account
			As sub. (3 months) 80%	As assoc. (9 months) 40%	
	£	£	£	£	£
Profit after tax					
group	3,500	2,000			
3/12 × 3,000			750		
associate					
9/12 × 3,000 × 40%				900	7,150
MI		25% (500)	20% (150)		(650)
	3,500	1,500	600	900	6,500
Transfer – realised on sale					
40% × 3,000 × 3/12	300		(300)		
	3,800		300		
Gain on sale	3,462				3,462
	7,262	1,500	300	900	9,962

Intercompany dividends

75% × 500	375	(375)			
40% × 1,000	400		(100)	(300)	
Dividends	(2,000)				(2,000)
Retained	6,037	1,125	200	600	7,962

(iv) Statement of movements on consolidated reserves for the year ended 31 December 1992:

	Parent	Subsidaries 1	2	Associate Subsidiary 2	Goodwill	Total
	£	£	£	£	£	£
1/1/92	16,500	7,500	5,600		(2,475)	27,125
Realised on sale						
(i) profits						
40% × 7,000	2,800		(2,800)			
(ii) goodwill						
1/2 × 1,100					550	550
Profit for year	6,037	1,125	200	600		7,962
Transfer – subsidiary to associate			(3,000)	3,000		
31/12/92	25,337	8,625	–	3,600	(1,925)	35,637

Situation 3 – loss of control and significant influence

There is one more partial disposal situation – loss of control and significant influence. You should, after having worked through the partial disposal situations in Examples 18.2 and 18.3 be able to adjust the numbers for this situation so as to account for the disposal gain under FRS 2. See Example 18.4.

EXAMPLE 18.4

H sells, on 30 September 1992, shares held in subsidiary 2, leaving H with a holding of 10%, in subsidiary 2 with no influence. The sale is for cash proceeds of £14,000. 80% – 70% = 10%, that is, the remaining holding is a trade investment.

(i) The FRS 2 gain on sale:

In the parent company:

The gain is sale proceeds less the cost of the shares sold:

	£
14,000 less (70/80 × 3,500) =	10,938
Tax at 25% =	(2,735)

In the consolidated accounts:

	£
Sale proceeds	14,000
Less: Net assets representing shares sold	
70% × (2,500 + 500 + 7,000 + [9/12 × 3,000])	(8,575)
Less: Goodwill paid on the shares now sold 70/80 × 1,100	(963)
None of the goodwill deducted above is added back as all of the goodwill on acquisition was written off to reserves at acquisition	–
	4,462
Tax – as above	(2,735)
	1,727

(ii) The consolidated balance sheet at 31 December 1992 (incorporating subsidiary 2 as a trade investment):

	£	£
Fixed assets 10,000 + 8,000		18,000
Fixed asset investment at cost 10/80 × 3,500		438
Net current assets 6,500 + 7,000	13,500	
Add: Dividends proposed by subsidiaries	500	
Add: Dividend receivable from trade investment (10% × 1,000)	100	
Less: Dividends payable to MI 25% × 500	(125)	
Add: Sale proceeds	14,000	
Less: Tax on gain on sale	(2,735)	
		25,240
		43,678
Ordinary share capital		6,000
Reserves – balancing item		33,928
MI – Subsidiary 1 25% × 15,000		3,750
		43,678

(iii) The consolidated profit and loss account for the year ended 31 December 1992:

	H	Subsidiary 1	Subsidiary 2 As sub. 80% 9m.	Consolidated p&l account
	£	£	£	£
Profit after tax	3,500	2,000		
9/12 × 3,000			2,250	
FII – dividend from subsidiary 2				
10% × 1,000	100			7,850
MI		25% (500)	20% (450)	(950)
	3,600	1,500	1,800	6,900
Transfer – realised on sale				
70% × 3,000 × 9/12	1,575	5,175	(1,575)	
Gain on sale	1,727			1,727
	6,902	1,500	225	8,627
Intercompany dividend				
75% × 500	375	(375)		
Dividends	(2,000)			(2,000)
Retained	5,277	1,125	225	6,627

(iv) Statement of movements on consolidated reserves for the year ended 31 December 1992:

	Parent	Subsidiaries 1	2	Goodwill	Total
	£	£	£	£	£
1/1/92	16,500	7,500	5,600	(2,475)	27,125
Realised on sale					
(i) profits					
70% × 7,000	4,900		(4,900)		
(ii) goodwill				963	963
Profit for year	5,277	1,125	225		6,627
Eliminated from					
consolidated reserves			(925)		(925)
				137	137
31/12/92	26,677	8,625	–	(1,375)	33,927
				rounding	1
					33,928

NOTE:

* Where the remaining holding is a trade investment, we are no longer concerned with either the remaining share of post-acquisition reserves or the remaining goodwill. Both these amounts are, accordingly, eliminated from consolidated reserves.

The problem of dividends paid by a subsidiary *before* the date of its disposal

In this situation, it follows that the parent must have received its share of the dividend and that the dividend cannot be in the net assets of the subsidiary on the date of its disposal.

In ascertaining the net assets of the subsidiary on the disposal date representing the shares sold follow the approach shown in Pro Forma 18.1.

PRO FORMA 18.1

	£
Net assets at the acquisition date:	
(i) Share capital	x
(ii) Reserves at acquisition	
– BVs	x
– FV adjustments	x
Increase in net assets since acquisition	
(iii) Post-acquisition reserves b/f	x
(iv) Profit for the current year before dividends, up to disposal date	x
	x
Deduct the whole of dividends paid by the subsidiary before the disposal date	(x)
The net assets of the subsidiary on the disposal date	x

Include the % representing the shares sold in the calculation of the gain or loss on disposal. See Example 18.5.

EXAMPLE 18.5

401

18

Holdings plc had acquired a 75% holding of 150,000 £1 ordinary shares in Subbat plc on 1 November 1980 for £700,000 at which date there was a credit balance on reserves of £200,000 in Subbat plc and the net assets of the company at fair values totalled £800,000. Holdings plc makes up its accounts to 31 October each year and the goodwill arising on consolidation was written off against reserves on 31 October 1981.

Acquisitive plc offered to purchase some or all of the shares in Subbat plc from Holdings plc with effect from 30 June 1991 on the following terms:

Offer 1 was to purchase 150,000 shares for £1,350,000.
Offer 2 was to purchase 100,000 shares for £720,000.

The following information was available for the year ending 31 October 1991 prior to the acceptance of either offer:

	Holding plc	Subbat plc
	£000	£000
Profit after tax	500	240
Dividends paid prior to 30 June	60	40
Dividends proposed	125	100
Profit retained	315	100
Retained profit brought forward	1,025	400

Holdings plc accounts for dividends on a cash received basis.

Assume a corporation tax rate of 35%.

Ignore inflation, indexation allowance and rebasing.

Calculate the gain or loss on disposal so as to comply with FRS 2 that will appear both in the accounts of Holdings plc and of the Holdings Group as at 31 October 1991 on the assumption that offer 1 was accepted and Acquisitive plc purchased 150,000 £1 ordinary shares in Subbat plc on 30 June 1991.

Workings

		£000
Parent company	Sale proceeds	1,350
	Cost of shares sold	(700)
		650
Tax at 35%		(228)
		422

Consolidated accounts:

	£000	£000
Sale proceeds		1,350
Less: Net assets representing shares sold		
share capital (150 × 100/75)	200	
Reserves at acquisition – BV	200*	
FV adjustment (800 – [200 + 200])	400	
Fair value of net assets at acquisition	800	
Post-acquisition reserves b/f		
(400 – 200*)	200	
Profit, before dividends, up to disposal date		
8/12 × 240	160	
	1,160	

Dividend paid before disposal date	(40)
	$1,120 \times 75\% = (840)$

Less: Goodwill paid on acquisition of shares now sold (700 less (75% × 800))	(100)
	410
Tax – as above	(228)
The FRS 2 gain for the consolidated accounts	182

EXAMPLE 18.6

Using the data in Example 18.5 prepare the following statements on the assumption that Acquisitive plc purchased 100,000 £1 ordinary shares in Subbat plc on 30 June 1991:

(i) a profit and loss account starting with the profit after tax figure for the year ended 31 October 1991, consolidating the results, of Holdings plc and Subbat plc, and
(ii) a statement of movement on reserves for the Group and Company.

Assume that the remaining (75% – 50%) 25% holding in Subbat plc is an associated undertaking.

Before you can prepare the profit and loss account, you will need to calculate the FRS 2 gain on disposal. Following the same approach as in Example 18.1 this will be as follows:

Parent company:	£000
Sale proceeds	720
Cost of shares sold (100/150 × 700)	(467)
	253
Tax at 35%	(89)
	164

Consolidated accounts	
Sale proceeds	720
Less: Net assets representing shares sold 1,120 [as in Example 18.1] × 50%	(560)
Less: Goodwill paid representing shares sold 100 × 50/75	(67)
Add: The goodwill paid deducted above but, remember again, only if there has been systematic amortisation against profits since acquisition – in this case nil	–
	93
Tax as above	(89)
	4

You can now prepare the consolidated profit and loss account for the year ended 31 October 1991 as follows:

	Holdings	Subbat plc 75% Sub 8/12	25% assoc. 4/12	Consolidated p&l account
Profit after tax	500			
Less: Intercompany dividend received from Subbat plc				
75% × 40	(30)			
	470			
240 × 8/12		160		
240 × 4/12 × 25%			20	
Gain on sale	4			
	474	160	20	654
MI		25% (40)		(40)
		120		614
Dividends from S				
75% × 40	30	(30)		
25% × 100	25		(25)	
	529	90		
Transfer – realised on sale 50/75 × 90	60	(60)		
	589	30	(5)	614
Dividends (60 + 125)	(185)			(185)
Retained	404	30	(5)	429

You can now put together a statement of the investments on group reserves during the year to 31 October 1991 as follows:

	Parent £000	Subsidiary £000	Associate £000	Goodwill £000	Total £000
1/11/90	1,025		–	(100)	1,075
75% × (400 – 200)		150			
Realised on sale:					
(i) Profit 50/75 × 150	100	(100)			–
(ii) Goodwill				67	67
Profit for year	404	30	(5)		429
Transfer: Subsidiary now asssociate		(80)	80		–
30/10/91	1,529	–	75	(33)	1,571

Deemed disposals

The FRS 2 basis of the calculation of the gain on disposal applies whether the cause of the undertaking ceasing to be a subsidiary undertaking is a direct disposal or a deemed disposal. Consider the situation in Example 18.7 dealt with in the 'Accounting solutions' section of *Accountancy* magazine.

EXAMPLE 18.7

At the beginning of the year a group had a 55% interest in a loss-making subsidiary. During the year the subsidiary made a 1 for 2 rights issue priced at £4 per ordinary £1 share. The group did not exercise its rights but sold them to a third party for £200,000. The third party then exercised those rights, as did other minority shareholders owning 40% of the remaining 45% of the company's share capital; therefore 95% of the rights issue was taken up. The subsidiary's share capital was £2m (ordinary £1 shares) and its net assets were £10m immediately prior to the rights issue. No goodwill arose on the original acquisition. How should the group account for the transaction?

This transaction is of the type categorised in paragraph 87 of FRS 2 – Accounting for Subsidiary Undertakings as a deemed disposal.

The group owned 55% of the share capital prior to the rights issue, that is, 1,100,000 shares. As it exercised no rights it also owned 1,100,000 shares following the issue.

The number of shares of the subsidiary in issue following the rights issue can be calculated as:

$2,000,000 + (2,000,000 \times 0.95 \times 1/2) = 2,950,000$ shares

The group's holding in the subsidiary has therefore been diluted from 55% to:

$$\frac{1,100,000}{2,950,000} = 37,29\%$$

The net assets of the company post-rights issue were:

$£10,000,000 + (950,000 \times £4)$
$= £13,800,000$

The group's balance sheet holding in the company was:

	£
Immediately prior to rights issue (accounted for as a subsidiary)	
55% of £10,000,000	5,500,000
Immediately after rights issue (accounted for as an associate)	
37.29% of £13,800,000	5,146,000
Reduction in share of net assets	354,000
Proceeds from sale of rights	200,000
Loss on disposal	154,000

Increase in interest or stake and accounting for fair value

FRS 2 deals exclusively with acquisition accounting. Under the standard, 'the date for accounting for an undertaking becoming a subsidiary undertaking is the date on which control of that undertaking passes to its new parent undertaking . . .'.

The following factors could indicate that the acquirer has gained control of the undertaking:

▶ the purchaser begins to direct the operating and financial policies of the acquired undertaking
▶ the purchaser begins to derive economic benefits arising from the undertaking
▶ the date on which the consideration is paid.

The Act's requirements for acquisition accounting

The Act, Schedule 4A paragraph 9, sets out the basic requirements for the consolidation of a subsidiary for the first time, as follows:

- ▶ The identifiable assets and liabilities of the acquired subsidiary should be included in the consolidated balance sheet at their fair values on the date of acquisition.
- ▶ The results of the acquired subsidiary, income and expenditure, should be brought into the consolidated financial statements from the date of the acquisition.
- ▶ Goodwill is derived by comparing the interest of the group in the adjusted capital and reserves of the acquired subsidiary with the acquisition cost of the group's interest in the shares of the new subsidiary.

These are points that you will be fully familiar with from Paper 10. Consider the simple example in Example 18.8.

EXAMPLE 18.8

Company 1 acquires 80% of Company 2 in September 1994. The acquisition cost amounted to £250,000 and, at the acquisition date, the share capital and reserves of the subsidiary were recorded in its books at £140,000.

A fair value exercise is carried out at the acquisition date and it is determined that fixed assets and stocks have values of £60,000 and £17,500 respectively in excess of their book values.

The adjusted share capital and reserves of Company 2 on the date of its acquisition are therefore £140,000 + £60,000 + £17,500 or £217,500.

Based on the numbers above, goodwill on consolidation would be £250,000 − (80% × £217,500) = £76,000.

Accounting for an increase in stake

The basic principles of accounting for acquisitions as dealt with under the Act and as set out above apply equally to increases in the original stake of the purchaser. FRS 2 gives us guidance on interpreting the requirements of the Act in this context. The main points to bear in mind are as follows:

Where you are dealing with 'piecemeal' acquisitions, under the Act you must assign fair values to the identifiable net assets of the acquired subsidiary as a one-off exercise *at the time the acquiree becomes a subsidiary*.

However, FRS 2 does state that, in special circumstances, not assigning fair values to the acquiree's net assets on the date of *each* prior purchase may result in accounting in a way that is not consistent with the way in which the investment has previously been treated in the consolidated accounts. This inconsistency may lead to the treatment required by the Act failing to give a true and fair view. This takes us into the S. 227 (6) true and fair override.

Failing to give a true and fair view

Two instances where accounting under the Act for prior holdings prior to the acquiree becoming a subsidiary might fail to give a true and fair view are:

- ▶ An acquisition of a further interest in an undertaking that has already been treated as an associate by the group, that is, included in the consolidated accounts under the equity method of accounting. In this instance if you were to assign fair values and calculate goodwill only once the acquiree becomes a subsidiary – applying the rules of the Act – the effect would be to reclassify the share of post-acquisition reserves of what was an associate as goodwill arising on the acquisition of what is now a subsidiary. This problem is dealt with in Example 18.11.
- ▶ A group restates an investment that subsequently becomes a subsidiary. In this instance the provision for diminution in value of the investment would result in an

increase in reserves and a creation of goodwill if the rules of the Act were to be applied. This problem is dealt with in Example 18.10.

In these instances, where the calculation of goodwill under the Act would be misleading, FRS 2 states that:

▶ Goodwill should be calculated as the sum of the goodwill arising from *each* purchase of an interest in the relevant undertaking, adjusted as necessary for any subsequent diminution in value.
▶ The goodwill arising on each purchase should be calculated as the difference between the cost of that purchase and the fair value at the date of that purchase of the identifiable net assets attributable to the interest purchased.
▶ The difference between the goodwill calculated using the true and fair override – as above – and that calculated under the Act must be shown in reserves.

Some further examples

There are four situations where an increase in a stake can give rise to a change in the status of an investment – an investment becomes an associate, an investment becomes a subsidiary, an associate becomes a subsidiary, and an increase in stake in an existing subsidiary.

The first of these situations is not dealt with here. Bear in mind, however, that SSAP 1 does require fair values to be assigned on the date of the acquisition of an associate and goodwill would have to be calculated when an associate is acquired.

Investment becomes a subsidiary

EXAMPLE 18.9 – APPLYING THE RULES OF SCHEDULE 4A PARAGRAPH 9 TO AN INVESTMENT BECOMING A SUBSIDIARY

The following takes place:

▶ Company 1 purchases 10% of Company 2 in 1985 for £50.
▶ The investment was subsequently revalued by Company 1 to £100.
▶ Company 1 purchases a further 50% of Company 2 in 1994 for £500 to bring its total holding in Company 2 to 60%.
▶ The identifiable net assets of Company 2 on the date of this second purchase are recorded in its books at £400 and the fair value exercise at this date indicates that the identifiable net assets of Company 2 on this date have a fair value of £700.
▶ The adjusted share capital and reserves on the date of the 50% purchase are, accordingly: share capital £100, reserves £600, including a revaluation reserve arising at this date of (700 – 400) £300.

Goodwill on consolidation would be calculated as follows:

	£
Consideration (50 + 500)	550
Less: Share of identifiable net assets acquired 60% × 700	(420)
	130

The minority interest, at the date Company 2 becomes a subsidiary of Company 1, would be 40% × 700 = £280.

Note that an adjustment would be required to reduce the value of the investment from its revalued amount of £100 to its original cost of £50, that is, DR revaluation reserve and CR Cost of investment with £50.

EXAMPLE 18.10 – INVESTMENT BECOMES A SUBSIDIARY BUT THERE HAS BEEN A PREVIOUS PROVISION FOR DIMINUTION IN VALUE

The following takes place:

▶ Company 1 purchased 10% of Company 2 in 1989 for £5,500 when the fair value of the net assets of Company 2 amounted to £50,000.
▶ Company 1 provided for a permanent diminution in value regarding its investment in Company 2 from £5,500 to £2,000.
▶ In 1994 Company 1 was able to purchase the remaining 90% of Company 2 for £20,000, at which time the fair value of the net assets of Company 2 amounted to £25,000.

In this example, if we were to apply the provisions of Schedule 4A paragraph 9 of the Act:

Consolidation goodwill would be:

	£
Consideration (5,500 + 20,000)	25,500
Less: Fair value of net assets at date Company 2 becomes a subsidiary – 100% × 25,000	(25,000)
	500

On consolidation:

▶ DR Cost of investment CR Reserves with £3,500 – restatement of investment to original cost.
▶ DR Reserves CR Goodwill £500 with the immediate write off of goodwill to reserves.
▶ The net effect in reserves will be a credit of £3,000.

The positive goodwill resulting above is effectively arrived at by reinstating the provision for permanent diminution in value and setting it off against the negative goodwill arising on the second purchase. The substance of the acquisition is (1) a holding loss on the first investment and (2) a discount on the purchase of the second investment. This substance is reflected by adopting the true and fair override as follows:

Consolidation goodwill would be:

	£
(1) 1st purchase £5,500 – (10% × £50,000)	500
(2) 2nd purchase £20,000 – (90% × £25,000)	(2,500)
Negative goodwill	(2,000)

On consolidation

▶ DR Cost of investment CR Reserves £3,500 with the restatement of the original investment to the original cost.
▶ DR Reserves CR Goodwill £2,500 with the reduction in net assets attributable to the original stake, that is 10% × (£50,000 – £25,000) from acquisition date to the date the company becomes a subsidiary
▶ DR Goodwill CR Reserves £2,000 with the transfer of negative goodwill to reserves.

Movements in reserves will be reflected as follows:

	£
Goodwill calculated under the Act, written off	(500)
Adjustment for true and fair override	2,500
Negative goodwill arising	2,000
Net write-back of provision for diminution in value (3,500 – 2,500)	1,000
	3,000

Associate becomes a subsidiary

In this instance it is important that you remember that the share of the associated company's post-acquisition results will have been included in the consolidated profit and loss account and in the carrying value of the associated company in the consolidated balance sheet under the equity method of accounting. Further goodwill will have been calculated on the acquisition of the associate and either written off immediately to reserves or systematically amortised following acquisition.

EXAMPLE 18.11 – AN ASSOCIATE BECOMES A SUBSIDIARY

The following takes place:

▶ Company 1 purchased 20% of the voting equity of Company 2 (its associate) in 1990 for £240 when the book (and fair) value of the net assets of Company 2 amounted to £1,000.

▶ The goodwill arising on this purchase was, accordingly, £240 – (20% × 1,000) = £40 and this was written off directly to reserves on acquisition.

▶ Company 1 purchased a further 50% of the voting equity of Company 2 in 1994 for £840 when the fair value of the net assets of Company 2 amounted to £1,500 – the book value of the net assets of Company 2 on the date of this purchase amounted to £1,360.

▶ On the date that Company 2 became a subsidiary it would have been included in the consolidated balance sheet at a carrying value, under the equity method, of:

	£
Share of net assets at acquisition	
20% × 1,000	200
Increase in share of net assets since acquisition	
20% × (1,360 – 1,000)	72
	272

▶ The fair value of Company 2's net assets on the date that it becomes a subsidiary is, as already stated, £1,500 made up as follows:

Share capital £100
Reserves £1,400 including a revaluation reserve arising on the date of the further 50% acquisition of £140, that is, £1,500 – £1,360.

Applying the provisons of Schedule 4A paragraph 9:

Consolidation goodwill would be:

	£
Consideration (240 + 840)	1,080
Less: Share of fair value of net assets 70% × 1,500	(1,050)
	30
Less: Goodwill previously written off	(40)
Negative goodwill	(10)

The minority interest would be 30% × 1,500 = £450

This method of calculating goodwill, reflecting 'form', has the effect of treating the post-acquisition reserves of Company 2 while it was an associate as a deduction from goodwill.

On consolidation:

▶ DR Reserves CR Carrying value of investment £72 being the elimination of share of post-acquisition reserves of the associate and the restatement of the original investment to its original cost.

▶ DR Goodwill CR Reserves £10 with the transfer of negative goodwill arising to reserves.
▶ Reserves are accordingly reduced by (72 – 10) = £62.
    This £62 can be explained as representing the difference between the carrying value as associate (£272) plus the cost of the increase in stake (£840), a total of £1,112, and the group's share of the net assets of the subsidiary after the acquisition of the controlling interest (70% × 1,500), £1,050

Applying the true and fair override:

Consolidation goodwill would be:

		£	£
Acquisition (1)	Cost	240	
	Less: 20% × 1,000	(200)	
			40
Acquisition (2)	Cost	840	
	Less: 50% × 1,500	(750)	
			90
			130
Goodwill already written off			(40)
Balance of goodwill			90

The minority interest would be, as before, 30% × 1,500 = £450.

In this situation, there is one further adjustment that will arise. There is a difference between the fair value of the net assets consolidated (£1,500) and the book value of the net assets on the date the associate became a subsidiary (£1,360). The difference of £140 has been dealt with above as follows:

▶ to the minority interest	30% × 140	= 42	
▶ in the goodwill calculation relating to the 50% purchase	50% × 140	= 70	
▶ the balance relates to the original stake of 20%	20% × 140	= 28	
		140	

The £28 above is post-acquisition as far as the original stake of 20% is concerned and should therefore be taken to revaluation reserve.

The net debit to reserves is as before, that is, £90 – £28 = £62

Increase of stake in an existing subsidiary

FRS 2 states that:

> when a group increases its interest in an undertaking that is already its subsidiary undertaking, the identifiable assets and liabilities of that subsidiary undertaking should be revalued to fair value and goodwill arising on the increase in interest should be calculated by reference to those fair values.

EXAMPLE 18.12 – INCREASE IN STAKE IN EXISTING SUBSIDIARY

The following takes place:

▶ Company 1 purchased a 60% interest in Company 2, its subsidiary, in 1988 for £25,000. The fair value of the identifiable net assets of Company 2 on the day of this purchase amounted to £30,000.
▶ Company 1 purchased a further 30% interest in Company 2 in 1994, to give it a total of a 90% interest in its existing subsidiary.

▶ The cost of the 1994 purchase was £20,000 and the fair value of the identifiable net assets of Company 2 on the date of this purchase amounted to £75,000.

▶ The increase in the fair value of the identifiable net assets of Company 2 between the date of the 1988 purchase and the 1994 purchase (75 – 30) £45,000 arises as follows:

– Retained profits   £10,000
– Fair value changes   £35,000

Consolidation goodwill would be:

	£	£
Acquisition (1) Cost	25,000	
Less: 60% × 30,000	(18,000)	
		7,000
Acquisition (2) Cost	20,000	
Less: 30% × 75,000	(22,500)	
		(2,500)
		4,500

The treatment of the fair value changes of £35,000 between the two purchase dates depends on whether or not the revaluation has been recorded by Company 2.

Group reorganisations

Changes in the organisational structure of individual companies are covered in Chapter 25. Here we will look, briefly, at group reorganisation. This may involve the setting up of a new parent company; changing the ownership of a subsidiary from one group company to another or transferring the business of one group company to another. All such changes are entirely within the group and will not therefore affect the totality of the group or consolidated accounts.

Reorganisation through the setting up of a new holding company

Such reorganisations are usually carried out by the exchange of shares. Thus, shareholders of Company 1 sell their shares to Company 2 in exchange for the shares of Company 2. In such a situation the combination could be accounted for as a merger as dealt with in Chapter 19, and there would be no need to assign fair values to the net assets of Company 1. If cash is paid for Company 1 shares, acquisition accounting and the fair value exercise, as dealt with in Chapter 20, must follow.

Shifting the ownership of shares in a subsidiary from one group company to another

There are three possible scenarios here:

1   A vertical group could be reorganised into one with a parent and fellow subsidiaries as follows:

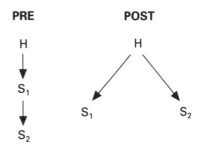

Such a reorganisation will be necessary if, for example, H wishes to dispose of S_1 while continuing to retain a controlling interest in S_2.

The reorganisation takes place by either H paying S_1 in cash (allotments of shares to subsidiaries are void) for its investment in S_2 or for S_1 to transfer its investment in S_2 to H as a dividend in specie. In either case, problems arise as to the value to be placed on the investment in S_2. Whatever the value assigned, there will be no effect on the group as a whole.

2   Transferring a sub-subsidiary from one subsidiary to another.

Such a reorganisation would result in:

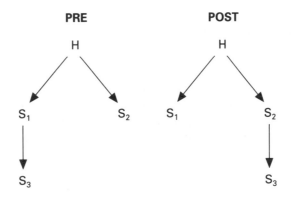

As with 1 above there will be no effect on the totality of the consolidated accounts.

3   Transferring a direct holding in a subsidiary to another subsidiary, the reverse of 1:

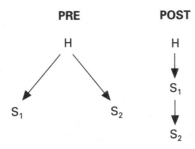

Where cash is the focus of consideration paid by S_1 to H there will be no difficulty in the accounting procedures involved although there is the question of whether or not H should recognise a gain or loss on "sale". If the consideration is in S_1 shares. In this situation S 132 of the 1985 Act, which gives partial relief from the S 130 requirement to second the premium on issue, comes into play. S 132 requires, in a group reorganisation, the amount to be taken to the share premiums account to represent "the minimum premium value" which is the excess of the book value of the investment over the nominal value of the shares issued by the acquired or transferee company.

Demergers

You will have read about the ICI demerger in 1993 and the proposed demerger of British Gas. In a demerger the purpose is to break up an existing group into two (or more) separate groups, effectively separating different operations.

1 H can transfer its holding in S to H shareholders as a dividend in specie. H shareholders are now shareholders of H and S and S is no longer a subsidiary of H.

2 H transfers an operation to a company newly formed for the purpose of the demerger; the new company issues, in exchange, shares to H shareholders.

3 H transfers its holding in S to a new company which issues its shares to H shareholders in exchange. S is now a subsidiary of the new company which is owned by some or all of the shareholders of H.

Aspects of group reorganisation have been examined under the old AFA syllabus and will be relevant to the examinations under the new Paper 13 syllabus. Follow the instructions of a question and think carefully as to whether the sale or purchase of shares has an accounting effect on the company or the shareholders of the company.

Summary

▶ This chapter deals with the accounting considerations of accounting for changes in the composition of the group. It covers the various disposal situations and also the impact of increasing a stake in an investment.

▶ As to disposals, the question of what should be reported as the gain on the sale is of importance as it has a direct impact on the profit of the year of disposal and it is in this context that you should interpret the make up of the FRS 2 gain.

▶ As to acquisitions, the increase of stake has a bearing on goodwill in respect of the total holding and the values to be assigned to a subsidiary's net assets in the consolidated accounts.

▶ Group reorganisations have been dealt with here on the basis that there is a change in the structure of a group.

▶ The chapter contains a number of worked examples and for this reason there are no self test questions attached to this chapter on the basis that you should now be in a position to adequately tackle exam style questions.

Suggested reading

FRS 2 – a commentary (Coopers & Lybrand)
An excellent survey and analysis of the requirements of the new Accounting Standard on accounting for subsidiary undertakings.

UK GAAP (Ernst and Young 3rd Ed)
This has a useful example dealing with step by step acquisitions and also covers the requirements and patterns of application that may arise under FRS 2.

Exam style question

1 *Grace plc – changes in the composition of a group*
At 30 September 1990, Grace plc had a 75% subsidiary, Barlow Ltd, and also held 30% of the share capital of Hornby Ltd, an associated company. Their summarised balance sheets at that date were as follows:

	Grace plc £000	Barlow Ltd £000	Hornby Ltd £000
Investment at cost in:			
Barlow Ltd	450	–	–
Hornby Ltd	210	–	–
Other net assets	1,690	1,000	800
	2,350	1,000	800
Share capital (£1 shares)	100	100	50
Reserves	2,250	900	750
	2,350	1,000	800

You are also informed that:

▶ Grace plc acquired its investment in Barlow Ltd many years ago when the reserves of Barlow Ltd were £500,000. The reserves of Hornby Ltd were £650,000 when Grace plc bought its 30% holding on 1 October 1988. No changes have taken place in the share capital of either company since Grace plc made its investments.

▶ Grace plc's accounting policy is to amortise goodwill on consolidation over 20 years.

▶ The following transactions have taken place during the year to 30 September 1991:
  – On 1 April 1991 Grace plc acquired a further 25,000 £1 shares in Hornby Ltd for £705,000 in cash.
  – On 1 July 1991 Grace plc sold its entire interest in Barlow Ltd for £1,100,000 in cash. The tax arising on this transaction was £83,000.

▶ The draft results of the individual companies in the period since 1 October 1990 were:

	Grace plc Year to 30 September 1991 £000	Barlow Ltd Year to 30 September 1991 £000	Hornby Ltd 6 months to 31 March 1991 £000	30 September 1991 £000
Turnover	4,000	5,400	2,500	3,000
Profit before tax	400	320	300	340
Tax	(140)	(112)	(105)	(119)
Profit after tax	260	208	195	221

Profits for Barlow Ltd evenly throughout the year.

▶ The results for Grace plc and Hornby Ltd at 30 September 1991 do not reflect the disposal of Barlow Ltd or the information below:
  – Grace plc's directors have now indicated that £70,000 of costs incurred and charged by Hornby Ltd in its draft results for the six-month period to 30 September 1991 related to the rationalisation of Hornby Ltd's operations upon it becoming a subsidiary. These costs should be provided in the balance sheet at 31 March 1991.
  – Hornby Ltd has now decided to write off a debtor balance of £40,000 of which £30,000 had been outstanding since 31 March 1991.
  – The rationalisation and bad debt costs referred to above are all allowable for taxation.

▶ Grace plc is a regular supplier to Hornby Ltd, and makes a pre-tax profit of 20% on the sales. Sales invoiced by Grace plc to Hornby Ltd in the six-month period to 30 September 1991 were £800,000. As a matter of policy Grace plc eliminated intragroup profit only when Hornby Ltd became a subsidiary: deferred tax on related timing differences is not required.

Hornby Ltd held the following amounts of stock at the prices invoiced by Grace plc:

	£000
At 1 April 1991	200
At 30 September 1991	450

Goods invoiced by Grace plc to Hornby Ltd in September 1991 at £150,000 were not reflected in Hornby Ltd's accounts at 30 September 1991 as they had not been delivered to Hornby Ltd.

Required:
Prepare the consolidated balance sheet of Grace plc at 30 September 1991 and the consolidated profit and loss account for the year then ended. Where applicable, assume a tax rate of 35%.

(20 marks)

All answers on pages 675–676.

Consolidated Accounts 5 – The Merger Method

CHAPTER

19

The ASC published ED 3 – Accounting for Acquisitions and Mergers, in 1971. The ED was an attempt to standardise methods of merger accounting that were developing at the time. The ED proposed that both the acquisition accounting method and the merger accounting method were acceptable methods of accounting for business combinations but also proposed that the two methods be mutually exclusive – that they were not alternatives in accounting for the same business combination. Thus, if certain criteria were met, a business combination should be accounted for as a merger; if not, as an acquisition.

Given the mechanics of merger accounting, ED 3 was considered by many to be in conflict with (the then relevant) Section 56 of the 1948 Act, which required the setting up of a share premium account where shares were issued at a premium. Based on the fact that there was no universal agreement as to the legal implications of merger accounting, the ASC decided not to convert ED 3 into an Accounting Standard.

The question of legality was reconsidered in the case of *Shearer* v. *Bercain Ltd* in 1980. The case was not primarily concerned with the accounting treatment of business combinations, but the judgement in the case appeared to confirm the following points:

▶ that a holding company should record an investment in a subsidiary in its own balance sheet at the fair rather than the nominal value of the shares issued
▶ a holding company should credit any excess of fair value over nominal value of shares issued as consideration for the purchase of the subsidiary to a share premium account.

The views of those commentators who questioned the legality of ED 3 appeared to be confirmed. Following *Shearer* v. *Bercain Ltd*, it appeared that any company that had adopted merger accounting in the past, may have been in contravention of the law. Following the court's decision in the case, the government consulted several interested parties and subsequently made it known that it considered that there were certain circumstances in which there should be no objection to a failure to set up a share premium account; in other words, the effect of Section 56 of the 1948 Act should be modified. New legislation to this effect appeared for the first time in Sections 36 to 41 of the 1981 Act – the 'merger relief' provisions of the 1981 Act. These sections stated that if a company secures at least a 90% holding in the equity of another company by means of an arrangement that includes the exchange of shares, Section 56 of the 1948 Act shall not apply to any premium on the shares that the company issues as (part of) the consideration that it gives for the shares that it receives. As to the precise accounting treatment that should be adopted when these sections applied, the law was silent; the government indicated that a future Accounting Standard should prescribe the accounting treatment to be adopted in the circumstances that fall within the scope of the merger relief provisions.

It was in response to these government comments, the old ED 3, the American approach as stated in APB Opinion 16, and an international exposure draft E 22 issued in 1981, that the ASC issued ED 31 – Accounting for Acquisitions and Mergers, in October 1982. As with ED 3, ED 31 stated that if a business combination satisfied all the conditions for a merger then merger accounting should be used; if not, acquisition accounting should be used. One of the main characteristics of a merger as defined in the new ED was that no significant resources should leave the group on the combination. In this event it was considered that two groups of shareholders have effectively pooled their resources, that is, they have merged. The new ED differed from the old in that it rejected the criteria of size and continuity in defining a merger situation. Thus a business combination would be accounted for as a merger under ED 31 even if one party was identifiably dominant and the management and business of the combining companies changed on combination.

The publication of ED 31 prompted 86 letters of comment to the ASC. In April 1984 it issued an SOI indicating the future strategy to be adopted on the subject of merger accounting. The conditions to be satisfied for a business combination to be accounted for as a merger were relaxed by the SOI. The statement indicated that the new standard would prescribe only the accounting treatment to be used on consolidation and that a holding company would be allowed flexibility in the way that it recorded its investment in subsidiaries in its own accounts.

SSAP 23 – Accounting for Acquisitions and Mergers, was issued in April 1985.

The Companies Act 1981 paved the way for the use of the merger method on consolidation by introducing relief from setting up a share premium account in certain circumstances. However, prior to the Companies Act 1989 there were no statutory restrictions on the use of merger accounting in the group accounts. Any restrictions as to the use of the merger method in group accounts were contained solely in SSAP 23. Merger accounting in group accounts is now dealt with in the Companies Act 1989. This Act preserves the current position that merger accounting be available as an option provided certain conditions are satisfied. In requiring that the use of merger accounting must accord with generally accepted accounting principles the 1989 Act effectively gives statutory backing to SSAP 23. The conditions of the Standard are generally more restrictive than in the new Act. The new rules as to the basis and method of preparing group accounts introduced by the 1989 Act are dealt with in Chapters 15 to 20. This chapter is concerned with SSAP 23 and the proposed revisions of SSAP 23 under ED 48.

The current SSAP 23 does not define a merger. It argues that merger accounting is an appropriate method of accounting for a business combination when certain conditions are satisfied. Essentially, merger accounting may be used in a combination where only limited resources leave the group. The ASC believed that a review of SSAP 23 could lead to improved accounting for business combinations.

The main points of the Standard

SSAP 23 should be regarded as standard accounting practice in respect of business combinations first accounted for in financial statements for accounting periods beginning on or after 1 April 1985. If a business combination satisfies all the merger conditions of the Standard, the group may use either merger or acquisition accounting to account for the business combination. If a business combination fails to satisfy any of the merger conditions of the Standard, the group must use acquisition accounting.

Thus merger accounting is optional when all the conditions are met, while acquisition accounting is mandatory if all the conditions are not met. This is justified by the ASC in that:

▶ There is no strong support for merger accounting being mandatory.
▶ Merger accounting is relatively new in the UK.
▶ The merger relief provisions of UK company law (as also the EC 7th Directive) are permissive rather than prescriptive.

▶ Companies who perceive themselves to be acquisitive regardless of the form of consideration offered may wish to account for their business combinations as acquisitions even though the merger conditions are satisfied.

▶ Acquisition accounting is considered to be the benchmark; merger accounting the exception. A Standard should not, therefore, prohibit acquisition accounting in any given situation. In merger accounting the consolidated accounts need not incorporate the fair values of the assets and liabilities of the subsidiary on the date of the business combination. In merger accounting the consolidated accounts for the period of the business combination should include the results of the subsidiary for the whole period regardless of the date of the combination. Goodwill on consolidation may arise under acquisition accounting but it does not arise under merger accounting. Differences on consolidation arise in merger accounting and these should be adjusted, on consolidation, against consolidated reserves. The Standard deals only with accounting in group accounts. Guidance is given in an appendix as to how a parent undertaking should account for a business combination in its own accounts and how it should account for distributions from pre-acquisition profits of subsidiaries.

The main differences between acquisition accounting and merger accounting

Merger accounting evolved in response to specific criticisms of acquisition accounting. It was argued that the latter produced unsatisfactory results when two or more companies combined by means of a share-for-share exchange. In such a situation, the following have been put forward as the disadvantages of acquisition accounting:

▶ The pre-acquisition reserves of the subsidiary are frozen or capitalised and cannot be distributed to the shareholders of the combined companies.

▶ One company may have to create a share premium account on shares issued as consideration.

▶ The combined group will have to recognise and, per SSAP 22, subsequently eliminate any goodwill on consolidation.

▶ The combined group will have to assign fair values to the assets and liabilities of the subsidiary on the date of the combination. This may result in an increased depreciation charge in the consolidated accounts.

Under merger accounting these disadvantages do not normally arise as the shareholders of the combining companies effectively pool their interests and the consolidated financial statements are simply the sum of the financial statements of the combining companies.

There are three main differences between the two methods of accounting for a business combination. First, in acquisition accounting the consolidated accounts will reflect only the post-acquisition results of the subsidiary acquired. In merger accounting the consolidated accounts incorporate the results of the combining companies as though they had always been combined, that is, even though a business combination may occur part of the way through the year the consolidated accounts reflect the full year's results of all combining companies (previous years' comparatives being re-stated). In acquisition accounting, consolidated reserves include those of the parent undertaking and only the group's share of the post-acquisition reserves of subsidiary undertakings. In merger accounting, consolidated reserves include those of the parent undertaking and the group's share of the total reserves, without distinction as to pre-acquisition or post-acquisition reserves, of subsidiary undertakings.

Secondly, in acquisition accounting the acquiring group accounts for the assets of the subsidiary acquired at cost to the acquiring group. Cost is determined by assigning fair values to the assets and liabilities of the subsidiary on the date of acquisition. In merger accounting the group does not re-state the assets and liabilities of the subsidiary on the date of the business combination. Merger accounting shows the position of the combining companies as if the companies had always been combined. As already stated, as a result of this difference, acquisition accounting is likely to lead to higher depreciation charges in the consolidated accounts than what would arise in merger accounting.

Thirdly, acquisition accounting usually gives rise to goodwill on consolidation. Goodwill does not arise in merger accounting. Any differences that arise in merger accounting between the nominal value of shares issued by one company on the combination and acquired by that company on the combination is not goodwill as defined in SSAP 22. These differences are adjusted for, on consolidation, against consolidated reserves.

These main differences will be familiar to you from Paper 10. To ensure that you can differentiate between the two methods, attempt Exam question 19.1 and check your own solution against the answer given.

EXAM QUESTION 19.1 – FRUIT PLC

On 1 January 1989 Fruit plc acquired all of the issued share capital of Vegetables plc in exchange for shares in Fruit plc.

Shares in both companies have a nominal value of £1 each and a market value at 1 January 1989 of £5 for a £1 Fruit plc share, and £2.25 for a £1 Vegetables plc share. The agreed terms were 1 ordinary share in Fruit plc for every 2 ordinary shares in Vegetables plc.

At 31 December 1989 the register of members of Fruit plc was correct but no entries had been made in the books of accounts of either company to record the exchange.

At 1 January 1989 the balance sheet of Vegetables plc was as follows:

	£	£
Ordinary shares of £1 each		765,000
Retained earnings		447,525
		1,212,525
Fixed assets		
Freehold premises		573,750
Plant and machinery at cost	316,965	
Less: Provision for depreciation	127,500	189,465
Quoted investments at cost		140,250
Net current assets		309,060
		1,212,525

At 1 January 1989 the quoted investments had a market value of £318,750; the freehold premises a market value of £828,750; the plant and machinery (which had an expected unexpired useful life of four years) a market value of £300,000. Vegetables plc advised that it was their regular practice to invest surplus cash on a short-term basis in quoted investments. Draft accounts prepared for the two companies at the end of their financial year on 31 December 1989 showed the following:

Profit and loss accounts for the year ended 31 December 1989

	Fruit plc £	Vegetables plc £
Profit before depreciation	568,310	437,070
Depreciation for the year	91,290	40,035
Trading profit	477,020	397,035
Profit on sale of investments	–	138,465
Profit before tax	477,020	535,500
Taxation	119,255	149,940
Profit after tax	357,765	385,560

Balance sheets as at 31 December 1989

	Fruit plc £	Vegetables plc £
Freehold premises	1,657,500	573,750
Plant and machinery at cost	653,055	316,965
Aggregate depreciation	(276,165)	(167,535)
Net current assets	249,390	874,905
	2,283,780	1,598,085
Ordinary shares of £1 each	1,275,000	765,000
Retained earnings	1,008,780	833,085
	2,283,780	1,598,085

Required:

a) Prepare draft accounts for 1989 for the consolidation on the basis that:

   (i) Merger accounting is applied.

   (ii) Acquisition accounting is applied – assume a policy of amortisation over ten years for any goodwill that arises. (Ignore any deferred taxation implications.)

                                             (12 marks)

b) Discuss the bases for computing the asset values and reserves in the financial statements that appear under the two alternatives

                                             (8 marks)

                                            (20 marks)

ACCA Level 3 AFA exam question, December 1989

Initial workings:

1   The consideration for the purchase of 100% of Vegetable ordinary shares to be settled by the issue of Fruit ordinary shares. As Fruit is to issue 1 ordinary share for every 2 Vegetable ordinary shares, Fruit will issue 765,000/2 or 382,500 ordinary shares:

	£
Nominal value £1	382,500
Premium £4	1,530,000
	1,912,500

2   Recording the cost of the subsidiary in the separate accounts of the parent undertaking:

You should always follow the guidance in the SSAP 23 appendix unless the question specifically asks you to do otherwise. Accordingly,

If the acquisition method is to be used on consolidation: £ £

DR Cost of subsidiary   1,912,500
CR Ordinary share capital   382,500
CR Merger reserve   1,530,000

If the merger method is to be used on consolidation: £ £
DR Cost of subsidiary   382,500
CR Ordinary share capital   382,500

3 Consolidation goodwill under the acquisition method: £ £

FV of the consideration: 1,912,500
Less: FV of the separable net assets acquired:
  Freehold property   828,750
  Plant and machinery   300,000
  Investments   318,750
  Net current assets   309,060
                                                                       (1,756,560)

                                                                          155,940

Goodwill amortised in 1989
  155,940/10 years   (15,594)

Unamortised goodwill 31/12/89   140,346

4 Consolidation difference under the merger method:

Cost		NV of Vegetable ordinary shares owned by Fruit
£		£
382,500	<	765,000

The difference of £382,500 must be credited to consolidated other reserves.

Answers to requirements

(a) *Consolidated balance sheet 31 December 1989*

	(ii) Acquisition method		(i) Merger method	
	Assign FVs to S net assetson date of S acq		*Do not* specifically assign FVs to S net assets on merger	
Intangible fixed assets	£	£	£	£
Goodwill		140,346		N/A
Tangible fixed assets				
Freehold	1,657,500		1,657,500	
	828,750		573,750	
		2,486,250		2,231,250
Plant & machinery	376,890		376,890	
Depreciation 300,000				
1/4 (75,000)	225,000		149,430	
		601,890		526,320
Net current assets				
	249,390		249,390	
	874,905		874,905	1,124,295
		1,124,295		
		4,352,781		3,881,865

Ordinary share capital

	1,275,000	
	382,500	
	1,657,500	1,657,500
Reserves	2,695,281	2,224,365
	4,352,781	3,881,865

Consolidated profit and loss account for the year ended 31 December 1989

	(ii) Acquisition method		(i) Merger method	
	£	£	£	£
Profit before depreciation				
	568,310			
	437,070			
		1,005,380		1,005,380
Depreciation				
	91,290		91,290	
	75,000		40,035	
		(166,290)		(131,325)
		839,090		874,055
Goodwill amortised		(15,594)		N/A
		823,496		
Profit on sale of investments:				
Sale proceeds	278,715		Sale Proceeds 278,715	
Cost to group			Cost to group	
(FV)	(318,750)	(40,035)	(BV) (140,250)	138,465
Profit before tax		783,461		1,012,520
Taxation	119,255			
	149,940			
		(269,195)		(269,195)
		514,266		743,325

	Acquisition method	Merger method
P/l reserves b/fwd	include only POST ACQ of S	include [group's share] of merger sub's reserves b/fwd
Retained	1,008,780	
Current	(357,765)	

	Acquisition method	Merger method
Fruit plc	651,015	651,015
Vegetable Ltd	– all pre acq	447,525
	651,015	1,098,540
P/l reserves	1,165,281	1,841,865
Merger reserve	1,530,000	N/A
Consolidation difference [CR to reserves]	N/A	382,500 *Include under consolidated other reserves*
	2,695,281	2,224,365

b) The different bases for computing asset values and reserves:

▶ Under the acquisition method, fair values are assigned to the subsidiary's net assets at the acquisition date. This can result in additional depreciation and a loss, as happens in (a) above, on the eventual sale of investments. Goodwill arises on consolidation and this, under SSAP 22, must be eliminated either immediately against reserves or systematically against profits. Under the merger method, given that there is a pooling of interests, as opposed to an acquisition, there is no goodwill and assets are brought into the consolidation at their existing book values. As a result, it is likely that consolidated profits will be lower under the acquisition method and consolidated net assets lower under the merger method.

▶ The consolidated profit and loss account for the year of the business combination will include only the (group's share of) post-acquisition results of the subsidiary under the acquisition method but will include the (group's share of) results of the subsidiary for the full year under the merger method.

Consolidated profit will tend to be lower under the acquisition method (in all years) given additional depreciation arising on the fair values of the subsidiary's fixed assets and, possibly, amortisation of goodwill.

▶ Consolidated reserves under the acquisition method will include only the (group's share of) post-acquisition reserves of the subsidiary. Under the merger method the (group's share of) all the reserves (pre and post-acquisition) of the subsidiary are included in consolidated reserves.

▶ Where the consideration includes shares issued by the parent undertaking S.131 may apply to the premium on these shares issued. It is legal for the parent undertaking not to record such premium in either the cost of the subsidiary or reserves. Where this is necessary for the merger method to be legally used on consolidation, it creates the problem of understated consolidation goodwill under the acquisition method. It is for this reason that the appendix to SSAP 23 recommends that the parent undertaking actually records the cost of the subsidiary as the fair value of the consideration and takes the premiums on issue to a separate 'merger reserve' (as in (a) above).

▶ Where no goodwill arises under the merger method of consolidation, a **consolidation difference** will arise in comparing the cost of the subsidiary as recorded by the parent with the nominal value of the subsidiary's shares owned by the parent. If the former is greater than the latter, the difference must be debited to (available) consolidated reserves. If the former is less than the latter, the difference must be credited to consolidated reserves.

The conditions that must be satisfied for a business combination to be accounted for as a merger

There are four merger conditions in the Standard. If the business combination satisfies all four conditions, the group may use either merger accounting or acquisition accounting in accounting for the business combination. Should any of the conditions fail to be satisfied the group must account for the business combination as an acquisition.

The four merger conditions are detailed below.

Offer to shareholders

The business combination must result from an offer both to the holders of all equity shares that are not already held by the offeror and to the holders of all voting shares that are not already held by the offeror.

The first condition means that a group may use merger accounting only if the business combination arises from a single offer. The Standard states that the definition of a single offer includes a number of separate offers that constitute in substance a composite transaction – for example, a takeover bid where a few of the offeree's shareholders accept an initial offer and the remaining shareholders accept a subsequent improved offer. The two offers effectively form a single transaction.

Further, under this condition, the offeror may have prior holdings of shares in the offeree (see below).

Ninety per cent holding

As a result of the offer to shareholders, the offeror must secure a holding of at least 90% of each class of equity shares of the offeree and must secure at least 90% of the votes of the offeree. See Examples 19.1 and 19.2.

EXAMPLE 19.1

The offeree company has two classes of equity shares:

$$
\begin{array}{ll}
200,000 \; £1 & \text{A shares} \\
300 \; £1 & \text{B shares}
\end{array}
$$

If the offeror company secures all of the A shares but none of the B shares it will have secured over 90% of the total equity capital of the offeree. In order for the merger conditions to be satisfied this is not sufficient. The conditions require the offeror company to secure at least 90% of each class of equity share capital. Therefore, the offeror company must secure at least 180,000 of the A shares and 270 of the B shares if the combination is to be accounted for as a merger.

EXAMPLE 19.2

The offeree company has

1	200,000	£1	A equity shares
2	300	£1	B equity shares
3	60,000	£1	C preference shares (voting)

(Each share, ordinary and preference, has one vote.)

If the offeror company secures at least 180,000 of the A shares and 270 of the B shares it will have secured at least 90% of each class of equity share.

For the merger conditions to be fully satisfied, however, the offeror company must also secure at least 90% of the offeree's votes – $90\% \times (200,000 + 300 + 60,000) = 234,270$ shares.

Prior holdings

Immediately before the offer to shareholders, the offeror must not hold more that 20% of any class of equity shares of the offeree and must not hold shares carrying more than 20% of the votes of the offeree.

ED 31 restricted prior holdings to 10%. The SOI relaxed the requirement from 10% to 20%. The working party decided on a 20% limit because a higher holding in the offeree would, per SSAP 1, have usually been accounted for as an associated company. SSAP 1 would have required the investing group to have assigned fair values to the share of the associate's net assets in this instance. Fair value accounting is inconsistent with merger accounting and it is for this reason that a 20% limit on prior holdings was decided on as one of the merger conditions.

Cash limits

Of the fair value of the total consideration given by the offeror for the equity share capital of the offeree not less than 90% must be in the form of equity share capital of the offeror; thus, up to 10% may be in any other form. Also, not less than 90% of the fair value of the total consideration given for voting non-equity share capital must be in the form of equity and or voting non-equity share capital of the offeror.

In ED 31 there was a 10% limit on prior holdings and a 10% limit on cash. The SOI that followed ED 31 proposed a 20% limit on prior holdings and a 20% limit on cash. In the standard there is a 20% limit on prior holdings and a 10% limit on cash. The EC 7th Directive differs from the Standard in this regard. It states that the cash element of the consideration should not exceed 10% of the nominal value of the shares issued. Examples 19.3 and 19.4 deal with the fourth condition for a merger under SSAP 23. The further restrictions introduced into UK company law via the 7th Directive are dealt with later in this chapter.

EXAMPLE 19.3

The offeree company has 200 £1 equity shares.

The offeror company has a prior holding of 38 of these shares, the fair value of the consideration for this holding being £38, paid in cash.

The offeror company secures the remaining 162 shares of the offeree by means of a share-for-share exchange. The fair value of the consideration for these shares is £162.

Fair value of total consideration = (38 + 162) £200.

For the business combination to satisfy the merger conditions, not less than 90% (£180) must be in the form of equity shares of the offeror company.

For this combination to satisfy the fourth merger condition the cash element of the prior holding would have to be £20 or less.

EXAMPLE 19.4

The offeree company has 200 £1 equity shares. The offeror company secures 100% of the share capital of the offeree company. The consideration amounted to:

1 cash   £25
2 equity of offeror company   £75 nominal value
                                 £275 fair value

For the fourth condition to be satisfied, at least 90% of the fair value of the total consideration – 90% (25 + 275) = £270 must be in the form of equity shares of the offeror company. The fact that the equity share capital issued forms less than 90% of the total of the nominal value of the shares issued plus the cash element of the consideration is not relevant in considering merger conditions per SSAP 23. This fact would, however, be relevant under the merger conditions introduced in the CA 1989 and, applying these rules to this example, the merger method cannot be used on consolidation.

Some additional points
▶ *Convertible stock* For the purposes of the merger conditions any convertible stock at the time of the offer is, normally, not regarded as equity. The only exception to this rule is where the convertible stock is converted into equity as a result of, and at the time of, the business combination.
▶ *The offeror* References to the offeror in the merger conditions include not just the offeror itself but also:

(i)   a parent undertaking of the offeror
(ii) a subsidiary of the offeror
(iii) a fellow subsidiary of the offeror
(iv) a nominee or nominees of (i) to (iii).

The procedures involved in merger accounting

In merger accounting, the parent undertaking will normally value its investment in the subsidiary in its own separate accounts at: the nominal value of shares issued as consideration, plus, where relevant, the fair value of any additional consideration. On consolidation, this amount is cancelled against the nominal value of shares acquired in the subsidiary company. One of two situations can arise:

▶ Where the carrying value of the investment is *less than* the nominal value of shares acquired in the subsidiary, the group should treat the difference as a reserve that arises on consolidation. Do not confuse this reserve with the 'merger reserve', which arises, initially, in the parent undertakings' separate accounts.
▶ Where the carrying value of the investment is *greater than* the nominal value of the shares acquired, the group should reduce its reserves by the amount of the difference.

All other items in the separate balance sheets of the combining companies are simply added together, taking account of, if applicable, any remaining minority interest involved.

As to reserves against which consolidation differences arising on a merger should be adjusted, the Standard does not specify any particular consolidated reserve. It would be appropriate, in the absence of any guidance to the contrary, to treat such differences as follows:

▶ If the difference arises because the carrying value of the investment is less than the nominal value of the shares acquired, the difference should be treated as a reserve arising on consolidation and disclosed under consolidated 'other reserves' in the consolidated balance sheet.
▶ If the difference arises because the carrying value of the investment is greater than the nominal value of the shares acquired the Standard requires that the group should reduce its reserves by the amount of the difference. The two main reserves in consolidated accounts are normally the revaluation reserve and the profit and loss account. The group may reduce its profit and loss account reserve by the amount of the difference, but, for the same reasons as dealt with in Chapter 5 as to the write-off of goodwill, there may be legal restrictions on the extent to which the group can reduce its revaluation reserve, and such a reserve should not be used for the elimination of this difference arising on consolidation.

The merger relief provisions of the Companies Act 1985

As mentioned in the introduction, the Companies Act 1981 introduced merger relief provisions that modified the effect of Section 56 of the Companies Act 1948, which required a company that issues shares at a premium to credit the excess above nominal value to the share premium account.

The merger relief provisions now contained in the 1985 Act apply only to individual companies, not groups. SSAP 23, in contrast, applies only to accounting in group accounts and does not apply to the accounts of individual companies. Thus, there is a fundamental difference between merger relief in the 1985 Act and merger accounting in SSAP 23. There is, however, a considerable overlap between the two concepts in that a holding company might use merger accounting in its group accounts and also use the merger relief provisions in its own separate accounts. It is this overlap that explains why the standard refers in detail to the merger relief provisions of company law in an appendix.

Section 131 of the 1985 Act provides that, subject to certain conditions being satisfied, where an issuing company has secured at least a 90% equity holding in another company, Section 130 of the 1985 Act shall not apply to any premium on shares that the issuing company includes in the consideration that it gives. This relief applies only to the premium on the shares issued by a parent company in that transaction that takes its holding to at least 90%. Thus, if the parent company already owned 70% and acquires the further 30% of the equity of a subsidiary, merger relief provisions apply only to the second transaction involving the 30% purchase.

The detailed conditions that must be satisfied for an issuing company to utilise the merger relief provisions are:

► The issuing or offeror company must have secured a 90% equity holding in the offeree company in pursuance of an arrangement.
► The consideration that the offeror company receives for the shares that it issues must be provided either by the issue or the transfer to the offeror company of equity shares in the offeree company, or by the cancellation of any such shares that the offeror company does not hold.
► Where the equity share capital of the offeree company consists of different classes of shares, the issuing company must secure at least 90% of each class.

There are important differences between the SSAP 23 merger conditions and the conditions for merger relief in UK company law. The former are more restrictive than the latter. As a result:

► If a business combination satisfies the merger conditions of SSAP 23 it will be eligible for merger relief under company law.
► If a business combination satisfies the conditions for merger relief in company law it will not necessarily satisfy the merger conditions of SSAP 23.

Thus, there could be a situation where the company qualifies for merger relief but the group must use acquisition accounting on consolidation. In such a situation the law allows the company to record its investment in a subsidiary to include only the nominal value of shares issued as consideration but the Standard requires the group to use fair values on consolidation. See Examples 19.5 and 19.6.

EXAMPLE 19.5

To illustrate a situation where merger relief is available in the accounts of the company but acquisition accounting is used on consolidation:

H makes an offer for all the ordinary shares of S. Before the combination H has net tangible assets of £3,000 and share capital of £3,000. S has net tangible assets with a book and fair value of £450, share capital of £300 and a balance on profit and loss account of £150. The consideration for the offer comprises £210 in cash and ordinary shares of H with a nominal value of £360 and a fair value of £540.

Clearly, merger relief is available under company law but the combination does not satisfy all the conditions for a merger laid down in SSAP 23 and is to be accounted for in the group accounts, per the standard, as an acquisition.

The summarised balance sheets of H and S before the combination and the consolidated balance sheet (acquisition accounting) after the combination would be as follows:

	H £	S £	Consol. £
Goodwill	–	–	120
Investment in S	570	–	–
Other net tangible assets	2,790	450	3,240
	3,360	450	3,360
Ordinary share capital	3,360	300	3,360
Profit and loss account		150	–
	3,360	450	3,360

Notes:

1 Goodwill on consolidation is ascertained as follows:

	£
Consideration recorded	570
Fair value of separable net assets acquired	(450)
	120

2 H records its investment in S at £570 which is calculated in accordance with the merger relief sections of the Act as follows:

	£
Cash	210
Nominal value of shares issued	360
	570

3 The other net tangible assets of H comprise the £3,000 pre-combination less the payment of cash in part consideration for the shares of S of £210 = £2,790.

4 The above example shows what happens in acquisition accounting when H records, given merger relief, the investment to include only the nominal value of shares issued as consideration.

If H had recorded its investment in S in accordance with the treatment recommended in the SSAP 23 appendix, the investment would have been recorded at (210 + 540) £750, that is, the fair value of the consideration given by H. H in this situation would not record share premium of (540 – 360) £180 but would set up a 'merger reserve' instead. This merger reserve would also be included in the consolidated balance sheet.

EXAMPLE 19.6

Facts as in Example 19.5: H is eligible for merger relief and the group uses acquisition accounting on consolidation *but* H records its investment in S at the fair value of the consideration given.

	H £	S £	Consol. £
Goodwill	–	–	300
Investment in S	750	–	–
Other net tangible assets	2,790	450	3,240
	3,540	450	3,540
Ordinary share capital	3,360	300	3,360
Merger reserve	180	–	180
Profit and loss account	–	150	–
	3,540	450	3,540

In this example, as H is eligible for merger relief and records its investment at fair values and uses acquisition accounting on consolidation, the merger reserve arises both in H and in the consolidated accounts. This is the treatment that is recommended in the SSAP 23 appendix.

The group, in this example could deal with the consolidation goodwill by either writing it off partly against the merger reserve and partly against profit and loss account reserves, or carry the consolidation goodwill forward and amortise it over its useful life.

If merger relief is not available to H and the shares issued are issued at a premium then a share premium account must be recorded by H, as required by S.130 of the Act.

The disclosure required by the Standard

The disclosure requirements of the Standard apply to all material business combinations whether they are accounted for in the group accounts as acquisitions or mergers. The items required to be disclosed by the Standard should be disclosed in the notes to the accounts (not the directors' report).

All business combinations

The acquiring or issuing company should disclose, in the year of the business combination:

▶ The names of the combining companies.
▶ The number and the class of securities that the company issued in respect of the combination.
▶ Details of any other consideration that the company gave in respect of the combination.
▶ The accounting treatment that the company adopted for the business combination.
▶ The nature and the amount of any significant accounting adjustments that the combining companies make to achieve consistent accounting practice.

For acquisitions

The consolidated financial statements should contain sufficient information about the results of subsidiaries acquired by the group during the year, that is, enough information to enable shareholders to appreciate the effect that the results of such subsidiaries have on the consolidated results.

The disclosure requirements for acquisitions are satisfied by disclosing (see Chapter 18):

▶ The results of the new subsidiary broken down into pre-acquisition and post-acquisition.
▶ The effective date of acquisition.

For mergers

The issuing company should disclose in the year of the combination:

▶ The fair value of the consideration given by the issuing company – this is even though the parent undertaking may have recorded the investment to include only the nominal value of shares issued.
▶ The amount of the current year's (group) profit, broken down into that which relates to the period before the merger and that which relates to the period after the merger.

► An analysis of the profit of the current year up to the effective date of the merger between that of the issuing company and the subsidiary.

► An analysis of the attributable profit of the previous year between that of the issuing company and that of the subsidiary.

Vendor placing and vendor rights

A problem may arise in a business combination where the acquiring company wishes to account for the business combination as a merger but the shareholders of the acquired company wish to receive cash as consideration for their shares. For the parent undertaking to account for the combination as a merger the consideration paid must, in the main, be in the form of the parent undertaking's equity shares. To resolve the conflict, to allow the parent company to issue its own shares as consideration and to allow the acquired company's shareholders to receive cash for the sale of their shares, vendor placing and vendor rights schemes have been devised. These are dealt with below.

Vendor placing

1   There is a business combination.
2   The acquiring company (A) wishes to use merger accounting on consolidation and therefore must pay for the target company (T) by the issue of its own shares rather than by paying cash to the target company's shareholders.
3   The shareholders of the target company, however, prefer to receive cash for the sale of their shares rather than shares of the acquiring company.
4   (A) offers shares in (A) to the (T) shareholders in exchange for their shares in (T). The offer satisfies the merger conditions of SSAP 23.
5   (A) arranges for a merchant bank (M) to buy (T) shares for cash from those (T) shareholders that would rather have cash than shares in (A).
6   (M) now exchanges these (T) shares for shares in (A) in accordance with (A)'s offer to (T) shareholders.
7   On completion of the offer (A) owns the shares of (T); (M) owns shares in (A).
8   (M) now places these (A) shares in the market normally by selling them to institutions such as pension funds or insurance companies.
9   The end result is that cash is transferred from these institutions, via (M), to the shareholders of (T). The institutions now own the shares issued by (A), which now owns the shares in (T). (A) has issued shares rather than paying cash for the (T) shares and may therefore use merger accounting on consolidation.

The substance of a vendor placing is a cash takeover and it has been argued that (A) in such a situation should account for the business combination as an acquisition not as a merger. The use of merger accounting in vendor placings is prohibited in the USA. In the UK, however, the main criterion (under SSAP 23) for merger accounting is whether material resources leave one or other of the combining companies, that is, (A) and (T). This does not happen in the sequence of events above and the Standard therefore would seem to allow a group to use merger accounting to account for the business combination.

In a vendor placing, the new shares issued by (A) will result in a dilution in percentage holdings of the existing (A) shareholders prior to the business combination. To avoid such dilution, the company may choose to go in for a vendor rights scheme instead.

Vendor rights

1   (A) offers (A) shares to (T) shareholders in exchange for their shares in (T). The offer complies with the merger conditions of SSAP 23.
2   (A) arranges for (M) to buy (T) shares for cash from those (T) shareholders who do not wish to receive shares in (A).
3   (M) exchanges these (T) shares with (A) for (A) shares in accordance with the terms of the (A) offer to (T) shareholders.
4   (A) now owns (T); (M) owns shares in (A). So far a vendor rights is no different from a vendor placing.
5   (M) sells the (A) shares it now owns to other shareholders of (A) on a pro rata basis.

After a vendor rights, cash will have been transferred from the shareholders of (A), via (M), to some or all of the shareholders in (T). (A) the company has issued shares rather than paying cash for (T) and may therefore use the merger method on consolidation.

As with vendor placing, so with vendor rights a group is prohibited from using merger accounting in the USA. Given, however, that no material resources have left the two companies involved, it would seem that the UK Standard allows a group to use merger accounting in a vendor rights situation.

Note, however, that if the proposals of ED 48 (see below) become standard accounting practice, it will no longer be possible to use the merger method of consolidation in either a vendor placing or a vendor rights situation.

Pre-combination profits

In merger accounting, the pre-combination profits of the subsidiary are normally available for eventual distribution to the shareholders of the parent undertaking, that is, dividends paid by the subsidiary out of pre-combination profits are normally treated by the parent undertaking as a revenue receipt. However, in some circumstances, the pre-combination profits of the subsidiary may be frozen, that is, they are not available for eventual distribution to the shareholders of the parent undertaking. Paragraph 3 of the Appendix to SSAP 23 states that where the new subsidiary pays a dividend out of pre-combination profits the parent undertaking should apply the dividend to reduce the carrying value of the investment to the extent that it is necessary to provide for a diminution in that carrying value.

In acquisition accounting, the pre-combination profits of the subsidiary are normally frozen, thus, they are not normally available for eventual distribution to the shareholders of the parent undertaking. The parent undertaking normally treats any such dividends that it receives as a capital receipt and credits such dividends against the cost of the investment in the subsidiary. However, in some circumstances the subsidiary's pre-combination profits may be available for eventual distribution to the parent undertaking's shareholders. This is exlained further in Chapter 16, see Pro forma 16.1.

Paragraph 3 of the appendix to SSAP 23 has already been mentioned above and applies generally to acquisition accounting. Paragraph 4 of the appendix states that where merger relief is available under the Act, but the parent undertaking records the investment in the subsidiary at fair value, it may need to credit to the investment the dividends that the subsidiary pays from its pre-combination profits. The question does then arise as to whether the parent undertaking can legally regard as realised an equivalent amount of the merger reserve arising on the recording of fair values. No firm ruling is available on this question and a company that wishes to treat an equivalent amount of the merger reserve as realised should seek legal advice.

Following on from the appendix, it could be argued that in some circumstances, dividends received by the parent undertaking out of pre-combination profits of the subsidiary need not be frozen or capitalised. Specifically, this may happen when the subsidiary makes post-combination profits. In these circumstances, the parent undertaking might not need to provide for a diminution in the value of its investment. See Chapter 16 for numerical examples illustrating the treatment of dividends paid by subsidiaries out of pre-combination profits.

The reasons for reviewing the current SSAP 23

The following points suggested that a review of SSAP 23 could lead to improved accounting for business combinations.

No definitions
The original Standard does not explicitly define either a merger or an acquisition. A definition of a merger that clearly distinguishes it from an acquisition is important in deciding under what circumstances it will be appropriate to use merger accounting, and in understanding why merger accounting is required for those business combinations.

Options available under the current Standard
Even though the current Standard lays down conditions that must be met before merger accounting may be used, the Standard does not require the use of merger accounting for any business combination that does meet the merger conditions. It is in this respect that the Standard was criticised as having too much flexibility in allowing a choice of method in certain circumstances.

Circumvention of the merger conditions of the current Standard
SSAP 23 has been further criticised in that the conditions which have to be met to allow the use of merger accounting have been ineffective in limiting the use of merger accounting. Thus:

▶ Combining businesses could make arrangements to circumvent the conditions if they perceived some benefit to themselves in using the merger method for a combination that would have been more appropriately accounted for by the acquisition method.
▶ Particularly, the condition limiting prior holdings in an acquired company could be negated by arrangement with friendly institutions.
▶ Further, the condition that not less than 90% of the fair value of the consideration should be in equity shares can be avoided by an arrangement whereby cash is paid by a third party, instead of by the acquiring company. This could be achieved by using vendor placing and vendor rights issues.

The development of the revised Standard

The ASC has decided that the conditions under which the alternative methods are to be used should be amended.

This is in the light of criticisms of the original Standard, further consideration of the objectives of financial reporting and of how to provide users of accounts with the most useful financial information in any particular set of circumstances. SSAP 23 also requires revision in the light of the legal changes introduced into the amended 1985 Act by the Companies Act 1989.

Changes as to definitions

The distinction between acquisitions and mergers that was drawn in the original Standard depended on whether substantial resources had left the group. Under ED 48, the level of resources leaving the group is held to be unsuitable as the main determinant in deciding what method of accounting to use because:

▶ A share-for-share exchange is an application of resources, the resources being measured by the fair value of the shares issued.

▶ A more useful distinction between acquisitions and mergers can be developed by considering the objectives of financial reporting and the information that would be available to the users of financial statements under different definitions of acquisition and merger with respect to the alternative accounting treatments.

▶ The use of these definitions should ensure that merger accounting will provide more useful information for all those business combinations that fit the definition of a merger, and acquisition accounting will provide better information for all other combinations.

▶ ED 48 proposes that any business combination that fits the definition of a merger be not merely permitted but be required to use merger accounting. All other business combinations are acquisitions and would be required to use the acquisition method of accounting.

(Business combinations that are mergers as defined in the ED will be rare and most combinations will be acquisitions.)

Definitions of acquisition and merger

The shortcoming of a lack of adequate definitions under the original Standard is overcome in the ED. Thus:

▶ *An acquisition* in the context of business combinations is the use of resources by an enterprise to obtain ownership or control of another enterprise. It is a transaction that requires both an acquiror and an acquiree.

▶ *A merger* in the context of business combinations is the coming together of two or more enterprises for the mutual sharing of the risks and rewards of the combined enterprise where no party to the combination can be identified as an acquiror or acquiree. There must be a substantially equal partnership with the pre-combination entities sharing influence in the new economic unit. If a dominant or a subordinate partner can be identified then the combination will be an acquisition regardless of the form of the consideration.

Any combination that is not a merger is an acquisition.

The circumstances when merger accounting or acquisition accounting are to be used

The definitions given above provide the general rules of when each method should be used. In ED 48 the ASC proposes to support the general rules with some additional conditions. These conditions will help to further refine in practice the definition of a merger given in the ED by identifying those combinations where there are acquirors or acquirees.

In particular, a combination should be treated as an acquisition except where *all* the following apply:

▶ none of the parties sees itself as acquiror or acquiree
▶ none of the parties dominates the management of the combined entity
▶ the equity shareholders of none of the parties have, or could have, disposed of a material part of their shareholdings, directly or indirectly, for shares carrying significantly reduced rights or any other non-equity consideration

- no minority interests of more than 10% of the equity remain in any of the enterprises to which an offer is made
- none of the combining parties is more than 50% larger than any other entity that is a party to the combination unless special circumstances prevent the larger from dominating the other(s)
- the share of the equity in the combination allocated to one or more parties does not depend on the post-combination performance of any of the businesses previously controlled by that party or parties.

Emphasis is placed on the substance of the combination rather than the form by which it is achieved.

The disclosure provisions of the original Standard are expanded in the ED to take account of the 1989 Act.

The mechanics of the acquisition and merger methods for business combinations

ED 48 describes the mechanics of the alternative treatments for business combinations in terms that are consistent with those of the original Standard. These were dealt with earlier, but are looked at again here.

Acquisition accounting

- The results of the acquired company are brought into the group accounts only from the date of acquisition.
- The identifiable assets and liabilities acquired are included at fair value in the consolidated accounts and are, therefore, stated at cost to the group.
- The fair value of the consideration given is set against the aggregate fair value of the net identifiable assets acquired and any balance that results is goodwill. SSAP 22 (Revised) prescribes how any such balances should be treated.

Merger accounting

- The financial statements of the parties to the combination are aggregated and prescribed as though the combining companies had always been together. Accordingly, although the merger may have taken place part of the way through the period:
  - the full period's results of the combining companies are reflected in the group accounts for the period
  - corresponding amounts are presented on the same basis.
- The accounting policies of the combining enterprises are adjusted to achieve uniformity.
- Differences between, on the one hand, the nominal value of the shares issued together with the fair value of any other consideration, and, on the other hand, the aggregate of the nominal value of the shares (and share premium account) of the other parties to the business combination are not goodwill, do not result from a fair value exercise, and should be shown as an adjustment to the consolidated reserves.
- Merger expenses are not to be included as a part of this adjustment but should be charged through the profit and loss account in the period in which they are incurred (unless charged to the share premium account).

Why acquisition accounting is appropriate for an acquisition as defined

The normal accounting treatment in a historical cost accounting model is to record an asset acquired at the amount of the resources applied to acquire it. There is no reason to depart from the normal rules of asset acquisition when accounting for an acquisition.

In acquisition accounting the company acquired is therefore recorded at the fair value of its identifiable net assets plus goodwill. This will be equal to the fair value of the consideration given for those assets. The profits of the group are brought into account only from the date of the combination and the history of the group is seen as the history of the acquiror with occasional asset additions when it acquires other enterprises.

Therefore, where there is an identifiable acquiror, acquisition accounting provides useful information that shows fairly the substance of the transaction and is the method that should be used.

Why merger accounting is appropriate for a merger as defined

Where neither an acquiror nor an acquiree can be identified, a business combination is a merger as defined by ED 48.

In these circumstances merger accounting will provide information that is more relevant and shows fairly the substance of the transaction. If no acquiror can be identified, the acquiror's perspective, on which fair value and acquisition accounting are based, will cease to have any meaning; indeed the acquiror's perspective could be applied only if the form of the business combination were elevated above its substance (and this, post ED 42 and ED 49 and now FRED 4, would not do).

A merger is a true mutual sharing of the risks and rewards of the combined enterprise. Therefore, the joint history of the enterprises that have combined will be relevant to the combined group's shareholders. This record will be provided by merger accounting because it treats the separate businesses as though they were continuing as before only now jointly owned and managed.

If acquisition accounting were to be used, it would focus artificially on the history of only one of the parties to the combination, which would lead to the loss of relevant information about the combined enterprise.

Deciding whether a business combination is an acquisition or a merger

The definitions dealt with above give the general rules for determining whether a business combination is an acquisition or a merger. It is important to record combining businesses according to the substance rather than the form of the transaction.

The circumstances that surround the transaction may be of use in indicating the nature of a business combination. The following (not individually conclusive) would need to be considered:

- the form by which the combination was achieved
- the plans for the combined enterprise's future operations, for example, if closures related more to one party than to the other
- the proposed corporate image, for example, name, logo, location of headquarters and principal operations
- where a plc is a party to a business combination the extent of communications with its shareholders is also likely to be relevant in determining the substance of the transaction.

Detailed conditions for a merger

The general rules that define acquisition and merger dealt with above are supported in ED 48 by detailed conditions, each of which must be met before a business combination can be accounted for as a merger. These conditions will help to refine further in practice the definition of a merger, and therefore an acquisition, by identifying those combinations in which there is an acquiror and an acquiree. Note, again, that the vast majority of business combinations will be acquisitions and only in rare circumstances will a combination fulfil all the detailed conditions to be treated as a merger.

The ED 48 conditions for business combinations

The detailed conditions, which, if all are met by a business combination, lead to merger accounting being required, are set out below:

▶ None of the parties sees itself as acquiror or acquiree.

▶ None of the parties dominates the management of the combined entity.

> In deciding whether one party to the combination dominates the management of the combined entity, both formal and informal management structures need to be considered. Thus the membership of the board and the identity of the chairman or managing director will be relevant, but so will the identity of any person or group who makes the key decisions or is involved in actively running the combined company.

▶ The equity shareholders of none of the parties have, or could have, disposed of any material part of their shareholdings, directly or indirectly, for shares carrying significantly reduced rights in the combined enterprise or any other non-equity consideration.

> Shares carry rights to votes and also to distributions. If any of these individual rights were significantly reduced or circumscribed the combination would fail to fulfil this condition.

> In deciding what part of a shareholding is material the figures should be considered in the context of the group rather than of the individual company.

> One form of non-equity consideration to which this condition relates is cash. The shareholders of any party will be considered to have been able to dispose of their shareholding for cash where any arrangement has been made in connection with the combination that enables shareholders to expect that any shares they receive in the combination or related arrangements may be exchanged or redeemed for cash other than by their individual market transactions that are not connected with the combination. Any assets distributed as part of the consideration count as an indirect form of payment in cash.

> If an enterprise has acquired an interest in any other enterprise in exchange for shares with significantly reduced rights or any other non-equity consideration within the two years prior to those enterprises combining, such shares or consideration should be taken as part of the consideration given to achieve the combination. It is, therefore, to be considered in deciding whether the form of the consideration for achieving that combination breaches the detailed conditions for merger accounting.

▶ No minority interests of more than 10% of the equity remain in any of the enterprises to which an offer is made.

▶ None of the combining parties is more than 50% larger than any other enterprise that is a party to the combination unless special circumstances prevent the larger from dominating the other(s).

> If any enterprise is more than 50% larger than any other enterprise in the combination then it will be presumed to dominate that other enterprise. The relative sizes of the enterprises that are party to a business combination should be judged by reference to the ownership interests, that is, by considering the proportion of the equity share capital they own or control in the combined enterprise. In certain circumstances voting and share agreements, blocking powers or other arrangements might mean that a party to the combination has more or less influence than can be construed from its relative size. These circumstances might rebut the presumption of dominant influence because of disparate sizes but the circumstances should be fully disclosed and explained.

▶ The share of the equity in the combination allocated to one or more parties does not depend on the post-combination performance of any businesses previously controlled by that party or parties.

Notes on the detailed conditions

The first condition relates to the perceptions of the enterprises that are party to the business combination. Where a party to a business combination believes it is being acquired, or believes it is acquiring the other, this precludes that combination being a mutual sharing in the risks and rewards of the combined enterprise.

The second condition concerns management dominance; it is impossible to have a substantially equal partnership in the new economic entity if the management of one party to the combination clearly dominates the others. Both formal and informal management structures should be considered. It will be necessary to look at the composition of management committees and of the board with regard to the proportionate shareholdings of the pre-combination enterprises. It will also be necessary to consider who is to be chair, who will make key decisions and how the combined enterprise is run.

The third condition precludes a business combination from being accounted for as a merger if the acquiror company offers the shareholders in the other parties shares with substantially reduced rights. The condition limiting the non-equity consideration that can be received, directly or indirectly, accords with the new rules introduced by the 1989 Act. In this Act, merger accounting is precluded in any combination where the non-equity consideration exceeds 10% of the *nominal value* of the shares issued. Under the proposed Standard, the limit stems from the concept of a merger as the mutual sharing of risks and rewards. Shareholders who receive non-equity consideration limit their continued interests in the combined enterprise.

The fourth condition limiting the size of any minority interest is also a requirement of the 1989 Act. Where a material minority remains the combination is not a mutual sharing by the shareholders of the pre-combination enterprises of the post-combination risks and rewards.

The fifth condition as to size follows from the fact that where one party in a business combination is substantially larger than the other parties it will be presumed that the larger party will or can dominate the combined undertakings. The effect of this limit is that the dominance of one party is presumed if it controls more than 60% of the equity in the combined enterprise.

The sixth condition is one that prevents a business combination being treated as a merger if the share of the equity in the combined undertaking allocated to a party depends on the post-combination performance of any of the businesses previously controlled by that party. This would preclude the use of 'earn-outs' or similar performance-related schemes in the arrangements to effect a merger. Consideration that is conditional in this way is inconsistent with the concept of a merger as the mutual sharing of the risks and rewards of the combined business.

Disclosure

Acquisitions and mergers

The following information should be disclosed in respect of all material business combinations, whether accounted for as acquisitions or mergers, in the financial statements of the acquiring or issuing enterprise that deal with the year in which the combination takes place:

▶ the names of the combining enterprises
▶ the number and class of the securities issued in respect of the combination, and details of any other consideration given

- the accounting treatment adopted for the business combination (that is, whether it has been accounted for as an acquisition or as a merger)
- the nature and amount of significant accounting adjustments by the combining enterprises to achieve consistency of accounting policies.

Acquisitions

The following disclosures should be made separately for each material acquisition and in aggregate for other acquisitions where these are material in total although not so individually. These disclosures do not relate to mergers.

The fair value of the consideration for each material acquisition during the period should be separately disclosed.

A table should be provided showing the initial book values and the fair values of each major category of asset and liability acquired in respect of each acquisition disclosed. The differences between these initial values and the fair values should be given for each major category of assets and liability together with an explanation of the reasons for these differences. Adjustments made as provisions for reorganisation costs should be identified. See also Chapter 20 on fair values in acqusition accounting as to the current thinking on the treatment of such provisions.

Movements on provisions related to acquisitions should be disclosed and analysed between amounts used, amounts released unused and amounts applied for another purpose. Sufficient details should be given to identify the extent to which the provisions have proved unnecessary. Where the fair value of the assets and liabilities, or the consideration, can be determined only on a provisional basis at the end of the accounting period in which the acquisition took place, this should be stated and the reasons given. Where there are subsequent material adjustments to such provisional fair value those adjustments should be disclosed and explained in the financial statements of the period concerned.

The date from which the results of material acquisitions in the period have been brought into the accounts should be disclosed.

Sufficient information should be given for each material acquisition in the period about the results of the subsidiaries acquired to enable shareholders to appreciate the effect of the acquisition on the consolidated accounts.

Mergers

In respect of each merger, the following information should be disclosed in the financial statements of the group for the period in which the merger takes place:

- the fair value and the composition of the consideration given by the issuing company
- an analysis of the current period's attributable results between those arising before and those arising after the effective date of the merger
- an analysis of the turnover and attributable results of the current period up to the effective date of the merger and of the previous period among that of the various parties to the merger
- the amount of net assets contributed by each enterprise and an explanation of any significant adjustments made to the net assets of any party to the merger as a consequence of the merger, with a statement of any resulting adjustments to consolidated reserves.

Concluding analysis

The original Standard on acquisitions and mergers, SSAP 23 was published in 1985 and began to attract criticism immediately. One of the aspects of the Standard most strongly criticised was that the conditions to be satisfied for the use of the merger method of accounting were too liberal with the result that the merger method was used for business combinations that were, in substance, acquisitions of one company by another. Notably, there was no size test, so that a large plc could bid for a small private company and, as long as the consideration was in shares, the chances were that merger accounting could be used. Critics also felt that the merger method should not be optional but should be mandatory for all business combinations that met the criteria laid down.

If these were easy criticisms to make, it should be remembered that when SSAP 23 was developed there were many ways to define a merger. ASC decided to base a merger on situations where material resources did not leave the group and decided not to make the merger method mandatory as, at the time, it was a relatively novel method in the UK. Certainly, recent experience has shown that the Standard introduced too much choice into accounting for business combinations where there should have been a single unequivocal rule. The ASC subsequently took the view that there was a clear need to tighten up the rules.

To summarise, briefly:

▶ merger accounting should be used for business combinations where no acquiror or acquiree can be identified
▶ the proposed standard is not intended to restrict the accounting treatment adopted for the internal restructuring of a group
▶ expenses of a merger should be charged to the profit and loss account unless they are taken to the share premium account.

The ED supplements the definition of a merger with six 'detailed conditions' the effect of which is to identify whether or not any features are present that would show that one party is an acquiror. If they are, then merger accounting would be ruled out. The ED stresses that it is important to record combining businesses according to the substance rather than the form of the transaction.

The methodology of merger accounting and of acquisition accounting does not change under ED 48. The application of the proposed Standard also does not change; it continues to apply to consolidated accounts leaving the accounting in the parent company to be determined by the framework of company law.

So, for example, a business combination might, under ED 48, need to be accounted for as an acquisition in the consolidated accounts, but company law might allow merger relief to the holding company. There is nothing inconsistent with this, although an important detailed point arises. There are two forms of merger relief in company law. Both provide that the premium need not be credited to the share premium account. Version one says that the premium can be disregarded altogether – so a company that uses this form would record the shares it issues and the investment acquired at the nominal value of the shares it issues. Version two says that the premium is recognised but credited to another reserve (usually called a 'merger reserve') instead of to the share premium account. Version one has normally been associated with merger accounting on consolidation and version two with acquisition accounting. However, some companies in recent years have adopted version one with acquisition accounting on consolidation, and this has come to be accepted. The effect has been that the cost of investment and the goodwill figure have been understated, although this has tended to have little effect when goodwill is written off to reserves. It now appears that as a result of the more prescriptive rules in the Companies Act 1989 it may no longer be possible to combine version one with acquisition investment and the full goodwill premium, would now require amortisation under ED 47.

This has been the topic of several examination questions and almost the whole point of question 1 in the Level 3 AFA paper in June 1990. No doubt, as the issue remains relevant, it will continue to feature in the examination.

Summary

▶ As long ago as the time of the issue of ED 3 it was recognised that acquisition accounting was not the appropriate response to a business combination which was, effectively, a pooling of interests. This chapter deals with the circumstances in which the merger method may be used and the main differences arising when compared to the use of the acquisition method of consolidation.

▶ The application of S.130 and S.131 of the Act is covered and the problem of merger relief applying to the parent undertaking where the acquisition method is used on consolidation is dealt with in detail.

▶ The chapter also deals with the introduction of new definitions as to acquisitions and mergers introduced into UK company law by the Companies Act 1989, the reasons for the proposed revision of SSAP 23 and the ED 48 proposals in this regard.

▶ Chapters 15 to 18 dealt in the main with acquisition accounting. This chapter deals mainly with merger accounting. The next chapter makes it clear that where there were initial problems as to the use of merger accounting the current focus is very much on the creative use that can be made of acquisition accounting. You need to consider the contents of this chapter together with the contents of the next chapter in assessing the relative merits or otherwise of using the one or the other method of accounting for business combinations.

Suggested reading

Accountants Digest No. 189 (ICAEW 1986)
and
UK GAAP (Ernst & Young 1990)
Chapter 4 is particularly relevant to the material covered in this chapter.

Manual of Accounting – Groups (Coopers & Lybrand Deloitte 1990)

Self test questions

1   Outline six areas of difference between the acquisition and merger methods of consolidation

2   Draw a diagram to indicate what happens in a vendor placing.

3   Summarise the six ED 48 conditions for a merger.

4   Hafiz plc acquires 95% of the voting equity of Salman Ltd for cash of £500, Hafiz plc 9% loan stock of £1,000, Hafiz plc £1 ordinary shares with a nominal value of £20,000 and premium on issue of £15,000. On the basis that Hafiz plc will incorporate Salman Ltd into its consolidated accounts using the merger method, record the purchase of shares in Salman Ltd in the separate accounts of Hafiz plc.

5   Facts are as in question 4 but, under SSAP 23, Hafiz plc decides to use the acquisition method to include Salman Ltd into its consolidated accounts.

   (a) Record the purchase of shares in Salman Ltd in the separate accounts of Hafiz plc taking advantage of S.131.
   (b) Identify the problem arising on consolidation.
   (c) Record the purchase of shares in Salman Ltd in the separate accounts of Hafiz plc following the guidance provided in the appendix to SSAP 23.

Exam style questions

1   *Macbeth plc and Duncan plc*

Macbeth plc, a grain wholesaler, has regularly supplied 20% of its sales volume to Duncan plc, a milling company. In 1980 there was a threat by a competitor to take over Duncan plc and, as a result of that, Macbeth plc had acquired a shareholding of 120,000 ordinary shares in Duncan plc, which it viewed as a long-term defensive measure. The threat was unsuccessful in 1980 but the directors of Macbeth plc have been aware of the recurring rumours of another takeover bid.

The directors of Duncan plc have been under a constant pressure, which they consider has made them too concerned with short-term results rather than being able to freely plan for the long-term development of their company. They have therefore approached Macbeth plc to enquire whether the company is interested in seeking to obtain a majority interest in Duncan plc.

The draft balance sheets of the two companies as at 31 December 1988 are set out below:

	Macbeth plc £000	Duncan plc £000
Fixed assets	2,624	1,792
Investment in Duncan plc	132	
Net current assets	1,056	864
	3,812	2,656
Ordinary share capital in shares of £1 each	2,560	1,920
Share premium account	12	
Profit and loss account	1,240	736
	3,812	2,656

You may assume that the assets and liabilities of Duncan plc are at fair values.

The draft profit and loss accounts indicated that the after-tax profit for 1988 for Macbeth plc would be £512,000 and for Duncan plc would be £320,000 and forecasts indicate that both companies will maintain these profit figures in 1989 and 1990.

The directors of Duncan plc have suggested two possible courses of action:

▶ for Macbeth plc to increase its holding to 480,000 ordinary shares by acquiring shares in the market and from institutional investors who were known to be in favour of the proposal on 1 January 1989, and then launch a bid for the balance of the shares on 1 January 1990.

The competitor currently holds 192,000 ordinary shares in Duncan plc and it is felt that even with a bid from Macbeth plc it would probably retain this holding.

▶ to attempt to acquire all shares other than those held by the competitor by making a bid on 1 January 1989.

The directors of Macbeth plc have been discussing these alternatives with the company's brokers who have given the following advice:

With regard to the proposal for Macbeth plc to increase the holding to 480,000 ordinary shares on 1 January 1989:

▶ They felt that it should be possible to acquire the additional 360,000 ordinary shares in the market on 1 January 1989.

With regard to making a bid for control on 1 January 1989:

▶ They thought that it would not be possible to acquire sufficient shares to gain control unless there was a combined cash option and share exchange offer.
▶ They stated that, as they understood that Macbeth plc did not have sufficient liquid resources within the company to finance a cash bid, they had identified certain financial institutions that were prepared to buy for cash any shares issued by Macbeth plc to the Duncan plc shareholders as consideration for the acquisition.
▶ They thought that the price/earnings ratios for the £1 ordinary shares in Macbeth plc, which was 10:1, and for the £1 ordinary shares in Duncan plc, which was 9:1, would continue at these levels.

The directors of Macbeth plc now wish to consider the likely impact on the annual financial accounts of the two alternatives and have requested the accountant to consider this aspect.

▶ *Alternative 1* Macbeth should acquire, for cash, ordinary shares to bring their holding up to 480,000 shares on 1 January 1989 at the current market price. The cash is to be raised by a rights issue at market value less a discount of 10%.

It should then issue sufficient ordinary shares at market value on 1 January 1990 to acquire sufficient additional shares to bring its total holding up to 1,728,000 shares. Of these, 750,000 shares would be covered by the agreement with the financial institutions whereby they would purchase the Macbeth plc shares from the Duncan plc shareholders.

▶ *Alternative 2* Macbeth should acquire sufficient ordinary shares on 1 January 1989 to bring its total holding up to 1,728,000 shares by issuing new shares in Macbeth.

Of these, 1,000,000 shares would have been covered by the agreement with the financial institutions, whereby they would purchase the Macbeth plc shares from the Duncan plc shareholders.

Required:
a) Assuming that Macbeth plc has chosen alternative 1:

(i) Prepare the balance sheet entries for Macbeth plc as at 31 December 1989 and 1990 applying the provisions of the Companies Act 1985 for:

▶ Investment in Duncan plc
▶ Share capital
▶ Share premium account.

(10 marks)

(ii) Explain how the balance sheet entries in (i) above would differ if the provisions of SSAP 23 were applied.

(5 marks)

b) Assuming that Macbeth plc has chosen alternative 1:

Explain whether it may use merger accounting to prepare accounts as at 31 December 1990.

(5 marks)

c) Assuming that Macbeth plc has chosen alternative 2:

Prepare the consolidated balance sheet for Macbeth plc and its subsidiary as at 31 December 1990 on the assumption that neither company declared a dividend in either 1989 or 1990.

(10 marks)

(30 marks)

ACCA Level 3 AFA exam question, June 1990

2   *Firebrand Ltd*

Firebrand Ltd, whose financial year end is 31 October, acquired, on 31 July 1989, 95% of Felix Ltd. Summary balance sheets as on 31 October 1989 for Firebrand Ltd and Felix Ltd are as follows:

	As on 31 October 1989	
	Firebrand Ltd before consolidation	Felix Ltd
	£000	£000
Fixed assets (all tangible)	2,150	625
Investment in Felix Ltd	950	–
Net current assets (Felix Ltd at fair value)	1,900	50
Long-term liabilities	(400)	–
	4,600	675
Share capital	1,000	200
Share premium account	500	–
Revaluation reserve	1,300	–
Profit and loss account	1,800	475
	4,600	675

The summary balance sheet for Felix Ltd as on 31 July 1989 was as follows:

	£000
Fixed assets (all tangible)	650
Net current assets (at fair value)	150
	800
Share capital	200
Profit and loss account	600
	800

In the three months to 31 October 1989, Felix Ltd made a profit of £25,000 and paid £150,000 in dividends to shareholders on the register as on 30 September 1989. Firebrand Ltd has credited its dividend received to a suspense account in current liabilities.

Firebrand Ltd made a first payment for the shares in Felix Ltd of £950,000 on 31 July 1989; the final price will depend on Felix Ltd's profits for the year to 31 July 1990. The maximum additional payment is £95,000 and present indications are that Felix Ltd will easily exceed its profit target.

Firebrand Ltd and Felix Ltd are in similar lines of business and both have built up valuable brands. Professional valuers have indicated that the current values are some £150,000 for Firebrand Ltd's brand names and some £50,000 for Felix Ltd's brand names. Also, professional valuations of the two companies' properties have disclosed a deficit compared with book value for Firebrand Ltd of

£50,000 as on 31 October 1989 and a surplus compared with book value for Felix Ltd of £120,000 as on 31 July 1989.

(Felix Ltd depreciates its properties at 2% per annum, straight line.)

The chairman of Firebrand Ltd has always felt it to be imprudent to carry intangible assets in the balance sheet and is intending to continue this policy following the acquisition of Felix Ltd. However, the new financial director of Firebrand Ltd is not necessarily of the same view.

Required:

a) Prepare a memorandum for the financial director of Firebrand Ltd, which he can present to the chairman, including:

(i) the summary consolidated balance sheet for Firebrand Ltd as on 31 October 1989 adopting the chairman's preferred accounting policy with regard to intangible assets

(ii) a brief description of the method of accounting for goodwill adopted in drawing up this consolidated balance sheet and its effects on realised profits

(iii) a brief explanation of the possible changes in accounting policies or treatment available to Firebrand Ltd.

State any assumptions you make.

(12 marks)

b) Indicate the further options that would be open to Firebrand Ltd in accounting for the acquisition of Felix Ltd, both in its own accounts and in the consolidated accounts, had the purchase consideration been wholly in ordinary shares, being 10p shares issued at £1 each.

State any assumptions you make.

(8 marks)
(20 marks)

Note: Ignore taxation

Based on ICAEW PE II exam question, December 1989

All answers on pages 677–681.

Consolidated Accounts 6 – Mergers, Acquisitions and Goodwill Continued

The practice of acquisition accounting has been dealt with in Chapters 16 to 18 and that of merger accounting in Chapter 19. Earlier chapters, Chapter 4 and Chapter 5, looked at the revaluation problem, goodwill and the problems arising in assigning fair values to the net assets of a subsidiary on the date of its acquisition. These chapters dealt with relevant aspects of UK company law and the thinking of the ASC in the context of mergers, acquisitions and goodwill. You should be aware of the background to the requirements of and the problems arising from SSAPs 22 and 23 and EDs 47, 48 and 53.

This chapter looks further at the issues dealt with in the chapters referred to above and also introduces the ASB's 1993 proposals on fair values in acquisition accounting and acquisitions and mergers. Current (as of June 1993) proposals on the former are now dealt with in an ASB Discussion Paper and proposals on the latter are now dealt with in FRED 6. These proposals of the ASB are part of a three-pronged attack to curb what are widely perceived to be abuses of acquisition and merger accounting. A third paper on goodwill has a publication date in late 1993.

Chapter 5 dealt with some of the problems arising from the application of the requirements of SSAP 22 on goodwill, including these five:

1   optional treatments and the resulting loss of comparability as to consolidated net assets and earnings arising
2   the treatment of goodwill when sold
3   the advantage that can be taken by a parent undertaking of merger relief when acquisition accounting is used on consolidation
4   the impact of 'provisioning' in a new subsidiary and the treatment of such provisions as charges against the subsidiary's pre-acquisition reserves
5   the treatment of deferred consideration.

The first problem was addressed by ED 47, which proposed that systematic amortisation be the only treatment for positive purchased goodwill. Prior to the issue of a paper on goodwill, the ASB is researching whether it is possible to prove that a goodwill investment maintains its value. How best or most appropriately to treat goodwill remains an outstanding topic on the agenda of the ASB.

The second problem was addressed in UITF Abstract 3 and is now resolved, re sold subsidiaries, in FRS 2 – see Chapter 18 regarding changes in the composition of a group.

Problem 3, that of merger relief used in conjunction with acquisition accounting, is partly resolved in that the Companies Act, as amended, requires disclosure of the accounting treatment adopted in the consolidated accounts. The ideal solution remains that recommended in the SSAP 23 appendix, which was outlined in Chapter 19. This would involve the parent undertaking in recording the cost of the subsidiary at the fair value of the consideration with any premium on the parent's shares issued as consideration taken, where it cannot be taken to share premium account, to a separate merger reserve.

The fourth problem is dealt with in detail in the Discussion Paper on fair values in acquisition accounting referred to above. The paper puts forward new proposals on the treatment of reorganisation and integration costs on the acquisition of a subsidiary and these are dealt with below. The essence of the new proposals is that *all* costs of reorganising acquired businesses should be charged against the post-acquisition profits of the subsidiary.

The last problem, the treatment of deferred consideration, was addressed in ED 53 and is expanded on in the fair value Discussion Paper.

Chapter 19 dealt with some of the problems arising from the application of the requirements of SSAP 23. David Tweedie, ASB chairman, has been reported (*Accountancy*, July 1993, p. 10) as calling the abuses of acquisition and merger accounting: 'the worst scam in UK accounting. If you want instant profits, merger accounting is for you.' If merger accounting is currently infrequently resorted to in the UK, there is some concern that it may be resorted to more frequently following the blocking of the main advantages of using acquisition accounting by the fair value Discussion Paper. FRED 6, however, now restricts the use of merger accounting to the very small number of cases that meet its strict definition of a merger, and there is also the view that merger accounting be prohibited altogether.

This chapter deals with the current ASB proposals on acquisitions and mergers. There will, of course, be changes as further FREDs and, finally, FRSs are issued on the subject. During 1994 ASB has issued FRED 7 on Fair values in Acquisition Accounting and a Discussion Paper on Goodwill and Intangible Assets. These are dealt with at the end of this chapter.

The Discussion Paper on fair values in acquisition accounting (and changes from ED 53)

When subsidiaries are first acquired, it is necessary that the parent measures the cost of what it is accounting for, that is:

▶ the cost of the investment in its own balance sheet
▶ the amount to be allocated between the separable or identifiable net assets of the subsidiary on the one hand and goodwill on the other hand for the purpose of the consolidated accounts.

The Discussion Paper is not principally concerned with the recording of the cost of the investment by the parent. SSAP 23 and the Act require this to be based on the fair value of the consideration, but they do not inform us as to how this is to be determined. ED 53 stated that the fair value of any parent securities issued as consideration should be based on the market price (or valuation, if not listed) of the security on the date the bid becomes unconditional.

The impact of merger relief has been dealt with above. This and other problems dealing with the fair value of the consideration paid will be dealt with in a future FRED. Here, as to consideration paid, we will look only at problems arising from deferred and contingent consideration. This section of the chapter is concerned mainly with assigning fair values to the net assets of subsidiaries on the date of acquisition and the treatment of reorganisation and integration costs.

It is this last area that has caused considerable controversy. Consider the following scenario. There is a business combination in the accounting period. The business combination is a (true) merger. SSAP 23 permits, as opposed to requires, the use of the merger method on consolidation. As with most business combinations, substantial costs are envisaged to be incurred for reorganisation and integration of the new subsidiary into the group. In merger accounting remember that we do not distinguish between pre-merger and post-merger reserves and that the results of the subsidiary for the whole of the year of combination will be included in the consolidated profit and loss account. Accordingly, provisions for reorganisation and integration costs, set up in the subsidiary, will pass through the consolidated profit and loss account. One way to avoid this (material) charge is to take advantage of the major shortcoming of SSAP 23 by opting to use the acquisition method of consolidation even though all the conditions for a merger are fully satisfied. In acquisition accounting remember that we do distinguish between pre-acquisition and post-acquisition reserves. Thus, only post-acquisition results of the acquired subsidiary pass through the consolidated profit and loss account. The issue of whether provisions for reorganisation and integration costs should be charged to either pre-acquisition or post-acquisition results of the acquired subsidiary now becomes crucial. Until recently it has been accepted practice for such provisions to be treated as pre-acquisition (and, therefore, a part of the fair value exercise in respect of the subsidiary's net assets at its acquisition date). Adopting this treatment results in such provisions reducing the fair value of the net assets of the subsidiary at acquisition date and increasing consolidation goodwill. The provisions will pass through consolidated profit and loss account only if goodwill is being systematically amortised, and, then, when amortised. The Discussion Paper seeks to outlaw this treatment in proposing that all such provisions be treated as charges against the post-acquisition reserves of the new subsidiary. It is useful in this context to note the proposals of FRED 6 on acquisitions and mergers. If the criteria for a merger are satisfied the merger method of consolidation must be used. This chapter is concerned with the issues arising from such a scenario. In being concerned with fair values, we are also concerned with revaluations, and we will be making reference in this chapter to the following additional ASB statements:

▶ Discussion Draft of Chapter 3 of the *Statements of Principles* – the elements of financial statements (see Chapter 1)
▶ Discussion Draft of Chapter 5 of the *Statement of Principles* – measurement in financial statements (see Chapter 1)
▶ Discussion Paper – the role of valuation in financial reporting (see Chapter 30).

The treatment of reorganisation costs

The Discussion Paper focuses on the exercise of identifying assets and liabilities and allocating fair values when a parent initially consolidates the net assets of a subsidiary into its consolidated balance sheet.

Assigning fair values to a subsidiary's net assets at its acquisition date has the following effects:

▶ it determines the values to be recognised from the assets and liabilities of the new subsidiary in the consolidated balance sheet, and
▶ it determines the amount to be recognised as consolidation goodwill.

Adopting what the Discussion Paper refers to as an 'acquirer's perspective' has led to the practice of liabilities recognised on acquisitions, including provisions for items taken into account by the parent in making its investment decision, such as reorganisation costs to be incurred after acquisition and even provisions for anticipated losses. The effect is to:

▶ *either* bypass the consolidated profit and loss account (if goodwill is written off immediately to reserves)
▶ *or* delay recognition in the consolidated profit and loss account over several periods (where there is systematic amortisation of goodwill).

This is because, as a result of treating such provisions as pre-acquisition, the debit for the provisions results in an increased debit for goodwill as opposed to a direct debit to the consolidated profit and loss account.

Arguments for treating reorganisation provisions as pre-acquisition or part of the fair value exercise on the acquisition of a subsidiary

The arguments are:

▶ The cost of the reorganisation is a part of the cost of the investment in the acquired business; it should not reduce post-acquisition results.

▶ Adopting an acquirer's perspective, decisions on the reorganisation of resources in the new economic grouping created by the acquisition should be reflected in the values assigned to the net assets acquired.

▶ Poorly managed businesses will cost less than efficient ones and the difference in cost should equate to the reorganisation costs necessary to make the (acquired) inefficient business more efficient.

▶ Concerns about potential abuses – for example, the release of provisions no longer considered necessary in subsequent periods in order to boost the earnings of such periods – can be dealt with through increased disclosure requirements.

Arguments against treating reorganisation provisions as part of the fair value exercise on the acquisition of a subsidiary

These are the arguments that influenced the ASB in arriving at its conclusions regarding the treatment of reorganisation costs as explained later in this chapter:

▶ Reorganisation is part of everyday management and not specific to a new acquisition, and it detracts from reporting financial performance if such costs are excluded from the consolidated profit and loss account.

▶ The results of post-acquisition periods will include the benefits of reorganisation and it is inappropriate to exclude the costs of the reorganisation from these results.

▶ Financial statements are focused on discrete periods in that they report performance for a particular period and position at a particular date and, therefore, post-acquisition expenditure on reorganisation of an acquired business should be treated as revenue or capital as normal.

▶ It is not appropriate to increase goodwill (by treating reorganisation provisions as pre-acquisition) in respect of a poorly performing business in need of reorganisation by providing at acquisition for expenses that do not relate to the obligations existing at the acquisition date.

▶ Reorganisation following an acquisition may be necessary in the acquirer's own business (for example, the closure of facilities that may now be duplicated in the acquired business) and such costs must pass through the consolidated profit and loss account; on this basis, costs of reorganisation arising in a new subsidiary should be dealt with in the same way.

▶ Over-generous provisioning, if treated as pre-acquisition, will result in increased distortion of post-acquisition results.

▶ Costs of reorganising businesses where there is no acquisition involved must be charged against profit and there is no good reason to create a bias in favour of acquiring businesses by permitting the acquirer scope for creating provisions and writing down asset values at acquisition and taking the benefit of the release of the provisions and the sale of reduced value assets in periods after acquisition.

The proposals of the Discussion Paper for reorganisation costs

Provisions for reorganisation costs (and provisions for future losses) following an acquisition should not be allowed as fair value adjustments at the acquisition date and should be dealt with through the profit and loss account. These proposals are intended to:

▶ better assist users in assessing trends in operating performance of both continuing and acquired operations from the date the new acquisition becomes a part of the

group
▶ assist users to better assess the effects of reorganisation of the group after the acquisition of a subsidiary
▶ reduce inconsistencies and reduce the areas of subjectivity in accounting for acquisitions.

The proposed framework for acquisition accounting

The Discussion Paper distinguishes between recording the elements of a purchase transaction and reporting post-acquisition performance. Accounting for an acquisition should therefore be looked at in two stages. The first stage is to determine the cost of the assets, liabilities and goodwill acquired – the fair value exercise. The second stage is to record the impact of the implementation of the purchaser's intentions as to the post-acquisition reorganisation and integration of the acquired business.

The first stage

The principles that apply in carrying out the fair value exercise are as follows.

Value to the business

The principle to be adopted for attributing fair values to the assets and liabilities of an acquired business is that of the value to the business. This is described in the ASB's Discussion Draft of Chapter 5 of the *Statement of Principles*, 'Measurement in financial statements'. The main points arising are as follows:

▶ The basic value to the business rule is to use replacement cost or recoverable amount, whichever is the lower.
▶ If the asset is worth replacing, use replacement cost.
▶ If it is not worth replacing but is worth keeping, use value in use (this is the present value of the net future cash flows that can be obtained by retaining the asset and using it as profitably as possible).
▶ If it is not worth keeping, use net realisable value.

Fair values assigned on this basis should be based on an evaluation of the acquired business before control passes to the acquirer.

Identifying and valuing the assets and liabilities

The policies and methods used for identifying and valuing the assets and liabilities of the acquired business should be those of the acquirer. Identifiable liabilities are restricted to those that should have been recognised in the accounts of the acquired business, prior to its acquisition, under the accounting policies of the acquirer business. Applying this principle, do not recognise any provisions for *subsequent* reorganisation of the new acquisition. However, despite this principle, assets and liabilities that have been identified in the acquired business but that are not normally recognised in accounts should be recognised on consolidation. Examples include pension surpluses or deficiencies, contingent assets, and tax losses.

In identifying assets and liabilities, remember the definitions of assets and liabilities included in the ASB's Discussion Draft of Chapter 3 of the *Statement of Principles*, 'The elements of financial statements' (see Chapter 1 of this textbook).

Fair value adjustments

Fair value adjustments, applying the principles above, could arise from the following:

▶ revaluation of fixed assets and stocks to replacement cost

- inclusion of subsidiaries held exclusively with a view to subsequent resale at net realisable values
- discounting of long-term borrowings to present value
- adjustments to bring accounting policies of the acquired business into line with the rest of the acquiring group
- adjustments to asset values arising from different estimates of net realisable value (for example, the carrying value of debtors).

A summary of the proposals for assigning initial fair values to particular categories of assets and liabilities acquired

Fixed assets
The fair value is the replacement cost of its service potential unless this exceeds its recoverable amount, in which case the fair value is the lower value.

Note: For fixed assets such as plant and machinery and properties specific to the business fair value will be depreciated replacement cost. For listed investments and certain types of property fair value should be based on current market value. For some assets the use of relevant price indices may be the most reliable means of estimating replacement cost.

In assessing recoverable amount at the date of acquisition the acquirer should not anticipate the accounting effects of any of its post-acquisition actions.

Stocks and work-in-progress
The fair value is the lower of replacement cost and net realisable value. Replacement cost is the current cost of bringing stocks to their present location and condition.

Subsidiary that is held exclusively with a view to subsequent resale
This asset will arise where a group of companies is acquired and where the group includes a subsidiary that is held by the acquirer exclusively with a view to subsequent resale. Such subsidiaries are dealt with in FRS 2 (see Chapter 15). The fair value is the estimated or actual net realisable value. Any initial estimate of fair value will normally be adjusted to actual net realised value within the period allowed for completing the investigation of fair values.

Note: Fair value is not the actual proceeds of sale if there are post-acquisition events such as changes in markets that affect the value of the subsidiary in the holding period and also if the proceeds have been reduced to achieve a quick sale. In both these situations the acquirer should record a post-acquisition profit or loss on sale.

Long-term receivables and payables
If these are subject to *variable* market rates of interest, their fair value is best represented by their historical carrying value. This is not, however, the case where there is long-term debt at fixed rates that are different from current rates and where there are long-term debtors and no compensation for the time to settlement by way of interest at current market rates. In such cases the fair value is the present value of the amounts payable or receivable using an appropriate current interest rate. If debt instruments are quoted, fair value is market value.

Any difference between fair values established by discounting and the actual amounts receivable or payable represents either a discount or a premium on acquisition, which should be dealt with in the acquirer's consolidated accounts, following FRED 3, as interest allocated to accounting periods over the term of the asset or liability at a constant rate based on their carrying amounts.

Pension fund or other post-retirement benefits surpluses or deficiencies
On the acquisition of a business its pension obligations should be evaluated by the acquirer. Any surplus or deficiency gives rise to an asset or liability in respect of the

prepayments or provisions that have accumulated in the acquired business under the requirements of SSAP 24.

Assets or liabilities that are recognised in the acquiring group's accounts would be reduced in post-acquisition periods when surpluses are actually recovered or deficiencies made good. This treatment, on the acquisition of a business, differs from the normal requirements of SSAP 24, which requires such variations to be recognised systematically over the average remaining service lives of the employees in the scheme.

Note, however, that any cost or credit for pensions that arises from a change in pension arrangements of an acquired scheme decided upon by the acquirers – such as improvements to benefits – should be dealt with as post-acquisition items.

The deferred tax problem

Any difference between fair values of identifiable assets and liabilities, arrived at as explained above, and their values for taxation purposes should be accounted for in accordance with the principles of SSAP 15 (see Chapter 7). Thus:

▶ Fair value adjustments do affect the carrying value of assets and liabilities but do not affect their values for tax purposes.

▶ As a result, fair value adjustments that are made on consolidation will give rise to subsequent differences between accounting profits and taxable profits as and when the adjusted value items pass through the consolidated profit and loss account.

▶ The Discussion Paper restricts the scope of fair value adjustments to those that are necessary to reflect the assets and liabilities of the acquired business at their value to the business.

▶ It is therefore logical, in accounting for the acquisition, to account for the deferred tax effects of fair value adjustments made on consolidation as if the adjustments had been made in the separate accounts of the acquired business at the date of acquisition.

▶ Fair value adjustments therefore give rise to potential deferred tax assets and liabilities on consolidation.

▶ These should be recognised if it is probable that they will crystallise.

How to deal with deferred tax arising on fair value adjustments is shown in Examples 20.1 (for stocks) and 20.2 (for depreciable fixed assets).

EXAMPLE 20.1 – DEFERRED TAX ARISING ON FAIR VALUE ADJUSTMENTS FOR STOCKS

The fair value of the stock of an acquired business exceeds its book value. When the stock is sold tax becomes payable on the difference between fair value and cost.

If stocks are carried in the books of an acquired business at £100 and included at fair value (being replacement cost) of £110 in the consolidated accounts of the acquirer and sold for £130 in the post-acquisition period, the consolidated profit and loss account will include a profit of (130 – 110) £20. The taxable profits in the separate accounts of the acquired company includes a profit of (130 – 100) = £30. If the tax rate is 25% tax of £7.50 is payable on this profit.

A deferred tax provision of £2.50 should be recognised in the consolidated accounts to match the fair value adjustment of £10.

Journals

1	DR Stocks	10	
	CR Revaluation reserve		10
2	DR Revaluation reserve	2.5	
	CR Deferred tax		2.5
3	DR Deferred tax	2.5	
	CR Tax charge in profit and loss account		2.5

EXAMPLE 20.2 – DEFERRED TAX ARISING ON FAIR VALUE ADJUSTMENTS FOR PLANT AND MACHINERY (AND OTHER DEPRECIABLE FIXED ASSETS)

An asset had an original cost of £22,500 and has been depreciated to £12,000. On the acquisition of the business that owns the asset the asset is revalued at £21,000, giving rise to a fair value adjustment of (21,000 – 12,000) £9,000. The tax written down value of the asset is £7,500.

The potential deferred tax liability, prior to revaluation, based on excess of capital allowances claimed over depreciation charged, is based on a timing difference of £4,500.

As the revaluation gives rise to a new timing difference, the potential deferred tax liability is based on a timing difference of (9,000 + 4,500) £13,500.

If the tax rate is 25% an additional deferred tax provision (debit to revaluation reserve) of £2,250 (based on the fair value adjustment of £9,000) should be recognised in the consolidated accounts if the application of SSAP 15 principles would result in a provision.

The tax effects of combining tax affairs in the enlarged group

Other than deferred tax arising from events or actions at acquisition, some tax effects of a business combination arise from post-acquisition events or actions. This is illustrated in Example 20.3.

EXAMPLE 20.3

An acquired company has provided for the deferred tax anticipated to crystallise on accelerated capital allowances. The acquirer company has accelerated capital allowances but has made no provision for deferred tax as no reversal is foreseen in the forecast period.

The acquirer company expects the deferred tax liabilities of the acquired company to be sheltered through the operation of group relief arrangements.

It follows that no deferred tax provision is required in the enlarged group. Any reassessment of the deferred tax liabilities of the group and/or the acquired company that is due to the post-acquisition management of the tax affairs of the enlarged group should be treated as a post-acquisition charge or credit in the acquirer's consolidated profit and loss account.

As to tax losses, the Discussion Paper proposes that when an acquisition takes place, tax losses that are recognised in the acquired company under SSAP 15 either as an asset or as a reduction in the deferred tax provision should be recognised on the same basis when the assets and liabilities of the acquired company are initially consolidated by the acquirer. However, it is rare for tax losses to be recognised as they usually do not satisfy the criteria of SSAP 15 as being recoverable. Even so, in an acquisition transaction, there may be evidence that unrecognised tax losses do have a realisable value. In this case an asset should be recognised at the amount expended on its acquisition. Any benefit from such tax losses that exceed their attributed values should be reported as post-acquisition tax credits in the profit and loss account. Such amounts may need to be explained in the accounts.

Second stage

This stage records the effects of the acquirer's plans for post-acquisition reorganisation and integration of the acquired business.

The fair value exercise described at the first stage above should not reflect the costs of any *future* plans the acquirer may have to change the activities of the enlarged

---

group. Specifically, the recognition of expected costs or losses that are not liabilities of the acquired business at the date of acquisition are not permitted as fair value adjustments. This is even though they may have been taken into account by the acquirer in its investment appraisal. Such costs should be reported in the profit and loss account of an acquiring group as incurred.

A problem may arise with provisions (for closure) that have been set up in the acquired company before the sale of the company. Referring back to Chapter 11 on reporting financial performance, remember that once a decision has been taken to sell an operation any consequential provisions should reflect the extent to which obligations have been incurred that are not expected to be covered by future operating profits or the disposal of its net assets.

The commitment to a sale and the establishing of provisions at such time can be entered into by the management of the acquired company before the completion of the acquisition. In this case a pre-acquisition provision is created where it would not have arisen had the acquisition not been a reality. The Discussion Paper suggests that an eventual FRS on the topic might require that decisions to reorganise operations taken before the date of acquisition at the request of or during negotiations with the acquirer should be treated as post-acquisition. There is also the proposal to further reduce the scope for subjective judgement, to create a rebuttable presumption that a decision taken within six months before the date of acquisition was a consequence of the future acquisition and that the effects be accounted for as post-acquisition.

The investigation period and goodwill adjustments

The first stage of accounting for an acquisition deals with the allocation of fair values to the identifiable net assets of a business acquired. Adjustments to these fair values and to purchased goodwill should be fixed by the date that the financial statements for the first full financial year following the acquisition are approved by the directors. Thereafter, any adjustments, other than corrections of fundamental errors, should be recorded as gains or losses when they are recognised. Disclosure should be made of any provisional fair values and subsequent adjustments.

Deferred and contingent consideration

Deferred consideration is consideration in any form that is determined precisely at the time of acquisition, either in value or as a number of shares, but where payment is delayed for a defined period.

Contingent consideration arises where the value of the consideration depends on uncertain future events, such as the future performance of the acquired company.

The Discussion Paper's proposals in this connection are as follows:

▶ Consideration to be satisfied in cash or by the issue of debt instruments should be provided as a liability. The fair value of contingent consideration is the expected value of the amount payable. Fair values are obtained by discounting to their present value the amounts expected to be payable in the future.
▶ The fair value of consideration to be satisfied by the issue of shares should be credited to shareholders' funds. The fair value of contingent share consideration should be based on its expected value.
▶ Re options to issue shares or cash:
  – if the acquirer has the option – the expected future consideration should be credited to shareholders' funds until the outcome is determined
  – if the vendor has the option – the expected future consideration should be accounted for as a liability until the outcome is determined.
▶ Contingent consideration may need to be revised as new estimates are made, with consequential adjustments continuing to be made to goodwill until the eventual amount is known.

▸ There should be disclosure of:
  - nature of the consideration
  - range of possible outcomes
  - basis on which amounts recognised have been measured
  - principal factors that affect the outcome
  - details of revisions to estimates and the reasons for them.

FRED 6 and the ASB's proposals for acquisitions and mergers

The major shortcomings of SSAP 23 and the way in which ED 48 sought to rectify these are covered in Chapter 19. This chapter, which looks at mergers, acquisitions and goodwill taken together, considers the proposals of FRED 6, which seek to restrict merger accounting to those business combinations for which acquisition accounting will not give a true and fair view. FRED 6 represents a relatively minor change from the ED 48 proposals, such changes as there are being in respect of definitions and the criteria for merger accounting.

A new definition of a merger

FRED 6 defines a merger as:

> A business combination which results in the creation of a new reporting entity formed from the combining parties, in which the shareholders of the combining entities come together in a substantially equal partnership for the mutual sharing of the risks and benefits of the combined entity, and in which no party to the combination in substance obtains control over any other, or is otherwise seen to be dominant, whether by virtue of the proportion of its shareholders' rights in the combined entity, the influence of its directors or otherwise.

Although the definition of a merger has been redrafted in FRED 6, its intent is unchanged from ED 48. The definition of an acquisition is amended in FRED 6 to clarify that all combinations are either mergers or acquisitions. Thus, an acquisition is defined as a business combination that is not a merger.

The new criteria for determining whether the definition of a merger is met

FRED 6 states that the following criteria should be used to determine whether a business combination is a merger. Note that the six conditions of ED 48 have now been redrafted as five criteria, as follows:

1. No party to the combination is portrayed as either acquirer or acquired, either by its own board or management or by that of another party to the combination.
2. All parties to the combination, as represented by the boards of directors or their appointees, participate in establishing the management structure for the combined entity and in selecting the management personnel, and such decisions are made on the basis of a consensus between the parties to the combination rather than purely by exercise of voting rights.
3. The relative sizes of the combining entities are not so disparate that one party effectively dominates the combined entity merely by virtue of its relative size. Such domination by the larger party would be contrary to the concept of a merger as a substantially equal partnership between the combining parties.
4. No more than an immaterial proportion of the fair value of the consideration received, under the terms of the combination or related arrangements, by shareholders of any party to the combination in exchange for equity shares, is

represented by non-equity consideration (or equity shares carrying substantially reduced voting or distribution rights). Where one of the combining entities has, within the period of two years prior to the combination, acquired equity shares in another of the combining entities, the consideration for this acquisition should be taken into account in determining whether this criterion has been met.

5   No equity shareholders of any of the combining entities retain any material interest in the future performance of part only of the combined entity.

Comment on FRED 6

There are perceived advantages to merger accounting. Thus, under such a method of consolidation:

▶ we are not concerned with the fair value exercise, which is central to acquisition accounting
▶ there is no consolidation goodwill
▶ earnings are brought in for the whole of the year of combination and all previous periods
▶ consolidated profits tend to be higher than in acquisition accounting
▶ consolidated capital employed tends to be lower than in acquisition accounting.

Despite these advantages and permission to use the merger method of consolidation under both SSAP 23 and the Act, where certain conditions were satisfied, it was acquisition accounting that allowed preparers more room for manoeuvre when it came to reporting performance and the effects of business combinations.

Much of this chapter has dealt with the problems of reorganisation and integration costs and how these can be manipulated to massage profits. It is following the tightening-up of the rules for acquisition accounting as suggested by the Discussion Paper on Fair Values in Acquisition Accounting that there may be a renewed interest in merger accounting. But, here too we have a tightening up of the rules. The FRED proposes that merger accounting be permitted, and more importantly, required, for those (rare) business combinations that meet its definition of a merger.

An alternative view to that put forward in the FRED argues the case for prohibiting merger accounting altogether, except for certain internal group restructurings. The case is built around the point that where merger accounting is a useful way of accounting for some business combinations, any advantage is offset by the lack of comparability that is inevitable if two widely differing methods continue to be allowed. Proponents of this view suggest that mergers are best accounted for under acquisition accounting with additional disclosures.

One change introduced by the FRED, in respect of acquisition accounting, is that there should be disclosure of:

▶ a summarised profit and loss account of the acquired company up to the date of acquisition
▶ a statement of total recognised gains and losses up to this date.

These disclosures provide the link between the acquired company's last balance sheet and the fair value table in the acquirer's accounts showing the net assets on acquisition.

The FRED is only one of three parts of the ASB's approach to accounting for business combinations. A second part, dealing with acquisition accounting, is dealt with above in the discussion on the ASB's Discussion Paper, Fair Values in Acquisition Accounting. The third part, dealing with goodwill, will, when issued, complete the picture.

1994 developments - FRED 7 on fair values and the ASB Discussion Paper on goodwill and intangible assets.

455

20

The development by the ASB of standard accounting practice as to accounting for business combinations is taken a stage further by FRED 7 which is based on the Discussion Paper on fair values in acquisition accounting and a Discussion Paper on goodwill and intangibles which takes the debate in this area beyond the proposals of ED 47 and ED 52 which were dealt with in Chapter 5.

FRED 7 and Fair Values in Acquisition Accounting

The main proposals of FRED 7 are:

▶ The fair values of an acquired entity's assets and liabilities should not be increased or decreased by changes that result from the acquirer's intentions for future actions involving the acquired entity.
▶ The fair values attributed to the acquired entity's liabilities should not include provisions for its future operating losses, or for reorganisation and integration costs expected to be incurred as a result of the acquisition.
▶ The fair values of identifiable non-monetary assets are normally measured at the lower of replacement cost and recoverable amount at the date of acquisition. Recoverable amount reflects the condition of the assets on acquisition but not any impairments resulting from subsequent events.
▶ The fair values of monetary amounts are based on the amounts expected to be received paid and discounted, if appropriate, to their present values.

▶ The main respects in which the proposals of the FRED 7 differ from those of the Discussion Paper on fair values are as follows:

▶ The FRED places greater emphasis than did the Discussion Paper on the principles for identifying and valuing the assets and liabilities assumed. Thus,
 – 'fair value' is no longer based on an acquirer's or an acquiree's perspective, but on the condition of the acquired assets at the date of acquisition, and does not reflect any impairments resulting from subsequent events: and
 – the principles for recognising liabilities have been clarified so as to be clearly based on establishing whether obligations, commitments or contingencies were in existence before the acquisition.
▶ The FRED does not include prescriptive anti-avoidance measures in the case of uncontested takeovers.
▶ The Discussion Paper proposal that, where an acquisition included a subsidiary held exclusively with a view to subsequent resale, its fair value should be determined on an aggregate basis and its results excluded from consolidation, has been modified to require a similar treatment for other business operations that are to be sold shortly after acquisition.
▶ The Discussion Paper developed a proposal to bring together the existing tax liabilities of both parties to an acquisition with minimal adjustments. Thus, the existing deferred tax balances of the combining entities, calculated under SSAP 15, were not to be adjusted to take account of the acquiree's different plans for capital expenditure, post-acquisition group relief arrangements and the like that might change the likelihood of deferred tax crystallising. The FRED proposes that the allocation of deferred tax balances relating to the acquisition should be determined on an overall group basis by following the principles of SSAP 15.

FRED 7 is one of three linked reforms designed to remove the abuses of acquisition accounting that have caused, as Graham Searjeant of The Times says, (23 May 1994) 'so much disillusion with auditing and played at least a passive role in some of the shocking corporate downfalls and collapses of recent years'. Its main object is to close gaping balance sheet holes into which sundry costs of acquisition could be dumped in order to improve reported profits after acquisition. Thus, typically, when a company is bought:

▶ the acquirer writes down the 'fair value' of its assets
▶ inconvenient costs such as depreciation are thereby cut
▶ the acquirer also make substantial 'provisions' for reorganisation, redundancies, factory closures and even anticipated future trading losses to cover the costs of turning the acquired business into what it really wanted
▶ all these write-downs and provisions turn much of the purchase price into 'goodwill' and will be written off against balance sheet reserves
▶ the costs, therefore, never appear in the acquirer's profit and loss account; unless provisions were later deemed unnecessary and written back as profit.

Under FRED 7, the provisions would be banned and any costs incurred after a business was bought would have to be charged in the acquirer's own accounts. Companies, however, argue that they plan reorganisation when they consider an acquisition and, to reflect the economic, business or commercial reality, the cost should count as part of the purchase cost. Some argue that it is not worth taking over a company unless it can be improved by reorganisation. The cost of this is fully worked out before arriving at an offer price. Some, in response to FRED 7, claim that the ASB's reforms in this area would tilt the so called 'level playing field' against bidders and cause business deals to be distorted by accounting issues.

The Discussion Paper on Goodwill and Intangible Assets

Previous chapters of this textbook have looked at the accounting treatment of goodwill under SSAP 22 and ED 47 in some detail. The Discussion Paper looks at four basic methods of accounting for purchased goodwill.

(i) Capitalisation and pre-determined life amortisation	(ii) Capitalisation and annual review	(iii) Immediate write off	(iv) Separate write off reserve

Under (i), purchased goodwill is capitalised, then amortised over a pre-determined finite life subject to a maximum of, for example, 20 years. Its remaining unamortised carrying value is assessed each year for recoverability.

Under (ii), purchased goodwill is capitalised, then amortised through the application of systematic annual review procedures to estimate the required annual amortisation charges. There may be years when the annual amortisation charge is zero.

Under (iii), purchased goodwill is eliminated against reserves immediately on acquisition. The subject of available reserves for this purpose is dealt with in Chapter 5.

Under (iv), purchased goodwill is transferred to a separate goodwill write-of reserve immediately on acquisition.

Two approaches have support among the board's members:
▶ a combination of (i) and (ii) above
▶ (iv) above.

Under the former, most acquisitions would be accounted for using 'capitalisation and pre-determined life amortisation'. However, in those special circumstances where purchased goodwill has an indetermined life believed to be greater than 20 years, it would be accounted for using 'capitalisation and annual review'.

The paper argues, in line with ED 52 as dealt with in Chapter 5, that the nature of purchased intangible assets is closely related to that of purchased goodwill and proposes that most purchased intangible assets should be subsumed within purchased goodwill for reporting purposes.

The following points were made at LSCA Technical Committee meetings in early 1994:

▶ The capitalisation and amortisation method should be rejected on the grounds that
   – the period of amortisation is often arbitrary;
   – the profit and loss charge is seen as double counting where goodwill is being maintained;
   – no deduction is allowed for the amortisation for UK tax purposes.

▶ The capitalisation with an annual review approach was seen as attractive but considered too complex for the majority of companies. 'Ceiling tests' in respect of the carrying amount of goodwill were considered far too complex for other than the most sophisticated companies. Simply put, under these ceiling tests the value of goodwill would be considered in the light of the present value of the cash flows generated by the acquired business. If this value was less than the purchase cost of the business acquired goodwill would be written down accordingly.

▶ The immediate write-off method was favoured because of its simplicity. The goodwill write-off reserve should be maintained separately and shown as a subset of the profit and loss account reserve.

▶ As to the treatment of intangibles it was agreed that goodwill can be attributed to a number of components such as, for example, brands, location, staff calibre and loyalty, product range, customer lists, future profitability... and an element for premium for control. It is convenient to bundle these components together for accounting purposes. However, intangibles that have a legal right that secures future benefits should be separately recognised where they can be valued objectively and pass a separability test.

It is this last point, that is the issue of brands et al, that has dominated many of the responses to this Discussion Paper. Interbrand, for example, points out that many brands, titles and patents can more easily be separated, licensed and traded than many conventional tangible assets that go unquestioned as recognised items in balance sheets.

The board's hostility to the matters of recognition of these other intangibles stems from the lack of agreed valuation standards. On this matter and the matter of method to be adopted for goodwill treatment, the board's views will be put forward, post the responses to the goodwill Discussion Paper, in an exposure draft to be published at a later date. Watch this space.

Summary

▶ This chapter brings you up to date (as of May 1994) with the ASB's proposals as to accounting for business combinations. The major part of the chapter deals with the problems of fair values in acquisition accounting (which has a bearing on purchased goodwill arising). The latter part of the chapter looks at the circumstances in which it is now proposed that merger accounting must be used.

▶ The most important change dealt with here, looking back on the ground covered in previous chapters, is the proposal that all reorganisation and integration costs be dealt with as charges against post-acquisition profit, removing what has been, up to now, a serious flaw in the prior rules as to acquisition accounting.

▶ A lot of detail is dealt with here and you should ensure that you are familiar with the proposals for the basis of arriving at fair values in what was referred to as the 'first-stage' of acquisition accounting.

▶ This chapter serves to remind you of the constantly evolving nature of the financial reporting environment. Some of what is dealt with here will change by the time we get to the issue of FRSs on these topics.

Suggested reading

Both the fair value and goodwill discussion papers and FRED 6 and FRED 7 are very recent and there is little to suggest for additional reading. Keep in touch with the accountancy press, particularly regarding company reports and the impact of these proposals in reporting financial performance.

Self test questions

1   What are the effects of establishing fair values on acquisition?

2   Acquisition accounting practices under existing accounting standards have been a source of confusion and criticism from within the financial community. Identify the prime target of such criticism and explain why it has given rise to confusion.

3   What are the main aims of the proposals presented in the Discussion Paper on fair values in acquisition accounting and FRED 7?

4   State the proposal of the fair value Discussion Paper and FRED 7 for treatment of reorganisation costs on the acquisition of new businesses.

5   What are the proposals of the fair value Discussion Paper and FRED 7 as to assigning initial fair values to:

a) fixed assets
b) stocks
c) long-term receivables and payables that do not bear interest at current market rates

in the net assets of the acquired business at acquisition?

Exam style question

1   *Miami plc*
    The board of Miami plc, a listed company that currently has no subsidiaries, is seeking to acquire the share capital of Vice Ltd for £35 million with effect from 1 January 1995. The shareholders of Vice Ltd wish to proceed and terms are being negotiated based upon an offer to the same value satisfied as to 75% in new ordinary shares in Miami plc and 25% in cash.

    The finance director of Miami plc has asked you, in your capacity as financial adviser to the company, for guidance on the accounting implications of the acquisition and has supplied you with the following estimated information.

Balance sheet at 31 December 1995:

	Miami plc	Vice Ltd
	£000	£000
Fixed assets	21,500	18,680
Other net assets	8,900	7,925
	30,400	26,605
Share capital	10,000	7,100
Share premium	2,200	–
Revaluation reserve	2,500	–
Profit and loss account	15,700	19,505
	30,400	26,605

Profit and loss account extracts for the year ended 31 December 1995:

	Miami plc	Vice Ltd
	£000	£000
Turnover	85,631	57,279
Gross profit	12,845	7,733
Profit before tax	1,924	1,142
Taxation	(596)	(388)
Profit after tax	1,328	754

You also establish that:

(i) Miami plc currently has share capital comprising 10,000,000 £1 ordinary shares. The market value is £2.20 per share at 1 January 1995.

(ii) Vice Ltd has share capital of 7,100,000 £1 ordinary shares.

(iii) Vice Ltd has a material business segment that is making substantial losses and it is decided by Miami plc that it be closed. As a consequence, the estimated information for Vice Ltd requires adjustment to reflect additional depreciation of £5,285,000 and redundancy and other provisions of £2,750,000. The need for a provision was identified at 1 January 1995 but no provision has been made for this reorganisation in the accounts above. The actual closure takes place in 1996.

(iv) The accounting policies of both companies are consistent except that Vice Ltd does not presently provide for warranty costs or deferred taxation. To achieve fully consistent accounting policies additional provisions would be required as follows:

	At 31 December	
	1994	1995
	£000	£000
Warranty costs	200	260
Deferred taxation	100	80

(v) The purchase of shares in Vice Ltd is not reflected in the Miami plc accounts above.

Required:

a) Calculate consolidation goodwill on the basis that all provisions identified at 1 January 1995 are treated as pre-acquisition.

b) Calculate consolidation goodwill on the basis that the reorganisation provisions identified in (iii) above are accounted for in line with the proposals in the ASB's Discussion Paper on fair values in acquisition accounting.

c) Assuming that consolidation goodwill is written off immediately on acquisition and that the cost of the subsidiary is recorded in Miami plc's own accounts in accordance with the guidance in the SSAP 23 appendix, prepare a summarised consolidated balance sheet for the Miami plc group of 31 December 1995. The capital employed section of the consolidated balance sheet should be prepared on the alternative bases that consolidation goodwill is calculated as, first, in (a) above, and second, in (b) above.

d) Prepare summary consolidated profit and loss accounts for the Miami plc group for the year ended 31 December 1995 on the alternative bases that consolidation goodwill is calculated as first, in (a) above and, second in (b) above.

(20 marks)

(Based on an ICAEW PE II exam question December 1987)

All answers on pages 681–683.

Associated Companies

Chapters 15 to 20 dealt with the treatment of subsidiary undertakings in consolidated accounts, with acquisition and merger accounting, and the preparation of and the problems arising in the preparation of consolidated accounts. This chapter deals with associated companies under SSAP 1 ('associated undertakings' under the Act). Where a parent controls its subsidiary undertakings and therefore consolidates all of the subsidiaries' earnings and net assets (with separate disclosure of minority interests therein) it exercises significant influence over its associates. With significant influence, as opposed to control, it would be inappropriate to consolidate the earnings and net assets of associates into the consolidated accounts. Such undertakings are better dealt with using what is called the equity method for their inclusion into the consolidated accounts.

Prior to the publication of SSAP 1, income from investments in which less than 50% of the equity was held by the investor, was restricted to the extent of dividends received or receivable from the investee, ignoring the profits earned but not distributed by the investee, on the ground that income should not be recognised until received or receivable. This principle did, however, lead to some distortion of the results of companies that conducted a material part of their business through the medium of other companies. With the decline of the importance of dividend yield given the growing importance of p/e ratios and eps amounts, several companies developed the 'associated company method' of including in income their share of the earnings from such investments, rather than only the dividends received and receivable. SSAP 1 was published to standardise accounting that had already begun to reflect 'equity accounting' for associated companies.

This chapter deals with the requirements of SSAP 1, the procedures involved in using the equity method of accounting for investments, the changes introduced by the Companies Act 1989, the proposed revision of SSAP 1 as set out in ED 50, the requirements of the ASB's interim statement on consolidated accounts relating to associates, and the problems arising as to a fair interpretation of consolidated profit and position where the equity method is used for undertakings in which the group exercises significant influence.

Alternative methods of accounting for investments

Before going on to consider the procedures involved in the application of the requirements of SSAP 1 and the problems that may, as a result, arise in the consolidated accounts, it is important to distinguish between accounting for investments in the separate accounts of the parent company and in the consolidated accounts of the investing group.

In the accounts of the investing company

An individual company will account for all its investments in the shares of other bodies corporate, be they holdings of shares in group companies, associated or related companies, or ordinary trade investments, using the 'cost method' of accounting.

Accordingly, all such investments will be included in the balance sheet, under the historical cost valuation rules, at the lower of their cost and net realisable value. The Companies Act 1985 requires that where there is a permanent diminution in value of any fixed asset, including investments, a provision for diminution in value must be made. The Act also states that where a fixed asset investment has temporarily diminished in value, a provision for diminution in value may be made. Thus, no investment may be included in the accounts at an amount that is in excess of its estimated recoverable amount.

Income from such investments, included in the profit and loss account, will comprise dividends received and receivable by the investing company. This accords with the accounting principle that only realised items be included in the profit and loss account. Such dividend income is distinguished between income from group companies, related companies and income from other fixed asset investments.

In the separate accounts of an investing company, investments are therefore classified according to type: group, related or other, but all investments are accounted for in exactly the same way. Alternative methods of accounting for investments are, therefore, relevant only where the investor is required to prepare consolidated accounts.

In the consolidated accounts of the investing group

A group may have investments in either what we may refer to as trade investments, or in associated undertakings, or in subsidiary undertakings. The essential difference between these holdings is in terms of the degree of influence exercised by the investing group: there is no influence over trade investments, significant influence over associates, and dominant influence over subsidiaries. The consolidated accounts properly reflect these varying degrees of influence by continuing to account for trade investments under the cost method outlined above and by including subsidiaries under the (full) consolidation method, as dealt with in the five preceding chapters. Neither of these methods is appropriate for associated companies in consolidated accounts, which seek to present the results of several companies as if they were a single entity. The appropriate method here is a 'one line consolidation', or use of the equity method of accounting for investments.

Definitions

SSAP 1 includes the following definition of an associated company:

> An associated company is a company not being a subsidiary of the investing group or company in which:
>
> (a) the interest of the investing group or company is effectively that of a partner in a joint venture or consortium and the investing group or company is in a position to exercise a significant influence over the company in which the investment is made; or
> (b) the interest of the investing group or company is for the long term and is substantial and, having regard to the disposition of the other shareholdings, the investing group or company is in a position to exercise a significant influence over the company in which the investment is made.

The Standard goes on to say that a shareholding of 20% or more would constitute a significant interest unless it could clearly be demonstrated otherwise. The opposite is presumed for a holding of less than 20%.

The Companies Act 1989 uses a new definition of associated companies, introducing an 'associated undertaking'. To comply with the current legislation, ED 50 defines an associate as an enterprise other than a subsidiary where the group:

- ▶ has a participating interest (see Chapter 15) and
- ▶ exercises a significant influence over operating and financial policies.

Significant influence

SSAP 1 permitted equity accounting in the income statement of the investor if the investor exercised significant influence over the investee. The Standard stated that it was essential that the investing group or company participates, usually through representation on the board, in commercial and financial policy decisions of the associated company, including the distribution of profits.

Whether or not significant influence is deemed to be exercised by the investor and, therefore, whether or not the investor takes credit for its share of earnings of the investee rather than dividends received or receivable, could have a material bearing on the investor's income and eps and significantly affect a proper appreciation of the accounts.

To clarify the situation as to indirect holdings in the associate, the Standard states that for the purposes of establishing whether or not significant influence is presumed to exist, the investment in the investee should be taken as the aggregate of the holdings of the investing company, together with those of its subsidiaries, but not its associates. Thus in an assumed situation where:

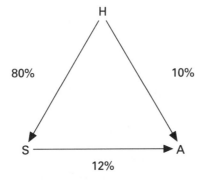

in order to arrive at the general presumption level of +/– 20% as to whether there is signficant influence over A, we look at:

(i)	the shares owned by H	= 10%
+ (ii)	the shares owned by S in A	
	which are deemed to be owned by H	= 12%
		22%

Having established this point, the 'effective' share of the earnings and net assets of A for incorporation into the consolidated accounts will be calculated as:

(i)	Direct	10%
+ (ii)	Indirect 80% × 12%	= 9.6%
		19.6%

Note the differences arising in (a) establishing whether or not there is a more than or less than 20% holding and (b) establishing the 'effective' share in the associate. SSAP 1 requires, where there are indirect holdings in an associate, separate disclosure of any minority interest arising in the associate. Thus, using the simple example above, the group accounts of H would include A as follows:

▶ In the consolidated profit and loss account:
  – the share of profit before tax and tax of the associate would be by reference to the *group* holding – the 10% owned by H plus the 12% owned by S, that is, 22%
  – the minority interest would be:
    (i) the 20% in the profit after tax of S, plus
    (ii) the minority interest, through S, in A – 20% × 12% = 2.4% in the profit after tax of A
  – group profit would therefore include 80% of S and (22% less 2.4%) 19.6% of A (the 'effective' share of the group in the profit after tax of A).
▶ In the consolidated balance sheet:
  – the carrying value would consist of 22% of the net assets of A, plus goodwill paid, less goodwill written off
  – the SSAP 1 note to the consolidated balance sheet should disclose the share of the net assets as consisting of group's share of 22% less minority interest therein of 2.4% = 19.6%.
  – the minority interest would include 2.4% of the new assets of A.

Last, as to significant influence, the Standard states that this involves participation in the financial and operating policy decisions of that company (including dividend policy) but not necessarily control of those policies. Representation on the board of directors is indicative of such participation but will neither necessarily give conclusive evidence of it nor be the only method by which the investing company can participate.

Accounting for income as required by SSAP 1

In the investing company's own accounts

Credit is taken in the investing company's own profit and loss account for (i) dividends received up to the accounting date of the investing company and (ii) dividends receivable in respect of periods ending on or before that date and declared before the accounts of the investing company are approved by the directors.

In the investing group's consolidated accounts

Credit is taken in the investing group's consolidated profit and loss account for the investing group's shares of profits less losses of associated companies (unless an associated company's results are omitted from the consolidated accounts on any of the grounds that would permit group accounts not to deal with a subsidiary).

Where an associated company itself has subsidiary or associated companies, the profits or losses to be dealt with in the investing group's consolidated accounts are its attributable proportion of the profits or losses of the group of which the associated company is parent.

If the effect is material, adjustments should be made to exclude from the investing group's consolidated accounts such items as unrealised profits on stocks. Where the SSAP is not specific in this regard it would be appropriate to account for provisions arising from the above as follows:

▶ eliminate only the group's share of the unrealised profit in the consolidated accounts
▶ if the parent has made the profit, the stock will be in the associate and, as the associate is not consolidated, will not appear, as such, in the consolidated balance sheet; accordingly you should: DR Parent's profits and CR Carrying value of the associate in the consolidated balance sheet, being elimination of the group's share of the unrealised profit

▶ if the associate has made the profit, the stock will be in the parent and will feature, as such in the consolidated balance sheet; accordingly you should DR share of associate's earnings and CR stock in the consolidated balance sheet, being elimination of the group's share of the unrealised profit.

The investing group's share of aggregate extraordinary items dealt with in the associated companies' accounts should be included with the group share of extraordinary items, unless material in the context of the group results in which case it should be separately disclosed. Where this is relevant under SSAP 1, note that it is unlikely to arise given FRS 3 definitions as to ordinary operations.

The investing group's share of aggregate net profits less losses retained by associated companies should be separately disclosed.

Associated companies' items such as turnover and depreciation should not be included in the aggregate amounts of these items disclosed in the consolidated accounts.

Accounting for value in the balance sheet as required by SSAP 1

In the investing company's own accounts the carrying value of an investment in an associate is at cost with disclosure as to market value, if relevant.

In the investing group's consolidated accounts the carrying value of an investment in an associated company is: the cost of the investment, less any amounts written off, plus the investing company or group's share of the post-acquisition retained profits *and* (other) reserves of the associated company, less any goodwill paid on acquisition subsequently written off.

Equity accounting for investments – procedure

Accounting for investments in associated companies as prescribed by SSAP 1, results in the investing group taking credit in its income statement for its share of the post-acquisition earnings of associated companies and an increase in the carrying value of the investment in its balance sheet by a similar amount. It is possible to break down this carrying value in the balance sheet as follows:

cost (share of net assets (fair value) acquired on the date of acquisition – representing the shares acquired plus/minus any goodwill paid on acquisition)

plus

share of retained post-acquisition profits and reserves (share of *increase* in net assets *since* acquisition)

= SSAP 1 carrying value (share of net assets of investee at balance sheet date + goodwill paid on acquisition)

SSAP 22 would require this carrying value to be reduced in respect of any goodwill paid written off since acquisition.

Share of net assets = share of (share capital plus reserves) = share of equity. Thus, the SSAP 1 carrying value in the balance sheet before any write-off of goodwill will always amount to the investing group's share of the equity of the associate plus any goodwill paid on acquisition. Hence the term equity accounting when applied to current practice applied to associated companies.

Journals

1. DR Investment in associate
   CR Cash/creditors
   being cost of shares acquired in associate

2. DR Investment in associate
   CR Investor consolidated revenue reserves b/f
   being share of post-acquisition retained revenue reserves of associate b/f

3. DR Investment in associate
   CR Investor consolidated profit and loss account for year
   being share of earnings of associate for the year

4. DR Investment in associate
   CR 'Other' consolidated reserves of investor
   being share of post-acquisition 'other' reserves of associate

5. DR Cash
   CR Investment in associate
   being dividends received from associate out of current year's profits

6. DR Debtors
   CR Investment in associate
   being dividends receivable from associate out of current year's profits

The balance *so far* on the investment in associate account will always represent the investor's share of the net assets of the associate at the balance sheet date plus the goodwill paid by the investor on acquisition.

7. DR Consolidated reserves
   CR Investment in associate with goodwill paid, written off since acquisition

Note, again, that equity accounting as set out above, does not apply to the investor's own separate accounts, but only to the investor's consolidated accounts, which would only be prepared if the investor had subsidiaries. In the investor's own accounts the journals would be:

1. DR Investment in associate
   CR Cash/creditors
   being cost of shares acquired in associate

2. DR Cash/debtors
   CR Investor profit and loss account
   being dividends received/receivable from associate

Given the relationship between cost plus share of retained post-acquisition reserves and share of net assets, where you are required to calculate the carrying value of an associated company for inclusion in a consolidated balance sheet, you may calculate the amount required in either one of the two ways indicated below:

Either	£	*or*	£
Cost	x	Share of separable net assets	x
Plus: Share of retained post-acquisition reserves	x	*Plus:* Goodwill paid (calculated in accordance with SSAP 22)	x
Less: Any goodwill paid written off since acquisition	(x)	*Less:* any goodwill paid written off since acquisition	(x)
	x		x

The 'or' alternative is also the disclosure note required as disclosure to support the carrying value of an associate in a consolidated balance sheet required by SSAP 1.

Associated companies and SSAP 22

SSAP 1 states that an investing group's interests in associated companies should be shown in the consolidated balance sheet as the total of:

▶ The investing group's share of the net assets other than goodwill of the associated companies, stated where possible after attributing fair values to the net assets at the time of acquisition of the net assets in the associated companies.
▶ The investing group's share of any goodwill in the associated companies' own financial statements.
▶ The goodwill paid on the acquisition of the net assets in the associated companies in so far as it has not already been written off or amortised.

The investing group should disclose the first item separately but may, and would show the second plus the third as one aggregate amount. The sum of the second and third items will always be the total of goodwill calculated as per SSAP 22.

Under SSAP 22, the investing group should eliminate the goodwill on acquisition from the value of associated companies in the consolidated balance sheet, preferably by immediate write-off against reserves.

Accounting for associates where the investing company does not prepare consolidated accounts

The investing company should account for its associates using the equity method of accounting by preparing a separate profit and loss account or by adding to its own profit and loss account in such a way that its share of profits of associates is not treated as realised for the purposes of the 1985 Act. To comply with the law in this regard, associates must be accounted for using the cost method of accounting in the separate accounts of an investing company. The share of associated earnings may be included in additional 'pro forma' accounts.

In the balance sheet of an investing company that does not prepare consolidated accounts, associates will be included at cost. However, a separate, pro forma balance sheet should be prepared incorporating associates under the equity method.

The problem of a significant level of debt

There is a problem, where the equity method is used, when there is a significant level of debt in an associate. It has been argued that the SSAP 1 basis of incorporating the value of an associate could lead to misinterpretation of ROCE and debt:equity ratios of the investor. This follows because, in so far as the value of the associate in the balance sheet amounts to the investor's share of the net assets of the associate, the investor's share of any debt in the associate is not separately included in the balance sheet, and is in effect, like pre-SSAP 21 finance lease commitments in the balance sheet of a lessee, off balance sheet finance. Thus both debt and capital employed are understated, giving rise to seemingly more favourable ROCE and debt:equity ratios.

As a counter to this misstatement arising, it has been proposed that equity accounting be, as it were, 'expanded', and instead of including associates in the investor's balance sheet at its share of net assets plus goodwill on acquisition, less goodwill written off, that this single value be broken down into the investor's share of the separate assets and liabilities of the associate and the whole of the premium arising on the acquisition. Further, that these separate amounts be aggregated with the like assets and liabilities of the investor in the balance sheet, that is, to consolidate the investor's share of the assets and liabilities of the investee or in effect what has been described as 'proportional consolidation'. In so doing, debt would be properly stated in the balance sheet and profitability ratios more realistic.

SSAP 1 does not have anything to say as to proportional consolidation. It simply requires, having used what may be termed the 'single line' equity method in the consolidated accounts that, if material, a separate note be included detailing information of an associate's separate assets and liabilities.

Thus, the Standard requires notes to the accounts for:

▶ a breakdown of the value of associates in the balance sheet comprising:

		£
(a)	group's share of separable net assets	x
(b)	goodwill paid on acquisition	x
	goodwill subsequently written off	(x)
		x

▶ the investor's share of the assets and liabilities of the associate, if material, to the group.

Summary

▶ This chapter explains why associates should be dealt with differently from subsidiaries in consolidated accounts and describes how it deals with the matter of significant influence, goodwill paid for associates, investors that have associates but no subsidiaries, and the distorting impact of the use of the one line equity method of SSAP 1 where there is material debt (and assets) in an associate.
▶ Where equity accounting is generally associated with associates, remember that it is also used, under FRS 2, for some situations where subsidiaries are excluded from consolidation (see Chapter 15). In both situations where the equity method is used, it has been criticised in that it allows manipulation given that assets and liabilities over which the group has signficant influence are effectively left off balance sheet.
▶ Another problem with the one line equity method is that we recognise profits of an associate in the consolidated profit and loss account as they accrue. It does not automatically follow that the parent can, individually, distribute such amounts. SSAP 1 is due to be revised. An Accounting Standard on this area now needs to reflect the impact of the amended 1985 Act and also the particular problems arising in respect of joint ventures. Given the increased tendency to do business through joint ventures, there is a clear need for greater guidance as to what is a joint venture and how it should best be reflected in financial statements.

Suggested reading:

The 1992–93 Survey of UK Reporting Practice (D J Tonkin and L C L Skerratt) includes a chapter on associated undertakings and joint ventures highlighting the problems arising under SSAP 1.

Self test questions

1   The summarised balance sheet of Gary Baldy plc as on 30 May 1994 is as follows:

	£000
Unamortised goodwill	200
Tangible fixed assets	1,650
Current assets	900
Current account with Gladys plc	150
Current liabilities	(700)
15% Debenture	(575)
Loan from Gladys plc	(255)
	1,370
Ordinary share capital	500
Preference share capital	100
Revaluation reserve	120
Profit and loss account	650
	£1,370

Gladys plc acquired 30% of the ordinary shares of Gary Baldy plc in 1980 at a cost of £180,000 when the revenue reserves of Gary Baldy Ltd were £220,000. The revaluation reserve of Gary Baldy plc relates to revaluations of tangible fixed assets as follows: surplus of £100,000 on the date of the acquisition of shares in Gary Baldy plc by Gladys plc; surplus of £20,000 after this date.

State the factors that need to be taken into account by Gladys plc in determining, in accordance with SSAP 1, accounting for associated companies, whether or not significant influence is exercised in relation to its investment in Gary Baldy plc.

2   Information as for question 1. Ascertain the carrying value of the investment in Gary Baldy plc to be included under 'shares in associated companies' in the consolidated balance sheet of Gladys plc as on 30 May 1994 assuming that significant influence is exercised and that Gladys plc has subsidiaries and prepares consolidated accounts.

3   On 31 March 1995 the London plc group acquired 30% of the 10,000 £1 ordinary share capital of Southend Ltd for £20,000. Extracts from Southend Ltd's profit and loss account for the year ended 31 December 1995 were as follows:

	£000
Profit before tax	124
Taxation	(64)
Profit after tax	60
Proposed dividends	(12)
Retained profit for the year	48
Retained profit brought forward	68
Retained profit carried forward	116

London plc has not yet accounted for the dividend receivable from Southend Ltd.

Ascertain the carrying value of the investment in the associated company in London plc's consolidated balance sheet as at 31 December 1995.

4   On 1 January 1993 Pimple plc purchased 40% of Simple Ltd. There was no goodwill on acquisition. On 1 January 1995, Simple Ltd acquired 75% of Dimple Ltd which was incorporated on that day. The summarised balance sheets of Simple Ltd and Dimple Ltd on 31 December 1996 are as follows:

	Simple Ltd	Dimple Ltd
	£	£
Investment in Dimple Ltd at cost	7,500	
Sundry net assets	47,500	32,000
	55,000	32,000
Share capital	20,000	10,000
Profit and loss account	35,000	22,000
	55,000	32,000

Calculate the amount at which the investment in Simple Ltd will be included in the consolidated balance sheet of Pimple plc at 31 December 1996.

5   Bingo plc owns 80% of Mongo Ltd and 30% of Vimto Ltd. Mongo Ltd owns 15% of Vimto Ltd. Vimto Ltd is an associated company of Bingo plc and is accounted for in Bingo plc's consolidated accounts under the equity method of accounting.

The profit and loss account of each company, for the year ended 31 December 1994, shows:

	Bingo plc	Mongo Ltd	Vimto Ltd
	£	£	£
Profit before tax	750	870	690
Tax	(300)	(340)	(270)
	450	530	420

Calculate the consolidated profit before tax for inclusion in the consolidated profit and loss account of the Bingo plc group for the year ended 31 December 1994.

Exam style questions

1   *Xanthos Ltd*

The separate summarised accounts for the year to 31 March 1991 of Xanthos Ltd and Ionic Ltd are given below.

	Xanthos Ltd	Ionic Ltd
Balance sheet at 31 March 1991:	£000s	£000s
Issued share capital (£1 ordinary)	2,000	1,000
Reserves and unappropriated profits	1,500	2,000
Long-term debt	2,000	8,700
Current liabilities	2,500	300
	8,000	12,000
Fixed assets	4,000	11,200
Investment in ionic	825	
Current assets	3,175	800
	8,000	12,000

	Xanthos Ltd	Ionic Ltd
Profit and loss account for the year ended 31 March 1991:		
Profit for the year after tax	950	3,000
Share of profits of Ionic	750	
Dividends paid	(1,500)	(2,000)
Profit retained for the year	200	1,000

1   Xanthos Ltd acquired 25% of the ordinary shares in Ionic Ltd in 1976, when Ionic Ltd reserves were £500,000, at a cost of £450,000.
2   In the accounts presented above, Xanthos Ltd has accounted for its investment using the equity method.
3   The long-term debt has interest attached at the rate of 10%.
4   Goodwill paid on acquisition is carried, where relevant, unamortised.

Required:

i)   Prepare the balance sheet at 31 March 1991 and the income statement for the year ended 31 March 1991 on the alternative bases that Xanthos Ltd accounted for its investment using:

a)   the cost method
b)   the equity method
c)   proportional consolidation
d)   full consolidation.

(15 marks)

ii)   Calculate for each of the methods above:

a) eps
b) ROCE
c) Debt:Equity

(6 marks)

iii) Prepare the SSAP 1 (1982 Revised) notes as to associated companies.

(2 marks)

iv)   Comment on the alternative bases of accounting for investments in the light of the differences revealed in (i) and (ii) above.

(7 marks)

ASSOCIATED COMPANIES

(30 marks)

2   *Horatio Ltd*

The fixed asset investments of Horatio Ltd comprise of shares in Sebastian Ltd and Arkwright Ltd. The shares in the investee companies were all purchased by Horatio Ltd in 1984. Percentage holdings, cost of purchase and reserves of the investee companies on the dates of acquisition are indicated to you as follows:

i)   Re: Sebastian Ltd

▶ 60% of the ordinary shares on 1 January 1984 for £950,000 when the reserves of Sebastian Ltd were £310,000.

▶ 30% of the ordinary shares and 40% of the preference shares on 30 September 1984 for £550,000 and £485,000 respectively when the reserves of Sebastian Ltd were £420,000.

ii) Re: Arkwright Ltd

▶ 35% of the ordinary shares on 30 June 1984 for £247,000 when the reserves of Arkwright Ltd were £102,000.

The summarised balance sheets and profit and loss accounts of the three companies as on and for the year ended 31 March 1991 are as follows:

Summarised profit and loss accounts for the year to 31 March 1991:

	Horatio Ltd £000	Sebastian Ltd £000	Arkwright Ltd £000
Profit on ordinary activities after taxation	600	360	200
Extraordinary items, net of taxation	(100)	40	110
	500	400	310
Preference dividends – paid	(30)	(30)	–
– proposed	(30)	(30)	–
Ordinary dividends – paid	(100)	(60)	(40)
– proposed	(200)	(80)	(80)
Profit retained for year	140	200	190
Profit brought forward	1,045	1,328	30
Profit carried forward	1,185	1,528	220

Summarised balance sheets as on 31 March 1991:

	Horatio Ltd £000	Sebastian Ltd £000	Akrwright Ltd £000
Goodwill	–	–	160
Fixed assets – tangible	2,675	1,925	1,180
Fixed assets – investments	2,232	–	–
Intercompany loans	100		(100)
Net current assets/(liabilities)	678	1,803	(620)
10% debentures	(500)	–	
	5,185	3,728	620
Ordinary share capital, shares of £1 each	3,000	1,000	400
Preference share capital, shares of £1 each	1,000	1,200	–
Reserves	1,185	1,528	220
	5,185	3,728	620

Additional information is provided to you as follows:

▶ Arkwright Ltd is an associated company, as defined in SSAP 1, of Horatio Ltd.
▶ All goodwill, whether arising in individual companies or in the group accounts, is to be wholly eliminated and written off directly to reserves.
▶ The summarised profit and loss accounts above include only those dividends that have been received. Credit has not been taken for dividends that are receivable at the year end. The preference dividends are payable on 30 September and 31 March each year.

Required:
Prepare a summarised consolidated balance sheet and a summarised consolidated profit and loss account for Horatio Ltd, its subsidiary company and its associated company as on and for the year ended 31 March 1991. Your answers should be supported by working schedules showing:

(i)   consolidation adjustments
(ii) movements on consolidated reserves during the year
(iii) minority interests, and
(iv) the carrying value of the associated company in the consolidated balance sheet.

(27 marks)
All answers on pages 683–688.

Overseas Transactions

Chapters 15 to 21 dealt with the treatment of investments, subsidiary and associated undertakings in consolidated accounts. This chapter deals with overseas transactions undertaken by individual companies and with accounting for overseas entities in consolidated accounts.

The subject of foreign currency translation has been on the agenda of the ASC since its formation in 1970. There have been a number of references to the accounting treatment of foreign currency in several of the statements published by the ASC since then. SSAP 2 identified the area as a significant matter for which different accounting bases are recognised and which may have a material bearing on financial statements. SSAP 6 stated that it presented many problems that were being studied with a view to the issue of a separate Accounting Standard. ED 16, which was published in 1975, gave some guidance on the accounting treatment of the revenue effects of translating foreign currencies. ED 21 – Accounting for Foreign Currency Transactions, was issued in 1977. It was not enthusiastically received and was not converted to Standard. A second ED on the subject, ED 27, was published in 1980. The draft was favourably received and formed the basis of the eventual Standard. SSAP 20 was published in 1983. It applies to all accounting periods beginning on or after 1 April 1983.

The requirements of the Standard relate to any enterprise that engages in foreign currency operations in either of the following ways:

▶ by entering directly into business transactions that are denominated in an overseas currency
▶ by conducting foreign operations through a subsidiary, associated company or branch whose operations are based in a country other than that of the investing company.

SSAP 20 and individual companies

General rules

The Standard requires in this regard that:

▶ All transactions in a foreign currency should be translated at the exchange rate on the date of the transaction – with the exception of those transactions that are entered into at forward rates and which are dealt with separately below.
▶ At the balance sheet date all non-monetary items that have already been translated at transaction dates above require no further translation with the exception of overseas equity investments, which are dealt with separately below.
▶ At the balance sheet date all monetary items should be retranslated at the closing rate – with the exception of those transactions that are entered into at forward rates and which are dealt with separately below.
▶ All exchange gains and losses, on settled and unsettled transactions, should be taken to the profit and loss account for the year as part of the profit or loss from ordinary operations – except where the offset procedure is applied, for which see below.

Forward rates

The general rule, as stated above, is for a company to translate an overseas transaction at the rate on the transaction date. A company may, however, when entering into such a transaction:

▶ *either* contract to settle the transaction at an agreed rate
▶ *or* hedge against any exchange risk involved and enter into a related or matching forward contract.

In the first case, the Standard states that the rate specified in such a contract should be used for translating the asset and creditor on the date of the transaction. No exchange difference will arise on settlement.

In the second case, the company may use either the rate on the date of the transaction or the forward rate specified in the forward contract. If the forward rate is used no exchange difference arises. Given an option, normal rules of consistency apply and an option, once taken, should be applied consistently to all transactions covered by forward contracts.

Example 22.1 illustrates the options available.

EXAMPLE 22.1

A UK company purchased goods overseas at a cost of US$200,000. The rate on the date of the transaction is US$1.5 = £1 and the rate on settlement three months later is US$1.2 = £1.

Applying the normal rules, the company would account for the overseas transaction as follows:

	£	£
DR Purchases US$200,000 @ 1.5	133,333	
CR Creditors		133,333
with transaction at rate on transaction date		
DR Creditors	133,333	
DR Profit and loss account	33,334	
CR Cash US$200,000 @ 1.2		166,667
with settlement of creditors at rate on date of settlement.		

If the purchase was entered into at an agreed settlement rate – say US$1.2 = £1, then the Standard would require this rate to be used for the translation of the transaction. Thus:

	£	£
DR Purchases US$200,000 @ 1.2	166,667	
CR Creditors		166,667
DR Creditors	166,667	
CR Cash US$200,000 @ 1.2		166,667
with transaction and settlement of the transaction at the agreed rate.		

Note that in this situation no exchange difference arises.

If the company entered into a contract to buy US$200,000 (£1 = $1.2) forward three months for delivery on the date of settlement, the Standard allows the company an option as to translation. Thus, the company may *either* use the normal rules and record the transaction on the date of the transaction giving rise to an exchange loss of £33,334 *or* use the forward rate, which would match the amount paid to purchase the currency, that is, £166,667, in which case no exchange difference would arise.

Whether or not a forward rate is used will influence whether or not an exchange difference is recognised. There is, however, no effect on the profit and loss account. If the transaction date is used, the profit and loss account is debited with cost of sales of £133,333 and the exchange loss of £33,334, a total of £166,667; if the forward rate is used, the profit and loss account is debited with cost of sales of £166,667.

One further point is relevant to this section. Forward rates must be used or may be used as illustrated in Example 22.1 in respect of *trading* transactions. SSAP 20 would not permit the use of the forward rate if there is no trading (that is, purchases on sales) involved. If, for example, a company buys currency forward for delivery in one year's time at a specified rate, and this contract does not relate to a trading transaction, the forward rate must not be used for translation. The contract could be accounted for in one of two ways. Firstly, as a speculative contract, in which case it must be revalued at the year end using the forward rate based on the period remaining until the existing maturity date. Alternatively, secondly, and perhaps more appropriately, the contract should be noted in the accounts as a contingency without setting up a debtor and creditor in the accounts.

Treatment of exchange differences

The Standard requires that all exchange differences, on both settled and unsettled transactions, be taken to the profit and loss account. This is even if, in the case of unsettled items, the transactions are not due to be settled for more than one year after the balance sheet date, that is, exchange differences on long-term debtors or creditors denominated in an overseas currency.

Exchange gains and losses taken to the profit and loss account will always be treated as part of the profit or loss from ordinary operations. Under FRS 3 you would need to distinguish exchange differences arising from continuing activities and those arising under activities classified as discontinued.

The Standard does, however, recognise that there may be exceptional circumstances where this treatment would not be prudent; specifically in those situations in which there are doubts as to the convertibility or marketability of the currency in question. Only in these exceptional circumstances might it be necessary to restrict exchange gains recognised in the profit and loss account. A company should, therefore, exclude the amount by which exchange gains in such situations exceed past exchange losses on the same items.

As is so often the case with Standards generally, when it comes to an area of some doubt as to treatment, SSAP 20 does not specify *how* the restricted profits should be excluded from the profit and loss account. It would appear to be the intention of the Standard that the monetary items involved should be translated at the closing rate and any excess gains taken to reserves until such time as they may, prudently, be recognised in the profit and loss account, for example, when doubts as to the convertibility of the currency involved no longer apply.

Such situations need to be distinguished from normal currency fluctuations or even post-balance sheet devaluations, which are regarded as non-adjusting post-balance sheet events and do not give rise to any restrictions on profit taken to the profit and loss account.

The exceptional case of foreign equity investments financed by foreign borrowings

As stated above, non-monetary items once translated on the date of the transaction, are not, normally, retranslated. There is one exception to this normal rule, and it arises where an overseas equity investment is financed by foreign currency borrowings.

An equity investment denominated in an overseas currency is regarded as a non-monetary asset and will be translated at the rate on the transaction date. No exchange gain or loss arises on this item as it is not, normally, subsequently retranslated. If such an asset is financed by a foreign currency loan the loan is regarded as a monetary item and having been initially translated at the transaction rate will be retranslated each year end at the closing rate. An exchange difference will arise on retranslation with movements in exchange rates.

Viewed in economic terms, it is probable that a company regards the overseas loan as a hedge against the exchange risk associated with the overseas equity investment, *regardless* of whether the investment existed before or after the loan was taken out. As no economic gain or loss is deemed to arise on exchange rate movements in these circumstances, the Standard argues that it would be inappropriate to recognise any accounting gain or loss. Therefore, where companies have such matched investments and loans they may *opt*, per the Standard, to treat the overseas equity investment as a monetary asset and retranslate the carrying amount at each year end at the closing rate. The exchange difference arising on retranslation should be taken not to the profit and loss account for the year, but direct to reserves. If this option is adopted, any compensating exchange difference on overseas loans must also be taken to reserves and offset against the movement on the investment.

The conditions that must apply before this offset is permitted are:

▶ In any accounting period, exchange gains or losses arising on the borrowings may be offset only to the extent of exchange differences arising on the equity investments.
▶ The foreign currency borrowings, whose exchange gains or losses are used in the offset process, should not exceed, in the aggregate, the total amount of cash that the investments are expected to be able to generate, whether from profits or otherwise.
▶ The accounting treatment should be applied consistently from period to period.

SSAP 20 recognises that companies usually manage their treasuries on a pool basis and finance groups of investments with a basket of loans, sometimes in different currencies. There is, therefore, no need that the hedge be in the same currency as the investment. Given several loans and investments denominated in an overseas currency, the offset procedure is carried out on an aggregate basis.

The following steps should help in carrying out the offset procedure of SSAP 20 when applied in the accounts of an individual company:

▶ *Step 1* Translate overseas equity investments at the transaction date.
▶ *Step 2* At each year end, consider the carrying value of the investments and ensure that each is expected to generate at least its original cost, either from profits or proceeds of sale.
▶ *Step 3* Assuming that step 2 is satisfactory, denominate the carrying amount in the appropriate foreign currencies and translate at closing rates.
▶ *Step 4* Ascertain the *net* exchange gain or loss on the translation in step 3.
▶ *Step 5* Calculate the *net* exchange difference on loans available for offset. If the exchange difference on the loans is the same as that on investments – that is, loss on loans and loss on investments, or gain on loans and gain on investments – there is no cover and the offset procedure cannot be used. If the exchange difference on the loans is opposite to the exchange difference on the investments – that is, loss on loans and gain on investments or gain on loans and loss on investments – there

is cover and the offset procedure may be used.

▶ *Step 6* The amount to be offset will be limited to the exchange difference on investments. Any excess of the exchange difference on loans is not used as a hedge against the exchange risk on investments and must be dealt with in profit or loss on ordinary operations.

It would make sense for an individual company to choose to apply the offset procedure where there are exchange losses on overseas borrowings that would otherwise be treated as realised losses in the company's profit and loss account.

SSAP 20 and realised and distributable profits

The 1985 Act requires that the amount of any item should be dealt with on a prudent basis and, in particular, that only profits realised at the balance sheet date shall be included in the profit and loss account. Realised profits are defined in Chapter 13 as those profits that are treated as realised in accordance with principles generally accepted with respect to the determination for accounting purposes of realised profits at the time when the accounts are prepared.

SSAP 20 requires all exchange gains on all transactions, at the *individual company level*, whether settled or unsettled, to be taken to the profit and loss account. In the context of the legal definition as to realised profits, it is difficult to argue that all exchange gains are realised, and it is necessary to find some point at which a logical distinction can be made.

The Standard identifies three different kinds of exchange gains on translation:

▶ those arising on settled transactions
▶ those arising on short-term monetary items
▶ those arising on long-term monetary items.

With the first there is no difficulty. Any such exchange gains are realised in cash terms and can be included in the profit and loss account to comply with company law.

With the second, exchange gains are not realised in cash terms, but their ultimate cash realisation can be assessed with reasonable certainty and they may be deemed realised and included in the profit and loss account to comply with company law.

It is with the third that there is a problem as such exchange gains will be unrealised at the balance sheet date. The Standard, however, argues that there is a need for symmetry in the treatment of exchange gains and losses. The one can be determined as objectively as the latter at the balance sheet date and it would be illogical not to include both in the profit and loss account. Exclusion from the profit and loss account would result in the statement not giving a true measure of a company's performance in a period. If one were to accept that there is an interaction between interest rates and currency movements and that interaction is taken into account in the making of a company's financial decisions, then only a symmetrical treatment of exchange gains and losses will fairly reflect the true results of currency involvement in the profit and loss account.

The Standard does not, however, invoke the true and fair override in arguing for this symmetrical treatment. Instead it invokes the section that explicitly permits a departure from the stated accounting principles where there are 'special reasons'. The special reason in this case is the necessity for the results to show a true and fair view based on the symmetry argument stated above. The company, in so departing, must give particulars of the departure, the reasons for it and its effect in a note to the accounts. To summarise, exchange differences are:

	Realised	Unrealised
Settled transaction	x	
Unsettled transaction		
1 Short-term monetary items	x	
2 Long-term monetary items		
(i) gains < losses	x	
(ii) gains > losses		x

The process of translation does not involve a departure from normal historical cost valuation rules and does not result in diminution in value of an asset for the purposes of the 1985 Act.

The Standard specifically excludes the question of distributable profits from its scope. A technical release did dwell on the matter but did not arrive at any precise conclusion. It stated that the question of distributability depends upon the interpretation of company legislation and should be resolved by individual companies with legal advice if necessary.

For the legal rules as to distributable profits see Chapter 13.

Two problems arise with the requirements of SSAP 20 in the context of distributable profits.

▶ The requirement of the Standard to take exchange gains on long-term monetary items to the profit and loss account could result in the inclusion of unrealised amounts in that account. Such unrealised gains are not legally distributable.

▶ Regarding the offset procedure, a loss on foreign currency borrowings could be considered a provision in company law and therefore a realised loss that would need to be deducted before arriving at a company's distributable profits. A compensating exchange gain on an overseas equity investment is not available for distribution. It may be appropriate for the directors of a company to take legal advice where the existence of a hedge would have to be taken into account in order to make a distribution. As the purpose of a hedge is to prevent any gain or loss arising it can be argued that a loss on such borrowings is not likely to be incurred and that therefore a loss on such borrowings need not be taken into account in ascertaining a company's distributable profits.

Following on from Chapter 13 you should be aware that the legal rules regarding distributable profits apply only to individual companies and not to groups. Totally different considerations apply to exchange differences that arise at the consolidation stage and these are now dealt with below.

SSAP 20 and consolidated financial statements

In order to incorporate the results and net assets of overseas subsidiaries or associates into the consolidated financial statements of the investing group, the results and net assets of such enterprises will need to be translated into the currency used for reporting purposes by the investing company.

Choice of method for translation

There are two commonly accepted methods of translation; the closing rate method and the temporal method. SSAP 20 recognises that each of these methods may be appropriate in certain circumstances. A choice between the methods is not left to the investing company, but depends on the financial and other operational relationships, which exist between the investing company and its individual foreign enterprises.

The closing rate method, which is also called the net investment method, will probably, in the UK, be used in the majority of cases. There are, however, certain specified circumstances where the temporal method *must* be used.

The closing rate or net investment method *must* be used where the investing company regards its foreign subsidiaries, associates or branches as separate businesses independent of, though they may be complementary to, the business of the investing company. In such (usual) situations the day-to-day business of the overseas enterprise will be managed with a regard to the overseas currency of the country of the overseas enterprise and the enterprise is likely to be financed wholly or partly in that currency. The acquisition of the overseas enterprise is not seen as an interest in the individual assets and liabilities of the enterprise but as a long-term investment in the net worth of the enterprise as a going concern. The investing company, though it will anticipate a stream of dividends, will not expect to realise its net investment unless the enterprise is liquidated or otherwise disposed of.

The above does not prohibit a degree of management control by the investing company. The main factor for consideration is the currency that is of most significance for each enterprise. This 'local currency' is that of the primary economic environment in which the enterprise operates and generates net cash flows.

In the UK it is most common for businesses to conduct their foreign operations through quasi-independent entities. The appropriate rate for translation of the results and net assets of such entities is the closing rate/net investment method.

There are, however, some situations where such quasi-independence does not apply. The affairs of the overseas enterprise may be closely interlinked with those of the investing company. In such situations it may not be appropriate to regard the overseas currency as the currency on which the overseas enterprise is dependent. In such situations the local currency of the overseas enterprise is deemed to be that of the investing company and the temporal method *must* be used for translation of the overseas results and net assets for incorporation into the consolidated accounts. The effect of using this method is that the separate legal structure of the overseas enterprise becomes irrelevant for accounting and the assets and liabilities of the overseas enterprise are treated as though they belonged, directly, to the investing company.

In respect of the method to use for translation, SSAP 20 does not lay down specific circumstances where the temporal method must be used. Each case must be considered separately in determining which currency is the local currency of each foreign enterprise. The Standard does, however, specify the factors to be taken into consideration in determining the dominant currency in order to ascertain whether the temporal method must be used. These factors are:

▶ The extent to which the cash flows of the overseas enterprise have a direct impact upon those of the investing company, that is, whether there are only occasional remittances such as dividends or whether there is a regular movement of cash between the investing company and the foreign enterprise.

▶ The extent to which the functioning of the enterprise is dependent directly upon the investing company, that is, whether day-to-day operations are managed locally or at head office; whether pricing decisions are taken on the basis of local conditions or whether they are a part of a global decision-making process.

▶ The currency in which the majority of the trading transactions are denominated, that is, whether the overseas currency or the currency of the investing company is used for the invoicing of goods and the payment of expenses.

▶ The major currency to which the operation is exposed in its financing structure, that is, whether the overseas enterprise is dependent on local sources of finance or whether the major part of the financing is in the currency of the investing company.

None of these factors on their own would require the use of the temporal method; a combination of these factors might make it necessary.

Once the decision to use a particular method has been taken, consistency would require that it will not normally be appropriate to change methods unless the circumstances of the group change so radically as to necessitate a change.

The Standard does suggest examples of situations where the use of the temporal method may be required. These arise where the foreign enterprise:

▶ acts as a selling agency, receiving goods from the investing company and remitting the proceeds back to the investing company, or
▶ produces a raw material or manufactures parts or subassemblies that are then shipped to the investing company for inclusion in its own products, or
▶ is located overseas for tax, exchange control or similar reasons to act as a means of raising finance for other companies in the group.

The closing rate/net investment method

As it is usual for most groups to set up quasi-independent entities to operate overseas, the closing rate/net investment method will normally be used for translation of the accounts of a foreign enterprise. This method is considered to be more likely to achieve the objective of translation stated in the Standard that consolidated statements should reflect the financial results and relationships as measured in the foreign currency financial statements prior to translation.

The general rules to be followed in using the method are:

▶ All amounts in the balance sheet of the foreign enterprise should be translated using the rate of exchange ruling at the balance sheet date: the closing rate.
▶ Amounts in the profit and loss account of the foreign enterprise should be translated using *either* the closing rate *or* an average rate for the period.
▶ All exchange differences arising on the retranslation of the opening net investment or on the use of an average rate to translate the profit and loss account should be taken to reserves, *not* to the consolidated profit and loss account for the year.

Pro forma 22.1 is the pro forma for the main working required in dealing with a number-based examination question including an independent overseas subsidiary. The working enables you to ascertain:

▶ £ values for the net assets of the subsidiary for inclusion in the consolidated balance sheet
▶ £ values for profits of the subsidiary for inclusion in the consolidated profit and loss account
▶ the consolidation stage exchange difference, the group's share of which is taken direct to consolidated reserves.

PRO FORMA 22.1

Translation of the balance sheet of an overseas subsidiary where the closing rate/net investment method is used (and a question provides 'full' information).

	$	Rate	£
Fixed assets – NBV	x	closing rate	x
Net current assets	x	closing rate	x
Loans	(x)	closing rate	(x)
	$x		£x
Ordinary share capital	x	acquisition rate	x

Reserves:

	$	Rate	£
(i) At acquisition	x	acquisition rate	x
(ii) Post acquisition b/f			
Year 1	x	average or closing rate for year	x
Year 2	x	average or closing rate for year	x
			x̄
Bal. item = Consolidation stage exchange difference b/f	–		x/(x)
Opening net assets	x	last year's closing rate	x
(iii) Profit for year	x	average or closing rate for year	x
Bal. item = Consolidation stage exchange difference for the year	–		x/(x)
	$x		£x

Note: Pro forma 22.1 applies where a question gives you 'full' information as to the reserves of the overseas subsidiary and exchange rates, that is, if the question indicates the post-acquisition reserves of the subsidiary for *each* year post-acquisition brought forward and the closing or average rates for *each* of these years. If such 'full' information is not given in a question, it will not be possible to ascertain the consolidation stage exchange difference b/f as in Pro forma 22.1 and you will need to adapt your working as shown in Pro forma 22.2.

PRO FORMA 22.2

Translation of the balance sheet of an overseas subsidiary where the closing rate/net investment is used (and a question does not provide 'full' information).

	$	Rate	£
Fixed assets – NBV	x	closing rate	x
Net current assets	x	closing rate	x
Loans	(x)	closing rate	(x)
	$x		£x
Ordinary share capital	x	acquisition rate	x
Reserves:			
(i) At acquisition	x	acquisition rate	x
(ii) Post acquisition b/f	x	Bal. item (see Note)	x
Opening net assets	x	last year's closing rate	x
(iii) Profit for year	x	average or closing rate for year	x
Bal item = Consolidation stage exchange difference for the year	–		x/(x)
	$x		£x

Note: In the case shown in Pro forma 22.2, as the question does not indicate either the post-acquisition reserves of the subsidiary brought forward for *each* year and/or the exchange rates for *each* of these years, it will not be possible to translate the post-acquisition reserves brought forward of the subsidiary. The £ value of these post-acquisition reserves is a balancing item. It will *include* the consolidation stage exchange difference brought forward (which cannot be separately ascertained).

Whether you have followed the approach in Pro forma 22.1 or Pro forma 22.2 you can now use the £ values ascertained as follows:

- Consolidate the £ values of the fixed assets, net current assets and loans of the overseas subsidiary.
- The minority interest is simply their share of the £ value of the net assets. This will include their share of the consolidation stage exchange difference.
- Goodwill on consolidation is: £

  Cost of subsidiary [at rate on date of its acquisition]   x

  Less:

  % of £ value of ordinary share capital plus reserves at acquisition   (x)

                                                                                                                  x

- Consolidated profits will include the group's share of the £ value of the subsidiary's post-acquisition reserves brought forward and for the year.
- *The group's share* of the balancing items representing the consolidation stage exchange differences is taken directly to consolidated reserves. SSAP 20 does not specify where in reserves these should be included. Best practice would be to take these exchange differences to a separate exchange difference reserve included in consolidated other reserves.

The earlier part of this chapter dealt with the situation where foreign borrowings are used by an individual company to hedge or finance foreign equity investments. A similar provision is also allowed in consolidated accounts whereby an exchange gain or loss on the foreign borrowings used to finance or hedge an investment in a foreign enterprise *may* be offset in reserves against the exchange difference arising on the net investment in that enterprise.

The theory behind this allowed offset procedure is that the group may have used foreign borrowings to finance new group investments or to provide a hedge against the exchange risk associated with existing group investments. Unless the offset procedure were allowed, exchange differences on the net investments would be reflected in consolidated reserves whereas exchange gains and losses on loans would be taken to the consolidated profit and loss account for the year. To the extent that these exchange movements match each other there is no economic exchange risk and it is therefore inappropriate to record an accounting profit or loss.

The conditions that must be met for the offset procedure to be used in consolidated accounts are the same as those that applied for an individual company, as previously set out, with the additional condition that the relationships between the investing company and the foreign enterprises concerned justify the use of the closing rate method for consolidation purposes.

There are, however, a number of differences between the offset allowed on consolidation and that allowed in the individual company. Only coincidentally will the offset on consolidation be the same as in the individual company's accounts. This is because:

- The offset in the individual company relates to all equity investments regardless of size or holding.
- In the individual company's accounts the amount available for offset is the exchange difference arising on the carrying value of the investment (which will include goodwill) translated at closing rates whereas, on consolidation, the amount

available for offset is the exchange difference arising on the opening net investment (which will exclude goodwill).

▶ In the individual company, only loans raised by the company are available for offset, whereas in the consolidated accounts loans raised by any group company may be included in the amount available for offset.

Areas of hyper-inflation

The Standard suggests that historical cost accounts translated using the closing rate method may not present a true and fair view of the financial position of an overseas enterprise if it operates in a country where a very high rate of inflation exists. In these situations the Standard requires that the local currency financial statements should be adjusted where possible to reflect current price levels before the translation process is undertaken. For obvious reasons, given the problems involved in price level accounting, the adjustments are not mandatory.

UITF 9, recently issued and effective for years ending on or after 23 August 1993, deals specifically with the application of SSAP 20 to subsidiaries operating in hyper-inflationary countries.

In such countries, defined as those where the cumulative rate of inflation over three years approaches or exceeds 100%, the UITF states that, as already noted per SSAP 20 above, the simple translation of the local currency financial statements may not give a true and fair view of the group's operations. The UITF proposes two alternative treatments:

▶ adjust the local currency accounts to reflect current price levels *before* translating them with the net gain on loss arising on the holding of monetary liabilities and assets being taken through the profit and loss account; or

▶ use a stable currency such as the US $ as the functional currency for preparing the company's accounts; if the transactions are not initially recorded in that currency, translate into that currency using the temporal method.

The temporal method

We have already dealt with the situations where the use of the temporal rate method would be required. The Standard does not include any details as to the mechanics of the method except to say that they are identical with those used in preparing the accounts of an individual company. Thus:

▶ All transactions should be translated at the rate on the transaction date (or an average rate for the period).
▶ Non-monetary assets should not normally be retranslated at the closing rate.
▶ Monetary assets and liabilities should be retranslated at the closing rate.
▶ All exchange differences arising should be taken to the consolidated profit and loss account as part of the profit or loss on ordinary operations (as opposed to direct to reserves as under the closing rate method).
▶ The offset procedure will not be applicable.

The steps indicated in Pro forma 22.3 should help in dealing with the mechanics of a temporal method translation.

Step 1 Reconstruct and translate the *opening* balance sheet of the overseas enterprise.

	$	Rate	£
Ordinary share capital	x	at acquisition	x
Reserves – pre-acquisition	x	at acquisition	x
– post-acquisition	x	Bal. item	x
Loans	(x)	closing rate at balance sheet date	(x)
	x		x
Fixed assets – NBV	x	at date of acquisition of fixed assets	x
Net current assets			
(bal. item in $ column)	x	closing rate at balance sheet date	x
	x		x

Stocks should, strictly, be translated at the rate on the date of acquisition.

The purpose of this step is to enable you to ascertain a £ value for reserves at this balance sheet date. In the event that this £ value is given to you in a question you can go directly to step 2.

Step 2 Translate the *closing* balance sheet using the same approach as above. Loans and net current assets would be translated at closing rates at the closing balance sheet date. You need a sterling value for post acquisition reserves at this date.

Step 3 Translate the profit and loss account for the year.

	$	Rate	£
Sales	x	average rate	x
Purchases	(x)	average rate	(x)
Opening stock	(x)	last year's closing rate (or rate on acquisition)	(x)
Closing stock	x	this year's closing rate (or rate on acquisition)	x
	x		x
Depreciation	(x)	at same rate as fixed assets	(x)
Expenses	(x)	average rate	(x)
	x		x
Taxation	(x)	average rate	(x)
Dividends – paid	(x)	actual rate	(x)
– proposed	(x)	closing rate	(x)
Retained for year	x		x
Post-acquisition b/f	x	per bal. item in opening B/S	x
Bal. item = exchange difference for year	–		x/(x)
Post acquisition c/f	$x	per bal. item in closing B/S	$x

Some problem areas in overseas group situations

The problems that may arise from intercompany transactions are dealt with below.

Intercompany trading transactions

An exchange difference will arise in either the investing company's accounts or in those of the overseas enterprise. Such an exchange difference should be reported in the accounts of the individual company in the same way as an exchange difference arising from an overseas transaction with third parties, that is, through the individual company's profit and loss account. On consolidation the net exchange differences will flow through into the consolidated profit and loss account. These differences reflect the risk of conducting business in a foreign environment; the fact that the overseas trading is not with third parties is irrelevant. The group's cash flow is affected and any exchange gain or loss is a genuine trading result. Such exchange differences will *not* be eliminated on consolidation.

Nevertheless a profit on intercompany transactions should be eliminated in the normal way on consolidation. See Example 22.2.

EXAMPLE 22.2

Group year end: 31 December. Overseas company (O) purchases goods from its UK parent company (UK) on 1 December. The goods cost (UK) £80,000 and were sold to (O) for £100,000. The goods remain in stock of (O) at the year end.

Relevant exchange rates are:	(O)= £1
1 December	10 = 1
31 December	9.5 = 1

Unrealised profit of (100,000 – 80,000) £20,000, included in the individual accounts of (UK) must be eliminated on consolidation.

(O) will translate its purchase into its own currency on the date of the purchase £100,000 @ 10 = (O) 1,000,000. This will be the amount of stock in the overseas subsidiary's balance sheet at its year end. This amount will need to be translated into £ at the year end for incorporation into the group balance sheet. This stock will appear in the consolidated accounts as follows:

	£
(O) 1,000,000 @ 9.5	105,263
Unrealised profit eliminated on consolidation	(20,000)
Stock value in consolidated balance sheet	85,263

The exchange difference of (105,263 – 100,000) £5,263 does not represent a further element of unrealised profit. It is part of the exchange risk involved in overseas operations.

Suppose the transaction went in the other direction, that is, Co. (O) sold goods that cost the company (O) 800,000 to Co. (UK) for (O) 1,000,000 and that (UK) retains these goods in stock at the year end.

	£
Cost of goods (O) 1,000,000 @ 10 =	100,000
Unrealised profit (O) (1,000,000 – 800,000) @ 10 =	(20,000)
Stock value in consolidated balance sheet	80,000

Intercompany dividends

Such dividends should be recorded in the accounts of the receiving company at the rate on the date when the dividend is declared or at the year end rate if the dividend is proposed at that date. The same rate should also be used to translate the dividend in the accounts of the paying company in order to ensure that the intercompany dividend is eliminated on consolidation. An exchange difference will arise if there is a change in the exchange rate between the declaration/proposal date and the date of actual payment. Any such exchange difference should be treated as a normal intercompany transaction and be included in the profit and loss account.

Intercompany loans

Two separate situations can arise:

▶ Loan from one group company to another in the local currency of the former company.
▶ Loan from one group company to another in a third currency, that is, not the local currency of the one or the other company.

In the first situation an exchange difference will arise in the accounts of the company to whom the loan is made. In the second situation an exchange difference will arise in the accounts of both companies.

The accounting treatment for such exchange differences is to take them to the profit and loss account of the individual company(s) involved, unless the loan is used to hedge or it would be imprudent to recognise a gain.

A special point can arise on such intercompany loans. The Standard makes a special provision for situations where an investment in an overseas enterprise consists not only of an equity stake but also long-term intercompany loans and intercompany trading accounts. The latter can in some instances be intended to be as permanent as equity. In these circumstances the loans and intercompany balances should be treated as being part of the investing company's net investment and any exchange differences on them should be dealt with as movements on *consolidated* reserves.

The standard does not permit exchange differences on such loans to be taken to reserves in the accounts of an individual company. This is because the concept of a 'net investment' is relevant only in a group and the individual company's accounts must reflect the results/net assets of that company as a single entity.

SSAP 20 and foreign branches

A foreign branch per SSAP 20 may be either a legally constituted enterprise located overseas or a group of assets and liabilities that are accounted for in foreign currencies. The factors to be considered for translation dealt with at the start of this chapter apply equally to the translation of foreign branches for incorporation into the accounts of an individual company.

The operations of a branch are normally integral to the business of the investing company and the temporal method will normally be required to be used for translation.

There may, however, be situations where a foreign branch should be accounted for using the closing rate/net investment method. The technical release that was issued with SSAP 20 gives the following examples where this method should be used:

▶ A hotel in France financed by borrowings in French francs.
▶ A ship or aircraft purchased in US$, with an associated loan in US$, which earns revenue and incurs expenses in US$.
▶ A foreign currency insurance operation where the liabilities are substantially covered by the holding of foreign currency assets.

In each of these situations, first, the local currency of the operation is different from that of the investing company and, secondly, the branch operates as a separate business with local finance, and therefore the closing rate/net investment method should be used.

Where this method is used, the net investment in the foreign branch is represented by the head office current account with the branch. The exchange difference on the opening net investment should be taken direct to reserves.

Disclosure

The Standard requires disclosure in the financial statements of the methods used in the translation of financial statements of foreign enterprises and the treatment accorded to exchange differences.

The following information should also be disclosed:

▶ For all companies/groups the net amount of exchange gains and losses on foreign currency borrowings less deposits, identifying separately, first the amount offset in reserves and, second, the net amount charged or credited to the profit and loss account.
▶ For all companies/groups, the net movement on reserves arising from exchange differences.

Gains or losses arising from trading transactions should normally be included under 'other operating income or expense'. Those arising from arrangements that may be considered as financing should be disclosed separately as part of 'other interest receivable/payable and similar income/expense'. Gains or losses that arise from events that themselves fall to be treated as extraordinary items should be included as part of such items.

Movements on reserves should disclose:

▶ the amount of the reserve at the beginning of the year and at the balance sheet date
▶ any amounts transferred to or from the reserve during the year
▶ the source and application of any amounts transferred.

Some criticisms of SSAP 20

There is little doubt that SSAP 20 has resulted in an improvement in the reporting of foreign currency transactions. We have moved a long way from the days in which a UK corporation could have changed its accounting policy in respect of translation three times in three years and reported, as a result of the change, improved results in each of these years. However, a number of criticisms remain.

Regarding forward contracts

The Standard contains insufficient guidance as to accounting for forward and similar hedging contracts. The use of forward rates regarding forward contracts is optional and this results in inconsistency of treatment between different companies. Further, the Standard does not deal with similar agreements such as currency swaps.

Regarding the offset procedure

There are three main criticisms here. First, the use of the cover method or offset procedure is optional; second, cover may cease to exist if the borrowings are not in the same currency as the investment; third, there can be inconsistent treatment in different companies and, within one company, from period to period.

It is worth noting here that, to be covered in a way that eliminates exchange risk completely, it is necessary for the borrowings to be in the same currency as the investment. It would help, in ensuring comparability, if exchange differences on borrowings are designated as economic hedges and, if so, taken to reserves from the designation date.

Regarding reserve accounting

As indicated previously in the chapter, exchange differences arising in situations where the use of the closing rate/net investment method of translation is justified, are taken, under SSAP 20, direct to reserves and not to the profit and loss account. This treatment is justified on the basis that the exchange difference arising does not affect group cash flows. It could be argued that such exchange differences pass, eventually, through the profit and loss account as they do become realised as dividends are paid or when the investment is sold. This last criticism does, however, need to be considered in the light of reporting financial performance under FRS 3 where there is adequate disclosure of exchange differences arising, wherever dealt with in the financial statements.

Regarding realised profits in individual companies – exchange losses

Paragraph 12 of Schedule 4 requires that items are determined on a prudent basis and that only profits realised at the balance sheet date be included in the profit and loss account. The treatment of exchange differences in this context has been dealt with earlier in this chapter.

As to exchange losses, S. 275 of the 1985 Act would appear to apply in that it requires, for the purposes of determining distributable profits, provisions to be treated as realised losses. It is generally accepted that exchange losses on settled transactions and on unsettled short-term monetery items and, on the ground of prudence, long-term monetary items should be regarded as realised. A problem arises on losses on long-term overseas borrowings taken direct to reserve in an individual company using the offset procedure in its own accounts. Should such losses be treated as realised?

One approach to answering this question is to consider the cash flows arising from the investment and related borrowings. Thus, if exchange losses taken to reserve for offset relate to borrowings that have been repaid, they should be treated as realised. The situation is not so clear-cut if the borrowings have not been repaid. If sufficient dividends will be received from the investment before the repayment of the borrowings, we could argue that there is a hedge and that the loss on the borrowings need not be treated as realised. If, however, insufficient dividends will be received prior to the repayment of the borrowings the loan may be considered not to be covered and, to that extent, the exchange difference arising should be regarded as a realised loss.

As a criticism of SSAP 20, we could argue that it is the purpose of an Accounting Standard to resolve areas that are open to interpretation such as the matter of losses here, and that it is a shortcoming of SSAP 20 that the ASC actually stated that, where the existence of a hedge needs to be taken into account in order to make a distribution, it may be appropriate for directors to seek legal advice (TR 504).

Summary

The first part of this chapter dealt with accounting for overseas transactions by individual companies. In this context you should now be able to:

▶ record overseas transactions
▶ ascertain exchange differences arising
▶ cope with alternative treatments where forward rates are applicable
▶ deal with the special case of overseas equity investments and the offset procedure in the accounts of an individual company
▶ account for all exchange differences arising
▶ discuss and quantify the effect of such exchange differences on the legally distributable profits of an individual company.

The second part of the chapter dealt with what may be called the consolidation stage of SSAP 20. In this context you should now be able to:

▶ decide on the appropriate method of translation to apply
▶ translate under the closing rate method
▶ translate under the temporal method.

The chapter also deals with some further problems arising on intercompany transactions, some points of interest as to foreign branches and with the disclosure required by the Accounting Standard.

Suggested reading

Accountants Digest No. 150

Advanced Financial Accounting (Samuels, Rickwood and Piper) See Chapter 12.

UK GAAP (Ernst and Young 1992)

Financial Reporting 1989–90 – A survey of UK Reporting Practice (Tonkin and Skerratt 1990)

Accounting for overseas operations (Westwick)

Self test questions

1   Define the two methods in consolidated accounts of currency translation specified in SSAP 20.

2   Explain the precise circumstances in which the use of each method is mandatory under SSAP 20.

3   Justify the treatment, in consolidated accounts, for overseas investment financed by overseas borrowing as prescribed in SSAP 20.

4   During the year ended 31 March 1992, Halogen plc sold goods to a Dutch company for Glds. 5 million. At the average exchange rate for each month, the sales amounted to £1 million. Halogen plc, however, entered into matching contracts to sell currency forward when received, and translated and recorded its sales at the rates specified per the forward contracts. The amount actually received by the company during the year ended 31 March 1992 amounted to £1.05 million.

Ascertain the exchange differences arising and explain how you would account for the transactions above so as to comply with SSAP 20 as at and for the year ended 31 March 1992.

5   Chlorine Ltd made a long-term loan to a supplier in Ruritania amounting to R 50 million in September 1991 when the exchange rate, £ to R, was £1 = R 25. At 31 March 1992, the exchange rate was £1 = R 20. At the balance sheet date there are, however, doubts as to the convertibility/marketability of the loan in question. Having taken these doubts into account, the directors consider that the loan will realise at least £2.1 million.

Explain how Chlorine Ltd should account for the loan above so as to comply with SSAP 20 as at and for the year ended 31 March 1992.

Exam style questions

1   *Cyrus plc*
    Cyrus plc operates in the UK and has one subsidiary, Darius Corporation, which operates overseas and the operating currency of which is the dinar or (D). Translation of the results and net assets of the Darius Corporation for incorporation into the sterling consolidated financial statements of the Cyrus plc group is effected using the closing rate/net investment method, and using the average rate for the year in the case of profit and loss account items.

a)   Cyrus plc purchased 900,000 of the (D) 10 ordinary shares of the Darius Corporation on 1 July 1989 when the profit and loss account of the overseas company amounted to (D) 1,500,000. There were no other reserves on this date.

b)   'Shares in related company' consist of 300,000 £1 ordinary shares in Xerxes plc, 40% of its voting equity capital, purchased when the reserves of Xerxes plc amounted to £187,500. Cyrus plc does exercise significant influence over the affairs of Xerxes plc. During the year ended 30 June 1991, Xerxes plc had pre-tax profits of £300,000, tax thereon of £120,000 and no extraordinary items. As on 30 June 1991, the retained reserves of Xerxes plc amounted to £450,000.

c)   The dividends from Xerxes plc, included in the profit and loss account of Cyrus plc, have been grossed up on the basis of the income tax basic rate of 30%. Cyrus plc has not taken credit, in its own accounts, for any dividend proposed by the Darius Corporation.

d)   During the year ended 30 June 1991, goods invoiced in sterling at £750,000 were sold by Cyrus plc to the Darius Corporation. Of these goods, £150,000 worth remained in the stock of the Darius Corporation as on 30 June 1991. Cyrus plc sells goods to its overseas subsidiary at cost plus 25%. During the year ended 30 June 1990, intercompany sales were £600,000 and the Darius Corporation had £120,000 worth of these sales in stock on this date. This stock was sold by the Darius Corporation in October 1990. Deferred taxation is provided, on consolidation, on provisions made for profit unrealised on such sales in the group accounts.

e)   Consolidation goodwill is eliminated, on acquisition, against reserves arising on consolidation.

f)   Rates of exchange were, (D) to £1: On 1 July 1989 = 9: Average for the year ended 30 June 1990 = 9.75: On 30 June 1990 = 10: Average for the year ended 30 June 1991 = 11: On 30 June 1991 = 12.

g)   The loan of £1,500,000 in the balance sheet of Cyrus plc as on 30 June 1991 is the sterling value of an overseas loan raised by Cyrus plc on 30 October 1990. The loan was raised in dollars – $ – and amounted to £1,500,000.

Rates of exchange were:

| 30 October 1990 | $1 | = £1 |
| 30 June 1991 | $1.5 | = £1 |

The offset procedure is used, as a matter of accounting policy, in the group accounts.

h) Summarised profit and loss accounts for the year ended 30 June 1991:

	Cyrus plc £000	Darius Corporation (D) £000
Turnover	10,500	33,000
Cost of sales	(8,400)	(24,750)
Distribution and administrative expenses	(1,200)	(3,900)
Income from shares in related company	45	
Interest payable	(200)	
Tax on profit on ordinary activities	(360)	(1,500)
Extraordinary profit/(loss)	150	(375)
Tax on extraordinary loss/(profit)	(45)	103
Dividends – proposed	(375)	(1,500)
Retained profit for the year	115	1,078

i) Summarised balance sheets as on 30 June 1991:

	Cyrus plc £000	Darius Corporation (D) £000
Tangible fixed assets	2,550	6,000
Cost of shares in group company translated at rate on date of acquisition	1,350	
Cost of shares in related company	450	
Stocks	2,250	7,500
Trade debtors	1,350	6,000
Amount owed by group company		1,500
Balance at bank	321	638
Trade creditors	(925)	(1,838)
Amount owed to group company	(125)	
Taxation and social security	(750)	(1,650)
Proposed dividends	(375)	(1,500)
ACT on proposed dividend	(161)	
Loan	(1,500)	
Deferred taxation	(204)	
Ordinary share capital	(3,000)	(12,000)
Revaluation reserve	(750)	
Profit and loss account	(481)	(4,650)

j) The rate of corporation tax is to be taken, where relevant, at 50%.

Required:

a) Prepare a summarised consolidated profit and loss account for the year ended 30 June 1991 incorporating the results of Cyrus plc, its overseas subsidiary and its related company. Accompanying notes are not required.

(12 marks)

b) Prepare a summarised consolidated balance sheet as on 30 June 1991 for the Cyrus plc group. Accompanying notes are not required.

(12 marks)

c) Prepare a statement of the movement on group reserves for the year ended 30 June 1991.

(6 marks)

(30 marks)

2   *Bough plc*

Bough plc is a holding company with three manufacturing subsidiaries in Canada. On 1 January 1991 it acquired a 30% holding in an American company, Branch Inc., for £5,000,000. The net assets in the balance sheet of Branch Inc. at 1 January 1991 were $21,000,000 and it was estimated that their fair value was

$28,000,000. The company has not yet adopted the Statement of Standard Accounting Practice on Accounting for Goodwill and is continuing to carry goodwill at cost.

The profit and loss account of Branch Inc. for the year ended 31 December 1991 showed:

	$
Profit from ordinary operations before tax	2,800,000
Tax	1,000,000
Profit on ordinary activities after tax	1,800,000
Dividend paid	750,000
Profit retained	1,050,000

The exchange rates were:

1 January 1991	$1.75 = £1
31 December 1991	$1.60 = £1

Required:

a) Show how the investment and translation reserve would appear in the balance sheet of Bough plc *and* in the consolidated balance sheet at 31 December 1991 on the basis that:

 (i) no currency borrowings were utilised to cover the investment
 (ii) specific dollar borrowings of £2 million were used to partially cover the investment.

 Where relevant, the offset procedure of SSAP 20 is to be used.
 Use the closing rate, with appropriate notes and supporting calculations

(15 marks)

b) Show the entries to record the income arising from the investment in the profit and loss account of Bough plc and in the consolidated profit and loss account for the year ended 31 December 1991.

 Use the closing rate, with appropriate notes and supporting calculations.

(5 marks)

c) Calculate the effect of the company's complying with each of the alternative methods allowed under the Statement of Standard Accounting Practice for goodwill.

(5 marks)

(25 marks)

All answers on pages 688–694.

The Preparation of Additional Reports

The preceding 22 chapters have dealt with, mainly, the financial statements of individual companies and groups and various problems as to measurement and disclosure therein. This chapter looks at additional reports, some of which are a part of an organisation's annual report and others that are quite separate.

Where the annual report will include the primary statements of FRS 3 (see Chapter 11) the balance sheet and the cash flow statement (see Chapter 12) and all supporting notes, the annual report is often expanded to include, for example, segment reports and value added statements. The former is governed by SSAP 25 and the latter put forward as useful information for inclusion in the annual report by the Corporate Report.

Other reports, separate from the annual report, such as profit forecasts, prospectus reports and reports re offers for sale, rights issues and conversion rights are also discussed in this chapter. A prospectus includes substantial amounts of accounting information that is usually contained in an accountants' report following on from a statement of adjustments made to actual data published by the company in previous years. Profit forecasts are made for a number of purposes, often to comply with Stock Exchange or City Code requirements in a given situation. All these additional reports are covered by the financial reporting environment paper.

The value added statement

Following the issue of the Corporate Report, a DTI consultative document, The Future of Company Reports (1977), expressed the view that publication of a value added statement (VAS) should be incorporated into company law and that its presentation should be standardised. However, as yet, there are no statutory or Stock Exchange requirements relating to the VAS. Nor has a FRED been issued on the subject.

The tendency to include value added statements in annual reports now appears to be waning. Possible reasons for the apparent decline in interest include the change in the economic and political climate. UK companies are now much less defensive about earning profits, and in the 1980s there was a major rise in the amount of profits earned. Also, since the statutory layouts for the profit and loss account came into force, formats 2 and 4 – which disclose turnover, raw materials and consumables, other external charges and staff costs – enable a measure of value added to be calculated. A further possible reason is the growing bulk of annual reports. It is likely that, as things are, the VAS, while providing useful information, especially when reporting to employees, is likely to stay out of the limelight (though not necessarily less relevant to your examination). A return to more difficult conditions for company profitability may, however, revive interest.

The Corporate Report stated that:

> The simplest and most immediate way of putting profit into proper perspective vis-à-vis the whole enterprise as a collective effort by capital, management and employees is by presentation of value added (that is, sales income less materials and services purchased). Value added is the wealth the reporting entity has been

able to create by its own and employees' efforts. This statement should show how value added has been used to pay those contributing to its creation.

Proponents of value added argue that there are advantages in defining income in such a way as to include the rewards of a much wider group than just the shareholders of a company. One can include shareholders and all suppliers of long-term and short-term loan capital together with employees and the government. The income of this team is called 'value added' and equals net profit with tax, interest and wages cost all added back. Morley points out that a frequent synonym for value added is 'wealth creation' and this may have encouraged many industrialists to link value added reports on wealth creation with remedial action to halt the UK's relative industrial decline.

The advantages of the VAS

Even though several advantages are claimed for the VAS, this should not hide the fact they are simply rearrangements of data that is available elsewhere in company reports. The advantages are:

▶ Because the VAS reflects a broader view of the company's objectives and responsibilities it improves the attitudes of employees toward their employers.
▶ It provides an alternative measure of performance and activity. The preparation of ratios from a VAS may be a useful means of interpreting that performance, for example, comparison of value added per employee ratios across divisions of a company, or with competitors, may be employed.
▶ It may be of assistance in the introduction of profit-sharing or productivity schemes based on value added. A significant number of companies have, in recent years, introduced profit-sharing schemes based on productivity increases as measured by value added or related ratios.
▶ It provides a good measure of the size and importance of a company and is superior to sales and capital in this respect. The sales figure may be inflated by large bought-in expenses, which are passed straight on to customers. Capital employed may be a poor indicator of the number of workers employed in a company.
▶ It reports a company's contribution to the national income and, therefore, is of value to the macro economist.

The disadvantages of the VAS

The disadvantages are:

▶ The VAS implicity treats a company as a team of co-operating groups; this attitude may be grossly at variance with the facts. It is the government that is the least natural member of the alleged team. It is not invited to join the team, it plays no part in team decision making and its share of value added is proportional to profits rather than value added.
▶ The inclusion of a VAS in an annual report can cause confusion with the earnings statement. What, for example, would a non-accountant infer on seeing that value added was rising when earnings were falling?
▶ It raises a new danger of inefficient management, since management may wrongly seek to maximise their company's value added. For example a company may currently buy in goods for £100, investigate the possibility of internal manufacture, and find that in the latter case the cost would be £80 in direct materials and £70 in direct labour. The value added maximiser would decide on internal manufacture so that value added would rise by £20. However, this £20 of added value would involve an extra £70 of wages and a fall in shareholders' earnings of £50.

▶ The last disadvantage is the most serious; the VAS is unstandardised and can be manipulated to produce almost any value added figure desired. For example, in 1975 the value added disclosed in the VAS produced by Allied Breweries Ltd was £379 million and the government's share 50%. In 1976 value added was £247 million and the government took 13%. This was not because both beer drinkers and the government had become abstemious, but because the company reclassified the special excise tax on alcohol as a bought-in cost rather than as part of the government's share of value added. Other problem areas are dealt with later in this section.

The basic form of a VAS

The format of a VAS is illustrated in Example 23.1.

EXAMPLE 23.1

Smiths Industries – VAS 1987

	1987 £000	%
Turnover	429,950	
Deduct		
Purchased materials and services	221,420	
Value added	208,530	
Utilised as follows:		%
Wages, pension contributions and employee benefits	135,368	64.9
Taxation	23,867	11.5
Interest	(3,449)	(1.7)
Dividends	14,030*	6.7
Minority interests	–	–
Depreciation	10,944	5.3
Retained profit (before extraordinary items)	27,770*	13.3
Value added	208,530	100.0

* Excludes dividend on shares issued after 1 August 1987.

Areas of non-standardisation and possible problem areas

Depreciation

A VAS can be framed as a report on net value added where depreciation is deducted as a part of bought-in costs. It can also be framed as a report on gross value added where depreciation is dealt with as an application, as above, of value added rather than a cost to be deducted in calculating value added. There are three reasons for reporting gross value added:

▶ Gross value added is a more objective figure than net value added as depreciation is more prone to subjective judgement than are bought-in costs. This point has special force if value added is to be added as a basis for some sort of productivity bonus to employees.
▶ The gross value added format involves reporting depreciation alongside retained profit. The resulting sub-total usefully shows the position of the year's value added which has become available for reinvestment. This ratio is less readily calculable from net VAS where depreciation is separated from retentions.

▶ The practice of reporting gross value added leads to a closer correspondence between value added and national income figures; economists generally prefer gross measures of national income to net ones.

There are, however, alternative arguments for preferring net value added and these are as follows:

▶ Value added as 'wealth creation' is overstated if no allowance is made for the wearing out or loss of value of fixed assets that occurs as new assets are created. As net value added is distributable while gross added value is not, net value added is a better denominator for distribution ratios such as payroll/value added.
▶ Net value added is a fairer base for calculating productivity bonuses than is gross value added, for example, a company's value added might rise after new capital has been invested in a major plant modernisation and employees may be given their share of this increase as a bonus. If that share is based on value added before depreciation, no recognition is given to the need for an additional depreciation charge. Providers of capital who deserve the credit for the increase in value added will not get it.
▶ Concepts of consistency and matching demand that depreciation be deducted along with bought-in costs to derive net value added. Depreciable fixed assets are also bought from outside suppliers and the cost of these should be matched with sales revenue over the assets' useful lives.
▶ Net value added involves no double counting. The double counting arises from the non-deduction of depreciation. Where one company buys a product from another, the seller's value added will be augmented. If the buyer discloses net value added, the buyer's value added will be diminished by the amount of the sale over the asset's useful life.
▶ Gross value added distorts the team concept. If depreciation is treated effectively as an application, suppliers of fixed assets are treated as honorary team members. This introduces inconsistency between classes of supplier.

The reason why most UK companies that have produced value added statements have reported gross value added is that they have followed the advice given in the Corporate Report. That document did not even mention the possibility of the alternative net value added format.

Taxation

Some companies have reported only tax levied on profits (corporation tax) under the heading applied to government. This practice has many advantages as it avoids the need to make subjective judgements as to which of the long list of government imposts should be regarded as a part of the government's share. Thus:

▶ It is possible that sales and bought-in costs could be included with VAT and VAT shown as an application to government.
▶ Applications to employees could be shown excluding PAYE and the PAYE shown as applied to government.

A further advantage of only including corporation tax in the applied to government amount is that the VAS would then be easier to reconcile with the earnings statement.

Non-trading charges and credits

These are items that do not readily fall into any one of the main headings in the VAS. They include items such as:

▶ investment income
▶ exchange differences
▶ extraordinary items.

Normally they are included in the value added statement, as illustrated in Example 23.2.

EXAMPLE 23.2

Imperial Chemical Industries Ltd, and Subsidiaries

Value Added Statement Year to December 31, 1977

Sources of Income		£ million
Sales		4,663
Royalties and other trading income		39
Less: Materials and services used		(2,866)
Value added by manufacturing and trading		1,836
Shares of profits of principal associated companies and investment income		96
Exchange loss on net current assets of overseas subsidiaries		(29)
Extraordinary items		(29)
Total value added		1,874
Disposal of total value added		
Employees		
Pay, plus pension and national insurance contributions	1,063	
Profit-sharing bonus	29	1,092
Government – corporate taxes, less grants		202
Providers of capital		
Interest on borrowings	107	
Dividends to shareholders	93	
Minority shareholders in subsidiaries	26	226
Reinvestment in the business		
Depreciation set aside	221	
Profit retained	133	354
		1,874

Associated companies

These may be dealt with in the VAS using either the 'cash' method or the 'equity' method.

If the cash method is used, dividends from associates would need to be included as a non-trading credit in arriving at total value added. If you adopt this procedure you must make sure that you *exclude* the share of earnings retained by the associate in the amounts retained by the group in applications.

If the equity method is used, the share of earnings of the associate would be included in total value added as a non-trading credit; the share of the tax of the associate would be included as paid to government; the share of earnings ultimately retained by the associate would be *included* in the amounts retained by the group.

Minority interests

As with associated companies, two treatments are possible.

▶ The minority interest in profits could be included in paid to providers of capital; group retentions would include only that of the parent plus share of subsidiaries' retentions.
▶ The dividends of subsidiaries attributable to minority interests could be included as paid to providers of capital; group retentions would include that of the parent plus the whole amount retained by subsidiaries, including the minority interest share.

Reporting to employees – an amplification of published financial statements

In many ways the VAS is an unsatisfactory innovation. It is easy enough to understand and prepare. Much is claimed for it but the claims are hard to pin down and verify. The benefits claimed are principally improvement in attitude, motivation and behaviour and these are remarkably difficult to substantiate.

The statement is largely, although not wholly, a rearrangement of information already disclosed in the company's profit and loss account and directors' report. For this reason many people consider it to be a mere cosmetic device to place less emphasis on the profit figure. Others would stress that presentation has an important role to play and that the arrangement of information in the value added statement provides a better means of understanding the contribution of a company to society. In particular, the inclusion of relevant percentages of value added by the side of items in the second part of the statement would make people aware of the respective shares of the various team members, one such team member being the employees of a company.

Segmental reporting

The result of legislation and standard-setting in recent years has been a trend towards financial reports that are user-oriented rather than preparer-oreinted. As stated by Belkaoui *et al.*, a lack of appropriate information promotes ignorance and uncertainty, causing both analysts and investors to make excessive allowances for errors in their forecast, thereby lessening the efficiency of the capital markets with consequently slower economic growth. The shift towards user needs has led to an increased attention being placed upon the importance of financial data in predictive processes. In the USA, the FASB, following the lead of the Trueblood Report, described the principal objective of financial reporting as providing information that would assist investors in predicting the amount, timing and certainty of future cash flows to the company. This aspect of disclosure is likely to be of increasing importance in the future on the basis that there is a case for increased disclosure by reporting, for example, the components of income, segmental information, interim information and forecast information. These areas of disclosure are important as current earnings statements invite an excessive emphasis on a single net earnings figure, the bottom line, though in the UK this has changed post-FRS 3. It is necessary to consider such increased disclosure if only to refute the claim, made by Clive Jenkins, that 'published accounts are utterly and absolutely useless'.

This section deals with the issue of segmental reporting, which came into prominence following a feature of business development that began in the 1960s, that is, the growth of diversified companies in which different segments of a company are subject to significantly different rates of profitability, degrees of risk, and opportunities for growth. An adoption of the decision usefulness approach, implies the disclosure of segmental information for diversified companies in order to provide the user with a better basis for an assessment of a company's past performance and future prospects.

The ASC set up a working party to draft a Standard on segmental reporting, or the breaking down in accounts of information between different business activities and different geographical areas. The issue was controversial in that an earlier working party had found that, where companies wished to limit disclosure in this respect on the grounds of the time and expense involved in its compilation, investment analysts wished for more detailed information on both business activities and geographical areas so as to better assess the different risks and economic trends to which a company is subject. Not surprisingly, there was support for segmental disclosure from groups of users of financial reports. Various market research studies have suggested that segmental reporting brings improvements in the efficiency of capital markets, providing further support for such additional disclosure.

ED 45 – Segmental Reporting, was published in November 1988. SSAP 25 was issued in June 1990.

Segmental information required to be disclosed by the Companies Act 1985

In the UK, company law now requires segmental information to be disclosed in the financial statements instead of in the directors' report, as was required by the 1948 Act.

The requirements of the 1985 Act

The Companies Act 1985 states that:

If in the course of the financial year, the company has carried on business of two or more classes that, in the opinion of the directors, differ substantially from each other, there shall be stated in respect of each class:

(a) the amount of turnover attributable to that class, and
(b) the amount of the profit or loss of the company before taxation which is in the opinion of the directors attributable to that class.

Additionally, the Act requires an analysis of turnover by geographical areas to be given where a company has supplied different markets. Prior to the Companies Act 1981, such a geographical analysis was provided only by listed companies as it was a Stock Exchange, though not a statutory, requirement.

Examples of turnover and profit analyses

1 **Allied-Lyons plc (31 March 1984)**

Divisional analysis of results:

1984	Beer £m	Wines spirits and soft drinks £m	Food £m	Central Companies £m	Group £m
Turnover	967.0	861.4	1,090.2	1.9	2.850.5*
Trading profit	77.7	66.9	53.2	(1.0)	196.8
Trading margin	8.0%	7.8%	4.9%	–	6.9%
Profit on disposal of properties and investments	12.3	1.0	0.3	(0.2)	13.4
Related companies	5.1	0.5	5.9	14.2	25.7
Investment income	1.2	–	–	0.3	1.5
	96.3	68.4	59.4	13.3	237.4
Finance charges	(11.2)	0.7	(9.3)	(22.7)	(42.5)
Profit before tax	85.1	69.1	50.1	(9.4)	194.9
1983					
Turnover	938.0	833.1	942.3	3.0	2,643.1*
Trading profit	68.3	65.1	38.5	0.2	172.1
Trading margin	7.3%	7.8%	4.1%		–
Profit on disposal of properties and investments	12.2	1.8	0.9	(0.6)	14.3
Related companies	6.1	0.3	5.4	13.0	24.8
Investment income	1.6	–	0.5	2.1	
	88.2	67.2	44.8	13.1	213.3
Finance charges	(11.9)	(5.6)	(7.7)	(28.5)	(53.7)
Profit before tax	76.3	61.6	37.1	(15.4)	159.6

* Excluding £70.0 million (£73.3 million) intragroup sales.

This divisional analysis is based on the management organisation of the group.

2 **Standard Telephones and Cables plc (31 December 1985)**

Effect of acquired companies and sales to principal customer shown.

	Turnover 1983 £m	Turnover 1982 £m	Profit on ordinary activities before taxation 1983 £m	Profit on ordinary activities before taxation 1982 £m
Turnover and profit on ordinary activities before taxation by activity:				
Telecommunications	406.5	322.0	52.9	49.6
International communications and services	245.3	112.9	23.8	5.8
Components and distributors	251.9	193.6	15.1	8.9
Residential electronics	16.9	–	0.4	–
	920.6	628.5	92.2	64.3

Acquired companies included in above	163.5	–	7.5	–

Turnover by geographical market:

United Kingdom	647.4	485.2
Continental Europe	39.0	41.9
The Americas	38.2	41.0
Asia and Australasia	99.1	53.8
Africa and Middle East	96.9	6.6
	920.6	628.5

Sales to British Telecom, the principal customer of the group, amounted to £305.4 million (1982: £239.0 million).

It should be noted that, if the directors are of the opinion that any of the above disclosures would be seriously prejudicial to the interests of the company, the information need not be given, but the fact of omission must be noted.

Comment

The 1985 Act compares with previous Companies Acts requirements in this area in the vagueness of its requirements.

Thus:

▶ The amount of information provided is largely at the discretion of the directors.
▶ Definitions of terms such as 'classes of business' and 'different markets' are not included. The Act provides no guidance as to what significantly different classes of business happen to be.

US practice, FASB 14

The US Standard on segmental reporting calls for information to be provided on each of three areas:

▶ the company's operations in different industries
▶ the foreign operations of the company and its export sales
▶ the major customers of the company.

The Standard acknowledges that no single system has developed for segmenting a company and that, therefore, the determination of a company's industry segments must depend to a considerable extent on the judgement of management. The Standard requires a company to present reports on each industry segment for which one or more of the following tests are satisfied during the accounting period:

▶ The segment's revenue is 10% or more of the combined revenue of all segments.
▶ The absolute amount of the segment's operating profit or loss is 10% or more of the greater of:
　－ the combined operating profit of all industry segments that did not incur an operating loss, or
　－ the combined operating loss of all industry segments that did incur an operating loss.
▶ The segment's identifiable assets are 10% or more of the combined identifiable assets of all industry segments.

In addition, the total revenue for all segments must be at least 75% of the revenue of the company as a whole. If this test is not satisfied, management has not identified an adequate number of reportable segments and the delineation of additional segments is necessary.

The US Standard represents a pioneering attempt to provide a rigorous basis for the disclosure of segmental information. Compared with the UK approach, as it is at the moment, it is prescriptive but not without problems, in that management discretion in the process of identifying segments is arbitrary.

SSAP 25 – the requirements

The Accounting Standard on segments is based on the principle that unless the financial statements of an enterprise contain segmental information, they do not enable the reader to make judgements about the nature of the different activities or of their contribution to its overall financial result.

The Standard aims to contribute to improved segmental reporting in two ways. Firstly, by providing guidance as to how the reportable segments should be determined and, secondly, by specifying the information to be disclosed.

Scope

The Standard will apply to all financial statements intended to give a true and fair view of the financial position and profit or loss of an enterprise. However, it is intended that certain of the information required by the Standard to be disclosed will have to be given only by:

▶ public companies or holding companies that have one or more public companies as a subsidiary; and

▶ private companies (and other enterprises) that do not satisfy the criteria, multiplied in each case by ten, for defining a medium-sized company under the Companies Act.

Where both parent company and consolidated financial statements are presented, segmental information is to be presented on the basis of the consolidated financial statements.

Comparative figures for the previous accounting period are to be given. However, on the first occasion on which a company provides segmental information, comparative figures need not be given if the necessary information is not readily available.

The exemption remains that where, in the opinion of the directors, the disclosure of any information required would be seriously prejudicial to the interests of the company that information need not be disclosed, but the fact that any such information has not been disclosed must be stated. In practice very few companies choose to take advantage of the exemption under the Companies Act and it is unlikely that this situation will change.

What is a reportable segment?

Information can be segmented in two main ways by class of business and geographically. SSAP 25 supports the provisions of the Companies Act 1985, which state that it is the directors' responsibility to determine the analysis of the segments. The Standard does not seek to override these provisions; instead it aims to provide guidance on factors that should influence the definition of segments. As it may be difficult to analyse a segment, the Standard states that a segment is normally regarded as material if:

▶ its third-party turnover is greater than 10% of the entity's total third-party turnover or

▶ its results, profit or loss, are greater than 10% of the combined results of all segments in profit or of all segments in loss, or

▶ its net assets are greater than 10% of the total net assets of the entity.

The basic guidance of the Standard is that directors should have regard to the overall purpose of presenting segmental information and the need for the readers of the financial statements to be informed where a company carries on operations in different classes of business or in different geographical areas that:

► earn returns on investment that are out of line with the remainder of the business, or
► are subject to different degrees of risk, or
► have experienced different rates of growth, or
► have different potentials for future development.

In determining whether or not a company operates in different classes of business the directors should take into account the following:

► the nature of the products or services
► the nature of the production processes
► the markets in which the products or services are sold
► the distribution channels for the products
► any separate legislative framework relating to part of the business.

In determining whether or not a company operates in different geographical segments the directors should take into account the following:

► expansionist or restrictive economic climates
► stable or unstable political regimes
► exchange control regulations
► exchange rate fluctuations.

This may result in companies having to reassess the geographical segments that they are currently disclosing, as in many cases this would appear to be based on geographical proximity; the Standard emphasises that 'although geographical proximity may indicate economic trends and risks, this will not always be the case'.

In establishing segments both for classes of business and for geographical areas, there is no single set of factors that is universally applicable, nor is any single factor predominant in all cases.

The company should define each of the reported classes of business and indicate the composition of each of the reported geographical segments. For each separate class of business and geographical segment, a company would be required to disclose:

► turnover
► results
► capital employed.

Turnover should be analysed between sales to external customers and sales between segments.

The geographical analysis of turnover is to be given with reference to its source (that is, where the products are manufactured) and to its destination (that is, where the customers are located) only if there is no material difference between them.

Results are the profit or loss before tax and minority interests. Profit or loss may be before or after accounting for interest. It is anticipated that in most situations the profit or loss before interest should be used. However, the profit or loss after interest is likely to be used in those companies where the earning of interest income or the incurring of interest expense is fundamental to the nature of the business; for example, companies in the financial sector.

Capital employed is not defined in the Standard. Generally it will be non-interest bearing operating assets less non-interest bearing operating liabilities. However, where interest income/expense has been included in arriving at the segmental results the related interest bearing assets/liabilities should be taken into account in determining the capital employed. The aim should be to relate the definition of capital employed to the definition of results so that a 'return on investment' type calculation can be performed (it is unlikely that any comparison between companies of such returns will be meaningful, given the fact that some companies incorporate fixed assets at valuation and others do not). Operating assets and liabilities that are shared by more than one segment are to be allocated, as appropriate, to those segments.

It is highly unlikely that different companies will interpret capital employed in the same way. Perhaps the best that can be achieved is for companies to settle on one definition of capital employed that is meaningful for their own company, and apply it consistently. In view of the fact that no definition is given for capital employed, the proposed Standard requires the method of calculating capital employed to be described.

The total of the information disclosed by segmental analysis should agree with the related totals in the financial statements. If they do not agree, a reconciliation between the figures is required.

Associated companies

A company should segmentally disclose, in its consolidated financial statements, the following information in respect of its associated companies:

▶ the company's share of the profits or losses of associated companies before accounting for taxation, and minority interests
▶ the company's share of the net assets of associated companies (including goodwill to the extent it has not been written off) stated, where possible, after attributing fair values to the net assets at the date of the interest in each associated company.

This disclosure should be of the aggregate information for all associated companies and should be shown separately in the segmental report.

The disclosure is required only if the results or assets of associated companies form a material part of the group's results or assets. For this purpose, associated companies form a material part of the reporting company's results if, in total, they account for at least 20% of the total results or at least 20% of the total capital employed by the reporting group (including the group's share of the results and net assets of the associated companies).

It may commonly be the case that the associated companies do not come within the scope of the proposed Standard and are therefore not disclosing segmental information in their financial statements. Where this is the case the investing company may be unable to obtain the necessary information to meet the requirement of the Standard as it does not control the associated company. The Standard recognises this problem by providing an exemption to the effect that the segmental information requirements do not apply where the company is unable to obtain the information.

Examples of a segmental report

Example 23.3 is reproduced from the appendix to SSAP 25.

EXAMPLE 23.3

Classes of business	Industry A		Industry B		Other industries		Group	
	1990	1989	1990	1989	1990	1989	1990	1989
	£000	£000	£000	£000	£000	£000	£000	£000
Turnover								
Total sales	33,000	30,000	42,000	38,000	26,000	23,000	101,000	91,000
Inter-segment sales	(4,000)	–	–	–	(12,000)	(14,000)	(16,000)	(14,000)
Sales to third parties	29,000	30,000	42,000	38,000	14,000	9,000	85,000	77,000
Profit before taxation								
Segment profit	3,000	2,500	4,500	4,000	1,800	1,500	9,300	8,000
Common costs							300	300
Operating profit							9,000	7,700
Net interest							(400)	(500)
							8,600	7,200
Group share of the profits before taxation of associated undertakings	1,000	1,000	1,400	1,200	–	–	2,400	2,200
Group profit before taxation							11,000	9,400
Net assets								
Segment net assets	17,600	15,000	24,000	25,000	19,400	19,000	61,000	59,000
Unallocated assets*							3,000	3,000
							64,000	62,000
Group share of the net assets of associated undertakings	10,200	8,000	8,800	9,000	–	–	19,000	17,000
Total net assets							83,000	79,000

Geographical segments

	United Kingdom		North America		Far East		Other		Group	
	1990	1989	1990	1989	1990	1989	1990	1989	1990	1989
	£000	£000	£000	£000	£000	£000	£000	£000	£000	£000
Turnover										
Turnover by destination:										
Sales to third parties	34,000	31,000	16,000	14,500	25,000	23,000	10,000	8,500	85,000	77,000
Turnover by origin:										
Total sales	38,000	34,000	29,000	27,500	23,000	23,000	12,000	10,500	102,000	95,000
Inter-segment sales	–	–	(8,000)	(9,000)	(9,000)	(9,000)	–	–	(17,000)	(18,000)
Sales to third parties	38,000	34,000	21,000	18,500	14,000	14,000	12,000	10,500	85,000	77,000
Profit before taxation										
Segment profit	4,000	2,900	2,500	2,300	1,800	1,900	1,000	900	9,300	8,000
Common costs									300	300
Operating profit									9,000	7,700
Net interest									(400)	(500)
									8,600	7,200
Group share of the profit before taxation of associated undertakings	950	1,000	1,450	1,200	–	–	–	–	2,400	2,200

Group profit before taxation									11,000	9,400

Net assets

Segment net assets	16,000	15,000	25,000	26,000	16,000	15,000	4,000	3,000	61,000	59,000
Unallocated assets*									3,000	3,000
									64,000	62,000
Group share of the net assets of associated undertakings	8,500	7,000	10,500	10,000	–	–	–	–	19,000	17,000
Total net assets									83,000	79,000

* Unallocated assets consist of assets at the group's head office in London amounting to £2.4 million (1989: £2.5 million) and at the group's regional office in Hong Kong amounting to £0.6 million (1989: 0.5 million).

Accountants' reports

This section of the chapter deals with the inclusion of an accountants' report in a prospectus. A prospectus is an invitation to the public to subscribe for, or to purchase shares or debentures in a company. There are a variety of circumstances in which prospectuses may be issued, the most common of which are those where a company is seeking admission to the Stock Exchange's Official List or its Unlisted Securities Market. The form and content of a prospectus may vary according to the circumstances in which it is issued.

The 1985 Act sets out the matters to be stated and the reports to be set out in a prospectus. The Act deals with the mandatory contents of a prospectus. The Auditing Practices Committee has issued an Auditing guideline on prospectuses and the reporting accountant.

The Act requires the prospectus to be produced by the directors of the company issuing the shares or debentures. It is they who bear, collectively and individually, full responsibility for the completeness and accuracy of the information given in the document, which includes a great deal of information on the company's affairs, and includes reports by 'experts' one of whom is the reporting accountant. The merchant bank or broker sponsoring the issue will organise the preparation of the document and take the lead in obtaining the various reports which the prospectus is required to contain.

The Stock Exchange's *Admission of Securities to Listing* – the Yellow Book – sets out the minimum information to be included in the accountants' report. The purpose of the report is to give possible investors financial information relating to the company concerned, which will assist them in making a decision as to whether to invest in it. Accordingly it is required to include an expression of opinion as to whether or not the financial information gives a true and fair view of the company's or group's state of affairs, profits and losses and sources and applications of funds for the preceding five years (or for the period since incorporation if that is a shorter period). Any other matters that the reporting accountant considers to be pertinent should also be dealt with in the report.

The reporting accountant may either be the company's auditor or may be another accountant, who must act with the auditor for the purposes of the work on the prospectus. The reporting accountant will need to review the financial statements that form the basis of the report to determine whether any adjustments are required for the purposes of the report. Thus the reporting accountant will need to consider:

▶ Material changes in accounting policies that may have been applied at any time during the period covered by the report and which may require the previously published information of any one year dealt with in the report to be adjusted in order to provide valid comparisons between financial statements prepared on the current basis.

▶ Material expenditure or revenue of a non-recurring nature may have arisen in circumstances that require such items to be eliminated from normal operations and disclosed separately as exceptional items.

▶ Material items that may have taken place after the publication of the audited financial statements of any one year may require adjustment to ensure that they are accounted for in the current period in the accountants' report.

▶ The appropriateness of all accounting policies as well as compliance with accounting standards and the consistency of their application is essential to ensure that all years' financial statements encompassed by the accountants' report are set out on the basis of current accounting policies.

Adjustments to previously published and audited financial statements for the purpose of the information to be included in the accountants' report

The Yellow Book states that 'in making a report the accountants should make such adjustments as are in their opinion appropriate for the purposes of the report'.

Thus, in the notes to the report as to turnover and operating costs in a prospectus document it was stated that:

> Turnover and operating profit for the two years ended 31 July 1982 include the results of a foreign exchange broking operation which was, in the main, closed in March 1982 and certain administration costs attributable to the then central management of the Group. The operating losses of these activities according to unaudited management accounts amounted to £1,227,000 in the year ended 31 July 1981 and £1,597,000 in the year ended 31 July 1982.

In considering whether any adjustments are required it is essential to bear in mind that the accountants' duty is to report on past losses and profits and not to attempt to forecast results in future conditions, which is the quite separate purpose of a profit forecast. Thus it would not normally be appropriate to adjust past losses or profits where a future charge for directors' or auditors' remuneration was expected to differ materially from that of the past. The report should, however, indicate that there has been a change in the level of such remuneration.

The form and content of the report

The Yellow Book sets out the Stock Exchange's requirements for a reporting accountants' report to the directors of a company and to the issuing house. When shares are being offered to the public for the first time, the principal contents of the report should be as follows:

▶ profits, losses, dividends, eps in respect of each of the three immediately preceding years

▶ movements on reserves not reflected in the statement of profits and losses (this is particularly important where items are taken direct to reserves in accordance with statue or standards)

▶ the balance sheets of the company and in the case of a group the consolidated balance sheets of the group at each year end over the period reported on

▶ the cash flow statements of the company or the group if it has subsidiaries in respect of each previous accounting period forming the basis of the report

▶ accounting policies

▶ any other matters that appear to be relevant for the purpose of the report.

The Stock Exchange's normal requirement regarding the maximum period of time between the date of the figures to be reported on and the date of the report may not have been satisfied. Thus a sixth period's date may need to be reported on where the latest financial period reported on by the company's auditors ended more than six months before the date of the prospectus or nine months in the case of a transaction on the USM.

The Yellow Book does not specify any particular format for the statement of adjustments, which should be that which is most appropriate to the circumstances in each case. It should, however, include details of, and the reasons for, the adjustments sufficient to reconcile the figures from the audited financial statements with the figures included in the accountants' report.

To sum up

A reporting accountant reports on the truth and fairness of the state of affairs, results and sources and applications of funds over a period of, normally, five years. The report differs from an audit report given that the latter is concerned with a true and fair view for the one accounting period being reported on.

These adjustments are dealt with in a statement of adjustments, showing how the audited profit and loss accounts, balance sheets and source and application of funds statements have been adjusted in order to arrive at the figures to be included in the report. The statement is submitted separately from the report; it is not a part of the prospectus, but it must be made available for inspection.

The following are the main reasons why adjustments may need to be made for the purposes of the report:

▶ The financial statements of the various years need to be adjusted so that the accounting policies are applied consistently from year to year. Adjustments may therefore need to be made, for example:
  - stock valuation, which would affect opening and closing stock valuations in each year
  - deferred taxation, which may need to be adjusted to bring it into line with the revised SSAP 15
  - goodwill previously carried as unamortised now to be adjusted for so that either immediately written off, or systematically written off
  - depreciation to ensure that realistic lives have been used, no supplementary depreciation has been charged without revaluation in the balance sheet, no 'split' depreciation charge has been made
  - exchange differences
  - charges against profit for finance leases capitalised.
▶ Adjustments may be required where there has been a fundamental error in any one year.
▶ Adjustments may be required for post balance sheet events of an adjusting nature.
▶ Given that the reporting accountant is required to state an opinion on the financial information reported on and that this information is intended to enable an appreciation of a trend of results and financial position, adjustments may be required if the trend of results would be misleading for any reason. It is therefore necessary to consider, for example, whether adjustments should be made to previous years' published audited accounts to take into account the effect of acquisitions and disposals of significant parts of the business/group during any one year; it will be necessary to consider how the effect of the change in the company's or group's operations can most appropriately be shown.

The Auditing Guideline states that except where merger accounting is adopted the acquisition or disposal of companies or businesses is not, normally, a reason to make adjustments to the audited financial statements for the years prior to the acquisition or disposal, which should remain as originally reported. However, where the acquisition or disposal is material, its effect should be disclosed within the accountants' report, and the most appropriate presentation of the results of the group as constituted at the date of the report may be by way of note setting out separately the relevant figures in respect of the acquisition or disposal.

Profit forecasts

When boards of directors are communicating with existing or potential shareholders, there are often circumstances in which they are responsible for ensuring that they provide all the information that the recipients of the communication need in making an informed judgement. In discharging this responsibility, the directors may consider it necessary to publish a forecast of the probable outcome of the current financial period and, sometimes, of the succeeding period as well.

It is important that you are aware of the fact that there are no requirements in the UK for companies to make or to publish profit forecasts. It is sometimes believed that directors, when they are making or are faced with a take-over bid, have to make a profit forecast. This is not so.

As a result of take-over activities, the City Code on take-overs and mergers requires directors using profit forecasts in take-over negotiations to have such forecasts examined by independent accountants and to publish an accountants' report thereon. In addition, the International Stock Exchange requests any profit forecast that is included in a prospectus document to be examined by independent accountants, and it regards the accountants' report thereon to be published in the prospectus. These requirements to publish the report have led to a general acceptance of a standardised short-form of report for publication, backed up by an unpublished long-form report.

The circumstances in which independent accountants may be approached to report on profit forecasts are usually one of the following:

▶ When a company proposes to publish a profit forecast in connection with a take-over or a merger that is subject to the published code of conduct (City Code) in such situations.

▶ When a company proposes to publish a profit forecast as part of a prospectus, or an offer for sale or other document which is subject to the rules and regulations of the International Stock Exchange.

▶ When accountants are appointed to carry out an investigation or a review of a company and the terms of the accountants' appointment include a review of profit forecasts.

In the first two situations above the reporting accountants would be required to prepare a report for publication (short-form report). In the third situation the report would be in greater detail and would not be intended for publication (long-form report). Long-form reports are sometimes additionally required in the first two situations.

In all situations, care must be taken to ensure that all parties concerned know what is meant by a profit forecast as opposed to a profit target or other forms of budget. A profit forecast is the level of profitability that the directors reasonably and honestly expect to achieve, whereas a profit target represents the profit level to which management may be striving. The City Code puts a strict interpretation on what constitutes a forecast:

It should be appreciated that even when no particular figure is mentioned certain forms of words may constitute a profit forecast. Examples are 'profits will be somewhat higher than last year'.

The division of responsibility in the preparation of a profit forecast

The sole responsibility for a profit forecast rests with the directors, who cannot be relieved of their responsibility by reporting accountants or financial advisers. Where the reporting accountants are also the auditors of the company, the directors must understand that there is no question of the profit forecast being audited by the auditors. In no circumstances can the reporting accountants prepare a profit forecast on behalf of the directors. If, in exceptional circumstances, the reporting accountants find it necessary to assist the directors to prepare a forecast, they must make it clear to the directors that the responsibility is the directors' alone.

It is not possible for reporting accountants to confirm and verify a profit forecast in the same way as they can confirm and verify financial statements. It is the accounting policies and calculations for the forecasts that they must examine and report on. They are required to satisfy themselves that the accounting bases and the calculations have been properly compiled on the footing of the assumptions made. As a result of their review they will be able to advise the company on what assumptions should be listed and the way in which they should be described. The reporting accountants will also want to satisfy themselves that the forecast is attainable. This means that they must form a judgement on the company's resources, particularly those relating to working capital, raw material supplies, manpower and management. They also need to form a judgement on the company's dependence on certain of its main customers. Their examination will therefore include examining the cash flow projections and assessing future viability.

There should be no restrictions on the scope of the work of reporting accountants. With a published report such restrictions would usually be unacceptable to the reporting accountant. In the case of investigations into unpublished forecasts reporting accountants should agree with their client any restrictions on the scope of their work beforehand and should satisfy themselves that such restrictions are acceptable.

Requirements of regulatory organisations

The City Code states:

> Shareholders shall have in their possession sufficient evidence, facts and opinions upon which an adequate judgement and decision can be reached, and shall have sufficient time to make an assessment and decision. No relevant information shall be withheld from them.

Although this implies that a profit forecast is desirable in take-over situations, the Code does not specifically require that there should be one. If the directors believe they can give adequate up-to-date information by other means, they are permitted to do so.

When a profit forecast is included in any circular to shareholders in connection with an offer, the Code requires:

▶ The accounting policies and the calculations for the forecast must be examined and reported on by auditors or consultant accountants.
▶ Any financial adviser mentioned in the document must also report on the forecasts.
▶ The accountants' report and (if there is an adviser) the adviser's report, must be contained in the document, and it must be accompanied by a statement that those making the reports have given their consent to the reports being published, and they have not withdrawn their consent.

▶ The assumptions (including the commercial assumptions) upon which the directors have based their profit forecast must be stated in the document.

▶ Wherever a profit forecast appears in relation to a period in which trading has already commenced, any previously published profit figures that are available in respect of any expired portion of that trading period, together with comparable figures for the preceding year, must be stated.

In addition the Code suggests that the following general rules should apply to the selecting and the drafting of assumptions:

▶ The reader should be able to understand the implications of the assumptions, so that he or she can be helped in forming a judgement as to the reasonableness of the forecast and the main uncertainties attaching to it.

▶ The assumption should be, wherever possible, specific rather than general, and definite rather than vague.

▶ All-embracing assumptions and assumptions relating to the general accuracy of the estimates should be avoided.

▶ The assumptions should relate only to matters that may have a material bearing on the forecast.

The International Stock Exchange rules require a prospectus to include a statement as to the financial and the trading prospects of the company or group, together with any material information that may be relevant to those prospects. This should include all special trade factors or risks that are not mentioned elsewhere in the prospectus, and that are unlikely to be known or anticipated by the general public, and that could materially affect profits.

The foregoing is not a requirement to issue a profit forecast. It is in fact a much wider requirement regarding trading prospects, and it is often interpreted as including the need to make a profit forecast although it does not necessarily do so. When, as frequently happens, a forecast is published, the rules state:

> Where a profit forecast appears in any prospectus the principal assumptions, including commercial assumptions, upon which the directors have based their profit forecast, must be stated. The accounting bases and calculations for the forecast must be examined and reported on by the auditors to the company, and any reporting accountants joined with the auditors in their report, and such report must be set out. The issuing house, or, in the absence of an issuing house, the sponsoring brokers must report in addition whether or not they have satisfied themselves that the forecast has been stated by the directors after due and careful enquiry, and such report must be set out.

The parts of a profit forecast

Reporting accountants should not normally undertake to review a profit forecast and to report to the directors on it, if it is intended to be published for any period beyond the date of expiry of the current accounting period. (For the purposes of unpublished reports, accountants may be asked to review and report on a forecast for a longer period ahead. If they accept such an assignment they must recognise the increasing uncertainties that underlie the assumptions made in preparing the forecast.)

As has been pointed out, a published forecast does not necessarily have to be expressed in monetary amounts. For forecasts to be informative, however, it is generally considered better to give monetary amounts, and the majority of forecasts now take the form of a pro-forma profit and loss account.

The City Code Practice says that 'there should be included where possible in forecasts of turnover, profit before taxation, taxation (when the figure is significantly abnormal), minority interests and extraordinary items (when either of these amounts is material).'

The International Stock Exchange rules do not include specific requirements as to the form of a published forecast. For this reason, forecasts in prospectuses are sometimes restricted to the 'estimated group profit before taxation'.

Because of the uncertainties attached to forecasting directors sometimes publish a range within which the actual profit is considered likely to fall. Alternatively, they sometimes specify that the forecast profit will be 'not less than' a certain amount. Sometimes the forecast is accompanied by an assessment of the possibilities associated with the basic assumptions. The City Code states: 'It may be helpful to indicate what the effect on the profit forecast would be if certain of the major assumptions were to prove to be wholly or partly invalid.'

It may be necessary in some circumstances to indicate the bases and the accounting policies adopted in preparing the forecast, if these cannot be ascertained from the accounting policies normally adopted.

The statement of assumptions should normally be regarded as an essential part of the published forecast. The only exception to this is likely to be where the forecast period has already expired, and it is not necessary to make assumptions about future events.

In their examination of a published forecast, reporting accountants will wish to be satisfied that it shows clearly:

▶ the period for which the forecast is made
▶ whether it is subject to any major uncertainties that should be disclosed
▶ whether the principal assumptions on which it is based are clearly stated.

It is the directors' responsibility to determine and to make reasonable assumptions about those unknown factors that could materially upset the ultimate realisation of their forecasts. These factors will often be determined by the size and the type of organisation and by the geographical areas in which it trades. Thus, political and world economic assumptions may be vital to a large organisation but relatively remote to a smaller one; industrial disturbances may not apply to a financial corporation; interest rates or the general availability of capital may be important to one group but not to another that has adequate capital; and the buying policies of major customers or even climatic conditions may be relevant.

Assumptions should not relate to the accuracy of the accounting and the forecasting systems.

Although reporting accountants have no responsibility for the assumptions, they will, as a result of this review, be in a position to advise the company both on the assumptions that should be listed and on the way in which these assumptions should be described.

If a forecast has been carefully prepared, the reasons for any difference from final results should be capable of being assessed and explained.

They should particularly be capable of being identified with an assumption that proved, in the event, to be wrong. The vital point is whether the forecast was honestly prepared and honestly presented, and not whether it was achieved.

EXAMPLE 23.4 – AN EXAMPLE OF A PROFIT FORECAST

I am now able to confirm a forecast of profit before taxation and extraordinary items for the year ending ....19....... in excess of £500,000. The basis on which it has been prepared, together with further details relating to the forecast, are set out in Appendix B.

Appendix B
The forecast of profit before taxation and extraordinary items of ABC plc and its subsidiaries for the year ending .... 19.... in excess of £500,000 has been compiled on the basis of the accounting policies normally adopted by ABC plc and its

subsidiaries. It includes results shown by published interim unaudited results for the six months to ....19..... The principal assumptions on which the directors have based their forecast are that:

(a) Sales for the remainder of the financial year will reflect normal seasonal patterns.
(b) There will be no new ventures or acquisitions during the remainder of the financial year.
(c) The operation of the group will not be materially affected by strikes or adverse weather conditions.
(d) There will be no material change in the economic climate currently being experienced, nor will the operations of the group be adversely affected by future Government action in the United Kingdom.

An example of a short-form accountants' report

Provided that the reporting accountants have no material reservations about the accounting policies and the calculations for the forecast, and have no reason to think that they are inconsistent with the stated assumptions, their short-form report for publication will be similar to that shown in Example 23.5.

EXAMPLE 23.5

We have reviewed the accounting policies and the calculations for the profit forecast (for which the directors are solely responsible) of ABC plc and its subsidiaries ('the group') for the year ending .... included in ....dated ....addressed to ....

The forecast includes results shown by (audited interim accounts) (unaudited interim accounts) (unaudited management accounts) for the .....months ended ....19.... In our opinion, the forecast, so far as the accounting policies and the calculations are concerned, has been properly compiled on the basis of the assumptions made by the directors set out in (the document). Also, it is presented, in our opinion, on a basis consistent with the accounting policies normally adopted by the group.

The reporting accountants and the financial advisers both have to give their consent to the issue of the document with the inclusion therein of their respective reports in the form and the context in which those reports appear. The letter of consent must therefore refer to the form and the context in which their report is included, and it will usually be in the form shown in Example 23.6.

EXAMPLE 23.6

We hereby consent to the issue to the shareholders of ABC plc of the circular dated ....19.... with the inclusion therein of our report dated ....19.... in the form and the context in which it is included.

Reports relating to rights issues

Companies issue securities for a variety of reasons, essentially in order to raise finance, but also to, for example:

▶ attain a listing on the Stock Exchange

- change the capital structure of the company
- increase the marketability of the shares of a company
- change the pattern of owners' control
- merge with another company.

This chapter has dealt with the role of the reporting accountant where a company issues a prospectus when it invites the public to apply for its shares or debentures. We now look at the role of an accountant where the company makes a rights issue, that is, where the right to take up the new issue is initially restricted to the existing shareholders of the company. The existing shareholders may decide to take up the rights, subscribe for the new shares and invest further in the company, or sell the rights to subscribe to a third party.

Because the rights to subscribe may be sold and, therefore, the general public can invest in the company, it is usual when making a rights issue to issue a prospectus. Existing shareholders will have to be informed and a document prepared. This will include listing particulars with regard to the company in accordance with the listing rules made under Part IV of the Financial Services Act 1986 and will have been delivered to the Registrar of Companies. The company will have made application to the Council of the Stock Exchange for the new shares to be admitted to the official list, before the rights issue document is distributed.

The rights issue document

The document will be addressed to the ordinary shareholders and others with conversion rights such as holders of convertible loan stock and will include the following:

- reasons for the rights issue, for example, financing of capital expenditure, provision of additional working capital, reduction of gearing
- a proposed timetable of events, for example, date for acceptance and payment, registration of renunciation and despatch of share certificates
- details of the rights issue such as the amount to be raised, number of shares to be issued and the basis, for example 1:4
- further supporting information such as details of working capital, indebtedness, directors' shareholdings, rights attaching to shares already in issue, UK taxation of dividends and underwriting expenses
- a recommendation by the directors that shareholders take up their entitlements and that the issue is in the best interests of the company and its shareholders.

Note again that even though a rights issue is an economical way of raising equity finance in that all that is required is a document to be sent to shareholders informing them of their right to subscribe for the rights issue at the stated price, given the possible involvement of the general public, it is usual to issue a prospectus.

Summary

This chapter dealt with first the expansion of the annual report in terms of additional statements such as the value added statements and segmental reports and second with the work of a reporting accountant, who may or may not be the company's auditor, in the preparation of a prospectus or other share circular and also of a profit forecast.

The additional statements need to be considered in the context of user needs:

- they provide different user groups with different information
- they present information in a format that might provide additional insights into a company.

Against this you need to consider the additional costs involved in their preparation.

As to accountants' reports, this chapter concentrates on the prospectus and the regulations of the Act and the Stock Exchange listing rules in this regard. The accountants' report will include a five-year summary, adjusted where appropriate for the trends disclosed to give a true and fair view. Such time-series are also dealt with in Chapter 29 in the different context of the voluntary disclosure of an historical summary as a part of the annual report of a company.

Profit forecasts are included in the prospectus of a company seeking a listing for its shares on the Stock Exchange and also in circulars issued in a take-over or merger situation. The forecasts are the sole responsibility of the directors. The role of the reporting accountant is two-fold. First to report on the accounting policies and calculations, and second to satisfy themselves that the forecast has been properly prepared on the footing of the assumptions made.

Suggested reading

Admission of Securities to Listing (The Yellow Book, Stock Exchange)

The Value Added Statement (Morley 1978)

Prospectuses and the reporting accountant (ACCA)

Development in Financial Reporting (Lee 1981)

The Corporate Report (ASC 1975)

Self test questions

1   The Corporate Report identified six main groups of people who might be interested in financial statements. List these groups.

2   What is 'value added', and what is a value added statement designed to show?

3   List the matters required by the Stock Exchange to be covered by an accountants' report in a prospectus to be issued by a company seeking a listing for its shares.

4   Provide reasons for preparing profit forecasts and indicate the problems that can arise in producing them.

5   From the data provided below prepare a value added statement for the year ended 31 December 1994, using the format illustrated in the Corporate Report.

Information for the year ended 31 December 1994:

	£000
Corporation tax on the profit for the year	280
Depreciation of plant and machinery	160
Proposed dividends	96
Loan interest paid and payable	40
Materials purchased for production	1,200
Salaries and wages	800
Sales	2,960
Purchase of services and overheads	240

Exam style question

1 *Pru Pereira*

'THIS CIRCULAR IS IMPORTANT – IF YOU ARE IN ANY DOUBT AS TO WHAT ACTION TO TAKE YOU SHOULD CONSULT YOUR STOCKBROKER, BANK MANAGER, SOLICITOR, ACCOUNTANT OR OTHER PROFESSIONAL ADVISER IMMEDIATELY.'

Your client, Pru Pereira, has recently received three such circulars:

a) Circular from Company A (20 February 1989):

Conversion of 8½% Convertible Unsecured Loan Stock 1995/2000

By notice given between 20 February 1989 and 25 February 1989 you are entitled to convert the whole or part (being £1 or a multiple of £1) of your Stock holding into Ordinary shares of 25p each of the Company and to require the Company to allot as at 25 March 1989 fully paid Ordinary Shares in exchange for and in satisfaction of such amount of Stock held by you as you may specify. The basis of conversion is £34.39 nominal amount of share capital for each £100 nominal amount of Stock and so in proportion for other nominal amounts of Stock. Shares representing fractional entitlements will be sold and the net proceeds in excess of £1 distributed to the person entitled thereto.

If you do not wish to exercise your conversion rights now there will be a further and final period in 1990 during which such rights may be exercised in accordance with the conditions permitted on Stock certificates.

On 19 February 1989, the last practicable date before the despatch of this circular, the middle market quotation on the Stock Exchange, London of the Ordinary Shares of the Company was 58p per Ordinary Share and of the Stock was 83p per £100 nominal of the Stock.

(12 marks)

b) Circular from Company B (1 March 1989)

Proposed purchase by the company of its own Preference Shares

. . . an announcement was made on 25 February 1989 of the proposal to purchase the entire issued preference Share Capital at a price of 75p per share together with dividends accrued to the date-of purchase. This represents an increase of more than 50 per cent over the mid-market price of the Preference Shares on the 24 February 1989.

(5 marks)

c) Circular from Company C (24 March 1989):

Proposed rights issue of Ordinary Shares

It was announced on 23 March 1989 that the Board proposed to offer 23,852,173 new Ordinary Shares by way of rights at 87p per Ordinary Share on the basis of one new ordinary share for every five ordinary shares held at the close of business on 3 March 1989. The issue, which has been underwritten by Dubash & Co. Ltd, will raise approximately £19.95 million (net of expenses).

Dividend

As will be seen from the summary of Group results, it is proposed to pay a final dividend of 4.36p per Ordinary Share in respect of the year ended 31 December 1988 on the existing Ordinary Shares making a total of 6.61p per share for the year.

The Directors expect, in the absence of any unforeseen circumstances, to recommend a maintained rate of total dividend for the year to 31 December 1989, amounting to 6.61p (net) per Ordinary share, on the Share Capital of the Company as increased by the rights issue. The total divided, with related tax credits at the current rate, would be equivalent to a gross dividend of 8.8133p per share for the year (1988: the same) which would represent a gross yield of 10.13 per cent on the issue price.

From the *Financial Times* dated 24 March 1989 you see that the ordinary shares of Company C were quoted at 109, down 10 from the previous day.

(13 marks)

Required:

Prepare notes on the advice you would give to Pru Pereira, who has consulted you after receiving the circulars above, stating clearly any assumptions you make regarding the circumstances of your client, *and* explaining the probable reason(s) for the Companies' proposals.

(Total 30 marks)
(*Based on ICAEW PE II July 1976*)

All answers on pages 694–697.

Share Valuation

The syllabus for Paper 13 includes sections on assessing the valuation of shares in unquoted companies and calculating and appraising the impact on 'profit reporting and balance sheet' of the available methods of valuation. You may, therefore, be examined on methods of valuing the whole undertaking either as a going concern, or for the purposes of a merger, or for a minority investment or for a total or partial liquidation.

It is important to establish, at the beginning, that there is no one exclusive method whereby you can place a value on a business or in the shares of that business. In the last analysis, the value of a share is the agreed level at which a vendor is prepared to sell and at which a purchaser is prepared to buy that share. In relation to quoted shares the Council of the International Stock Exchange states that Stock Exchange quotations are not directly related to the value of a company's assets or to the amount of its profits and that these quotations cannot form a fair and equitable or even rational basis for compensation. The Stock Exchange registers the actions and opinions of private and institutional investors all over the world; these are the result of hope, fear, guesswork, investment policy and many other considerations. In considering therefore the alternative bases that may be taken into account in valuing the shares of a business all one can do is to determine a range of values within which a successful bid may be made.

Alternative bases for valuing shares include:

► the dividend yield basis
► the price/earnings (p/e) ratio basis
► the assets basis on either a going concern or break-up basis.

Again, it must be stressed that none of these methods will enable you to arrive at a precise value per share; considered together they will indicate a range of values within which an existing shareholder may sell or an intending shareholder will be prepared to purchase shares.

It is also important to consider the circumstances in which you may be called upon to value shares in an examination situation. Thus you may be faced with a valuation question dealing with:

► transfer of shares in an unlisted company
► valuation of shareholdings in a merger or takeover situation
► the issue of shares to the public
► the purchase by a company of its own shares.

A share is defined in *Borland's Trustee* v. *Steel Brothers* (1901) as:

> A share is the interest of a shareholder in a company measured by a sum of money for the purpose of liability in the first place and of interest in the second but also consisting of a series of mutual covenants entered into by all the shareholders.

Questions on share valuation in this paper are likely to be combined with requirements dealing with calculations of key statistics, for example, eps and aspects of interpretation of accounts that are dealt with in Chapter 28 and Chapter 29. Such questions will therefore require a broad understanding of various financial matters, will not have any one 'correct' answer and will test you on the underlying principles involved.

Different valuation bases

The valuation bases dealt with above that are more or less relevant to a given valuation situation will essentially depend on whether the shares being valued are in an unlisted company or in a plc and, further, whether the purchase or sale under consideration is of a minority or a majority holding. The important distinction between listed and unlisted holdings is that the shares of the latter are not freely marketable. The important distinction between minority and majority holdings is that the latter enables control and would usually involve the payment of a control premium.

Situation 1: An unlisted company (minority holding)

The main interest of an investor in such a holding will be in the expectation of a steady stream of dividends. The investor has little or no control over the earnings or assets of the company. The most appropriate basis for valuation is therefore that of the dividend yield or dividend capitalisation basis.

Situation 2: A listed company (minority holding)

Intending investors would look first to annual dividend income and secondly to capital growth from the holding of such an investment. A minority holding in a listed company would therefore be valued on the basis of both the dividend yield basis and the p/e ratio basis. Given the two separate and different valuations obtained, the relative importance of each would depend on the individual requirements of a particular investor. If the investor were concerned with capital growth the p/e ratio provides an indication of the extent to which the market has taken into account future growth prospects in placing a value on a share. The higher a current p/e ratio the greater the presumption that the market has already taken into account future growth potential in the current share price; the lower the p/e ratio the greater the presumption that the market anticipates a future decline in eps.

Situation 3: Majority holdings in listed or unlisted companies

Given the control acquired by an investor through the purchase of such a holding it follows that the dividend yield basis of valuation is of less significance and the value of shares should be ascertained in terms of the asset worth and earnings potential of the company.

Assets basis: attributable values

The value of a share is simply determined by dividing the total value of the net assets of the company by the number of ordinary shares in issue. If there are any preference shares or debentures in issue it is important to remember to deduct these from the value of the net assets and to also deduct, where relevant, any premium payable on redemption.

The one problem area that arises on this basis is to arrive at a separate value for goodwill. This could be valued at a number of years' purchase of the 'super profits' of a business, or the surplus of profits actually earned over and above those that may reasonably be expected of the capital employed in the company. The questions of how many years' purchase and what represents a normal yield for the capital employed in a business are questions of judgement. The basis of the calculation would be:

	£
Average maintainable profits	x
Less: Normal yield on capital employed	(x)
'Super profits'	x

Number of years' purchase thereof = value placed on goodwill.

Assets basis: capitalised earnings

One way to avoid the problem of a separate valuation for goodwill in using the assets basis is to arrive at a value for the business as a whole in terms of its total assets including goodwill by ascertaining the rate of return an investor would expect from an investment in the selling company and capitalising the earnings of the selling company by this rate. Given that the earnings of the selling company represent a return on investment for a purchaser, the purchaser values the net assets, including goodwill, on the basis of what they generate in terms of earnings. In so far as information is available, you could arrive at alternative valuations using discounting techniques, as follows:

▶ Ascertain the average maintainable earnings of the company before interest on long-term debt and dividends. Include investment income on long-term investments but exclude investment income on investments that merely represent temporary investment of surplus funds. Charge a market rent on freehold properties. Adjust directors' remuneration to reflect commercial considerations. Possible adjustments for stock, R & D, depreciation.
▶ Capitalise using, as indicated, discounted or undiscounted rates of return.
▶ Add the market value of the investments that represent the temporary investment of surplus funds and the market value of any freeholds.
▶ Deduct the market value of any debentures and/or preference shares.
▶ This equals the value of the ordinary share capital, which when divided by the number of ordinary shares gives the value per ordinary share.

Price/earnings ratio basis

For listed companies one would use this basis in placing a value on a majority holding by multiplying the eps of the vendor company by the p/e offered (price offered/eps of the vendor company). The p/e offered would be higher than the actual p/e of the vendor company to take account of the fact that a suitable 'control premium' needs to be paid by the purchaser in seeking a controlling interest. Put another way vendor shareholders must be offered a suitable 'exit p/e ratio' to persuade them to part with their shares to the purchaser rather than to sell them in the open market.

In terms of maximising eps of the purchaser company's shareholders, where shares of the purchasing company are offered for shares of the vendor company, there will be an increase in eps attributable to these shareholders after the purchase if the 'p/e offered' is less than the p/e of the purchasing company; such an offer is hardly likely to be acceptable to the shareholders of the vendor company. There will be no change in the relative eps position of the purchaser company's shareholders if the p/e offered equals the p/e of the purchasing company. There will be dilution in the eps available for the purchaser company's shareholders if the p/e offered is greater than that of the purchasing company. Such an offer would, therefore, be made only if combined earnings as a result of the combination were anticipated, given synergy, to increase. Bear in mind that the form of the consideration offered could of itself affect the acceptability of an offer price.

Unlisted companies do not have a p/e ratio but the basis may none the less be used in arriving at an alternative valuation for such a majority holding by multiplying the eps of the vendor company by a suitably reduced p/e of a similar listed company to take into account the disadvantage of a lack of marketability as to shares in unlisted companies.

Situation 4: Valuation for a share issue

Even though it may appear that a majority valuation basis would be appropriate for this situation it must be remembered that although substantial amounts of the capital of the company that is seeking a listing will be on offer it will be applied for in a large number of minority applications. The shares should be issued at a discount to the p/e ratio of a similar listed company and should also offer a dividend yield in excess of that available on similar listed companies.

Some definitions

In dealing with this part of the syllabus it is essential that you are familiar with the financial terms as stated in the stock exchange daily official list. These terms are defined below.

Dividend yield relates the dividend per share to the market price of that share expressed as a percentage. It is a measure of the dividend or income return on an investment. It is useful in that it can be compared with the yields available on alternative forms of investment. It may be calculated in terms of the Actual rate of dividend × Nominal value (NV) per share/Market value (MV) per share. Where the share does not have a MV, the value of the share may be ascertained using the dividend yield basis as amounting to NV per share × Actual rate of dividend/Investor's required rate of income return. In order to compare dividend yields with the yields available on alternative investments such as government securities, local authority bonds and debentures the gross rate of dividend should be dealt with above.

Dividend cover relates dividends paid to the profits available for the payment of those dividends. For a shareholder it is an indication of the security available for the continuing payment of dividends. Cover = eps/dividend per share (net).

Price/earnings or p/e ratio This has been referred to in the previous section and relates eps to the market price of a share expressed as an inverted ratio. It is sometimes referred to as the 'earnings multiple' given that it represents the number of years it would take to recover the price paid for a share in terms of current eps. Using the p/e ratio the price of a share may be expressed as eps × p/e. This implies that the share price will change only where there is a change in eps, which is obviously not so in reality. None the less this principle of determining the value of a share is used extensively in share valuation.

Market capitalisation represents the MV of the issued capital of a company. Thus Market capitalisation = Number of shares × Share price. It does not represent the asset worth of the company.

Further points regarding minority holdings

As already stated, the appropriate basis for valuation of such a holding of shares is that of the dividend yield. The value of a share using this basis is:

$$\text{NV} \times \frac{\text{Actual dividend (gross)}}{\text{Investor's required rate of return as dividend (gross)}}$$

Where information is available, it is more realistic to use expected rates of future dividends and, where possible, to build in growth to the valuation.

The size of the minority holding being acquired is also of relevance in that an investor may be prepared to accept a lower rate of return, that is, pay more for the shares for the advantages that follow from a holding in excess of a certain percentage. These advantages follow from a holding of:

▶ More than 15% – the 1985 Act gives holders of not less than 15% in aggregate of a class of shares the power to apply to the court to have any variation in rights attaching to the shares cancelled.
▶ More than 20% – 'significant influence' (see Chapter 21).
▶ More than 25% – this enables a shareholder to block a special resolution.

Obviously, and of relevance to shares in unlisted companies, the greater the restrictions attaching to the transferability of shares, the higher would be an investor's required rate of return and the lower the price an investor would be prepared to pay. See Example 24.1.

EXAMPLE 24.1

Company X currently pays a dividend of 18p per £1 share, that is, a net dividend at the rate of 18%. An intending purchaser of a minority holding in the company requires a rate of return of 15%, gross, on his investments. The basic rate of income tax is 25%. The value of the shares is:

$$£1 \times \frac{(18 \times 100/75)}{0.15} = £1.6$$

If growth is indicated as to the dividends – say 7% – use the formula:

$$\text{Price} = £1 \times \frac{\text{Current dividend} + (1 + \text{growth rate})}{(\text{Required rate} - \text{growth rate})}$$

Therefore, the price or value would be:

$$£1 \times \frac{(18 \times 100/75) = 24 \times (1 + 0.07)}{(0.15 - 0.07)}$$

i.e. £3.21

At this price, the investor's current yield would be

$$\frac{24}{321} = 7.5\%$$

In those situations where you are called upon to value either preference shares or debentures always use the dividend yield basis as above.

Further points regarding majority holdings

As already stated, an investor wishing to acquire a majority holding will acquire control over the earnings of the company and, therefore, over the dividends paid out of such earnings. It is not, therefore, appropriate to value such holdings on the basis of the dividend yield.

As the purchaser would also acquire control over the disposition of the assets of the company, it would be appropriate to value the shares in terms of both the net assets and the earnings of the company.

Assets basis of valuation

You could value the net assets underlying the shares on the basis of both attributable values and in terms of the earnings generated by those assets.

Attributable values

Under this method the value of the shares is the sum of the total value of the assets representing those shares; for ordinary shares this is equal to the value of the ordinary share capital plus the reserves of the company. Obviously the value of the net assets will vary depending upon whether you are called to value them on the basis of going concern or break up values. In any event, a valuation on this basis should provide you with a value at the lower end of the range of values to be put on the shares. It is improbable that a vendor would accept lower value. A question may lead you into adjustments to be made to balance sheet values. Look out for the following and make adjustments to the reserves of the company in the balance sheet accordingly:

▶ revaluations
▶ changes in value arising from changes in accounting policy
▶ adjustments for off balance sheet finance.

Note that such a valuation excludes goodwill, which will need to be separately considered.

Assets valued on the basis of the earnings that they generate

EXAMPLE 24.2

If the attributable values of the net assets of the company happen to be £150,000 and current maintainable annual earnings £40,000 before tax and an investor requires a yield or return on an investment, pre-tax, of 15%, the value to be placed on the net assets would be the capitalised earnings of the company, that is, £40,000 × 100/15 = £266,667. This method eliminates the need to consider goodwill separately. The investor pays goodwill, as defined by SSAP 22, of £116,667 (266,167 – 150,000).

As with the attributable values calculation, adjustments may be required in terms of:

▶ remuneration of directors
▶ effect on earnings of changes in accounting policy
▶ anticipated growth in earnings.

Where you undertake to value shares on this basis problems will arise where the company has freehold properties, investments, preference shares and debentures (see Example 24.3).

EXAMPLE 24.3

Facts as in Example 24.2 except that the company has investments in its net assets at a book value of £30,000 and investment income is £3,500 per annum. The market value of the investments is £40,000. The company also has preference shares in issue of £15,000 and 10% debentures of £10,000.

	£
Maintainable profit	40,000
Add: Debenture interest 10% × 10,000	1,000
Less: Investment income	(3,500)
Adjusted earnings, pre-tax	37,500
Capitalised at 15%	x 100/15
	= 250,000
Add: Market value of investments	40,000
	290,000
Deduct: Preference share capital, yield in line with market rates, therefore NV	(15,000)
Deduct: Debentures, yield in line with market rates, therefore NV	(10,000)
Value of net assets representing ordinary shares	265,000

The earnings or p/e ratio basis of valuation

A company may be valued on this basis using either an accounting rate of return or a p/e ratio.

In a takeover situation, the company to be taken over may be valued in terms of required rates of return on either the basis of the existing return on capital employed of the purchaser company *or* a similar listed company (information on which is provided in the question) or on the basis of the p/e ratio of the purchaser company or similar listed company (information on which is provided in the question). An accounting rate of return, or capitalising the (adjusted) earnings of the vendor company, by the required return on capital employed of the purchaser company, may well be more appropriate than the p/e approach to the valuation of shares in a small unlisted company. The procedure is as in Example 24.3.

Where p/e information is provided, or information is provided to enable you to calculate eps and therefore a p/e, a value for shares to be purchased is arrived at as follows:

Value per share = eps of vendor company × p/e (of similar listed company)

In any event, before arriving at a value, the earnings of the vendor should be adjusted in the light of any relevant post-acquisition information provided in a question. You should reduce the p/e of a similar listed company in the calculation above to reflect the lack of a market for shares in an unlisted company.

Report writing

Share valuation questions in an examination will usually require you to write a report. You should deal with, in the report, the following:

▶ The circumstances of the valuation exercise.
▶ The point that there is no such thing as one value to be arrived at; one is concerned with establishing a range of values for negotiation.
▶ The fact that there are alternative bases of valuation and what these are.
▶ The fact that different bases of valuation are more or less relevant in different circumstances; applying more relevant bases to the particular circumstances of the valuation.

▶ Arriving at a range of values, taking account of all information given in the question.

▶ Noting the importance of the form of consideration, that is, cash, loan stock, shares and, possibly, having an effect on the value of the shares being valued.

▶ Arriving at a conclusion comparing positions of interested parties prior to and post the sale/purchase of shares at a price within the range of values arrived at.

Summary

This chapter deals with the basic principles involved in the valuation of shares in private companies. It sets out alternative valuation bases and identifies the circumstances where one or other basis may be more or less relevant in arriving at a value that is acceptable to the different parties involved. The chapter includes some definitions as to financial terms and should be generally borne in mind when you come to later chapters dealing with the interpretation of accounts.

Final level accounting papers have, traditionally, usually included questions involving the writing of reports and this chapter outlines, in broad terms, the steps that you should follow in report writing regarding share valuation.

Suggested reading

Accountants Digest No 52 – The statutory valuation of unquoted shares

Advanced Financial Accounting (Lewis, Pendrill and Simon)

Self test questions

1   Outline the situations in which the valuation of a business may be required.

2   Fink Ltd is a profitable private company. Its profits over the last five years have ranged from £3,000 to £34,000 and the maintainable profit is reasonably taken to be £30,400. The book values of the company's net assets are currently £60,000 and their net realisable value £220,000. The listed shares of a similar company sell at a p/e of 10.

Value the company on the basis of its earnings.

3   Information as in question 2 and you are additionally informed that an expected normal rate of return on net assets for a company like Fink Ltd is 10%. Value the company in terms of its net assets where goodwill is to be valued at four years' purchase of 'super profits'.

4   If net dividends are £6,000, the number of ordinary shares is 100,000, the market price per share is £1.50 and the rate of ACT is 3/7, what is the dividend yield?

5   Why is the p/e ratio an important tool in the valuation of shares?

Exam style questions

1   *Fig plc*
    You act in the capacity of financial adviser to a number of companies. One of them, Fig plc, whose managing director is not familiar with finance, has asked you to explain some financial terms which he does not understand and has also asked you to assist him in obtaining certain information. An extract of the letter received from the managing director of Fig plc is as follows:

    I should be grateful if you would briefly explain the following matters:

    (1) For ordinary shares quoted in the *Financial Times*, the following particulars:

Company	Price	+ or −	Dividend Net	Cover	Yield Gross	P/E
x	x	x	x	x	x	x

    (2) This extract from the quotations page of the *Financial Times*:

    'Price/earnings ratios are calculated on "net" distribution basis ...; bracketed figures indicate 10 per cent more difference if calculated on "nil" distribution. Covers are based on "maximum" distribution.'

    In addition could you please inform me where I might obtain the following information:

    a)   daily share prices for any share quoted on the International Stock Exchange, London
    b)   recent dividends and rights issues of UK listed companies
    c)   copies of the financial statements of my competitors, which include both public and private companies in the UK.

    Required:
    Draft a letter in reply.

    (20 marks)

2   *Hari Kumar*
    The directors of Hari Kumar plc, a large listed company, are engaged in a policy of expansion. Accordingly, they have approached the directors of Leyton Ltd, an unlisted company of substantial size, in connection with a proposed purchase of the business of Leyton Ltd.

    The directors of Leyton Ltd have indicated that the shareholders of Leyton Ltd would prefer the form of the consideration for the purchase of their shares to be in cash and you are informed that this is acceptable to the prospective purchasing company, Hari Kumar plc.

    The directors of Leyton Ltd have now been asked to state the price at which the shareholders of Leyton Ltd would be prepared to sell their shares to Hari Kumar plc. You have been asked to advise the directors of Leyton Ltd in this regard.

    In order that you may be able to do so, the following details have been extracted from the most recent financial statements of Leyton Ltd.

Balance sheet extracts as on 30 June 1991:

	£000
Purchased goodwill unamortised	7,500
Freehold property	15,000
Plant and machinery	30,000
Investments	7,500
Net current assets	6,000
10% debentures	(15,000)
Ordinary shares of £1 each	(20,000)
7% preference shares of £1 each	(6,000)
Share premium account	(10,000)
Profit and loss account	(15,000)

(Amounts in brackets indicate credit balances.)

Profit and loss account extracts for the year ended 30 June 1991:

	£000
Profit before interest payments and taxation	9,000
Interest	(1,500)
Taxation on ordinary activities	(3,000)
Extraordinary items, net of related taxation	750
Dividends paid – preference	(420)
– ordinary	(1,500)
Profit retained for the year	3,330

(Amounts in brackets indicate charges or appropriations.)

The following further information is also supplied to you:

1 Profit before interest payments and taxation for the year ended 30 June 1990 amounted to £12 million and for the year ended 30 June 1989 amounted to £15 million.
2 The share premium account arose on the issue of ordinary shares at a premium.
3 The preference share capital can be sold independently, and a buyer has been found to purchase these shares at 90 pence each. The price is acceptable to the existing preference shareholders of Leyton Ltd.
4 Hari Kumar plc has agreed to purchase the 10% debentures of Leyton Ltd at a price of £110 for each £100 of the debentures.
5 The current rental value of the freehold property is £2.25 million per annum and a buyer is available on the basis of offering an 8% return to the freeholder.
6 The investments owned by Leyton Ltd have a current market value of £11.25 million.
7 Leyton Ltd has disclosed a contingent liability of £1.5 million in the notes to its financial statements as at 30 June 1991.
8 Leyton Ltd is engaged in operations substantially different from those of Hari Kumar plc. The most recent financial data relating to two listed companies that are engaged in operations similar to those of Leyton Ltd are indicated below.

	NV per share	Market price per share	P/E	Net dividend per share	Cover	Yield
Ranpur plc	£1	£3.50	11.3	12 pence	2.6	4.9
Manners plc	50 pence	£1.25	8.2	4 pence	3.8	4.1

Required:
Write a report, addressed to the directors of Leyton Ltd, advising them of the principles of share valuation, and, in terms of these principles, advise them as to the alternative valuations that could be placed on the ordinary shares of Leyton Ltd, including as appendices to your report, supporting schedules indicating how you have arrived at these alternative valuations.

(30 marks)

Answers to all questions on pages 697–700.

Changes in Organisational Structure – Single Companies

The changes in organisational structure that are dealt with in this chapter are the changes following from, first, the purchase by a company of its own shares and, second, capital reduction under Sections 135, 425, 426 and 427 of the 1985 Act.

A major change in company law, introduced by the 1981 Act, was the provision to allow companies to purchase or redeem their own shares. This has proved popular in practice, and several hundred companies have taken advantage of the new rules. These are mainly private companies, although some public companies have also purchased their own shares, invariably in situations where the market value of the shares is substantially less than their underlying net asset value.

Prior to the publication of the 1981 Act, it had been a long-held principle of English law that a limited company should not be permitted to buy its own shares. This was established by the case of *Trevor* v. *Whitworth* (1887), which stated that for a limited company to buy its own shares would amount to an unauthorised reduction of capital. The basic principle was incorporated into the 1980 Act, which included a general prohibition subject to specified exemptions.

In 1962, the Jenkins Committee considered the possibility of extending the circumstances in which a company could purchase its own shares, but rejected any extension of the then existing exemptions on the basis that there was at that time considerable support for the existing position. In following years, however, there developed an increasing interest in relaxing the general prohibition to the benefit of the company and its shareholders and, at the same time, continuing to protect the position of creditors and others interested in the company. Thus the Wilson Committee, which reviewed the financial institutions of the City, recommended in an interim report in 1979, that consideration should be given to permitting small firms to issue redeemable equity shares as a means of enabling them to raise capital without parting permanently with family control.

In 1980, the principal advantages of allowing a company to purchase its own shares were considered by Professor Gower in a Green Paper. The 1981 Act permitted a company, for the first time in UK company law, to purchase its own shares, whether redeemable or not. These provisions are now dealt with in the Companies Act 1985.

This chapter deals with more than just the purchase and redemption of own shares. To place the topic in perspective it is necessary, initially, to consider the disclosure requirements of the 1985 Act in respect of the share capital and reserves of a company. The chapter also deals with, given the related nature of the topic, the situations in which a company may or may not give financial assistance, to third parties, for the purchase of the company's shares.

This chapter is also concerned with capital reduction schemes under S. 135 of the 1985 Act.

Where most of the rest of this book is concerned with accounting for the profitable operation of a company, this part of Paper 13 is concerned with a loss-making, contracting, failing company. The options that are open to such a company are stark. Liquidation may be the only feasible solution unless a scheme or arrangement can be devised to the mutual benefit of the creditors and the members of the company. The whole purpose of such a scheme or arrangement would be to reorganise the capital of the company so as to eliminate existing losses, to raise further capital for future requirements and return the company to profitability.

Accounting for cessation is dealt with in Chapter 26, which deals with the dissolution of companies.

The disclosure requirements of the Act in respect of share capital and reserves

The notes to the accounts dealing with share capital

PRO FORMA 25.1

Called up share capital	1991	1990
	£	£
Authorised:		
Number of ordinary shares of xp each	x	x
Number of x% (now x% + tax credit) redeemable preference shares of xp each	x	x
	x	x
Allotted, called up and fully paid:		
Number of ordinary shares of xp each	x	x
Number of x% (now x% + tax credit) redeemable preference shares of xp each	x	x
	x	x

Details as to redemption of redeemable shares should follow.

Details as to allotments during the year should follow.

Details of directors' interests in shares and debentures may be included in the notes or in the directors' report.

Contingent rights to the allotment of shares:

The company has granted options in respect of the following shares

Type	Number of shares subject to options	Period of option	Price per share
x	x	x	£x

(Note that if directors' interests in shares, including options, are disclosed in the notes instead of in the directors' report, the name of the directors concerned must also be disclosed.)

Some further points on shareholdings

Both the Act and the Listing Agreement of the Stock Exchange require disclosure in respect of shareholders' interests. These requirements are dealt with in turn below.

Statutory requirements

Comprehensive disclosure of directors' interests in the share capital of a company was required by the Companies Act 1967. The 1985 Act allows a company to publish this information by way of notes to the accounts or in the directors' report.

The 1967 Act required members to notify a quoted company if their interest in the voting share capital amounted to 10% or more of the nominal value. This proportion is now reduced to 3%.

The Listing Rules

The International Stock Exchange requires details of any substantial interests (3% or more of a company's voting share capital) to be disclosed in the directors' report. The amount of the interest should be disclosed (or, if there is no single interest in excess of 3%, a statement of that fact). The information to be disclosed should relate to a date not more than one month prior to the date of the notice of meeting.

In order to assess the influence that shareholders have, an 'analysis of shareholdings' is a useful form of additional disclosure. Several companies disclose such information as a separate statement in their published accounts.

This additional information is useful in that:

▶ It provides an indication of the degree to which share prices are likely to be susceptible to fluctuations resulting from substantial changes in the holdings of institutional investors.
▶ It provides useful information to shareholders of companies previously under state control that have now been privatised.

At the present time, users of such of this information as is currently available, face two disadvantages:

▶ The widespread use of nominee holdings can obscure the true ownership.
▶ Given that companies can choose what to disclose, comparability is difficult.

It has been suggested that this is a problem area that should be resolved by the accounting profession, possibly in the form of a SORP. The following classification of categories could provide a useful basis for any future standardisation in this area: charities, banks, insurance companies, pension funds, investment trusts, other financial companies, industrial and commercial companies, public sector, overseas sector, nominee and trustee companies, other.

It would appear to be a sensible development for details of directors' shareholdings – which are required to be disclosed by company law; details of substantial shareholdings – which are required to be disclosed by the Stock Exchange; and analysis of shareholdings – currently voluntarily disclosed, to be brought together into one statement either as a note to the accounts or as an appendix to the directors' report.

The notes to the accounts dealing with reserves

The Act does not require any distinction to be drawn between the distributable (realised) and non-distributable (unrealised) reserves of a company. This is dealt with in greater detail in Chapter 13 on distributable profits. It may, however, be argued that disclosure of the distributable and non-distributable reserves of a company enhances a true and fair view and, in some cases, if not disclosed, could result in a true and fair view not being shown.

The Act does require disclosure of the movements on reserves during the year – see Pro forma 25.2. SSAP 6 (Revised) suggested (see Chapter 11), that a statement of the movement on reserves should immediately follow the profit and loss account for the year or, if not, that disclosure is made in the notes to the profit and loss account, as to where in the accounts such a statement can be located. FRS 3 requires disclosure of the movements on reserves to support the statements of recognised gains and losses and movements on shareholders' funds.

PRO FORMA 25.2

Statement of movement on reserves:

	Share premium account £	Capital redemption reserve £	Revaluation reserve £	Other £	Profit and loss account £	Total £
At 1 January 199Z	x	x	x	x	x	x
Premium on allotment	x					x
Capitalisation issue	(x)					(x)
Purchase/redemption of own shares		x				x
Revaluation surpluses			x			x
Transfer of realised amounts			(x)		x	
Exchange differences			x	x or	x	x
Retained profit for year					x	
At 31 December 199Z	x	x	x	x	x	x

(Note that the disclosure above as to movement on reserves, in the published financial statements of the group, are required separately for the group *and* the parent company.)

Further notes:

► Included in the revaluation reserve is £x (199Y £x) in respect of surpluses on the annual revaluation of investment properites.
► Included in the group profit and loss account is an amount of £x (199Y £x) in respect of profits retained in X Ltd, the remittance of which is subject to approval by the (country's) authorities.
► The amount of the reserves of (parent company) that may not legally be distributed under Section 264 of the Companies Act 1985 is £x (199Y £x).

(Note that the last item is obviously not required for the group and is disclosure that is relevant to the parent company only.)

The relevant provisions of the Act in respect of the redemption and purchase, by a company, of its own shares

Regarding redemption and purchase generally

S. 159 – Power to issue redeemable shares

This Section allows companies to issue redeemable equity shares, that is, those specifically redeemable under the terms of the issue. It re-enacts S. 145 of the 1981 Act, which in turn replaced the narrower authority to issue redeemable preference shares contained in S. 58 of the 1948 Act.

In order to issue redeemable shares, a company must have authority to do so in the articles. Redeemable shares may not be redeemed unless they are fully paid and the terms of redemption provide for payment on redemption. A company may not issue redeemable shares if there are no non-redeemable shares in issue, that is, the Act prevents a company from redeeming its whole share capital.

S. 160 – Financing of redemption

Redeemable shares may be redeemed only out of distributable profits of the company or out of the proceeds of a fresh issue of shares made for the purpose of the redemption. (Private companies, see below, may finance a redemption or purchase out of capital.)

Any premium payable on redemption must be paid out of distributable profits. The share premium account may be utilised only if:

▶ there is a new replacement issue, and
▶ the shares to be redeemed or purchased were themselves issued at a premium, and even then only to the lower of:
  – the aggregate of the premium received by the company on the issue of the shares redeemed
  – the current amount of the company's share premium account (including any premium on a new replacement issue)
  – the proceeds of the new replacement issue.

All shares redeemed are cancelled on redemption, but the redemption is not to be taken as reducing the company's authorised share capital.

S. 162 – A company limited by shares or limited by guarantee and having a share capital

A company limited by shares or limited by guarantee and having a share capital may, if authorised to do so by its articles, purchase its own shares. The rules as to redemption, as specified in Sections 159 and 160, apply equally to purchase with the one exception that the terms and manner of purchase need not be determined by the articles of the company. The power to purchase shares must, however, be contained in the articles.

A company may not purchase its own shares if, as a result of the purchase, there would no longer be any member of the company holding shares other than redeemable shares.

This Section reverses the long-established rule in *Trevor* v. *Whitworth* (1887). The facility to purchase its own shares is complementary to the power to issue redeemable shares.

A company may purchase its own shares by way of either a market or an off-market purchase. A purchase by a company of its own shares is off market if the shares are:

▶ *either* purchased otherwise than on a recognised stock exchange
▶ *or* purchased on a recognised stock exchange but are not subject to a marketing arrangement on that stock exchange.

For an off-market purchase, the terms of the proposed contract must be authorised by a special resolution of the company.

For a market purchase, there must be authority by the company in general meeting. The authority must specify the maximum number of shares authorised to be acquired, determine both the maximum and minimum prices that may be paid for the shares, and specify a date on which the authority is to expire.

S. 170 – The capital redemption reserve

Where the shares of a company are redeemed or purchased wholly out of the company's distributable profits, the amount by which the company's issued share capital is diminished must be transferred to a capital redemption reserve.

Where the shares are redeemed or purchased wholly or partly out of the proceeds of a new issue, and the proceeds are less than the nominal value of the shares redeemed or purchased, only the difference must be transferred to a capital redemption reserve. (This does not apply if a payment is made out of capital by a private company to effect a purchase or redemption of its own shares, for which see below.)

The capital redemption reserve can be applied only by the making of a bonus issue of shares.

Redemption or purchase of own shares financed out of capital – private companies only

S. 171

A private company may, if so authorised by its articles, make a payment for redemption or purchase of its own shares otherwise than out of its distributable profits or the proceeds of a fresh issue of shares, that is, out of capital. Such a payment is referred to as the permissible capital payment. This Section does not increase the powers of redemption or purchase, but extends the funds available. It is available only to private companies and presupposes that the funds available from the alternative sources of financing – that is, distributable profits – and the proceeds of a new issue are insufficient for the purpose of redemption or purchase of own shares.

For a private company to make a payment out of capital to redeem or purchase its own shares, it must first utilise all available distributable profits. After such a payment has been made for such a purpose, such a company cannot have any distributable profits remaining in its balance sheet. The permissible capital payment referred to above is shown in Pro forma 25.3.

PRO FORMA 25.3

	£	£
Cost of purchase or redemption		x
Less:		
(i) All available distributable profits	(x)	
(ii) Proceeds, if any, of a new replacement issue	(x)	
		(x)
Permissible capital payment		x

Where a permissible capital payment is made, two situations are possible:

▶ *either* the permissible capital payment plus the proceeds of a new issue are less than the nominal value of the shares redeemed or purchased
▶ *or* the permissible capital payment plus the proceeds of a new issue are greater than the nominal value of the shares redeemed or purchased.

In the first case, the difference must be transferred to the capital redemption reserve. In the second case the excess may be applied to reduce the amount of any capital redemption reserve, or share premium account, or any unrealised profits standing to the credit of any revaluation reserve or fully paid share capital of the company.

The conditions that must be met by a private company to make a payment out of capital to purchase or redeem its own shares are as follows:

▶ The payment out of capital must be approved by a special resolution of the company.

▶ The company's directors must make a statutory declaration specifying the amount of the permissible capital payment, and stating that they have formed the opinion that there will be no grounds on which the company would then be unable to pay its debts for the year immediately following the payment.

▶ The directors' statutory declaration must have annexed to it a report addressed to the directors by the company's auditors stating that:
  – they have inquired into the company's state of affairs
  – the permissible capital payment has been properly determined
  – they are not aware of anything to indicate that the opinion expressed by the directors in their declaration is unreasonable in all the circumstances.

▶ The special resolution must be passed on, or within the week immediately following the date on which the directors make their statutory declaration. The payment out of capital must be made no earlier than five nor more than seven weeks after the date of the resolution.

▶ Within the week immediately following the date of the resolution for payment out of capital the company must cause to be published in the *Gazette* a notice:
  – stating that the company has approved a payment out of capital for the purpose of acquiring its own shares
  – specifying the amount of the permissible capital payment
  – stating that the statutory declaration of the directors, and the relevant auditors' report thereon, are available for inspection at the company's registered office
  – stating that any creditor of the company may at any time within the five weeks immediately following the date of the resolution for payment out of capital, apply to court for an order prohibiting payment.

▶ The company must also either cause a notice to the same effect to be published in an appropriate national newspaper or give notice in writing to each of its creditors.

▶ The company must deliver to the Registrar of Companies a copy of the statutory declaration of the directors and of the auditors' report thereon.

An example of the disclosure required to be made in the accounts where a company purchases its own shares

Extracts from the Directors' Report and Notes to the Accounts of the Lincroft Kilgour Group plc (30 September 1983) follow.

Directors' Report

> Purchase of own shares. During the year the Company purchased and cancelled 221,918 of its own ordinary shares of 10p each, being 4.63% of the issued ordinary share capital at 30th September 1982. The aggregate consideration paid was £127,228 (note 25). The shares were purchased because the prices paid were substantially less than the net asset value per share at the relevant time.

Notes to the accounts

24. Called up share capital	Number	1983	1982
Authorised:			
Ordinary shares of 10p	7,500,000	£750,000	£750,000

		Number	£
Issued and fully paid:			
Ordinary shares of 10p each			
At 1st October 1982		4,791,918	479,192
Transfer to capital redemption reserve in respect of shares purchased for cancellation during the year (note 25)		221,918	22,192
At 30th September 1983		4,570,000	457,000

25. Reserves

	Capital redemption reserve £	Revaluation reserve £	Profit and loss account £
Company			
At 1st October 1982	–	–	959,480
Called up share capital:			
Transfer on cancellation of own shares purchased	22,192	–	–
Cost of own shares purchased	–	–	(127,228)
Profit and loss account:			
Retained profit for the year	–	–	346,555
At 30th September 1983	22,192	–	1,178,807

Bookkeeping for the purchase and redemption of own shares

This section deals with the bookkeeping involved where companies redeem or purchase their own shares.

EXAMPLE 25.1

Purchase or redemption financed wholly out of distributable profits:

Balance sheet of company before purchase/redemption:

	£
Ordinary share capital (£1 each)	500
Share premium account	250
Revaluation reserve	100
Profit and loss account	400
Sundry net assets	1,250

The company wishes to purchase 300 of its ordinary shares at par. The finance for the purchase is to be made available wholly out of funds representing available distributable profits.

Journal entries:

	£	£
1 DR Ordinary share capital	300	
CR Cash		300
2 DR Profit and loss account	300	
CR Capital redemption reserve		300

Balance sheet of company after purchase:

	£
Ordinary share capital	200
Capital redemption reserve	300
Share premium account	250
Revaluation reserve	100
Profit and loss account	100
Sundry net assets	950

Capital (share capital plus non-distributable reserves) = £850 both before and after the purchase.

EXAMPLE 25.2

Purchase or redemption financed partly out of distributable profits and partly out of the proceeds of a new issue; purchase or redemption of shares at a premium:

Balance sheet of company before purchase/redemption as in Example 25.1.

The company wishes to purchase 300 of its ordinary shares at a premium of 10p per share. The shares were originally issued at a premium of 50p per share. The finance for the purchase is to be made available partly by a new replacement issue of 100 £1 ordinary shares at a premium of 20p each and the balance out of distributable profits.

Journal entries:

	£	£
1 DR Cash	120	
CR Ordinary share capital		100
CR Share premium capital		20
2 DR Ordinary share capital	300	
CR Cash		330
DR Share premium account	30	
3 DR Profit and loss account	180	
CR Capital redemption reserve		180
(300 – 120)		

Balance sheet of company after purchase:

	£
Ordinary share capital	300
Capital redemption reserve	180
Share premium account	240
Revaluation reserve	100
Profit and loss account	220
Sundry net assets	1,040

Capital before the purchase (500 + 250 + 100) = £850

Capital after the purchase (300 + 180 + 240 + 100) = £820

Capital has been reduced to the extent of the share premium payable on the purchase, which has been debited to the share premium account.

Note that the premium payable on the purchase is debited to share premium account only because:

▶ there is a new replacement issue
▶ the shares to be purchased were originally issued at a premium

and that even then the amount to be debited to the share premium account must be restricted to the lower of:

▶ the premium originally received on the shares to be redeemed
▶ the current balance on the share premium account, including any premium on a new replacement issue
▶ the proceeds of the new replacement issue.

None of these restrictions applies in this example. If any one of them did apply, then any excess of share premium payable, over and above what may be debited to share premium account, would have to be debited against distributable profits.

EXAMPLE 25.3

Purchase or redemption financed partly out of distributable profits, partly out of the proceeds of a new issue and partly out of capital; permissible capital payment plus the proceeds of the new issue is *less than* the nominal value of the shares purchased or redeemed:

For a payment to be made out of capital for the purpose of a purchase or redemption, the company must be a private company.

Balance sheet of (private) company before the purchase as in Example 25.1.

The company wishes to purchase 400 of its £1 ordinary shares at a premium of 60p each. The finance for the purchase it to be made available first out of available distributable profits, second out of a new replacement issue of 100 £1 ordinary shares at a premium of 10p each, and the balance out of capital.

The procedure for accounting for the purchase/redemption of shares where part of the financing is out of capital is as follows:

First, calculate the permissible capital payment as follows:

		£
Cost of purchase		640
Less:		
(i) All available distributable profits	(400)	
(ii) Proceeds of new issue	(110)	
		(510)
Permissible capital payment		130

Second, compare the permissible capital payment plus the proceeds of the new issue with the nominal value of the shares purchased or redeemed:

130 + 110 compared with 400

Either the former is less than or greater than the latter. If the former is less than the latter the difference must be credited to a capital redemption reserve.

Difference = 400 − 240 = £160

Third, set out journal entries to record the bookkeeping involved:

		£	£
1	DR Cash	110	
	CR Ordinary share capital		100
	CR Share premium account		10
2	DR Ordinary share capital	400	
	CR Cash		640
	DR Profit and loss account (premium payable)	240	
3	DR Profit and loss account	160	
	CR Capital redemption reserve		160

For a payment to be made out of capital, the company must first utilise all its available distributable profits. The premium payable on the purchase is therefore charged to the profit and loss account without recourse to the rules illustrated in Example 25.2 as to debiting this premium payable to share premium account.

Journal 3, the transfer to the capital redemption reserve, is the difference ascertained in the second step above.

Fourth, prepare the balance sheet after the purchase:

	£
Ordinary share capital	200
Capital redemption reserve	160
Share premium account	260
Revaluation reserve	100
Profit and loss account	–
Sundry net assets	720

Fifth, compare capital before and after the purchase:

Capital before the purchase (500 + 250 + 100)   = £850
Capital after the purchase (200 + 160 + 260 + 100)   = £720

The reduction in capital of £130 amounts to the permissible capital payment, and for a private company in a purchase or redemption of own shares situation, is the extent to which the capital of the company may legally be reduced after the purchase or redemption.

EXAMPLE 25.4

Purchase or redemption financed partly out of distributable profits, partly out of the proceeds of a new issue and partly out of capital; permissible capital payment plus the proceeds of the new issue is *greater than* the nominal value of the shares purchased or redeemed:

Facts as in Example 25.3 except that the cost of the purchase of the 400 ordinary shares amounts to £840.

First, calculate the permissible capital payment as follows:

		£
Cost of purchase		840
Less:		
(i) All available distributable profits	(400)	
+ (ii) Proceeds of new issues	(110)	
		(510)
Permissible capital payment		330

Second, compare the permissible capital payment plus the proceeds of a new issue with the nominal value of the shares purchased or redeemed.

330 + 110 compared with 400

The former is greater than the latter and the excess of £40 may be applied to reducing the company's 'capital' after the purchase.

Third, set out journal entries to record the bookkeeping involved:

		£	£
1	DR Cash	110	
	CR Ordinary share capital		100
	CR Share premium account		10
2	DR Ordinary share capital	400	
	CR Cash		840
	DR Profit and loss account	400	
	DR 'Capital'	40	

The premium payable on the purchase is taken to the profit and loss account without recourse to the rules illustrated in Example 25.2 as to the treatment of such a premium. As the company has only £400 available as distributable profit, the balance of the premium payable of £40 is debited, as in the journal above, against capital. This surplus amount will always be the excess ascertained in the second step above.

Fourth, prepare the balance sheet after the purchase:

	£
Ordinary share capital	200
Share premium account (250 + 10 − 40)*	220
Revaluation reserve	100
Profit and loss account	–
Sundry net assets	520

* The excess of £40 debited against capital has been debited above against the share premium account. The law does not specify any specific order of write-off against capital.

Fifth, compare capital before and after the purchase:

Capital before the purchase (500 + 250 + 100) = £850
Capital after the purchase (200 + 220 + 100) = £520

The reduction in capital of £330 amounts to the permissible capital payment and, for a private company in a purchase or redemption of shares situation, is the extent to which the capital of the company may legally be reduced after the purchase or redemption.

There are some further points that you should bear in mind in accounting for the purchase or redemption by a company of its own shares. These are as follows:

▶ The excess of the permissible capital payment plus the proceeds of a new issue over the nominal value of shares purchased or redeemed, where the financing is partly out of capital, is debited to capital only where the company has actually made a payment out of capital.

Thus, if the permissible capital payment is nil, and the proceeds of a new issue are £200, and the nominal value of shares redeemed or purchased is £180, one cannot take such an excess of £20 to the debit of capital.

▶ Distributable profits for the purposes of this section are as defined in the relevant sections of the 1985 Act and have been dealt with in Chapter 13. One small complication may arise in this connection. It may be that a company has realised amounts held in unrealised reserves, for example, additional depreciation on the revaluation of fixed assets not yet transferred from revaluation reserves to profit and loss account reserves. Such realised amounts are distributable, and may be utilised in situations where premium payable on purchase or redemption needs to be charged against distributable profits.

► Section 180 of the 1985 Act re-enacts Section 62 (2–4) of the 1981 Act. It provides for the treatment of redeemable preference shares issued prior to the 1981 Act provisions on redeemable shares coming into force (that is, prior to 15 June 1982), to be under Section 58 of the 1948 Act. Thus, where a company redeems any such redeemable preference shares, any premium payable by the company on the redemption may be taken to the debit of the share premium account without concern as to whether or not there is a new replacement issue and whether or not the shares were originally issued at a premium.

► Given that shares redeemed or purchaed by a company must be cancelled on redemption or purchase, it is unlikely that there will be any need for the item 'Own shares' in the pro forma balance sheet (B III 6 in Format 1). Do not allow the existence of this item in the pro forma balance sheet to confuse what is very straightforward bookkeeping in this area.

► An examination question may ask you to discuss the advantages and disadvantages of the Act now allowing a company to purchase its own shares.

The further problem of financial assistance, provided by a company, to third parties, for the purchase of the company's shares

So far, we have dealt with the legal rules relating to a purchase or redemption by a company of its own shares. This section deals with the law as far as it relates to the giving of financial assistance by a company, to third parties, in order that the third parties may purchase the shares of the company. The new sections of the 1985 Act in this regard re-enact sections 42–44 of the 1981 Act, which themselves constituted a radical revision of the law relating to the giving of financial assistance by a company for the purchase of its own shares or those of its holding company, formerly contained in Section 54 of the 1948 Act. What started as one section in 1948, became three sections in 1981 and are now eight sections in the 1985 Act.

S. 151 applies to both public and private companies. The general rule is that it is not lawful for a company or any of its subsidiaries to give financial assistance, directly or indirectly, for the purpose of that acquisition before or at the same time or after the acquisition takes place. If a company acts in contravention of this section, it is liable to a fine and every officer of it who is in default is liable to imprisonment or a fine or both.

S. 152 defines 'financial assistance'.

S. 153 sets out the transactions that are not prohibited by S. 151, that is, a company may give financial assistance in the following situations:

► If the company's principal purpose in giving the assistance is but an incidental part of some larger purpose of the company and is given in good faith by the company.

► A distribution of a company's assets by way of dividend or a distribution in the course of the company's winding up.

► A reduction in capital confirmed by order of the court.

► A redemption or purchase of own shares.

► Where the lending of money is part of the ordinary business of the company.

► The provision by a company, in accordance with an employees' share scheme, of money for the acquisiton of fully paid shares in the company or its holding company to be held by them by way of beneficial ownership.

S. 154 sets out special restrictions for public companies. A public company may give financial assistance only in the circumstances where the general prohibition against the giving of such assistance does not apply and if the net assets of the company are not thereby reduced *or*, if the net assets are reduced, the assistance is provided out of distributable profits. Thus a public company may give financial assistance for the purchase of its own shares only in situations listed above and, even then, the assistance must be in the form of a recoverable loan or, if not, out of available distributable profits.

3. 155 relates to private companies only and sets out the rules relating to the giving of such financial assistance by private companies. Thus, S. 151 does not relate to private companies, and such companies may give financial assistance if the company has net assets that are not thereby reduced *or*, to the extent that they are reduced, the assistance is provided out of distributable profits.

The giving of such assistance under this section must be approved by special resolution of the company in general meeting. The directors of the company proposing to give the financial assistance must make a statutory declaration (S. 156). This should:

▶ contain particulars of the financial assistance to be given and the business of the company
▶ identify the person to whom the assistance is to be given
▶ state that the directors have formed the opinion that the company will be able to pay its debts.

The directors' statutory declaration must have annexed to it an auditors' report addressed to them and stating that:

▶ they have enquired into the state of affairs of the company
▶ they are not aware of anything in the directors' declaration being unreasonable.

The statutory declaration and auditors' report must be delivered to the Registrar of Companies.

There is protection for minorities in that a dissenting minority may apply to court for the cancellation of the special resolution authorising the giving of financial assistance.

Relevant sections of company law in schemes of capital reduction

It is a basic rule of company law that the share capital of a company provides a fund to which creditors can look for settlement of their debts. Any scheme that involves the reduction of the capital of a company must, therefore, have the sanction of the court. This sanction is necessary not only to protect the interests of creditors but also those of members whose rights may be varied as the result of such a scheme. You need to bear the following sections of the Act in mind in dealing with capital reductions and reorganisations.

Section 135

Section 135 provides for reduction of capital by a company. Thus, 'subject to confirmation by the Court, a company limited by shares or a company limited by guarantee and having a share capital may, if so desired by its articles, by special resolution reduce its share capital in any way'.

In particular a company may:

- ► extinguish or reduce the liability on any of its shares in respect of share capital not paid up
- ► either with or without extinguishing or reducing liability on any of its shares, cancel any paid up share capital that is lost or unrepresented by available assets
- ► either with or without extinguishing or reducing liability on any of its shares, pay off any paid up share capital which is in excess of the company's wants.

The first situation would apply where a company has in issue partly paid share capital. The company can, in this situation, extinguish the uncalled share capital effectively making the partly paid shares fully paid shares. The third situation would arise where the company has surplus cash, perhaps as a result of a sale of the major part of its business that is returned to shareholders. In the second situation a detailed scheme of reorganisation would need to be formulated. This chapter is concerned with such a situation.

Section 425

If, on the reconstruction of a company, any compromise or arrangement is proposed between the company and its members and creditors, this section must be used. The essential feature of Section 425 is that the scheme must be a 'compromise or an arrangement'. Under Section 425, a reconstruction must result in a reasonable chance of returning the company to profitable operations; otherwise it may be preferable for the creditors if the company were to be liquidated.

Section 425 states that:

- ► Where a compromise or arrangement is proposed between a company and its creditors or members, the court may on the application of the company or any creditor or member or liquidator order a meeting of the creditors or members, as the case may be.
- ► If a majority in number representing 75% in value of the creditors or members present and voting either in person or by proxy, agree to any compromise or arrangement, it is binding on all members of that class of creditors or members, if sanctioned by the court.

Sections 425 to 427 allow businesses to be transferred to a newly formed company that may acquire either the net assets or the share capital of the old company. There must be approval by at least 75% of each class of member and creditors and court approval must be obtained.

S. 110 of the Insolvency Act 1986 can also be used in a reconstruction that involves the formation of a new company. The main points here are:

- ► court approval is not required
- ► a special resolution is required
- ► the existing company goes into voluntary liquidation
- ► the business is sold to a newly formed company in exchange for the issue of the new company's shares to the shareholders of the old company
- ► any dissenting shareholder can notify the liquidator either not to carry out the scheme or to have the dissenting shares purchased at a price determined by agreement.

The basic principles underlying a scheme of capital reduction

A scheme of capital reorganisation or reduction is normally recommended in three situations:

▶ The company is in financial difficulty and cannot raise further capital without changing its capital structure. A capital reduction scheme must ensure that a viable company is the end result.
▶ The company may wish to reorganise its share capital for commercial reasons, for example:
  − the company may need to vary class rights (which can be achieved using a Section 425–427 reorganisation)
  − the company may organise an external reorganisation to prevent a takeover.
▶ The company may wish to return surplus funds to its shareholders without incurring an ACT liability. This can be achieved by the company purchasing its own shares as dealt with earlier in this chapter.

Where the share capital of a company is lost or unrepresented by available assets the only alternative to a scheme of capital reorganisation would be to wind up the company. Thus the scheme must produce a viable result and provide evidence that after the reorganisation the company will be able to trade profitably and remunerate its capital providers. All adverse factors giving rise to the necessity to reorganise must be eliminated and, given the involvement of the court, the scheme must be fair to all parties. The purpose of the scheme is to make available the capital of the company to write off negative balances on profit and loss account, write off fictitious assets, revalue assets on a going-concern basis, reorganise the capital structure of the company in line with the actual assets of the company and to provide for any costs associated with the scheme.

Given that there is loss of capital it is obvious that the major part of this loss must be borne by ordinary shareholders. Preference shareholders may bear some part of the loss but would normally be compensated for this by either a higher rate of dividend, and/or as a part of the scheme, a new issue of shares. Any arrears of preference dividends on cumulative preference shares would usually be cancelled. In exceptional circumstances, where the loss cannot be fully borne by ordinary shareholders and what the preference shareholders could reasonably be expected to bear, part of the loss may be borne by debenture holders and creditors. New shares would normally be issued for amounts written off debts, or creditors may agree to defer their claims by accepting short-term loan stock for part of the amounts due to them.

Section 135 deals only with the reduction of share capital. If as a part of the scheme it is necessary to vary the rights of shareholders, for example, the dividend rights of preference shareholders or to come to a satisfactory arrangement with creditors the provisions of Section 425 become relevant. As most schemes of capital reorganisation usually involve both a reduction of share capital and a variation of rights of shareholders and creditors it is important that you appreciate what these rights are, particularly as shareholders are hardly likely to accept a scheme unless they would be better off than with the result of the alternative situation of liquidation.

For preference shareholders, prima facie, the dividend is cumulative. If, therefore, there are arrears that have accumulated prior to the scheme they would need to be cancelled in return for some form of compensation. As a general rule, preference shares have no priority as to return of capital and, therefore, when the company is wound up, rank *pari passu* with ordinary shares. If the preference shares are given priority as to return of capital in a winding up by the articles, they will not share in any surplus.

Ordinary shares have only a residual interest in the profits and net assets of a company.

Debenture holders are limited to suing for principal and interest and to petition for a compulsory winding up order unless their debt is secured, in which case they can apply for an order of foreclosure or sell the security under the authority of the debentures or of the court. It would be unusual therefore for debenture holders to share in any loss in a scheme of capital reorganisation.

The main features of a scheme of capital reduction, following on from the above are, therefore:

▶ The ordinary shareholders bear most of the loss; this follows from the fact that they would stand to lose the most in the event of a liquidation and stand to gain the most in the event of successful operations after the scheme.

▶ Preference shareholders may bear a part of the loss but would expect to be compensated either by a higher rate of future dividend and/or a new issue of equity shares without consideration.

▶ Any arrears of preference dividends payable would normally be cancelled and compensated by the issue of new equity shares without consideration.

▶ Debenture holders and creditors may bear a part of the loss in exceptional circumstances but must be issued with new equity shares, without consideration, for the amounts written off; creditors may be willing to accept short-term loan stock for some of the amounts due to them.

▶ The scheme must be fair to all parties, must have the agreement of all parties concerned, must eliminate all adverse factors and the end result must be viable, that is, there should be evidence that, after the scheme, the company will return to profitable operations.

▶ Given the importance of evidence that the company will return to profitability it is important to consider further working capital requirements; the court would normally expect existing members and directors to subscribe for new shares in order to provide support for the scheme.

Devising a scheme

An examination question in this area will probably require you to devise a scheme of capital reorganisation on the basis of background information provided, possibly in the form of a requirement to write a report to the directors or a substantial ordinary or preference shareholder. There can be no one correct answer to such a question and your answer should try to demonstrate a grasp of the underlying principles. Pro forma 25.4 provides an outline of the approach that you should adopt if asked to provide a report to an interested party on whether or not to vote for the scheme.

PRO FORMA 25.4

Set up the report headings as usual:

Report

To:

From:

Re: proposed scheme of capital reduction

Date:

(a) Paragraph 1 – General introduction: background to the current situation of the company; alternatives available either liquidation or voting for a scheme of capital reduction, legal references, that is, Section 135 and 425.

(b) Paragraph 2 – Consider the likely outcome if the company were to be liquidated – who would get what? – all calculations being presented as an appendix to the report.

(c) Paragraph 3 – Suggest a scheme of capital reorganisation adopting the following procedures in an appendix:

(i) Ascertain the existing loss as follows:	£
– accumulated debit balance on profit and loss account	x
– deficit on assets	x
– gain on assets	(x)
– cancellation of loans *by* directors	(x)
– *value* of any shares issued as compensation to preference shareholders or debentures holders	x
– costs of the scheme	x
– balance, to round up to an easily divisible sum – say, for contingencies	x
Amount to be made available out of capital	x

(ii) Decide how the loss should be allocated:

First, against ordinary shareholders' funds, that is:

	£
– any credit balances on reserve, for example a share premium amount	x
– reduction of nominal value of ordinary shares	x
Second, if necessary, and if acceptable to preference shareholders, reduction in nominal value of preference shares	x
Third, and only as a last resort, reduction in value of amounts owing to debenture holders and/or creditors	x
Amount made available out of capital to make good existing loss	— x

The steps above involve a restructuring of the existing balance sheet of the company. It may be useful to summarise the effects of your scheme so far by listing the adjustments proposed in a capital reduction or reorganisation account as follows:

Capital reorganisation account

Utilisation of amount available	£	Amount made available	£
Credit to:		Debit to:	
Assets: deficits	x	Share premium account	x
Ordinary share capital: new		Ordinary share capital	x
shares issued as compensation	x	Preference share capital	x
Creditors: costs	x	Debentures/creditors	x
Balance for contingencies		Directors' loans	x
c/f as reserve arising on scheme	x	Assets: gains	x
	x		x

(d) Paragraph 4 – Given that the whole purpose of the scheme is to return the company to profitability and that funds are required for this purpose suggest, in the light of information in the question, how such funds should be raised; you could consider the sale of investments, sale and leaseback of properties, factoring of debtors, availability of loans and new issues of shares to be subscribed for by existing members and directors.

(e) Paragraph 5 – If information is provided as to estimates of future earnings indicate the extent of participation in such earnings by the party to whom you are reporting.

(f) Paragraph 6 – Provide a conclusion in the light of all the information now available.

The second supporting question to this chapter, Tree plc, takes you through the procedures you would need to follow in first suggesting and second implementing a scheme of capital reorganisation.

Summary

This chapter deals with what may be termed 'internal reorganisation' within a single company. It covers:

▶ the disclosure requirements of the Act as to share capital and reserves
▶ the legal provisions as to the purchase by a company of its own shares
▶ the bookkeeping involved in a situation where a company purchases its own shares
▶ the problems of financial assistance provided by a company for the purchase of its shares
▶ the circumstances in which schemes of capital reduction may be resorted to
▶ the principles underlying such schemes
▶ devising a scheme.

Suggested reading

Advanced Financial Accounting (Lewis, Pendrill and Simon 1981)
Modern Financial Accounting – G.A. Lee (1981)

Self test questions

1   Beep Ltd, which has a share premium account of £20,000 and a profit and loss account of £30,000 wishes to purchase 80,000 of its own full paid £1 ordinary shares at a premium of 10p per share without making a new issue of shares. Calculate the permissible capital payment.

2   Fluffy plc purchases 400,000 of its own ordinary shares for £600,000. These shares were originally issued at a premium of 25p each. The current balance on the share premium account is £200,000. The purchase is financed partly out of the proceeds of a fresh issue of 200,000 £1 preference shares at a premium of 10p each. What is the maximum amount that may legally be debited to share premium account?

3   Puff plc has a balance on its profit and loss account of £400,000. It purchases 200,000 of its own £1 ordinary shares at a premium of 20p per share, financed partly out of the proceeds of a new issue of 80,000 £1 preference shares at par. Calculate the balance on the profit and loss account after the purchase.

4   Barnaby Ltd has share capital (£1 ordinary shares) of £250,000 and a negative balance on its profit and loss account of £(120,000). The company has proposed a capital reduction scheme that involves:

▶ the write-off of £45,000 of goodwill
▶ the revaluation of property to £150,000 from £125,000
▶ a reduction for ordinary shareholders of 70p per share
▶ the elimination of the negative balance on profit and loss account.

Ascertain the reserve arising after implementation of the scheme.

Exam style questions

1   *Planets plc*
The companies listed below wish to purchase their own shares in accordance with the provisions of the Companies Act 1985. Details of the share capital and sundry reserves of each company are provided to you as follows:

	Planets plc £000	Saturn plc £000	Neptune Ltd £000	Pluto Ltd £000	Mars plc £000
Called up share capital	500	200	5,000	2,000	400
Reserves:					
Share premium account	–	20	500	500	–
Revaluation reserve	100	–	–	–	120
Profit and loss account	300	50	50	5,000	40
	900	270	5,500	7,500	560

1   Planets plc wishes to purchase 20,000 shares of £1 each at a price of 90p per share through a market purchase. At the same time it is issuing to a merchant bank 13,000 shares at a price of £1 each, payable in cash.
2   Saturn plc plans to purchase 100,000 shares of £1 each. The shares were originally issued at a price of £1.10 each. The cost of the purchase, £1.50 per share, is to be financed by a new replacement issue of 100,000 £1 shares at a price of £1.30 per share.
3   Neptune Ltd, a private company, intends to purchase 1 million shares of £1 each at a price of £1.10 per share. The shares were originally issued at par. The company plans a new replacement issue of 850,000 shares of £1 each at par.
4   Pluto Ltd, also a private company, wishes to purchase 1 million shares of £1 each for £1.60 per share. The shares were originally issued at £1.50 per share. The company plans a new replacement issue of 500,000 shares of £1 each at £1.70 per share.
5   Mars plc proposes to purchase 200,000 50p shares from a venture capital trust at a 5% discount on the current market price of £2 per share. The shares purchased will then be issued to the company's founders at 75p per share.

Required:
Comment, with reasons, on whether the intended transactions of each company listed above are permitted under the Companies Act 1985 and, if so:

(i)   Prepare the necessary journal entries for each company for all the share transactions proposed.
(ii) Draft the revised shareholders' funds for each company after the proposed share transactions.
(iii) Where appropriate for any of the companies in the question, calculate the permissible capital payment.   (20 marks)

2 *Tree plc*

Tree plc has been operating in the scrap metal business for many years. The company is under pressure from its bankers and other creditors and the directors wish to consider reorganisation.

The summarised balance sheet of Tree plc as on 30 September 1991 is as follows:

	£000	£000	£000
Capital and reserves			
Share capital			
Ordinary shares of £1 each fully paid			1,500
7% Preference shares of £1 each fully paid			500
			2,000
Profit and loss account			(352)
			1,648
Fixed assets			
Patents and research & development			500
Land and buildings (freehold)			700
Plant and machinery			100
			1,300
Current assets			
Stock		1,200	
Debtors		830	
Investments at cost (market value £220,000)		150	
Cash in hand		10	
		2,190	
Creditors falling due within 1 year			
Bank overdraft and short-term loans	(1,140)		
Trade and other creditors	(148)		
Directors' loans	(140)		
Debenture interest	(14)		
	(1,442)		748
			2,048
Creditors due after more than 1 year			
7% debenture secured on land and buildings			(400)
			1,648

The following information is given:

1 Assets whose value has been impaired are to be written down or written off as appropriate.
2 The estimated costs of the reorganisation are £50,000.
3 Of the trade and other creditors, £15,000 relates to arrears of two weeks' wages, £25,000 to VAT and £12,000 to Scrap Metal Dealers Association, the balance being trade creditors.
4 Accruals for expenses in September of £60,000 have not been included.
5 If the reorganisation took place, an estimated £90,000 would be required for new processing equipment.
6 The bank would require part payment of its overdraft and short-term loans before agreeing to the scheme. Preliminary negotiations suggest that a 40% reduction would be acceptable.
7 Preference dividends are three years in arrears.

8 The values of certain assets on a going concern basis are as stated below:

   a) Patents are worth £140,000.
   b) An alternative use exists for the scrap metal yard as a car park, hence the value of the land and buildings is estimated to be £900,000.
   c) Present plant and machinery is worth only £10,000.
   d) Stock being unprocessed scrap is worth £800,000.
   e) Debtors include an estimated £40,000 bad debts.

9 A floating charge is held by the bank.

10 There is a general willingness on the part of the shareholders and directors to forego part of their capital and their loans and to subscribe further equity capital, while ensuring that trade creditors are paid in full.

11 The debenture holder is willing to provide further secured funds.

Required:

Prepare for consideration of the directors of Tree plc:

a) Your estimated state of affairs, assuming a liquidation with assets realised on a forced sale basis, making such assumptions as you consider appropriate.

   (9 marks)

b) Your suggested scheme of reorganisation.   (10 marks)

c) The balance sheet following your scheme.   (7 marks)

Note:

Marks will be awarded primarily for principles and presentation.   (26 marks)
Workings are required.

All answers on pages 700–704.

Accounting for Cessation and Dissolution of Companies

Chapter 25 dealt with changes in the organisational structure of single companies and examined the law and accounting procedures involved in situations where companies purchase their own shares and where, as an alternative to liquidation, companies decide on a scheme of capital reduction or reorganisation. This chapter deals with two further aspects of change in the organisational structure of companies. First we look at schemes of amalgamation or absorption, and second we look at the dissolution of companies and explain the major features and legal processes by which a company may be wound up under the Insolvency Act 1986, covering administrative receivership and voluntary and compulsory liquidation.

Where a capital *reorganisation*, as dealt with in the previous chapter, involves leaving the company in existence but with an altered capital structure involving changes in the rights of shareholders and possibly creditors, a company *reconstruction*, as dealt with in this chapter, may be described as involving a scheme where either an existing company is amalgamated with or absorbed by another existing company or one where a new company is formed to take over the net assets of one or more existing companies. Amalgamations may be dealt with under either Sections 425–427 of the Act or under Section 582 of the Act. Schemes of amalgamation under Sections 425–427, involving changes in the rights of members or creditors, would require the sanction of the court to:

▶ transfer to a transferee company the undertaking of a transferor company
▶ issue shares or debentures of the transferee company to the shareholders or debenture holders of the transferor company
▶ dissolve the transferor company without winding it up.

For such schemes to be sanctioned by the court they must be approved by a majority in number representing more than 75% in value.

Reconstruction can also be brought about under the winding up provisions of Section 582, which will involve putting the transferor company into voluntary liquidation, the sale of its net assets to a transferee company with shares of the transferee company as consideration for the transferor company's shareholders. As a new company is formed under such schemes the new company will include the reconstructed capital and revised net asset values in its accounts. Such schemes have an advantage over those using Sections 425–427 in that they avoid legal costs (although liquidation costs will be incurred).

This chapter, in that it is concerned with the dissolution of companies, is also concerned with the procedure of company liquidation. The procedure for initiating the liquidation of a company is governed by the provisions of the Insolvency Act 1986 and those of the Insolvency Rules 1986. Some of these provisions apply to compulsory liquidation under a winding-up order made by the court, while other provisions apply only to voluntary liquidations, which are initiated by a winding-up resolution passed by a general meeting of the company.

Scheme of reconstruction (1) – closing off the books of the transferor company; opening up the books of the transferee company

In such schemes, where one or more companies are effectively taken over by a new (or existing) company it will be necessary to close off the accounts of the old company (or companies) including the showing of the distributions to the old company's shareholders and preparing the opening (or adjusted) balance sheet of the new company.

To close off the books of the transferor company or companies you will be concerned with the following accounts:

▶ realisation account, which will record the assets to be transferred, the consolidation received for such assets and the profit or loss on realisation that accrues to sundry members

▶ separate accounts for creditors, which are either paid off or assumed by the transferee company (in which case they are a part of the purchase consideration for the assets taken over)

▶ bank account, which will record the inflows and outflows of cash as a result of the reconstruction

▶ purchaser's account, which will record the consideration due from the transferee company and the way in which it is distributed among the members and creditors of the transferor company

▶ sundry members' account, which will record the amounts due to and received by (in the form of cash or debentures or shares of the transferee company) shareholders of the transferor company.

A simple example to illustrate the bookkeeping involved

Example 26.1 shows the bookkeeping for closing off the books of the transferor company and opening up the books of the transferee company.

EXAMPLE 26.1

	£
The balance sheet of A Ltd of 31 December 1994 is summarised as follows:	
Fixed assets, intangible – goodwill	8,250
Fixed assets, tangible　– land and buildings	61,875
– plant and machinery	46,200
Stock	24,750
Debtors	17,325
Cash	1,100
Creditors	(42,350)
Overdraft	(55,550)
9% debentures	(8,250)
	53,350
Ordinary share capital of £1 each	165,000
7% cumulative preference shares of £1 each	5,500
Share premium account	5,500
Profit and loss account	(122,650)
	53,350

Preference dividends are two years in arrears and the company has employed a new management team to take advantage of an upturn in trading conditions. The new finance director has produced a corporate plan that includes a scheme of reconstruction as follows:

▶ A Ltd is to go into voluntary liquidation and a new company, B Ltd, is to be formed to acquire the old company. The consideration for the takeover is to be satisfied in the form of shares and debentures of the new company.

▶ The land and buildings are to be sold and new premises leased. The lease will fall to be classified as an operating lease and the sale proceeds for the land and buildings are expected to be £82,500. The proceeds are used in part to repay the 9% debentures.

▶ B Ltd is to take over the plant and machinery at book value plus £3,300. Stock and debtors are to be taken over by B Ltd at book values.

▶ Of the creditors, £3,850 that are preferential are to be paid off by A Ltd in full and in cash, while the remaining creditors are to be paid 60p in the £ in cash with the balance being discharged by the issue by B Ltd of 10% debentures.

▶ The ordinary shareholders are to receive one fully paid £1 ordinary share in B Ltd for every five ordinary shares held in A Ltd. They also agree to purchase, for cash, two £1 ordinary shares, at par, in B Ltd for every 15 ordinary shares held in A Ltd.

▶ Existing goodwill is considered to be worthless.

▶ The preference shareholders are to receive one fully paid £1 ordinary share in B Ltd for each preference share held in A Ltd. In addition, while agreeing to waive any entitlement to arrears of preference dividend, the preference shareholders are to receive a £100 10% debenture for every 200 preference shares held.

▶ The scheme will cost A Ltd £2,750 and B Ltd £1, 375.

Close off the books of A Ltd and open up the books of B Ltd.

In the books of A Ltd

Realisation Account

	£		£
Assets taken over at book values:		Bank – sale of land and	82,500
Plant and machinery	46,200	buildings	
Stock	24,750	Purchaser's account –	
Debtors	17,325	purchase consideration	56,650
Assets sold at book values:		Sundry members' account	
Land and buildings	61,875	– loss on realisation	13,750
Bank – costs	2,750		

Creditors' account

	£		£
Preferential creditors paid	3,850	Balance sheet	42,350
Other creditors paid	23,100		
Purchaser's account			
– 10% debentures issued	15,400		

Bank and cash account

	£		£
Balance sheet	1,100	Balance sheet	55,550
Realisation account –			
sale of land and buildings	82,500	9% debentures paid	8,250
Sundry members' account –		Preferential creditors paid	3,850
balance	9,900	Other creditors paid	23,100
		Realisation account – costs	2,750

Purchaser's account

	£		£
Realisation account	56,650	Creditors – 10% debentures issued	15,400
Made up:		Sundry members' account	
– ordinary shares		(33,000 + 5,500 + 2,750)	41,250
to ords 165,000/5 =	33,000		
to prefs 5,500/1 =	5,500		
– debentures			
to creditors	15,400		
to prefs 5,500/200 × 100	2,750		
	56,650		

Sundry members' account

	Preference £	Ordinary £		Preference £	Ordinary £
Profit and loss account		122,650	Share capital	5,500	165,000
Goodwill		8,250	Share premium account		5,500
Purchaser's account					
ordinary shares	5,500	33,000			
debentures	2,750				
Realisation account					
loss		13,750	Bank – to balance	2,750	7,150

In the books of B Ltd

Purchase of business account

	£		£
Bank – costs	1,375	Assets taken over at fair values:	
Ordinary share capital			
(33,000 + 5,500)	38,500	Plant and machinery	49,500
10% debentures		Stock	24,750
(15,400 + 2,750)	18,150	Debtors	17,325
Negative goodwill	33,550		

The issue of ordinary shares for cash would raise $165,000 \times {}^2/_{15} = £22,000$.

Assessment

Any assessment of such a scheme should take account of the position of members and creditors before and after the scheme. The following points can be made:

▶ Preference shares have been eliminated. This will allow a more flexible dividend policy, but this involves greater risk for the old preference shareholders.
▶ There is an increase in the value of debenture debt, which will result in an increase in interest to be paid and covered.
▶ Even though control is retained by the old ordinary shareholders, they have had to make a material cash injection to maintain this control.
▶ The overdraft has been eliminated and this will remove any restrictions imposed by the bank.
▶ Future profits will need to cover the rental on the lease of land and buildings.

Scheme of reconstruction (2) – amalgamation and absorption

These schemes can be distinguished from mergers, dealt with in Chapter 19, in that one or more parties to the combination will here be liquidated. In such schemes two or more companies transfer their assets and liabilities to a new company in exchange for the new company's shares. The accounting procedures are similar to those illustrated in the scheme of reconstruction (1) above.

The bookkeeping involved in the scheme of reconstruction for amalgamation and absorption is illustrated in Example 26.2.

EXAMPLE 26.2

A Ltd and B Ltd agreed to amalgamate. A new company, C Ltd, was formed to take over the assets and liabilities of a A Ltd and B Ltd. The balance sheet carrying values at the date of amalgamation and the agreed values for amalgamation were:

	A Ltd		B Ltd	
	Balance sheet	Agreed values	Balance sheet	Agreed values
	£	£	£	£
Land and buildings (NBV)	5,800	7,000	8,000	10,000
Plant and machinery (NBV)	4,400	4,200	4,000	4,100
Investment in E Ltd at cost	3,500			
Stock	1,000	900	2,000	1,800
Debtors	4,800	4,500	1,000	900
Cash at bank	1,200	1,200	1,100	1,100
Creditors	(3,700)	(3,600)	(2,600)	(2,600)
	17,000		13,500	
Ordinary shares £1 each	6,000		3,500	
Profit and loss account	11,000		10,000	
	17,000		13,500	

Under the terms of the agreement:

▶ The investment in E Ltd would be sold before the amalgamation at a price of £6,120.
▶ The values as shown and included in this agreement shall be used to decide the respective interests in the new company C Ltd.
▶ Goodwill for amalgamation purposes shall be recorded as:
  – A Ltd £1,580
  – B Ltd £500
▶ The capital of C Ltd shall consist of 26,000 £1 ordinary shares issued at a price to meet the consideration for A Ltd's and B Ltd's net assets.

Based on the above:

The value of the consideration is:

	A Ltd	B Ltd
	£	£
Goodwill	1,580	500
Land and buildings	7,000	10,000
Plant and machinery	4,200	4,100
Stock	900	1,800
Debtors	4,500	900
Cash at bank	7,320	1,100
Creditors	(3,600)	(2,600)

		21,900	15,800

with combined values of £37,700 the 26,000 £1 ordinary shares of C Ltd are effectively being issued at £1.45 each, that is, at a 45p premium.

Closing the books:

Realisations accounts:

	A Ltd £	B Ltd £		A Ltd £	B Ltd £
Land and buildings	5,800	8,000	Creditors	3,700	2,600
Plant and machinery	4,400	4,000	Purchaser's account	21,900	15,800
Stock	1,000	2,000	(consideration)		
Debtors	4,800	1,000			
Cash at bank	7,320	1,100			
Sundry members' account (profit)	2,280	2,300			
	25,600	18,400		25,600	18,400

Alternatively, separate accounts could have been opened for creditors.

Sundry members' accounts:

	A Ltd £	B Ltd £		A Ltd £	B Ltd £
Purchaser's account (shares in C Ltd)	21,900	15,800	Ordinary shares	6,000	3,500
			Profit and loss account	11,000	10,000
			Profit on investment	2,620	
			Realisation profit	2,280	2,300
	21,900	15,800		21,900	15,800

Purchaser's (C Ltd) account:

	A Ltd £	B Ltd £		A Ltd £	B Ltd £
			Sundry members'		
Realisation account	21,900	15,800	account	21,900	15,800

Where there are more transactions involving the movement of cash, including part settlement of the consideration in cash, it may be appropriate to produce separate bank accounts.

As a result of the amalgamation of A Ltd and B Ltd through the medium of a new company it is necessary to prepare the opening journal for the company: (*Note*: A similar journal would be required to integrate the assets of the two old companies if C Ltd already existed and the scheme was one of absorption.)

	Debit £	Credit £
Goodwill	2,080	
Land and buildings	17,000	
Plant and machinery	8,300	
Stock	2,700	
Debtors	5,400	
Cash at bank	8,420	
Creditors		6,200
Ordinary share capital		26,000
Share premium:		11,700

In an amalgamation these balances would also represent the opening balance sheet of C Ltd, unless further shares have been issued to raise cash outside of the amalgamation transactions. This would not be the case in an absorption where the journal would give the adjustments to the balance sheet of the existing company before the absorption took place.

Assessment

As with other capital structure changes assessments should be made by considering the relative positions of shareholders and creditors before and after the implementation of the scheme. In Example 26.2 there are no long-term creditors/debenture holders or preference shareholders, but in other cases these parties may exist and their positions should be considered in any assessment, with particular attention given to periodic income and capital repayment.

In the situation in Example 26.2 the creditors do not appear to have been specifically dealt with; they should ensure that the risks involved in obtaining settlement of the outstanding debt are not increased unless the likelihood of future profitable trading makes such an increase acceptable. The realisable value of assets offering cover for the creditors in the new company appears to be as good as in the old companies and there is no obvious reason to consider that the scheme would be considered unacceptable to them.

The position of the ordinary shareholders is slightly different. The shareholders' assets backing is probably not significantly changed – although the realisable value of the assets may change through amalgamation – but their relative level of control has changed. This is particularly important for the old shareholders of B Ltd. Before the amalgamation they had full control over the use of the assets of their company; now they have a relatively high percentage interest in the combined business, 42%, but they have conceded control to the old A Ltd shareholders, who have 58% of the shares of C Ltd. This may be acceptable if their share of the future profits of the combined business are in excess of those achievable as a separate company. Such a position is likely to increase the market value of their investment. It is likely that such positions will exist because it is one of the main reasons companies choose to combine their resources. Any forecast of profitability, as a combined business and as separate entities, should be used in an assessment of the 'fairness' of any scheme of amalgamation or absorption.

Company liquidation

In a liquidation the powers of a company's directors to manage its affairs are superseded by those of the liquidator, the company is wound up and its operations as a going concern are terminated. The company's assets are realised by the liquidator so that its debts and liabilities are satisfied so far as possible. Any surplus of assets is distributed to the members of the company. In some circumstances, where the assets of the company do not realise sufficient sums to discharge its debts and liabilities in full, the liquidator may recover contributions from present and former members of the company. There are compulsory and voluntary winding-up situations. A compulsory winding-up is where the court makes an order for the company to be wound up. A voluntary winding-up results from the passing of a resolution in a general meeting of members that the company be wound up.

Winding-up orders

There are seven grounds that may be relied on by the company or its directors or its creditors or contributories as petitioners. There is also one special ground that can be relied on only by the Secretary of State for Trade and Industry. Most petitions are presented by creditors and present and former shareholders (contributories) of the company on two grounds:

▶ the company is unable to pay its debts
▶ it is just and equitable that the company be wound up.

Under the Insolvency Act 1986 a creditor may prove that a company cannot pay its debts by serving a written demand on the company, in the prescribed form, requiring the company to pay the debt it owes the creditors and by the company neglecting to pay the debt within three weeks. The amount of the debt must be more than £750.

When a winding-up order is made against a company the Official Receiver becomes its liquidator until another person is appointed. The Official Receiver will decide whether to call meetings of the company's creditors and contributories to resolve the question of the appointment of a liquidator in his place and whether to constitute a liquidation committee to supervise the liquidator's conduct of the winding up.

When the court has made a winding-up order the Official Receiver may require persons connected with the company to make a statement of the company's affairs, verified by affidavit. This must be in the prescribed form and contain particulars of:

▶ the company's assets, debts and liabilities
▶ the names and addresses of the company's creditors
▶ the nature and dates of the creation of any securities for the debts and liabilities of the company
▶ the preferential debts of the company
▶ the estimated surplus or deficiency of the company's assets to satisfy its preferential and other debts and liabilities
▶ the names and addresses of the company's shareholders
▶ the number, nominal values and classes of shares held by them and the amounts called up.

A liquidator, other than the Official Receiver, must be a qualified insolvency practitioner. The liquidator is entitled to remuneration for services rendered, which may be either a fee or a percentage of the assets realised. The functions of the liquidator are to:

▶ collect and realise the assets of the company
▶ discharge the expenses of the liquidation and the debts and liabilities of the company out of the above and any additional assets that are available
▶ distribute any surplus to the members or contributories of the company.

A liquidation is concluded when the company is dissolved or when its assets are completely disposed of by the remaining proceeds of the realisation of its assets being paid into the Insolvency Services Account at the Bank of England.

Preferential claims

Some debts and liabilities of a company in liquidation must be satisfied in full before payments can be made for non-preferential claims. Preferential debts are payable out of assets comprised in a floating charge if the remaining assets of the company are insufficient to meet the preferential claims. There are seven classes of preferential debts as follows:

1 Sums due to the Inland Revenue for deductions of income tax.
2 VAT payable by the company to the Customs and Excise for the period of six months before the date of the administration order.
3 Contributions under the Social Services Act 1975 in respect of employees of the company.
4 Contributions under the Social Services Act 1975 in respect of an occupational pension scheme or as premiums under the state pension scheme.
5 Remuneration owing to employees in respect of the period of four months before the date of the administration order, but not exceeding, per person, such amount as prescribed for the time being by the Secretary of State.
6 Amounts owing to employees for payments claimed under the Employment Protection Act 1975.
7 Amounts the company has been ordered to pay to former employees under the Reserve Forces (Safeguard of Employment) Act 1985.

Secured debts

A secured creditor may pursue any one of the following four courses of action in a company's liquidation:

1 The security may be surrendered to the liquidator and the creditor renounces the right to be paid out of the proceeds of the security and ranks in the same way as other creditors.
2 The secured creditor may include particulars of the security and of its valuation in a proof submitted to the liquidator and may then prove in the winding-up for the excess of the amount secured over the valuation of the security.
3 The secured creditor can obtain possession of the secured property, realise it and discharge the debt out of the proceeds of sale and then prove as an unsecured creditor in the winding up for any deficiency.
4 The secured creditor need not prove for any part of the debt in the liquidation. If the liquidator wishes to recover the asset comprised in the security it can be redeemed only by payment of the whole amount owing to the creditors.

Distribution to members

If a company is wound up in a solvent condition any remaining assets must be distributed among the members or shareholders of the company. This distribution is in proportion to the nominal value of their shares. If premiums were paid on the issue of shares, they are not repayable when a company is wound up. Note that the memorandum or articles of association of the company may vary the normal rules for distribution of assets to shareholders but this is by express provision and cannot be inferred. The most common variation found in articles of association is one providing for the repayment of arrears of preference dividends in priority to any distribution to other shareholders.

Voluntary winding up

A company is voluntarily wound up by its members in general meeting passing:

▶ *either* a special resolution, which need not give any reason for the company to go into liquidation
▶ *or* an extraordinary resolution, given that it cannot continue its business by reason of its liabilities

In the first case the voluntary winding up is controlled by the members without interference by its creditors, and in the second case, where the company is believed to be insolvent, control over the proceedings will be shared between members and creditors.

Both resolutions must be passed by a three-quarters majority of the total votes cast on the resolution, although the notice period will differ, being 21 days for the passing of a special resolution and 14 days for the passing of an extraordinary resolution.

Such liquidations may be initiated as either a members' or a creditors' voluntary winding up. A members' voluntary winding up is defined in the Insolvency Act 1986 as one where the the directors have, within the five weeks before the winding-up resolution is passed, made a statutory declaration as to the company's solvency at a board meeting and have, in that declaration, stated that after making a full examination of the company's affairs they have formed the opinion that the company will be able to pay its debts in full within a period specified in the declaration and not exceeding twelve months from the date on which the winding-up resolution is passed. If no such declaration of solvency is made before the winding-up resolution is passed, the winding up is a creditors' voluntary winding up.

If it appears to a liquidator, during a members' voluntary winding up, that the company's debts will not be paid during the period of the solvency, the liquidator is bound to take steps to convert the liquidation into a creditors' voluntary winding up.

In a creditors' voluntary winding up the company must:

▶ call a meeting of its creditors
▶ send notices of the meeting to each creditor
▶ advertise the meeting in the *London Gazette* and at least two newspapers circulating in the locality.

The directors must prepare a statement of the company's affairs in the prescribed form, showing details of the company's assets, debts and liabilities, the names and addresses of its creditors and any securities held and a verification of the affidavit by one or more of the directors.

Conversion of a voluntary into a compulsory liquidation

The persons who may petition the court to order the winding up of a company that is already in voluntary liquidation are the same as those that may apply for a compulsory winding up of a company that is not in liquidation. The Official Receiver can also petition for a company in voluntary liquidation to be wound up under an order of the court. The petitioner must prove that one of the statutory grounds for making a winding-up order, as dealt with above, exists.

As a last point, the functions of the liquidator in a voluntary winding up are stated in the Insolvency Act 1986 to be 'winding up the company's affairs and distributing its assets' and are essentially the same as those of the liquidator in a compulsory winding up.

Summary

This chapter outlines the procedures to be followed in company reconstructions and amalgamations as distinct from mergers. One situation looked at was that of a company with accumulated losses that was reconstructed by the formation of a new company to take over its undertaking. Another situation looked at the amalgamation of two existing companies by the formation of a new company to take over their undertakings. The bookkeeping involved is, first, the closing off of the books of the transferee company or companies, and second, the opening up of the books of the transferor company. As such reconstructions will involve liquidation of the transferee companies this chapter also deals with the dissolution of companies under the Insolvency Act 1986. The section on liquidation deals with both compulsory and voluntary liquidations and, in the latter situation, with both a members' and creditors' winding up.

Suggested reading

The mechanics of accounting for a reconstruction scheme are illustrated above and require no further reading. For a more thorough examination of the law and procedures involved in company liquidations refer to the Guide and Practice Series: *Insolvency Law – Company Liquidations, Volume 1 The Substantive Law* and *Volume 2 The Procedure*, both by Robert Pennington (1987).

Self test questions

1 In devising a scheme of reconstruction, which sections of the 1985 Act are relevant to any arrangements with the company's creditors, and in what respect?

2 How does an amalgamation differ from a merger?

3 Describe the items that pass through the realisation account in a scheme of reconstruction or amalgamation.

4 Distinguish between a compulsory and a voluntary winding up.

5 Distinguish between a members' and a creditors' voluntary winding up.

Exam style questions

1 *Fulbright Ltd*

Fulbright Ltd is a company that was incorporated on 30 September 1994, to purchase the ordinary share capital of two existing companies. Rhodes Ltd and Inlac Ltd. The initiative for the business combination was taken by the board of directors of Rhodes Ltd. Fulbright Ltd was incorporated with an authorised share capital of 50 million ordinary shares of 50p each. Two million 50p ordinary shares were issued, fully paid, on 30 September 1994.

You are presented with the following information as to the liabilities, assets and profits of Rhodes Ltd and Inlac Ltd.
Draft accounts to 1 April 1995:

	Rhodes Ltd	Inlac Ltd
	£	£
Fixed assets at net book value	12,000,000	11,000,000
Net current assets	5,000,000	1,000,000
	17,000,000	12,000,000
Ordinary share capital – fully paid shares of 50p each	4,000,000	800,000
Unappropriated profits	3,000,000	1,200,000
10% debentures 2001/6	8,000,000	6,000,000
8% convertible loan stock	2,000,000	4,000,000
	17,000,000	12,000,000
Fair values of fixed assets on 1 April 1995	15,570,000	14,280,000
Profit after all expenses and taxation for the year to 30 September 1994	950,000	495,000
Estimated profit after taxation, for the year ended 30 September 1995, but before interest on the convertible loan stock	1,050,000	515,000

The convertible loan stock is convertible into ordinary shares as follows: that of Rhodes Ltd on the basis of one ordinary share for each £1 of stock and that of Inlac Ltd on the basis of two ordinary shares for each £1 of stock. Full conversion is to take place on 1 April 1995.

The proposal for the business combination, which is to take place on 1 April 1995, after the conversion of convertible loan stock as above, is that the same number of new 50p ordinary shares in the new company, Fulbright Ltd, should be issued to the shareholders of Rhodes Ltd and Inlac Ltd respectively. The number of ordinary shares to be issued by Fulbright Ltd to the shareholders of the two existing companies is to be determined as follows:

▶ One new 50p ordinary share of Fulbright Ltd for each ordinary share of the existing company with the lower net asset value.

▶ The shareholders of the existing company with the higher net asset value are to receive the same number of ordinary shares.

▶ The value of the ordinary shares to be issued by Fulbright Ltd is to be calculated in terms of the fair values of the net assets of the existing company with the lower net asset value.

▶ The shareholders of the existing company with the higher net asset value are to receive, in addition to new ordinary shares in Fulbright Ltd, 15% debentures of Fulbright Ltd, issued at par, so that the value of the total consideration received by the ordinary shareholders of this company is equal to the fair value of its net assets on the date of the business combination.

Neither of the existing companies records the fair values of their fixed assets in their separate balance sheets. Had such fair values been incorporated, the additional depreciation arising for the six months to 30 September 1995, would have been £220,000 for Rhodes Ltd and £190,000 for Inlac Ltd.

Fulbright Ltd is to account for its subsidiaries using the merger method of consolidation if the conditions of SSAP 23 – Accounting for Acquisitions and Mergers, are satisfied in respect of the use of the merger method, and the acquisition method if not.

Fulbright Ltd has other trading activities, and makes a profit after expenses and tax, but before interest, of £475,000 for the year to 30 September 1995.

Corporation tax is to be taken, where relevant, at 35%.

The accounts of all group companies are prepared to 30 September each year.

Required

a) Calculate the number and value of shares to be issued by Fulbright Ltd to the shareholders of Rhodes Ltd and to the shareholders of Inlac Ltd.   (6 marks)

b) Calculate the earnings per share for both Rhodes Ltd and Inlac Ltd, basic and fully diluted, for the year to 30 September 1994.   (4 marks)

c) Present a summarised (individual company) balance sheet for Fulbright Ltd, as on 1 April 1995, immediately after the business combination, and accounting for the cost of the investment in the two subsidiaries in accordance with the guidance given in the Appendix to SSAP 23.   (5 marks)

d) Present a summarised consolidated balance sheet for the Fulbright Ltd Group, as on 1 April 1995, immediately after the business combination.   (7 marks)

e) Present a summarised consolidated profit and loss account for the Fulbright Ltd Group for the year ended 30 September 1995.   (5 marks)

f) Calculate the basic earnings per share of the Fulbright Ltd Group for the year ended 30 September 1995.   (3 marks)

(Total 30 marks)

2   *Corinth plc*

Corinth plc commenced operations several years ago as a shipbuilding company and subsequently diversified its operations by manufacturing rigs for use in oil exploration and recovery. After initial success in its diversified operations, the company experienced financial setbacks and, for the last several years, has traded at a loss. Accordingly, with the approval of its members and the agreement of its creditors, the company has decided to reorganise its business. In future years, the company will trade under the name of Corinth (1993) plc and revert entirely to its original business of shipbuilding as from 1 July 1993.

The summarised balance sheet of Corinth plc as on 30 June 1993 indicates:

	£
Development costs	100,000
Patents	30,000
Yards at net book value	320,000
Equipment at net book value	120,000
Stocks	40,000
Debtors	20,000
Trade creditors	(10,000)
Arrears of preference dividends	(20,000)
Bank overdraft	(90,000)
	510,000
100,000 ordinary shares of £4 each	400,000
60,000 5% cumulative preference shares of £1 each	60,000
Profit and loss account – accumulated losses	(80,000)
6% secured debenture repayable in 1995	130,000
	510,000

You are provided with the following further information:

▶ All of the equipment of Corinth plc can be used, interchangeably, for both shipbuilding and rig construction.

▶ Corinth plc has two yards, one of which was designed specifically for the construction of rigs. This latter yard, with a net book value of £160,000, is to be sold for £42,000 prior to the creation of Corinth (1993) plc. The sale has not been recorded in the summarised balance sheet of Corinth plc above.

▶ The development expenditure was incurred on the design and testing of prototype oil rigs. The patent rights, which have a further ten years to run, relate to Corinth plc's unique design of an oil rig.

▶ Stocks worth £30,000 are for shipbuilding and the remainder of the stocks have no value. The debtor for £20,000 represents the final payment due for the sale of an oil rig, the purchaser of which has recently gone into liquidation.

▶ The 6% debenture is secured over Corinth plc's assets by a floating charge.

The scheme of reorganisation is to be as follows:

1   The authorised and issued ordinary share capital of Corinth (1993) plc is to be set at £200,000. The existing ordinary shareholders of Corinth plc are to receive one partly paid £2 ordinary share in Corinth (1993) plc for every one of their ordinary shares in Corinth plc. £1 of the Corinth (1993) plc ordinary shares to be issued is to be treated as fully paid up and the balance of £1 per ordinary share is to be paid for by the ordinary shareholders of Corinth plc to Corinth (1993) plc on 1 July 1993.

2   The preference shareholders of Corinth plc are to exchange their shares for a new issue of 10% £1 cumulative preference shares in Corinth (1993) plc in the ratio of one new preference share for every two existing preference

shares. All arrears of preference dividend are to be cancelled.

3   Unsecured trade creditors are to be discharged by cash payments of 20p in the £.

4   The bank overdraft in the books of Corinth plc, *after* any necessary adjustments, is to be fully discharged by a debenture issue at 8% interest to be secured on Corinth (1993) plc's yard.

5   The 6% debenture of £130,000 in the books of Corinth plc is to be fully discharged as part of the purchase consideration for the business of Corinth plc as on 30 June 1993.

6   The debit balance on the profit and loss account is to be eliminated and all assets useful to the new company are to be transferred at book values.

Required

a) Prepare the journal entries necessary to close off the books of Corinth plc as on 30 June 1993.   (19 marks)

b) Prepare the balance sheet of Corinth (1993) plc as on 1 July 1993.   (6 marks)

(25 marks)

All answers on pages 704– 708.

The Major Features of Reconstructions, Mergers and Takeovers

Chapters 25 and 26 dealt with changes in the organisational structure of individual companies and also with their dissolution. Chapters 15 to 22 dealt with various aspects of consolidated accounts following the combination of two or more businesses under common control. This, relatively short, chapter deals with the major features of reconstructions, mergers and takeovers. We will look here at the main reasons for business combinations, the role of the Stock Exchange, the Mergers and Monopolies Commission and the EC in relation to the control and regulation of takeovers and mergers in the public interest, the obligations on directors during takeover bids and the ways in which the rights of a minority are protected.

Where growth is often the result of the expansion of the original business it is also achieved by the acquisition of existing enterprises as going concerns followed by reorganisation. There are many strategies that are possible where two or more enterprises combine. Thus an undertaking may acquire its main supplier(s) or customer(s), that is vertical integration; or, alternatively, business of a similar nature to that of the acquirer company may be acquired, that is, horizontal integration, where the acquired businesses may, for example, be in different geographical areas. Further, a company may diversify into activities that are different from that of its existing business.

For whatever reasons businesses combine, there are essentially, to use the terminology of the previous chapter, two forms of business combination – absorption and amalgamation. This will hold true whether or not any of the combining businesses are wound up and lose their separate legal entities. So, too, there are essentially two methods of satisfying the consideration for absorptions or amalgamations – that is, cash and debt capital of the acquirer on the one hand, and equity capital of the acquirer on the other – or some combination of the two. Where we can try to distinguish, as in Chapter 26, between terms such as merger, amalgamation, absorption, acquisition and takeover, the terms all apply to the common situation of two or more businesses coming together.

Acquisitions and mergers, where shares of businesses are purchased, give rise to parent–subsidiary undertaking relationships and these in turn give rise to the additional preparation of consolidated accounts, as dealt with in Chapters 15 to 22.

An absorption may be described as a situation where, on the acquisition of an undertaking, the original proprietors are displaced, the purchased company goes out of existence and its assets are incorporated into the acquirer company.

An amalgamation may reasonably be described as a situation where businesses that are similar in size merge their identities in a new, larger undertaking. There are two ways in which this can be achieved. One is to form a new company to which existing companies sell their undertakings for shares in the newly formed company, followed by the liquidation of the transferee companies. The other is where a new company is formed to take over the shares of existing companies, which continue in existence as subsidiaries.

The UK has a substantial mergers and acquisitions industry. In 1992 there were 1,152 acquisitions of UK companies with a total value of £19,747 million (Cameron, 1993). This market is regulated by a number of mechanisms that provide protection for investors. Thus, all intermediaries involved are required to be licensed under the

Financial Service Act. The institutions and bodies that govern takeover activity in the UK include:

▶ The Stock Exchange, which regulates the listing of shares and the disclosure requirements, acquisitions and disposals of listed companies.
▶ The Monopolies and Mergers Commission, which looks into whether an acquisition restricts competition and can advise whether an acquisition is against the public interest.
▶ The Takeover Panel, which publishes the *City Code on Takeovers and Mergers* and seeks to ensure fair and equal treatment of all shareholders involved in the takeover of a public company.

In Chapter 2 we looked at company law harmonisation throughout the EC. The main instrument used in the harmonisation programme has been the Directive. The 3rd and 6th Directives contain various technical provisions regarding mergers and demergers of plcs. The draft 10th Directive deals with cross-border mergers of plcs. There is also a draft European Company Statute, which would allow two or more companies based in at least two member states to form a European company, a 'Societos Europa', or SE, either by merging or forming a joint parent company, or by forming a joint subsidiary. An SE would be governed by the provisions of the (draft) European Company Statute in relation to its accounts, employee participation, share capital, internal procedures and regulations. In matters such as formation, issue of shares, changes in share capital, insolvency and the rights of members and creditors, the law of the member state in which the SE is registered would apply. Given disagreements as to the proposed employee participation provisions in the statute and the possibility that an SE can change the law applicable to it by simply moving its registered office, the draft has yet to be finalised.

The draft 13th Directive on takeovers and other general bids proposes the minimum requirements for the conduct of takeover bids so that the equality of treatment of affected shareholders is ensured. The UK has objected to these proposals on the ground that their adoption would result in a loss of flexibility in the decisions of the Takeover Panel

Why should companies combine?

The reasons why one company might seek to combine with another include:

▶ The purchase of undervalued assets through the purchase of the shares of a company currently listed at a relatively low price in a dull market or the practice of asset stripping.
▶ The effects of economies of scale or synergy so that, effectively, $2 + 2 = 5$.
▶ Combination can achieve the elimination of competition and therefore the generation of larger profits and better rates of return on capital employed. The elimination of competition represents a danger to the public at large. It is for this reason that some mergers can be referred to the Monopolies and Mergers Commission.
▶ A combination that results in diversified activities can reduce risk in that expected earnings may be less variable than the separate earnings of individual businesses.
▶ The acquisition of a management team through the acquisition of their employer company.
▶ The acquisition of brands.
▶ External growth through acquisition may be cheaper than attempting organic or internal growth.

The question as to whether or not one company should combine with another, the investment decision, falls in the province of Paper 14 and financial strategy. It is, however, interesting to note here that the usual financial and economic reasons suggested for business combination (see, for example, Meeks, 1977) have been found, in practice, not to be of prime importance and that the most important determinant of mergers among large corporations would appear to be managerial desire to protect their position, reduce the uncertainties of their employment, and perhaps increase their remuneration.

Directors' duties in a takeover situation

Directors' duties are owed to the company as a whole and arise out of both statute and common law. Thus directors have:

▶ a fiduciary duty to act honestly and in good faith
▶ a duty to exercise skill and care, and
▶ a statutory duty.

Statute does not specifically deal with takeovers and mergers. It does, however, deal with relationships between successful bidders and dissenting minority shareholders and other aspects of successful offers (CA 1985, Part XIII A).

Takeovers and mergers involving public companies are governed by the City Code on Takeovers and Mergers, issued by the Council for the securities industry. This is a general guide as to the principles and practices that should be followed. The Takeover Panel has issued, as an adjunct to the City Code, rules governing substantial acquisitions of shares. Directors are expected to observe the spirit as well as the letter of these rules.

The Stock Exchange *Yellow Book*, Section 6, contains specific provisions relating to acquisitions and mergers. There are different requirements imposed in different situations, depending on the size of the transaction and the identity of the parties involved. In some circumstances shareholders approval is a pre-requisite. Directors duties in these situations is dealt with further below.

The City Code on Takeovers and Mergers

The Code is applied by a panel. It has no statutory force but is backed by the authority of the Stock Exchange and the Issuing Houses Association. The listing agreement requires listed companies to adhere to the Code.

Its purpose is to regulate the processes of takeovers and mergers and it contains principles and rules relating both to the conduct of the parties to takeovers and mergers and to the disclosure of information. Its main information requirements are outlined below.

General principles and specific rules

The general principles of the Code are:

▶ 'All shareholders (of the same class) of an offeree company must be treated similarly' and given adequate information to decide upon the merits of a bid.
▶ All documents issued in connection with a bid should be drafted with the same care as the Companies Act requires of a prospectus.
▶ No relevant information should be withheld from shareholders and they should be given sufficient advice, information and time to enable them to reach a properly informed decision.

- After an offer has been communicated to the board of directors of an offeree company no action can be taken by the directors without the approval of shareholders in general meeting. Thus, shareholders must be given the chance of deciding on the merits of a bid for themselves.
- The oppression of a minority is not acceptable. Thus, a parent undertaking cannot take decisions as to the takeover of one of its subsidiaries in such a way that the minority interest in such a subsidiary is unfairly treated.
- If control (here 30% or more of the voting rights) is required, a general offer to all other shareholders is normally required.

Sale and purchase agreements, due diligence and public offers

A target company will normally require some indication of the price to be offered by the acquirer before entering into negotiations. At this stage, the acquirer will require more information than will be publicly available from such sources as published accounts. The target may release information not generally available, but it would be usual in this case for the target to request a letter of confidentiality, in which the acquirer will undertake not to use the information except for the purpose of assessing the investment, and not to release the information to any third party except for the advisers to the acquirer. This information could include customer lists, budgets, management accounts and product information.

Due diligence and the sale and purchase agreement

Any agreement as to terms will be subject to negotiation of the sale and purchase agreement, and it would be usual at this stage for an acquirer to insist that any agreement be subject to a detailed investigation, due diligence, of the target. A due diligence exercise will address such questions as:

- What are the major risks that the target is exposed to?
- Are there any undisclosed liabilities (off balance sheet finance) or contingent liabilities?
- Is there a proper statement of control and is information fully available to management to make decisions?
- What are the sources of profits?
- Is reported profit a true reflection of financial performance?

A sale and purchase agreement cannot be entered into if the target is a public company and it will not usually be possible to carry out a due diligence investigation in this situation. For public company targets an acquirer will seek to acquire as many of the target's shares as possible before the share price begins to reflect the interest. The following percentages are relevant in the build-up of the stake:

- Company law requires public disclosure of a holding of 3% or more.
- The Takeover Panel restricts the rate at which a stake of 15% may be built up.
- As mentioned above, the Takeover Panel defines control of a company as a holding of 30% or more of its voting shares. Once this point has been reached the purchaser must make a cash offer for the remaining equity shares.

Further, the Code stipulates that:

- to acquire a controlling interest in a plc an investor must make an offer to all its shareholders
- the offer must be publicly announced and followed by the issue of an offer document to all the shareholders within 28 days

▶ the final closing date for acceptances is limited to 60 days after the posting of the offer document.

The acquirer will appoint a team of professional advisers to guide on the requirements of the Code.

Other factors

Paper 13 is not specifically concerned with the pricing of a bid and the effects of a successful bid on a purchaser company's share price. You should, however, be aware of factors other than those dealt with above in the making of a takeover decision. The purchaser will obviously be concerned with the purchase price and whether the acquisition will be worth that price. Share valuation principles, as dealt with in Chapter 24, will be relevant here. In practical terms, service contracts for key personnel will need to be considered.

Factors affecting the acquiring company

Directors of the acquirer company will need to gauge the reaction of the shareholders of the company to the bid. Where it will not always be necessary to seek the approval of shareholders in making a bid such approval may be necessary under the rules of the Stock Exchange if the consideration to be paid includes a major issue of the acquirer company's shares. Chapter 10 of the Consultation Draft listing rules deals with acquisitions and disposals by a listed company and will replace parts of Section 6 of the *Yellow Book*. Chapter 10 lists five categories of transactions:

▶ *Class 3 transactions* are acquisitions and disposals where percentages are less then 5%. No announcement is required unless consideration for an acquisition is satisfied by the issue of securities for which listing is being sought.
▶ *Class 2 transactions* are where acquisitions and disposals are for 5% or more but less than 15%. An announcement is required.
▶ *Class 1* describes an acquisition or disposal of 15% or more but less than 25%; these require an announcement and a circular.
▶ *Super Class 1* describes an acquisition or disposal of 25% or more; these transactions require an announcement, a circular and also the approval of shareholders in general meeting.
▶ *Reverse takeovers* describe an acquisition by a listed company where any percentage ratio is 100% or more, or which would result in a material change of management or change in shareholders control of the listed company. When a reverse takeover is announced the Stock Exchange will suspend listing of the company's securities pending the meeting at which shareholders' approval is sought. If approval is given the listing is cancelled. If approval is not given, the listing is restored. In any event the company will need to prepare a Super Class 1 circular and listing particulars.

Chapter 11 of the Consultation Draft provides certain safeguards against directors or substantial shareholders taking advantage of their position.

The impact of a bid on the share price of the acquirer company must be considered bearing in mind the responsibility of directors to protect the interests of shareholders.

Factors affecting the target company

A bid may be resisted by the defensive tactics of the target's board of directors or, ultimately, rejected by the target's shareholders who do not sell their shares. Where differences of opinion arise as to whether or not to accept the bid, the City Code governs the conduct of the bid. Some of the principles and rules of the code have been dealt with above. Directors may contest a bid on the following grounds:

▶ there is no advantage to shareholders in the company being taken over
▶ there may be strong opposition among employees
▶ founder members, with influence over other members, may oppose the bid
▶ the terms of the bid may not be acceptable
▶ initial rejection can lead to a higher bid.

In contesting the bid the directors of the target might follow this course of action:

▶ Prepare a profit forecast to show that shareholders are best advised not to sell their shares.
▶ Attempt to have the bid referred to the Monopolies and Mergers Commission.
▶ Locate a 'white knight' to make a more favourable takeover bid.
▶ Counter-bid for the acquirer company.
▶ Plan a management buy-out.

The Monopolies and Mergers Commission

The Office of Fair Trading is empowered under the Monopolies and Mergers Act as modified by the Fair Trading Act 1973 to examine all mergers and takeovers over a certain size and, if they conclude that a merger or takeover is not in the public interest, will refer the bid to the Monopolies and Merger Commission. As a result of an investigation by the Commission the bid may be withdrawn, or it may proceed but with conditions attached in respect of, for example, prices to be set or employment practices.

Summary

This chapter concludes our examination of the changes in the organisational structure of both individual companies and groups. It accepts that the terms acquisition, merger, takeover, absorption and amalgamation are used interchangeably, but attempts to distinguish between them. It outlines the role of the Stock Exchange, the Monopolies and Mergers Commission and the Takeover Panel in the regulation of mergers and takeovers and also deals with the impact of EC directives and statutes in this respect. The reasons why companies seek to combine are listed and the duties of directors of companies taking over or taken over by other companies explained.

It is unlikely that the contents of this chapter will be the subject of a whole question in Paper 13 and for this reason, in that it supports by way of additional information the relevant examinable areas of consolidation and reconstruction, no exam standard questions follow the chapter.

Suggested reading

A Practitioner's Guide to the Stock Exchange Yellow Book (Westminster Management Consultants 1993)

This is a comprehensive review of the requirements of the *Yellow Book*. Chapter 7 by Stuart Evans of Simmons & Simmons deals with acquisitions, disposals, takeovers and mergers and transactions with related parties.

Advanced Financial Accounting (Lewis, Pendrill and Simon 1981)

Chapter 11 on business combinations links up the reasons for combining with methods of combining and the preference for a group structure.

Acquisitions in the UK (Graves, 1993) This short article in the *European Handbook 1993* provides useful information on selecting and approaching a target.

Self test questions

1 Outline some of the reasons why companies may wish to merge with or take over other companies.

2 Although few guidelines are provided, by either the Office of Fair Trading or the Monopolies and Mergers Commission, for the basis on which mergers are recommended for reference to the Commission or for the criteria applied in determining whether a merger is likely to contravene the public interest, state what these bases or criteria are likely to be.

3 The City Code represents an attempt at self-regulation by the City in the conduct of merger and takeover transactions. Identify the two principal means designed by the Code to protect the interests of individual shareholders.

4 The City Code is a statement of principles, rules and practice notes. Summarise the main requirements of the Code.

5 Outline the work of the Takeover Panel.

All answers on pages 708–709

Earnings per Share and Other Stock Market Ratios

This and subsequent chapters address that part of the syllabus dealing with analysing and appraising financial and related information. Subsequent chapters will deal with financial analysis in the context of the demand for and sources of information, trend analysis, corporate failure prediction and the limitations of ratio analysis. This chapter deals mainly with what was, until recently, the primary performance indicator, earnings per share (eps) and, while looking at the role of the Stock Exchange, briefly at other stock market ratios.

SSAP 3 was issued in 1972, amended in 1974 and, following the issue of FRS 3 in 1992, amended again in 1992. It indicates precisely the procedures to be followed in the calculation of eps. As SSAP 3 was published well before the accounting standard on acquisitions and mergers – see Chapter 19 – it does not deal with the different treatment that should be applied to shares issued by a parent company for a merger as opposed to an acquisition and there remains a case for a further revision of SSAP 3 in this regard.

In terms of examination emphasis, this is an important chapter in that the topic may be examined either as a topic on its own or as a part of a question dealing with any of the areas listed below:

▶ share valuation
▶ capital reduction schemes
▶ interpretation of accounts
▶ accountants' reports
▶ profit forecast.

Investors in shares that are listed on the Stock Exchange depend upon various ratios that are an aid to comparing the relative merits of alternative investments based upon the dividends and earnings of a company. These further ratios are also dealt with in this chapter.

Earnings per share defined

Earnings per share is defined in SSAP 3 as:

> The profit in pence attributable to each equity share, based on the consolidated profit of the period after tax and after deducting minority interests and preference dividends, but before taking into account extraordinary items, divided by the number of equity shares in issue and ranking for dividend in respect of the period.

The standard applies to listed companies and requires that they disclose the following:

▶ Basic eps calculated on the 'net' basis for the current and preceding accounting periods and disclosed on the face of the profit and loss account. If calculations on the 'nil' basis are materially different they should, additionally, be disclosed.

► Fully diluted eps, if appropriate, and where the difference between it and basic eps is more than 5% of basic eps. The corresponding amount for the previous period should not be shown unless the assumptions on which it was based remain applicable.
► Equal prominence should be given to disclosure of basic and fully diluted eps.
► The basis of calculation for eps, together with the amount of earnings and the number of shares taken into consideration in its calculation.

FRS 3 has amended the SSAP 3 definition above. As has already been stated in Chapter 11 here, eps must be calculated as the profit in pence attributable to each equity share, based on the profit for the year *after* taxation, minority interests and *extraordinary items* (if any) and after deducting appropriations in respect of preference shares, divided by the number of equity shares in issue and ranking for dividend in respect of the period.

Given that eps is now to be calculated after extraordinary items, this represents a change from SSAP 3, which is amended accordingly by FRS 3 in this respect.

The FRS allows alternative bases for calculating eps provided that the basic eps required by the standard is given at least as much prominence as the alternative and there is a reconciliation between the two figures and the reason for showing the alternative is explained.

The essential point arising here is not so much the fact that eps is now to be based on earnings *after* extraordinary items but that, given the effective abolition of extraordinary items by FRS 3, there will be *no* extraordinary items. Further, items that would previously have been excluded from eps as extraordinary will now be included as exceptional. It is this last point that is behind the alternative eps permitted by FRS 3.

All references to eps in this chapter are to eps as defined by SSAP 3 but amended by FRS 3. No reference is made to extraordinary items, on the basis that they will not arise.

Basic eps

This section breaks down the definition of eps and deals with some of the problems that may arise in ascertaining which profits and what number of ordinary shares to include in the calculation.

Profits on earnings

These are consolidated profits including, where relevant, share of earnings of associated undertakings, after taxation and minority interests and after deducting preference dividends.

Taxation

The tax on profit on ordinary activities dealt with in the profit and loss account could include any of the following items:

	£000
Corporation tax on income at x%	x
Less: Relief for overseas taxation	(x)
Overseas taxation	x
Under/(over) provisions in previous years	x/(x)
Tax suffered on FII	x
Transfers to/(from) deferred taxation	x/(x)
Irrecoverable advance corporation tax	x
Associated companies	x
	x

Where such a tax charge will include elements that are constant, in that they do not vary with the proportion of profit distributed by way of dividend, the charge may include an element that varies according to the profit distributed and which would be absent if no distributions were made. The component of the tax charge that may be classified as variable, as opposed to constant, is irrecoverable ACT. As eps is calculated after taxation, and as taxation could include irrecoverable ACT, the dividend policy of a company which may give rise to irrecoverable ACT can have a bearing on the eps calculation. This has given rise to alternative bases of calculating eps. The 'net basis' based on 'net earnings', that is, earnings after deducting the whole of the tax on profit on activities regardless of the make-up of the tax charge and the 'nil basis' based on 'nil earnings', that is, earnings after deducting all items of tax on profit on ordinary activities except, where it arises, irrecoverable ACT. SSAP 3 requires that eps be calculated on a net basis and that it additionally be disclosed on a nil basis, if materially different.

An argument in favour of the net basis of calculating eps is that users of accounts would wish to consider all relevant information in appraising a company's performance and that any additional tax arising from a company's dividend policy is relevant information. The ASC justified the SSAP 3 requirement that eps be calculated on a net basis on the ground that it 'takes account of all relevant facts including the additional tax liabilities inherent in the dividend policy pursued by the company, for which the directors should be no less accountable to shareholders'.

As to nil earnings and eps as these are, effectively, net earnings plus any irrecoverable ACT included in the tax on profit on ordinary activities, any such irrecoverable ACT is effectively treated as an appropriation as opposed to a charge. Treating irrecoverable ACT as an appropriation means that nil eps is not influenced by a company's dividend policy; hence the term nil.

It has been argued that as the nil basis produces a figure for eps that is not dependent upon a company's dividend policy, it is more comparable between companies. SSAP 3 requires that nil eps be disclosed in addition to net eps if materially different. Materiality in this context is not quantified. The *Financial Times* in its share information service states that 'p/e's are calculated on the net distribution basis, earnings per share being computed on profit after taxation and unrelieved ACT where applicable; bracketed figures indicate 10% or more difference if calculated on nil distribution'.

Preference dividends

The earnings dealt with in eps are those that are attributable to equity shares. Where preference shares are in issue it is necessary to eliminate preference dividends. In most cases this is relatively straightforward, but complications may arise where a question distinguishes between cumulative and non-cumulative preference shares. You should deduct preference dividends to arrive at earnings available per equity share as follows:

► *Cumulative preference shares* Deduct the preference dividend for the year only (do not deduct arrears relating to previous years), whether or not a dividend is declared. It may be that in doing so you will create a loss resulting in a loss per equity share.
► *Non-cumulative preference shares* Deduct the preference dividend for the year only, but only if the dividend is declared; such preference dividends will not be declared if there are insufficient profits available.

The effect of business combinations

The effect of a business combination on earnings available for eps is not fully dealt with in SSAP 3 and you need to refer also to SSAP 23 on acquisitions and mergers (see Chapter 11) to appreciate the effect on consolidated earnings of different methods of consolidation. If the acquisition method is used, relevant earnings must include only the post-acquisition earnings of a subsidiary combined with in the year. Where the merger method is used, relevant earnings must include the whole of the earnings of a subsidiary combined with in the year, regardless of the date of the business combination.

The number of equity shares to be used in the basic eps calculation

The denominator of the eps calculation depends upon the number of equity shares in issue and ranking for dividend in the period. The value of the denominator may change during an accounting period for several reasons. There may, for example, be an issue of new equity at full market price, a bonus, scrip or capitalisation issue, a rights issue at less than full market price, a share-for-share exchange, shares issued on the conversion of convertible loan stock in the period or options exercised in the period and the purchase by the company of its own shares during the period. The effects of each of these on the number of shares to be included in the basic eps calculation are dealt with in turn.

Issue of new equity shares at full market value

Such shares must be time apportioned to arrive at the weighted average number of shares for the eps calculation. An example of this is shown in Example 28.1.

EXAMPLE 28.1

1 January: Number of ordinary shares in issue	100
1 March: New issue at full market value	24
31 December: Number of ordinary shares in issue at the year end	124
Weighted average number = 100 + (10/12 × 24)=	120

Such new issues of shares do not have a distorting effect on the comparability of previous years' eps and no adjustment is required to be made to the corresponding years' eps amounts disclosed as comparatives.

Bonus issue

As a general rule, use the year end number of shares and apply a factor to previous years' eps to put them on a comparable basis, as shown in Example 28.2.

EXAMPLE 28.2

1 January: Number of ordinary shares in issue	100
1 June: Bonus issue of 1:4	25
31 December: Number of ordinary shares in issue at the year end	125

The number of shares for the basic eps calculation is 125.

All previous years' eps would need to be restated by applying the factor, given a bonus value of 1:4, of 4/5.

Some care needs to be taken if a bonus issue takes place after other issues. Thus, using the data in Example 28.2, if a new issue for cash at full market value of 24 shares is made on 1 March, the number of shares for the basic eps calculation is not (100 +

$[10/12 \times 24] + [124/4])$ 151. This is because the bonus shares attaching to the 24 shares issued on 1 March cannot be assumed to be in issue from before that date. The correct calculation is shown in Example 28.3.

EXAMPLE 28.3

1 January: Number of shares in issue	100		
1 June bonus issue thereon 1:4	25		
		$125 \times 2/12$	21
1 March: New issue for cash at full market value	24		
1 June bonus issue thereon 1:4	6	30	
		$155 \times 10/12$	129
31 December: Weighted average number of shares for basic eps			150

The effect of a bonus issue made during a year is to reduce the basic eps for that year. This amount is not comparable with the basic eps for previous years. Accordingly, in order to be made comparable, the basic eps of previous years needs to be restated on the assumption that the bonus shares issued in the current year were in issue for all previous years. This is achieved by applying a factor to the basic eps of previous years, as previously stated, as follows:

▶ if the current year's bonus issue was 1:4 then 4/5
▶ if the current year's bonus issue was 1:3 then 3/4
▶ if the current year's bonus issue was 1:10 then 10/11.

Rights issue

As a rights issue is always made at a price below the current market value of a share, such issues combine the effects of both an issue for cash and, effectively, given the reduced price of issue, an issue by way of a bonus. Accordingly, the rules in both situations above need to be applied in calculating the weighted average number of shares for the basic eps calculation. A question must provide you with the following information:

▶ the actual cum-rights value of the shares on the last day so quoted
▶ the rights issue price.

You would normally be expected to work out the theoretical ex-rights value to ascertain the bonus element in the rights issue. This is easily done, as outlined below and shown in Example 28.4.

Assume a convenient number of shares; if the rights issue is 1:4 then 4, if 1:5 then 5 etc. Ascertain the actual cum-rights value of this number. Add to this value the value of the rights share taken up at the rights issue price. The theoretical ex-rights value is the theoretical value of the holding after the rights issue divided by the number of shares after the rights issue.

EXAMPLE 28.4

A company has 500 shares in issue on 1 January and makes a rights issue of 1:5 on 30 September. The actual cum-rights value on the last day the shares are so quoted is 90p per share. The rights shares are issued at 60p per share and are fully taken up. First ascertain the theoretical ex rights price as follows:

	Number	£
Assumed number	5 @ 90p	4.50
Rights issue (1:5)	1 @ 60p	0.60
	6	5.10
	£5.10/6 = 85p	

Once the theoretical ex-rights value has been determined, the procedure to ascertain the weighted average number of ordinary shares is as follows:

▶ Start with the number of shares before the rights issue and uplift by the factor actual cum-rights value/theoretical ex-rights value (to take into account the bonus element in the rights issue).
▶ Time apportion the adjusted number up to the date of the rights issue.
▶ Add to the uplifted, time apportioned number of shares the total number of shares after the rights issue time apportioned from the date of the rights issue to the year end.

1 January	$500 \times 90/85 \times 9/12$	397
1 October (1:5)	100	
	600	$\times 3/12$	150
Weighted average number of shares		547

As in the bonus issue example (Example 28.3), given the bonus element in the rights issue, previous years' basic eps are no longer comparable with that of the current year. Accordingly, for comparative information, previous years' basic eps, as previously stated, need to be adjusted by the factor theoretical ex-rights value/actual cum-rights value (effectively assuming that the bonus shares issued as a part of the rights issue were in issue for all previous years).

Share-for-share exchange

Where such shares are issued for the purchase of a trade investment, associated undertaking or subsidiary accounted for as an acquisition (as opposed to a merger), they need to be time apportioned from the 'effective date of the acquisition', that is, the date that the earnings from the investments are included in the profit and loss account. This is the date that control passes. The procedure is exactly the same as in the issue for cash at full market value situation above, and there is no need for any restatement of previous years' basic eps. If, however, there is a share-for-share exchange resulting in a merger where the subsidiary is accounted for using the merger method of consolidation, you need to go beyond SSAP 3 and take into account the effects of SSAP 23 and accounting for mergers. As the earnings of a subsidiary consolidated using the merger method are included in the profit and loss account for the full year in the year of combination, it is not appropriate to time apportion the shares issued as consideration for the merger from the date of the merger. To do so would result in not comparing like with like, and the shares issued are taken as being in issue for the whole year regardless of the actual date of their issue. Comparative earnings need to be restated in the consolidated profit and loss account in a merger consolidation to include the earnings of the merger subsidiary for the whole of the previous year. This SSAP 23 requirement has a bearing on the basic eps of the previous year(s) included as a comparative in the current year. The previous year(s)' basic eps need to be restated to take into account the merger subsidiary's earnings for the previous year(s) and the number of shares issued by the parent as consideration for the merger in the current year. See Example 28.5.

EXAMPLE 28.5

	1994 £000	1993 £000
Consolidated earnings of H Group excluding merger in 1994	4,700	4,150
Earnings of merger subsidiary, combined with on 1 June 1994 consolidated for the full year	750	625
	5,450	4,775
Parent company number of ordinary shares at 1 January	25,000	25,000
Issued as consideration for the merger on 1 June 1994	10,200	
	35,200	25,000

The basic eps for the year ended 31 December 1994 is £5,450/35,200 = 15.5p. Earnings include the earnings of the merger subsidiary for the full year and the number of shares includes the shares issued as consideration, without time apportionment, for the full year.

The basic eps for the year ended 31 December 1993 would have been previously stated as £4,150/25,000 = 16.6p. The 1993 comparative basic eps for inclusion in the 1994 accounts would need to be restated to £4,775/(25,000 + 10,200) so as to = 13.6p.

Shares issued on conversion of convertible loan stock and shares issued on the exercise of options during the period

The shares actually issued will be in accordance with the terms of conversion of convertible loan stock (CLS) and the exercise of options, for example, 150 ordinary shares for every £100 nominal of CLS and an option to purchase 1,500 ordinary shares at a stated price on or within stated dates. The number actually issued will be included in the basic eps calculation on a time apportioned basis from the date of issue to the year end. This is shown in Example 28.6.

EXAMPLE 28.6

A company has 1,700 ordinary shares in issue on 1 January. Also in issue on this date are £1,000 of 11% CLS and options to purchase 750 ordinary shares at 75p per share. The terms of conversion of the CLS were that 150 ordinary shares were to be issued for every £100 nominal of the CLS. Holders of the convertible loan stock converted all their stock in accordance with these terms on 1 April and the holders of the options exercised their right to purchase ordinary shares on 1 August.

1 January	1,700	× 3/12	425
1 April issued on conversion 1,000 × 150/100	1,500		
	3,200	× 4/12	1,067
1 August issued on exercise of options	750		
31 December	3,950	× 5/12	1,646
Weighted average number of shares			3,138

The terms of conversion and exercise would, normally, also make reference to adjustments to the shares issued on eventual conversion and exercise for any bonus issues and rights issues made by the company between the date of the issue of the CLS and options and the date of their eventual conversion and exercise. This is to enable CLS and option holders to maintain their relative positions vis-à-vis other existing shareholders of the company. The number of shares to be issued on conversion and exercise would now need to be uplifted to take into account any bonus issues and rights issues made by the company between the relevant dates, as shown in Example 28.7

EXAMPLE 28.7

This example uses data as in Example 28.6. The company issued the 11% CLS before issuing the options. After the date of the issue of the 11% CLS, but before the date of the issue of the options, the company made a bonus issue of 1:3 shares held on that date. After the date of the issue of the options, the company made a rights issue of 1:5 shares held on that date. The actual cum-rights price of the company's shares immediately prior to the rights issue was 90p per share and the theoretical ex-rights value 85p per share. The terms of conversion and exercise included reference to adjustment for the number of shares to be issued for previous bonus issues and rights issues made by the company.

1 January (assume including bonus and rights shares)		1,700 ×3/12	425
1 April issued on conversion			
1,000 × 150/100 =	1,500		
	×		
Adjustment for bonus issue	4/3		
	×		
Adjustment for rights issue	90/85		
	= 2,118		
		3,818 × 4/12	1,273
1 August issued on exercise of options	750		
Adjustment for bonus issue	–		
(bonus issue made before options were issued)			
	×		
Adjustment for rights issue 31 December	90/85 = 794		
		4,612 × 5/12	
			1,922
Weighted average number of shares			3,620

Note: Always adjust the numbers of shares issued on conversion of CLS/exercise of options, whether or not you are asked to do so in a question.

Purchase of own shares

The shares purchased must be included in the basic eps calculation time apportioned from the beginning of the year to the date of purchase. This is illustrated by Example 28.8.

EXAMPLE 28.8

1 January: Number of ordinary shares in issue	1,800	× 5/12	750
31 May: Number of own shares purchased by the company	(750)		
31 December	1,050	× 7/12	613
Weighted average number of ordinary shares			1,363

Losses

Where relevant earnings for the basic eps calculation are negative, a loss per ordinary share is calculated and disclosed.

Fully diluted eps

Where a company has in issue any form of security that does not, at present, rank for ordinary dividends but may do so in future – for example, convertibles, warrants or options – the effect on eps of these securities becoming entitled to earnings is called 'full dilution'. As eps is used by analysts to make share investment decisions, it is its predictive character that is important. Thus, if any factors exist that may make basic eps unrepresentative of future trends, they should be incorporated into this calculation.

Circumstances in which a fully diluted eps calculation is required

There are three factors that may make current basic eps unrepresentative of future trends:

▶ classes of ordinary share not presently ranking for dividend but which will do so in the future
▶ convertible loan stock or convertible preference shares
▶ options or warrants to subscribe for ordinary shares.

Where a company has in issue, for any part of the period, any of these securities, it must calculate and disclose, in addition to basic eps, fully diluted eps.

When fully diluted eps need not be disclosed

The standard sets out three situations in which fully diluted eps need not be disclosed. These are:

▶ if basic eps is a loss per share
▶ if, as may turn out, fully diluted eps is greater than basic eps – according to the standard, conversion and option rights would not be exercised in such an event (this exception has been criticised because of the lack of the realism of the previous assumption, and the standard's assertion about likely investors' behaviour)
▶ if the dilution is not material, that is, less than 5%.

The calculation of fully diluted eps

The intention in disclosing fully diluted eps is to show the eps that would have resulted if all potential shares had been issued at the beginning of the period (or date of issue of the security giving rise to such shares, if later). Account needs to be taken of any possible effect of such shares on both available earnings and the number of shares over which earnings will eventually be spread.

Shares in issue but not ranking for dividend until a later period

This is explained by Example 28.9.

EXAMPLE 28.9

Relevant earnings amount to £100.

Relevant number of ordinary shares in issue and ranking for dividend amount to 1,200. In addition, during the year to 31 December, the company issued 1,000 ordinary shares on 1 January but these shares did not rank for dividend until the period beginning the following 1 January.

The basic eps is £100/1,200 = 8.3p. The fully diluted eps is £100/(1,200 + 1,000) = 4.5p.

CLS

The effect of assuming that conversion of CLS takes place at the beginning of the period (or date of issue of the CLS, if later) is twofold. There is, first, an effect on earnings in terms of an interest saving and, secondly, an effect on the number of shares to bring into account, as shown in Example 28.10.

EXAMPLE 28.10

Relevant earnings for the period to 31 December amounted to £750. The relevant number of ordinary shares for the basic eps calculation amounts to 9,500. There were £800 12% CLS in issue at the beginning of the period on 1 January, all of which were convertible, 150 ordinary shares for every £100 nominal of CLS, on 31 July of the following period. Corporation tax is taken at 35%.

	£
Basic earnings	750
Adjustment for 12% CLS: add interest paid, net of tax, 12% × 800 × 0.65	62
Fully diluted earnings	812
Basic number of shares	9,500
Adjustment for 12% CLS: maximum issuable on conversion 800 × 150/100	1,200
	10,700

Basic eps £750/9,500 = 7.9p

Fully diluted eps £812/10,700 = 7.6p

(The dilution is 0.3p, is 3.8% of basic eps, is immaterial, and would not be disclosed.)

In a period where CLS is converted, wholly or partially, during the period, there is an effect on both basic eps and fully diluted eps for the period. This is shown in Example 28.11.

EXAMPLE 28.11

The facts are as in Example 28.10. The CLS was fully converted on 31 July of the current period and there were 9,500 ordinary shares in issue before the conversion.

Basic number of ordinary shares:			
1 January	9,500	× 7/12	5,542
31 July issued on conversion 800 × 150/100	1,200		
31 December	10,700	× 5/12	4,458
			10,000

Weighted average number basic eps = £750/10,000 = <u>7.5p</u>

Fully diluted earnings:	£
As for basic earnings	750
Adjustment for 12% CLS: add interest paid, net of tax, 12% × 800 × 7/12 × 0.65	36
	786

Fully diluted number of ordinary shares:	
As for basic eps	10,000
Adjustment for 12% CLS: add 7/12 × 1,200	700
(only 5/12 of 1,200 is included in the basic number)	
Fully diluted number	10,700

Fully diluted eps £786/10,700 = <u>7.3p</u>

(Again, the dilution is immaterial, and would not be disclosed.)

One last problem remains on this area: that of bonus issues and rights issues of shares made by the company between the date of the issue of the CLS and the date of their eventual exercise. In ascertaining either the number to be issued on actual conversion, or the number issuable on eventual conversion, an uplift is required for a bonus issue in the relevant period (6/5 where the bonus issue is 1:5, 5/4 where the bonus issue is 1:4, and so on) and for a rights issue in the relevant period (actual cum-rights value/theoretical ex-rights value of that rights issue). See Example 28.12.

EXAMPLE 28.12

Taking the facts as in Example 28.10 and assuming the company made a bonus issue of 1:2 shares in a previous year (included in the 9,500 shares for the current year), the fully diluted eps for the current year would be based on a maximum of 800 × 150/100 × 3/2, that is, 1,800 shares issuable on eventual conversion to give a fully diluted eps of £812/(9,500 + 1,800) = 7.2p. (The dilution is now, 7.9 less 7.2, that is, 0.7, is 8.9% of basic eps of 7.9p, is material, and must be disclosed.)

Options or warrants to subscribe

Unlike the instance of CLS, where it was possible to quantify the effect of conversion, in terms of interest no longer payable, on the earnings of a company, it is not possible to quantify the exact effect on earnings of the exercise of options. To estimate such an effect, you should simply assume that the proceeds receivable by the company would be invested in $2\frac{1}{2}$% Consols so as to earn interest, net of tax, from the beginning of the period (or the date of issue of the options, if later). Thus, you must be given information relating to the proceeds receivable (number of options @ option price), yield available on investment in $2\frac{1}{2}$% Consols at the beginning of the period (or date of issue of the options, if later) or the market value of the $2\frac{1}{2}$% Consols on the relevant date(s) in which case the yield available is simply 2.5/market value. This is illustrated in Example 28.13.

EXAMPLE 28.13

Relevant earnings for the period to 31 December amount to £1,800. Relevant number of ordinary shares for the basic eps calculation amounted to 12,000. The company had issued 4,500 options to purchase ordinary shares at a given price of 70p per share in a previous year. The options are exercisable in the following year. The yield available on $2^{1}/_{2}\%$ Consols on 1 January of the current year is 9.5% and corporation tax is to be taken at 35%.

	£
Fully diluted earnings:	
As for basic earnings	1,800
Adjustment for options (4,500 × 70p) × 9.5% × 0.65	195
Fully diluted earnings	1,995
Fully diluted number of shares:	
As for basic number	12,000
Adjustment for options: add back maximum shares issuable	4,500
	16,500

Basic eps £1,800/12,000	=	15.0p
Fully diluted eps £1,995/16,500	=	12.1p

(The dilution is material and must be disclosed.)

As in the case of CLS, in a period where options are either wholly or partially exercised, both basic eps and fully diluted eps must be calculated and an adjustment, uplift, is required to the number of shares actually issued on actual exercise or issuable on eventual exercise of the options for any bonus issues or rights issues within the relevant period.

Disclosure in the financial statements

The standard requires that the basis of calculation for eps be disclosed.

A suggested note to the financial statements

The calculation of basic earnings per ordinary share is based on profit before extraordinary items, after deducting preference dividends of £x (1993 £x) and on x number (1993 x number) of ordinary shares being the weighted average number of ordinary shares in issue and ranking for dividend during the year.

The fully diluted earnings per ordinary share is based on x number (1993 x number) of ordinary shares, allowing for the full exercise of outstanding share purchase options (see Note x) and adjusted profit of £x (1993 £x) after adding interest deemed to be earned from investing the proceeds of such share options in 2½% Consols.

Earnings per share on the nil basis are xp (1993 xp). This calculation is based on adjusted profits of £x (1993 £x) after adding irrecoverable advance corporation tax and on x number (1993 x number) of ordinary shares.

A suggested examination approach to dealing with the numbers

It is important when answering examination questions on this topic to set out your workings clearly. These would deal with, first, relevant earnings, and secondly, relevant numbers of ordinary shares.

Earnings

These would be set out as shown in Pro Forma 28.1.

PRO FORMA 28.1

	Current year £	Preceding year £
Profit after tax and minority interest	x	x
Preference dividends	(x)	(x)
Earnings for basic eps	x	x
Adjustments:		
Interest, net of tax, on convertible loan stock:		
(i) re converted in year: for period while in issue	x	generally not applicable, see note (4) below
(ii) re outstanding at y/e: for whole year, unless issued in year in which case for period in issue only	x	
Interest, net of tax, on assumed investment of proceeds receivable on exercise of options in 2½% Consols at the beginning of year or date of issue of options if issued in year	x	
Earnings for fully diluted eps	x	N/A

Notes

1   ED 36 proposed that eps be calculated both before and after extraordinary items. The revised SSAP 6 has no requirement in this regard. Extraordinary items will no longer arise under FRS 3 and this standard permits additional disclosure of eps on an alternative basis.

2   SSAP 3 requires that eps be calculated on the net basis, that is, after deducting all of taxation for the year, i.e. profit after tax is profit after deducting the whole of the tax on ordinary profits for the year, as disclosed in the profit and loss account, regardless of what it comprises.

   The standard does, however, also require eps to be calculated on a nil basis if this is materially different from eps on a net basis. Nil eps will become relevant only if there is included in the tax charge irrecoverable ACT. Earnings, for eps on a nil basis, are earnings as for net eps plus any irrecoverable ACT included in the tax charge for the year.

3   Preference dividends to be deducted are as follows:

   a) *Non-cumulative preference shares* Deduct the preference dividend for the year only if a dividend is declared. Dividends will not be declared if there are insufficient profits available.

b) *Cumulative preference shares* Deduct the preference dividend for the year only (do not deduct arrears of previous years) whether or not a dividend is declared. It may be that in doing so you will create a loss per ordinary share.

4   Fully diluted eps must be calculated where there are circumstances giving rise to dilution unless any of the three conditions noted above apply. You are not required to disclose fully diluted eps as a comparative if the circumstances relating to dilution have changed in the current year, that is, if the company issues options or convertible loan stock in the current year or if the company is in the position where, in the current year, options are exercised or CLS is converted by holders of options or owners of CLS.

5   When companies issue CLS or options, the terms of conversion or exercise usually include adjustment for any bonus issues or rights issues of shares made by the company between the dates of issue of the convertible loan stock or options and their eventual conversion or exercise. Earning may have to be adjusted to take such terms into account.

a) re CLS: there is *no* further effect on earnings for fully diluted eps.
b) re options: *both* the price and the number of options will change. The proceeds receivable remain the same.

This is shown by Example 28.14.

EXAMPLE 28.14

A company issues 100 options to purchase ordinary shares of £1 each on 1 January 1994. The options are exercisable at a price of 110p per share.

On 30 June 1994 the company makes a bonus issue of 1 ordinary share for every 5 ordinary shares on that date.

On 30 October 1994 the company makes a rights issue of 1 ordinary share for every 10 ordinary shares held on that date. The actual cum-rights price is 140p per share and the theoretical ex-rights price is calculated at 130p per share.

The yield available on $2^1/2$% Consols as on 1 January 1994 is 10%. Corporation tax is to be taken at 35%.

Had the company not made the bonus or rights issues of shares the add-back to earnings to arrive at fully diluted earnings would be:

$100 \times 110p \times 10\%$, net of tax at 35% $\times 0.65 = £7.2$

As the company has made a bonus and a rights issue subsequent to the issue of options but before the exercise of the options, the add-back to earnings to arrive at fully diluted earnings would be:

Number of options – originally –	100
Adjusted to take account of bonus issue	$\times 6/5$
Adjusted to take account of rights issue	$\times 140/130$
	$= 129.2$
Price of options – originally –	110p
Adjusted to take account of bonus issue	$\times 5/6$
Adjusted to take account of rights issue	$\times 130/140$
	$= 85.1p$

| Proceeds receivable on eventual exercise of options therefore 129.2 × 85.1p | = £110 |

Interest on assumed investment in 2$\frac{1}{2}$% Consols on 1 January 1994 10% × 110	= £11
Less tax @ 35%	£(3.8)
	= £7.2

that is, the same as would have been added book had there been no bonus or rights issue of shares during the year. Remember, therefore, that where such issues are made, it is *both* the number and the price of options that have to be adjusted. Alternatively, adjust neither.

6   For consolidated accounts and business combinations during the year the following rules apply:

a) If the subsidiary acquired during the year is accounted for using the acquisition method: earnings should include the group's share (that is, after minority interest) of the post-acquisition profits of the subsidiary only.

b) If the subsidiary acquired during the year is accounted for using the merger method: include the group's share (that is, after minority interest) of the profits of the subsidiary for the whole year, regardless of the date of the business combination. Also, for the comparative eps of the previous year, earnings should include the group's share of the results of the merger subsidiary for the whole of the previous year despite the fact that the business combination arises in the current year.

Number of ordinary shares

Example 28.15 deals with various adjustments that you may have to make in respect of number of ordinary shares in eps calculations.

EXAMPLE 28.15

This example shows the calculation for 100 shares in issue on 1 January; 50 shares are issued on conversion of CLS on 31 March; 100 shares are issued for cash at full market value on 30 April; there is a bonus issue of 1:5 shares on 30 July; 100 shares are issued as consideration for an 'acquisition' subsidiary on 30 August, and 140 shares are issued as consideration for a merger subsidiary on the same date; and there is a rights issue (actual cum-rights value 140p; theoretical ex-rights value 130p) on 31 October. The weighted average number of shares would be ascertained as follows:

At beginning of year (1 January)	100	
Bonus thereon (1:5)	20	
		120 × 3/12 × 140/130 = 32
Issued on conversion of convertible loan stock (31 March)	50*	see note (2)
Bonus thereon (1:5)	10	
		60
		180 × 1/12 × 140/130 = 16
Issued for cash at full MV (30 April)	100	
Bonus thereon (1:5)	20	
		120
		300 × 4/12 × 140/130 = 108

Issued re 'acquisition' subsidiary (30 August)	100	
	400 $\times 2/12 \times 140/130 = 72$	
Issued re 'merger' subsidiary (30 August)	140 $\times 12/12 \times 140/130 = 151$	
Rights issue (1:10) 31 October	54	
At 31 December	$(594 - 140) \times 2/12$	76
		455

The basic eps of the previous year would have to be restated by first, taking account of the current year's bonus issue, 5/6, and secondly, taking account of the current year's rights issue, 130/140.

Notes

1. Re bonus issue: Adjust all holdings of shares prior to the bonus issue for the bonus issue. Thus, if the bonus issue was made on 28 February only the shares at 1 January would be adjusted.

2. Re shares issued on conversion: The number to be issued would take account of all bonus issues and rights issues of shares made by the company between the dates of the issue of the convertible loan stock and their eventual conversion.

   Uplift re bonus issues – if 1:4 – 5/4
   1:5 – 6/5 etc.

   Uplift re rights issues – $\dfrac{\text{Actual cum-rights value of that rights issue}}{\text{Theoretical ex-rights value}}$

   No uplift has been made for the current year's bonus or rights issues re the 50 shares issued on conversion as the issues were made after conversion of the loan stock.

3. Re rights issues: uplift all holdings *prior* to the date of the rights issue by the factor actual cum-rights value to theoretical ex-rights value.

4. Re business combinations: time apportion shares issued for an 'acquisition' but not for a 'merger'.

5. If options are exercised in the year the same principles as in note 2 would apply.

NUMBER OF ORDINARY SHARES FOR FULLY DILUTED EPS

As for basic eps	455
Add back:	
(i) re shares issued on conversion of convertible loan stock in year $50 \times 6/5 \times 140/130 \times 3/12$ (i.e. the additional number that would have been included if the conversion was at 1 January)	16
(ii) re shares issuable on eventual conversion of CLS outstanding at year end Number issuable $\times 6/5 \times 140/130$ (Uplifts would also be required re bonus or rights issues in previous years after the issue of the CLS.)	x
(iii) re options Number issuable uplifted for relevant bonus issues and rights issues	x
	x

The usefulness and limitations of eps

Earnings per share is frequently cited as a financial accounting ratio that is widely used in shareholder investment decisions. It is used in conjunction with the price earnings (p/e) ratio in order to estimate the share price. As the p/e ratio is defined as current market price per share/eps, the estimated share price is p/e ratio × eps. Investment analysts estimate an appropriate value for p/e ratio rather than use the current market estimate. Earnings per share is also used in the dividend model approach to share valuation.

However used, eps implies interfirm comparisons. Therefore, it is important that eps figures be both reliable and comparable. The difficulties that arise in the computation of the components of profits, the tax system and number of shares in issue have, in part, been dealt with in the preceding sections of this chapter. SSAP 3 deals only with the latter two of the three areas of difficulty referred to as other accounting standards are concerned with particular profit components. Herein lie the limitations of eps. Thus, as has already been noted, the classification of items as extraordinary or ordinary could and did have a material impact on disclosed eps. Prior to FRS 3 deferred tax provided affected the tax charge and thus eps. To get around the problems of non-comparability arising through taxation, analysts ascertain 'fully taxed earnings' and, therefore a fully taxed eps and p/e ratio based on these earnings, on the basis deferred tax is fully provided for.

Where accounting for deferred tax prior to the revised SSAP 15 did create problems re comparability, the revised standard has resulted in some improvement. The same could be said of the revised standard on extraordinary items as evidenced by the treatment of bad debt provisions in different ways by different banks in 1987. Further problems arose in respect of comparability in more recent years given, pre FRS 3, inconsistent treatment of costs of restructuring and costs of closure. These problems are dealt with in Chapter 11 on reporting financial performance.

The more relevant question is not so much what is the usefulness and what are the limitations of eps, but whether it is possible to encapsulate, in a single number, the totality of the performance of an entity in a period. Some would argue that it is the duty of accountants to come up with such a number. The opposite view, as indicated by the essential thrust of FRS 3, is that we need to adopt a broader perspective in reporting financial performance, and overreliance on a single performance indicator can be misleading. These points are highlighted in self test question and answer number 5 in Chapter 11.

Other stock market ratios

Some of these ratios were dealt with, briefly, in Chapter 24 in the context of share valuation. They are dealt with again in this chapter in the context of analysing and appraising financial and related information.

One advantage of a company going public is that it is easier for it to raise new equity capital as a listed company. In making informed decisions as to the returns available on their investment, investors would refer to information that is available from published stock market information and in ratios that can be derived from this information.

Earnings per share and the price earnings ratio

The p/e ratio is the relationship between eps and share price. If you assume that the p/e ratio will not vary significantly over time, it follows that if eps changes, the p/e ratio will change accordingly (see Example 28.15).

EXAMPLE 28.15

Rai plc achieved an eps of 10p in 1994 and had a share price of £2 per share. Its p/e ratio would have been 20. If the company's eps increases to 12.5p in 1995 and on the basis that its p/e ratio might be expected to remain at 20, its share price ought to increase to (12.5p × 20) = £2.5 per share.

The p/e ratio is a reflection of the market's view of the company's future prospects. In one sense it is simply the number of years it would take an investor to recover an investment in the shares of the company in terms of the current eps of the company. In another sense, a company that has a high p/e ratio relative to other similar companies is an indication of factors such as an expectation of increasing earnings, or less risk attaching to the shares.

Of course, the p/e ratio will change over time and the reasons for this will depend on factors such as:

▶ change in investors' confidence given the changing political and economic climate
▶ improving prospects for a company will result in an increase in its share price, which is a reflection of future rather than current earnings, and an increase in share price will result in a higher p/e ratio
▶ changes in interest rates, in that, for example, rates may go up, capital may move away from equity into fixed interest capital, share prices may fall and the p/e ratio also fall as a result.

Maggie Urry (1993) stated in an article in the *Financial Times* that 'The introduction of Financial Reporting Standard 3 will make fundamental changes to the way earnings per share are calculated, and will therefore affect the p/e, often regarded as the most important investment ratio'.

FRS 3 brings clearly into focus the fact that the p/e ratio is only one measure of company performance and that we should look also at other measures such as yield, cash flow, asset value, balance sheet strength and judgements on the quality of management.

Dividend cover and yield

An investment in shares will yield dividend income. Existing and intending investors would find it useful to have information on the level of earnings distributed and retained and the risk of a company not being able to maintain the level of its dividend. The dividend cover calculation provides this information. It is the number of times that the current dividend can be paid out of current earnings. The higher the cover, the greater the proportion of earnings being retained by the company. The market's expectations of what the company will do with these earnings will have a bearing on the price of the company's share. Dividend cover is calculated as:

$$\frac{\text{Maximum earnings available for dividend for ordinary shareholders}}{\text{Actual level of dividend for ordinary shareholders}}$$

The dividend yield, referred to in Chapter 24, is simply the gross dividend per share/market price per share. It is usually stated gross so that investors can compare it with other gross yields available on an investment in other securities.

Investors might also find it useful to determine the earnings yield of a company, that is:

$$\frac{\text{eps (grossed up for the basic rate of income tax)}}{\text{Market price per share}}$$

Summary

Earlier chapters have dealt with specific areas of a company's position and financial performance. Subsequent chapters will deal with the analysis and appraisal of this information. This chapter deals with one aspect of performance, eps and other stock market ratios, which can assist investors in making informed decisions as to an investment in the shares of a company. Earnings per share involves, at times, fairly complex calculations and this chapter sets out the problems that can arise in determining, first, the earnings for eps and, second, the number of ordinary shares to include in the calculation. The many examples included in the chapter should enable you to deal with the practical problems that can arise in an examination question on the calculation of either basic or fully diluted eps.

Post-FRS 3 there has been much discussion as to the usefulness of eps. Is it reliable? Is it the ultimate answer as to performance? Are there other aspects of performance that ought also to be examined in arriving at conclusions as to performance? These questions are also addressed in this chapter.

Leading into the chapters that follow, this chapter also looks into other stock market ratios, such as dividend and earnings yield, dividend cover and the price earnings ratio.

Self test questions

1   The share information of the *Financial Times* is published, every Tuesday to Saturday, so as to include:

Stock	Price	+/−	1993 High	Low	Market Capitalisation	Yield gross	P/E ratio

Briefly, explain the various headings.

2   Explain how eps may be used to judge the returns that a company achieves for its equity shareholders.

3   The eps of three listed companies for the year ended 31 December 1984 are as follows:

	Ash plc	Oak plc	Lime plc
Basic eps	50p	64p	(76)p
Fully diluted eps	34p	90p	(64p)

Indicate which company or companies must disclose fully diluted eps in addition to basic eps.

4   Compare and contrast 'net', 'nil', 'fully taxed' and 'maximum' earnings.

Exam style question

1   *Haas plc*
The draft profit and loss accounts of Haas plc disclosed earnings available for ordinary shareholders as follows:

For the year ended 30 June 1992, *losses* of £215,000
For the year ended 30 June 1993, *profits* of £385,000

As on 30 June 1991, Haas plc had 4,500,000 ordinary shares of £1 each. £1,500,000 of 12% convertible loan stock and options in issue to subscribe for 800,000 ordinary shares of £1 each at a price of £1.50 per share.

During the year ended 30 June 1992:

1 All of the options to subscribe for ordinary shares were exercised on 1 July 1991.

2 The company made a bonus issue of 1 ordinary share for every 5 ordinary shares held on 1 January 1992.

During the year ended 30 June 1993:

1 £500,000 of the convertible loan stock was converted on 31 October 1992 in accordance with the terms of the debenture trust deed, which were:

'100 ordinary shares of £1 each for each £150 of debentures converted and that the shares issued on conversion should be adjusted to take into account any previous bonus issue and/or the bonus element in any rights issue of shares between the date of the issue of the convertible loan stock and the date of its conversion.'

2 During the year, the company acquired a controlling interest, 90%, in the ordinary shares of Chernoff Ltd. The business combination satisfies the criteria of SSAP 23, the Companies Act and ED 48 as to the use of the merger method on consolidation, and this method is used to consolidate the subsidiary into the group accounts. The earnings of Chernoff Ltd, after all taxation and preference dividends were as follows:

For the year ended 30 June 1992, *profits* of £670,000
For the year ended 30 June 1993, *profits* of £321,000

The consideration paid by Haas plc for the shares in Chernoff Ltd consisted of 4,500,000 ordinary shares of Haas plc which were issued to the selling Chernoff Ltd shareholders on 1 June 1993.

The results of Chernoff Ltd are not included in the earnings of Haas plc indicated above.

Corporation tax for the year ended 30 June 1992 is to be taken at 45% and for the year ended 30 June 1993 at 40%.

Required
a) Calculate the earnings per share of the Haas plc group as it would be disclosed in the group financial statements as on and for the year ended 30 June 1993, including the comparative information for the immediately preceding year. You are not required to prepare a note relating to the basis of the calculation.

(13 marks)
b) State briefly, the main changes proposed in FRED 6 in accounting for subsidiaries in the consolidated accounts using the merger method.

(7 marks)

(20 marks)

All answers on pages 709–711.

Financial Analysis – The Interpretation of Financial Statements and Other Information in the Annual Report of Companies

Previous chapters have dealt with an extensive examination of the financial and legal aspects of company accounting in so far as they affect the individual parts of a company's financial statements. This chapter deals with the interpretation of the financial statements and other information in the annual report, such as the historical summary, taken as a whole. Of all the information that is available to users other than the management of a company the annual report is the most detailed, the most regularly produced and the most publicised. The accounts are also solemnly stated by the company's auditors to give a true and fair view. They are, accordingly, used for a variety of purposes:

▶ for forecasting the level of dividends
▶ for computing the price/earnings ratio (as dealt with in Chapter 28)
▶ for arriving at conclusions as to the solvency, liquidity and profitability of a company.

Necessarily this chapter must start with the different users of a company's annual report and their different information needs. Where, as Lewis, Pendrill and Simon (1981) point out, relatively little is known as to the decision models used by different user groups, it is clear, at a general level, that different groups make different use of the different information provided by companies in their financial statements. It is therefore essential when we are dealing with the interpretation of accounts to bear in mind the viewpoint of the particular users involved in the exercise. Equity shareholders will be concerned with returns on their investment and the inherent risks involved; suppliers will be concerned about whether or not they will receive payment, and so on.

Our interpretation of accounts will start with what is termed univariate analysis. Applying this analysis, only one ratio at a time is calculated and analysed. The alternative approach, when we consider several ratios at once, what is known as multivariate analysis, is examined in Chapter 30 when we look at the limitations of ratio analysis and corporate failure prediction.

In Chapter 14 we looked at the effects of changing prices and the different ways in which these could be reflected in financial statements. Chapter 30, which deals with the limitation of ratio analysis, will look at the calculation of ratios from financial statements prepared under alternative systems of accounting and their utility as the source of information for the interpretation of a company's performance, liquidity and overall financial health.

Where ratios are one means of appraising the financial well-being of a company we need also to look at the trend of results and position over a number of years. Trend analysis was dealt with in Chapter 23 when we looked at the accountants' report in share circulars. This chapter looks at the usefulness, and also at the limitations, of trend analysis in the context of the additional and voluntarily disclosed information that companies sometimes make available in the form of an historical summary of key data over the past five or ten years.

Although the annual report is an important source of information for users, there are other sources, such as: interim statements, circulars on acquisitions, documents issued in a contested bid, company newsletters, catalogues and sales information literature, the annual general meeting, the Registrar of Companies, Extel Cards, Datastream, government statistical publications and specialist and trade publications. These are also dealt with in this chapter.

Users of accounts and their different information needs

You should be familiar with *The Corporate Report*, which was published in 1976. This identified six main groups of users of a company's published information. These groups and their main interests in such information are:

▶ *Investors* – present and potential, who will be concerned with dividends, profitability, market price, security and risk of investment.
▶ *Creditors* – present and future, who will be concerned mainly with assessing whether a company can pay its debts and, therefore, also with security, profitability, reliability and underlying assets.
▶ *Management* – will be concerned with market share, market price, dividends, profitability and, as employees, pension returns.
▶ *Employees* – will be concerned with the security of their employment, their working environment, pension returns, value added and market price.
▶ *Government* – as a user group the government will be concerned with the profitability of companies, dividends, reliability of information, environmental concerns and underlying assets.
▶ *Other* – users such as public environmental groups, consumer protection groups, neighbours and local government will be concerned with factors affecting the environment, market forces, profitability and underlying net assets.

Where each user group will have its own specific requirements as to information for interpretation, there may be some overlapping requirements and the same financial ratios may be used by different groups.

Sources of information

Before going on to consider ratio analysis and trend analysis, it would be useful to be aware of the different sources of information for different users. In an examination context these are limited to the question being attempted but, in practice, data collection is an ongoing process and financial institutions have data gathering systems, which continuously collect data that could be relevant. These range from published accounts to daily clippings from newspapers. A useful classification of sources is:

▶ *Facts*: published accounts; industrial/commercial association reports; government and Department of Trade publications; tailored questionnaire; interfirm comparisons; previous research; prospectus/offer documents; the press; Dunn & Bradstreet, Extel etc.; stockbrokers and other institutional publications.
▶ *Opinion*: investment journals; reports in the press; interview with key company personnel; World Bank, EC, OECD, etc.; economic surveys and forecasts; tailored questionnaire.
▶ *Judgement*: attitudes towards risk and return; interpretation of objectives.

Ratio analysis

You will be familiar with the definitions and calculation of ratios from your Paper 10 studies. Holmes and Sugden (1986) suggest that we look at the analysis of a report and accounts in stages, as follows:

▶ Make a cursory examination of the balance sheet and profit and loss account to get a general idea of company size, structure and profitability. Look at the historical summary, if there is one, to determine whether the company is growing, cyclical, stagnant or declining. Any segmented analysis would be useful in breaking down turnover by activity and geographically. Reports to employees may be enclosed with the accounts and these may help in giving you a general picture before you get down to detail.

▶ Review the chair's statements and directors' report for points of interest; go through the balance sheet and profit and loss account 'line by line', read each accompanying note and mark unusual points arising. Check the statement of accounting policies for anything out of the ordinary and check the auditors' report for any qualification or reservation.

▶ Trends and ratios should now be determined and calculated as pointers to performance and, possibly, warnings as to impending disaster.

▶ The final stage is the interpretation of the trends and ratios and it would be useful to be able to compare performance with that of similar companies or with the average for the industry. Other sources of information, as mentioned above should be consulted.

Methods of relating items of information

There are four different ways in which items of information in the accounts can be related to each other.

▶ *Horizontal analysis* is a line-by-line comparison of the current year's accounts with those of the previous year. The percentage changes could reveal important messages as to a company's performance, but the analysis tends to be of greater value in prompting further lines of enquiry – for example, why has turnover increased but the gross profit decreased?

▶ *Trend analysis* is horizontal analysis extended over several years. Trend analysis as indicated by the historical summary is dealt with, in more detail, later in this chapter.

▶ *Vertical analysis* is conducted by preparing 'common size' balance sheets and profit and loss accounts, where each balance sheet item is expressed as a percentage of the balance sheet total and each profit and loss account item as a percentage of sales or earnings.

▶ *Ratios* are determined by comparing different items in the accounts with one another for the same period.

Using ratios

There is much evidence to show that ratio analysis has been a developing subject since the beginning of this century and most of those still used today were available before World War II. Such ratios still provide an accepted framework for analysing a company and form a major tool for fundamental analysis.

One of the leading authorities on the use of ratio analysis in the UK is the Centre for Interfirm Comparison. They use ratios to show:

▶ *How* overall performance of the business compares with other firms, by using ROCE.

▶ *Why* it differs, by using suitable subsidiary ratios.

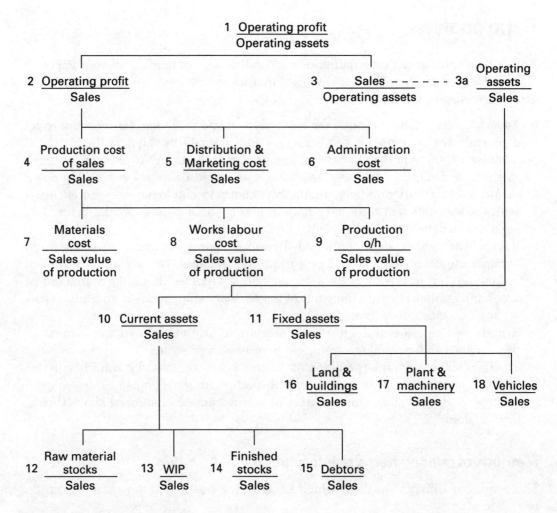

Figure 29.1 Pyramid of ratios

This can be done by using a pyramid of ratios, as shown in Figure 29.1. The pyramid focuses on the profitability of a company. Other ratios will focus on liquidity, on financial structure and on stock market performance. A possible classification of ratios is:

▶ Profitability ratios – analyse the returns made on sales and capital invested.
▶ Activity ratios – analyse how effectively the company is using its resources.
▶ Growth ratios – analyse the economic position of the firm in the industrial segment and economy generally.
▶ Gearing ratios – analyse the extent to which long-term debt is used as a source of finance.
▶ Liquidity ratios – analyse the ability of the company to meet short-term liabilities.
▶ Valuation ratios – analyse corporate performance in terms of wealth creation, that is, the ability to create market values that are in excess of cost to the company. Clearly of great importance in a subject which assumes maximising the value of the firm and of shareholder wealth.

A checklist of available ratios

The most likely exam question will require candidates to prepare ratios without specifying which ones. It is therefore necessary to establish some checklist of ratios from which the crucial (and appropriate) ones can be selected for any particular question.

ROCE

There is a major definition problem here, which is particularly significant since it is widely used as the major ratio to assess performance. The concept is that it captures all aspects of corporate performance in one single ratio.

The following are key points to watch out for in exam questions:

▶ Use an earnings definition that is appropriate to the capital definition. A typical capital definition would be:

Issued ordinary capital
+ Reserves
+ Preference shares
+ Minority interests
+ Loan capital
+ Tax provision
+ Bank overdraft (this is generally variable and if small can be excluded, or alternatively an average over several years can be used)
− Intangible assets

Thus if the bank overdraft is included then earnings must be before bank interest.

▶ Ensure that it is clear what ROCE is being measured. The capital above is the capital of the business. An alternative is to examine return on shareholders' capital employed. This is sometimes called return on net worth. This would be net income available for equity ÷ book value of equity.

▶ Use market values of assets, if these are available, rather than historic cost. This gives a better measure of economic performance and a possible guide to opportunity cost. It may be necessary to use both book and market values and to score marks by comparing them.

▶ When considering use of capital it is usual to take earnings before tax. When considering return on net worth take net income (earnings) after tax.

▶ Be careful with dates. If profits and major cash flows take place unevenly then an average of opening and closing figures should not be used.

Particular problems in calculation and use are likely to be:

▶ Raising of new capital makes ROCE difficult to establish. Although capital can be time weighted, it takes time to deploy resources.

▶ Valuation – historical cost, revaluation, depreciation problems.

▶ Special earnings factors, for example, leases, rentals, sale or lease-back – are profits 'normalised'?

▶ Valuation of intangibles – it is usual to exclude these, but goodwill is included. If in any doubt then note the point to the examiner.

The significance of the ROCE figure might also have to be stated in an answer. Suggest to the examiner some or all of the following:

▶ It is regarded as an important measure of management performance.
▶ If low, there could be a bid at a premium.
▶ If a new management takes over when ROCE is low, expect an improvement in eps.
▶ High ROCE suggests a substantial lead over competitors.
▶ Beware consistently high ROCE – competitive entry into the segment might occur.
▶ The ultimate implication of poor ROCE is winding-up, but this has costs.
▶ Trend of ROCE and interfirm comparison provide an indication of relative performance.

Profit margin

This is usually trading profit divided by turnover. However, again there is a definition problem, because of particular costs that might be very misleading. A good working basis is:

Group profit before tax
+ Depreciation
+ Interest charges
+ Directors' emoluments
+ Exceptional items
− Investment income

The company profit margin can be used to:

▶ project forward to make both short-term and tentative long-term estimates of gross trading profits
▶ compare with similar companies to see scope for improvement and the danger of increased competition.

The projecting forward of profit margins is more reliable if recent observed margins are fairly stable. High variability in margins makes projection difficult.

Operating gearing

The profit level will be more variable depending on the degree of operating gearing (DOG). This measures the responsiveness of profits to changes in variable costs and sales. It is also known as trade gearing or cost gearing.

$$\text{DOG} = \frac{\text{Turnover} - \text{Variable Costs}}{\text{EBIT}}$$

Where EBIT = earnings before interest and tax.

The numerator might be readily identified as contribution in some questions.

For example:

Turnover = £3.5 m

Variable costs = £2.2 m

EBIT = £560,000

$$\text{thus DOG} = \frac{3.5 - 2.2}{0.56} = 2.32$$

This indicates that if the cost–volume–profit relationship is linear, a 1% change in activity (that is, turnover) will result in a 2.32% change in EBIT.

The higher the DOG, the higher the variability of EBIT associated with variability in activity. Be prepared to point out that DOG affects business risk, which is the extent of the variability in EBIT. It should also be appreciated that the higher the proportion of costs that are fixed then the greater the DOG.

Sales to capital employed

Just as the profit margin examines that part of return on capital which comes from sales, so the sales to capital employed considers the extent to which sales are generated by the assets. It is usually measured as asset turnover by taking:

$$\frac{\text{Turnover}}{\text{Operating assets}}$$

Note that operating assets exclude trade and other investments.

The ratio can be sub-divided into categories of assets over sales, for example, fixed assets, current assets, net current assets and so on.

Generally in exam questions improved ROCE may well be accounted for by improving asset turnover; however, be prepared to make contrary comment that a high ratio may indicate too narrow an asset base and a need for further capital to finance sales. Rather more obviously of course, low ratios indicate underemployment of assets, and comment can be made of possibly poor management.

Stock turnover

This is a particularly useful activity ratio. Ideally the ratio should be cost of sales divided by average inventory value so as to avoid distortions caused by changing profit margins. However, usually only turnover is available and this will have to be used. Note also that an average of the opening and closing values will be best if inventory is not consistent.

When comparing different companies in a seasonal business then the year-end dates should be roughly the same so as to be comparable.

The ratio can be sub-divided into separate ratios for raw materials, work in progress and finished goods. In an exam this would be worthwhile only to highlight a very dramatic change in turnover, probably a fall, due to an increase in one particular category.

Average collection period

This is another particularly important ratio for examination purposes. It is usually calculated as average debtors divided by average daily sales. For this purpose average daily sales is found as turnover divided by 365 (or some examiners specify 360 days). Although technically it is an activity ratio it is often associated with liquidity analysis since it essentially indicates how long, on average, that working capital is tied up in debtors. In particular look out for increases in this, associated with cash flow problems. High days in debt (or low turnover ratios) are not in themselves indications of poor performance. It all depends on the terms of trade and what is usual in that industry. Trend is particularly important in the exam.

Gearing ratios

High gearing means that a substantial proportion of capital is provided by long-term debt, which must be paid a prior charge amount of fixed interest. The level of gearing has an effect on the relative variability of shareholders' return, whether measured by earnings or dividend. This should be described in the exam as financial risk. Care must be taken to avoid too many general statements such as 'gearing is very high'. Different industries have different levels of gearing, as do different companies, and the theoretical analysis of gearing is a most contentious area. Companies will find it easier to increase gearing if they have stable earnings patterns and substantial and marketable fixed assets to act as security. Property companies tend to be highly geared, service industries to be low geared. Cyclical industries are also typically lowly geared. The market normally allocates an approximate gearing level for a particular industry and companies will find it difficult to go beyond this level.

Measuring gearing

The usual measure in theoretical questions is the market value of debt divided by the market value of equity, that is VD/VE. However in practical situations there is often no 'market value' of debt, or if there is then other debt is unquoted. It is sometimes possible in exam questions to calculate an approximate market value by using current debt yields. However, in practice it is usual to use book values of debt, and even book values of equity. Two approaches are used: one considers balance sheet values and the other the profit and loss account.

Total debt:total assets

This is called the debt ratio and measures total debt as a proportion of total assets. Debt here would include all current liabilities.

Interest cover

This is found as EBIT divided by interest charges and indicates the extent to which interest payments are covered by earnings. An elaboration of this would be to use fixed charge cover, in which lease payments were included with debt interest since they are a prior charge for what is effectively a source of finance. It is usual to add the fixed charges to the numerator in this calculation.

Liquidity ratios

The main ratios to use are:

▶ the current ratio (also known as the working capital ratio)
▶ the quick ratio (or acid test)
▶ cash flow cover – this is cash flows divided by fixed cash outflows. This focuses on the financing effect on liquidity. Cash inflows are probably approximated by:

EBIT + interest payments + lease payments + depreciation

Fixed cash outflows are fixed charges + Preference dividends (I–T) where T is the tax rate.

Liquidity ratios focus on immediate liquidity and in particular any shortage of working capital. The current ratio is: current assets divided by current liabilities. Beware of making broad observations about this in the exam. It is trend and comparison that matters, not an absolute figure. The acid test focuses on very liquid assets, for example, (current assets – inventory) divided by current liabilities. If debtors are particularly high, with an unusually high number of days' turnover in debtors then this can be reduced to a 'normal' level in the acid test.

Be aware that these ratios are very easy to manipulate, for example, reducing debtors and creditors by the same amount improves these ratios.

Investment ratios

In some ways these are the most important ratios in that they reflect the market perception of the firm. The most important is the p/e ratio. This is the current share price divided by the eps. It may well represent the premium that the market is paying over the historic book values, although these may be so out of date as to be useless. This and other stock market ratios were dealt with in Chapter 28.

Time series

Examination questions dealing with interpretation of accounts sometimes require an evaluation of a time series in the form of a five-year or ten-year summary included as part of the annual report of a company. This section deals with some suggestions as to what should be included in such a summary and some brief comments on the points that should be raised when interpreting the information normally included in such summaries.

A suggested layout

Five-year summary:

Year	1	2	3	4	5
	£	£	£	£	£
Turnover	x	x	x	x	x
Operating profit	x	x	x	x	x
Profit on ordinary activities before tax	x	x	x	x	x
Dividends	x	x	x	x	x
	x	x	x	x	x
Assets					
Fixed assets	x	x	x	x	x
Net current assets	x	x	x	x	x
Creditors due after more than one year	x	x	x	x	x
Provisions for liabilities and charges	x	x	x	x	x
Net assets	x	x	x	x	x
Financed by:					
Shareholders' funds	x	x	x	x	x
Minority interest	x	x	x	x	x
	x	x	x	x	x
Key statistics					
eps	p	p	p	p	p
Dividend per share	p	p	p	p	p
Dividend cover	times	times	times	times	times
Return on shareholders' funds	%	%	%	%	%
Return on assets	%	%	%	%	%
Share price – high	p	p	p	p	p
– low	p	p	p	p	p
Annual rate of inflation	%	%	%	%	%

Points to note in commenting on the summary

You should note the following:

► The practice of including five-year time summaries in published financial statements is not required by law, accounting standard or Stock Exchange rule, although it is recommended for listed companies.
► The company is therefore at liberty to select those figures which, over the period, seem to portray the business in a favourable light.
► There is no new information provided in such a time series, which simply makes selected historical data more accessible to the public.
► In a period of inflation the amounts included in the time series are likely to rise continually and to convey an impression of progress and growth. Therefore, the relevance of disclosing, in key statistics, the annual rate of inflation.
► Even when the index is applied to correct for inflation, the figures in the time series must be analysed with caution. The net profit for the year may not be analysed and include undisclosed one-off exceptional items. Hence the relevance of disclosing such items separately in the time series.
► Further points that may be made as to the possibility of a misleading impression being created are:
  - interest charges may not be specified; investment income may not be distinguished from trading profits
  - revaluations of fixed assets may have been made making comparison imperfect

between net profit figures before and after the revaluation (given additional depreciation after the revaluation).

▶ You need to ensure that dividends of previous years have been adjusted to take into account subsequent bonus or rights issues of shares. Adjustments would also be required of eps for the same reason.

▶ As to balance sheet amounts, current assets will be comparable from year to year but fixed assets, given revaluations, need not be.

▶ In all cases, ratio analysis will play an important part in appriaising the performance of a company over the period of years in the summary. Changes from year to year would need to be carefully analysed with reference to the points raised above.

▶ Changes in the composition of a group will affect the comparability of different years in the time series. Generally:
  – for acquisitions where the consideration is (mainly) cash, comparability is not affected by the exclusion of the acquired subsidiary's results prior to its acquisition
  – for acquisitions where the consideration is (mainly) in the form of the parent's equity, you will not be able to compare like with like unless you include the results of the acquired subsidiary for the years prior to its acquisition
  – for disposals there is no loss of comparability and there is no need to exclude results of a sold subsidiary prior to disposal
  – for discontinued operations there is a loss of comparability and results of discontinued operations prior to discontinuance ought to be highlighted.

▶ Changes in accounting policy over the period of the time series will also affect comparability and you should always remember the importance of consistency in an analysis of results and position of a company over time.

The audit use of financial analysis

Audit evidence is obtained in part by carrying out audit tests, which may be classified as 'substantive'. These are defined as those tests of transactions and balances, and other procedures such as analytical review, which seek to provide audit evidence as to the completeness accuracy and validity of the information contained in the accounting records or in the financial statements. The auditors may rely on appropriate evidence obtained by substantive testing to form an opinion, provided that sufficient of such evidence is obtained. Such analytical review procedures include studying significant ratios, trends and other statistics and investigating any unusual or unexpected variations.

Unusual or unexpected variations, and expected variations that fail to occur should be investigated. Explanations obtained should be verified and evaluated by the auditors to determine whether they are consistent with the auditors' understanding of the business. Explanations may indicate a change in the business of which the auditors are not aware in which case the auditors should reconsider the adequacy of the approach adopted for the audit. Atternatively, they may indicate the possibility of misstatements in the financial statements, which may mean that the auditors will have to extend testing to determine whether the financial statements do include material misstatements.

Summary

This chapter deals with financial analysis in the context of ratio analysis and trend analysis. Any assessment of a company must include both a look at a company's performance in previous years and a comparison with other companies. The use of percentages and various ratios is of help in assessing trends and may highlight aspects of a company's published information that may merit closer scrutiny.

Operating ratios are concerned with the profitability of a company without taking into account the financing of activities. They include the following:

► trading profit/turnover
► trading profit/capital employed
► turnover/capital employed
► stocks/turnover
► trade debtors/turnover
► trade creditors/turnover
► working capital/turnover.

Financial ratios are those that measure the financial structure of the company and show how it relates to trading activities. They include the following:

► gearing, as dealt with above
► the leverage effect, that is, the percentage change in earnings available to ordinary shareholders brought about by a 1% change in EBIT
► operational gearing, as dealt with above.

Liquidity ratios are those that examine the ability of the company to meet its short-term obligations out of its short-term resources. They include the following:

► the current ratio
► the quick or acid test ratio.

Cash flows should also be considered in any examination of liquidity.

Investment ratios were dealt with in Chapter 28.

The chapter also looks at the historical summary in the annual report, its possible forms and some problems that may arise in interpreting the trends disclosed. The chapter concludes with a short section on the relevance of financial analysis to auditors in search of evidence.

Suggested reading

Interpreting Company Reports and Accounts (Holmes and Sugden 1986)

Advanced Financial Accounting (Lewis, Pendrill and Simon 1981)

Modern Financial Accounting (Lee 1981)

Self test questions

1 Identify and state the basis of calculation for four profitability ratios.

2 Identify and state the basis of calculation of the two main liquidity ratios.

3 Identify and state the basis of calculation of three working capital-based ratios and the basis of calculating the debtor's collection period, the stock holding period and the trade credit period.

4 Identify and state the basis of calculation for three capital structure ratios.

---

5   Say what you understand by the term 'overtrading', and identify the symptoms that might indicate that a company is overtrading.

Exam style questions

1   *TexMex plc*

Mr Jon Thorburn-Levy has recently received a copy of the Annual Report of TexMex plc and its subsidiaries for the year ended 31 December 1989. The Annual Report includes, for the first time, a series of significant figures for the previous five years. The five year historical summary is reproduced as follows:

	1985 £000	1986 £000	1987 £000	1988 £000	1989 £000
PROFIT AND LOSS ACCOUNT					
Turnover	2,000	2,250	2,500	2,800	3,200
Net profit before interest and tax	150	180	200	235	330
Net profit after tax	60	75	80	85	130
Net profit for the year	80	55	80	75	150
Dividends (ordinary)	40	40	60	60	90
Earnings per share (p)	15.0	18.8	13.3	14.2	13.0
BALANCE SHEET					
Fixed assets	750	800	850	1,500	2,200
Net current assets	450	500	650	550	1,200
Ordinary share capital (£1 shares)	400	400	600	600	1,000
Reserves: non distributable	200	200	300	800	1,200
Reserves: distributable	100	115	135	150	210
Loan capital	300	300	300	600	600

You are additionally informed that:

▶ During the year ended 31 December 1987, TexMex plc issued 200,000 £1 ordinary shares at a premium of £0.50 each in order to acquire a subsidiary.

▶ During the year ended 31 December 1988 the group revalued its fixed assets upwards by £500,000 and issued £300,000 of 15% debentures. 10% debentures were in issue prior to 1988.

▶ During the year ended 31 December 1989, TexMex plc issued 400,000 £1 ordinary shares at a premium of £1 each, in order to acquire a subsidiary.

▶ Over the five years ended 31 December 1989, the average Index of Retail Prices for each year was:

1985	270
1986	301
1987	323
1988	343
1989	360

The data included in the five years' summary above has not been adjusted to reflect the effects of general price changes.

Required:
Write a report to Mr Jon Thorburn-Levy, evaluating the five-year historical summary of TexMex plc and its subsidiaries in the light of the notes that accompany it.

(20 marks)

2 *Mr John York*
Mr John York is a wealthy client of your firm and is considering buying some ordinary shares in Stone plc, a listed company with subsidiaries in the UK and overseas.

He has recently received a stockbroker's circular in relation to Stone plc and is confused by certain of the statistics provided, in particular the following:

	Years ended 31 December		
	1984	1985	1986
Profit/(loss) before tax (£ million)	(2.3)	(0.5)	4.7
Earnings/(loss) per share (p)	(9.4)	2.8	6.2
Dividends per share (p)	0.2	2.8	3.1
Net assets per share (p)	128	154	117

Mr York is obtaining copies of the annual report and accounts for the relevant years and has sought your guidance on interpreting the statistics. In particular he has indicated that while he understands the trend in profit before tax, he finds it difficult to understand the relationship between the four sets of statistics and the changes in the relationship from year to year.

Required:
Write a letter to Mr York suggesting possible alternative explanations for the changing relationships indicated by the above statistics and where in the annual report and accounts support may be found for these explanations.

Your letter should clearly identify and deal separately with the relationship between

(i)   profit/(loss) before tax and earnings/(loss) per share
(ii) earnings/(loss) per share, dividends per share and net assets per share
(iii) movements in net assets per share from year to year.

ICAEW PEII exam question July 1987

All answers on pages 711–715.

Financial Analysis Continued

Chapter 29 dealt essentially with the interpretation of financial statements and with trend analysis. This concluding chapter of the textbook looks at the problems users may have in interpreting financial information, and we will look at these:

▶ the impact of changing prices in interpreting accounts
▶ the effects of revaluation and the role of valuation in financial reporting
▶ the effectiveness of current proposals for dealing with related-party transactions
▶ corporate failure prediction
▶ the auditor and the going concern
▶ limitations of ratio analysis
▶ current proposals as to further disclosure in accounts.

Before addressing these aspects of the Paper 13 syllabus it would be useful to look back to the ground covered in previous chapters and to reconsider the arbitrary nature of profit and how easily different accounting policies can manipulate profit. Thus, we have already considered the several matters listed below and their impact on profit and net asset measurement and the comparison of one company with another. In spite of more than two decades of standard setting, informed users need to weigh the alternative results arising from, for example:

▶ the constant pitting of prudence against accruals
▶ different methods of depreciation
▶ alternative approaches to accounting for development costs; to capitalise or not to capitalise
▶ providing for deferred taxation by way of full as opposed to partial provision
▶ the use of the temporal as opposed to the closing rate/net investment method of translation for the net assets and results of overseas entities
▶ the different ways of accounting for different leases
▶ decisions to capitalise or not to capitalise borrowing costs
▶ decisions of whether or not to capitalise intangible assets such as brand names
▶ the accounting treatment decided on in respect of purchased goodwill and questions as to whether or not the expenditure incurred represents an asset of the purchaser company
▶ different methods of accounting for business combinations
▶ the treatment decided on for the accounting of pension fund surpluses
▶ the issue of off balance sheet financing
▶ window-dressing transactions.

The impact of different methods of accounting for the above is obviously important to individuals who have to take decisions about and based on annual reports of companies. Finance directors have to decide on particular accounting procedures to adopt, auditors frequently have to advise on such decisions, loan officers of lending institutions must assess the creditworthiness of corporations that use different (and equally acceptable) accounting policies, and investors have to interpret accounts as an input into their decision as to whether or not to invest in particular companies.

Elsewhere in your studies at the Professional Stage, you will cover the efficient market hypothesis (EMH) and the capital asset pricing model (CAPM). Efficient market research is concerned with how capital markets operate and with an assessment of their performance. EMH describes the operation of capital markets and it would be helpful if you were to bear the hypothesis in mind when studying this chapter. In an efficient market the prices of all securities reflect all available information and prices change rapidly to reflect new information. The efficiency of markets will therefore depend on the availability of information about companies and the quality of analysis made available by analysts and investment managers. This chapter looks at some of the factors that will have a bearing on that analysis.

The impact of changing price levels

Accounting for the effects of changing price and the mechanics of CPP and CCA were dealt with in Chapter 14. Some of the shortcomings of the historical cost convention of accounting, which were discussed in that chapter, include the points that, if prices were increasing, historical cost profits were overstated, resulting in a more favourable reporting of return on capital employed, given that historical cost balance sheet values are understated. Example 30.1 enables you to compare the three alternative accounting systems of HCA, CPP and CCA to calculate ratios under each of the three systems and to comment on the differences arising and the usefulness of the information derived.

EXAMPLE 30.1 – COMPARING HCA, CPP ACCOUNTING AND CCA

The summarised consolidated profit and loss account and consolidated balance sheet of Duccio plc and its subsidiaries, prepared under the historical cost accounting (HCA), current purchasing power accounting (CPP), and the current cost accounting (CCA) bases are presented to you as follows.

Consolidated profit and loss account for the year ended 30 June 1994:

	HCA £000	CPP £000	CCA £000
Turnover	7,500	7,725	7,500
Cost of sales	(5,250)	(5,358)	(5,250)
Gross profit	2,250	2,367	2,250
Other operating expenses	(1,500)	(1,650)	(1,500)
Depreciation adjustment			(75)
Cost of sales adjustment			(35)
Monetary working capital adjustment			(29)
	750	717	611
Income from shares in associated companies	75	71	68
Interest – overdraft	(30)	(32)	(30)
– debentures	(169)	(174)	(169)
Gearing adjustment			26
Gain in net monetary liabilities		23	
Profit on ordinary activities, pre-tax	626	605	506
Tax on ordinary activities	(263)	(263)	(263)
Profit on ordinary activities, post-tax	363	342	243
Minority interest	(38)	(37)	(30)
	325	305	213
Extraordinary gains, net of taxation	75	78	75
Profit for the financial year	400	383	288
Dividends	(262)	(268)	(262)

	HCA	CPP	CCA
Retained profits for the year	138	115	26

Consolidated balance sheet as on 30 June 1994:

	HCA £000	CPP £000	CCA £000
Fixed assets: Property, plant and equipment	3,750	4,875	5,925
Depreciation thereon	(1,631)	(2,333)	(2,959)
	2,119	2,542	2,966
Shares in associated companies	450	518	563
	2,569	3,060	3,529
Current assets:			
Stocks	750	759	758
Debtors	1,125	1,125	1,125
Bank	825	825	825
	2,700	2,709	2,708
Current liabilities:			
Overdraft	(150)	(150)	(150)
Creditors	(675)	(675)	(675)
Corporation tax	(179)	(179)	(179)
Proposed dividends	(150)	(150)	(150)
ACT payable	(65)	(65)	(65)
	(1,219)	(1,219)	(1,219)
Net current assets	1,481	1,490	1,489
Total assets less current liabilities	4,050	4,550	5,018
Debenture loans	(1,125)	(1,125)	(1,125)
Deferred tax	(150)	(150)	(150)
	2,775	3,275	3,743
Preference share capital – 10%	375		375
Ordinary share capital	1,500		1,500
Share premium account	188		188
Current cost reserve			885
Profit and loss account	337		218
Group's share of post-acquisition reserves of associates	150		262
Equity shareholders' interest	2,550	2,975	3,428
Minority interest	225	300	315
	2,775	3,275	3,743

You are also provided with the following additional information:

▶ The general price level, as measured by the Retail Price Index, increasing during the year to 30 June 1994 by 6%. During the same period, the average prices of physical fixed assets increased by 10% and those of stocks by 5%.
▶ The preference shares are of £1 each and the ordinary shares are 25p each. There have been no changes in share capital, or loans, during the year to 30 June 1994.
▶ Debentures carry an average interest rate of 15%.
▶ Equity shareholders' interest in the CPP balance sheet has not been analysed as such an analysis is of little relevance under this method of accounting.

Required
a) Calculate *six* significant accounting ratios for the Duccio plc group from *each* of the three sets of accounts for the group drawn up under the different accounting conventions above.

b) Comment, briefly, on the position indicated by *each* of the three sets of ratios calculated in (a).

c) Comment on the usefulness to users of financial statements of *each* of the three alternative sets of figures calculated in (a).

a) **Significant ratios**

		HCA	CPP	CCA
1	**Gross profit/Turnover**			
	2,250/7,500	30%		
	2,367/7,725		30.6%	
	(2,250 − COSA of 35)/7,500			29.5%
2	**Trading profit/Turnover**			
	750/7,500	10%		
	717/7,725		9.3%	
	611/7,500			8.1%
3	**Current assets/Current liabilities**			
	2,700/1,219	2.2		
	2,709/1,219		2.2	
	2,708/1,219			2.2
4	**Return on capital employed**			
	(Capital employed here taken as shareholders' funds, minority interest debtors and deferred tax. Return here taken as pre-tax profit + debenture interest.)			
	(626 + 169)/(2,775 + 1,125 + 150)	19.6%		
	(605 + 174)/(3,275 + 1,125 + 150		17.1%	
	(506 + 169)/(3,743 + 1,125 + 150)			13.5%
5	**Post-tax return on equity shareholders' funds**			
	(400 − 38)/(2,550 − 375)	16.6%		
	(383 − 38)/(2,975 − 375)		13.3%	
	(288 − 38)/(3,428 − 375)			8.2%
6	**Proprietory ratio**			
	Shareholders' funds/Shareholders' funds + MI + debtors + DT			
	2,550/4,050	0.6		
	2,975/4,550		0.7	
	3,428/5,018			0.7

b) **Comment on the position shown by the three sets of ratios**

(i) **HCA**

Both the gross margin and the trading profit to turnover show, in absolute terms, satisfactory percentages suggesting efficient management. The financial structure in the balance sheet appears sound, with the current ratio in excess of 2 and a proprietary ratio (shareholders' funds to fixed and net current assets) in excess of 0.5.

The return on capital employed, at almost 20%, is also satisfactory, again in absolute terms. It is almost twice the percentage of trading profit to turnover, given that turnover is almost twice the net assets (fixed assets + net current assets) employed in the business.

The return on equity funds is nearly as much, at 16.6%. This is because of the high gearing ratio, indicating that in a year of poor results there could be a drastic fall in the return on equity funds.

(ii) **CPP**

With the lowish rate of inflation of 6%, the differences between HCA and CPP ratios are not significant. Ratios 1, 2, 3, and 6 will not be significantly different in any event as they are computed predominantly on funds flows and monetary items in the balance sheet. Only ratios 4 and 5 are significantly different when compared with HCA. This fact arises from the effects of a reduction in the numerator (profit) because of disproportionate increases in deprecation charges on older fixed assets and of an increase in the denominator (capital) through upward revaluation of fixed assets in CPP.

The gap between pre-tax and post-tax returns is further widened by the charging of historical cost taxation against the CPP profit.

It is important to appreciate that the actual numbers in the HCA and CPP columns are not comparable as they are expressed in different units of measurement; only the ratios arising from the two different sets of accounts can be meaningfully compared.

(iii) CCA

In relation to CCP, the use of this system of accounting results in a sharper effect on the results and return ratios (1, 2, 4, and 5). This is because *specific* price changes have risen faster than *general* price changes. The cost of sales adjustment is not offset by any increase in reported turnover and the depreciation adjustment is larger than the corresponding adjustment in the CPP accounts.

Whereas the monetary working capital adjustment has no counterpart in CPP, the gearing adjustment in CCA can be said to have a counterpart in CPP in the shape of the gain on the holding of monetary liabilities in those accounts.

Tax remains based on HCA profits and the profitability ratios are substantially reduced as revenues have been charged with the current costs of generating those revenues. It is possible to compare both numbers and ratios with HCA and CCA as the numbers are in the same unit of measurement in both sets of accounts.

c) Usefulness

It is generally accepted that historical cost accounts are insufficient in reflecting the effects of changing prices in that profitability is overstated, asset values understated and trends distorted. The debate on which method to adopt when accounting for the effects of changing prices has so far generally been expressed in terms of a choice between the two alternatives of CPP accounting and CCA.

In CPP accounting, all items in the accounts are expressed in pounds of the same date – 'constant pounds', a stabilised measuring unit. This is achieved by restating all non-monetary assets by reference to the relevant change in a general price index. CPP accounting can therefore be regarded as a type of historical cost accounting that adjusts for general inflation. This system of accounting has a fundamental disadvantage in that input prices specific to a company may fluctuate independently of general prices and the relevant CPP asset amounts may bear no relationship to the underlying asset values.

The principal usefulness of CCA is in the disclosure of current cost operating profit and the identification of holding gains. The profitability ratios calculated under this system are meaningful in that they serve as a useful basis for comparison of the results of similar companies. Asset values are based on specific price changes relevant to individual companies. The principal disadvantage of the system is that it does not take into account the effect of general price changes and therefore suffers from the same disadvantage as HCA in that the results of one year are not truly comparable with those of another.

The ASC Handbook on accounting for the effects of changing prices states that a company may determine its reporting objective based on its perception of the users of its accounts. Thus, it may be considered that for many shareholders and owner/managers the CPP system will be the most useful. Managers and employees, however, may consider shareholders to be only one of the many stakeholders in the company. They may consider the company's major objective as being one of perpetuating its existence by maintaining its ability to produce similar quantities of goods as those produced at the current time. To such users CCA is much more relevant and useful.

The Handbook proposed that information as to both general and specific price changes be disclosed in a 'real terms' statement that is able to provide both a profit figure based on CCA concepts and a figure of real gains after allowing for inflation. Such a statement, disclosing as it will HCA, CPP and CCA type profits, is most useful as various users can draw on the information presented depending on the use to which they wish to put the information, and the nature and circumstances of the company. Such a statement would eliminate the reduced usefulness of HCA in times of changing prices and also eliminate the reduced utility of the particular, though not universal, usefulness of CPP and CCA systems considered individually.

The effects of revaluation and the role of valuation in financial reporting

In Chapter 4 we looked at the revaluation problem and the proposals of ED 51 in this regard. Where companies revalue on a selective basis the fact of revaluation gives rise to an adverse earnings effect when compared with the earnings of companies that do not revalue. We also looked, in Chapter 4, at the practice – no longer permitted under SSAP 12 – of split depreciation. The ASB issued a discussion paper on the role of valuation in financial reporting in 1993. The discussion paper describes why the present system of irregular asset valuations is unsatisfactory and sets out the options for reform.

It would be unusual for a historical cost accounting system to be found in its pure form in the UK. Assets are carried at the lower of cost and net realisable value and UK company law does not attempt to impose a pure historical cost accounting system permitting companies to use what it calls the alternative accounting rules and allowing companies to apply these rules selectively enabling companies to revalue only particular assets. Other aspects of company law deem current value information to be of sufficient relevance so as to require:

▶ an indication in the directors' report of the difference between market value and book value of land and buildings held as fixed assets
▶ disclosure of information about the market value of listed investments where it differs from the amount shown in the financial statements
▶ disclosure of the replacement cost of stock where it differs materially from the balance sheet amount.

The fact that, in addition to the disclosures above, several companies have moved towards marking to market and preparing their financial statements on what is termed the modified historical cost system creates problems in the interpretation of company results as follows:

▶ There is little consistency in revaluation practice. Further, where revaluations are undertaken, they are undertaken irregularly leading to difficulties in comparisons of companies one with another. Revaluations affect not only the balance sheet but also the profit and loss account. This is one reason, as dealt with in Chapter 11, why FRS 3 requires companies that follow the modified historical cost convention to prepare a statement of historical profit.
▶ Under the modified historical cost convention we measure profit by comparing sale proceeds with the original cost or revalued amount of the asset sold and, in so doing, we recognise gains and losses at the time of the sale of the asset as opposed to at the time the change in value takes place. This can lead to difficulties in obtaining a clear picture of a company's economic performance during a period. Two such difficulties are dealt with below:
  – if long-term assets such as land banks are held at historical cost or out-of-date revaluation and prices have increased materially during the period the asset is held, the profit recorded when the land is finally used for building will include, as asset strippers have fully appreciated, the holding gains relating to past years and not simply the current profit margin

- companies can sell assets held for many years, whenever they wish to create an improvement in reported profits.

▶ Under present practice there are times when a loss of value of fixed assets other than investment properties is not recorded where it is considered probable that the loss will subsequently reverse; that is, we do not provide for temporary diminutions in value. Property companies that bought or revalued at the peak of the property boom continue to carry the assets at these values in spite of the fact of the considerable fall in their present value. This problem could be relieved if there was a requirement for such assets to be regularly revalued.

▶ The gearing ratio, as dealt with in Chapter 29, is considered important by several user groups. There could be considerable distortion here between companies that do revalue (higher equity) and those that do not (lower equity). Users would need to rely on note disclosure to obtain a true impression of a company's debt:equity ratio.

▶ Merger accounting for a business combination was dealt with in Chapter 19. If companies were required to regularly revalue their assets the differences between the acquisition and merger methods of consolidation in the treatment of asset valuations and of future profitability would be significantly reduced.

In the light of these problems there are three options available:

▶ a return to historical cost accounting
▶ a move to a full current value system
▶ continue with the present modified historical cost system, but attempt to remove some of the anomalies as outlined above.

The ASB, in its discussion paper on the role of valuation, considers a return to historical cost accounting inappropriate to user needs. It also suggests such a move would be contrary to the trend of accounting development in the UK. A change to a full current value system would require a long period of experimentation and learning before it could successfully be introduced. For these reasons the Board proposes to continue with the present system but to provide better guidance on those assets where value changes indicate changes in a company's financial strength. Thus, we can expect the Board to pronounce on the revaluation of properties, the revaluation of quoted investments and the revaluation of commodity stock and long-term stock where there is a market of sufficient depth. Before it does, such assets will continue to create problems in interpreting the results and position of different companies and indeed, in any one company, one year to another.

Related party transactions

Such transactions are relevant to and create problems for interpretation in that they could have a significant effect on the results and/or position of a company. It is for this reason that related party transactions are dealt with not only in the Companies Act but also in the requirements of the Stock Exchange and (currently) FRED 8. When we interpret accounts we assume that the company, its owners and other parties that enter into transactions with the company are separate and that all transactions between them are on an arm's length basis. The existence of related party transactions may not be easy to identify as the related party relationship may not be readily apparent and, further, even if there is a related party transaction it may be at nil charge such as management services provided by one group company to another.

FRED 8

FRED 8, which deals with the disclosure of related party transactions, was issued in March 1994 with the objective of improving the quality of information provided in financial statements. In the specific context of this chapter, the ED justifies its proposal for the disclosure of related party relationships as it is 'considered necessary to enable users to make informed decisions on the reporting enterprise'.

FRED 8 requires the disclosure of:

▶ all material related party transactions, and
▶ the name of the party controlling the reporting entity and, if different, that of the ultimate controlling party whether or not any transactions between the reporting entity and those parties have taken place.

Two or more parties are related parties when for all or part of the financial period:

▶ one party has either direct or indirect control over the other party, or
▶ one party has the ability to influence the financial and operating policies of the other party, or
▶ the parties are subject to common control from the same source, or
▶ one of the parties is subject to control and the other to influence (as in the second point above) from the same source.

The FRED states that reporting control relationships and related party transactions draw the attention of users to the possibility that those statements may have been affected by the relationship.

Who are related parties?

The following are deemed to be related parties of the reporting entity:

▶ its ultimate or intermediate parent undertaking or undertakings, subsidiary undertakings and fellow subsidiary undertakings
▶ associates and joint ventures of itself or any of the undertakings above
▶ the investor or venturers in respect of which the reporting entity is an associate or joint venture
▶ directors of the reporting entity and the directors of its parent undertaking and members of the immediate family of such directors
▶ pension funds for the benefit of employees of the reporting entity or of any entity that is a related party of the reporting entity.

The following are presumed to be related parties unless there is evidence to the contrary:

▶ a person owning or able to exercise control over 10 per cent or more of the voting rights of the reporting entity
▶ the key management of the reporting entity and members of their immediate family
▶ partnerships, companies, trusts or other entities in which directors, persons controlling 10 per cent or more of voting rights and key management have a controlling interest
▶ each person acting in concert so as to exercise control or influence over the reporting entity
▶ an entity managing or managed by the reporting entity under a management contract.

What should be disclosed?

Material transactions undertaken with a related party should be disclosed irrespective of whether a price is charged. The disclosure should include:

▶ the names of the related parties
▶ a description of the relationship between the parties
▶ a description of the transactions
▶ the amounts involved
▶ the amounts due to or from related parties at the balance sheet date
▶ any other elements of the transactions necessary for an understanding of the financial statements.

Transactions with related parties may be disclosed on an aggregated basis.

Examples of related party transactions

Examples of related party transactions that require disclosure by a reporting entity in the period in which they occur include:

▶ purchases or sales of goods or property and other assets
▶ rendering or receiving of services
▶ agency arrangements
▶ leasing arrangements
▶ transfer of research and development
▶ licence agreements
▶ provision of finance
▶ guarantees and the provision of collateral security
▶ mangement contracts.

The Companies Act and Stock Exchange requirements relating to related party transactions

The Companies Act requirements involving related party transactions focus on the disclosure of details relating to directors and persons connected with them. Connected persons include a director's spouse and infant children, companies with which the director is associated, the trustee of a trust of which the directors or connected person is a beneficiary and any partners of a director or connected person. Statute requires disclosure of the capital held by directors and connected persons, transactions with a company in which directors or connected persons have mutual interests and of the amounts and terms of the transactions involved.

The Stock Exchange defines directors or substantial shareholders or associates of such persons as Class IV parties. Class IV transactions involving such parties such as the acquisition or disposal of assets by the company result in the company having to issue a Class IV circular to all shareholders.

Other related party disclosures required by statute include subsidiary and associated undertakings and the name of a company's ultimate parent undertaking must be included in the notes to the accounts. Both the Act and the Stock Exchange require the disclosure of options granted to directors and their immediate families.

Current related-party disclosures concentrate on directors and connected persons, substantial shareholders, subsidiary and associated undertakings and, under FRED 8, parties related by economic dependence. The extent to which such parties influence or even control the financial and operating policies of a company is most relevant to a user in interpreting that company's results and financial position.

Corporate failure prediction and some limitations of ratio analysis

Ratio analysis, as dealt with in Chapter 29, is a widely used approach for interpreting company accounts. Ratios summarise results and relationships which are important for an appreciation of the critical indicators of business performance; for example, the ratio of profit to net assets or capital employed. Further, ratios are particularly useful in assessing the performance of different companies of different size where the aggregate amounts of, say, turnover and net assets are materially different in each company. Ratios assist in predicting the future and it is important to note that, to be meaningful, ratios must consistently be stated and compared with ratios for previous years or with those of competitor companies. In the previous chapter reference was made to the Centre for Inter-firm Comparisons. However, there are limitations to the usefulness of ratio analysis, particularly in predicting business failure, which include:

▶ difficulty of comparisons between companies where each adopts different accounting policies
▶ difficulty of comparison between company's operating in different geographical areas with different methods of financing
▶ lack of access to internal or management accounts
▶ problems of survival, imminent collapse and cash flow crises are not immediately made obvious from the univariate approach to ratio analysis (see below for multivariate analysis)
▶ ratios, based on published financial statements (without reference to sequential analysis) will not highlight the differences between different parts of the company
▶ ratio analysis can reflect only what is reported in the accounts and may give rise to distortions if there is material off balance sheet financing; the analysis is only as good as the data on which it is based
▶ the distorting effects of material acquisitions and disposals of businesses will need to be taken into account in assessing ratios
▶ ratios should be seen as the starting point for areas that need further investigation and should be used together with other sources of information and analytical techniques.

Predicting Corporate failure

This is a particularly specialist form of ratio analysis whereby financial ratios are used to give a discriminant analysis. This is an analysis that discriminates between companies that have failed (gone into liquidation) and those that have not. Statistical techniques are used to construct a model which best discriminates between these two classifications. This model is then applied to firms in the market with a view to predicting whether or not they are likely to fail.

The major techniques are:

▶ regression analysis – which uses the past to predict the future
▶ discriminant analysis – which produces an index that allows classification in some a priori group.

Discriminant analysis

This process has three steps:

▶ Establish mutually exclusive group classifications. Each group is distinguished by a probability distribution of the characteristics.
▶ Collect data.

► Derive linear combinations of the characteristics that 'best' discriminate between the groups (that is, minimises the probability of misclassification). The classic work was done by:

- Beaver (1966) in the USA
- Altman (1968) in the USA
- Taffler (1982) in the UK.

Altman (1968)

Altman used a sample of 66 manufacturing firms, of which half went bankrupt. Using financial statements one period prior to bankruptcy, 22 financial ratios were calculated, of which five were found to contribute most to the prediction model.

The discriminant function was:

$$Z = 0.012X_1 + 0.014X_2 + 0.033X_3 + 0.006X_4 + 0.999X_5$$

where X_1 = working capital/total assets   (%)
       X_2 = retained earnings/total assets   (%)
       X_3 = EBIT/total assets   (%)
       X_4 = MV of equity/book value of debt   (%)
       X_5 = sales/total assets   (times assets are turned over)

Note: the use of Z as the 'score' for this model.

The mean Z score for bankrupt firms was – 0.2599 and for non-bankrupt firms it was 4.8863. The 'cut-off' value of Z chosen was 2.675. Thus a firm with a mean score of less than 2.675 was classified as bankrupt.

The model correctly classifies 95% of the sample, and applying the model to data from two to five years prior to bankruptcy, correctly classified 72% of the initial sample.

The position in the UK

Most research in the UK has been done by Taffler. In the UK the evidence is that corporate failure can be nearly 100% predicted one year before bankruptcy and powerful predictions made up to five years before.

An analysis of share prices of failed companies suggests analysts perceive corporate distress on average at least five years before failure.

Taffler and Tisshaw (1977) applied Altman's multiple discriminant analysis to companies in the UK and tested the predictive value of 80 different ratios in different combinations. The best results were obtained when four ratios were combined after weighting to reflect their significance in analysing corporate failure. The ratios used and their weightings are as follows:

► Profit before tax: Current liabilities (53%), which according to Taffler and Tisshaw 'is a profitability measure indicating the ability of a company to cover its current liabilities through its earning power. If it has a low or negative value, its downside risk is clearly greater than that for the average company.'

► Current assets: Total liabilities (15%), which according to the authors 'is related to the conventional current ratio, and is a measure of the working capital position of the firm. The greater the ratio, the sounder the enterprise'.

► Current liabilities: Total assets (18%), which according to the authors 'measures the company's current liabilities position and is a financial leverage ratio. The greater its magnitude, the more serious the problems the company has to face in financing the cost of its debt and the acquisition of new debt'.

► Immediate assets less current liabilities: Operating costs less depreciation (16%), which according to the authors 'calculates the time for which the company can finance its continuing operations from its immediate assets, if all other sources of short-time finance are cut-off, and in a ratio relatively new to the accounting literature' – a so-called no credit interval.

Taffler has further adapted the Z score technique and developed the PAS Score, which evaluates company performance in relation to other companies in the industry and also incorporates changes in the economy.

Failure can also be explained (Argenti) by looking at other factors such as:

▶ defects in company management and the inability to respond to change
▶ management mistakes such as high gearing, overtrading and project failure
▶ creative accounting to disguise reduction in market share.

While empirical studies provide evidence for the conclusion that firms avoiding bankruptcy had stronger ratios in areas of significant analysis than firms that did not survive, Argenti has drawn attention to three limitations of ratio analysis, which call into question the usefulness of financial ratios in predicting failure and that caution should be exercised in accepting the conclusions suggested by financial ratios in this regard. Thus:

▶ ratios may indicate areas of weakness, but it is doubtful that collapse could be predicted on the basis of these ratios alone
▶ their value is impaired by inflation
▶ given creative accounting to mask serious difficulties there have been several well-publicised cases where the first sign of imminent bankruptcy was made evident only on the actual day of bankruptcy.

Some current developments

The major frauds and financial collapse of the recent past have given rise to demands for companies to strengthen their control over their business and their public accountability. Many firms that have failed have not had their accounts qualified on a going-concern basis, suggesting that the profession has failed in its duty to the investing public. In *Accounting for Change* Austin Mitchell and others refer to Polly Peck, Sock Shop, Coloroll, Parkfield, British and Commonwealth, Sound Diffusion, Rush & Tomkins, and Johnson Mathey as examples of companies that failed soon after receiving unqualified audit reports. In 1992 the draft report of the Cadbury Report on Corporate Government was published. It called for directors to report explicitly on whether a business is a going concern and for auditors to report on this statement.

As David Gwillim (1993) has pointed out:

> ... it would appear that auditors' knowledge of their client company, their powers of access to internal information including forecast information, and their direct relationship with company management should mean that they are uniquely placed to make judgemental decisions about the likelihood of company survival. It is this 'inside' nature of the information contained in a going-concern qualification that greatly enhances its value to users of financial statements.

The Cadbury committee's final report recommends that all listed companies registered in the UK should comply with a code of best practice and that the Stock Exchange should require companies, as a continuing obligation of listing, to state in their annual report whether they comply with the code. The key elements of the code include:

▶ division of responsibilities at the head of the company
▶ sufficient non-executive directors to carry significant weight in the board's decisions
▶ a schedule of key matters reserved for full board decision

- full disclosure of directors' total emoluments, with separate figures for salary and performance-related pay
- audit committees composed solely of non-executives to scrutinise figures and appoint auditors
- the board to report on the effectiveness of the company's system of internal control
- as dealt with above, the directors to report that the business is a going concern and auditors to report on this statement.

Other improvements in the quality of financial reporting are included in the ASB's discussion paper proposing an operating and financial review. Where the chairman's report in the annual report of many listed companies does include details as to operations and financing there has until now been no guidance as to precisely what should be covered in such a review. The proposals are that such a review be fair in that it should be a balanced and objective statement focusing on matters of significance and presented so as to provide an understanding of the financial circumstances of a business. It should cover operating results, the group's financial needs and resources and a commentary on shareholders' return and value.

The going concern and the auditor

The Going Concern guide-line was issued in August 1985 closely followed by the Insolvency Act 1986. A draft APB statement was published in 1992 and a further draft was published in December 1993. The Insolvency Act increased directors' responsibility for corporate trading by making them more accountable to creditors in the event of a liquidation if it could be proved that either:

- The directors carried on the business in a fraudulent manner with the specific intention of defrauding creditors, or
- There was wrongful trading, that is the company was trading whilst insolvent, taking on creditors without any realistic expectation of paying them for the goods or services supplied.

The concept of fraudulent trading has existed for some time in statute. However, it proved very difficult to prove faudulent intent. The concept of wrongful trading moves away from a dependence on attitudes to one of fact.

In some ways the Insolvency Act 1986 focussed statutory attention upon the going concern concept and has put the auditor under greater pressure. For small practices, the argument exists for suing the auditors in the event of liquidation, on the following grounds:

- It could be decided that as the auditor was a trusted professional adviser of the company and the directors relied upong the auditor for guidance, the absence of a going concern qualification misled the directors and therefore positively encouraged the wrongful trading to continue and also encouraged creditors to continue their support in the belief that the company woud 'pull through'.
- In many small practices the partners of the audit practice take a keen interest in their clients and have a close working relationship with them.
- Auditors may give advice to the directors about a variety of difference matters and may actually get involved in the day to day decision making for the business. This is an undesirable situation as it obviously compromises the auditor's independence and the image thereof. However, there is a thin dividing line between a close adviser and a shadow director. The Insolvency Act 1986 in section 214 states that if a company trades whilst insolvent, i.e. wrongful trading, the directors can be held personally liable for all corporate debts in the event of corporate failure; this extends to shadow directors.

The approach of the going concern concept must be an active one. There should be adequate evidence on all audit files to support the audit conclusion regarding the suitability of the going concern concept as a basis for the preparation of the financial statements.

It is now suggested that the auditor's duty should be to form an opinion on the going concern concept for one year from the date the directors approve the financial statements.

With many small businesses, solvency will often be the most critical audit area on the balance sheet and therefore, almost by definition, the audit of a small company must involve the active review of the going concern concept.

Audit procedures

The auditor should determine the scope of his work during the planning stage of every audit. He should identify and evaluate high risk areas and then decide the most appropriate way of planning audit emphasis on the problem areas identified.

The identification of high risk areas specific to the company and to the year in question can be achieved by:

▶ Analytical review of the financial statements and more importantly the monthly management accounts.
▶ Discussions with management about trading difficulties experienced during the year and the company's future prospects.
▶ A review of trade media and other environmental statistics to evaluate the future prospects of the market.

There are of course indicators which the auditor should be careful to note. These can be divided into two main areas:

a) Indicators that a company may be unable to pay its debts

   i) Recurring operating losses;
   ii) Financing to a considerable extent out of overdue creditors;
   iii)Heavy dependance on short term finance for long term needs;
   iv) Low liquidity ratios;
   v) Overgearing;
   vi) Non-compliance with statutory capital requirements;
   vii)Deterioration of relationship with bankers.

   The list is not intended to be exhaustive and each company will have unique indicators.

b) Indicators that raise questions about the continuation of business

   i) Loss of key personnel;
   ii) Work stoppages or other types of industrial action;
   iii)Loss of key franchise or patent;
   iv) Excessive reliance on the success of new product;
   v) Loss of principal supplier
   vi) Frequent failure of enterprises in the same industry;
   vii)Technical developments which render a key product obsolete.

The auditor should search carefully to determine whether any or a combination of the indicators exist.

The simple existence of key indicators may not mean that the company is in difficulty, as management may be able to show mitigating factors, e.g.

► the company may be able to restructure its debts
► it may be able to sell fixed assets without affecting operations
► alternative markets may be found
► new products may be developed
► the company may be able to replace key personnel by internal promotion.

The APB have recently published the following statements on the evidence gathering process in the new draft SAS.

► The auditors shoud request from the directors an adequate written assertion confirming the directors' considered view as to whether it is appropriate for them to adopt the going concern basis in preparing the financial statements. The auditors should consider the following factors in deciding whether in their view the written assertion is adequate:
  - (where there are matters indicating that it may be inappropriate to adopt the going concern basis in preparing the financial statements) whether the assertion so obtained is supported by the directors with an explanation of these matters and any relevant assumptions; and
  - whether the assertion has been made having regard to circumstances which the directors consider may occur during a period of at least one year from the date they approve the financial statements.

► The auditors should make enquiries of the directors, and examine appropriate available financial and other information. The auditor's aim should be to assess the adequacy of the means by which the directors have arrived at their considered view as to whether it is appropriate for them to adopt the going conern basis in preparing the financial statements.

► The auditors should plan and perform procedures specifically designed to identify any material matters which could indicate concern as to the directors' considered view as to whether it is appropriate for the directors to adopt the going concern basis in preparing the financial statements. They should evaluate the results of these procedures together with their other audit evidence (such as their knowledge of the company, its industry and possible developments therein). The auditors should determine and document the extent of their concern (if any) as to the appropriate of the going concern basis.

Reporting implications

Audit reporting has now (see Chapter 3) been considerably changed with the issue of the new audit reporting standard in May 1993. This will be effective for all period ends after 30 September 1993.

With regard to going concern the APB have made the following points.

► If any uncertainty exists which could affect the company's ability to continue as a going concern, other than when an opinion is disclaimed through limitation in scope, the auditors should decide whether the disclosures in the financial statements of the matter giving rise to this uncertainty are adequate to give a true and fair view.

► If the disclosures in the financial statements of the matters giving rise to an uncertainty which could affect the company's ability to continue as a going concern are adequate to give a true and fair view, the auditors should draw attention to the matters in their report, and refer to the financial statement disclosures. Such added emphasis will be required even if the recoverability and classfication of recorded assets or the amount and classification of liabilities are not in question. However if the disclosure made is not adequate, the auditors should give an 'except for' or 'adverse' qualification in their audit report in respect of the inadequate disclosures, and should explain the matter in their report.

- ▶ If the auditors disagree with the presumption that the company is a going concern, they should give an 'adverse' audit opinion and should provide in their audit report such additional information as they consider necessary and are able to provide.
- ▶ A total disclaimer of opinion should be issued in those rare instances when:
  - there are factors which result in limitations in the work undertaken by the auditors; and
  - as a result of the limitations, the auditors are unable to obtain evidence which may reasonably be expected to be available to them to support the director's view that the company is a going concern, and which they consider necessary in order to form an opinion.
- ▶ In rare circumstances, in order to give a true and fair view, the directors may have prepared financial statements on a basis other than that of a going concern. If the auditors consider this other basis to be appropriate in the specific circumstances, and if the financial statements contain the necessary disclosures, the auditors should not qualify their audit report in this respect. Their report should, however, draw attention to the basis of preparation and to the note to the financial statements concerning this basis.

Example of an extract from notes to the Financial Statements and effect on the auditor's report

The company meets its day to day working capital requirement through an overdraft facility which, in common with all such facilities, is repayble on demand. The company's bank overdraft as at the balance sheet date was £Am, which lies within its agreed facility of £Bm as at the balance sheet date. In view of their relationship with the company's bankers, the directors consider it reasonable to rely on the continuation of the overdraft facility.

The company's bankers are due to consider the renewal of the bank overdraft facility on (date). There is always the possibility that the facility may not be renewed at a level adequate for the company's requirements. The nature of the company's business is such that there can be considerable variation in the timing of cash inflows. The directors have prepared projected cashflow information covering the year ended 11 months from the date on which they approved the financial statements. On the basis of this cashflow information, other financial information covering the period thereafter and discussions with the company's bankers, the directors consider that it is likely that facilities adequate for the company's requirements will be forthcoming on the facilities renewal date. On this basis, the directors consider it appropriate to prepare the financial statements on the going concern basis.

Auditor's Report to the Shareholder of XYZ Limited
We have audited the financial statements on pages ... to ... which have been prepared under the historical cost convention and the accounting policies set out on page ...

Respective responsibilities of directors and auditors
As described on page ... the company's directors are responsible for the preparation of financial statements. It is our responsibility to form an independent opinion, based on our audit, on those statements and to report our opinion to you.

Basis of Opinion
We conducted our audit in accordance with Auditing Standards issued by the Auditing Practices Board. An audit includes examination, on a test basis, of evidence relevant to the amounts and disclosure in the financial statements. It also includes an assessment of the significant estimates and judgements made by the directors in the preparation of the financial statements, and of whether the accounting policies are appropriate to the company's circumstances, consistently applied and adequately disclosed.

We planned and performed our audit so as to obtain all the information and explanations which we consider necessary in order to provide us with significant evidence to give reasonable assurance that the financial statements are free from material misstatement, whether caused by fraud or other irregularity or error. In forming our opinion we also evaluated the overall adequacy of the presentation of information in the financial statements.

Fundamental uncertainty: going concern

In forming our opinion, we have considered the adequacy of disclosures made in the financial statements concerning the inherent uncertainty as to the continuation and renewal of the company's bank overdraft facility. The company meets its day to day working capital requirements through this overdraft facility which, in common with all such facilities, is repayable on demand. At the year end the overdraft amounted to £Am, which lies within the facility of £Bm currently agreed with the company's bankers. However, the nature of the company's business is such that there can be considerable variation in the timing of cash inflows.

Details of the circumstances relating to this inherent uncertainty are described in the extract from notes to the financial statement. We consider that, in view of the matters referred to above and in this extract, there is a significant level of concern as to the appropriateness of the going concern basis. However, our opinion is not qualified in this respect, and on the basis of our discussions with the directors and other information of which we have become aware during our audit we consider that it is appropriate for the directors to prepare financial statements drawn up on the going concern basis.

Opinion

In our opinion the financial statements give a true and fair view of the state of the company's affairs as at 31 December 19... and of its profit for the year then ended and have been properly prepared in accordance with the Companies Act 1985.

Example of an unpublished assertion from the Directors

Set out below is an illustrative example of the form of assertion that auditors might obtain from the directors in relation to SAS 130.2. The assertion could be in the form of a letter from the directors addressed to the auditors, or might be included within the letter of representation.

Going Concern

The considered view of the directors of A Limited (the company) is that, after making enquiries, the directors have a reasonable expectation that the company has adequate resources to continue operations for the foreseeable future. For this reason the directors continue to adopt the going concern basis in preparing the financial statements for the year ended...

The directors have reached this conclusion having regard to circumstances which they consider may occur during a period of at least one year from (date the directors approve the financial statement), and in the light of a number of considerations. The key factors are (set out below) (contained in the attached schedules which show the development of our views through our discussions with the auditors of the company, and for which we are responsible).

Key Factors
Forecasts and borrowing requirements
The forecasts for the next .... months prepared by the directors show that the available borrowing facilities exceed the peak borrowing requirements by a margin of £X.X thousand; furthermore, the forecast borrowing requirement can be met without breaching covenants or other borrowing restrictions.

Summary

This chapter deals with some further aspects of financial analysis. Where in Chapter 29 we were concerned with what is termed univariate analysis, where only one ratio at a time is calculated and analysed, here we look at some of the limitations of this analysis. We looked accordingly at the impact of changing prices and different accounting systems to deal with these and the effects on the interpretation of accounts and also at the importance of identifying and disclosing transactions with related parties.

The chapter covers the alternative approach to analysis, known as multivariate analysis, and its use as a tool in predicting company failure. The general conclusions that can be drawn from the above are that the usefulness and relevance of ratio analysis to users would be improved by increasing the uniformity of the practice of financial reporting and adopting current value accounting. The chapter also looks to the overall improvement in financial reporting practice that is intended to follow compliance with the proposals of the Cadbury Report and its code of best practice and the ASB's discussion paper on operating and financial review. Thus, directors are now expected to explain their responsibilities for preparing accounts, to report on the company's system of internal control, to report that the business is a going concern, to include a commentary on operating results, present a review of the company's financial needs and resources and include a commentary on shareholders' return and value. All of this is intended to contribute to an improvement in the financial reporting environment, which is the subject matter of Paper 13. Lastly, keeping pace with changes in the world of auditing (SAS 130–draft) the chapter deals with the going concern, its assessment and relevance to the audit opinion.

Suggested reading

Going, going, gone – four factors which predict (Taffler and Tisshaw 1977)
This is a useful article on predicting company failure, once the basis for an examination question.

Z scores and the going concern basis (Inman 1991)
A useful article in the ACCA *Students' Newsletter*.

Predicting corporate failure (Argenti)
This article provides a detailed analysis of company failures.

Self test questions

1   Outline the main shortcomings of ratio analysis.

2   Indicate what Z scores are designed for.

3   What are the advantages and the main disadvantages of historical cost accounting?

4   Provide examples of possible related parties under FRED 8.

5   What is the disclosure proposed by FRED 8 as to related party transactions?

Exam style questions

1   *Ratios*
    An accounting ratio is a means of measuring the relationship between two figures.

    Required
    a)   Define the following ratios and indicate what is measured by them:

         (i)   return on capital employed
         (ii) stock turnover
         (iii) gearing.

                                                                    (3 marks)

    b)   Explain the usefulness and limitations of accounting ratios for an external financial analyst, with particular reference to the above where appropriate.
                                                                    (7 marks)
                                                                   (10 marks)

                              (*ICAEW PEI, November 1988, exam question*)

2   *Stock Exchange regulation*
    One of the aims of Stock Exchange regulation in relation to the annual report and accounts of listed companies is to provide a more comprehensive picture of a company's background.

    Required
    a)   Illustrate how this is achieved by comparing the Stock Exchange disclosure requirements in relation to directors with those of the Companies Act 1985
                                                                    (6 marks)

    b)   Outline why the Stock Exchange needs to impose additional disclosure requirements.   (4 marks)

                                                                   (10 marks)

                              (*ICAEW PEI, November 1988, exam question*)

                              Answers to all questions on pages 715–717.

Answers to End of Chapter Questions

CHAPTER 1 *Self test questions*

1   *Assets* are rights or other access to future economic benefits controlled by an entity as a result of past transactions or events.

   Liabilities are an entity's obligations to transfer economic benefits as a result of past transactions or events.

   Equity is the ownership interest in the entity. It is the residual amount found by deducting all liabilities of the entity from all of the entity's assets.

2   An item should be recognised in financial statements if:

   ▶ the item meets the definition of an element of financial statements and
   ▶ there is sufficient evidence that the change in assets or liabilities inherent in the item has occurred (including, where appropriate, evidence that a future inflow or outflow of benefit will occur) and
   ▶ the item can be measured at a monetary amount with sufficient reliability.

3   The principle of 'value to the business' can be illustrated by:

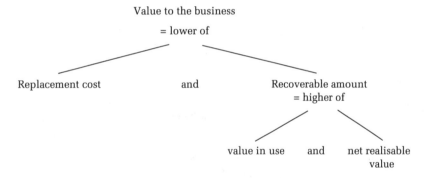

4   The principle of the 'relief value of a liability' can be illustrated by:

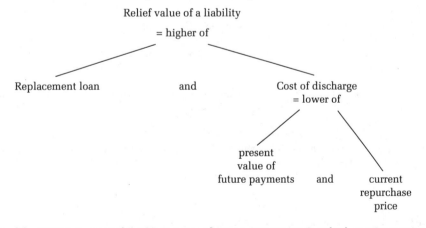

5   The main role of the UITF is to assist the ASB in areas where an Accounting Standard or a Companies Act provision exists (including the requirement to give a true and fair view) but where unsatisfactory or conflicting interpretations have developed or seem likely to develop. In such circumstances it operates by seeking a consensus as to the accounting treatment that should be adopted. Such a consensus is reached against the background of the ASB's declared aim of relying on principles rather than detailed prescription.

CHAPTER 1 *Exam style question*

1   Your answer should have made the following points:

▶ Information has the quality of reliability when it is free from error and bias and where it can be relied upon by users to represent that which it either purports to or could reasonably be expected to represent.

▶ If information is relevant but unreliable its recognition may be potentially misleading; for example, if factored debts are sold back to a company without proper documentation it would be misleading to leave them in current assets without making a provision.

▶ To be reliable, information must be accounted for and presented in accordance with its substance, as opposed to merely its legal form; for example, if invoices are held as part of a financing arrangement they should be reported as such in the accounts.

▶ In some cases the measurement of the financial effects of items could be so uncertain that enterprises generally would not recognise them in accounts; for example, if long-term contracts involve projects that involve risk and where the company has little prior experience, profit recognition should be delayed until there is reasonable certainty as to outcome.

▶ Uncertainties should be recognised by the exercise of prudence in the preparation of accounts.

▶ The exercise of prudence should not create hidden reserves or excessive provisions or the deliberate understatement of assets or the deliberate overstatement of expenses.

▶ To maximise the usefulness of information provided to users, preparers have to achieve a balance between relevance and reliability while considering how best to satisfy the economic decision-making needs of users.

CHAPTER 2 *Self test questions*

1   The IASC has *two* objectives. The first is to provide standards – this is very important to affiliated countries that do not have the time, money or expertise to develop their own standards. The second is to harmonise the numerous national standards – this recognises that the IASC is not likely to be able to get countries with resources to produce their own standards to adopt the IASs and that the way forward is to try to ensure that these national standards are consistent with each other and the IASs.

2   The national standard-setting process in the UK is not a model of the regulating processes in other countries. See the section of this chapter that describes other countries' standard-setting processes; they are clearly very different, although the ASB's new process is closely aligned to the American system.

3   Arguments put forward to support global harmonisation of financial reporting would be based on the benefits to users and preparers of such global harmonisation:

▶ *Investors* Would help individual and corporate investors make decisions on international investment decisions.

▶ *Multinational companies (MNCs)* Several advantages including ease of preparation of group accounts and simpler internal management control across national borders.

▶ *Governments of developing countries* Would save time and money if they could adopt universally recognised methods of accounting. Would also help such governments control activities of MNCs; MNCs could not hide behind foreign misunderstood accounting practices.

▶ *International Accounting Firms* Would make accounting and auditing much easier if similar accounting practices existed throughout the world.

▶ *Tax authorities* Easier to assess the tax liabilities of investors, including MNCs, who receive income from overseas sources. (Note, however, that it is often the tax authorities who regulate in such a way as to cause the differences they would like to see eliminated.)

4   The United Nations is a global organisation, often working on behalf of developing countries. The European Commission is a regional organisation, working to standardise practices within the developed European Community.

5   The IASC prefers immediate write-off but permits capitalisation in specific circumstances. Under US GAAP capitalisation is compulsory for borrowing costs attaching to certain assets. Under UK GAAP such costs may either be capitalised or immediately written off.

CHAPTER 2 *Exam style question*

1   *Revenue recognition*
     a)   'Revenue' may be defined as the gross inflow of cash, receivables, or other consideration arising in the course of the ordinary activities of an enterprise from:

▶ the sale of goods
▶ the rendering of services
▶ the use by others of enterprise resources yielding interest, royalties and dividends.

Revenue from sales or service transactions should be recognised when the 'requirements as to performance' set out below are satisfied, provided that at the time of performance it is not unreasonable to expect ultimate collection.

In a transaction involving the sale of goods, performance should be regarded as being achieved when the following conditions have been fulfilled:

▶ The seller has transferred to the buyer the significant risks and rewards of ownership.
▶ No significant uncertainty exists regarding:

– the consideration to be derived from the sale
– costs incurred or to be incurred in producing or purchasing the goods
– the extent to which goods may be returned.

In a transaction involving the rendering of services, performance should be measured either under the 'completed contract method' or under the 'percentage of completion' method, whichever relates the revenues to the work accomplished.

No significant uncertainty should exist regarding:

▶ Consideration derived from rendering the service.
▶ The costs incurred or to be incurred in rendering the service.

b) i) *Bill and hold sales* Revenue should be recognised even where there has been no physical delivery so long as there is every expectation that delivery will be made. However, the item must be on hand, identified and ready for delivery to the buyer at the time the sale is recognised rather than there being simply an intention to acquire or manufacture the goods in time for delivery.

ii) *Guaranteed sales* Recognition of revenue in such circumstances will depend on the substance of the agreement. In the case of normal retail sales – for example, a chain store offering 'money back if not completely satisfied' – it may be appropriate to recognise the sale but to make a suitable provision for returns based on previous experience. In other cases the substance of the agreement may amount to a sale on consignment, that is, a shipment is made whereby the recipient undertakes to sell the goods on behalf of the shipper. In this event revenue should not be recognised until the goods are sold to a third party.

iii) *Publication and record subscriptions* Revenue received or billed should be deferred and recognised either on a straight-line basis over time, or, where the items shipped vary in value from period to period, revenue should be based on the sales value of the item shipped in relation to the total sales value of all items covered by the subscription.

iv) *Advertising and insurance agency commissions* Revenue should be recognised when the service is completed. For advertising agencies, media commissions will normally be recognised when the related advertisement or commercial appears before the public, as opposed to production commission which will be recognised when the project is completed.

Insurance agency commissions should be recognised on the effective commencement or renewal dates of the related policies. In some circumstances the commission may be adjusted depending upon the claims experienced in respect of the policies written by the agent. In those cases where it is expected that the policy will need servicing during its life, the commission or a relevant part thereof may be recognised over that period.

v) *Financial service commissions* A financial service may be rendered as a single act or may be provided over a period of time. Similarly charges for such services may be made as a single amount or in stages over the period of the service or the life of the transaction to which it relates. Such charges may be settled in full when made or added to a loan or other account and settled in stages. The recognition of such revenue should therefore have regard to:

▶ whether the service has been provided for once and for all, or is on a continuing basis
▶ the incidence of the costs relating to the service
▶ when the payment for the service will be received.

In general, commissions charged for arranging for granting loans or other facilities should be recognised when a binding obligation has been entered into. Commitment, facility or loan management fees that relate to continuing obligations or services should normally be recognised over the life of the loan or facility having regard to the amount of the obligation outstanding, the nature of the services provided and the timing of the costs relating thereto.

vi) *Franchise fees* Such fees may cover the supply of any combination of initial and subsequent services, equipment, know-how, and so on. Frequently, the determination of such matters and the allocation of the franchise fee thereto is difficult and requires considerable judgement. As general guidance, the following methods of fee recognition may be appropriate:

▶ The portion of the initial franchise fee that relates to tangible assets should be recognised when the items are delivered.
▶ The portion that applies to future services should be deferred and recognised as revenue when the services are rendered.
▶ If continuing fees receivable under the agreement are inadequate to cover the cost and a reasonable profit level for the continuing services, recognition of some or all of the initial franchise fee should be delayed.

CHAPTER 3   *Self test questions*

1   The matters that an auditor should consider before accepting an appointment to a new client are:

▶ client desirability
▶ client background
▶ solvency of the company
▶ history of the company
▶ reasons for changing auditors
▶ source of introduction
▶ ethical capability of the practice to perform the work
▶ technical ability of the practice to perform the work
▶ logistical resources of the practice to perform the work to a proper standard.

2   The purpose of a letter of engagement is to formally clarify the relationship between the auditor or accountant and the client. It is not to be confused with a contract, as consideration is not specified. However, it should clearly explain the responsibility accepted by the auditor and the responsibilites to be taken on by the client.

3   The quality controls that should be found within a firm of auditors follow the normal control structure contained within the Operational Standard.

▶ Personal controls – adequate training.
▶ Authorisation controls – restriction on signing of the firm's name.
▶ Physical controls – custody of working papers.
▶ Recording – standardised working papers.
▶ Management – proper planning procedures.
▶ Organisation controls – practice procedure manual.
▶ Supervisory controls – formal file reviewing procedures.
▶ The segregation of duties – adequate independence procedures, splitting audit work from accountancy work.

4   Audit can be controlled on a day-to-day basis if the following are implemented:

▶ planning memorandums
▶ standardised working papers
▶ regular meetings
▶ staff training
▶ practice procedure manual
▶ review of working paper files.

CHAPTER 3   *Exam style questions*

1   a) There are two main factors that have increased the importance of quality control within audit firms:

▶ If the work is to be performed efficiently and costs are to be minimised, the audit techniques must be designed to gather *relevant* evidence. The systems-based audit was developed to improve the speed of the audit process and improve the quality of the evidence.

Profits will not be maximised if the firm has to perform additional work rectifying poor audit work.

▶ The audit environment is becoming increasingly more risky. The public's expectations of the skill and care to be exercised by auditors are becoming greater. The increasing complexity of business in general means that there is a greater chance of material errors going undetected and the possibility of legal action being taken against the firm.

   b) The main procedures that should be instigated to maintain the quality of audit work are as follows:

▶ Personnel controls
   – There must be a strict system of recruitment. Specialist personnel staff should be in charge of this area.
   – The firm should have a well-defined training policy so that all staff trainees and qualified personnel are kept as up to date as possible with all technical developments. This objective may be achieved by: in-house training courses; contracted-in continuing professional education courses; regular technical update memos to all staff.
▶ Physical controls – There should be very strict control over the storage and movement of audit files. The files will contain highly confidential information which, if not securely maintained, may lead to accusations of insider dealing. If the files were lost this would cause severe problems for the following year's audit.

- ▶ Authorisation controls – It must be made very clear to all staff as to who may sign documents in the firm's name. Usually this is restricted to partners.
- ▶ Supervisory controls – All audit files must be reviewed by the senior staff in charge of the audit before the audit report is written and signed. In many firms a further reviewing process has been introduced – the cold or technical review – sometimes referred to as a post-audit review. This is where the technical committee will select completed audits at random to ensure that the quality of work is being maintained. If any consistent failures are identified, corrective action will be taken, such as special training course.
- ▶ Segregation of duties – It is important that staff involved in day-to-day accounting or bookkeeping for a particular client are not involved in the audit of that client.
- ▶ Organisation charts – Audit firm procedures and techniques should be formalised in a procedure manual. For individual audits there should be a planning memorandum that explains the duties of each member of the audit team.
- ▶ Management controls – There should be controls to ensure that the work is performed expeditiously. This will mean that Gantt charts will be necessary – in extreme cases network analysis may be employed.

c) The UK accounting bodies have instigated the following main procedures to ensure that the quality of work is maintained and improved:

- ▶ The establishment of the APC and the issue of auditing standards and guidelines.
- ▶ The establishment of the Joint Disciplinary Council. The JDC includes non-accountants on the board of enquiry.
- ▶ Restriction of Practising Certificates – members require post-qualification experience before a Practising Certificate is issued. Practising certificates are issued for one year and not for life and members must reapply each year.
- ▶ There is a requirement of a minimum of 40 hours' continual professional education per year if the practising certificate is to be renewed.
- ▶ The establishment of a Practice Advisory Service whereby members can obtain advice on difficult matters of principle.
- ▶ The provision of update courses by the Association, which are taken around the country providing members with the opportunity to attend lectures on current topical developments.

d) i) *Effect of peer review on the standard of audit work.*

With the increased risk of litigation the quality of audit work is a critical factor for any practising firm. Whilst the matters outlined in c) above have gone some way to increasing the overall quality of work, peer review by another firm would be a very strong incentive for the firms to ensure compliance with the internal quality controls within the practice. The peer review would also serve as a good detective control over any lapses, so that they can be corrected in a timely manner.

ii) The acceptability of peer review, however, is quite another matter. In the UK, professional firms are very competitive and the idea of giving one firm the opportunity to inspect the internal procedures and working papers of another firm would probably be very difficult to accept. Currently, peer review of a sort takes place in joint audits and group audits where primary and secondary auditors are involved. This is acceptable because both firms have been appointed by the client company.

Every major practice in the UK has very individual accounting techniques, of which they are very possessive and to which they are very loyal. It may, therefore, be difficult for one firm to make an objective judgement about another firm's techniques and procedures, for example, conflicts over sample size, acceptable error rate, level of compliance or substantive testing.

In the US peer review is almost a mandatory check. However, in the UK, peer review of the manner described in the question is unlikely to be implemented. In *Accountancy* magazine for March 1987 Branden Gough of Coopers & Lybrand stated that he thought that peer review by an institute-employed panel of accountants was a workable idea.

2 a) Considering the three points raised in the statements:

i) The decision in the Caparo case suggests that auditors have a liability for negligence to the company being audited and shareholders as a body (but not individual shareholders). Auditors have no liability to third parties, as they do not have a contractual relationship with them (that is, the third parties have not paid any consideration to the auditor). So, the Caparo case strictly limits the persons to whom an auditor is liable. As this reduces auditors' risk, they will be able to reduce their audit work (to maintain the same potential liability to claims) and this will result in a lowering of the assurance that the accounts are correct. However, if the auditors have carried out audits and have not detected material errors that were later uncovered, their reputations and the confidence that companies and investors place on their work will be adversely affected. As a result, auditors are likely to lose audit work to competitors. Because of the potential loss of reputation and work, auditors will be careful to ensure their work is of a high standard and so the decision in the Caparo case is unlikely to result in a serious decline in audit standards.

ii) Professional indemnity insurance (PII) will mean that auditors will be able to use their insurance to pay any claims for negligence, provided they are not above their liability limit and so this development may mean that auditors will be less careful in their work as they will not have to pay for their mistakes. However, professional indemnity insurance will probably cover only the cost of claims against the auditor and the legal costs of both parties. The cost of the time spent by firms' employees will probably not be covered by the insurance, and so there will be a net cost to auditors which they will want to avoid (by maintaining the quality of audit work and minimising the rise of claims). Also, major claims against auditors will lead to the loss of time of partners and senior staff spent in obtaining evidence and defending the firm. Partners would prefer that this time is spent on providing a good service to existing clients and developing the business and so they will want to keep claims to a minimum.

If auditors make claims against their PII, this will probabaly increase their PII premiums and this will be a deterrent to allowing auditing standards in the firm to fall.

For the person claiming against the auditors, the existence of PII gives them more confidence that a successful claim will be met. Without PII the auditors may have inadequate funds to meet a claim (they may deliberately transfer assets to other individuals to minimise the cost of claims) and so the financial consequences of meeting a claim may be small. This may lead to a poor standard of audit work.

PII may result in a small reduction in the quality of audit work, but the effect of claims against the auditor, both in terms of increased PII premiums and on their reputation as auditors, are likely to maintain the standard of their work. For the company making a claim against the auditors, the effect of PII is that a successful claim should be fully met, and unscrupulous auditors would not be able to 'walk away' from claims against them.

It should be noted that for a number of years ACCA has required all members with a practising certificate to have PII.

iii) The compulsory registration of auditors under the Companies Act 1989 is unlikely to have much effect on auditors in the short term. ACCA has said that all their members with practising certificates will be entitled to become Registered Auditors. Only those members carrying out a few audits with no practising certificate will be disadvantaged by this change.

The new rules of registration of auditors limits auditors to members of the Association of one of the three UK chartered accounting bodies. Although this appears to create a monopoly, if any unqualified person was allowed to carry out an audit (that is, a 'free for all' situation) there would certainly be a substantial reduction in the quality of audit work.

The change to Registered Auditors will ensure that all are competent to carry out audit work. All will have practical experience monitored by the supervisory body and all will have studied and passed the exacting examinations set by the body.

Limiting auditors to members of the four accounting bodies would appear to create a monopoly, but a large number of firms carry out audit work and there is plenty of competition between them. Also, it appears that audit work is less profitable than some other services provided by firms of accountants and this suggests that the apparent monopoly is not creating excessive prices. Professional firms carry out types of work other than audits (for example, management consultancy, taxation, receivership and liquidations) and if they thought audit work was becoming more profitable they would transfer their resouces into that area. However, many of the large audit firms are reducing audit work as a proportion of their total activity and this confirms the suggestion above that auditing is less profitable than their other activities.

Summarising the discussion above, I believe the development of registered auditors will improve the quality of audit work (because they will be properly trained from a practical and academic viewpoint) and the evidence is that this apparent monopoly is not leading to an increase in auditors' fees and profits (in real terms).

b) The factors which I believe will increase the standard of audit work include:

i) The requirement for auditors to undertake educational studies while they hold a practising certificate. These studies include attending courses and working on study material. This should ensure that auditors' knowledge is kept up to date.

ii) The Association is proposing that under the new registration regime, the work of auditors will be checked periodically, with a maximum period between checks of five years. The existence of these checks should ensure that auditors maintain the quality of their work and that they keep up to date with current developments.

iii) The Joint Disciplinary Scheme (JDS) is a means whereby the four accounting bodies can investigate and take action against auditors where there is an allegation of poor work. This body includes members who are not accountants and so it is seen to be more independent that a body composed only of accountants. Also, as the JDS is composed of members from four accounting bodies (and not one body) this will deter any accounting body from trying to hide any unfavourable reports about members' work.

iv) The new regime of developing accounting standards under the Accounting Standards Board (ASB) should ensure that accounting standards are more independent. The new ASB includes members from outside the accounting profession. This will make accounting standards more independent and less subject to amendments which will be beneficial to accountants, although not to the users of accounts.

v)   A body similar to the ASB is being proposed to replace the Auditing Practices Committee. Currently, the Auditing Practices Committee comprises auditors alone, and the change should ensure that the views of companies and investors are seen to be taken into account.

vi)   The development of the risk-based approach to auditing should improve the quality of audit work, feeding to auditors performing more work where the risk is high and less work where it is low. Provided auditors assess the risk correctly, this should ensure that there is a proper examination of contentious areas and that the auditor gives a correct audit opinion.

vii)   Publicity about legal claims against auditors and financial scandals adversely affect the reputation of auditors, and this leads to the firms concerned losing work and being less successful in gaining new work. The publicity about cases of major frauds by proprietors of investment businesses has had an adverse effect on the reputation of auditors, particularly the auditors of these businesses. The effect of both legal claims and financial scandals will reduce the profits of the auditing firm, and so auditors will be careful in maintaining the quality of their audit work in order to minimise the risk of claims against them.

c)   In conclusion, I believe that the Caparo decision and the requirement for compulsory professional indemnity insurance could lead to a small reduction in the standards of audit work. However, the new requirement for registered auditors should improve the standard of auditors, and the factors cited in part (b) above should have a positive effect on the standards of audit work.

Overall, I believe there is little or no evidence that the standards of audit work are deteriorating, and it is more likely that standards are improving (because of the compulsory registration of auditors and the factors cited in part (b) above).

3   a)

14 December 1992

To: Senior partner

From: A.N. Auditor

Subject: Quality control procedures

Further to your recent request on the above matter, my suggestions and comments are that the following matters should be considered, and appropriate action should be taken in relation to:

i)   When accepting appointment or re-appointment as auditor, the firm should consider whether it is sufficiently independent and competent to perform the audit.

ii)   Staff should be aware of, and comply with, the principles of independence, objectivity, integrity and confidentiality, set out in the ethical statements issued by the Chartered Association of Certified Accountants.

iii)   Staff should have the appropriate skills and competence to perform the work:

►   training of staff, both from a day-to-day work and a technical viewpoint
►   a technical library
►   a procedures manual for audit work, standard checklists and standards for the preparation of audit working papers.

iv)   The work of staff on audits should be monitored. Before commencing an audit, an audit planning memorandum should be prepared, the staff should be briefed, and the progress of the audit should be monitored by either the partner or manager responsible for the audit. The audit work should be properly recorded and reviewed by the manager, and then the partner.

For large audits, there should be a brief report of the performance of each member of the audit team, which should be discussed with that person. If audits are small, it would be more appropriate to review the work of each member of the firm's audit staff at regular intervals, say every six months.

v)   A post-audit review of a sample of audits should be carried out at regular intervals. A sample of audits should be taken for each partner (or manager, if it is a large firm) and the audit working papers should be studied by a panel of partners and managers from other offices who are not involved in the audits being reviewed. This review panel should make a report on their findings and give a general assessment of the standard of the audit work, note any errors of weaknesses found and suggest action that should be taken to improve the quality of the audit work. For instance, it could suggest that there should be more detailed checks to determine whether stock should be valued at net realisable value (that is, when it may be worth less than cost), or it could recommend that less work is carried out in certain areas where there is a low risk of errors occurring.

If you require any further information or explanation of the points raised in this memorandum, please do not hesitate to contact me.

b)   *Audit committees*

i)   Audit committees normally comprise non-executive directors of public companies. A few public companies in the UK have audit committees. As pointed out in the question, since 1978 all public companies in the USA have had to have an audit committee as a condition of listing on the New York Stock Exchange.

ii) There are no formal requirements for the duties of an audit committee, but they can include:

- ▶ reviewing the financial results shown by the management accounts and those presented to shareholders.
- ▶ recommending improvements in management control
- ▶ helping the external auditors obtain all the information they require, and helping to resolve any difficulties they may experience
- ▶ dealing with any significant reservations of the auditors about the final accounts, the management and the company's records
- ▶ assisting in maintaining a satisfactory working relationship between the external auditors and management, and the external and internal auditors
- ▶ ensuring that there is adequate review of interim statements, rights circulars and other financial information prior to their distribution to shareholders
- ▶ being responsible for recommending the appointment or removal of the external auditors, and fixing their remuneration
- ▶ being available for consultation with the external auditors at all times and, if necessary, without the presence of the company's management.

iii) The advantages of audit committees are:

- ▶ There is a body to which the external auditors can report, who are independent of the executive management. This could be helpful where unlawful acts have been carried out, or were proposed, by the executive directors, or where the executive directors were proving unhelpful to the auditor or obstructive, or where there is a dispute between the executive directors and the auditors. The audit committee could help to resolve the problems without the auditors having to take the serious step of reporting the matter to the shareholders, either in their audit report or at the AGM.
- ▶ The audit committee may be a deterrent to executive directors carrying out unlawful acts or acts not in the interests of the shareholders.
- ▶ The existence of an audit committee should make the non-executive directors more aware of their duties and responsibilities.

The disadvantages of audit committees include:

- ▶ As they are not compulsory in the UK, it is probable that the firms that most need them (that is, those with a dominant chief executive) will not have them. This is because the dominant chief executive will prevent them from being set up. A compulsory requirement for audit committees, like that in the USA, would overcome this limitation.
- ▶ It is unusual for the work of audit committees to be made public and so it is not clear how much work they do, or their effectiveness.
- ▶ The audit committee could hamper executive flair. The brilliant idea may appear to contravene accepted rules. The success of some companies mainly derives from the actions of a dominant chief executive, whose actions may be limited by the audit committe thus damaging careful plans and the successful development of the company.

iv) Unless audit committees are made compulsory for listed companies in the UK (as in the USA), it appears that they will have limited value.

Even in the USA, it appears that the value of audit committees is questionable. The value of audit committees would be better appreciated if details of their work were available. However, some of their work would be confidential and publication of other work could prejudice relations between the auditor and the company's management, or affect the shareholders' confidence in the auditor or management. Despite the confidentiality and other problems, companies should at least publish the duties and responsibilities of the audit committee in their financial statements and indicate the frequency of its meetings.

Without a compulsory requirement for audit committees in listed companies and without more details of their work being published they are of only limited value.

CHAPTER 4 *Self test questions*

1 Under the Companies Act 1985, a company is in breach of the specific requirements of the law if it fails to depreciate any fixed asset that has a limited useful economic life.

Despite this legal requirement an accounting standard is necessary in order to deal with the practical aspects of depreciation, for example:

- ▶ the problem of revaluation (dealt with in ED 51)
- ▶ the problem of revision of estimated lives
- ▶ the problem of provisions for permanent diminution of value
- ▶ the problem of alternative methods of depreciation
- ▶ the problem of capitalised borrowing cost (dealt with in ED 51)
- ▶ the problem of enhancement costs (dealt with in ED 51).

2 Where an asset is revalued, SSAP 12 requires depreciation to be based on the revalued amount. Depreciation so calculated can be broken down into:

- depreciation based on historical cost
- depreciation based on the revaluation surplus

On the basis that depreciation based on the revaluation surplus distorts the comparability of accounts, given that not all companies revalue all of their fixed assets, some commentators argued that the depreciation charge be split, that is, depreciation based on historical cost to be charged against earnings and depreciation based on the revaluation surplus to be charged against the revaluation surplus in revaluation reserve.

SSAP 12 however, argues that the accounting treatment in the profit and loss account should be consistent with that in the balance sheet. 'Split depreciation' would result in:

- hybrid accounts failing to give a true and fair view
- confusion for users
- users not being able to relate the depreciation charge in the profit and loss account with the carrying amount of the asset in the balance sheet.

3   The net book value of the asset at 1 January 1994 is 2,400 less [(2,000)/10yrs × 3] = £1,800
Annual depreciation after 1 January 1994 will be (1,800 – 400)/5 yrs = £280.

4   The value of investment properties in the balance sheet of Justin plc as at 31 March 1995 is:

(6,500 + 5,100 + 2,900 = £14,500

5   The depreciation charge on the buildings of Justin plc for the year ended 31 March 1995 is:

	£000
Main office	15
Office let to subsidiaries	25
Short leasehold investment property	15
	55

Note that leaseholds of less than 20 years remain investment properties but must be depreciated.

CHAPTER 4   *Exam style question*

1   *Jupiter Ltd*

(a) *Note x: Tangible fixed assets*

	Land and buildings £000	Plant and machinery £000	Fixtures fittings and equipment £000	Total £000
Cost or valuation				
1 November 1990	390	525	395	1,310
Surplus on revaluation	400			400
Additions		128	8	136
Disposals		(6)		(6)
31 October 1991	790	647	403	1,840
Depreciation				
1 November 1990	(60)	(400)	(125)	(585)
Adjustment on revaluation	60			60
Charge for the year	(10)	(68)	(95)	(173)
Eliminated in respect of disposals		6		6
31 October 1991	(10)	(462)	(220)	(692)
Net book value				
At 31 October 1991	780	185	183	1,148
At 31 October 1990	330	125	270	725

Cost or valuation at 31 October 1991 is represented by:

Valuation in 1990	790			790
Cost		647	403	1,050
	790	647	403	1,840

Land and buildings were revalued on the basis of an open market valuation for existing use on 1 November 1990, by C. Star, Chartered Surveyor.

If land and building had not been revalued they would have been included at the following amounts:

	1991 £000	1990 £000
Cost	390	390
Aggregate depreciation based on cost	(67)	(60)

Land and buildings consist entirely of freehold property.

Workings:

1 Land and buildings

	Land £000	Buildings Factory £000		Salesroom £000		Total £000
Cost	60	150		180		390
Depreciation to 1/11/90	–	(30)	10 yrs	(30)	7½ yrs	(60)
NBV 1/11/90	60	120		150		330
Revaluation surplus	340	120		–		460
At valuation 1/11/90	400	240		150		790
Depreciation y/e 31/10/91	–					
240/40 years		(6)				
150/37.5 years				(4)		(10)
NBV 31/10/1991	400	234		146		780

2 Plant and machinery

	Plant and machinery £000	Motor vehicles £000	Total £000
Cost	475	50	525
Depreciation to 1/11/90	(365)	(35)	(400)
NBV 1/11/90	110	15	125
Additions	100	28	128
	210	43	253
Depreciation y/e 31/10/91			
475/10 years	(47.5)		
100/10 years × 6/12	(5)		
(50 – 6)/4 years		(11)	
6/4 years × 6/12		(0.75)	
28/4 years × 6/12		(3.5)	(67.75)
Disposal			
Cost		(6)	(6)
Depreciation (5 + 0.75)		5.75	5.75
NBV 31/10/91	157.5	27.5	185.0

3 Fixtures fittings and equipment

	Furniture and fittings £000	Computer equipment £000	Total £000
Cost	100	295	395
Depreciation to 1/11/90	(40)	(85)	(125)
NBV 1/11/90	60	210	270
Additions		8	8
Depreciation y/e 31/10/91			
100/5 years	(20)		
295/4 years		(73.75)	
8/4 years × 6/12		(1)	(94.75)
	40	143.25	183.25

b) *The arguments for and against including tangible fixed assets at revalued amounts*

The revaluation of fixed assets in historical cost financial statements is acceptable in the eyes of standards and the law; the former make many references to its results, and the latter specifically allows it.

The arguments for historical cost accounting seem to be that:

▶ it is more objective than systems based on current values
▶ consequently, it is easier to audit

► it is cheaper because the figures are already recorded
► it sticks to the ancient purpose of stewardship accounting by showing what was actually spent on the asset.

All these advantages are compromised by revaluations. What is worse, for ad hoc revaluations (as allowed and practiced in the UK), companies can choose whether to revalue, which assets to revalue, how to revalue and how often to revalue.

This leads to inconsistency from year to year and lack of uniformity from company to company. As it is usual for depreciation figures to be revised, companies have a very wide choice of asset values, reserve figures and profit figures. As stated by Christopher Nobes in his monograph, *Depreciation problems in the context of historical cost accounting*, there is little justification for this given the ability to provide supplementary valuations in note form. If an individual company is prepared to sacrifice the benefits of historical cost, it should be required to use a standard system such as, perhaps, CCA. If not, strict historical cost should be followed, supplemented by notes or supplementary statements on current values. The present UK position is remarkably disorganised. Revaluation (modified historical cost accounts) contributes considerably to the difficulty of comprehension of, and comparisons of, financial statements by users. It brings many unresolved problems and diverse practices in its wake, for example, depreciation and disposals.

The effect of permitting ad hoc revaluations is a lack of consistency of treatment. A company that does selectively revalue its fixed assets will suffer higher depreciation charges and report a lower gain (sale proceeds less book value) in the year of disposal compared with a company that does not revalue its fixed assets.

One way to eliminate the distortion of revaluation arising from additional depreciation charged against profits following revaluation is to split the depreciation charge. Split depreciation is legal, reasonably 'good' and, depending on interpretation, not outlawed by the original SSAP 12. The revised SSAP 12, however, requires that a split depreciation charge be prohibited and, if a company does revalue its assets, that the depreciation charge in the profit and loss account be based on the revalued amount – what is referred to as the articulation concept. The principal advantage of the split depreciation charge is that only historical cost depreciation is charged against profits, ensuring consistency, and the additional depreciation on revaluation taken direct to reserves.

As to disposals, unless any remaining relevant part of the revaluation reserve were re-credited to gains on disposal, the total debits to profit and loss account over the life of the asset would exceed its cost. It is this fact that lay behind the ED 36 proposals as to calculating and recognising in reported profits the profit or loss on a sale of a previously revalued fixed asset in terms of sale proceeds less depreciated historical cost of the sold asset.

The effect of the ED 36 proposal in this regard is to ensure that total charges against profits from date of revaluation to date of sale would be the same for companies that do and do not revalue their assets. The fundamental distortion problem of additional depreciation charged in *each* year after revaluation is not resolved.

The revised SSAP 6 does not require a company to recognise profits/losses on disposal of revalued assets as proposed by ED 36, permitting the alternative procedure of recognising in the profit and loss account the difference between sale proceeds and carrying value of the asset on the date of sale. It is this latter approach that was proposed by ED 51 and is now standard accounting practice under FRS 3.

Summarising, the main advantages of revaluation of fixed assets are that assets are included in the balance sheet at a more realistic value than historical cost and depreciation, in that it is charged on the revalued amount, results in a more meaningful figure of profit than in strict historical cost accounts. As to these points there is little argument. The disadvantages of revaluation arise in the main from the use of modified historical cost accounts. As dealt with above, such hybrid accounts result in distortion when it comes to comprehension and comparison of financial statements in respect of first depreciation charges and second profit and loss arising on eventual sale. The full advantage of revaluing fixed assets will not be realised until a coherent and universally applicable requirement in this regard is introduced as standard accounting practice.

CHAPTER 5   *Self test questions*

1   Goodwill arising on Kiwi plc's purchase:

	£000	£000
Consideration 200,000 × £1.10		220
Less: Fair value of separable net		
Patents	20	
Plant	138	
Net current assets	30	(188)
Goodwill		32

---

2   ED 47 states that the amortisation period should be determined by identifying and evaluating the factors that gave rise to the goodwill, for example:

- ▶ customer awareness
- ▶ reputation for quality
- ▶ marketing and distribution skills
- ▶ technical know-how
- ▶ established business connections
- ▶ management ability
- ▶ level of workforce training.

The ED suggests that the following be taken into account in determining the life of such advantages:

- ▶ the foreseeable life of the business
- ▶ expected changes in products, markets or technology
- ▶ the expected future period of service of key individuals
- ▶ expected future demand
- ▶ legal, regulatory or contractual factors affecting the useful life.

However, the life should not exceed 20 years unless the directors can justify a longer period in which case the life should not exceed 40 years.

3   The advantages and disadvantages attaching to each of the two alternative treatments permitted under SSAP 22 as to goodwill are:

		Immediate write-off	*Systematic amortisation*
i)	Re profit and loss account	No earnings effect	Adverse earning effect
ii)	Re statement of recognised gains and losses	Not a recognised loss	Included as a recognised loss in the statement
iii)	Re balance sheet	Reduced net worth	No immediate reduction in net worth on acquisition
iv)	Re individual companies and legally distributable profits	As with systematic amortisation, the impact is spread over economic useful life. This is because goodwill must, by law, ultimately result in a realised loss	The impact is spread over economic useful life

4   There are 2 views based on alternative conclusions as to the nature of goodwill:

Not an asset

- ▶ Goodwill is the result of accounting for an acquisition.
- ▶ It is merely the residual after comparing the worth of the consideration with the worth of the net assets acquired.
- ▶ It may be paid for but is replaced sooner rather than later by internally created or non-purchased goodwill, which we do not recognise.
- ▶ Unlike other assets, it is inseparable from the business.

For these reasons it should not be carried as an asset but eliminated, on acquisition, against available reserves

Asset

- ▶ Even though inseparable, it is similar to other fixed assets.
- ▶ It is paid for in the anticipation of future benefits.
- ▶ It would appear to meet the definition of an asset as set out in the ASB's Statement of Principles.
- ▶ The cost should be deferred and matched against the future benefit.

For these reasons it should be capitalised and systematically amortised over its economic useful life.

5   In the 19th century a company's assets were mainly tangible and its balance sheet was essentially a statement as to its worth. In this century the intangible assets of a company have frequently turned out to be more valuable than its tangible assets.

Many acquiring companies that have acquired valuable brands argue that either to show a weaker balance sheet position following immediate write-off, or to hit the profit and loss account by amortising the asset, are not appropriate accounting investments on the basis that the brands are not wasting assets. It is from this view that the practice of assigning a value to and capitalising brands has arisen in the UK. In a report commissioned by the ICAEW in 1989 the London Business School concluded that to allow brands, whether acquired or internally created, to be included in the balance sheet would be unwise. K Wild and H Everitt in an article titled 'The accountancy perspective in the UK' make the following points:

▶ Putting brand values in the balance sheet is legal.
▶ Valuing brands is demonstrably possible.
▶ However, the values are less objective than cost and the values assigned to tangible fixed assets such as property.
▶ If we were to disclose brand values as a note to the accounts, the additional information is likely to be helpful.
▶ Limiting the information to note form recognises the different quality of the information and leaves the balance sheet in conventional and less confusing form.
▶ There are doubts as to whether the values disclosed are useful and meaningful and the disclosure of such information should come with a 'health warning'.
▶ Supplementary information can be provided, as an alternative, in the form of an economic (as opposed to historic cost) balance sheet and profit and loss account which would include a consistent revaluation of all the elements in the financial statements.

CHAPTER 5 *Exam style questions*

1 *Scotty plc*
  a) The fair value of Sulu Inc. at 1 October 1989:
    i) *Redundancy costs*
    It is usual, on the acquisition of a new subsidiary, to reorganise the activities of the subsidiary to bring them into line with the rest of the group. Provisions set up for such reorganisation – the £380,000 for redundancies – give rise to an accounting problem on consolidation given that the cost has to be allocated as a charge to either the pre-acquisition or the post-acquisition reserves of the subsidiary. On the basis that the need for the provision was identified at the date of acquisition (and, therefore, taken account of in setting the value of the consideration paid) it is appropriate that the provision be taken into account in arriving at the fair value of the subsidiary at the acquisition date, that is, treated as a charge against the pre-acquisition reserves of the subsidiary even though the costs were actually incurred after acquisition. Note, however, that under FRED all provisions set up on the acquisition of a new subsidiary should be charged against post-acquisition reserves.

    ii) *The investment in plant and machinery*
    The proposed investment of $300,000 in plant and machinery has no effect on the fair value of Sulu Inc. at the date of its acquisition. Had the purchase taken place prior to acquisition the effect on net assets would be nil in so far as fixed assets would increase and cash decrease by the same amount.

    iii) *Professional fees and directors' time and expenses*
    It is appropriate to treat the professional fees of £30,000 in respect of the acquisition as a part of the cost of the purchase and, accordingly, Scotty plc should include this amount as a part of the cost of its subsidiary in its own accounts. There is no justification for treating the £20,000 estimated as the cost of time and expenses incurred by the directors in negotiating and completing the deal as a part of the cost of acquisition of the subsidiary. This amount should be expensed in the normal way, that is, as part of staff costs and other expenses. In any event neither the £30,000 nor the £20,000 have an effect on the fair value of Sulu Inc. at 1 October 1989.

    iv) *Stocks*
    It is usual practice, on the acquisition of a subsidiary, to change the accounting policies of the new subsidiary where relevant to bring them into line with those of the rest of the group. The impact of such changes in the subsidiary should be dealt with as part of the fair value exercise at acquisition. Accordingly, the fair value of Sulu Inc. at 1 October 1989 should be increased by $150,000.

    The fair value of Sulu Inc. of 1 October 1989 can now be calculated as follows:

	$000
Net assets at 30 September 1989 per question	4,370
Less: per (i) above, provision for redundancy costs	(380)*
Add: per iv), increase in value of stock on change of accounting policy	150
	4,140

    *Note the alternative FRED 7 proposal

  b) Calculation of unamortised consolidated goodwill in the consolidated balance sheet at 30 June 1990:

	£000
Cost – the fair value of the consideration paid	
Scotty plc ordinary shares (5,000 @ 25p each) NV	1,250

[*Note*: The premium on issue (1,500 – 1,250) of £250
is not credited to share premium account as S.131
relief applies. Accordingly, Scotty plc may either exclude
the £250,000 from both the cost of the subsidiary and reserves
or include the £250,000 in both the cost of the subsidiary and
reserves in which case the £250,000 would be credited, in line
with the guidance in the SSAP 23 appendix, to a separate
merger reserve.]

	£000
Scotty plc ordinary shares, premium on issue to merger reserve	250
Cash paid on completion	750
Cash payable – deferred consideration – certain to be paid and therefore provided for at the date of acquisition of the subsidiary	200
	2,450
Professional fees re (a) iii) above	30
	2,480
Less: Fair value of separable net assets acquired (per (a))	
90% × $4,140 @ 1.8	(2,070)
Consolidation goodwill	410
Amortised in year to 30 June 1990	
410/3 years × $^9/_{12}$	(102)
Unamortised goodwill for the consolidated balance sheet at 30 June 1990	308

c) The note to the accounts relating to earnings per share:

i) Earnings

	Basic		Fully diluted	
	Net	Nil	Net	Nil
	£000	£000	£000	£000
Group profit after tax	1,614	1,614	1,614	1,614
Irrecoverable ACT	–	200	–	200
Adjustment re options				
3,250 × £0.18 × 2.5/27 × 0.65	–	–	35	35
	1,614	1,814	1,649	1,849

ii) Number of ordinary shares	£000
At 1 July 1989	47,500
Issued (as consideration for Sulu Inc.) at 1/10/89	
5,000 × 9/12	3,750
Basic number	51,250
Adjustment re options	3,250
Fully diluted number	54,500

The basic eps would be:
i) net £1,614/51,250   3.1p
ii) nil £1,814/51,250   3.5p
(more than 10% different and, therefore, assumed to be materially different).

The fully diluted eps would be:
i) net £1,649/54,500   3.0p
ii) nil £1,849/54,500   3.4p
(Less than 5% different when compared with basic eps and, therefore, the dilution is considered immaterial.)

Note to the accounts
The basic earnings per share for the year ended 30 June 1990, calculated on a net basis, based on earnings of £1,614,000 and a weighted average number of ordinary shares in issue of 51,250 amounts to 3.1p. The basic earnings per share calculated on a nil basis, taking into account the incidence of irrecoverable ACT in the year amounts to 3.5p. Fully diluted earnings per share taking into account the effects of the share options outstanding during the year, is not disclosed as the dilution is considered immaterial.

2   *Casscadura plc*
a) Although SSAP 13 distinguishes between pure and applied research, the accounting treatment laid down is the same for both types of research, which are considered to be part of the normal continuing activities of the company. Neither pure nor applied research can be expected to

produce benefits in any one particular accounting period; such expenditure is incurred because it is required to maintain the company's business and competitive position. For this reason there is no justification for deferring such expenditure and the costs must be written off as incurred. The original SSAP 13 did not require any specific disclosure of such costs written off in the period (although the international standard – IAS 9 – does). The revised SSAP 13 requires the disclosure of all research and development costs incurred in the year. Note, however, that some enterprises are exempt from this disclosure.

The expenditure on the project to develop the drug to treat cancer can clearly be categorised as applied research, in that commercial possibilities have not yet been identified, and should accordingly be charged in arriving at profit on ordinary operations for the year ended 30 June 1991 and be separately disclosed as an exceptional item if material.

b) Expenditure on development is generally undertaken when there is a reasonable expectation that specific commercial success and future benefits will accrue from the work. This would appear to be the case with the new tranquilliser being developed by the company.

SSAP 13 (Revised) lays down the general rule that development expenditure should be written off as incurred. As an exception, if the directors so wish, the company may defer such expenditure and match it against related revenue of future periods but only if the criteria set out in SSAP 13 (Revised) for the carry forward of such costs are satisfied. In the main these criteria are designed to ensure that such costs are not carried forward unless there is reasonable certainty of their recovery in future accounting periods.

Where conditions for deferring development costs are satisfied, and a decision to defer is made, two further questions arise. First, at what point should amortisation commence, and, second, over what period and on what basis should the expenditure be amortised?

The standard assumes, for the sake of simplicity, that the expected future benefits of the deferred development expenditure begin to arise on commencement of the production process. It lays down that the amortisation of development costs should commence at the same time.

As to the period of amortisation, the standard states that development costs must be allocated, on a systematic basis, to each accounting period by reference to:

▶ the sale or use of the product or process, or
▶ the period over which the product or process is expected to be sold or used.

This requires a commercial assessment of the product, of the pattern of its use, involves predictions and gives rise to areas of potential uncertainty. One acceptable method would be to write off the costs over a number of years based on market forecasts of sales on a straight-line or weighted average basis. Thus the accumulated development costs of £3,600,000 should begin to be amortised in the year to 30 June 1991 giving rise to amortisation in the year of either 2.25/(15 + 7.5) or 1.5/(12 + 3), that is, 10% of £3,600,000 or £360,000.

The standard would require disclosure of the movements on development costs during the year and the accounting policy notes of the company should specify the basis adopted for amortisation.

c) Given that the considerations involved in deciding on a deferral of development costs involve considerable speculation into the future, the standard requires that deferred development expenditure should be reviewed at the end of each accounting period. Where the circumstances that originally justified deferring the costs no longer apply, the costs must be written off to the extent considered irrecoverable through the profit and loss account as part of profit on ordinary operations (as an exceptional item, where material). Once written off the costs should not be reinstated unless the circumstances relating to the write-down no longer apply in a later year. The company should accordingly write off the previously carried forward costs of £15,000,000 and disclose such a charge as an exceptional item in the year.

CHAPTER 6 *Self test questions*

1   Stock is considered to be a high risk area for the following reasons:

▶ It is very vulnerable to management manipulation. Frequently auditors will not have sufficient knowledge or experience to be able to recognise damaged or obsolete stock and will have to rely on management representations to a certain extent.
▶ The valuation of stock is often very subjective and again management representations will be very important.
▶ Stock is not usually part of the double entry process. Unlike an item such as purchases in the profit and loss account, which is an accumulation of transactions throughout the year, stock is counted at the year end, valued and debited to the balance sheet and credited to the trading account.
▶ It is often a very material item on the balance sheet of manufacturing companies.
▶ An error in stock will have a pound-for-pound effect on profits.

2   Auditors should do the following before a stocktake:

▶ *Plan* As with any other stage in the audit process, auditors must plan the work. This can be divided into two parts:

- *Determination of the scope of work* This involves finding out about the nature of the stock and identifying any critical stock areas, such as the need for a specialist, the number and location of branches which may need to be visited.
- *Strategic planning* This will mean making decisions as to the number of staff, the stocktake dates, the appointment of a specialist.
▶ *Ascertain the stocktaking instructions* The client will have drafted written stocktaking instructions, which the auditor will read and discuss with the client.
▶ *Evaluation* At the full evaluation stage the auditor will need to review the controls built into the stocktaking instructions. These controls will be the normal examples of internal control as contained in the Internal Control Guideline within the Operational Standard.
▶ *Recommendations* The auditor must assess the effectiveness of the stocktaking instructions several months before the stocktake date, and recommend to the management improvements, usually in the form of a letter of weakness, giving management adequate time to incorporate all agreed improvements.

3   When planning attendance at a stocktake, auditors should consider the following:

- ▶ nature of the stock
- ▶ need for a specialist
- ▶ location of stock
- ▶ value of stock – branches within the company
- ▶ past experience of stocktaking
- ▶ timing of stocktake
- ▶ staff to attend the stocktake.

4   The primary purpose of auditors attending the stocktake is to enable them to carry out compliance testing. They will observe whether the agreed procedures are being applied as prescribed.

5   When auditors attend a stocktake they should do the following:

- ▶ observe that the controls within the stocktaking instructions are being adhered to
- ▶ test counts of stock counted and stock to be counted by the stock count team
- ▶ inspect goods to make notes of any obsolete or damaged stock
- ▶ gather cut-off details such as goods received notes to be followed up after the stocktake
- ▶ ensure exclusion of third-party stock.

6   Auditors need to attend a stocktake in order to confirm the existence of stock and that it has been accurately counted. The Practice Monitoring Unit at the Association regard the attendance at a stocktake to be a very important part of the audit process.

7   Cut-off procedures are those procedures that are implemented by the client in order to ensure that no assets are double counted and no liabilities are omitted. For all sales made before the year end goods must either have been despatched or excluded from the stocktake. For all deliveries made before the year end an accrual should be made for the relevant liability if the invoice has not been received and posted by the year end.

8   After the stocktake auditors should do the following:

- ▶ follow up all test counts
- ▶ ensure exclusion of damaged or slow-moving stock
- ▶ perform cut-off tests as in 7 above and 14 below
- ▶ ensure that all stock sheets have been accounted for
- ▶ investigate any significant differences between the physical stockcount and the stock record.

9   Costs can be defined as being all costs incurred in bringing the product to its present condition (direct material, direct labour and attributable overheads) and location (carriage and insurance).

10   Net realisable value can be defined in one of two ways:

- ▶ *For raw materials and finished goods* The estimated disposal proceeds that will be realised from the sale of the product in the ordinary course of business, less any selling expenses.
- ▶ *For work in progress* The estimated disposal proceeds that will be realised from the sale of the finished product in the ordinary course of business, less estimated costs of completion and selling expenses.

11   Auditors will do the following when verifying the cost of raw materials in a manufacturing company:

- ▶ select a sample of raw material from stock records
- ▶ assuming a FIFO basis, analyse the stock between the relevant goods received notes
- ▶ agree the stock cost from goods received notes to suppliers' invoices
- ▶ test-check the casts and extensions of the raw material stock record.

12   Auditors will do the following to check the net realisable value of raw materials in a manufacturing company:

- ▶ identify slow-moving, obsolete and damaged stock and ensure that adequate provision is being made to adjust to the relevant scrap value
- ▶ check that the finished product into which the raw material is being incorporated is sold at a gross profit during the post-balance sheet period.

If the finished product is sold at a gross profit the auditor can assume that the net realisable value of the raw material is higher than cost and therefore cost will be used as the basis of balance sheet valuation.

13 Auditors should check the net realisable value of a finished product by:

▶ identifying slow-moving, obsolete and damaged finished products and ensuring that adequate provisions are made to reduce valuation
▶ checking the after-date sale proceeds and if higher than cost, cost will form the basis of the balance sheet valuation.

14 Auditors would check the accuracy of the purchase cut off procedures in the following ways:

▶ Selecting a sample of goods received notes to ensure completeness of population by checking sequential numbering.
▶ Matching the goods received notes with the corresponding invoices to ensure that full provision for the liability has been made within the financial statements at the year end. If no invoice has been received an estimate of the liability should be accrued.
▶ Similarly, purchase invoices should be matched to goods received notes before the year end.
▶ The above test should be repeated after the year end.

15 If goods are returned after the year end during the post-balance sheet period the following adjustments should be made:

DR	Sales	XX	
CR	Returns provision		XX
DR	Stock in balance sheet	XX	
CR	Stock in profit and loss		XX

The stock adjustments should be done at the lower of cost and net realisable value.

16 To adjust standard cost to actual cost all adverse variances should be added and all favourable variances should be deducted from the standard. However, it would be imprudent to add adverse variances to the standard cost if these adverse variances were caused by inefficiency or wastage. To do so would be to increase the value of stock and therefore increase the net worth of the company because of inefficiency.

17 Auditors would verify standard cost by doing the following:

▶ agree material usage to product specification
▶ review management's past accuracy in producing product specifications
▶ once the usage has been determined, check standard cost of each type of raw material to suppliers' price lists
▶ the labour hours per product will be incorporated within the product specification but can be checked to time and motion studies
▶ the labour rate will be agreed with union agreements
▶ the final standard cost calculated will be agreed to the standard costing cards.

18 Auditors must consider the following when verifying the attributable overheads included within the stock valuation:

▶ that the correct overheads have been included within the attributable overhead definition
▶ that the overhead is being absorbed on the basis of normal production activity levels.

19 A long-term contract is usually one that will extend for a period exceeding one year. However, a duration exceeding one year is not an essential feature of a long-term contract. Some contracts with a duration shorter than one year should be accounted for as long-term contracts – those that are sufficiently material to the activity of the period and that not to record turnover and attributable profit would lead to a distortion of the period's turnover and results, such that the financial statements would not give a true and fair view.

20 Auditors should verify long-term contracts in the following ways:

▶ Ascertain, evaluate and compliance test the system of internal control relating to:
   – the authorisation of invoices for material and time records for wages
   – the recording and accounting controls over the allocation of cost to the various contracts.

Most of the compliance testing will be performed at the interim audit.

▶ At the year end auditors:
   – discuss the contracts with the directors to ascertain whether there are any foreseeable problems
   – inspect the contracts to confirm the contract prices
   – perform analytical review, checking costs to date for various areas of each contract to the individual contract budgets
   – visit sites (where relevant) to confirm the degree of completion of the work in progress; it may be necessary to require assistance from an independent expert
   – check the component parts of the attributable profit calculation
   – agree costs to date to contract account

- agree estimated total cost to budget; this needs to be checked carefully: (review management's past estimating success; compare budget to date with actual to date; review completed contracts to determine level of rectification costs)
- agree estimated profit to contract price less estimated total costs
- review post-balance sheet events to ensure that the contracts are continuing according to plan
- check cut-off procedures ensuring that all costs incurred before the year end have been accrued; this can be achieved by agreeing delivery notes to after-date invoices and generally reviewing after-date invoices especially from subcontractors
- request inclusion within the letter of representation
- check that the long-term contracts have been properly disclosed in accordance with the Companies Act and SSAP 9 (Revised).

CHAPTER 6 *Exam style question*

1   *Athos Ltd*

a) *Balance sheet amounts at 31 July 1991 under the provisions of SSAP 9*

Assumption: Attributable profit is recognised on long-term contracts for the first time in the year to 31 July 1991 and on a cost-based as opposed to a value-based approach.

Contract	A	B	C
	£ 000	£ 000	£ 000
Tender value	1,700	2,100	875
Costs to date	(910)	(1,500)	(222)
Future costs to complete	(545)	(495)	(666)
Estimated profit/(loss)	245	105	(13)
Percentage complete – costs to date/total estimated costs	62.54%	75.19%	25.00%
Foreseeable loss – provided for in full			(13)
Attributable profit –			
62.54% × £245	153		
75.19% × £105		79	

Long-term contracts:

				Balance sheet value £ 000
Costs to date	910	1,500	222	
Foreseeable loss			(13)	
Attributable profit	153	79		
	1,063	1,579	209	2,851
Progress payments received and receivable	(757)	(1,579)	(200)	(2,536)
	306	–	9	315

Creditors – payments on account:
Excess progress payments on Contract B (1,650 – 1,579)   £71
Debtors – amounts receivable on Contract B (1,650 – 1,600)   £50

b) Profit and loss and balance sheet amounts for the year ended 31 July 1991 under the provisions of the revised SSAP 9

Using a cost-based approach – assumption above – turnover is recognised as 'an appropriate proportion of total contract value', that is, the percentage of the total contract value completed in the year; the cost of sales is the cost incurred in reaching that stage of completion so as to result in the reporting of results that can be attributed to the proportion of work completed.

Contract	A	B	C	Profit and loss account
	£000	£000	£000	£000
Turnover				
62.54% × 1,700	1,063			
75.19% × 2,100		1,579		
25.00% × 875			219	2,861
Cost of sales				
62.54% × 1,455	(910)			
75.19% × 1,995		(1,500)		
25.00% × 888			(222)	(2,632)
Additional provision			(10)	(10)
Gross profit	153	79	(13)	219

	A	B	C	Balance sheet value £ 000
Long-term contracts:				
Costs to date	910	1,500	222	2,632
Costs transferred to cost of sales	(910)	(1,500)	(222)	(2,632)
–	–	–	–	
Creditors – payments on account in excess of turnover		71		
Provision			10	
Debtors – trade		50		
Recoverable on long-term contracts – turnover in excess of payments on account	306		19	

c) *The background to the development of the revised SSAP 9 and the likely practical advantages and disadvantages of its provisions to preparers and users of financial statements*

In November 1986 the ASC published ED 40, which proposed a revision to SSAP 9 – Stocks and Work in Progress. The main reason for the proposed revision of the accounting standard was to remove the apparent conflict with the Companies Act 1985 in respect of the balance sheet presentation of long-term contracts.

Paragraph 27 of SSAP 9 required long-term contract work in progress to be entered in a balance sheet at 'cost plus any attributable profit, less any foreseeable losses and progress payments received and receivable'. Conversely, the Companies Act 1985 requires that 'the amount to be included in respect of any current asset shall be its purchase price or production cost' or its net realisable value if lower. The conflict, therefore, arose in respect of the profit element.

Practices adopted to deal with the conflict in published accounts did vary, but most companies invoked the true and fair override to justify the inclusion of the profit element. There were, however, two problems with this approach. First, that the true and fair override should not be used as a general solution, but only in the specific circumstances of a particular company. Second, even where it is invoked, its use requires particulars of departure, along with reasons and effect, to be disclosed in the notes of the accounts. Opinion was divided on the practicability of providing adequate disclosure of 'the effect of the departure', but the balance of opinion among preparers was that no meaningful information could be provided. In seeking to eliminate the profit element from the balance sheet value of long-term contracts, ED 40 removed both the problem of departure from the Act and the seemingly intractable problem of attempting to quantify the effect of the departure. These are the main results of the revised SSAP 9.

A second reason for the development of the revised standard arises from the fact that SSAP 9 did not address the problem as to how contract sales revenue and related costs should be reported in the profit and loss account. In many cases this was not derived from a formal integration of revenue, cost and balance sheet accounting. International practice, as set out in IAS 11, takes an alternative approach, which ED 40 put forward for use in the UK. Under this approach revenue is recognised as the contract activity progresses. The costs incurred in reaching the stage of completion are matched with this revenue, resulting in the reporting of results which can be attributed to the proportion of work completed. The revised SSAP 9 achieves standardisation of disclosure in this respect.

A third reason for the development of the revised standard arose from the view that SSAP 9, in distinguishing short-term from long-term contracts, and in not permitting profit to be recognised on short-term contracts until completion, was too prudent. ED 40, in proposing a revised definition of long-term contracts, seemed to permit a company with mainly long-term contracts to account for any of its short-term contracts in the same way, that is, using a percentage of completion method as opposed to the completion method of recognising profits on contracts. The revised SSAP 9 includes a revised definition of a contract to achieve this.

The provisions of the revised standard are advantageous to preparers of accounts in that there is no conflict with the requirements of the Act and no need to quantify the effect of departure, in the view of the DTI, the attributable profit recognised. The disadvantage arises in the additional work that this will involve. *Accountancy* reported that companies with long-term contracts were examining the position but fully agreed with SSAP 9 on the principle of including profit on long-term work in progress. There was perhaps a general reluctance to move away from SSAP 9, which was regarded as good accounting practice, and some would have preferred to continue with the present true and fair override or even a change to the Companies Act.

From the viewpoint of users of financial statements, the provisions of the revised standard are advantageous in that they result in more informative reporting of results and consistency of profit and loss treatment. Financial statements will reflect a similar treatment for similar contracts and the adoption of the revised standard would require the restatement of comparable amounts in previous years. Turnover will be meaningful for contracting companies while there is no change in the determination of attributable profits. There are, however, disadvantages in that the reclassification of some part of the SSAP 9 long-term contract balances as debtors may be misleading and make it difficult for users to appreciate a company's exposure to long-term contracting activities.

CHAPTER 7 *Self test questions*

1 Corporation tax on income is ascertained on the basis of fiscal rules as opposed to accounting rules for the pre-tax profit included in the profit and loss account. This gives rise to an effective tax rate that differs from the corporation tax rate. Other reasons for the difference arise from accounting for tax under UK accounting standards. Thus, under SSAP 8 the tax charge may include irrecoverable ACT and under SSAP 15 (Revised) only a partial as opposed to a full provision is made for deferred tax.

2 The different basis of arriving at profits for tax purposes derives from two main sources:

▶ Certain types of income are tax free and certain types of expenditure are disallowable, giving rise to 'permanent' differences between taxable and accounting profits. Permanent differences also arise where there are tax allowances with no corresponding amount in the accounts.
▶ There are items that are included in the financial statements of a period different from that in which they are dealt with for tax purposes, giving rise to timing differences. Thus, revenues, gains, expenditure and losses may be included in financial statements either earlier or later than they enter into the computation of profit for tax purposes, for example, accelerated capital allowances, development costs capitalised and trading and capital losses.

Accordingly, the following points arise:

▶ permanent differences will always result in an effective rate of tax which differs from the corporation tax rate
▶ timing differences may or may not result in an effective tax rate which differs from the corporation tax rate, depending on whether or not deferred tax is provided and, if so, on the extent to which it is provided.

3 If deferred is not provided – nil provision – the effective rate of tax will be different from the actual corporation tax rate. If it is fully provided – comprehensive allocation – timing differences will not give rise to a difference between the effective and corporation tax rates.

However, such tax is provided for in accordance with SSAP 15 (Revised) only if it is probable that a deferred tax asset or liability will crystallise in future periods. Because the SSAP 15 (Revised) provision is based on an assessment of what will actually be the position – partial provision – this third basis of accounting for deferred tax is held to be preferable. Accordingly, there will, usually, be a difference between the effective and actual corporation tax rates given standard accounting practice regarding deferred tax.

4 The 'flow through' approach involves accounting only for the tax that is actually payable for each year. Deferred tax arising each year is left alone to flow through into the actual tax payable in a future year. 'Comprehensive allocation' involves providing in each year for the future tax effects of all timing differences arising in the year. The 'partial provision' approach is based on providing in each year, for the tax effects of only those timing differences arising in the year, which will crystallise in future years.

5 If you account for pension costs in a pension plan where there is no external funding, the annual cost recognised under SSAP 24 would have to be provided for each year under provisions in the balance sheet. Similar provisions would arise in accounting for other post-retirement benefits under UITF 6.

Such provisions represent, in deferred tax terms, future tax recoverable on tax which is effectively prepaid when the provisions are set up. These provisions will tend to be ever increasing and any reduction will tend to be more than matched with new provisions being made.

If the deferred tax (recoverable in the long term) on such provisions is accounted for under the partial provision approach of SSAP 15 (Revised) it is unlikely, given the relatively short time frame involved in looking at setting up a partial provision, that any deferred tax will be recognised in respect of such provisions.

It is for this reason that FRED 2 permits full provision to be made for the tax recoverable on such pension and other post-retirement benefits provisions

1 *Deftax Ltd*

 a) Deferred tax provision at 30 June 1990 and 1991 and deferred tax to be included in the tax on profit on ordinary activities for the year ended 30 June 1991 so as to comply with the requirements of SSAP 15 (Revised):

 (All amounts in £000)

 i) Full potential deferred tax:

	30 June 1990			30 June 1991	
	Payable	Recoverable		Payable	Recoverable
	£000	£000		£000	£000
Accelerated capital allowances	350		− 67	283	
Provision for deferred repairs		60	+10		70
Interest payable		−	+6		6
	350	60		283	76
	(60)			(76)	
	290			207	
	35%			30%	
	101.5			62.1	

 Full potential deferred tax payable on accelerated capital allowances alone amounts to: at

30 June 1990 – 350 @ 35%	122.5	
30 June 1991 – 283 @ 30%	84.9	

 ii) Deferred tax that would have been included in the tax on profit on ordinary activities for the year ended 30 June 1991 if a full provision for deferred tax had been made:

	£000
At 1 July 1990 290 @ 35%	101.5
Reduction in opening provision given a change in the rate of tax (and the use of the liability method)	(14.5)
	87
At 1 July 1990 re-stated 290 @ 30%	
Release of provision in year	(24.9)
At 30 June 1991	62.1

 The total deferred tax for the year would, therefore, have amounted to a credit in the tax on profit on ordinary activities for the year ended 30 June 1991 of (14.5 + 24.9) = £39.4.

 iii) Provision (partial) required at 30 June 1990:

 Taking accelerated timing differences in isolation:

	Capital allowances > Depreciation (tax benefit)	Depreciation > Capital allowances (adverse tax effect)	Cumulative timing difference
Forecast y/e	£000	£000	£000
30/6/91		(67)	(67)
30/6/92	170		103
30/6/93		(92)	11
30/6/94		(73)	(62)
30/6/95		(60)	(122)

 Based on the maximum cumulative reversing timing difference foreseen, taking this one timing difference in isolation, the provision required at 30 June 1990 is 122 @ 35% = £42.7.

Taking all (trading) timing differences together:

(tax benefit = +; adverse tax effect = −)	1991 £000	1992 £000	1993 £000	1994 £000	1995 £000
Accelerated capital allowances					
Capital allowances > Depreciation (benefit)		170			
Depreciation > Capital allowances (adverse)	(67)		(92)	(73)	(60)
Provision for deferred repairs					
Decrease (benefit)		16	12		6
Increase (adverse)	(10)			(15)	
Net effect of all timing differences	(77)	186	(80)	(88)	(54)
Cumulative net effect	(77)	109	29	(59)	(113)

The deferred tax provision required at 30 June 1990, based on the maximum cumulative reversing timing differences foreseen is 113 @ 35% = £39.55.

iv) Provision (partial) required at 30 June 1991:

Taking accelerated capital allowances in isolation:

	Capital allowances > Depreciation (tax benefit)	Depreciation > Capital allowances (adverse tax effect)	Cumulative timing difference
Forecast y/e		£000	£000
30/6/92		(96)	(96)
30/6/93		(70)	(166)
30/6/94		(68)	(234)
30/6/95	140		(94)

Based on the maximum cumulative reversing timing difference foreseen, taking this one timing difference in isolation, the provision required at 30 June 1991 is 234 @ 30% = £70.2.

Taking all (trading) timing differences together:

	1992 £000	1993 £000	1994 £000	1995 £000
Accelerated capital allowances				
Capital allowances > Depreciation (benefit)				140
Depreciation > Capital allowances (adverse)	(96)	(70)	(68)	
Provision for deferred repairs				
Decrease (benefit)	16	12		6
Increase (adverse)			(15)	
Interest				
Paid (benefit)	6	6	6	6
Payable (adverse)	(6)	(6)	(6)	(6)
Net effect of all timing differences	(80)	(58)	(83)	146
Cumulative net effect	(80)	(138)	(221)	(75)

Based on the maximum cumulative reversing timing differences foreseen, the deferred tax provision required at 30 June 1991 is 221 @ 30% = £66.3.

v) The deferred tax included in tax on profit on ordinary activities for the year ended 30 June 1991:

On re-statement of opening provision given a change in the rate of tax (given the liability method of accounting for deferred tax)

		£
$5/35 \times 39.55 =$	Credit	5.65
Provision for year – comparison of restated opening provision – 113 @ 30% = £33.9 with the closing provision of £66.3	Debit	32.40
	Net debit	26.75

b) Disclosure notes:

i) Accounting policy:
Deferred tax is provided for under the liability method of accounting for deferred tax to the extent that a liability to future tax on the reversal of the net tax effects of timing differences, taken together, is expected to crystallise. To the extent that no tax effect is expected to crystallise, no provision is made.

ii) Movements on the deferred tax provision during the year to 30 June 1991:

	£000
At 1 July 1990	39.55
Release of deferred tax provision on a change in the rate of corporation tax from 35% to 30%	(5.65)
At 1 July 1990 restated	33.9
Deferred tax provided in year	32.4
At 30 June 1991	66.3

iii) Deferred tax provided in the financial statements, and the total potential liability including the amounts for which provision has been made are as follows:

Principal categories of timing difference	Full potential deferred tax		Provision made		Provision not made	
	1991 £000	1990 £000	1991 £000	1990 £000	1991 £000	1990 £000
Accelerated capital allowances	84.9	122.5	70.2	42.7	14.7	79.8
Other	(22.8)	(21.0)	(3.9)	(3.15)	(18.9)	(17.85)
	62.1	101.5	66.3	39.55	(4.2)	61.95

iv) If deferred tax had been fully provided for, the reported amount of tax on profit on ordinary activities would have been reduced by (and reported earnings increased by) 39.4 + 26.75 = £66.15.

CHAPTER 8   *Self test questions*

1   No contributions are paid out of the company and Leroy's pension benefit is defined even though, as it is based on his salary in his final year of employment, it is yet unknown. Leroy's pension is, therefore, an unfunded defined benefit scheme.

2
	£m
Regular cost	2.5
Variation – deficiency £5m/10 years	0.5
	3.0

3   The profit and loss account charge for pension cost for Furtado plc for the ten years to 31 December 2004 will be:

£1.5m + (£15m/10 years) = £3m

For the year ended 31 December 1995:

	£m	£m
DR Profit and loss account	3.0	
CR Cash (£5m + £1.5m)		6.5
DR Prepayment	3.5	

4   The pension cost of Bunty plc of the year ended 31 December 1994:

£100m − (£600m/12 years) = £50 million

5   The four ways in which a pension fund surplus may be applied are:

▶ for the benefit of the employee by increasing the benefits payable as pensions
▶ for the benefit of the employer by a long-term reduction in contributions (and therefore, cost)
▶ for the benefit of the employer by the employer taking a short-term contribution holiday
▶ for the benefit of the employer by the employer clawing back the contributions paid from its pension scheme.

The last two ways give rise to an accounting problem.

The SSAP 24 treatment in a contribution holiday situation is to spread the benefit of the surplus forward over average remaining service lives of existing employees. The SSAP 24 treatment when the company takes a cash refund from its pension scheme is either:

i)   DR cash
     CR pension cost

as and when the refund is received or, more in line with the SSAP 24 treatment of variations generally,

ii)   DR cash
      CR deferred income

and release the deferred income to the profit and loss account over average remaining service lives of existing employees.

CHAPTER 8   *Exam style question*

1   MEMORANDUM
     To: Managing Director
     From: Chief Accountant
     Re: Accounting for pension costs
     Date:
     The effect on the results for the year ending 31 December 1988 of adopting SSAP 24 and contrasting the effect with other currently available accounting treatments for the pension costs:

Many companies have, until now, simply charged the contributions payable to the pension scheme as the pension cost in each accounting period. In order to comply with SSAP 24, it will be necessary to consider whether the 'funding plan' provides a satisfactory basis for allocating the 'pension cost' to particular accounting periods.

As, from the viewpoint of the employee, a pension may be regarded as deferred remuneration, from the viewpoint of the employer it is part of the cost incurred in obtaining the employee's services. The accounting objective of SSAP 24 therefore requires employers to recognise the cost of providing pensions on a systematic and rational basis over the period during which they benefit from the service of employees. Consequently, the charge against profits may differ from the contributions paid or payable in an accounting period. The standard states that the method of providing for pension costs should be such that the normal or regular pension cost is a substantially level percentage of the current and expected future pensionable payroll. The long-term regular cost of the company has been indicated by the company's actuaries to be £1 million per annum.

An experience surplus is part of the ongoing process of revising the estimate of the ultimate liabilities that will fall on the employer. In line with SSAP 24, any effect on the cost should normally be taken into account by adjusting the current and future costs charged in the accounts and should not be treated as a prior year adjustment.

In accordance with the accounting objective, the normal period over which the effect of material surpluses should be spread is the expected remaining service lives of the current employees in the scheme.

If the company were to simply charge the contributions payable as the pension cost in each period the effect on the results for the year ending 31 December 1988 (and, for tutorial purposes, for later years) would be:

All amounts in £000s

	88 £	89 £	90 £	91 £	92 £	93 £	94 £	95 £	96 £	97 £	98 £	99 £	TOTAL £
Pension cost	600	nil	360	960	960	960	960	960	960	960	960	960	9,600

Alternatively, the company could continue to pay £1.2 million in 1988 and treat that amount as pension cost for the year. In this case:

	88 £	89 £	90 £	91 £	92 £	93 £	94 £	95 £	96 £	97 £	98 £	99 £	TOTAL £
Pension cost	1,200	nil	nil	720	960	960	960	960	960	960	960	960	9,600

The above treatments would be acceptable under SSAP 24 if the surplus arose as a result of a significant reduction in the number of employees but not as the result of a closure of a material business segment. Assuming that this is not the reason for the surplus, SSAP 24 would require the effect to be spread over average remaining lives. Thus the annual pension cost should be £1,000 less £2,400/12 years or £800 per annum.
Accordingly, the effect on results would be:

	88 £	89 £	90 £	91 £	92 £	93 £	94 £	95 £	96 £	97 £	98 £	99 £	TOTAL £
Pension cost	800	800	800	800	800	800	800	800	800	800	800	800	9,600

(Movements on pension provision,

91 to 99 (960 – 800) × 9	1,400	88 (800 – 600)	200
		89 (800 – nil)	800
		90 (800 – 360)	440
	1,440		1,440

Only £360 would be paid in 1990 as £600 has already been prepaid in 1988.)

(Note: If the surplus arises as the result of a significant reduction in the number of employees covered by the company's pension scheme it may not be appropriate to defer recognition of the pension cost credit which should be dealt with as part of the exceptional item arising on the closure.)

Lastly, if the company were to deal with the surplus by way of a refund from the pension scheme under the provisions of the Finance Act 1986, the company may, under SSAP 24, recognise the refund in the period in which it occurs.

By way of conclusion, the SSAP 24 treatment seeks to avoid the volatility that may be involved in charging against profits the contributions actually made in the year, which in the case of a contribution holiday would be nil.

CHAPTER 9   *Self test questions*

1   Adjusting events are post balance sheet events that provide additional evidence of conditions existing at the balance sheet date. They include events that because of statutory or conventional requirements are reflected in financial statements.

A contingency is a condition that exists at the balance sheet date where the outcome will be confirmed only on the occurrence or non-occurrence of one or more uncertain future events. A contingent gain or loss is a gain or loss dependent on a contingency.

2   TR 603 defines off balance sheet finance as: 'the funding or refinancing of a company's operations in such a way that, under legal requirements and existing accounting conventions, some or all of the finance may not be shown on its balance sheet.'

3   The reasons for entering into transactions that can give rise to off balance sheet finance include:

    1   to maintain a low level of gearing
    2   to prevent high gearing, which is seen as an indication of the need for new finance by way of a rights issue with an adverse effect on share price
    3   to match borrowings with the cost of non-income generating assets, which are in the process of being developed and remove both the asset and the liability from the balance sheet.
    4   to place activities with high gearing ratios such as financial services off balance sheet perhaps by treating such activities as being conducted by dissimilar subsidiaries to be excluded from consolidation.

4   A quasiy subsidiary of a reporting entity is a company, trust, partnership or other vehicle which, though not fulfilling the definition of a subsidiary, is directly or indirectly controlled by the reporting entity and represents a source of benefit inflows or outflows for that entity that are in substance no different from those that would arise were the vehicle a subsidiary.

Such vehicles can give rise to off balance sheet finance in that (assets and) liabilities transferred to them by the investor company would not feature in the investor's consolidated balance sheet as such vehicles are not subsidiaries and, legally, are not consolidated.

FRED 4 proposes that the assets, liabilities, profits, losses and cash flows of a quasi subsidiary should be included in the group accounts of the group that controls it in the same way as if they were those of a subsidiary.

5   The three possible ways of reflecting sale and repurchase transactions in the accounts of an entity under FRED 4 are:

    1   as a secured loan by showing the asset and the liability in the balance sheet
    2   a sale
    3   where a new asset arises, by recording the fair value of the new asset, together with any new liability arising.

CHAPTER 9   *Exam style question*

The effect on key ratios and performance measures are detailed below.

Return on capital employed

Whether capital employed is defined as shareholders' funds plus all debt (total assets) or as total long-term funds, the omission of assets and corresponding liabilities will lower the value of the denominator and hence raise the return on capital employed.

This distorts the true position because the assets remain under the control of the company (or group) and remain part of the operating capacity through which profits are generated.

Gearing

Debt: Debt plus equity – There will be a decrease in both the numerator and the denominator by the same absolute amount and, thus, a decrease in the gearing percentage.

Debt: Equity – The numerator will decrease but the denominator will remain unchanged, giving an even more marked decrease in the gearing percentage.

Working capital

This may be measured either gross (equivalent to current assets) or net (by reference to current assets net of current liabilities). In either event, reclassication of a subsidiary as an associate company (or subsidiaries excluded from consolidation but accounted for under the equity method) will result in omission of that subsidiary's assets and liabilities from the balance sheet. This would be despite the fact that the working capital omitted would still be part of the operating capacity of the group.

Profit before tax

Many off balance sheet schemes do not affect net profits. Where the equity method is used instead of consolidation, the group's share of the subsidiary's (or effective subsidiary's) profits is included in pre-tax profit. If, however, a subsidiary was transformed into an associate by putting 50% of the equity in the hands of a friendly third party, only 50% of the associate's profits or losses would be included in pre-tax profits rather than the 100% that would appear in the case of a subsidiary.

Further, in a scheme of stock financing where the loan secured on the stock is repaid as the stock is sold, pre-tax profit could be distorted, if not affected in net terms. This is because the whole of the cost of repayment might be charged to cost of goods sold in operating profit rather than making a sub-division into the true cost of the stock sold and the element of interest charged on funds provided.

Note: Re off balance sheet schemes generally, even with full disclosure (without recognition) it would be difficult to judge the current and future performance of a group carrying out such transactions.

CHAPTER 10 *Self test questions*

1   Accounting policy:
Leased assets:
Where assets are financed by leasing agreements that give rights approximating to ownership – finance leases – the assets are treated as if they had been purchased outright. The amount capitalised is the present value of the minimum lease payments payable during the lease term.

The corresponding leasing commitments are shown as obligations to the lessor. Depreciation on the relevant assets is charged to the profit and loss account over the lease term.

Lease payments are treated as consisting of capital and interest elements, and the interest is charged to the profit and loss account using the [state method] method.

All other leases are operating leases, and the annual rentals are charged to the profit and loss account on a straight-line basis over the lease term.

2   Cash flow summary – actuarial post-tax method of recognising gross earnings:

Period	NCI at start of period £000	Cost/tax £000	Rentals £000	Average NCI in the period £000	Profit taken out of the lease £000	NCI at end of period £000
1/94	–	(5,000)	800	(4,200)	(227)	(4,427)
2/94	(4,427)		800	(3,627)	(196)	(3,823)
			1,600		(423)	
1/95	(3,823)		800	(3,023)	(163)	(3,186)
2/95	(3,186)		800	(2,386)	(129)	(2,515)
			1,600		(292)	
1/96	(2,515)	(123)	800	(1,838)	(99)	(1,937)
2/96	(1,937)		800	(1,137)	(61)	(1,198)
			1,600		(160)	
1/97	(1,198)	(232)	800	(630)	(34)	(664)
2/97	(664)		800	136	7	143
			1,600		(27)	
1/98	143	(314)	(171)		(9)	(180)
2/98	(180)			(180)	(10)	(190)
1/99	(190)	178		(12)	12	rounding error
Cost		(5,000)	6,400		(7)	
Tax		(491)				
				Profit	909	

Taxation for 1994 35% × (1,600 less 1,250) 123
1995 35% × (1,600 less 938) 232
1996 35% × (1,600 less 703 314
1997 35% × (1,600 less 2,109 178 benefit

3   Summarised profit and loss accounts

	1994	1995	1996
	£000	£000	£000
Gross earnings	651	449	246
Taxation Corporation Tax	(123)	(232)	(314)
Deferred tax	(105)	75	228
Profit after taxation	423	292	160

Gross earnings are simply 100/65 of profit after taxation, which is the 'profit taken out of the lease' per the cash flow summary; deferred tax is a balancing item.

4   Amounts receivable under financial lease obligations: (in £000)
1994 – Capital repayment – (1,600 less 651) £949
Balance sheet debtor – (5,000 less 949) £4,051
1995 – (1,600 less 449) 1,151 (4,051 less 1,151) £2,900
1996 – (1,600 less 246) 1,354 (2,900) less 1,354) £1,546

5   It used to be common practice in dealing with profits or losses on sale and leaseback transactions in the financial statements of a seller/lessee to recognise the profit or loss immediately as an extraordinary item in the profit and loss account. Following SSAP 21, in accounting for the profit or loss on such a sale, regard must be had to i) the leaseback in terms of finance or operating leases and ii) whether or not the transaction was at arm's length.

If the leaseback results in a finance lease, the seller continues to enjoy all the rewards and bears the risks of ownership. Given no change in this regard, it would be inappropriate to account for any profit or loss on the sale immediately. Such amounts relate to the remaining period of use of the asset and should be spread over such periods. The depreciation on the asset would then be consistent with the carrying value of the asset before the leaseback.

If the leaseback results in an operating lease, profit or loss on the sale should be recognised immediately if the transaction is at arm's length, but not otherwise. In the latter case, selling price will be either above or below market value, resulting in either higher than current market rentals or lower than current market rentals. The profit/loss on the sale should be related to these above or below market rentals in the profit and loss account each year.

The rules may be summarised as follows:

▶ If sale proceeds are greater than fair value: spread this amount of the gain over the period to the next rent review, but recognise the balance of the total profit on the sale immediately.

▶ If sale proceeds are less than fair value: recognise the loss in full if the loss is a result of a poor bargain, but otherwise spread the loss over the period to the next review so that it is matched in the profit and loss account with the lower than market rental.

CHAPTER 10 *Exam style questions*

1   *Thexton M. Thexton*

AR Countants & Co
Owen House
London EC1

29 November 1993

Thexton M. Thexton
112 Auditors' Avenue
London WY 240

Dear Mr Thexton

Accounting for lease income by lessor companies

Thank you for your recent letter requesting clarification as to the application of the accounting policy of your client company in arriving at income in the profit and loss account based on the net cash investment in the lease during each period. I would make the following points by way of reply:

1   *General principles underlying income recognition by lessors*

The accounting standard on leasing, SSAP 21, requires that income from finance leases be allocated over the lease term in such a manner as to produce a constant periodic rate of return on the net cash investment in the lease. The principle underlying this requirement is sometimes referred to as the investment period principle. The objective is to apportion gross earnings, or the finance charges relating to a lease, in such a way that income is properly matched with expense. There are two methods available to achieve such an apportionment, the 'actuarial post-tax method' and the 'investment period method'.

The basis of the actuarial post-tax method is that the lessor's anticipated after-tax net profit is removed from the lease cash flows in such a way that it represents a constant periodic rate of return on the lessor's net cash investment in the lease.

The allocation of gross earnings to each accounting period is then derived from working backwards from a forecast and loss account based on the forecast lease cash flows.

2   *Application of general principles in the hypothetical situation of Michael plc – see example attached (per question).*

i)   The first step would be to construct a table so as to ascertain the net cash investment in each period and the amount of profit to be taken out of the lease in each period. For Michael plc this would be as follows:

Period	NCI at beginning of period	Capital cost	Rental	Tax	Average NCI during period	Profit taken out of lease	NCI at end of period
	£	£	£	£	£	£	£
12/92		(54,000)	9,450	–	(44,550)	(3,506)	(48,056)
6/93	(48,056)		9,450		(38,606)	(3,038)	(41,644)
						6,544	
12/93	(41,644)		9,450		(32,194)	(2,534)	(34,728)
6/94	(34,728)		9,450		(25,278)	(1,989)	(27,267)
						4,523	
12/94	(27,267)		9,450	(1,890)	(19,707)	(1,551)	(21,528)
6/95	(21,528)		9,450		(11,808)	(929)	(12,737)
						2,480	
12/95	(12,737)		9,450	(3,071)	(6,358)	(500)	(6,858)
6/96	(6,858)		9,450		2,592	203	2,795
						297	
12/96	2,795			(3,957)	(1,162)	(91)	(1,253)
6/97	(1,253)				(1,253)	(99)	(1,352)
						190	
12/97	(1,352)			1,358	6 rounding	(6)	nil
						6	
	Cost	(54,000)	75,600			14,040	Profit
	Tax	(7,560)					

Tax:

For the year ended

				£
30/6/1993	(18,900 – 13,500)	× 35%	1,890	payable
30/6/1994	(18,900 – 10,125)	× 35%	3,071	payable
30/6/1995	(18,900 – 7,594)	× 35%	3,957	payable
30/6/1996	(18,900 – 22,781)	× 35%	1,358	recoverable

ii)   It is now possible to construct summary profit and loss accounts for each of the years ended 30 June to 1996 as follows:

	1993 £	1994 £	1995 £	1996 £
Rentals	18,900	18,900	18,900	18,900
Capital repayment	(8,832)	(11,942)	(15,085)	(18,443)
Gross earnings	10,068	6,958	3,815	457
Tax – Corporation Tax	1,890 DR	3,071 DR	3,957 DR	1,358 CR
Deferred tax	1,634 DR	636 CR	2,622 CR	1,518 DR
Profit after tax	6,544	4,523	2,480	297

iii)   Amounts to be included as debtors in the balance sheets as at each year end can now be determined as follows:

	Balance sheet debtors		**Post-tax rate of return**
y/e 30 June 1993	(54,000 – 8,832)	= £45,168	£6,544/45,168 = 14%
y/e 30 June 1994	(45,168 – 11,941)	= £33,226	£4,523/33,226 = 14%
y/e 30 June 1995	(33,226 – 15,085)	= £18,141	(£2,480/18,141 = 14%
y/e 30 June 1996	(18,141 – 18,443)		
	(less rounding)		

I hope that this explains matters. If you have any further points on which you need clarification please write again.

Yours sincerely,

2 *Troon plc*

a) Explanation of the accounting treatment adopted and schedule of charges and credits to the profit and loss account:

Fixed asset 1: It is inappropriate to recognise the whole of any profit or loss on the sale in the year of sale. The company continues to enjoy the rights and bear the risks of ownership following the sale and subsequent finance leaseback of the asset. Any gain on the sale should be spread over the period of the finance lease. Tutorial note – There are two ways in which this may be achieved:

▶ *either* i) The company could account for the disposal
    – eliminate the asset
    – ascertain the gain on disposal and recognise the gain over the eight-year lease term
    – capitalise the asset leased back at the fair value to the lessor (the sale price)
    – depreciate the capitalised asset and account for the finance charges arising.

▶ *or* ii) The company could retain the sold asset in the books and continue to depreciate it as before. The sale proceeds would be credited to finance lease creditors in the balance sheet and finance charges accounted for as normal.

However accounted for, the net effect on profits would be the same and any 'gain' on the 'sale' would effectively be spread over the period of the finance lease. The latter procedure – ii) above – would seem to be more in keeping with the spirit of ED 42 and ED 49 and, now, FRED 4.

Fixed assets 2, 3, 4 and 5: The asset should be eliminated and any profit or loss on sale should be recognised in full in the year of sale given the operating leaseback unless the transaction is not at arm's length.

▶ If sale proceeds are greater than fair value, this part of the gain should be spread over the period to the next rent review.
▶ If sale proceeds are less than fair value, three situations need to be distinguished:

  1 if the loss is the result of a bad bargain it should be recognised in full in the year of sale
  2 if the transaction is not at arm's length, the lower than normal sale proceeds will be matched with lower than normal rentals and it is appropriate to spread the loss over the period to the next rent review, effectively charging an arm's length rental against profits
  3 if a profit arises on sale (fixed asset 5) it should be recognised wholly in the year of sale.

b) Schedule to disclose charges and credits to the profit and loss account for the year ended 31 December 1991:

	£000
Depreciation – Fixed asset 1 only – 1st option –	
on value of capitalised asset – 1,500/8 years	187.5
– gain recognised 380/8 yrs	(47.5)
	140

2nd option – on original cost, i.e. as before – 10% × 1,400 = 140

Finance charges – Fixed asset 1 only	£000
Total = (250 × 8) less 1,500 = 500	
Total sum of digits = (8 + 1)/2 × 8 = 36	
1991 allocation = 8/36 × 500	111
Lease rentals – Fixed assets 2, 3, 4 and 5 – (170 + 155 + 150 +60)	535
Profit on sale – Fixed asset 1 – as dealt with under 1st option in depreciation above	
– Fixed asset 2 – 480 less 420 – arm's length gain	(60)
– 500 less 480/2 yrs – non arm's length	(10)
– Fixed asset 3 – 410 less 450 – loss recognised in full	40
– Fixed asset 4 – 400 less 487 = 87/2 yrs	44
– Fixed asset 5 – 138 less 130 – gain recognised in full	(8)

c) Schedule to disclose the finance lease obligation in the balance sheet at 31 December 1991:

		£000
Capital cost – sale proceeds		1,500
1991 rental		(250)
1991 finance charge – as in (a)		111
Finance lease obligation as at 31 December 1991:		1,361
Creditors: less than one year – 1992 rental	250	
– 1992 finance charge 7/36 × 500	(97)	
		153
Creditors: more than one year – the balance		1,208
		1,361

CHAPTER 11 *Self test questions*

1 According to David Tweedie, chair of the ASB, Martians walking down the street are extraordinary; everything else is ordinary.

2 Schedule to show how Pongo Ltd would be dealt with in the FRS 3 consolidated profit and loss account of the Pingo Plc group for the year ended 31 December 1994.

	Continuing operations 1994 £000	Discontinued operations 1994 £000	Continuing operations 1993 £000	Discontinued operations 1993 £000
Turnover	x	4,700	x	25,500
Operating expenses	(x)	(5,800)	(x)	(22,000)
		(1,100)		
Release of 1993 provision		2,000		
Operating profit		900		3,500
Provision for loss on operations to be discontinued $(2,000 + 1,500 + 300 - 1,100)$				(2,700)
Loss on termination $(1,500 + 350 - 900)$		(950)		
Release of 1993 provision		700		
Profit on ordinary activities before taxation		650		800

3 Revaluation and subsequent sale of revalued assets and their impact on FRS 3 financial statements:

a) Calculations:

	£000
Cost 1/1/90	800
Depreciation to 1/1/92 $800 \times \%_0$	(32)
NBV 1/1/92	768
Revaluation surplus	432
At valuation 1/1/92	1,200
Depreciation 1992 1,200/48 years	(25)
Depreciation 1993 1,200/48 years	(25)

(Additional depreciation charged in *each* year $(25 - 16) = 9$)

NBV 1/1/94	1,150
Sale proceeds February 1994	(2,000)
Sale proceeds less NBV on date of sale	850

Prior to FRS 3 there were two approaches to reporting a gain on the disposal of a previously revalued fixed asset. Either approach was permissible under SSAP 6.

Under what was called the 'income approach' (first put forward in ED 36), the gain on sale to be reported in the profit and loss account of the year of sale was 'sale proceeds less depreciated historical cost' which amounted to:

	£000
i) sale proceeds less NBV on date of sale	850
ii) the revaluation surplus on the date of revaluation	432
	1,282

The alternative approach, what was called the 'value approach' (as put forward in ED 51) differed from that above in that the gain reported in the profit and loss account was restricted to i) above only ii) above being dealt with within reserves.

Pre FRS 3, when the focus as to performance was concentrated on the profit and loss account, the approach adopted, given a choice, could have had a material impact on reporting financial performance as was.

Post FRS 3, in terms of assessing financial performance, we look not only at the profit and loss account but, taken together, also at:

▶ the statement of recognised gains/losses
▶ reconciliation of movements on shareholders' funds
▶ [if modified historical cost accounts are prepared] the statement of historical profit.

In this context, it is no longer that important what is reported in the profit and loss account and what is dealt with within reserves. Accordingly, FRS 3 requires that the gain on sale of a revalued asset be calculated and reported in the profit and loss account (exceptional item) under the 'value approach'. The extent to which the revaluation surplus becomes realised is dealt with in the statement of historical profit.

Given that one effect of using the modified historical cost convention is an impact on earnings compared with companies preparing accounts under strict historical cost, FRS 3 requires that companies using the former convention disclose a statement of historical profits or a reconciliation of profit actually arising with what it would have been had there been no revaluation of fixed assets.

In 1992 and 1993 the reason for the difference between the two profit numbers would be the additional depreciation (£9,000 per year) charged since revaluation. In 1994 the reason for the difference would be previous years' recognised gains (the revaluation surplus of £432,000) now realised on sale (432,000 − 9,000 − 9,000) £414,000.

FRS 3 reporting should, accordingly, be more useful to different users, given the more complete information set provided and a better basis for the analysis of accounts.

4   The changes to company accounts triggered by the new FRS 3 accounting standard will have a significant impact on companies' results and the whole attitude of analysts has recently been under scrutiny.

The new rules of FRS 3 will ensure that a company produces much clearer figures. These will need to be analysed by users, depending on what they themselves need to know, and it is this which clearly leaves room for debate, that is, can one single earnings figure 'do everything' or not?

The problem arises given that earnings per share figures are likely to fluctuate more widely under the new system than the old. The Rank Organisation, for example, has said that under the new accounting standard, which takes effect in June 1993, its 1992 earnings per share would have been 6.8p rather than the 37.8p it reported. This is because the new system provides that extraordinary items, previously taken below the line, now have to be included in earnings for earnings per share. Thus, distorting factors such as:

▶   costs of rationalising the business
▶   costs of disposing of operations
▶   profits/losses on sale of revalued assets

will now all be included in the earnings per share number.

City analysts James Capel has stressed that users of accounts should not rely on the sub-totals shown in the new-style profit and loss account any more than on the new volatile earnings figure.

ASB's view is that the perception that accounts could be broken down into one magic earnings per share figure should itself be broken. Only then, it argues, will people really start analysing figures with some rigour and beneficial results.

The opposite view, taken for example by Professor Skerratt of Manchester, is that the absence of a bottom line brings the profession into disrepute and that it is the function of the profession to produce these judgements. There are two routes which the analysts/preparers of accounts can follow. One is to produce their own methodology to deal with a changing world (FRS 3 permits additional disclosure of earnings per share on an alternative basis). The other is to criticise those who are trying to achieve change as Hoare Govett did in its note 'Tweedie: Descent into chaos'. They argued that Hanson's earnings for 1992, using a variety of reasonable bases were down 11, 6, or 2 per cent, or up 1, 2, 3, 8 or 10 per cent.

The BZW approach is perhaps the constructive one with which to end this discussion. It says it will begin publishing its own earnings figure alongside the reported earnings in its circulars. The figure will be reached by taking published operating profit, subtracting net interest, tax, preference dividends and adding back tax and minority interests attributable to fixed asset and business disposals, closures and restructuring. The three exceptional items which FRS 3 requires to be disclosed separately on the face of the profit and loss account will therefore be excluded from this alternative earnings per share calculation.

What is clear is that the information available will now need to be tailored for different users.

CHAPTER 11 *Exam style questions*

1 **Pringle Ltd**

	£000
Initial workings	
Cost 1/1/89	875
Depreciation to 1/1/91 ($^2/_{10} \times 875$)	(175)
NBV 1/1/91	700
Revaluation surplus	340
At valuation 1/1/91	1,040
Depreciation for 1991 (1,040/8 yrs)	(130)

[Additional depreciation, that is depreciation
based on revaluation compared with
depreciation based on historical cost,
(130 – [875/10 yrs]) amounts to £42,000]

NBV 31/12/91	910
Revaluation surplus	290
At valuation 1/1/92	1,200
Depreciation for 1992 (1,200/7 yrs)	(171)
[Additional depreciation (171–87) amounts to £84,000]	
NBV 31/12/92	1,029

	£000
The 'income approach' gain is two-fold:	
Sale proceeds less NBV on date of sale (1,450 – 1,029)	421
plus	
The whole of the revaluation surplus on the date of revaluation (340 + 290)	630
	1,051

The 'value approach' gain does not include the revaluation surplus and consists only of sale proceeds less NBV on the date of sale, that is £421,000.

a) Movements on reserves for the year ended 31 December 1991 and 1992:

i) On the basis that there is no revaluation, that is strict HCA

	Revaluation reserve £000	Profit and loss account £000	Total £000
At 1/1/91	–	5,678	5,678
1991 Profit			
– before depreciation		110	
– depreciation 875/10 yrs		(88)	
	–	22	22
At 31/12/91	–	5,700	5,700
At 1/1/92	–	5,700	5,700
1992 Profit			
– before depreciation		95	
– depreciation 875/10 yrs		(87)	
	–	8	8
At 31/12/92	–	5,708	5,708

ii) On the basis that there is revaluation, that is modified HCA:

	Revaluation reserve £000	Profit and loss account £000	Total £000
At 1/1/91	–	5,678	5,678
Revaluation	340	–	340
1991 Profit			
– before depreciation		110	
– depreciation (1,040/8 yrs)		(130)	
	–	(20)	(20)
Transfer, realised through use	(42)	42	–
At 31/12/91	298	5,700	5,998
At 1/1/92	298	5,700	5,998
Revaluation	290	–	290
1992 Profit			
– before depreciation		95	
– depreciation (1,200/7 yrs)		(171)	
	–	(76)	(76)
Transfer, realised through use	(84)	84	–
At 31/12/92	504	5,708	6,212

Following from the movements on reserves above, the points arising are:

▶ Revaluation of assets gives rise to an additional depreciation charge and, therefore, an adverse earnings impact.
▶ The revaluation reserve is, initially, an unrealised (although recognised) surplus.
▶ The revaluation reserve becomes realised through use (and, eventually, on sale – see (2) below).
▶ The extent of the revaluation reserve that becomes realised through use is the additional depreciation, arising from revaluation, that has been charged against profit.
▶ As this part of the revaluation reserve is now realised it is transferred to realised reserves (as proposed under ED 51).
▶ As a result there *is* an effect on 'earnings' but *no* effect on 'legally distributable profits'.
▶ Looking at 1992:

	strict HCA £000	modified HCA £000
Earnings	8	(76)
Legally distributable profit	5,708	5,708

b)

	£000
The gain arising on disposal	
Strict HCA [1,450 – (‰ × 875)]	925
The ED 36 income approach, as above	1,051
The ED 51/FRS 3 value approach, as above	421

Movements on reserves during 1993 would now be:
i) On the basis that there is strict HCA:

	Revaluation reserve £000	Profit and loss account £000	Total £000
At 1/1/93	–	5,708	5,708
1993 Profit			
– before gain		33	
– gain on sale		925	
At 31/12/93	–	958	958
	–	6,666	6,666

ii) On the basis-that there is modified HCA – ED 36 income approach:

	£000	£000	£000
At 1/1/93	504	5,708	6,212
Reinstatement of amounts previously transferred out of revaluation reserve	126	(126)	–
	630	5,582	
1993 Profit			
– before gain		33	
– gain on sale – SP less NBV		421	
– revaluation surplus		454	454
	(630)	630	–
		1,084	
At 31/12/93	–	6,666	6,666

iii) On the basis that there is modified HCA – FRS 3 value approach:

	£000	£000	£000
At 1/1/93	504	5,708	6,212
1993 Profit			
– before gain		33	
– gain on sale – SP less NBV		421	
	–	454	454
Transfer, realised on sale	(504)	504	–
At 31/12/93	–	6,666	6,666

Following from the movements on reserves above, the comment points arising are:

▶ Whether or not we revalue an asset there will be an effect on reported profits in the profit and loss account in the years of sale of an asset.
▶ If we revalue, reported profits in the profit and loss account will differ depending on whether we use the 'income' or 'value' approach in arriving at the gain on sale to be included in the profit and loss account.

▶ Whether or not we revalue and, if we revalue, however, we account for the gain on sale, there will be no effect on legally distributable profit.

▶ Looking at 1993:

	strict HCA	modified HCA 'income' approach'	modified HCA 'value' approach
	£000	£000	£000
Earnings	958	1,084	454
Legally distributable profit	6,666	6,666	6,666

Tutorial note: Why does FRS 3 now require the 'value' approach to be used in reporting the gain on disposal of a previously revalued asset in the profit and loss account of the year of sale?

Prior to FRS 3, the whole emphasis, in reporting the financial performance of an entity, was on its profit and loss account. Therefore, the issue of what to pass through the profit and loss account and what to include in reserves was crucial. As to the profit on sale of a previously revalued asset the debate, prior to FRS 3, was what to do with the revaluation surplus and the question of whether or not it should be reported as income in the profit and loss account.

The 'income' approach, as put forward in ED 36, argued in the affirmative and, under this approach, the revaluation surplus was included, as part of the gain on sale, in the profit and loss account of the year of sale.

The 'value' approach, however, argued that the profit on sale to be reported in the profit and loss account should be based on the value exchange arising on sale of the asset, that is, sale proceeds less net book value on the date of the sale. Any balance on the revaluation reserve, now realised on sale, should be transferred to realised reserves within reserves. This was the approach proposed in ED 51 and it is the required approach of FRS 3.

Where advocates of the 'income' approach might have argued that the adopting of the 'value' approach might have resulted in 'lost' information for users, this will no longer be the case under the more complete information set now demanded by FRS 3.

Under the standard, where the emphasis on performance moves away from only the profit and loss account to an expanded set of primary statements about performance, the 'value' approach will not result in 'lost' information. This is because the revaluation element of the gain on sale will have been dealt with:

▶ in the statement of recognised gains in the year of revaluation and
▶ in the statement of historical profit – see 3 below – in the year of sale.

c) The FRS 3 note of historical cost profits:

	1993	1992	1991
	£000	£000	£000
Reported profit on ordinary activities	454	(76)	(20)
Realisation of property revaluation gains of previous years	504	–	–
Difference between a historical cost depreciation charge and the actual depreciation charge of the year calculated on the revalued amount	–	84	42
Historical cost profit	958	8	22

2 *Rabbit plc*

Profit and loss account for the year ended 31 March 1994

Notes	Continuing operations £000	Discontinued operations £000	Total £000
1(b) & 3 Turnover	297,000	40,500	337,500
Cost of sales	(207,509)	(33,781)	(241,290)
Gross profit	89,491	6,719	96,210
Distribution costs	(47,587)	(8,398)	(55,985)
Administration expenses	(14,678)	(937)	(15,615)
Other operating income		200	200
Operating profit (loss)	27,226	(2,416)	24,810
2 Provision for loss on operations to be discontinued		(440)	(440)
Reorganisation and restructuring costs	(550)		(550)
	26,676	(2,856)	23,820

Interest payable and similar charges	(877)
4 Profit on ordinary activities before taxation	22,943
5 Tax on profit on ordinary activities	(12,748)
Profit on ordinary activities after taxation	10,195
Transfer to stock replacement reserve	(135)
8 Dividends	(6,750)
Retained profit	3,310
9 Earnings per share	5.7p

Statement of total recognised gains and losses for the year ended 31 March 1994

	£000
Profit for the financial year	10,195
Unrealised gain on revaluation of freehold land	1,200
Discount on issue of debentures written off against share premium	(300)
Total recognised since last report	11,095

Note of historical cost profits and losses

	£000
Reported profit on ordinary activities before taxation	22,943
Difference between a historical cost depreciation charge and the actual charge based on revalued amounts	120
Historical cost profit before taxation	23,063
Historical cost retained profit after taxation and appropriations	3,430

Balance sheet as at 31 March 1994

Notes		£000	£000
	Fixed assets		
10	Tangible assets		19,762
	Current assets		
	Stocks (800 – 90 + 55,407)	56,117	
11	Debtors	78,734	
		134,851	
	Creditors: amounts falling due within one year		
12	Bank overdraft	10,832	
	Trade creditors	37,980	
	Taxation (11,700 + 1,350)	13,050	
	Other creditors (1,845 + 2)	1,847	
	Accruals (882 + 225)	1,107	
	Proposed dividends	4,050	
		68,866	
	Net current assets		65,985
	Total assets less current liabilities		85,747
	Creditors: amounts falling due after more than one year		
13	12% debenture stock		6,000
			16,832
	Provisions for liabilities and charges		
15	Deferred taxation	9,112	
	Provision for loss on operations to be discontinued	440	9,552
	Capital and reserves		
16	Called-up share capital	45,000	
17	Share premium account	12,400	
17	Revaluation reserve	5,300	
17	Stock replacement reserve	135	
17	Profit and loss account	7,360	70,195
			85,747

Notes to the financial statements

1 *Accounting policies*
   a) The financial statements have been prepared in accordance with recognised standards of accounting practice.
   b) Turnover is based on sales less returns and excludes value added tax.
   c) Stocks have been valued at the lower of cost and net realisable value.
   d) Deferred tax is provided for on all timing differences except where the tax is not likely to become payable in the future.
   e) Depreciation has been provided on all tangible fixed assets except on freehold land.

2 *Acquisition and discontinued operations*
   There were no significant operations acquired at the year end in the UK. There was no resulting payment for goodwill.
       The discontinued operations related to the selling agency branch which ceased operations on 9 May 1994 but before these financial statements were approved. Provision has been made for the loss on termination as follows:

	£
Direct closure costs	720,000
Less: Operating profit up to cessation	280,000
	440,000

3 *Segmental analysis*
   The turnover and profit has been contributed by the company's principal activity, which is the sale of goods by mail order.

Geographical analysis:	Turnover	Profit/(loss)
	£000	£000
By origin: UK	297,000	26,676
France	40,500	(2,856)
	337,500	23,820

The above profit (loss) represents 'Profit or loss on ordinary activities before taxation' but excluding net interest.

4 Profit on ordinary activities before tax is arrived at after accounting for:

	£000
Depreciation	743
Directors' remuneration	322
Auditors' remuneration	39
Staff costs	25,560
Exceptional bad debts	900
Hire of equipment	207
Interest on bank overdraft	877
Loss on disposal of equipment	33
Profit on translation of foreign currency balances	(200)

5 *Taxation*

	£000
UK Corporation tax on profits at 33%	12,600
Transfer to deferred tax	112
Underprovision in previous year	36
	12,748

The above provision includes tax attributable to the exceptional items. (Details to be disclosed where clearly given.)

6 *Details of employees*
   Staff costs:

	£000
Wages and salaries	18,120
Social security costs	4,065
Other pension costs	3,375
	25,560

Average number of employuees:

	No.
Distribution	2,124
Administration	1,416
	3,540

7	Directors' remuneration	£000
	Fees	14.5
	Other emoluments	224
	Pensions	42.5
	Compensation for loss of office	41
		322

Chairman's emoluments		£18,000
Chief executive's emoluments		£36,500
Other directors' emoluments in bands of £5,000		No.
£0 – 5,000		2
£15,0001 – 20,000		3
£25,001 – 30,000		4
One director waived emoluments of £3,000		

8	Dividends	
		£000
	Interim paid – 1.5p per share	2,700
	Final proposed – 2.25p per share	4,050
		6,750

9   Earnings per share is based on earnings of £10,195,000 and 180 million ordinary shares in issue throughout the year.

10   Tangible assets

	Freehold land and buildings	Equipment and vehicles	Total
Cost of valuation:	£000	£000	£000
At 1/4/93	17,797	5,738	23,535
Revaluation	1,200		1,200
Additions		292	292
Disposals		(158)	(158)
At 31/3/94	18,997	5,872	24,869
Depreciation:			
At 1/4/93	1,822	2,610	4,432
Eliminated on disposals		(68)	(68)
Charge for the year	203	540	743
At 31/3/94	2,025	3,082	5,107
Net book value:			
At 1/4/93	15,975	3,128	19,103
At 31/3/94	16,972	2,790	19,762

The freehold land has revalued during the year by chartered surveyors. A provision for deferred taxation is not considered necessary. No depreciation has been provided on freehold land.

11	Debtors	£000
	Trade debtors (77,400 – 254)	77,146
	Loans to employees to purchase the company's shares	600
	Prepayments	988
		78,734

12   The bank overdraft is secured on the freehold property.
13   The 12% debenture stock was issued at the year end to finance certain acquisitions. The debentures are secured with a floating charge and are redeemable in 2003.
14   There is a contingent liability of £420,000 in respect of bills of exchange discounted which have not yet matured.

15	Deferred taxation	
	On accelerated capital allowances:	£000
	At 1/4/93	10,350
	Transfer from profits	112
	At 31/3/94	10,462
	Deduct: ACT recoverable	1,350
		9,112

16 *Called-up share capital*

	Authorised £000	Issued and fully paid £000
Ordinary shares of 25p	75,000	45,000

17 *Reserves*

	Share Premium account £000	Revaluation reserve £000	Stock replacement reserve £000	Profit and loss account £000
At 1/4/93	12,700	4,100	-	4,050
Discount on issue of debenture	(300)			
Transfer from profits for the year			135	
Revaluation of freehold land		1,200		
Retained profit for the year				3,310
AT 31/3/94	12,400	5,300	135	7,360

18 *Reconciliation of movements in shareholders' funds*

	£000
Profit for the financial year	10,195
Dividends	(6,750)
Retained profit	3,445
Other recognised gains and losses relating to the year (net)	900
Net increase in shareholders' funds	4,345
Opening shareholders' funds	65,850
Closing shareholders' funds	70,195

Workings

1

	Cost of sales £000	Distribution costs £000	Administration expenses £000
Closing stock	(800)		
Obsolete stock	90		
Balance	242,000		
Accruals – Agents commission		855	
– Audit			5
Provision for doubtful debts		20	
Salaries and wages		17,892	7,668
Directors' emoluments		57	265
Other expenses		11,289	7,184
Hire of equipment			207
Depreciation – Property		131	72
– Equipment		360	180
Audit fees			34
Bad debts		1,003	
Agents' commission		24,345	
Loss on disposal		33	
	241,290	55,985	15,615

2

Corporation tax	£000		£000
		Balance b/f	7,900
Cash paid	7,936	Prov. for year	12,600
ACT rec.	900	Under-prov.	36
Bals c/f		ACT rec.	1,350
– ACT pay	1,350		
– C.T.	11,700		

Deferred tax			£000		£000
		ACT rec.	1,350	Bal b/f	10,350
		Bal. c/f	9,112	Prov. for year	112

3

Disposal a/c	£000		£000
Cost		Depreciation	68
		Proceeds	57
	158	Loss	33

FINANCIAL REPORTING ENVIRONMENT

CHAPTER 12 *Exam style questions*

1   *Nero plc*
    Cash flow statement for the year ended 31 December 1992:

	£000	£000
Operating activities		
Ordinary operating activities (Note 1)	257	
Extraordinary item	(40)	
Net cash inflow from operating activities		217
Returns on investments and servicing of finance:		
Interest paid (46 + 5 − 15)	(36)	
Dividends received from associates		
((250 + (60 − 15) − (280 + 10))	5	
Dividends paid by Nero plc (40 + 15 − 30)	(25)	
Dividends paid to minority interest (55 + 15 + 36 − 95)	(11)	
Net cash outflow from returns on investments and servicing of finance		(67)
Taxation:		
Corporation tax paid on ordinary activities		
((40 + 5) + 10 + 92 − (50 + 10))	(87)	
Corporation tax on extraordinary item	14	
Tax paid		(73)
Investing activities:		
Payment to acquire tangible fixed assets		
(328 − 245 − 5 − 64)	(14)	
Receipts from sales of tangible fixed assets	25	
Purchase of subsidiary undertaking of cash and cash equivalent acquired		
(Notes 6, 7)	92	
Net cash inflow from investing activities		103
Net cash inflow before financing		180
Financing		
Repurchase of ordinary shares (2 + 16)	18	
Expenses of share issue	5	
Capital repayments under finance leases		
((50 + 30) + 245 − (60 + 195))	70	
Net cash outflow from financing (Notes 4, 5)		93
Increase in cash and cash equivalents (Notes 2, 3)		87
		180

Notes to the cash flow statement

1   **Reconciliation of operating profit to net cash inflow from ordinary operating activites:**

	£000
Operating profit	253
Depreciation:	85
Loss of sale of fixed assets (50 − 25 − 5)	20
Increase in stocks (370 − 310 − 24)	(36)
Increase in debtors (285 − 215 − 18)	(52)
Decrease in creditors (135 − 150 + 28)	(13)
	257

2   **Analysis of changes in cash and cash equivalents:**

	£000
Balance at 1 January 1992	(55)
Net cash inflow	87
Balance at 31 December 1992	32

3   **Analysis of the balances of cash and cash equivalents as shown in the balance sheet:**

	1992 £000	1992 £000	Change in year £000
Cash at bank and in hand	32	10	22
Overdraft		(65)	65
	32	(55)	87

4 **Analysis of changes in financing during the year:**

	Share capital (including premium) £000	Finance lease obligations £000
Balance at 1 January 1992	290	80
Cash flows from financing	(23)	(70)
Issued for non-cash consideration	182	
Premium on purchase of own shares	16	
Finance leases entered into during year		245
Balance at 31 Dec 1992	465	255

5 **Major non-cash transactions:**
During the year, fixed assets were acquired for £245,000 under finance leases. Part of the consideration for the purchase of a subsidiary undertaking during the year was in the form of shares. Further details are set out below.

6 **Purchase of subsidiary undertaking – Polanski Ltd:**

	£000
Net assets acquired:	
Fixed assets	64
Stocks	24
Debtors	18
Cash	112
Creditors	(28)
Corporation tax	(10)
	180
Minority interest	(36)
Goodwill	58
	202
Satisfied by:	
Shares issued (market value)	182
Cash	20
	202

The subsidiary undertaking acquired during the year contributed £W to the group's net operating cash flows, paid £x in respect of net returns on investments and servicing of finance, paid £Y in respect of taxation and used £Z for investing activities.

7 Analysis of the net inflow of cash and cash equivalent in respect of the acquisiton of Polanski Ltd:

	£000
Cash consideration:	20
Cash acquired	(112)
Net inflow	92

2 *Proserpina plc*
Proserpina plc group – Cash flow statement for the year ended 31 October 1992:

	£000	£000
Operating activities (Note 1)		7,848
Returns on investment and servicing of finance		
Interest paid	(174)	
Dividends received	48	
Dividends paid by Proserpina plc (240 + 600 − 267)	(573)	
Dividends paid to minority interest (1,997 + 60 + 226 + 452 − 2,519 − 75)	(141)	
		(840)
Taxation		
Corporation tax paid (2,738 + 80 + 2,830 − 2,655 − 89)		(2,904)
Investing activities		
Payments to acquire tangible fixed assets (1,977 + 10,969 − 7,642 − 1,228)		(4,076)

Net cash inflow before financing		28
Financing		
Proceeds of share issue (Note 3)	1,511	
Repayment of loans (Note 3)	(790)	
		721
Increase in cash and cash equivalents (Note 2)		749

Notes to the cash flow statement

1   Reconciliation of operating profit to net cash inflow from operating activities:

	£000
Operating profit	6,955
Depreciation	1,977
Increase in stocks (7,245 – 6,100 – 393)	(752)
Increase in debtors	
(6,410 – 1,235 – 7,211 + 2,746 – 211)	(499)
Increase in creditors (1,920 – 1,690 – 63)	167
	7,848

2   Analysis of changes in cash and cash equivalents during the year:

	£000
Cash at bank and in hand at 1 November 1991	165
Net cash inflow	749
Exchange gain	39
Cash at bank and in hand at 31 October 1992	953

3   Analysis of changes in financing during the year:

	Share capital (including premium) £000	Loans £000
Balance at 1 November 1991	8,000	1,410
Cash flows from financing	1,511	(790)
Reduction in debtor for called up share capital not paid	(1,511)	
Exchange loss		382
Balance at 31 October 1992	8,000	1,002

CHAPTER 13 *Self test questions*

1   The rules, briefly, are these:

▶ Under S. 263, which applies to all companies except investment and insurance companies, a company may distribute its accumulated realised profits less its realised losses.

▶ If a company is a plc, it must additionally comply with S. 264, which following S. 263, further restricts the distributable profits of a plc to the extent that it has net unrealised losses. This is to ensure that, after the distribution, the net assets of the company are at least as much as its share capital and non-distributable reserves.

▶ S. 265 applies to investment companies only. Such companies, which are plcs, may distribute its accumulated realised revenue profits less its accumulated realised and unrealised revenue losses subject to a capital maintenance test as either under S. 264 above or so as to ensure that, after distribution, the assets of the company are at least 150% of its liabilities.

2   The three main conclusions of TR 481 on determining realised profits are as follows:

▶ A profit that is required by an Accounting Standard to be recognised in the profit and loss account should, normally, be treated as a realised profit. (For example, attributable profit on long-term contracts.)

▶ A profit may be recognised in the profit and loss account in accordance with an accounting policy that is not the subject of an Accounting Standard (or that is contrary to an Accounting Standard). Such a profit will normally be a realised profit if the accounting policy is consistent with the concepts of accruals and prudence.

▶ If, in special circumstances, a company cannot give a true and fair view without including an unrealised profit in its profit and loss account, the Act requires a company to include that unrealised profit. (For example, net exchange gains on the translation of long-term overseas borrowings.)

3   The amount transferred to the revaluation reserve is:
240 – (200 – 40) = £80

This amount becomes realised through use to the extent of the additional depreciation charged since revaluation. At 31 December 1995, this would be:

	£
Based on revalution (240/8 yrs)	30
Based on original cost ((200 – 40)/8 yrs)	(20)
Additional depreciation	10

The legally distributable profits of 31 December 1995 are:

	£
Profit available before 1995 depreciation	70
Less: 1995 depreciation, as above	(30)
Add: Realised extent of revaluation reserve, as above	10
	50

4   The maximum legally distributable profits of Pingo plc at 30 June 1994 are:

	£
The balance on profit and loss account	1,080

Note: Attributable profit included above is deemed to be realised; the exchange differences taken to reserves, applying the offset procedure of SSAP 20, are deemed to be unrealised. Therefore:

Unrealised items included above	Nil
Realised items not included above	Nil
S. 264 profits available for distribution	1,080

5   The maximum legally distributable profit of Pongo plc is:

	£
Accumulated realised profits	75
Less: Accumulated realised losses	(9)
Less: Net unrealised losses	Nil
(unrealised profits > unrealised losses)	
	66

CHAPTER 13 *Exam style question*

1   *Tower plc*

a) The Companies Act 1985 imposes conditions that companies must satisfy before they can make distributions. Some of these conditions apply only to public companies and special provisions apply to investment companies (and insurance companies).

S.263(1) – Any company, whether public or private, may make a distribution only out of 'profits available for the purpose'.

S.263(3) – For any company other than an investment company (or an insurance company) profits available for distribution are the company's accumulated realised profits that have not previously been either distributed or capitalised, less its accumulated realised losses in so far as they have not been previously written off in either a reduction or reorganisation of capital.

The origin of these profits and losses may be either revenue or capital. The exact meaning of the term 'realised' is not defined in the Act. The Act merely gives an indication of the interpretation of the term. It states that references to realised profits are to such profits as fall to be treated as realised profits in accordance with principles generally accepted with respect to the determination for accounting purposes of realised profits at the time when accounts are prepared.

S.264(1) – In addition to the condition that it can make a distribution only out of profits available for the purpose, a public company can make a distribution only to the extent that the distribution does not reduce the amount of the company's net assets below the aggregate of its called up share capital plus its undistributable reserves, that is, the share premium account, the capital redemption reserve, the excess of accumulated unrealised profits over accumulated unrealised losses and any reserve that the company, for any other reason, is prohibited from distributing.

The effect of this additional condition is that a public company can make a distribution provided only that it has net realised profits available after it has provided for any net *unrealised* losses.

S.265(1) – An investment company may make a distribution at any time out of those of its accumulated realised revenue profits that have not previously been either distributed or capitalised, less its accumulated revenue losses, whether or not these are realised and only in so far as they have not previously been written off in either a reduction or reoganisation of capital. Further, an investment company may make a distribution only to the extent that the distribution does not reduce the amount of the company's assets below 150% of the aggregate of its liabilities.

b) Tower plc
    S.263 test – accumulated realised profits less accumulated realised losses:

	£ 000
Profit and loss account	2500
Revaluation reserves – realised amounts -	
Buildings – 2% × £350,000	7
Plant and machinery – 15% × 100,000	15
Fixtures and fittings – 20% × (100,000)	(20)
	2,502

S.264 test – no effect – as the company has no net unrealised losses.

The maximum legally distributed profits of Tower plc amount therfore to £2,502,000.

Notes:
1   The deficit on fixtures and fittings is not treated as a realised loss given that the directors consider that the value of the remaining fixed assets not revalued is at least equal to their net book amounts. The deficit does, however, become realised, as do surpluses, through continued use of the assets and, to this extent, is taken account of in the S.263 test above.
2   Development costs capitalised have not been treated as a realised loss on the ground that there are 'special circumstances' that justify the directors deciding not to treat the costs as a realised (revnue) loss. In this situation the note to the accounts that states the reasons for capitalising development costs must also state that development costs have not been treated as a realised (revenue) loss. In addition, the note must state the justification the directors used for adopting this treatment.

Book Ltd
S.263 test – accumulated realised profit less accumulated realised losses:

	£000
Retained profit	55
Write down of investment in Worm Ltd to 60% of £50,000	(10)
Realised extent of the current cost reserve	13
	58

The S.264 test does not apply to Book Ltd.
The maximum legally distributable profits of Book Ltd amount therefore to £58,000.

Notes:
The profit element of £6,000 included in long-term work in progress and therefore in retained profit does not result in a departure from the statutory requirement that only realised items be included in the profit and loss account. Calculated, as it is, in accordance with SSAP 9, such an amount is properly included in the profit and loss account and no adjustment is necessary to ascertain the maximum legally distributable profits of the company. The company may, however, be departing from the statutory valuation rules in relation to current assets and may therefore have to note the departure from the Act in this respect. In any event the maximum legally distributable profits of the company are not affected.

Holdings plc
As an investment company, Holdings plc is bound by the normal S.264 rule for a plc, but may choose instead to apply the S.265 test. This will allow it to distribute even if it has large *capital* losses (which are not so important for this type of company). However, it will be forbidden by its articles to distribute capital profits.

		£ 000
S.264 test: Net assets	5,355	
Undistributable reserves:		
Share capital	650	
Share premium	325	
Net unrealised profit	75	(1,050)
Maximum distribution under S.264		4,305
S.265 test: Gross assets (5,667 + 2,681)		8,348
Less: 1.5 × liabilities (1,793 + 936 + 264 = 2,993)		4,490
'Excess assets'		3858
Realised revenue profits		2,666
Realised revenue losses		(10)
Unrealised revenue losses*		(17)
Maximum distribution, as less than excess:		2,639

* (It may be that these can be set first against unrealised revenue profits, as there is no *net* unrealised loss; however, it has been deducted here on the grounds of prudence.)

It has been assumed that Holdings plc realises investments in order to pay the dividend. If it pays out its cash (£147) and takes out an overdraft, the liabilities figure rises and the 'excess assets' become 147 + 2/3 × (3,858 − 147) = 2,621, which would further limit the distribution under this section.

As Holdings plc has the choice between S.264 and S.265, I consider that it can rely on S.264 and distribute the whole of its revenue account. It is not clear where the unrealised items would have been debited and credited, but *assuming* that net unrealised profits would be credited to a separate reserve (net unrealised losses, if any, passing through revenue account), the distributable profits would be:

Realised revenue profits	2,666
Realised revenue losses	(10)
	2,656

The net unrealised revenue reserve of £123 (which is apparently distributable under S.264) would not be distributed on grounds of prudence.

c) As stated in SSAP 16, the amount of profit that a company may prudently distribute depends not only on its profitability but also on the availability of funds. When determining distribution policy, consideration must be given to factors not reflected in profits, such as capital expenditure plans, changes in the volume of working capital, the effect on funding requirements of changes in production methods and efficiency, liquidity and new financing arrangements.

While noting that there is no difference between historical cost accounts and current cost accounts when it comes to the amount of profit that a company may legally distribute, see Holdings plc above, the news release issued with SSAP 16 emphasised that the distribution of profit may be assessed more easily by using current cost information. It stated that CCA provided for management a means of setting aside funds required to maintain the physical assets representing the operating capability of the business. Thus, the current cost profit attributable to shareholders would be the maximum amount which could be paid out as dividends without eroding shareholders' investment in the net operating assets of the business. Even so SSAP 16 stated that the other factors noted above would still need to be considered.

In commercial and practical terms, a company would have constraints in making a maximum distribution in that it would be restricted by:

▶ cash flow considerations
▶ the desirability of ploughing profits back into the business
▶ the possibility of loss-making periods and the desirability of maintaining the level of dividend payments
▶ the effects of price changes.

Distributions are not influenced only by the Act. They may also be subject to any enactment, or any rule of law or any provision in the memorandum or articles of association that may restrict either the amounts available for distribution or the circumstances in which a distribution may be made. Investment companies, for example, are restricted by their memorandum and articles of association from distributing realised capital profits. It is important therefore for the directors to know the memorandum and articles, as well as the statutory rules, before making a distribution. In conclusion, it is also important to bear in mind that a company may not lawfully pay a dividend if, as a result, the company could become either insolvent or have insufficient working capital to carry on its business. Thus, directors should not only refer to the 'relevant accounts' when they authorise a dividend but should also take into account the company's results since the date on which those accounts were drawn up.

CHAPTER 14 *Exam style question*

1 *Muirfield Ltd*

REPORT

TO: The directors of Muirfield Ltd

FROM: AR Countants & Co

RE: The effects of changing prices

DATE: 31 July 1991

---

a) **The shortcomings of historical cost accounts in a period of changing prices**

Inflation has imposed a severe test on historical cost accounting as a reliable basis for reporting results and financial positions of companies. While the Accounting Standards Committee does not assert that historical cost accounting is 'wrong', it does believe that it has serious limitations in times of changing prices. When prices are rising these include:

▶ reported results may be distorted as a result of the matching of current revenues with costs incurred at an earlier date

▶ the amounts reported in a balance sheet in respect of assets may not be realistic up-to-date measures of the resources employed in the business

▶ calculations to measure returns on capital employed may be misleading

▶ as holding gains or losses attributable to price level changes are not identified, management's effectiveness in achieving operating results may be concealed

▶ there is no recognition of the loss that arises through holding assets of fixed monetary value and the gain that arises through holding liabilities of fixed monetary value

▶ a misleading impression of the trend of performance overtime may be given because no account is taken of changes in the real value of money (although this is also true of current cost information unless it is expressed in units of constant purchasing power).

b) **How the effects of changing prices may most appropriately be reflected in the financial statements of the company:**

Some companies have attempted to mitigate a number of the limitations of historical cost accounting by adopting a modified historical cost convention.

However, most companies that use this convention undertake revaluations comparatively infrequently and do not revalue all their assets. The result of this is that many of the limitations of pure historical cost accounting remain.

Some of the limitations of historical cost accounting can be remedied by supplementing it (or replacing it) with information on the effects of changing prices on the results and financial position of the company. Such information can:

▶ indicate profitability on a basis that makes allowance for the maintenance of operating or real financial

▶ capital giving a more up-to-date indication of current operating results and management performance

▶ indicate more realistic, up-to-date amounts in respect of assets

▶ make allowance for the effects of changing prices on monetary items

▶ provide a more realistic indication of trend information.

The debate on which method to adopt when accounting for the effects of changing prices has generally been expressed in terms of a choice between two methods. These are, CCA or current cost accounting, in which adjustments are made for *specific* price changes, and CPP or current purchasing power accounting, in which adjustments are made for changes in the *general* level of prices.

Although the debate has often been expressed in terms of a straight choice between CCA and CPP, the effects of changing prices, both specific and general, can really be fully reflected only by combining the two methods and disclosing the effects of these changes in an 'adjusted earnings statement'.

c) **Adjusted earnings statement for Muirfield Ltd for the year ended 30 June 1991 under the real terms system:**

		£000	£000
Historical cost profit for the financial year			95
Deduct:	Cost of sales adjustment	(35)	
	Depreciation adjustment	(58)	
	Monetary working capital adjustment	(8)	
		(101)	
Add:	Gearing adjustment	27	
	Realised holding gains		(74)
	Operating profit		21
Add:	Unrealised holding gains arising during year (38 – 4)	34	
	Realised holdings gains	74	
	Total holding gains		108
			129
Deduct:	inflation adjustment to shareholders' funds 4.6% × 431		(20)
Real holding gains (108 less 20 = 88)			——
Total real gains			109

Appendix: quantifying the effects of changing prices: (all amounts in £000)

1   Realised holding gains:
     i) COSA – using the averaging method

	£	£
Closing stock	235 × 138/141	230
Less:		
Opening stock	(150) × 138/115	(180)
	85 less	50 = £35

     ii) Depreciation adjustment – CC depreciation calculated, for simplicity, on the basis of year end current cost of fixed assets

	£
CC depreciation = 90 × 987.5/600	148
HC depreciation	(90)
	58

2   Unrealised holdings gains:

		£
i) re stocks: at 30 June 1991 (235 × 147/141) less 235 =	10	
at 30 June 1990 (150 × 126/115) less 150 =		14
Unrealised holding gains arising in yaer		4

	£
ii) re fixed assets:	
NBV b/f – HCA – 330 × 812.5/600 = 447 × 987.5/812.5 =	543
Depreciation for the year	(148)
	395

		£
Unrealised holding gain brought forward (447 – 330)	=	117
Unrealised holding gain for year (543 – 447) = 96 less		
(depreciation adjustment for year per 1 ii) above) 58	=	38

3   Current cost of shareholders' funds at the beginning of the period:

	£
Historical cost – per question	300
Unrealised holding gains – on stocks	14
– on fixed assets	117
	431

CHAPTER 16 *Self test questions*

1   The main objective and purpose of consolidated accounts, to quote FRS 2:

For a variety of legal, tax and other reasons undertakings generally choose to conduct their activities not through a single legal entity but through several undertakings under the ultimate control of the parent undertaking of that group. For this reason the financial statements of a parent undertaking by itself do not present a full picture of its economic activities or financial position. Consolidated financial statements are required in order to reflect the extended business unit that conducts activities under the control of the parent undertaking.

2   It has always been a requirement, first under SSAPs 14 and 23 and then under FRS 2, to bring the net assets of a subsidiary into the consolidated accounts at their fair value rather than their book value. This is also a legal requirement under Schedule 4(A) to the Act. The purpose of the fair value exercise is simply to establish a starting point as to the questions – what is the value of the amount paid by the group as consideration and what is the value of the underlying net assets required? The answers have a direct bearing on consolidation goodwill.

3   We need to adjust for intra-group transactions in the conslidated accounts. FRS 2 states that 'intragroup transactions may result in profits or losses being included in the book value of assets to be included in the consolidation.' The FRS requires the elimination, in full, of all such profits and losses because, for the group as a whole, no profits or losses have arisen.

4   The requirements of FRS 2 in relation to accounting periods and dates are:

The financial statements of all subsidiary undertakings to be used in preparing consolidated financial statements should have the same financial year end and be for the same accounting period as those of the parent undertaking of the group. Where the financial year of a subsidiary undertaking differs from that of the parent undertaking of the group interim financial statements for that subsidiary undertaking prepared to the parent undertaking's accounting date should be used. If this is impracticable, earlier financial statements of the subsidiary undertaking may be used, provided they are prepared for a financial year that ended not more than three months earlier.

5   The FRS 2 requirements on minority interests, to quote FRS 2, are:

Minority interests in total should be reported separately in the consolidated balance sheet and profit and loss account. When an entity becomes a subsidiary undertaking the assets and liabilities attributable to its minority interest should be included on the same basis as those attributable to the interest held by the parent and other subsidiary undertakings. The effect of this for an acquisition is that all the subsidiary undertaking's identifiable assets and liabilities are included at fair value as required by the Act. No goodwill should be attributed to the minority interest.

Further, debit balances should be recognised and, if appropriate, provided against.

CHAPTER 16 *Exam style questions*

1   *Delta Ltd*

Amounts to be included in the consolidated balance sheet of Delta Ltd as on 30 November 1995:

	£	£
Sundry net assets (W.3)		534,900
Ordinary share capital		230,000
Revenue reservers (W.7)		165,620
Goodwill - negative (W.7)	39,480	
positive (W.7)	(13,781)	25,699
Minority interest (W.5)		113,581
		534,900

(As an alternative, the goodwill arising arising on the acquisition of Echo Ltd could be written off against consolidated revenue reserves.)

Workings		Delta Ltd	Echo Ltd	Foxtrot Ltd
1	Number of shares	230,000	180,000	240,000
	Split		2:1	
			360,000	
2	Nominal value		£1	25p	50p
		£	£	£
	Share capital	230,000	90,000	120,000
	Revenue reserves/1/12/94	103,900	31,350	56,250
	Capital reserve/1/12/94			20,000
	Profits for year to 30/11/95	37,300	25,500	27,600
	Revaluation 30/5/95			32,000
	Net assets	371,200	146,850	255,850
	Less:			
	Cost of Delta Ltd	(52,000)		
	Cost of Echo Ltd	(31,000)		
	Cost of Foxtrot Ltd	(156,000)		
	Consolidated net assets	132,200	146,850	255,850

3   Consolidated net assets for the consolidated balance sheet – £534,900

4 Percentage holdings

		Echo Ltd	Foxtrot Ltd
Group:			
30/4/93	81/180	45%	
30/6/95	192/240		80%
31/8/95	45/360	12.5%	
		57.5%	
Minority interest		42.5%	20%

5 Minority interest for the consolidated balance sheet

	£
Echo Ltd 42.5% × 146,850	62,411
Foxtrot Ltd 20% × 255, 850	51,170
	113,581

6 Consolidated revenue reserves

		£
Delta Ltd (103,900 + 37,300)		141,200
Echo Ltd (31,350 + 25,500) =	56,850	
45% × (56,850 − 24,800)		14,423
12.5% × 25,500 × 3/12		797
Foxtrot Ltd 80% × 27,600 × 5/12		9,200
		165,620

7 Goodwill

			£	£
–	Purchase of Echo Ltd			
	30/4/93	Cost	52,000	
		Less:		
		45% × (90,000 + 24,800)	(51,660)	
				340
	31/8.95	Cost	31,000	
		Less:		
		12.5% × (90,000 + 31,350 + 9/12 × 25,500)	(17,559)	13,441
				13,781
–	Purchase of Foxtrot Ltd			
	30/6/95	Cost	156,000	
		Less:		
		80% × (120,000 + 56,250 + 20,000 + 32,000 + [7/12 × 27,600)	(195,480)	(39,480)

2 *Bell Ltd*

Bell Ltd Group
Consolidated profit and loss account for the year ended 30 September 1995

	£
Turnover	5,610,700
Cost of Sales	(3,744,490)
Gross profit	1,866,210
Administration cost	(1,046,020)
Operating profit	820,190
Share of associated company profit	88,450
Profit on ordinary operations before taxation	908,640
Tax on profits on ordinary operations	(344,074)
Profit on ordinary activities after taxation	564,566
Minority interest (see note)	(39,201)
Group profit of which £473,060 is dealt with in the separate accounts of Bell Ltd.	525,365
Proposed dividend	(380,100)
Profit for the financial year	145,265

Movement on group reserves for the year ended 30 September 1995

	Company £	Subsidiary £	Associate £	Total £
1 October 1994	298,570	–	27,959	326,529
Retained in year	92,960	39,932	12,373	145,265
30 September 1995	391,530	39,932	40,332	471,794

Consolidation schedules

1   Group holdings:

Book Ltd.   Acquired 1/1/92

$$\frac{269,500 \times 100}{550,000} = 49\%$$

Candle Ltd   Acquired 1/7/95

$$\frac{264,600 \times 100}{420,000} = 63\%$$

2   Consolidated profit and loss account:

	Bell Ltd. £	Book Ltd. 49% £	Candle Ltd. 63% £
Turnover	4,865,300	–	745,400
Cost of sales	3,352,170	–	392,320
Gross profit	1,513,130	–	353,080
Administration (W.1)	807,860	–	238,160
Operating profit	705,270	–	114,920
Share of associate company profit	–	88,450	
Provision for corporation tax (W.2)	(286,110)	(22,177)	(35,787)
	419,160	66,273	79,133
Minority interest	–	–	(29,279)
Inter Company dividends (W.3)	53,900	(53,900)	(9,922)
	473,060	12,373	39,932
Proposed dividend (362,000 × 1.05)	(380,100)		
	92,960		
Retained profit b/f (W.4)	298,570	27,959	–
carried fwd.	391,530	40,332	39,932

Workings [W1–4]

1   Administration costs - Candle Ltd:
990,640 - 38,000 = 952,640 × 3/12 = £238,160

2   Provision for Corporation Tax:
Book Ltd. 45,260 × 49% = 22.177
Candle Ltd. 129,850 + (35% × 38,000) = 143,150 × 3/12 = £35,787

3   Inter company dividends
Book Ltd. 20p × 550,000 × 49% = 53,900

Candle Ltd. 63,000 × 63% × 3/12 = 9,922

This post-acquisition dividend is not receivable by the parent but by previous shareholders.

4   Retained profit b/f:
Bell Ltd. 49% × (106,430 - 49,370) = 27,959

Note:
The treatment of the dividend paid before acquisition by the subsidiary is one of a number of alternative treatments. The disclosure of this item might be:

	£
Minority share of profits	29,279
Post-acquisition dividend paid to vendors	9,922
	39,201

The dividend proportion of this would be posted to cost of control account.

CHAPTER 17 *Exam style question*

1   *Hellenic Ltd*

   a) Consolidated balance sheet at 30 September 1993

      i)   Group structure

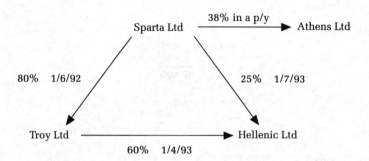

      ii) Relevant percentages

		Troy Ltd		Hellenic Ltd	
Group	– direct	80%		25%	
	– indirect	–		(80% × 60%)	48%
		80%		73%	
Minority interest		20%		27%	

      iii) Reserves of subsidiaries on the date of acquisition

Troy Ltd: 1 June 1992

	£		£ Pre		£ Post
1/10/91 (balancing item)	18,000		18,000		
y/e 30/9/92	(36,000)	8/12	(24,000)	4/12	(12,000)
1/10/92	(18,000)				
y/e 30/9/93	52,000				52,000
	34,000		(6,000)		40,000
Group's share 80%			(4,800)		32,000

Hellenic Ltd: piecemeal acquisition

1/4/93 80% × 60% =	48%				
1/7/93	25%				
y/e 30/9/93	12,800	6/12	6,400	6/12	6,400
Group's share 48%			3,072		3,072
y/e 30/9/93	12,800	9/12	9,600	3/12	3,200
Group's share 25%			2,400		800
Total group's share re Hellenic Ltd			5,472		3,872

      iv) Goodwill on conslidation

	£	£	£
Cost in Troy Ltd		107,200	
Less: NV of SC (80%)	96,000		
Less: Share of pre-acq losses	(4,800)		
		(91,200)	
			16,000
Cost in Hellenic Ltd – direct		24,400	
indirect 80% × 51,040		40,832	
		65,232	
Less: NV of SC (73%)	52,560		
Add: Share of pre-acq profits	5,472		
		(58,032)	
			7,200
			23,200

v) Minority interest		£	£
Troy Ltd: NV of SC (20%)			24,000
share of reserves 20% × 34,000			6,800
			30,800
Hellenic Ltd: NV of SC (27%)		19,440	
share of reserves 27% × 12,800		3,456	
		22,896	
Less: cost in Hellenic Ltd 20% × 51,040		(10,208)	
			12,688
			43,488

vi) Athens Ltd: Value for consolidated balance sheet	£	£
Share of net assets on 30/9/93, excluding goodwill		
38% × (146,400 − 7,500)		52,782
Add: Goodwill paid on acquisition		
cost	45,500	
share of separable net assets on date of acquisition 38% × (109,700 − 7,500)(38,836)		
		6,664
Less: Goodwill eliminated per SSAP 22		(6,664)
		52,782

vii) Consolidated reserves:

	£
Sparta Ltd	187,000
Troy Ltd	32,000
Hellenic Ltd	3,872
Athens Ltd 38% × (57,400 − 20,700)	13,946
	236,818
Less: Goodwill written off − (23,200 + 6,664)	(29,864)
	206,954

Summarised consolidated balance sheet as on 30 September 1993

Sundry net assets	84,800	+ 154,000	+ 437,000	
Less: cost of investments				
Hellenic		(51,040)	(24,400)	
Troy			(107,200)	
Athens			(45,500)	
	84,800	102,960	259,900	447,660
Associated company				52,782
				500,442
Ordinary share capital				250,000
Reserves				206,954
Minority interest				43,488
				500,442

CHAPTER 18 *Exam style question*

1   *Grace plc*

A calculation as to the gain on disposal of Barlow Ltd:

	£		
Sale proceeds		1,100	
Less:			
Net assets sold on 1/7/91	1,000		
Net assets at 30/9/90			
Increase in 9 months to 1/7/91 9/12 × 208	156		
	1,156 × 75%	(867)	
		233	
Tax, as given		(83)	
		150	

A calculation for goodwill paid regarding Hornby Ltd:

	£
Cost		705
Less: Net assets 30/9/90	800
Add: 6 months to 1/4/91	195
	995
Less: Provisions (70 + 30) × 0.65	(65)
	930 × 50%	(465)
		240

Amortised in year 240/20 × 6/12 = 6
Unamortised (240 − 6) = 234

A summarised consolidated profit and loss account for the year ended 30 September 1991:

	Grace	Barlow (9 months)	Hornby Assoc (6 months)	Hornby Sub (6 months)	Good will	Consoli dated P&L account
Profit before tax	400	240				
(300 − 70 − 30) × 30%			60			
(340 + 70 − 10)				400		
PURP 20% × 450	(90)					
20% × 150	(30)					
Goodwill written off					(6)	974
	280	240	60	400	(6)	974
Tax	(140)	(84)				
(105 − 35) × 30%			(21)			
119 − 4 + 25 [(35% × 10) (35% × 70)]				(140)		(385)
	140	156	39	260	(6)	589
MI		25% (39)		20% (52)		(91)
	140	117	39	208	(6)	498
Transfer	117	(117)				
	257	–	39	208	(6)	498
Exceptional item net of tax	150					150
Associate now subsidiary			(39)	39		
	407	–	–	247	(6)	648
b/f	2,250					
(900 − 500) × 75%		300				
(750 − 650) × 30%				30		2,580
Transfer	300	(300)				
	2,957	–	–	277	(6)	3,228

Summarised consolidated balance sheet at 30 September 1991:

	£
Net assets 30/9/90 (1,690 + 800)	2,490
Profit for year to 30/9/91 − increase in net assets:	
Per question 260 + [195 + 221]	676
Adjustments:	
PURP (90 + 30)	(120)
Bad debts 40 × 0.65	(26)
Goodwill − unamortised	234
Cash 1,100 − 705	395
Tax on gain on disposal	(83)
	3,566
Ordinary share capital	100
Reserves	3,228
MI 20% × (800 + 195 + 221 − 26)	238
	3,566

1   Six areas of difference between the acquisition and merger methods of consolidation are:

▶ Acquistion accounting involves goodwill, merger accounting does not, giving rise instead to a 'difference' arising on consolidation.

▶ Fair values are assigned to the subsidiary's net assets at acquisiton in acquisition accounting; fair values of either the consideration paid by the parent undertaking or the net assets of the subsidiary at combination date are irrelevant in merger accounting.

▶ Acquisition accounting distinguishes between the parent combination and the post combination reserves of a subsidiary, merger accounting does not.

▶ Consolidated net assets are likely to be higher in acquisition accounting whereas consolidated earnings are likely to be higher in merger accounting.

▶ Provisions set up on the combination with a new subsidiary will pass through the consolidated profit and loss account in merger accounting but not necessarily in acquisition accounting.

▶ Movements on reserves will differ under the two methods.

2   Your diagram to indicate what happens in a vendor placing might look like this:

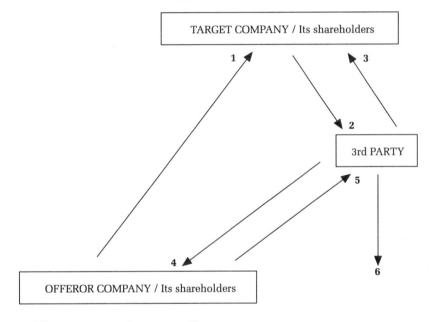

1 Offeror company makes merger offer

2 Target company shareholders sell their shares to the 3rd party for cash

3 3rd party pays cash for Target company's shares

4 3rd party transfers the Target company's shares to the Offeror company

5 Offeror company pays consideration to 3rd party in line with merger offers in 1

6 3rd party places offeror company's shares with investors

3   The six ED 48 conditions for a merger are:

▶ None of the parties sees itself as acquirer or acquiree.

▶ None of the parties dominates the management of the combined entity.

▶ Equity shareholders of the combining parties do not dispose of (a material part of) their shareholdings for non-equity consideration (ruling out vendor placings and vendor rights).

▶ The minority interest must not exceed 10%.

▶ None of the accounting parties is more than 50% larger than any other party to the combination.

▶ The share of equity in the combination allocated to the parties does not depend on past combination performance (ruling out contingent deferred consideration).

4   The purchase of shares in Salman Ltd will be recorded in the separate accounts of Hafiz Ltd as follows:

	£	£
DR Cost of investment in Salman Ltd	21,500	
CR Cash		500
CR 9% Loan Stock		1,000
CR Ordinary Share Capital		20,000

5   a)   The journal would be the same as in answer 4.
    b)   The cost of the subsidiary is not the fair value of the consideration. Consolidation based goodwill based on this cost will be understated. SSAP 22 requires disclosure of the fair value of the consideration.

		£	£
c)	DR Cost of investment in Salman Ltd	36,500	
	CR Cash		500
	CR 9% Loan Stock		1,000
	CR Ordinary Share Capital		20,000
	CR Merger reserve		15,000

In this case, consolidation goodwill will not be understated. The merger reserve can be utilised for the write off of the goodwill. Where the net effect on consolidated reserves cannot be different, following the guidance in the Appendix to SSAP 23 does result in more fair disclosure.

CHAPTER 19 *Exam style questions*

1   *Macbeth plc and Duncan plc*
    a) i)   On the basis that Macbeth plc has chosen alternative 1 and applying the provisions of the Companies Act 1985 (S.130 and S.131):

Investment in Duncan plc

		£000
1/1/89 - per question		132
Cost of purchase of 360,000 Duncan plc ordinary shares	(W.2)	540
31/12/89		672
Cost of purchase of 1,248,000 Duncan plc ordinary shares	(W.3)	936
31/12/90		1,608

Share capital

		£000
1/1/89 - per question		2,560
Rights issue	(W.2)	300
31/12/89		2,860
Shares issued as consideration for the purchase of 1,248,000 Duncan plc ordinary shares	(W.3)	936
31/12/90		3,796

Share premium account

		£000
1/1/89 - per question		12
Premium on shares issued as rights issue	(W.2)	240
31/12/89		252
Premium on shares issued on consideration for the purchase of 1,248,000 Duncan plc ordinary shares	(W.3)	–
31/12/90		252

Workings [W1–3]
Note that all numbers and values are in 000s.

W1

	Macbeth plc	Duncan plc
eps	£512	£320
	2,560	1,920
	= 20.00p	16.67p
P/E - per question	10	9
Price (eps × P/E)	£2.00	£1.50

(Note: it is assumed that these prices remain constant through 1989 and 1990 regardless of any further issues of shares during these two years.)

W2

Re the purchase of 360 Duncan plc ordinary shares on 1 January 1989 for cash:

The cost to Macbeth plc is 360 × £1.50 = £540.

FINANCIAL REPORTING ENVIRONMENT

Macbeth plc raises this £540 by a rights issue of its own shares at market value less 10% (90% × £2.00 = £1.80). Therefore, Macbeth plc issues 540/1.80 = 300 ordinary shares of £1.80 each to raise the £540. The NV of the shares issued is therefore (300 × £1.00) £300 and the premium on issue (300 × £0.80) £240. S.130 applies to this premium, there is no relief under S.131 and the premium must, therefore, be recorded as share premium account.

W3

The purchase of 1,248 Duncan plc ordinary shars on 1 January 1990:

The consideration is to be entirely in the form of Macbeth plc ordinary shares.

As the value of the Duncan plc ordinary shares purchased is (1,248 × £1.50) £1,872, the number of Macbeth plc ordinary shares, value £2.00 each, to be issued as consideration is 1,872/2 = £936.

The nominal value of these shares issued would be 936 × £1 = £936 and the premium on issue 936 × £1 = £936.

This purchase results in Macbeth plc owning 90% of the Duncan plc ordinary shares. As the consideration includes Macbeth plc ordinary shares, S.131, relief from S.130, applies to the premium on these shares issued and Macbeth plc 'shall not' record such premium as share premium account. The accounting entry to record the purchase of the 1,248 Duncan plc ordindary shares, in the books of Macbeth plc would, accordingly, be as follows:

	£	£
DR Investment in Duncan plc	936	
CR Ordinary share capital		936

ii) The extent to which the balance sheet entries in i) above would differ, if the guidance in the appendix to SSAP 23 were applied:

If alternative 1 were adopted, Macbeth plc would have to use the 'acquisition method' of consolidation (see (b) below). In this case we have the situation where 'merger relief' applies to a parent company but where the 'acquisition method' is used on consolidation.

If, taking advantage of 'merger relief', the parent company were to record the cost of a subsidiary as in i) above (£1,608), goodwill on consolidation, based on this cost would be understated.

Accordingly, the guidance in the SSAP 23 appendix advises that if 'merger relief' applies to the parent company and the 'acquisition method' is used on consolidation, the parent company should record the cost of its subsidiary as amounting to the fair value of the consideration. If the premium on any of the parent company's shares issued as consideration cannot be taken to share premium account, under S.131, it should be taken, instead, to a separate unrealised reserve called a 'merger reserve'.

Thus, the balance sheet entries in i) above would differ as follows:

The investment in Duncan plc would include cost of purchase of the 1,248,000 Duncan plc shares of £1,872,000 and not £936,000. The premium of £936,000 on the Macbeth plc ordinary shares issued as consideration for this purchase would be credited to a merger reserve. The cost of the subsidiary would therefore be (1,608 + 936) £2,544,000.

The *share capital* of Macbeth plc would remain unchanged as would the *share premium account.*

b) Whether or not Macbeth plc may use the merger method of consolidation under alternative 1:

Both SSAP 23 and the Companies Act 1985 would require a holding of at least 90% of the equity of the subsidiary before the merger method could be used on consolidation. Macbeth plc does own 90% of the equity of Duncan plc.

Under SSAP 23, prior holdings are permissible in the subsidiary but only up to and not including 20% of the subsidiary's equity. As Macbeth plc's prior holdings in Duncan plc (6.25% + 18.75%) amount to 25%, the merger method of consolidation cannot be used and the acquisition method must be used. (Note that the Companies Act 1985 is silent as to prior holdings in this respect.)

As to the consideration, under SSAP 23, we would look at the fair value of the total consideration - £2,544,000 (see (a) ii) above). Assuming that the cost of the prior holding of 120,000 shares of £132,000 consisted wholly of cash, the cash element of (132 + 540) of £672,000 is more than 10% of the fair value of the total consideration and the merger method of consolidation cannot be used.

Under the Companies Act 1985 one would look to the consideration for the 'merger offer'. No more than 10% of the NV of the parent undertaking's equity shares issued as consideration for this offer can be in a form other than the parent undertaking's equity shares - see (c) below for an illustration of the application of this restriction.

Accordingly, as not all the conditions of both SSAP 23 and the Companies Act 1985 in this respect are satisfied the merger method cannot be used on consolidation and the acquisition method must be used.

c) The consolidated balance sheet of Macbeth plc and its subsidiary at 31 December 1990 (alternative 2):

It is first necessary to establish the cost of the subsidiary as it would be recorded by Macbeth plc

The merger offer is for 1,608,000 Duncan plc ordinary shares with a value of £2,412,000. The consideration for this purchase is to be satisfied by an issue by Macbeth plc of its own ordinary shares.

Macbeth plc will therefore issue (2,412/2) 1,206,000 £1 ordinary shares at a premium of £1 each. The premium of £1,206,000 will not be recorded as S.131 applies to the premium. The cost of the subsidiary, as recorded by Macbeth plc will therefore be (132 + 1,206) £1,338,000 (the fair value of the consideration would be [1,338 + 1,206] £2,544,000).

The merger method may be used in consolidation as Macbeth plc owns 90% of Duncan plc's equity, the prior holding is less than 20% and

i)   re SSAP 23 – 132 is < 10% × 2,544, and

ii) re CA 1985 – there is no non-equity included in the consideration for the merger offer.

The consolidated balance sheet at 31 December 1990, using the merger method (assuming no change in fixed assets since 31 December 1988 and that retained profits result in an increase in net current assets):

Consolidated balance sheet at 31 December 1990

	£000	
Fixed assets (assuming no change since 1988)	2,624 + 1,792	4,416
Net current assets	1,056 + 864	
Increase 1989	512 + 320	
Increase 1990	512 + 320	
	2,080 + 1,504	3,584
		8,000
Ordinary share capital	2,560 + 1,206	3,766
Share premium account		12
Consolidated difference on merger	1,388 < 1,728	390
Profit and loss account 1,240 + 512 + 512		
+ (90% × [736 + 320 + 320])		3,502
Minority interest 10% × (1,792 + 1,504)		330
		8,000

2 Firebrand Ltd

a) Memorandum

i)   Summary consolidated balance sheet as on 31 October 1989:

	£
Tangible fixed assets (2,150 - 50) + (625 + 120 – 0.6)	2,844,400
Net current assets (1,900 + 142.5) + 50	2,092,500
Long-term liabilities	(400,000)
Provisions and other charges	(95,000)
	4,441,900
Share capital	1,000,000
Share premium account	500,000
Revaluation reserve (1,300 – 50)	1,250,000
Profit and loss account (balancing item)	1,652,180
Minority interest 5% × (675 + 120 – 0.6)	39,720
	4,441,900

The profit and loss account is explained as follows:

	£
Firebrand Ltd (per question)	1,800,000
Dividend from Felix Ltd restricted to share of post-acquisition profits of Felix Ltd – £25 less additional depreciation of 2% × 120 × 3/12 i.e. 90% × (25 – 0.6)	23,180
Consolidation goodwill written off	(171,000)
	1,652,180

ii) A brief description of the method of accounting for goodwill adopted:

		£
Consolidation goodwill arising on the purchase of Felix Ltd is arrived at as follows:		
Cost – initial consideration paid		950,000
– deferred consideration likley to be paid		95,000
		1,045,000
Less: fair value of separable net assets acquired:		
Tangible fixed assets (650 + 120)	770,000	
Net current assets	150,000	
	920,000 × 95%	(874,000)
		171,000

The goodwill arising on consolidation has been written off (following the chairman's preferred accounting policy) immediately against consolidated reserves. As neither the share premium account nor the revaluation reserve are available, it has been written off to profit and loss account.

Accordingly, there is no charge for amortisation of goodwill against consolidated reported profits and therefore no earnings effect. Consolidated net assets are, of course, less than they might otherwise have been. As the write-off arises only on consolidation there is no effect on the realised profits of either the parent or the subsidiary as individual companies.

iii) A brief explanation of the possible changes in accounting policies or treatment available to Firebrand Ltd:

As the brands of Felix Ltd are acquired, and assuming them to be separable, they may be included in the consolidation goodwill calculation and under intangible fixed assets in the consolidated balance sheet. This would result in a decrease in the consolidation goodwill and an increase in minority interest. If such brands are capitalised, they should be amortised over their economic useful life. By contrast, the brands of Firebrand are 'home grown' and in line with recent ASC proposals (ED 52) should not be included under intangible fixed assets.

Goodwill on consolidation may, instead of being written off, be carried forward and systematically amortised. Where, at present, companies have a choice of writing off goodwill to reserves or amortising it over economic useful life, the ASC has proposed (ED 47) the removal of the write-off option requiring companies to amortise goodwill over a maximum of 20 years unless it can be demonstrated that a longer period is suitable.

b)   The options available to Firebrand Ltd had the purchase consideration been wholly in shares of 10p each issued at £1 each:

In Firebrand Ltd's own accounts:

The fair value of the consideration would be £1,045,000. Merger relief would apply to shares issued by Firebrand Ltd as the initial consideration. Accordingly, Firebrand Ltd could record its investment:

		£	£
either	DR Investment in subsidiary	104,500	
	CR Provision		9,500
	CR Share capital		95,000
or	DR Investment in subsidiary	1,045,000	
	CR Provision		95,000
	CR Share capital		95,000
	CR S.131 or merger reserve		855,000

In Firebrand Ltd's consolidated accounts:

Under SSAP 23, the conditions for the use of the merger method are satisfied. Accordingly, the merger method may, but need not necessarily, be used on consolidation.

If the merger method were used on consolidation, the cost of the investment would be £104,500. Fair value would not be assigned to the net assets of the subsidiary, no distinction would be made between pre-combination and post-combination reserves of the subsidiary and no goodwill would arise on the combination. A consolidation difference would arise between the cost of the subsidiary and the nominal value of shares owned. This would be credited to reserves.

If the acquisiton method were used on consolidation, Firebrand Ltd might have recorded the investment under either of the two alternatives illustrated above. Under the first alternative, a consolidation adjustment would be necessary to uplift the cost of the investment to fair value. This would be necessary to calculate the goodwill arising.

Under the second alternative, fair value is already recorded in the books of the parent company. In either event, goodwill arising can be written off against the S.131 or merger reserve. Fair values must be assigned to the subsidiary's net assets on the date of the acquisiton, and pre-acquisition reserves of the subsidiary would be frozen or capitalised.

CHAPTER 20 *Self test questions*

1   The effects of establishing fair values on the acquisition of a subsidiary are threefold:

   ▶ it determines the cost of the acquisition for the parent
   ▶ it determines how the purchase consideration should be allocated in arriving at the initial carrying amounts of the identifiable assets and liabilities of the acquired undertaking in the consolidated accounts of the acquirer
   ▶ the difference between the fair value of the consideration and the fair value of the (underlying) identifiable net assets acquired determines the amount to be recognised as consolidation goodwill.

2   Adopting what has been termed an 'acquirer's perspective' has led to the past practice of liabilities recognised at acquisition including provisions in respect of items taken into account by the acquirer in making its investment decision, such as costs relating to post-acquisition reorganisations or

anticipated future losses. Treating such provisions as pre-acquisition results in such provisions bypassing the consolidated profit and loss account if goodwill is written off immediately to reserves. This is because the treatment results in a reduction of fair values of identifiable net assets at acquisition and an increase in goodwill. If such goodwill is written off to reserves at acquisition the provisions will not pass through the consolidated profit and loss account.

3 The main aims of the proposals presented in FRED 7 are to:

▶ assist users to assess trends in operating performance of continuing and acquired businesses from the date the new acquisitions enter the group
▶ assist users to assess the financial effects of activities to develop and re-shape the enlarged group after an acquisition
▶ reduce inconsistencies by narrowing areas of subjectivity.

4 The recognition of expected costs or losses that are not liabilities of the acquired business at the date of its acquisition are not permitted as fair value adjustments even though they were identified at the acquisition date and taken into account by the acquirer in its investment appraisal. Such costs should be reported in the profit and loss account of an acquiring group as incurred.

5 The proposals of the fair value Discussion Paper and FRED 7 for assigning initial fair values in the net assets of the acquired business at acquisition are:

a) Fixed assets – The fair value at the date of acquisition is the replacement cost of its service potential unless that exceeds its recoverable amount in which case it is necessary to reflect the lower value.
b) Stocks – The fair value is the lower of replacement cost and net realisable value. Replacement cost is the cost at which the stock would have been replaced by the acquired company.
c) Long-term receivables and payables – Where these do not bear interest at current market rates they should be discounted to their present value.

CHAPTER 20 *Exam style question*

1 *Miami plc*
a) Consolidation goodwill on the basis that all provisions identified at 1 January 1995 are treated as pre-acquisition. This was accepted practice until the ASB fair value discussion paper.

Fair value of the consideration:

	£000	£000
Cash (25%)		8,750
Miami plc ordinary shares (75%)		
Nominal value 26,250/2.2	11,932	
Premium £11,932 × £1.2	14,318	
		26,250
		35,000
Less:		
Fair value of identifiable net assets at 1 January 1995:		
Per balance sheet (26,605 – 754)	25,851	
Reorganisation provisions (5,285 + 2,750)	(8,035)	
Other provisions (200 + 100)	(300)	
		(17,516)
		17,484

b) Consolidation goodwill on the basis that the reorganisation provisions are treated as post-acquisition.

This is the proposed practice of the ASB Discussion Paper on fair values in acquisition accounting.

	£000	£000
Fair value of the consideration (as in (a))		35,000
Less:		
Fair value of identifiable net assets at 1 January 1995:		
Per balance sheet (as in (a))	25,851	
Other provisions	(300)	
		(25,551)
		9,449

---

c) Consolidated balance sheet at 31 December 1995:

	£000
Fixed assets (21,500 + 18,680 – 5,285)	34,895
Other net assets (8,900 – 8,750 + 7,925 – 2,750 – 260 – 80)	4,985
	39,880

	Either £	Or £
Share capital (10,000 + 11,932)	21,932	21,932
Share premium account	2,200	2,200
Revaluation reserve	2,500	2,500
Merger reserve	14,318	14,318
Profit and loss account (per (d))	16,414	8,379
Goodwill written off (per (a)/(b))	(17,484)	(9,449)
	39,880	39,880

d) Consolidated profit and loss account for the year ended 31 December 1995:

	(a) Reorganisation provisions treated as pre-acquisition £000	(b) Reorganisation provisions treated as post-acquisition £000
Turnover (85,631 + 57,279)	142,910	142,910
Gross profit (12,845 + 7,733)	20,578	20,578
Profit before tax (1,924 + 1,142)	3,066	3,066
Increase in provision for warranty costs	(60)	(60)
Reorganisation provisions	–	(8,035)
	3,006	(5,029)
Tax (596 + 388)	(984)	(984)
Decrease in deferred tax provision	20	20
	(964)	(964)
Profit/(Loss) for year	2,042	(5,993)
Brought forward – Miami only (15,700 – 1,328)	14,372	14,372
	16,414	8,379

CHAPTER 21 *Self test questions*

1 Factors to be taken into account in determining whether or not significant influence is exercised:
An associate is defined in SSAP 1 as an investment in which the investing company's or group's interest is:

▶ *either* that of a partner in a joint venture or consortium and the investing company or group is in a position to exercise significant influence over the associated company
▶ *or* long-term, substantial, and having regard to the other shareholdings, the investing company or group is in a position to exercise a significant influence over the associated company.

There is a general presumption that there is significant influence if the investor holds 20% or more of the equity voting rights and that there is no significant influence if less than this amount is owned.
    Significant influence may, none the less, be exercised with a holding of less than 20%; no significant influence may exist even with a holding of more than 20%. What is important is the disposition of the other shareholdings.
    In order to arrive at the general presumption level, you need to take into account:

▶ the percentage owned by the investor company
▶ the whole of the percentage owned by any subsidiaries (but not other associates) of the investor.

The fact that the effective share of the investing group may be less than 20% is of no relevance.
    Further, the standard states that the exercise of significant influence involves participation in the financial and operating policy decisions of the investee company but not necessarily control over those policies. Representation on the board of directors of the investee company is indicative of such participation, but will neither necessarily give conclusive evidence of it, nor be the only method by which the investing company can participate.

2 The carrying value of the investment in Gary Baldy plc in the consolidated balance sheet of Gladys plc on 20 May 1994:

This may be calculated in either one of two ways and, in either case, is the value after eliminating, per SSAP 22, goodwill paid on acquisition.

Either

			£000
Cost			180
Plus: share of retained post-acquisition reserves			
Profit and loss account	$30\% \times (650 - 220)$		129
Revaluation reserve	$30\% \times 20$		6
			315

Less: Positive goodwill paid written off		
or		
Add: negative goodwill credited to reserves		
Cost	180	
Less: $30\% \times$ (OSC + reserves at acquisition		
– goodwill of 200 written off against		
reserves at acquisition)		
$30\% \times (500 + 220 + 100 - 200)$	(186)	6
		321

Or

	£000
Share of separable net assets representing ordinary shares:	
$30\% \times (1,370$ less goodwill of 200 less preference share capital of 100)	321
Share of separable net assets representing preference shares	–
Add: positive goodwill	
or	
Less: negative goodwill	(6)
	315
Less: positive goodwill	
or	
Add: negative goodwill	6
	321

3   The carrying value of the investment in the associated company in London plc's consolidated balance sheet as at 31 December 1995:

	£
Cost	20,000
Plus: share of profit after tax (post acquisition)	
$30\% \times 60 \times {}^9/_{12}$	13,500
Less: dividend – treated as wholly out of post-acquisition profits	
$30\% \times 12$	(3,600)
	£29,900

4   The amount at which the investment in Simple Ltd will be included in the consolidated balance sheet of Pimple plc at 31 December 1996:

$40\% \times (47,500 + 32,000 - [25\% \times 32,000]) = £28,600$

5   The consolidated profit before tax for inclusion in the consolidated profit and loss account of the Bingo plc group for the year ended 31 December 1994:

$750 + 870 + (45\% \times 690) = £1,930.5$

$30\% + 15\% = 45\%$
A MI of $20\% \times 15\% = 3\%$ will need to be disclosed for Vimto Ltd's profits.

CHAPTER 21 *Exam style questions*

1   *Xanthos Ltd*

		Cost	Equity	Proportional consolidation	Full consolidation
		£000s	£000s	£000s	£000s
i)					
	Income statement for the year ended 31 March 1991:				
	Xanthos	950	950	950	950
	Ionic				
	(a) Dividend	500	–	–	–
	(b) Share of earnings	–	750	750	–
	(c) Total earnings	–	–	–	3,000
		1,450	1,700	1,700	3,950
	MI (75% × 3,000)				(2,250)
	Earnings before dividend	1,450	1,700	1,700	1,700
	Balance sheet as at 31 March 1991:				
	Ordinary share capital	2,000	2,000	2,000	2,000
	Reserves	1,125	1,500	1,500	1,500
	MI	–	–	–	2,250
	Long-term debt	2,000	2,000 +2,175	4,175	10,700
	Current liabilities	2,500	2,500+75	2,575	2,800
		7,625	8,000	10,250	19,250
	Fixed assets	4,000	4,000 +2,800	6,800	15,200
	Goodwill	–	– + 75	75	75
	Investment in Ionic	450	825	–	–
	Current assets	3,175	3,175 +200	3,375	3,975
		7,625	8,000	10,250	19,250
				(*See* W3)	

ii)

	Cost	Equity	Proportional consolidation	Full consolidation
eps	$\dfrac{1,450}{2,000}$	$\dfrac{1,700}{2,000}$	$\dfrac{1,700}{2,000}$	$\dfrac{1,700}{2,000}$
	= 72.5p	85p	85p	85p
ROCE	$\dfrac{(1,450+200)}{5,125}$	$\dfrac{(1,700+200)}{5,500}$	$\dfrac{(1,700+417.5)}{7,675}$	$\dfrac{(3,950+1,070)}{16,450}$
	= (32,19%)	(34.54%)	(27,58%)	(30.51%)
Debt: Equity	$\dfrac{2,000}{3,125}$	$\dfrac{2,000}{3,500}$	$\dfrac{4,175}{3,500}$	$\dfrac{10,700}{5,750}$
	= (64%)	(57.14%)	(119.28%)	(186.08%)

iii)

	£
SSAP 1 disclosure note	
Share of net assets (equity) 25% × (1,000 + 2,000)	750
Goodwill on acquisition (*see* W2)	75
	825

Share of debt of associate 25% × 10% long-term debt of 8,700 = £2,17.5

iv)

In so far as there are several methods of accounting for an investment in another company in the accounts of the investor, it is important in establishing the most appropriate method to ascertain the degree of control and the degree of influence that is exercised over the decisions of the investee. Clearly, where control is not exercised over the investee, it is inappropriate to consolidate income and net assets and quite absurd to describe a 'minority' interest in such income and net assets. It is, however, relevant to appreciate that no difference arises in eps regardless of choice between the equity accounting alternatives and full consolidation procedures. There is only a difference in presentation of income.

The choice therefore in deciding on the most appropriate method of accounting for an investment over which only significant influence but not control is exercised over the investee, boils down to one between the cost method and the alternative equity accounting procedures.

Under the cost method, eps is understated in so far as only dividends received from the investee are included in income. The shareholders of the investor are given no indication of the extent to which their investment in the investee has appreciated in terms of the underlying net assets of the investee. In this sense the eps indicated under the equity alternatives provides a far more meaningful indicator of performance as far as the investor is concerned.

Exactly the same point can be made in terms of ROCE where return and capital employed are understated under the cost method. As far as this measurement is concerned, however, there is a point to be made distinguishing between the equity accounting alternatives. As the investor's share of debt in the investee is effectively 'off balance sheet' in the equity column, the ROCE is favourable compared with the ROCE in the proportional consolidation column. Proportional consolidation procedures, in so far as they incorporate the investor's share of debt of the investee result in a more meaningful calculation of the primary ratio.

If, however, you were to view the equity column results together with the SSAP 1 disclosures that are now required, the users of the investor's accounts could quite easily re-calculate the ROCE of the investor to arrive at the same conclusion as that indicated in the proportional consolidation column.

Thus,

Equity column	SSAP 1 note information	Restated results corresponding to those in the proportional consolidation column
1,900 *add* additional interest	217.5 =	2,117.5
5,500 *add* additional debt	2175	7,675

and it could be satisfactorily argued that SSAP 1 would result in a true and fair view of the results of an investor.

Essentially the same points could be raised as to the debt: equity ratio. In so far as debt is understated in the equity column, the SSAP 1 note enables re-calculation to reflect the true position as far as gearing is concerned.

Workings (W.1–4)

1 Reserves in the cost method balance sheet

		£000
per question – equity method		1,500
Less: share of post-acquisition earnings		
i.e. post-acquisition retained	2,000 – 500 = 1,500	
Add: Dividends	2,000	
Post-acquisition earnings	3,500 × 25%	(875)
		625
Add: Dividends received 25% × 2,000		500
		1,125

2 Goodwill

	£000
Cost	450
Less: net assets acquired	
25% (1,000 + 500)	(375)
Goodwill	75

3 Share of separate assets and liabilities

		£000
FA	25% × 11,200	2,800
CA	25% × 800	200
CL	25% × (300)	(75)
Long-term debt 25% × (8,700)		(2,175)
Goodwill		75
SSAP 1 value – equity method		825

4 SSAP 1 value – equity method

	£000		£000
Cost	450	Dividends received	
		25% × 2,000	500
Share of post-acquisition earnings		B/S – equity method	825
1 b/f (1,000-500) × 25%	125		
2 year 3,000 × 25%	750		

(Note, per the question, the goodwill is carried unamortised and therefore included in the carrying value above.)

2 *Horatio Ltd*

Summarised consolidated balance sheet as on 31 March 1991:

	£000
Tangible fixed assets (2,675 + 1,925)	4,600
Shares in associated company (W.1)	161
Loan to associated company	100
Net current assets (W.2)	22,593
10% Debentures	(500)
	6,954
Ordinary share capital	3,000
Preference share capital	1,000
Reserves (W.3)	1,981.2
Minority interest (W.4)	972.8
	6,954

Summarised profit and loss account for the year ended 31 March 1991:

	Horatio Ltd £000	Sebastian Ltd £000	Arkwright Ltd £000	Consolidated £000
Profit on ordinary activities after taxation	600			
Less: intercompany dividends received				
40% × 30	(12)			
90% × 60	(54)			
35% × 40	(14)			
	520	360	–	880
Income from shares in associated company, after taxation				
35% × 200			70	70
				950
Intercompany preference dividends				
40% × (30 + 30)	24	(60)		(36)
	544	300	70	914
Minority interest		10% (30)		(30)
	544	270	70	884
Extraordinary items, net of taxation	(100)			
90% × 40		36		
35% × 110			38.5	
(25.5)				
Intercompany ordinary dividends				
90% × 140	126	(126)		
35% × 120	42		(42)	
Group profit 'dealt with'	612	180	66.5	858.5
Dividends – preference	(60)			
– ordinary	(300)			(360)
Retained for year	252	180	66.5	498.5
Profit brought forward (W.3)	1,045	883.2	(25.2)	1,903
				2,401.5
Consolidated adjustments: goodwill written off (W.1 and W.5)				
re: Arkwright Ltd				(127.3)
re: Sebastian Ltd				(293)
				1,981.2

Workings (W.1–5)

W.1 Associated company, carrying value in the consolidated balance sheet

	£000	£000
Either: Cost	247	
Plus: share of retained post acquisition reserves		
(35% × (220 – 102)	41.3	
		288.3
Less: goodwill written off		
247 less 35% (400 + 102 – 160)		127.3
		161

Or:

Share of net assets (excluding goodwill)	
35% (620 – 160)	161
Plus: goodwill paid – as above	127.3
Less: goodwill written off	(127.3)
	161

W.2 Consolidated net current assets	£000
Per balance sheets (678 + 1,803)	2,481
Add back proposed dividends of Sebastian Ltd (30 + 80)	110
	2,591
Less: Sebastian Ltd dividends payable to M.1	
60% × 30	(18)
10% × 80	(8)
	2,565
Add: dividend receivable from Arkwright Ltd	28
	2,593

W.3 Consolidated reserves	£000
Brought forward – Horatio Ltd	1,045
Sebastian Ltd i) 60% × (1,328 – 310)	610.8
ii) 30% × (1,328 – 420)	272.4
Arkwright Ltd 35% × (30 – 102) – losses	(25.2)
	1,903
Less: consolidated adjustments, goodwill on consolidation written off	
i) re. Arkwright Ltd (see W.1)	(127.3)
ii) re. Sebastian Ltd (see W.5)	(293)
For the year – Horatio Ltd, including dividends received	140
Dividends receivable:	
From Sebastian Ltd 40% × 30	12
90% × 80	72
From Arkwright Ltd 35% × 80	28
Sebastian Ltd – share of retained profits 90% × 200	180
Arkwright Ltd 35% × 190	66.5
Consolidated reserves carried forward	1,981.2

W.4 Minority interest	£000
ordinary shares 10% × (1,000 + 1,528)	252.8
preference shares 60% × 1,200	720
	972.8

W.5 Consolidation adjustment, goodwill re. Sebastian Ltd

	£000	£000
i) Re. 1/1/84 purchase		
cost of ordinary shares	950	
60% (1,000 + 310)	(786)	
		164
ii) Re. 30/9/84 purchases		
Cost of ordinary shares	550	
30% (1,000 + 420)	(426)	
		124
Cost of preference shares	485	
NV of preference shares 40% × 1,200	(480)	
		5
Written off, on consolidation, direct to reserves		293

CHAPTER 22 *Self test questions*

1   Under the closing rate/net investment method the amounts in the balance sheet of a foreign enterprise should be translated into the reporting currency of the investing company using the rate of exchange ruling at the balance sheet date. Amounts in the profit and loss account of a foreign enterprise should be translated at the closing rate or at an average rate for the accounting period. The one selected is to be applied consistently. All exchange differences arising are taken on consolidation directly to reserves.

Under the temporal rate method all monetary items are translated at closing rates giving rise to exchange differences recognised through the profit and loss account while all non-monetary items are translated at the rate on the date of purchase.

2   In most cases an investing company will regard its foreign enterprises as separate businesses that are independent from the business of the investing company. In these situations the day-to-day business operations of the enterprise are managed with regard to the currency of the country in which the enterprise operates and the enterprise is likely to be financed in that currency. The acquisition of the foreign enterprise is a long-term investment in the net worth of the business as a going concern, and the investing company has no specific interest in the individual assets and liabilities of the enterprise. While the investing company may anticipate a stream of dividends from the investment, it will not expect to realise a share of the net investment unless it liquidates the business or disposes of the investment. In the UK it is most common for businesses to conduct their foreign operations through such quasi-independent entities. The closing rate/net investment method must be used.

   In those situations, however, where the affairs of a foreign enterprise are closely interlinked with those of the investing company, it no longer seems appropriate to regard the foreign currency as being that on which the foreign enterprise is dependent. In these circumstances, the local currency of the foreign enterprise is deemed to be that of the investing company, and the temporal method must be used. The effect its to treat the assets and liabilities of the foreign enterprise as though they belonged directly to the investing company.

   The standard specifies a number of factors that need to be taken into consideration in determining the dominant currency and therefore the method to be used. The temporal method should be used where:

▶ the cash flows of the enterprise have a direct impact on those of the investing company
▶ the functioning of the enterprise is dependent directly upon the investing company
▶ the majority of trading transactions are denominated in the currency of the investing company
▶ the majority of the financing is in the currency of the investing company and is obtained through or guaranteed by that company.

Thus the temporal method would usually be required where the overseas enterprise:

▶ acts as a selling agency receiving goods from the investing company and remitting back the proceeds of sale
▶ produces raw material for inclusion in the investing company's product
▶ is located overseas for tax, exchange control or similar reasons to act as a means of raising finance for other companies in the group.

3   The justification of the treatment prescribed for an overseas equity investment financed by foreign borrowings is that the group may have used foreign borrowings to finance new group investments or to provide a hedge against the exchange risk associated with existing group investments. Without this offset, exchange fluctuations on the net investment would be reflected in reserves, whereas exchange gains and losses on the loans would be taken to the consolidated profit and loss account. To the extent that these exchange movements match each other, there is no economic exchange risk, and it is therefore inappropriate to record an accounting profit or loss. For such an offset procedure to apply it is relevant that:

▶ the closing rate method is used
▶ the exchange gains or losses on foreign currency borrowings are offset only to the extent of the exchange differences on the overseas net investments
▶ the foreign currency borrowings used in the offset process should not exceed the cash that the net investments are expected to be able to generate, whether from profits or otherwise
▶ the accounting treatment is applied consistently from period to period.

4   Under SSAP 20, Halogen plc may initially record the sales (and debtors) at either the rates on the date of the transaction – per the question, average rates – that is, £1,000,000 or at the rate specified in the matching forward contract, that is, £1,050,000.

   Had the company opted to record the sales and debtors at £1,000,000, the debtor, on receipt, would give rise to an exchange gain of £50,000. This would be credited to trading profit as other operating income. Had the company opted to record the sales and debtors at £1,050,000, the debtors would eventually be settled at this amount and no exchange difference would arise.

   Regardless of the option adopted, there will be no effect on the total amount credited to the profit and loss account as arising from the foreign currency transaction.

   Given alternative permissible treatments, it is important that the accounting policies of the company specify the treatment adopted. Where an exchange difference on such a transaction does arise, it would not be separately disclosed unless it were material, and then as exceptional.

5   Chlorine Ltd should include the loan in its balance sheet at its present estimated realisable value which is:

R 50,000,000/20 = £2,500,000 less, in order to write down to recoverable amount, £400,000 = £2,100,000.

There is, therefore, a gain on retranslation of £500,000 (R 50 million/20 less R 50 million/25) and a required provision of £400,000. This is required under SSAP 20, given doubts as to the convertibility/marketability of the loan receivable. The company should include the net gain of £100,000 (as interest) in the profit and loss account.

   Having included, per the accounting standard, the gain in the profit and loss account, the company will have departed from the legal rule that only profits realised at the balance sheet date should be included in the profit and loss account. Accordingly, the company should disclose:

▶ reason for the departure – special reason – symmetry of accounting treatment of all exchange differences, losses and gains.

▶ effect of departure – the (net) gain on retranslation of overseas loans included in the profit and loss account.

CHAPTER 22 *Exam style questions*

1   *Cyrus plc*
W.1
i)   Associated company for the consolidated balance sheet

	£000
Share of separable net assets	
40% × (750 + 450)	480
(*Note:* share capital = 300 × 100/40 = 750)	
Plus:	
Goodwill paid 450 less (40% × [750 + 187.5])	75
Less:	
Goodwill paid, written off since acquisition	(75)
	480

ii) Share of post-acquisition reserves brought forward

	£000	£000
At acquisition		187.50
Post-acquisition brought forward – Bal. Item		161.25
For the year:		
Profit before taxation	300	
Taxation	(120)	
	180	
Dividends (70% × 45) × 100/40	(78.75)	101.25
Retained carried forward		450

Therefore the group's share of the retained post-acquisition reserves brought forward
= 40% × 161.25 = £64.5.

W.2
Provision for unrealised profit (PURP)

	PURP	CT = 50%	DT
30 June 1990			
120 × 25/125	24		12
Increase for the year ended 30 June 1991	6		3
30 June 1991 150 × 25/125	30		15

W.3

*Translation of balance sheet of overseas subsidiary and
the consolidated balance sheet of 30 June 1991 (per b) of question)*

	Darius		Cyrus	Adjust	CBS
	D000	Closing rate/ net inv method	£000	£000	£000	£000
Fixed assets	6,000	12	500	2,550	–	3,050
Assoc. Co.					W1	480
Stocks	7,500	12	625	2,250	W2 (30)	2,845
Debtors	6,000	12	500	1,350		1,850
Intercompany receivable	1,500	12	125¢			–
Bank	638	12	53	321		374
Creditors	(1,838)	12	(153)	(925)		(1,078)
Intercompany payable				(125)¢		–
Tax	(1,650)	12	(138)	(750)		(888)
Prop. Div. – sub	(1,500)	12	(125) – Payable to M.I 25% × 125			(31)
– parent			(375)			(375)
ACT payable				(161)		(161)
Loan				(1,500)	W4	(1,000)
Deferred tax				(204)	W2 15	(189)
	16,650		1,387			4,877

	Darius D000	Closing rate/ net inv method	£000	Cyrus £000	Adjust £000	CBS £000
Ordinary share capital	12,000	9	1,333			3,000
Reserves:					Bal. item	1,530
i) At acq.	1,500	9	167			
ii) Post acq. b/f	2,072	9.75	213			
Exch. diff. b/f	–		(156)			
Net assets b/f	15,572	10	1,557			
iii) For the year	1,078	W6	109		Minority interest	
Exch. diff. for year	–		(279)		W5	347
	16,650		1,387			4,877

W.4
Re-translation of overseas loan in Cyrus

				£000	
	$1,500	30/10/90	1	1,500	
		30/6/91	1.5	1,000	CBS
			Gain	500	

W.5
Minority interest for the consolidated balance sheet

$$25\% \times 1,387 = £347,000$$

W.6
Darius profit for the year

	D000		£000
Retained profit	1,078		
Add: Proposed dividend	1,500		
	2,578	11	234
Less: Proposed dividend	(1,500)	12	(125)
	D1,078		109

W.7
Consolidation goodwill

	£000
Xerxes – see W.1 -	75
Darius 1,350 less [75% × (1,333 + 167)]	225
	300

W.8
Consolidation stage exchange differences and offset:

	£000		£000
Loss on overseas subsidiary		Gain on overseas loan	
75% × (156 + 279)	326	500 – restricted to	326

The excess gain on the loan of £174,000 must be dealt with as interest in the consolidated profit and loss account for the year.

a) and c) The consolidated profit and loss account for the year ended 30 June 1991 and movements on reserves:

	Cyrus £000	Subdis. Darius D000	Average	£000	Assoc. Xerxes £000	Consol. adj. £000	CPL a/c £000
Turnover	10,500	33,000	11	3,000		(750)	12,750
Cost of sales	(8,400)	(24,750)	11	(2,250)		750	(9,906)
PURP W2	(6)						
	2,094			750			2,844
Dist/admin	(1,200)	(3,900)	11	(355)			(1,555)
	894			395			1,289
Income from associate 40% × 300					120		120
							1,409
Interest payable	(200)						
W8	174						
	(26)						(26)
	868	–		395	120	–	1,383

Tax

per question   (360)   (1,500)   11   (136)

                 14   (Remove tax suffered on associate dividend

                         30% × 45)

                 3   D Tax on PURP W2

                (343)

40% × 120				(48)	(527)
	525		259	72	856
Minority interest		25% (65)			(65)
		194			791
Extraordinary (net)	105				
(272) × 75%					
@ 11			(19)		86
	630		175	72	877
Intercompany dividends					
75% × 125	94		(94)		
Dividends 45 = Gross					
70% = 31 = net	31		(31)		
	755		81	41 –	877
Dividends	(375)				(375)
Retained	380		81	41 –	502

B/F

     481

     (115)   366

         PURP b/fwd   (24)   W2

         D Tax thereon   12

                       354

Subsidiary 75% × 213					278
(W3)		160	64	(300)	
			W1	W7	
P/L reserves	734	241	105	(300)	780
Revaluation reserve	750				750
Ex difference	–	–	–	W8	Nil
	1,484	241	105	(300)	1,530
					CBS

2   *Bough plc*

(a)   i)   If no currency borrowings were utilised to cover the investment:

Parent co.

The parent company would have an overseas equity investment but no overseas loan. The overseas equity investment would be recorded at cost at the rate on the acquisition date and not retranslated. Accordingly, no exchange difference would arise in the individual company, which would show:

     Investment in Branch Inc. – cost –   £5,000,000

     Translation reserve

Consolidated accounts

Branch Inc., assuming significant influence, would be classified as an associated company and included in the consolidated balance sheet of Bough plc under the equity method of accounting for investments. The carrying value of the associated company for the consolidated balance sheet at 31 December 1991 would be.

			£	£
Cost 1/1/91	$8,750,000	@ 1.75	5,000,000	
31/12/91		@ 1.60	5,468,750	5,468,750
	Exchange gain		468,750	

Plus, share of retained post-acquisition reserves

         $1,050,000 × 30% @ 1.60   196,875

                                                   5,665,625

Less, goodwill paid to the extent written off   –

                                                   5,665,625

(*Note:* The carrying value could, alternatively, be ascertained as follows):

		£	£
Share of FV of separable net assets:			
At acquisition:			
1/1/91	$2,800,000 × 30% @ 1.75	4,800,000	
31/12/91	@ 1.60	5,250,000	5,250,000
	Exchange gain	450,000	
Since acquisition – post-acquisition reserves:			
	$1,050,000 × 30% @ 1.60		196,875
			5,446,875
Plus, goodwill paid on acquisition			
($8,750,000 less (30% × $28,000,000)			
= $350,000			
1/1/91	$350,000 @ 1.75	200,000	
31/12/91	@ 1.60	218,750	218,750
	Exchange gain	18,750	
			5,665,625

The translation reserve in the consolidated accounts would be CR £468,750

ii) If currency borrowings of £2,000,000 were used to cover the investment:

(Assuming that the offset procedure of SSAP 20 is applied at both individual company and group levels.)

Parent co.

The cost of the investment in Branch Inc., $8,750,000 (£5,000,000 @ 1.75), would be retranslated at the year end rate and the exchange difference taken to the translation reserve (exchange difference reserve).

$8,750,000	1/1/91 @ 1.75	5,000,000
	31/12/91 @ 1.60	5,468,750
	Exchange gain	468,750

The loan of £2,000,000 would have been recorded, initially, at the rate entered into and, subsequently retranslated at the year end rate. The exchange difference arising given use of the offset procedure, would be taken direct to reserves for offset against the (opposite) exchange difference on the cost of the investment.

£2,000,000 @ 1.75 = $3,500,000

		£
1/1/91 $3,500,000 @ 1.75		2,000,000
31/12/91	@ 1.60	2,187,500
	Exchange loss	187,500

Thus, the parent company balance sheet at 31 December 1991 would include:

			£
i)	Investment in Branch Inc.	DR	5,468,750
ii)	Loan	CR	2,187,500
iii)	Translation reserve	CR	281,250
	(468,750 – 187,500)		

Consolidated accounts

Branch Inc. would be included in the consolidated balance sheet under fixed asset investments at the same carrying value as in (a)i) above, that is £5,665,625. The exchange gain on retranslation of net assets of £468,750 would be taken direct to consolidation reserves.

The overseas loan would be included in the consolidated balance sheet at £2,187,500 and the exchange loss of £187,500 taken direct to consolidated reserves for offset against the exchange gain on the retranslation of the investment leaving a balance on the reserve of CR £281,250.

b) Income arising from the investment:

Parent Co. (Cost method) Dividend received and receivable

	£
$750,000 × 30% @ 1.60	140,625

Consolidated accounts (Equity method)

Share of profit before tax to be included under income from fixed asset investments:

$2,800,000 × 30% @ 1.60		525,000

Share of tax to be included in the tax on profit on ordinary activities:

$1,000,000 × 30% @ 1.60		187,500

Share of profit retained in associate to be disclosed:

$1,050,000 × 30% @ 1.60		196,875

c) The effects of complying with the requirements of SSAP 22:

Goodwill will arise only in the consolidated accounts. As shares, as opposed to net assets, are purchased, no goodwill will arise in the separate accounts of the investor company.

If goodwill is written off immediately on acquisition, the investment will be held in the consolidated balance sheet at 31 December 1991 at:

Share of FV of separable net assets:

– per NOTE in (a)i above		5,446,875
(exchange gain of £450,000 CR to reserves)		

Plus, goodwill paid, on date of acquisition,

$350,000 @ 1.75		200,000

Less, goodwill paid, written off immediately on acquisition   (200,000)

5,446,875

If the goodwill is written off systematically over, say, 10 years:

			$
1/1/91	350,000	1.75	200,000
Amortisation (1/10)	(35,000)	1.60	(21,875)
Exchange difference	–	gain	18,750
	$315,000	1.60	196,875

The investment will be held in the consolidated balance sheet at 31 December 1991 at:

Share of FV of separable net assets	5,446,875
Plus, unamortised goodwill	196,875
	5,643,750

The consolidation translation reserve would be credited with gains of £450,000 on the separable net assets and £18,750 on the goodwill.

[Note: you could, quite reasonably, have taken goodwill at the rate on the date of acquisition and not retranslated it subsequently. In this case, no exchange difference would arise on the goodwill.

CHAPTER 23 *Self test questions*

1   The six groups of people who might be interested in financial statements are:

i)   present and future potential investors
ii)   creditors, present and potential
iii)   management
iv)   employees, past, present and future
v)   government, for example, Customs and Excise, Inland Revenue
vi)   others such as local government and public environmental groups.

2   Value added may be described as the wealth created by a business producing finished goods that can be sold for more than the cost of bought-in goods and services.

   The value added statement is designed to show the amount of value added by operations during a year (sales less bought-in materials and services consumed) and the application of this value added in remunerating maintenance and expansion of assets.

3   The Stock Exchange requires the following to be covered by an accountants' report in a prospectus to be issued by a company seeking a listing for its shares:

▶ a profit and loss account for each of the five completed financial years prior to the issue of the prospectus
▶ a balance sheet at the end of the last accounting period, each of the previous four years and at the beginning of the five year period
▶ cash flow statements for each of the five years
▶ accounting policies

▶ other relevant matters

▶ whether or not the financial information gives a true and fair view.

4   The reasons for preparing a profit forecast include:

▶ the need for information to guide future decision making

▶ usefulness in share valuation exercises

▶ therefore included in prospectuses and takeover or merger circulars

▶ relevance in forecasting future dividends.

The problems that can arise in producing a profit forecast are:

▶ given the subjectivity involved, management can manipulate the data included in arriving at the forecast

▶ some users may mistake the forecast for a commitment as opposed to an estimate

▶ forecasting can be imprecise given, for example, fluctuating exchange rates, interest rates and inflation

▶ forecasts may be arrived at in terms of desirable as opposed to achievable targets.

5   Value added statement for the year ended 31 December 1994

	£000
Sales	2,960
Less: Bought in goods and services (1,200 + 240)	(1,440)
Value added	1,520

Applied:

	£000
Employees	800
Government	280
Providers of capital (96+40)	136
Reinvested in the business:	
depreciation	160
profit retained	144
	1,520

CHAPTER 23 *Exam style question*

1   *Pru Pereira*

Notes on the advice to be given to Pru Pereira

a)   COMPANY A

Options available   i)   Convert now
                     ii)   Convert next year
                     iii) Hold to maturity between 1995 and 2000

If she were to convert now:

	£
Market value of £100 loan stock	83.00
Market value of shares issued on conversion (£34.39 × 58p/25p)	(79.78)
Loss on conversion	£3.22

Other points:

If the loan stock is sold on the market at £83, the gross proceeds will be reduced by transaction costs and any CGT liability which might arise. No transaction costs are incurred on conversion, and no CGT liability will arise until the shares received on conversion are sold.

If she were to convert next year:

No information is available as to the conversion terms next year. It is probable that a lower number of shares would be issued per £100 stock on the basis that the share price may be expected to increase over time.

It will be necessary to forecast the anticipated growth (or fall) in the share price vis-à-vis conversion terms.

If she were to hold to maturity:

No further options for conversion exist between 1991 and 1995. It must be assumed that the company has the option to determine the redemption date at any time between 1995 and 2000. We assume that the current price of 83 reflects redemption yields required on bonds of this risk type and degree of security. Holding till redemption must depend on the view taken as to the movement on the price of the company's shares.

Income position:

At present, the income return on the loan stock is $8.5\% \times 100/83 = 10.2\%$

This needs to be looked at in the light of average yields available on term loans and debentures. Get a clerk to check on the FT Actuaries Index. The 10.2% includes the premium attaching to conversion rights.

After conversion, the shareholder will receive dividends. Whereas the dividend yield is likely to be less than the present interest yield on the loan stock, it may be expected that dividends will grow over time. With no conversion, the rate of interest will remain unchanged.

Advise Pru to wait until next year for the further and final time that conversion rights may be exercised.

Reasons for company's proposals:

▶ The reason for publication of the circular is to remind holders of their rights under the original offer document.

▶ Conversion may lead to dilution in earnings per share, but it will result in an improvement in gearing ratios.

b) COMPANY B

Options available   i)   oppose resolution
                     ii)   support resolution

The purchase of shares will normally require an ordinary resolution, requiring 50% of the votes of those attending and voting at the meeting.

It would appear that the purchase was not anticipated by the market because the price would have risen to approximately the purchase price. As the purchase provides a substantial gain, although liable to CGT, the proposal should be accepted.

Reasons for the company's proposal:

▶ The company may have surplus funds which it wishes to utilise.

▶ It is most likely that the company is contemplating replacement of its preference share capital with a debenture issue. This is because debenture interest is tax deductible, whereas preference dividends are not.

c) COMPANY C

Options available   i)   sell all rights
                     ii)   sell sufficient rights to raise cash to purchase remainder
                     iii)   take up rights paying out of own resources.

In theory, the price at which a rights issue is priced is irrelevant, providing the market correctly anticipates the return which the proceeds will earn. As a rights issue is priced at a discount on current market price, the price is bound to fall after the issue is made. The amount of the fall will depend on the market's expectations of future earnings.

Market expectations:

Dividend per share – year to 31.12.88	6.61p
Market value per share 23.3.89	119p
Net yield	5.55%
Gross yield (at 25%)	7.40%

	£	£
Market value of 5 shares before rights issue 5 × 119p		5.95
Market value of 6 shares after rights issue 6 × 109p	6.54	
Paid for rights	0.87	
		5.67
Loss in value		0.28

Although the company forecasts the same dividend per share on the increased share capital, the market seems to have discounted this by marking the shares down by 10p. If the market had believed the forecast, it would be expected that the original price would have been maintained.

Other points:

▶ Pru may not wish to increase her holding.
▶ If she wishes to increase her holding, she can avoid transaction costs by taking up the rights issue.
▶ The sale of rights, nil paid, would not give rise to a CGT liability as the value of rights is less than 5% of the market value of the existing shares.

Reason for the company's proposals:

▶ It is probable that the company needs funds to finance expansion or an increase in working capital due to inflation.

CHAPTER 24 *Self test questions*

1 The situations in which the valuation of a business may be required are:

▶ for taxation purposes, for example inheritance tax
▶ for insurance purposes where management may prudently wish to insure a business
▶ where there is to be a transfer of ownership
▶ in partnerships, where there is a change in the partnership.

2 The value of Fink Ltd on the basis of its earnings is:

£30,400 × 10 × [say] 75% = £228,000

The p/e of the similar listed company has been reduced to take account of the lack of marketability of the shares in a private company.

3 The valuation of Fink Ltd in terms of its net assets is calculated as follows:

Super profits are maintainable profits of £30,400 less the normal return of (10% × £220,000) £22,000 = £8,400. The value of the company in terms of its net assets is now £220,000 + (£8,400 × 4) = £253,600.

4 The net dividend per share is £6,000/100,000 = 6p. The gross dividend is 6 × 100/70 = 8.57p. The dividend yield is 8.57/150 × 100 = 5.7%.

5 The p/e ratio is an important tool in the valuation of shares because it is an indication of the number of years' earnings that are purchased by an investor – that is, it is an earnings multiple and enables an investor to compare an investment with alternatives. Bear in mind, however, that it is based on current earnings, whereas an investor buys into future earnings. It is for this reason that companies having an anticipated earnings growth have a high p/e ratio compared with companies having earnings that are considered risky by the market. Also bear in mind the impact of FRS 3.

CHAPTER 24 *Exam style questions*

1 *Fig plc*
Your letter of reply should read something like this:

P.S. Pringle & Co.,
TM House,
Barbican,
London EC2Y 8DR

17 December 199X

The Managing Director,
Fig plc,
DD House,
Barbican,
London EC2X 7SR

Dear Sir,

Thank you for your recent letter asking for an explanation of some financial terms and assistance in obtaining certain information.
        In response to your specific enquiries:

1. Re ordinary shares listed in the *Financial Times*:

COMPANY – The name of the company for which further particulars are disclosed. Companies are conveniently grouped by function, e.g. Motors and Aircraft or Mining.

PRICE – The mid-market price of each share of the company at the end of the previous day's trading. Unless otherwise indicated prices are in pence and denominations are 25p. The listings also indicate the price of each of the company's shares 'ex dividend' or 'ex rights' as the case may be.

Indication is also made when there has been a bid for the company and where the price is 'ex scrip or share split'. Some of these terms may require further explanation and, should this be the case, I would be happy to write again to elaborate.

+ OR –: This indicates, in pence, the movement in the mid-market price of the share from the opening to the closing price during the previous day's trading.

DIVIDEND NET – As with estimated price/earnings ratios and covers these are based on latest annual reports and accounts and, where possible, are updated on half-yearly figures. Whenever a company makes a distribution it must pay advance corporation tax equal to 25% of the gross amount of the dividend. Shareholders receive dividends net of advance corporation tax.

COVER – This indicates the number of times the dividend per share is covered by the earnings per share. See 2. below for a more detailed explanation of cover.

YIELD GROSS – This is the gross dividend, that is, before deducting the advance corporation tax payable by the company in respect of the dividend, to the price of a share. It provides a useful measure in comparing the return on an investment in the shares of a company in terms of dividends with the return on alternative investments.

P/E – This is the price to earnings ratio and is simply the price of a share divided by the earnings per share in respect of that share. It is sometimes also referred to as the earnings multiple since it indicates the number of years that it would take to recover an investment in the shares of a company at their current price given subsequent earnings equal to the current earnings per share.

2. Re extract from the quotations page of the *Financial Times:*

The advance corporation tax (ACT) paid by a company on the dividends that it has paid is available for offset against the company's basic corporation tax liability in computing its mainstream liability. The company therefore has a debtor for ACT which can, for tax purposes, be recovered without time limit. Recovery will, however, depend on the sufficiency of taxable profits in future accounting periods. This possiblity is recognised in an accounting standard, SSAP 8, which adopts the prudence concept and requires that, where such ACT cannot be recovered in the next accounting period, the unrelieved ACT should be written off against current profits as what is termed irrecoverable ACT. The question now arises as to whether such irrecoverable ACT should be seen as part of the cost of the dividend with no effect on the earnings of the company or as part of the tax charge with a consequent effect on the earnings of the company.

The argument in favour of treating it as part of the cost of the dividend is based on the premise that the irrecoverable ACT arises only as a result of the dividend policy adopted by the company and should therefore be shown as an appropriation. This is what is known as the NIL BASIS of ascertaining earnings, that is, excluding that part of the tax charge that varies depending upon the dividend policy adopted by the company.

The argument in favour of treating it as part of the tax charge, what is known as the NET BASIS of ascertaining earnings, is the one supported by SSAP 8. Earnings per share may therefore be calculated either on the basis of net or nil earnings. The relevant accounting standard on the topic, SSAP 3, requires that it be calculated on the basis of net earnings but that disclosure should desirably be made where it differs materially on the basis of nil earnings.

P/E ratios indicated in the *Financial Times* are calculated on the basis of net earnings. Material differences – 10% or more – arising from the use of nil earnings are indicated by bracketed figures.

There is a third basis for ascertaining earnings, which is relevant to the calculation of dividend cover that was briefly dealt with in 1. above, and that is the MAXIMUM BASIS. For a company in which irrecoverable ACT does not arise, dividend cover is based on profit after tax, minority interests and preference dividends but before extraordinary items divided by the net ordinary dividend. In situations in which irrecoverable ACT does arise, and the greater the dividend the greater would be the irrecoverable ACT, investment analysts have devised the maximum distribution basis for computing dividend cover. It is based on profit or earnings after the tax charge that would arise if the whole of the available profit, after such a notional tax charge, were distributed by way of dividend.

3. Re daily share prices for any share listed on The International Stock Exchange, London:

Such information may be obtained from:

▶ SEDOL – the stock exchange daily official list
▶ any reputable broker
▶ Datastream
▶ national newspapers, for important shares only.

The above would also apply re information as to dividends and rights issues.

4. Re copies of financial statements of competitors:

These may be obtained from:

▶ the Registrar of Companies – all incorporated companies are required by law to 'deliver' accounts
▶ special companies that provide such a service
▶ the company itself.

Should you require any further explanations or information please do not hesitate to ask.

Yours faithfully,

2   *Hari Kumar*
REPORT
FROM: AR Countants & Co.
TO: The directors of Leyton Ltd
DATE: 30 September 1991

The principles of share valuation and the alternative valuations that could be placed on the shares of Leyton Ltd.

General
It is important to establish at the outset that there is no one exclusive method for placing a value on a business or on the shares of that business. In the last analysis, the value of a share is the agreed level at which a vendor is prepared to sell and a purchaser is prepared to buy those shares. In considering, therefore, the alternative bases that may be taken into account in valuing the shares of a business all you can do is to determine a range of values within which a successful bid may be made.

Alternative basis for valuing unlisted shares
The alternative bases include:

▶ the dividend yield basis
▶ the price/earnings ratio basis
▶ assets bases on the basis of either the going concern or on a break-up basis.

In arriving at a decision for the relative worth of the share values obtained under each of these bases, you must take into account the fact that yours is an unlisted company and that we are called upon to arrive at a valuation for what amounts to a majority holding. In these circumstances, the value of £2.38 per ordinary share on the dividend yield basis, explained in Appendix 1, is not appropriate. The buyer of the shares will acquire control and therefore exercise control over both the assets and the earnings of your company. Only a minority shareholder would be primarily concerned with this basis of valuation being concerned in the main with a stream of dividend income.

Appropriate bases of valuation in the particular circumstances of the sale of the business to Hari Kumar plc
Given that Hari Kumar plc will acquire control of the business through the purchase of a majority of the ordinary shares of your company, it would be more appropriate to value these shares on the basis of the worth of the underlying net assets and also on the basis of the earnings potential of your company.

As indicated in Appendix 2, the value per ordinary share in your company, using the basis of the attributable values of the net assets of your company amounts to £2.97. It is important to appreciate that, even though account has been taken of the independent sale of the preference shares and the purchase of the 10% Debentures by Hari Kumar plc and current values of existing assets and the contingent liability, this value is arrived at after taking into account your existing goodwill. Were this to be eliminated the value would fall to £2.60 per share.

A purchaser of a controlling interest would also be interested in the earnings potential of your company. A value per ordinary share on the p/e ratio basis would amount to £1.99. The basis of this calculation is set out in Appendix 3.

Advice and recommendations
There is a wide range of values derived from the three alternative bases above. While it may be argued that you should not advise your shareholders to sell their shares at a value below the net asset worth per share, which is the highest of the alternative valuations, Hari Kumar plc may not be prepared to accept this valuation. It is based on the market value of the freehold property. If we were to value the company excluding the property gain and the intangible of goodwill the value of the assets would more closely approximate the valuation arrived at on the two alternative bases.

It is also instructive to point out that the profits of Leyton Ltd appear, from the data provided for the last two years, to be decreasing.

A starting point for negotiations could be the net asset worth per ordinary share as disclosed by your most recent balance sheet, that is, (51,000 less 6,000)/20,000 = £2.25. You would then have some room to manoeuvre based on the potential value of the freehold property and a move to alternative premises without a loss of profits. These considerations may outweigh your decreasing profitability and the fact that the share valuation on the p/e basis is based on the p/e's of listed companies and should have been discounted to take account of the disadvantages of holding unlisted shares.

APPENDIX 1 (Basic rate of income tax assumed at 30%)
Valuation on the basis of the dividend yield:

Net dividend on ordinary shares	£1.5 million
Dividend per share £1.5 million/20 million	= 7.50 pence
Gross dividend (10/7 × 7.5)	= 10.71 pence
Rate of dividend = 10.71p /100p	= 10.71%

Investor's required rate of return based on average gross dividend yield of the two comparable listed companies (4.9 + 4.1)/2 = 4.5%.
Value per share £1 × 10.71/4.5 = £2.38
(Note that the yields indicated in the question are gross yields. Thus for Ranpur plc – (12p × 10/7)/350p = 4.9%.)

APPENDIX 2
Valuation on the basis of attributable values of assets:

	£000
Goodwill	7,500
Property revalued (2,250 × 100/8)	28,125
Plant	30,000
Investments at market value	11,250
Net current assets	6,000

Contingent liabilities	(1,500)
10% Debentures at premium of 10%	(16,500)
Preference shares at sale price	(5,400)
	59,475

Value per share – 59,475/20,000   £2.97

APPENDIX 3

Valuation on an earnings basis – p/e ratio basis:

Capitalised using a p/e ratio of a similar listed company. Taking the average of the two similar listed companies for which data is provided:

(11.3 + 8.2) = 9.75

Therefore value = 20.4p × 9.75 = £1.99 per share.

CHAPTER 25 *Self test questions*

1 The permissible capital payment for Beep Ltd is:

	£
Cost 80,000 × £1.10	88,000
Less: available distributable profits	(30,000)
	58,000

2 The maximum amount that may be debited to Fluffy plc's share premium account:

£100,000, being the lower of the premium on original issue: (400,000 × 25p) £100,000; balance on share premium account after the new issue: (£200,000 + [200,000 × 10p]) £220,000; and proceeds of the new issue of £220,000.

3 The balance on Puff plc's profit and loss account is:

	£
	400,000
Less: premium on purchase	
200,000 × 20p	(40,000)
Less: transfer to capital redemption reserve	
200,000 – 80,000	(120,000)
	240,000

4 The reserve arising after implementation of Barnaby Ltd's capital reduction scheme is:

Capital reduction account

	£000		£000
Profit & loss account	120	Property	25
Goodwill	45	Share capital	
Reserve arising	35	250 × 70p	175

CHAPTER 25 *Exam style questions*

1   *Planets plc*

There must be authority in the articles of the company for a company to purchase its own shares. The financing of the cost of the purchase in the case of a plc must be out of the distributable profits of the company and/or out of the proceeds of a new replacement issue. As the total cost of the proposed purchase is £18,000 and the proceeds of the new replacement issue amount to £13,000, and there are sufficient distributable profits to cover the balance, as indicated by the balance on the company's profit and loss account, the transactions would be permitted under the Companies Act 1985.

Saturn plc

The plan for the company to purchase its own shares is, as above for Planets plc, permitted under the Companies Act 1985, that is, out of the distributable profits and/or the proceeds of a new replacement issue. Given that the shares to be purchased are to be purchased at a premium, the premium payable may legally be paid out of the proceeds of the new replacement issue. Thus the premium payable on the purchase may be dealt with against share premium account if the shares were originally issued at a premium, but only to the lower of the premium originally received and the current balance on the share premium account (including any premium on a new replacement issue) and the proceeds of the new issue.

Neptune Ltd

A private company may finance the cost of the purchase of its own shares not only out of distributable profits and/or the proceeds of a new replacement issue, but also out of funds representing capital. No payment may be made out of capital unless distributable profits are fully utilised to finance part of the cost of the purchase. The company therefore may purchase its own shares as proposed in accordance with the law by making what is called a permissible capital payment to finance the balance of the cost of the purchase.

Pluto Ltd

No legal restrictions would apply in this situation regarding purchase by the company of its own shares given that the proceeds of a new replacement issue on more than sufficient distributable profits to finance the cost of the purchase.

Mars plc

As no new replacement issue of shares is proposed, and because there are insufficient distributable profits held by the company, and because, being a plc, no payment can be made out of capital, the proposed purchase of own shares is not permitted under the Companies Act 1985.

i)   Journal entries:

	Planet plc		Saturn plc		Neptune Ltd		Pluto Ltd	
	£000	£000	£000	£000	£000	£000	£000	£000
DR Cash	13		130		850		850	
CR Share capital		13		100		850		500
CR Share premium account				30				350
with proceeds of new issue								
DR Share capital	20		100		1,000		1,000	
CR Cash		18		150		1,100		1,600
CR Capital redemption reserve		2	–		–		–	
DR Share premiums account			10		50		500	
DR profit and loss account	–		40		50		100	
with purchase of own shares								
DR Profit and loss account	5		–		–	–	150	
CR Capital redemption reserve		5		–		–		150
	(20–13–2)						(1000–850)	

with amount legally required to be transferred to Capital redemption reserve to maintain capital of the company.

ii)   Revised shareholders' funds:

	Planet plc	Saturn plc	Neptune Ltd	Pluto Ltd	Mars plc
	£000	£000	£000	£000	£000
Called up share capital					
(500 + 13 – 20)	493				
(200 + 100 – 100)		200			NO
(5,000 + 850 – 1000)			4,850		CHANGE
(2,000 + 500 – 1,000)				1,500	
Share premium account	–				
(20 + 30 – 10)		40			
(500–50)			450		
(500 + 350 – 500)				350	
Capital redemption reserve					
(2 + 5)	7	–	–	150	
Revaluation reserve	100	–	–	–	
Profit & loss account					
(300 – 5)	295		–		
(50 – 40)		10			
(50 – 50)				–	
(5,000 – 100 – 150)				4,750	
	895	250	5,300	6,750	

iii)   A permissible capital payment arises in Neptune Ltd:

		£000	£000
The PCP =	Cost of purchase of		1,100
	Less:		
	1 All available distributable profits	(50)	
	2 Proceeds of new issue	(850)	
			(900)
			200

As the PCP + the proceeds of the new issue (200 + 850) is greater than the NV of the shares purchased of £1,000, the excess of £50 is written off against 'capital' of the company, in the answer as to journals, against share premium account

---

2   *Tree plc*

For the consideration of the directors of Tree plc:

a) Statement of affairs as at 30 September 1991

	Note	Book value £000	Estimated to realise £000
Assets			
Not specifically pledged:			
Patents and R&D	1	500	–
Plant and machinery		100	10
Stock		1,200	800
Debtors		830	790
Investments		150	220
Cash		10	10
		2,790	1,830
Specifically pledged:			
Land and buildings	2	700	900
			2,730
Due to secured creditors		(414)	(414)
			2,316
Liabilities			
Preferential:			
Wages		(15)	
VAT		(25)	
			(40)
			2,276
Floating charge:			
Bank overdraft and short-term loans		(1,140)	(1,140)
			1,136
Unsecured creditors:			
Trade and other creditors		(148)	
(148 + 60–15–25)			(168)
Directors' loans		(140)	(140)
			828
Provision for costs of liquidation, say			(50)
			778

Notes:

1   The patents are indicated to be worth £140,000 on a going-concern basis. They are assumed to have a nil value on a forced sale.
2   The land and buildings are indicated as having an alternative use value of £900,000. It is assumed that this value would be realised on a forced sale.

If the company were to be liquidated, creditors and shareholders of the company could expect to receive:

	£000
Debenture holders	414
Preferential creditors	40
Bank	1,140
Trade and other creditors	358
Preference shareholders **	500
Ordinary shareholders – the balance	278
	2,730

The assets of the company would realise sufficient amounts to enable creditors of the company to be paid in full, the surplus being available for shareholders.

** When a company is wound up, arrears of dividends are not payable unless declared. Prima facie, preference shares have no priority to return of capital and will rank *pari passu* with ordinary shares. It is usual, however, for the articles to give preference shareholders such priority and it is assumed above that this is the case with Tree plc.

b) **Suggested scheme of reorganisation**

The first step would be to ascertain the total amount to be made available by the scheme:

	£000
Debit balance on profit and loss account to be eliminated	
(352 plus the accrual for September expenses of 60)	412
Loss on patents (500-140)	360
Land and buildings (see note)	–
Plant and machinerey (100-10)	90
Stocks (1,200-800)	400
Debtors	40
Investments at market value (220–150)	(70)
Preference dividends in arrears (see note)	105
Waiver of directors' loans	(140)
Provision for reorganisation costs	50
	1,247
Contingency – say	28
	1,275

Notes:

1   No surplus is recognised on the land and buildings as the alternative use value, while appropriate for a discontinuance valuation, is not appropriate for a going concern valuation for which existing use values are applicable.

2   As the scheme must be acceptable to all parties, the preference dividend for the last 3 years – 7% × £500,000 × 3 – is provided for above. It is normal for such arrears to be cancelled in return for some form of compensation usually an issue of ordinary shares (see below).

The second step would be to allocate the loss:

As noted in (a) above, it is the ordinary shareholders who would bear the whole of any loss in the event of a liquidation, and it is, therefore, only appropriate that the ordinary shareholders bear the whole of the loss arising on reorganisation. This is greater than the loss that the ordinary shareholders would suffer on liquidation but one may reasonably assume that the scheme will return the company to profitability and that the ordinary shareholders would accept the current situation in the hope of better things to come.

On the basis of the reasoning above, the loss of £1,275,000 will be borne entirely by the ordinary shareholders, resulting in a reduction in the value of each £1 share to 15p.

The restructuring of the existing balance sheet would result in:

	£000
Debit to:	
Ordinary share capital	1,275
Investments	70
Directors' loans	140
Amount made available by the scheme	1,485
Applied as follows:	
Credit to:	
Ordinary share capital – shares issued as compensation to	
preference share capital for preference dividends in arrears	105
Profit and loss account – elimination of debit balance	
including accrual for September expenses	412
Realignment of assets to going concern values (360+90+400+40)	890
Provision for reorganisation costs	50
Reserve arising on scheme	28
	1,485

Before you can proceed to the post scheme balance sheet, consideration needs to be given to the additional funds required by the company. This is easily ascertained as a balancing item on the cash account as follows:

	£000
Bank overdraft and short-term loans per pre-scheme balance sheet	1,140
Trade and other creditors to be paid off in full (168+40)	208
Debenture interest to be paid	14
Costs of reorganisation to be paid	50
New processing equipment to be purchased	90
	1,502
Cash in hand per pre-scheme balance sheet	10
Sale of investments	220
Maximum overdraft/loans carried forward 60% × 1,140 = 684 – say	672
Therefore additional finance required – the balancing item	600
	1,502

ANSWERS TO CHAPTER 25

Given that ordinary shareholders are willing to subscribe further equity capital and that the debenture holder is willing to provide further secured funds and that the gearing of the company may remain within acceptable bounds it is proposed that:

1 Ordinary shareholders take up a new issue of 2.67 million ordinary shares of 15p each to raise £400,000.
2 Existing 7% debenture to be converted into a 10% debenture and an additional 10% debenture of £200,000 be raised. There is sufficient security in the going concern value of the land and buildings.
3 The 15p ordinary shares be consolidated into shares of £1 each following the scheme.

c) **Balance sheet of Tree plc following the scheme:**

	£000	£000
Fixed assets		
Patents		140
Land and buildings		700
Plant and machinery (10+90)		100
		940
Current assets		
Stocks	800	
Debtors	790	
	1,590	
Creditors falling due within 1 year		
Bank overdraft and short-term loans	(672)	
		918
		1,858
Creditors falling due after more than 1 year		
10% debenture secured on land and buildings		(600)
		1,258
Ordinary shares of £1 each fully paid (225 + 105 + 400)		730
7% Preference shares of £1 each fully paid		500
Reserve arising on reorganisation		28
		1,258

CHAPTER 26 *Self test questions*

1 Where Section 135 allows a company to reduce its share capital, there will be occasions when a company in financial difficulties will wish to vary the rights of its members and creditors. The provisions of the Act that permit a company to do this are contained in Section 425-427. Where the company seeks to vary the rights of creditors (and members) by the transfer of a business to a newly formed company for the purpose it must under Sections 425-427 obtain the approval of a 75% majority of each class affected. As the permission of the court is required before such schemes can proceed there is protection for creditors.

2 An amalgamation involves the absorption of two or more companies by the creation of a new business to take over their undertakings. The transferor companies are wound up and no longer exist after the scheme. In a merger it is the shares of one or more companies that are purchased by the issue of shares in the purchaser company. The purchased companies are subsidiaries of the purchaser company and will be consolidated into its consolidated accounts.

3 The realisation account is debited with the book value of assets of the business that are taken over by the purchaser company. It is best to deal with creditors separately. The account is credited with the value of the purchase consideration including, where creditors are excluded above, creditors taken over by the purchaser company. The account should include costs borne by the transferor company and any balance on the account represents a profit or loss on realisation which is attributable to the ordinary shareholders of the transferor company.

4 A compulsory winding up is one where a winding up order is made by the order of the court on a petition made by the company itself or its directors or its creditors or its contributories. A voluntary winding up is initiated by the passing of a winding-up resolution by a general meeting of the company.

5 A members' voluntary winding up is one where the directors have made a statutory declaration of the company's solvency at a board meeting before the passing of the winding-up resolution. If no such declaration is made the winding up is a creditors' voluntary winding up, under which the creditors may appoint their own nominee or liquidator.

CHAPTER 26 *Exam style questions*

1   *Fulbright Ltd*

   a) **The number and value of shares to be issued by Fulbright Ltd**

      Supporting information: (all amounts in £000)

      1   **Number of shares in issue after conversion of CLS:**

	Rhodes	Inlac
50p ordinary shares in issue 1/4/95	8,000	1,600
50p ordinary shares issued on conversion of CLS		
£2,000 1 share for each £1	2,000	
£4,000 2 shares for each £2		8,000
In issue after conversion of CLS	10,000	9,600

      2   **Net asset values:**

	Rhodes	Inlac
Fixed assets at FV	15,570	14,280
Net current assets	5,000	1,000
10% debentures	(8,000)	(6,000)
	12,570	9,280

      3   **Shares to be issued by Fulbright:**

	Rhodes	Inlac
Number (000)	9,600	9,600
Value	9,280	9,280
Value per share	9,280/9,600 = 96.67p	

      4   **15% debentures to be issued by Fulbright to Rhodes shareholders:**

FV of Rhodes net assets	12,570
Value of Fulbright shares issed	(9,280)
15% debentures to be issued	3,290

      5   Fair value of net assets taken over (12,570 + 9,280)   21,850

Fair value of Fulbright shares issued (9,280 × 2)	18,560
15% debenture of Fulbright issued	3,290
	21,850

      6   The combination with Inlac would fully satisfy the conditions of SSAP 23 for the use of the merger method on consolidation. The combination with Rhodes would have to be accounted for as an acquisition as the non equity form of the consideration, 3,290, is greater than 10% of the FV of the total consideration of 12,570.

      7   S. 131 of the Act would apply to the shares issued by Fulbright. As the merger method is used on consolidation of Inlac, 'Cost of Inlac' will be the NV of the shares issued, that is, 4,800. The premium on the issue is ignored. As the acquisition method is used on consolidation of Rhodes, 'Cost of Rhodes' must be the FV of the consideration, that is, 12,570 and the premium on the 9,600,000 Fulbright shares issued – 9,600,000 × 46.67p = 4,480 – will be taken in the Fulbright balance sheet not to a share premium account but to a S. 131 or 'merger' reserve.

   b) **Basic and fully diluted EPS**

		Rhodes Ltd £000	Inlac Ltd £000
Earnings for the year to 30/9/94		950	495
Adjustment for CLS			
£2,000 × 0.08 × 0.65		104	
£4,000 × 0.08 × 0.65			208
Fully diluted earnings:		1,054	703
Number of ordinary shares 30/9/94 (000s)		8,000	1,600
Issuable on conversion (000s)		2,000	8,000
Fully diluted number (000s)		10,000	9,600
Basic eps	950/8,000	11.9p	
	495/1,600		30.0p
Fully diluted eps	1,054/10,000	10.5p	
	703/9,600		7.3p

c) **Fulbright Ltd summarised balance sheet on 1 April 1995**

	£000
Fixed asset investments: shares in group companies	
Cost of shares in Rhodes Ltd	12,570
Cost of shares in Inlac Ltd	4,800
Net current assets	1,238*
15% debenture	(3,290)
	15,318
Ordinary share capital – (9,600 × 2) shares of 50p each	10,600*
Merger reserve	4,480
Profit and loss account (475 × 6/12)	238
	15,318

* The net current assets include 1,000 representing the original issued share capital, plus the increase in net current assets arising from the trading of Fulbright during the period, that is, 475 × 6/12 = 238. The ordinary share capital represents the original issued share capital of 1,000 and the further issues made in respect of the two business combinations arising in the period.

d) **Fulbright Ltd Group summarised consolidated balance sheet on 1 April 1995**

	£000
Fixed assets (15,570 + 11,000)	26,570
Net current assets (5,000 + 1,000 + 1,238)	7,238
15% debenture	(3,290)
10% debenture (8,000 + 6,000)	(14,000)
	16,518
Ordinary share capital	10,600
Merger reserve	4,480
Profit and loss account (1,200 + 238)	1,438
	16,518

Consolidated reserves are those of the parent and the merger subsidiary. The reserves of the acquisition subsidiary are capitalised (pre-acquisition reserves). There is no consolidation goodwill arising on the acquisition subsidiary, and no consolidation difference arising on the merger subsidiary.

e)/f) **Fulbright Ltd Group summarised consolidated profit and loss account for the year to 30 September 1995 and Basic eps**

			£000	£000
Fulbright Ltd	–	trading activities	475	
		interest on 15% debenture for 6m		
		3,290 × 0.15 × 0.65 × 6/12	(160)	
				315
Rhodes Ltd	–	acquisition subsidiary, post-acquisition		
		only: 1,050 × 6/12		525
Consolidation				
adjustment	–	additional depn, in post-acq. period		(220)
Inlac Ltd	–	merger subsidiary, full year	515	
		interest on 8% CLS for 6m		
		4,000 × 0.08 × 0.65 × 6/12	(104)	
				411
				1,031

Number of ordinary shares 1 October 1994	2,000,000
9,600 re Rhodes Ltd × 6/12	4,800,000
9,600 re Inlac Ltd	9,600,000
	16,400,000
Basic eps £1,031,000/16,400,000	6.3p

2 *Corinth plc*

a) Journal entries to close off the books of Corinth plc as on 30 June 1993:

		£000	£000
1	DR Bank	42	
	CR Yards		160
	DR Realisation account	118	
	with sale of surpluse yard at a loss		

2 DR Realisation account   130
   CR Development costs   100
   CR Patents   30
   with assets which do not represent value for Corinth (1993) plc

3 DR Realisation account   30
   CR Stocks   10
   CR Debtors   20
   with write down to realisable value of stocks and debtors

4 DR Realisation account   310
   CR Yards   160
   CR Equipment   120
   CR Stocks   30
   with sundry assets to be transferred to Corinth (1993) plc

5 Note as to purchase consideration: £000

i) Ordinary shares to be issued – 100,000 shares of £2 each,
£1 paid up, issued to ordinary shareholders of Corinth plc   100
i) Preference shares to be issued – 30,000 10% shares of £1
each issued to preference shareholders of Corinth plc   30

iii) Re discharge of bank overdraft   £000
Overdraft per question   90
Discharge of 6% debentures   130
Payment of trade creditors (0.2 × 10)   2
    222
Cash received on sale of yard   (42)
Cash received from Corinth (1993) plc   (132)
    48

therefore £48,000 of 8% secured debentures to be issued to discharge the overdraft   48
iv) Discharge of existing 6% debenture by Corinth (1993) plc   130
v) Part payment of creditors by Corinth (1993) plc   2
    310

DR Corinth (1993) plc   310
CR Realisation account   310
with the purchase consideration paid by Corinth (1993) plc for assets taken over from Corinth plc

6 DR Creditors   10
   CR Bank – part payment   2
   CR Realisation account   8
   DR Arrears of preference dividends   20
   CR Realisation account   20
   with settlement of trade creditors and cancellation of arrears of preference dividends

7 DR Preference share capital   30
   CR Corinth (1993) plc   30
   with purchase consideration paid to preference shareholders of Corinth plc

8 DR Preference share capital   30
   CR Realisation account   30
   with reduction in preference share capital

9 Realisation account:

	£000		£000
Yards	160	Corinth (1987) plc purchase consideration	310
Equipment	120	Creditors – agreed reduction	28
Stocks	30		
Losses – re yard	118		
Write-offs			
dev. costs	100	Preference shareholders – reduction	30
patents	30		
stocks	10	Ordinary shareholders – loss on realisation	220
debtors	20		
	588		588

	£000	£000
DR Ordinary shareholders	220	
CR Realisation account		220
with loss on realisation		

	£000	£000

10	DR Ordinary shareholders	80	
	CR Profit and loss account		80
	with transfer of balance on profit and loss account		

11	DR Bank	130	
	CR Corinth (1993) plc		130
	with cash paid by Corinth (1993) plc re discharge of debentures		

12	DR 6% debentures	130	
	CR Bank		130
	with discharge of 6% debentures		

13	DR Bank	48	
	CR Corinth		48
	with issue of debenture in discharging overdraft		

14	DR Ordinary share capital	100	
	CR Corinth (1993) plc		100
	with ordinary shares in Corinth (1993) plc issued to existing shareholders		

15	DR Preference share capital	30	
	CR Corinth (1993) plc		30
	with preference shares in Corinth (1993) plc issued to existing shareholders		

Supporting schedules

Ordinary shareholders:	£000			£000
Profit and loss account – B/S	80	per B/S		400
Realisation account – loss	220			
Corinth (1993) plc	100			

Preference shareholders	£000			£000
Corinth (1993) plc	30	per B/S		60
Realisation account – reduction	30			

Corinth (1993) plc:	£000			£000
Realisation account – consideration	310	Preference share capital		30
		Ordinary share capital		100
		Bank – 8% debenture		48
		– re creditors		2
		– 6% debenture		130

b)   Corinth (1993) plc: Balance sheet as at 1 July 1993

	£000	£000
Tangible fixed assets:		
Yard		160
Equipment		120
		280
Current assets:		
Stocks	30	
Creditors: amounts falling due in less one year		
Bank overdraft	(32)	(2)
		278
Creditors: amounts falling due after more than one year:		
8% debenture		(48)
		230
Ordinary share capital: 100,000 £2 shares		200
Preference share capital: 30,000 10% cumulative £1 shares		30
		230

CHAPTER 27 *Self test questions*

1   Reasons why companies may wish to merge with or take over other companies are: economies of scale; economies of vertical integration; elimination of inefficiencies; tax efficiency through the acquisition of companies with unutilised tax losses; combining complementary resources; to defend against takeover by another company, and managerial drive for growth.

2   Among the criteria that determine the likelihood of a merger being referred for investigation and the probability of it being found to be detrimental to the public interest are:

▶ the size of the companies involved
▶ whether the bid is being defended by the offeree company
▶ the likelihood or otherwise of the bid resulting in reducing competition by increasing market share in a particular business sector
▶ acquisitions by overseas companies
▶ the commercial and financial performance of the companies involved.

3 The two principal means by which the City Code seeks to protect the interests of individual shareholders are:

▶ the inclusion of provisions to ensure that shareholders of the offeree company have sufficient information and time to properly consider the terms of a bid and its likely effects if successful
▶ the inclusion of provisions to ensure that shareholders of the offeree company are treated equally.

4 The main requirements of the City Code are:

▶ an offer must be made in a prescribed form
▶ information in offer documents that are mailed to shareholders must be accurate and is scrutinised by the Takeover Panel
▶ partial offers require the consent of the Takeover Panel
▶ 'insider dealing' must not occur and proposed offers must not be kept secret
▶ acquisitions over 30% must be followed by a full takeover bid
▶ if a bid is withdrawn, the bidders cannot bid again for the same company for a period of twelve months.

5 The work of the Takeover Panel includes:

▶ the vetting of offer documents, circulars and announcements
▶ ruling as to interpretation of the City Code
▶ investigations into possible cases of insider dealing.

CHAPTER 28 *Self test questions*

1 'Stock' will indicate the name of the company; the most actively traded stocks will be indicated.

'Price' is the mid-market price at the close of business at the end of the previous day's trading. It is cum-dividend unless indicated as xd in which case it is ex-dividend.

'+/−' indicates the movements in price for the previous day's trading.

'High/Low' refers to the highest and lowest prices of which the company's shares have been listed during the year.

'Market capitalisation' is the price of a share × the number of shares that a company has in issue.

'Yield gross' is the gross dividend yield that is grossed up for the basic rate of income tax.

'P/E ratio' is the price per share/eps.

Note that eps is not shown but that it can be derived from the information above as price per share/price earnings ratio.

2 Earnings per share, taken on its own is not particularly informative. It needs to be looked at in the following context:

▶ It should be used as a basic for comparing the results of a company over a period of time.
▶ It should not be used to compare the earnings of one company with another, as different companies will have different numbers of shares. To compare the earnings of different companies it is more appropriate to consider the p/e ratio and earnings yields.
▶ To be useful, eps must be calculated consistently. This is the main problem arising post FRS 3, as earnings for eps may now include one off items that were previously excluded from the eps calculations.
▶ In judging returns you should also look at the impact of any future dilution in eps, given that a company may have securities in issue that are convertible at some later date into ordinary shares of the company.

3 Only Ash plc must disclose fully diluted eps in addition to basic eps. Oak plc has fully diluted eps that is greater than basic eps, and Lime plc has basic eps that is a loss per share.

4 'Net' earnings are earnings after deducting the whole of the tax charge. If irrecoverable ACT is included in the tax charge, it is treated as a cost of dividends paid by the company. 'Nil' earnings will differ from 'net' earnings in that any irrecoverable ACT included in the tax charge is excluded in

arriving at earnings for eps on a 'nil' basis. Irrecoverable ACT is treated as an appropriation of as opposed to charge against earnings. 'Fully taxed' earnings are the notional earnings of a company on the basis of a full provision for the tax effects of all timing differences arising in the year. 'Maximum' earnings are the earnings on which dividend cover calculations are based. They are the total earnings available for distribution to ordinary shareholders less any irrecoverable ACT that may arise if these earnings were distributed in full.

CHAPTER 28 *Exam style question*

1   *Haas plc*

		1993	1992
a)	Calculation of earnings per share		

Basic earnings per share:

	1993	1992
£674/11,127	6.1p	
Comparative as previously stated – £(215)/6,360		(3.4)p
as restated – following the merger on 1 June 1993 – £388/10,860		3.6p

Fully diluted earnings per share:

	1993	1992
£758/12,060	6.3p	N/A

Workings

1 Earnings

	£000	£000
Arising on merger on 1 June 1993	385	(215)
90% × 670		603
90% × 321	289	
Earnings for basic eps	674	388

Adjustments for dilution:

re CLS converted in year £500 × 12 × 4/12 × 6	12
re CLS outstanding for full year £1,000 × 12 × 6	72
Earnings for fully diluted eps	758

Number of ordinary shares (in 000s):

1/7/91	4,500
1/7/91 issued on exercise of options	800
	5,300
1/1/92 bonus issue 1:5	1,060
Original number for the 1992 eps	6,360
Add: shares issued on merger on 1/6/93, deemed to be in issue for all previous years	4,500
Adjusted number for the 1992 restated eps	10,860

1/7/92 6,360 × 4/12	2,120
31/10/92 issued on conversion of CLS	
500 × 100/150 × 6/5 = 400 + 6,360 = 6,760 × 8/12	4,507
	6,627
1/6/93 issued on merger 4,500 no time apportionment	4,500
Number of ordinary shares for basic eps	11,127

Adjustments for dilution:

re CLS converted in year – add back 400 × 4/12	133
re CLS outstanding for full year £1,000 × 100/150 × 6/5	800
Number of ordinary shares for fully diluted eps	12,060

b) ED 48 and the proposed amendments to SSAP 23:

The SSAP 23 definition of a merger (essentially where no resources leave the group) was criticised as follows:

▶ the standard did not require that all combining entities be of a similar size
▶ it was possible for share exchanges to qualify for merger relief under the CA 1985 but not to qualify as a merger under SSAP 23
▶ the merger accounting criteria of SSAP 23 have now been superseded by the EC 7th Directive and its incorporation into the amended CA 1985
▶ the standard allowed choice as to the use of the merger method and there were easy means (e.g. vendor placings) of getting round its provisions.

ED 48 now proposes that the merger method of consolidation *must* be used where:

▶ no one party sees itself as acquiror or acquiree
▶ no party dominates the management of the combined entity
▶ no equity shareholder of any of the parties involved disposes of a material shareholding for shares carrying reduced rights or any other non-equity consideration
▶ there is no minority interest of more than 10% in any subsidiary undertaking
▶ no combing party is more than 50% larger than any other party to the combination (unless special circumstances prevent the larger from dominating the other(s)).

ED 48 is now superseded by FRED 6.

CHAPTER 29 *Self test questions*

1 The basis of calculation for four profitability ratios is:

a) Return on capital employed $= \dfrac{\text{Earnings before interest and tax}}{\text{Shareholders' funds plus debt}}$

b) Fixed asset turnover ratio $= \dfrac{\text{Sales}}{\text{Fixed Assets}}$

c) Gross profit margin $= \dfrac{\text{Sales} - \text{Cost of sales}}{\text{Sales}}$

d) Net profit margin $= \dfrac{\text{Earnings before interest and tax}}{\text{Sales}}$

2 The basis of calculation of the two main liquidity ratios is:

a) Current ratio $= \dfrac{\text{Current assets}}{\text{Current liabilities}}$

b) Quick ratio $= \dfrac{\text{Cash and near cash}}{\text{Current liabilities}}$

(also known as the liquid ratio or acid test ratio)

3 Three working capital-based ratios are calculated as follows:

a) Debtors turnover ratio $= \dfrac{\text{Sales}}{\text{Trade debtors}}$

b) Stock turnover ratio $= \dfrac{\text{Cost of sales}}{\text{Stock}}$

c) Creditors turnover ratio $= \dfrac{\text{Cost of sales}}{\text{Trade creditors}}$

Debtor's collection period (days) $= \dfrac{\text{Trade debtors}}{\text{Sales}} \times 365$

Stock holding period (days) $= \dfrac{\text{Stock}}{\text{Cost of sales}} \times 365$

Trade credit period (days) $= \dfrac{\text{Trade creditors}}{\text{Cost of sales}} \times 365$

4 The three capital structure ratios are:

a) Gearing ratio $= \dfrac{\text{Long-term debt} + \text{bank overdraft} + \text{preference capital}}{\text{Shareholders' funds}}$

b) Interest cover ratio $= \dfrac{\text{Earnings before interest and tax}}{\text{Interest liabilities}}$

c) Dividend cover ratio $= \dfrac{\text{Earnings after tax and interest}}{\text{Dividends}}$

5   A company that is overtrading is likely to be a successful company that is under-capitalised for working capital; that is, the company will be financing long-term expansion out of short-term resources. The symptoms that may suggest overtrading are:

▶ a high ROCE
▶ the company taking longer than usual to pay its creditors
▶ weak liquidity ratios.

The solution is to fund long-term expansion out of long-term capital.

CHAPTER 29 *Exam style questions*

1   *TexMex plc*

REPORT

To: Mr Jon Thorburn-Levy
From: AR Countants & Co
Re: Evaluation of the five-year historical summary of TexMex plc
Date: 15 January 1994

a) *General*

The practice of including in financial statements a five-year time series of significant figures, while common today, is not required by law or by any Accounting Standard or Stock Exchange rule. A company or group is, therefore, at liberty to select those figures which, over a short span of years, show the business in a favourable light. In a period of inflation, such figures are likely to rise continuously and to convey a superficial impression of progress and growth. As a rule, relevant price index numbers are not provided and the casual reader has no means of knowing whether the impression of continuous growth is real or not.

Even where an index is applied to correct for inflation, the figures in a time series must be interpreted with caution:

▶ profits may not be analysed and may contain undisclosed extraordinary items
▶ even if extraordinary items are disclosed, without a detailed breakdown it is not always certain that the disclosed amounts really are extraordinary in their context
▶ interest charges may or may not be specified and investment income may or may not be distinguished from trading profits
▶ there may have been a revaluation of fixed assets in one year, increasing depreciation charges thereafter and making comparison of profits before and after the revaluation imperfect
▶ dividends, if stated in money terms, need to be related to the number of shares in issue at the relevant time
▶ material acquisitions and disposals have a bearing on a proper appreciation of a trend of results.

b) *Calculations*

	1985	1986	1987	1988	1989
RPI – average	270	310	323	343	360
	£000	£000	£000	£000	£000
Turnover at historical cost	2,000	2,250	2,500	2,800	3,200
Turnover at average 1989 level	2,667	2,691	2,786	2,939	3,200
Cumulative growth	–	0.9%	4.5%	10.2%	20%
Turnover/net assets – times	1.7	1.7	1.7	1.4	0.9
Net PBIT:					
Historical cost	150	180	200	235	330
Average 1989 level	200	215	223	247	330
Cumulative growth	–	7.5%	11.5%	23.5%	65%
Pre-tax profit/turnover	7.5%	8%	8%	8.4%	10.3%
Pre-tax profit/net assets	12.5%	13.8%	13.3%	11.5%	9.7%
NP after tax/equity funds	8.6%	10.5%	7.7%	5.5%	5.4%
Net profit/equity funds	11.4%	7.7%	7.7%	4.8%	6.2%
Dividends – historical	40	40	60	60	90
– average 1989 level	53	48	67	63	90
Dividend per share (adjusted)	13.3p	12p	11.1p	10.5p	9p
eps – historical	15p	18.8p	13.3p	14.2p	13p
Average 1989 level	20p	22.5p	14.8p	14.9p	13p
Loan capital/equity funds	0.4	0.4	0.3	0.4	0.2

FINANCIAL REPORTING ENVIRONMENT

---

c) *Comment*

The first impression conveyed by the figures in the summary is one of continuous growth in turnover, profits and net assets. Turnover has risen over the five-year period by 60%, profit before interest and tax by 120%, net profit after tax by 117%, net profit for the year by 88% and net assets by 183%.

Further analysis suggests a less impressive achievement:

i) The general level of retail prices increased by 33% in the period. Adjusting for inflation, the gains become: turnover 20% and pre-tax profit 65%. The group has grown in real terms, but not as remarkably as would appear without adjustment.

ii) Much of the growth is due to the acquisition of two new subsidiaries. The effect of these was to expand net assets, up to £2.8 million from £0.9 million. There is insufficient information to assess the effects of the two acquisitions on the group's turnover and profits, but it is reasonable to assume that they account for much of the growth therein.

iii) Dividends per share remained constant at 10p for the first four years falling back to 9p in the last year. In real terms they declined by 32.5%, that is, from 13.3p to 9p. Earnings per share has also fallen in real terms, by 35% from 20p to 13p.

iv) Analysis of profit and loss account figures shows a fairly consistent rate of profit to turnover, despite the higher depreciation charges owing to fixed asset revaluations. This trend is offset by a declining rate of turnover of net assets.

v) Analysis of the post-tax profit shows a declining rate of return on equity funds, while the net profit for the year, *including extraordinary items*, shows considerable fluctuation relative to equity funds. The nature of the extraordinary items is not stated and one does not know whether the historical figures have been tampered with by changing the classification of items.

d) *Conclusion*

It would appear that the group's performance for the first four years has been adequate, but there are disquieting symptoms arising in the last year. This may have something to do with the acquisition of the subsidiary in 1989. Consolidated results may only include a small part of the subsidiary's year, or the holding may have been acquired at an inflated price. Informed judgement can only be made on the basis of the 1990 results.

2 *Mr John York*

AR Countants & Co
100 Owen Street
London EC4 XY
7 July 198X

Mr John York
20 Bull Street
London EC2 JZ

Dear Mr York

Re: Stone plc, explanations for the changing relationships indicated by selected financial statistics relating to the company and an indication as to where in the annual accounts support may be found for these explanations

In response to your request for guidance on interpreting the relationship between the selected four sets of statistics of Stone plc over a three year period, I would make the following points:

1 Profit/(loss) before tax and earnings/(loss) per share

Earnings per share is calculated on the basis of earnings after taxation, minority interests and preference dividends, divided by the number of shares in issue and ranking for dividend in the accounting period.

The fact that a company discloses a trend of increasing profit before taxation, minority interests and preference dividends does not therefore necessarily result in a similar trend of increasing earnings per share. The 1984 amounts are both negative. The 1985 amounts disclose a loss before tax and positive earnings per share. There are several possible reasons for this:

i) Tax for the year is a credit giving rise to a profit after tax. The credit may have arisen through utilisation of tax losses brought forward, release of deferred tax provisions to the profit and loss account, ACT previously considered irrecoverable and written off now written back.

ii) The pre-tax losses may have arisen through the consolidation of loss-making subsidiaries with substantial minority interests. The minority share of loss-making subsidiaries would be added back resulting, possibly, in positive group earnings for earnings per share.

iii) Preference dividends for the year may have been reduced perhaps as a result of purchase or redemption of the shares by the company.

Where the company moves from pre-tax losses to pre-tax profits in 1986, there has been only a slight improvement in earnings per share. Again the reasons can be derived from a closer inspection of the tax charge for the year and by determining whether:

i) There have been any changes in the composition of the group and whether the number of shares have increased through share-for-share exchanges.

ii) There has been a capital reorganisation resulting in a change in the number of ordinary shares in issue.

iii)   There have been bonus or rights issues of shares made by the company, conversion of convertible loan stock or exercise of options resulting in increased numbers of shares.

Information to support these explanations may be found in:

i)   The notes to the financial statements, particularly those dealing with:
   - earnings per share indicating the basis of calculation
   - changes in the composition of the group
   - taxation and deferred taxation
   - share capital
ii)   The Chairperson's statement and Directors' report dealing with the principal activities and business review of the group.
iii)   The five-year summary in which earnings and earnings per share of previous years may have been restated to take account of mergers, bonus issues, rights issues and capital reorganisations.

2   Earnings/(loss) per share, dividends per share and net assets per share
Increase in earnings per share would normally result in an increase in net assets per share. To the extent that the company pays out dividends, such distributions would result in a decrease in net assets per share.

There are, however, factors other than current earnings per share which affect the dividend capacity of a company. Thus, in 1984 the company paid a dividend even though there was a loss per share. This is legally permitted so long as the company makes the distribution out of accumulated net realised profits.

In 1985, the company distributed its earnings per share in full, but reported an increase in net assets per share. Possible explanations for this are:

i)   The company may have reported significant one-off exceptional gains in the year.
ii)   The company may have revalued its fixed assets during the year. Such gains would be taken direct to reserves and would not be reflected in the earnings per share for the year.

In 1986 the company retained half of its earnings per share but reported a 24% decrease in net assets per share. Possible explanations for this are:

i)   Some assets may have been written off direct to reserves. Thus, the company may previously have been carrying goodwill in its balance sheet and, in line with the accounting standard on goodwill, may have eliminated such existing goodwill by writing it off directly against reserves. The company may also have revalued its tangible fixed assets downwards and taken the deficit to revaluation reserves.
ii)   Loss making subsidiaries may have been disposed of for less than the book value of their net assets.

Information to support these explanations may be found in:

i)   The Chairperson's statement and the Directors' report where there may be explanations of the dividend policy of the company and its dependence on earnings per share and effect on net assets per share.
ii)   The Notes to the accounts dealing with:
   - the statement of movement on reserves would indicate assets written off directly against reserves and revaluation gains, as would the notes on fixed assets
   - the movements on provisions would support the explanations for a reduction in net assets per share
   - changes in the composition of the group would indicate material acquisitions and disposals of a subsidiary and the contribution paid or received and any goodwill arising
   - share capital would explain any movement in the number of shares.
iii)   The cash flow statement would indicate amounts paid or received and the effects of the acquisition or disposal of subsidiaries.
iv)   The five-year summary. Note, however, that financial statistics extracted from the accounts of each year may not be meaningfully comparable one year to another. There may have been changes in accounting policy, material acquisitions and disposals, changes in the number of ordinary shares so as to render any comparison, without restatement of previous years, of little use. The form and content of the summary is not regulated by either statute, Stock Exchange rule or accounting standard. What is included is entirely at the discretion of the directors. Properly prepared, it could be the support for many of the explanations dealt with above.

3   Movements in net assets per share from year to year
The worth of the net assets of a company increases through either retention of earnings, or injections of capital, or capital appreciation of assets, or through the purchase of subsidiaries.

The net assets per share of Stone plc increased in 1985 and reduced to less than 1984 levels in 1986. The possible explanations for this are:

i)   An increase in the number of shares as a result of a bonus issue in 1986.
ii)   An issue of shares for cash in 1985.
iii)   The making of or the releasing of provisions; asset revaluations.
iv)   Subsidiaries acquired during a period accounted for either at fair values on the date of combination (acquisition) or at book values (merger). The elimination of any merger reserve in the accounts of the holding company on consolidation of a merger subsidiary.

v)   The treatment of goodwill arising on acquisition.

Support for these explanations may be found in:

i)   The cash flow statement, which will indicate transactions that have a funds flow effect and those that do not. Share issues for cash would be reflected in the statement but not bonus issues.

ii)   The Chairperson's statement and Directors' report dealing with significant changes in fixed assets.

iii) Notes to the accounts dealing with fixed assets, provisions, share capital, movement on reserves and accounting policies dealing with basis of consolidation and goodwill.

iv)   The five-year summary for, possibly, restated net assets per share to take account of mergers and acquisitions and revaluations and changes of accounting policy, for example, goodwill, all of which can have a distorting effect on a comparison of net assets over a period of years.

In conclusion, if you require any further guidance as to the points raised above, please get in touch.

Yours sincerely,

CHAPTER 30 *Self test questions*

1   Financial ratios, in that they provide measures of the profitability and liquidity of a company, help in directing attention to those areas of operations that require further analysis. They can be compared only against the ratios of the preceding period, budgeted ratios for the current period and ratios of other similar companies. The comparison is appropriate only when the basis of calculation is consistently applied. Their main shortcomings arise from the application of different accounting policies by different companies and, in the context of multinationals, in different countries, the lack of uniformity and comparability of accounts that result and the impact of inflation on the numbers included in the calculations.

2   As described by Inman, 'Z scores attempt to replace various independent and often unreliable and misleading historical ratios and subjective rule-of-thumb tests with scientifically analysed ratios which can reliably predict future events by identifying benchmarks above which "all's well" and below which there is imminent danger.'

3   Historical cost accounting has been widely practised for a long time, is familiar, is a cheap valuation method for preparers and is deemed to be relatively objective and, therefore, reliable. The main disadvantage of the system is that it results in financial statements lacking the property of comparability not only between different companies but also between different assets owned by the same company. Further, it allows companies to decide when to sell assets to realise profits or losses and therefore to manage income.

4   Under FRED 8, related parties would include:

   ►   other companies and undertakings in the same group
   ►   associated undertakings
   ►   directors or officers of the company and its holding company and members of their immediate family
   ►   a company or person owning 10% or more of the company's voting rights, and members of the immediate family of such a person
   ►   partnerships, companies, trusts or other entities in which anyone falling into the two categories immediately above has a controlling interest or significant influence
   ►   the other party in a management contract.

5   FRED 8 proposes disclosure of the following:

   ►   the name of the related party
   ►   the relationship between the parties
   ►   the extent of the ownership interest, in percentage terms, if any, in or by the related party
   ►   the nature of the transaction
   ►   the amounts involved either in percentage or monetary terms
   ►   the amount due to or from the related party at the balance sheet date
   ►   the basis on which the transaction price was determined
   ►   any other information necessary for a full understanding of the transaction.

CHAPTER 30 *Exam style questions*

1   *Ratios*
   a) Definitions
      i)   *Return on capital employed* This is the relationship of profit (pre or post tax) to capital employed expressed as a percentage. It can be calculated in terms of the total capital employed or in terms of shareholders' funds plus long-term borrowings or in terms of shareholders' funds. In the first case, the return is the profit before all interest and dividends; in the second,

after interest on short-term borrowings but before all other interest and dividends; in the third, after all interest but before all dividends. In terms of capital employed as ordinary shareholders' funds, the return available is after deducting preference dividends.

ii) *Stock turnover* This is cost of sales/stock. The ratio measures the number of days stock held. It is a measure of efficiency. Stocks consist of raw materials and consumables, purchased components, work in progress, finished goods, goods for resale and payments on account. Where cost of sales is available, it should be used; if not, the sales figure may be used. Many analysts take the average of opening and closing stocks which has a smoothing effect.

iii) *Gearing* Financial gearing can be defined in a multiplicity of ways the two most common being:

► Debt: Equity, also called leverage, or the relationship of fixed interest capital to ordinary shareholders' funds.

► The percentage of capital employed (total assets) financed by borrowings or Total debt: Total debt plus shareholders' funds.

Preference share capital may be included as either debt or equity depending on the use to which the ratio is put.

b) The usefulness and limitations of accounting ratios for an external financial analyst

Accounting ratios are merely a means of presenting information in the form of a ratio or percentage. They are of use in that they assess in simplified form the trading results and financial position of the company as shown by the accounts. They are, however, only of value if they are used as a basis of comparison either internally (with the company's results of previous periods) or externally (with the results of other companies in a similar industry). For example, the statement that a retail company has a stock turnover ratio of four in the current period is of little use in itself. When compared with the previous period or with other companies in the same trade, it takes on a meaningful value.

Return on capital employed This is useful in that it is the most important measure of profitability. From the viewpoint of the analyst it is useful in that:

► it serves as a guide to the company in assessing possible acquisitions and in starting up new activities

► where the figure is lower than the cost of borrowing, increased borrowings will reduce eps unless the extra money can be used in areas where the ratio is higher than the company's average.

It has limitations in that one needs further segmental information to ascertain which are the more or less profitable segments of the business. Also, the ratio may be distorted where one company revalues asssets. Thus, for such a company capital employed will be increased and the return, given additional depreciation, will decrease. Further, to fully understand the ratio it needs to be broken down into first, profit margins and, second, the efficiency of asset utilisation, both of which contribute to or detract from the overall profitability of the company.

Stock turnover This is an operating ratio and provides the analyst with information as to the efficiency of working capital management. Well-run companies try to carry the minimum stock required for a satisfactory running of the business. This minimises interest costs and the costs of storage. A rising stock ratio without any special reason is regarded as bad news reflecting lack of demand for goods and/or poor stock control. The use of the ratio has limitations in that the ratios vary enormously with the nature of the business. Additionally, the use of average stocks, while having a smoothing effect, does dampen the effect of a major change in stocks over the period.

Gearing These ratios are particularly useful in calculating the 'leverage effect' or percentage change in earnings available to ordinary shareholders brought about by a 1% change in earnings before interest and tax.

Ratios are useful in that they:

► indicate trends and significant changes
► provide an indication of future trends
► indicate areas where financial control or investigation are required
► are not expressed in money terms and are therefore not affected by inflation.

The limitations of accounting ratios arise in that:

► they should be used only as a guide to areas of further investigation; they are not definitive
► they are subject to manipulation, for example, as a result of off balance sheet finance.

Looked at individually, a ratio is of little meaning. A ratio is meaningful only when compared with the results of other ratios to derive the broader picture. Thus, a worsening position indicated by one ratio may be compensated by an improving position indicated by another.

In comparing ratios, one year to another or one company to another, it is important to be consistent in the bases of their computation so that one is comparing like with like.

Lastly, one should look at ratios over a period of time to establish patterns of long-term growth or otherwise.

2 *Stock Exchange regulation*

a) Comparison of Stock Exchange disclosure requirements in relation to directors with those of the Companies Act 1985

The Act requires disclosure in relation to directors as follows: s

- ▶ The names of persons who were directors of the company at any time during the year.
- ▶ Directors' (those who held office at the year end) interests in shares and debentures of the company.
- ▶ Average weekly number of persons, including directors, employed by the company.
- ▶ Directors' remuneration including emoluments waived by (number of) directors.
- ▶ Transactions with directors.

For a more comprehensive picture, the continuing obligations of the Stock Exchange for listed companies additionally require disclosure of:

- ▶ The unexpired period of the service contract of each director proposed for re-election at the AGM.
- ▶ Beneficial and non-beneficial interests of directors in shares and debentures of the company.
- ▶ Between the year end and a date not more than one month prior to the date of the notice of the meeting changes, (or that no changes) in the interests of directors in the shares of the company.
- ▶ Emoluments waived by (numbers of) directors.
- ▶ Particulars where any shareholder (including directors) has waived any dividends.

b) Reasons for the imposition of additional disclosure requirements by the Stock Exchange

The Stock Exchange maintains a very firm control over all listed companies through its continuing obligations for listing.

A principal object of continuing obligations is to secure immediate release of information which might reasonably be expected to have a material effect on market activity in, and prices of, securities. Such information includes both regularly recurring matters such as dividends and interim figures and exceptional matters. The guiding principle is that information that is expected to be price-sensitive should be released immediately it is the subject of a decision. Until that point is reached, it is imperative that the strictest security within the company is observed.

It is argued that there is a need for an imposition of disclosure requirements over and above those required by the Act in order to ensure a fair and orderly securities market. By following the additional regulations of the Stock Exchange, directors should ensure that dealings do not take place between parties one of whom does not have price-sensitive information in the possession of the other. It would be damaging to the company's relationship with its shareholders if there were an apparent unreadiness to disclose information at the proper time. Additional disclosure is required by the Stock Exchange as to:

- ▶ notification of dividend payments and changes in capital structure
- ▶ notification of significant events
- ▶ some parts of the financial statements, for example, directors should disclose, in the directors' report, an explanation of material differences between the trading results and any published forecast made by the company
- ▶ interim accounts.

Given wider share ownership and investment by persons having no inside knowledge of a company other than its published accounts, there is a greater need for investor protection.

Given the greater separation of ownership and management, it is important that there are additional requirements for more detailed information to be made available to shareholders.

Bibliography

Argenti, J.   'Predicting corporate failure', *Accountants Digest*, 138

Arden, M.   Legal opinion in *The Forward to Accounting Standards*. ASB, London, 1993

ASC   *The Corporate Report*. ASC, London, 1975

Bogie, D.J.   *Bogie on Group Accounts*, 3rd edn, edited by J.C. Shaw. Jordan, Bristol 1973

Cameron, S.   'Company law harmonisation – its effect on UK law and its future', in the *UK Regional Handbook*. Capital, London, 1993

Carsberg, B. and Hoke, C.   *The Reporting of Profits and the Concept of Realisation*. ICAEW, London, 1989

Chapping, D. and
Skerratt, L.C.L.   *Applying GAAP 1993/94 – A Practical Guide to Financial Reporting*. Accountancy Books, ICAEW, London, 1993

Coopers & Lybrand
Deloitte   *Accounting Guides: Reporting Financial Performance – A Commentary on FRS 3*. Gee, London, 1992

Coopers & Lybrand
Deloitte   *Manual of Accounting – Companies*. Tolley Publishing, 1990

Coopers & Lybrand
Deloitte   *Manual of Accounting – Groups*. Tolley Publishing, 1990

Dearing, R.E.   Chairman's statement, cited in a review of *The State of Financial Reporting*, November 1991

Ernst & Young   *Accounting for Pension Costs – The Implementation of SSAP 24*. Ernst & Young, London, 1989

Ernst & Young   *UK GAAP*. Longman, London, 1992

Graves, R.   'Acquisitions in the UK', in LSCA *European Handbook 1993*. Capital Publishing, London 1993

Gwilliam, D.   'The auditors' on-going concern', *Accountancy*, January 1993, pp. 70, 72

Inman, M.L.   'Z scores and the going concern review', *ACCA Students' Newsletter*, August 1991

IPA Stitt   *Deferred Tax Accounting*. ICAEW, London, 1985

Lewis, R., Pendrill, D.
and Simon, D.S.   *Advanced Financial Accounting*. Pitman, London 1981

Loveday, G.   'ED 40 – what about the balancing figure?' *Accountancy*, June 1987

LSCA   *The European Handbook 1993*. Capital, London, 1993

Meeks, G.   *Disappointing Marriage: A Study of the Gains from Merger*. Cambridge University Press, Cambridge, 1977

Michell, G.   'Happy Birthday ISAC', *Capital Account*, June 1993

Mueller, G.G. — 'Accounting practices generally accepted in the United States versus those generally accepted elsewhere', *International Journal of Accounting*, Spring, 1968

Munson, R.J. — 'Deferred taxation', in Skerratt and Tonkin (eds) *Financial Reporting 1985–86: A Survey of UK Published Accounts*. London, ICAEW, 1986

Murphy, J. (ed) — *Brand Valuation: Establishing a True and Fair View*. Hutchinson Business Books, London, 1989

Napier, C.J. — *Accounting for the Cost of Pensions*. ICAEW, London, 1983

Pennington, R. — *Insolvency Law – Company Liquidations, Vol. 1 The Substantive Law. Vol. 2 The Procedure*. Jordans, Bristol, 1987

Purvis, S.E.C., Gernon, H., and Diamond, M.A. — 'The ISAC and its comparability project', *Accounting Horizons*, June 1991

Rutteman, P. — 'Where has all the goodwill gone?' *Accountancy*, August 1987

Skerratt, L.C.L. and Tonkin, D.J. — *Financial Reporting 1985–86: A Survey of UK Published Accounts*. ICAEW, London, 1986

Skerratt, L.C.L. and Tonkin, D.J. — *Financial Reporting 1989–90: A Survey of UK Reporting Practice*. ICAEW, London, 1989

Taffler, R.J. and Tisshaw, H., — 'Going, going, gone – four factors which predict', *Accountancy*, March 1977

Thompson, G. — 'The crunch comes for international harmonisation', *Accountancy*, October 1992

Tonkin, D.J. and Skerratt, L.C.L. (eds) — *Financial Reporting 1987–88: A Survey of UK Reporting Practice*. ICAEW, London, 1988

Tonkin, D.J. and Skerratt, L.C.L. (eds) — *Financial Reporting 1992–93: A Survey of UK Reporting Practice*. ICAEW, London, 1993

Urry, M. — 'Change in ruling will devalue p/e ratios', *Financial Times*, 1993

Wainman, D. and Brown, H. — *Leasing: The Accounting and Taxation Implications*, 2nd edn. Guild Press, London, 1980

Weetman, Adams, and Gray, — *Certified Research Report 33 – Issues in International Harmonisation*. CAET, 1993

Westminster Management Consultants, — *A Practitioner's Guide to the Stock Exchange Yellow Book*. Westminster Management Consultants, London, 1993

Wilkins, R.M. — *Group Accounts – The Fundamental Principles, Form and Content*, 2nd edn. ICAEW, London, 1979

Wilkins, R.M. — 'Pension surpluses in company accounts', in Skerratt and Tonkin (eds) *Financial Reporting 1986–87: A Survey of UK Published Accounts*. ICAEW, London 1987

Woolf, E. — 'Goodwill: SSAP 22 is the best answer', *Accountancy*, August 1987

Glossary

Accounting concepts
The broad basic assumptions which underlie periodic financial statements of business enterprises.

Accounting bases
The methods developed to apply accounting concepts to financial transactions.

Accounting policies
The specific accounting bases adopted by companies in preparing their financial statements.

Assets
The rights or other access to future economic benefits controlled by an entity as a result of past transactions or events.

Articulation
This follows where financial statements interrelate, are consistent and thus collective and enable analysis and interpretation.

Analytical review
This consists of audit procedures which systematically analyse and compare related figures, trends, ratios and other data with the aim of providing evidence to support the audit opinion.

Accelerated capital allowances
The timing differences that arise from the availability of capital allowances in tax computations that are in excess of the related depreciation charges in financial statements.

Actuarial post tax method
A method used by the lessor so that the anticipated after tax net profit is removed from the lease cash flows in such a way that it represents a constant periodic rate of return on the lessor's net cash investment in the lease.

Actual exercise of dominant influence
The operating and financial policies of the undertaking influenced are set in accordance with the wishes of the holder of the influence and for its benefit, whether or not those wishes are explicit.

Activity ratios
These analyse how effectively the company is using its resources.

Conceptual framework
A theory of accounting against which the practical problems of accounting can be objectively tested.

Capitalisation of borrowing costs
The practice of not recognising such costs in the profit and loss account of the period when incurred and including such costs as part of the total cost of assets carried forward in the balance sheet.

Cut-off
Procedures that are implemented by business enterprises to ensure that no assets are double counted and no liabilities are omitted.

Comprehensive allocation
Also called the full provision approach to accounting for deferred tax. This is based on the principle that the financial statements of one period should recognise the tax effects, current or deferred, of all transactions arising in that period.

Call option
This occurs where the seller is given an option to purchase.

Control
The ability to direct the financial and operating policies of an undertaking with a view to gaining economic benefits from its activities.

Consolidated accounts
These are intended to report the activities, assets and liabilities of the group as if they were those of a single entity.

Closing rate/net investment method
This must be used where the investor regards the overseas entity as separate from, and independent of, the business of the investor company.

Derecognition
This should follow when items cease to meet recognition criteria.

Development costs
These arise from the moment there is a reasonable expectation that specific commercial success and future benefits will accrue from the work. Under SSAP 13, they may be capitalised.

Deferred tax
This arises from the tax effects of timing differences.

Defined benefit pension schemes
Those in which the rules specify the benefits to be paid and the scheme is financed accordingly.

Defined contribution pension schemes
Those in which the benefits are directly determined by the value of contributions paid in respect of each member.

Direct method
The method of disclosing cash flows from operating activities that requires the gross operating cash receipts and payments from/to customers/suppliers to be reported on the face of the cash flow statement.

Dominant influence
This requires that a parent undertaking has a right to give directions on the operating and financial policies of a subsidiary undertaking which the subsidiary undertaking's directors are obliged to follow whether or not they are for the benefit of the subsidiary undertaking.

Deferred consideration
Consideration in any form that is determined precisely at the time of acquisition, either in value or as a number of shares, but where payment is delayed for a defined period.

Dividend cover
This relates dividends paid to the profits available for the payment of these dividends.

Dividend yield
This relates the dividend per share to the market price of that share and is expressed as a percentage.

Due diligence exercise
This is undertaken when an acquirer insists that any agreement be subject to a detailed investigation.

Extraordinary items
These include 'Martians walking down the street'.

Equity
This is the ownership interest in the entity; it is the residual amount found by deducting all liabilities of the entity from all of the entity's assets.

Experience surpluses or deficiencies
Those parts of the excess or deficiency of the actuarial value of pension fund assets over liabilities that arise because events have not coincided with previous actuarial assumptions made.

Equity method
This brings into the consolidated accounts the investor's share of earnings and, in the consolidated balance sheet, records the investor's share of net assets to the extent not previously written off.

Financial performance
This is now reported not only in terms of a profit and loss account but also in terms of total recognised gains and losses whether dealt with in the profit and loss account or directly within reserves.

Funding
In pensions this gives rise to:
funding plans: the timing of payments in an orderly fashion to meet the future cost of a given set of benefits.
funded schemes: future liabilities to pension benefits are provided for by the accumulation of assets held externally to the employer company's business.

funding levels: the proportion at a given date of the actuarial value of the liabilities for pension benefits that are covered by the actuarial value of the assets.

Finance leases
The substantial transfer to the lessee of all the risks and rewards of owning an asset.

Financial capital maintenance
The view that the capital of a company consists of its shareholders' funds and it is the value of these that needs to be maintained.

Gains
Increases in equity, other than those relating to contributions from owners.

Goodwill
The difference between the value of a business as a whole and the aggregate of the fair values of its separable net assets. It may be positive or negative.

Growth ratios
These analyse the economic position of a company in the industrial segment and economy generally.

Gearing ratios
These analyse the extent to which long term debt is used as a source of finance.

Horizontal analysis
A line by line comparison of the current year's accounts with those of the previous year.

Investment properties
These are interests in land and buildings where construction work and development have been completed which are held for their investment potential, any rental income being negotiated at arm's length.

Investment period principle
The lessor should allocate its gross earnings on the basis of its net cash investment using either the investment period method or the actuarial post tax method.

Indirect method
The method of reporting cash flows from operating activities which involves starting with the net cash flow from

operating activities on the face of the cash flow statement.

Liabilities
An entity's obligations to transfer economic benefits as a result of past transactions or events.

Losses
Decreases in equity other than those relating to distributions to owners.

Linked presentation
Under FRED 4 this gives rise to disclosure of the gross amount of an asset and the gross amount of the (related) liability deducted from this amount.

Liquidity ratios
These analyse the ability of the company to meet short term obligations out of short term resources.

Modified historical cost convention
The convention of preparing accounts on the basis of historical cost, modified by the revaluation of selected assets.

Merger relief
Relief, given under S131 of the CA1985, from the requirement (S130) to record the premium on shares issued as share premium account.

Merger method
An alternative to the acquisition method of consolidation.

Mabgeblichkeitsprinzip
The (German) authoritative principle which requires tax returns to be based on figures published in financial statements.

Money purchase schemes
Pension schemes where the pension benefit is equivalent to the annuity which can be purchased with the accumulated contributions of employer and employee together with interest earned.

Managed on a unified basis
This arises if the whole of the operations of the undertakings are integrated and they are managed as a single unit.

Merger
This arises where shareholders of combining entities come together in a

substantially equal partnership for the mutual sharing of the risks and benefits of the combined entity. No party to the combination obtains control over any other or is seen to be dominant.

Market capitalisation
This represents the market value of the issued share capital of a company.

Multivariate analysis
Several ratios are calculated and analysed at the same time.

Net earnings
In the context of eps these take account of all the elements of the tax charge in arriving at earnings for the eps calculation.

Nil earnings
In the context of eps these take account of only those elements of the tax charge that do not vary with the level of dividend payments and will not include irrecoverable ACT as an expense for eps purposes.

Off balance sheet finance
The funding or refinancing of a company's operations in such a way that, under legal requirements and existing accounting conventions, some or all of the finance may not be shown on its balance sheet.

Offset procedure
This may be used under SSAP 20 when foreign borrowings are used to finance new overseas investments or to provide a hedge against the exchange risk associated with existing overseas investments.

Put option
The buyer is given an option to sell.

Physical capital maintenance
The view that capital is a physical measure, such as operating capability, and profit should be recognised only after maintaining that physical state.

Participating interest
An interest in shares, held for the long term, for the purpose of securing a contribution of activities by the exercise

of control (in the case of a subsidiary) or influence (in the case of an associate).

Prospectus
An invitation to the public to subscribe for or to purchase shares or debentures in a company.

Profit forecasts
These are included in the prospectus of a company seeking a listing for its shares and also in circulars issued in a takeover or merger.

Price earnings ratio
This relates eps to the market price of a share expressed as an inverted ratio.

Permissible capital payments
These arise where private companies purchase or redeem their own shares other than out of distributable profits or the proceeds of a new issue of shares.

Preferential claims
Some debts and liabilities of a company in liquidation must be satisfied in full before payments can be made for non-preferential claims.

Profitability ratios
These analyse the returns made on sales and capital invested.

Quasi subsidiaries
These could be companies, trusts, partnerships or other vehicles that, though not fulfilling the definition of a subsidiary, are directly or indirectly controlled by the reporting entity and are, in substance, no different from subsidiaries.

Reserve accounting
The practice of taking the results of transactions directly to reserves, bypassing the profit and loss account.

Relevant information
This is information that is useful to assess past predictions and to formulate predictions for the future and that which shows all the suitable aspects of a transaction.

Reliable information
This is free from material errors and bias, faithfully represents what it purports to

represent, complies with the substance over form concept, is neutral, shows the exercise of prudence and includes all relevant aspects.

Recognition
Recognition of items should follow if the definition of an element of financial statements has been met, there is evidence that the changes in assets and liabilities inherent in the item have occurred and if they can be measured at a monetary amount with sufficient reliability.

Regular cost
The consistent ongoing pension cost recognised under the actuarial method used.

Realised profits
Those that fall to be treated as realised in accordance with principles generally accepted.

Real terms
The system of accounting under which both financial and physical concepts of capital are combined to reflect the effects of all price changes affecting a company.

Related party relationships
These arise where one party exercises control or significant influence over another party or the assets or resources of the other party, or, such parties are subject to common control or significant influence from the same source.

Split depreciation
The practice, not permitted under SSAP 12, whereby depreciation following revaluation is split so that the amount based on historical cost is charged to the profit and loss account; the additional amount based on the revaluation surplus is taken to the debit of revaluation reserves.

Securitised assets
These arise where one company sells its assets to a buying company that finances the purchase by issuing debt securities.

Super Class 1
Transactions describing acquisitions or disposals of 25% or more require an announcement, a circular and also the approval of shareholders in general meeting.

Timing differences
These originate in one period and reverse in one or more subsequent periods. They give rise to a tax effect on the tax liability of one year and an opposite tax effect on the tax liability of a subsequent year(s).

Trend analysis
Horizontal analysis extended over several years.

Undertaking
A body corporate or partnership or an unincorporated association carrying on a trade or business with, or without, a view to profit.

Univariate analysis
Only one ratio at a time is calculated and analysed.

Value to the business
The lower of, on the one hand, replacement cost and, on the other hand, the higher of net realisable value and economic value.

Value added
The wealth the reporting entity has been able to create by its own and employees' efforts.

Value added statements
These should show how value added has been used to pay those contributing to its creation.

Vertical analysis
This is conducted by preparing `common size' balance sheets and profit and loss accounts where each balance sheet item is expressed as a percentage of the balance sheet total and each profit and loss account item is expressed as a percentage of sales.

Valuation ratios
These analyse corporate performance in terms of wealth creation.

Window dressing
The term applied to the reversal after the year end of transactions entered into before the year end, the substance of which is to alter the appearance of a company's balance sheet.

Index

Evaluation form – Textbooks 1995 edition

We are interested in knowing what you think of our products and would appreciate it if you could spend a few minutes completing the following questionnaire.

Please tick the appropriate box where necessary

Paper No. _____   **Paper title** _____

Are you a

Student ☐   **Lecturer** ☐

Have you purchased other CAEP products

Textbooks ☐   **Revision Texts** ☐   **Open Learning Packages** ☐

What do you think are the best features of this textbook?

_____

_____

_____

_____

What improvements need to be made?

_____

_____

_____

_____

How does the textbook compare with other textbooks or manuals you have used on your course?

_____

_____

_____

Did you find any errors? If so, we apologise and would greatly appreciate it if you could list them below with the relevant page number or attach a photocopy.

_____

_____

_____

_____

If you would like to receive more information on CAEP's products please supply your name and address.

_____

_____

_____

Please return your completed questionnaire to the address overleaf.

Thank you for your help

Please detach here

3rd fold

2 1

Customer Services
Certified Accountants Educational Projects Ltd
FREEPOST
29 Lincoln's Inn Fields
London
WC2A 3BR

1st fold

2nd fold

No glue or sticky tape required

4th Fold

ACCA Textbooks–Open Learning–Revision

ORDER FORM Please indicate month and year of exam diet you are sitting e.g. 12/94, 6/95 etc.

STAGE	MODULE	PAPER		EXAM DIET	TEXTBOOKS Product	TEXTBOOKS No	TEXTBOOKS Price	TEXTBOOKS Charge	OPEN LEARNING PACKAGES Product	OPEN LEARNING PACKAGES No	OPEN LEARNING PACKAGES Price	OPEN LEARNING PACKAGES Charge	REVISION TEXTS Product	REVISION TEXTS No	REVISION TEXTS Price	REVISION TEXTS Charge
Foundation	A	1	Accounting Framework		T01		15.95		L01		95.00		R01		9.95	
		2	Legal Framework		T02		15.95		L02		95.00		R02		9.95	
	B	3	Management Information		T03		15.95		L03		95.00		R03		9.95	
		4	Organisational Framework		T04		15.95		L04		95.00		R04		9.95	
Certificate	C	5	Information Analysis		T05		17.95		L05		100.00		R05		9.95	
		6	Audit Framework		T06		17.95		L06		100.00		R06		9.95	
	D	7	Tax Framework		T07		17.95		L07		100.00		R07		9.95	
		8	Managerial Finance		T08		17.95		L08		100.00		R08		9.95	
Professional	E	9	Information for Control and Decision Making		T09		18.95		L09		115.00		R09		9.95	
		10	Accounting and Audit Practice		T10		18.95		L10		115.00		R10		9.95	
		11	Tax Planning		T11		18.95		L11		115.00		R11		9.95	
	F	12	Management and Strategy		T12		18.95		L12		115.00		R12		9.95	
		13	Financial Reporting Environment		T13		18.95		L13		115.00		R13		9.95	
		14	Financial Strategy		T14		18.95		L14		115.00		R14		9.95	

TEXTBOOKS Sub Total £ ___ Postage £ ___ Total £ ___

OPEN LEARNING PACKAGES Sub Total £ ___ Postage £ ___ Total £ ___

REVISION TEXTS Sub Total £ ___ Postage £ ___ GRAND TOTAL £ ___

Postage UK: Textbooks: add £3.50 for first book, plus £2 for each extra:
Revision: £2 for first, £1 for each extra: **Open Learning:** £5 for first package, £3.50 for each extra:
Europe (inc ROI): Textbooks: £5 for first, £4 for each extra: **Revision:** £3 for first, £1.50 for each extra:
Open Learning: £20 per package. **Rest of the World: Textbooks: (airmail):** £7.50 for first, £5 for each extra:
Revision: £5.50 for first, £2.50 each extra: **Open Learning:** £20 per package.
Prices are subject to change and may vary following any new VAT legislation.

CUSTOMER DETAILS

Students Registration No. _____

Access/Mastercard/Visa/Switch Account Number _____

Switchcard Version No. ___ Expiry Date ___

Order Ref. _____

Name _____

Invoice Address _____

_____ Post Code _____

Country _____ Telephone _____

VAT No (Only if a firm or personally registered) _____

Delivery Address (if different) _____

_____ Post Code _____

Country _____ Telephone _____

ORDER TAKEN BY _____ Date _____

Please send to CAEP Ltd. PO Box 66 Glasgow G41 1BS or Fax to 041 309 3998 Credit Card Hotline: 041 309 3999

TB2-OF-94A